UFOs and Government
A Historical Inquiry

Michael Swords
Robert Powell
Clas Svahn
Vicente-Juan Ballester Olmos
Bill Chalker
Barry Greenwood
Richard Thieme
Jan Aldrich
Steve Purcell

ANOMALIST BOOKS
San Antonio * Charlottesville

The UFO History Group:
Michael Swords, primary content author for United States chapters
Robert Powell, project administrator, editor, and author
Clas Svahn, primary author for Sweden
Vicente-Juan Ballester Olmos, primary author for Spain
Bill Chalker, primary author for Australia
Barry Greenwood, author and content consultant
Richard Thieme, author and content consultant
Jan Aldrich, primary content consultant
Steve Purcell, primary photo illustration editor

The UFO History Group would also like to thank William Murphy, Thomas Tulien, and Franklin Woodward for their help and advice during the project.

Cover design: Seale Studios

AnomalistBooks.com

Anomalist Books
5150 Broadway #108
San Antonio, TX 78209

This book is dedicated to Loren Gross
in appreciation for his long years of collegial friendship
and his valuable historical contributions to UFO research.

Contents

Foreword

Those of us who have devoted an alarming portion of our lives to the reading of UFO literature know how awful much of it is. Those whose intellectual curiosity further encompasses mainstream history and science often find themselves wincing at the way UFO writers—not excluding, by the way, many who present themselves as skeptics—have of drawing big conclusions from little evidence. Not surprisingly, the results range from the amateurish and implausible to the paranoid and conspiratorial, and end up being of little more than anthropological interest.

Still, let us be fair. One need not be crazy to wonder at the disconnect between deeply puzzling UFO sightings and oddly apathetic official responses. From the earliest days of the UFO controversy, outside observers—and some inside ones—could only surmise that a presumably alert U.S. government tasked to protect the nation's safety must be secretly in the know. Could it really be as little alarmed as it appeared about mysterious sights and events that were sparking speculation, even by some scientists, about visitation from elsewhere?

It wasn't as if the phenomena were no more than, say, ambiguous light sources glimpsed by individuals possessed of excessive imagination and dubious probity. Countless sober witnesses spoke of what to all appearances were structured craft, observed under decent viewing conditions (sometimes at close range) and displaying performance characteristics of a sort that ought to have given anyone concerned with aviation security a bracing case of the chills. And worse, fresh sightings of such things were being recorded daily. Some came from instrumented trackings, others from multiple and independent witnesses on the ground, in the air, or both. How reasonable was it to believe that everybody must be radically—and curiously consistently—mistaken?

The first English-language books on UFOlogy, which saw print in 1950, took as their themes (1) the reality of visitors from space and (2) the strong likelihood that the American government kept that reality hidden behind a high wall of classification. One book, Donald Keyhoe's *The Flying Saucers Are Real*, held that the Air Force drew its conclusions from sightings by its own pilots and from believable civilian observers. The other, Frank Scully's *Behind the Flying Saucers*, put forth a more fantastic allegation, that the military had recovered alien wreckage and bodies.

A number who embraced (1) rejected (2), but both views would prove durable. If Scully's story collapsed after a famous *True* expose in 1952, crashed-disc rumors would persist on UFOlogy's fringes into the late 1970s and the revival of interest in the now-celebrated Roswell, New Mexico, incident of July 1947. Since then, a mass of crash/retrieval tales has circulated and captured the popular imagination. Long dismissed as an absurd fabrication, even Scully's yarn concerning a crash with dead humanoids at Aztec, New Mexico, is now back up for discussion in some quarters.

If aspects of Roswell-related testimony (as painstakingly collected by civilian field investigators over the past three decades) seem intriguing, albeit yet unproved, and the belated official explanations remain less than persuasive, one cannot say as much of comparable claims which have gone nowhere. Today, UFOlogy's more cautious proponents spurn them, though these stories—along with suspect related documents alleged to be of official provenance—still wind up the impressionable even as they try the patience of the rest of us.

Quite aside from limitations of evidence, the problem with the notion of recovered discs is one most thoughtful analysts find insurmountable. If the U.S. government had access to a highly advanced otherworldly technology from reverse-engineered spacecraft, yes, it *could* keep that a secret. It is indeed true, an often-heard lazy contrary argument notwithstanding, that some secrets are successfully kept over extended periods of time. One can reasonably argue, moreover, that if the assorted rumors and testimonies are in any way true, the secrets *haven't* been kept.

The problem, however, is that no such episode could have occurred outside history. Decades of concealment cannot hide the consequences—technological, political, military, diplomatic, and other—of the intrusion into the normal course of human events of radically disruptive knowledge that abruptly pushes science forward by decades or centuries. At the least, applications of that suddenly acquired explosive information would show up everywhere from new weapons and transportation systems to computers to household appliances. Yet the history of technology demonstrates a deliberate, linear, step-by-step progression of knowledge and application. It does not require, in other words, the injection of what amounts to otherworldly magic into the process.

Reading the cover-up literature, one notices how little many of the writers know about how history works and why history after the end of World War II, when the UFO phenomenon entered popular consciousness, happened as it did—pretty much, in short, as if no one had ever reported an unidentified flying object. Not only do UFOs have no visible part of that history, they are unnecessary to it. That is an interesting story in itself. How could something of such potential official (and other) consequence have been pushed so far to the official (and other) margin?

In what is sure to be an enduring work of historical UFO inquiry, *UFOs and Government* tackles this question using the tools of the scholar: thorough documentation, scrupulous analysis, and speculation tethered tightly to the recoverable record. The authors can't resolve every issue, naturally. Grand cover-up theories aside, secrets and classification are genuine concerns and authentic barriers to historical understanding. So is the loss of documents by design, carelessness, apathy, or routine disposal. Where contemporary documents are unavailable, we are dependent upon the fallible memories of humans.

Nonetheless, the evidence points overwhelmingly, at least in the case of American officialdom, to something less like UFOs vs. conspiratorial plotters than like UFOs vs. bungling bureaucrats. In my reading of the often frustrating, depressing, and infuriating mishandling of what future historians may judge the most vital scientific question of the 20th Century, one is initially tempted to think of category errors and to charge the Air Force, the Condon Committee, and others of falling victim to Type 2—the sort that has the investigator thinking that nothing interesting is going on while in fact something is.

Sad to say, from all we can infer, the reasoning (to the extent that reasoning ever impinged on dismissive impulses) never rose to the level of that kind of intellectual error. Perhaps that was because so little actual investigation was pursued. In its recounting of dramatically anomalous sightings, this book makes mordantly clear what wasn't being explained all the while. With a few scattered, honorable exceptions in which genuine curiosity was expressed and real study urged (and, on rarer occasion, practiced), even the most intriguing UFO reports seldom got more than the bum's rush out of the building. The subject would be left to the few individual scientists who dared to identify themselves with the Great Taboo and to lay UFOlogists forced to operate with no resources to speak of.

On the American side of this official history, heroes, if not entirely nonexistent, are hard to come by. The non-ignoble comprise some of the early Sign personnel, those University of Colorado project members who dared challenge the bullying, execrable Edward Condon, and—at least at their best moments, but not, alas, all of their moments—Capt. Edward Ruppelt and astronomer/Blue Book consultant J. Allen Hynek. (Ironically, in their later years the first would openly reject UFOs while the second would resolutely champion them.) The villains, those who quashed the work that needed to be done, are many. Robertson, Menzel, and Condon, though, will live on in particular infamy. The reader will come to know them and others all too well in the pages that follow.

While *UFOs and Government* revisits an often unhappy history, the reading of it is far from an unhappy experience. The authors, eloquent, intelligent, sophisticated, and conscientious, provide us with the first credible, comprehensive overview of official UFO history in many years, superseding such notable earlier works as Edward Ruppelt's *The Report on Unidentified Flying Objects*, David

Jacobs's *The UFO Controversy in America*, and Larry Fawcett and Barry J. Greenwood's *Clear Intent*. Most of the current volume (and thus most of the commentary above) deals with U.S. military and intelligence responses to the UFO phenomenon, but it also features richly informative chapters that expand the story across the international arena. If you're looking for an example of a nation that dealt productively with the UFO reports that came its official way, you will take heart in the chapter on the French projects.

From here on, every responsible treatment of UFOs and government will have to cite *UFOs and Government* prominently among its sources. New facts about old issues will inevitably emerge, of course, and one day no doubt a revised and expanded edition will be possible and necessary. In the meantime, however, this is the real story as accurately as it can be reconstructed in the second decade of the new century. I expect to keep my copy close at hand and to return to it often. While it cannot be said of many books, UFO-themed or otherwise, this is among the essential ones. Stray from it at your peril.

Jerome Clark
Minnesota
February 2012

Preface

This book is a work of history. It describes the ways that human beings handled the UFO mystery. In this, it is unlike the vast majority of other writings about UFOs that focus upon claims and the phenomenology. This book's focus is, rather, on the way major governments dealt with the mystery and the problems that it gave them. The sources of our information are the governments and their military and intelligence organizations themselves. The story that emerges from those formal documents is surprising and fascinating, and needs to be told. Although the book's theme centers upon the responses and policy decisions of the intelligence communities, there must be significant space given to key UFO incidents, as they are what initiated the government reactions. In all these "encounters," the book will base its descriptions upon primary documents, just as it does each of its remarks about governmental actions, policies, and even internal debates. A serious attempt has been made to place all information in a solid scholarly context with well-cited descriptions of the exact source materials used.

The book is heavily U.S.-focused, though not entirely so. This is for many reasons. Rightly or wrongly, many countries took their lead on how to respond to the UFO phenomenon from the United States, and, in particular, the U.S. Air Force. Whether it was clearly true or not, the expression of the UFO phenomenon seemed to center more so upon the United States than in other countries, particularly in its early post-World War II days. Despite the awareness that many intelligence community documents have either been lost or are still to be released, those currently available to the scholarly community are mainly from U.S. sources as well. Thankfully those available resources, plus outstanding sources from other countries, form a fertile and powerful base upon which to build the book, and hopefully many others to come.

The formation of this project was accidental but perhaps inevitable. Robert Powell, the Research Director of the Mutual UFO Network, had the idea that the subject of UFOs needed some serious scholarly writing; perhaps a few "essays" or "white papers," making clear the stand of colleagues who had researched this subject in depth. He persuaded his board of directors to fund travel expenses for six persons to meet and talk about such a project. For that catalysis, all of us in what came to be known by ourselves as the UFO History Group are grateful. From that meeting, and over four years of consistent work, came the History Group team and this book. Everyone has contributed, whether by writing chapters or notes, massive editing or small, reference finding and illustrations, and the constant patient lead of Robert Powell bringing it together.

This book, as you will read, is primarily chronological. It chooses its beginning in World War II with the "foo fighter" phenomenon, and follows the U.S. path up through the Colorado Project era and, in a piecemeal fashion, beyond. This is not merely to be conventional. It is a decision based upon available documentation. Without such documentation the writing would be merely speculative. After the "U.S. Chronology" chapters are complete, the book shifts focus to several non-U.S. governmental responses to the phenomenon. The very best UFOlogist-scholars were asked to write the Spanish, Australian, and Swedish chapters, and we should all be thankful for their contributions. Because of available documentation (and latent interest), shorter pieces on other governments' involvement have been added. The similarities and differences in their dealings with the phenomenon are fascinating. This is particularly true of the French program, based within their space agency. In contrast, the Canadian and British governments' reactions to the UFO phenomenon were quite similar to—and closely linked with— that of the United States. Their story does not provide a unique perspective of dealing with the phenomenon and is therefore not covered in this work.

This was not an easy book to create. That is perhaps why someone has not already done so. Dr.

Preface

David Jacobs's *The UFO Controversy in America* has stood for 35 years as the only really serious scholarly history. Dr. Thomas E. Bullard's recent *The Myth and Mystery of UFOs* is an intellectual tour-de-force, if not precisely a history. Jerome Clark's *The UFO Encyclopedia* is a rich mine of historical articles written in encyclopedia style. Persons actually wishing to know something about the field of study, rather than merely be entertained by it, should read these books. But the one non-governmental resource that made this history possible was Loren Gross. An indefatigable chronicler of information, Gross privately published over many years, a year-by-year, date-by-date, listing of UFO facts, news, documents—all referenced. It was a heroic effort. It made the gleaning and bringing together of many disparate social, cultural, and phenomenological threads come about in a richer, more illuminated way. This book could not have been written without his labor. And it is to him that it is dedicated.

Michael Swords, writing for the UFO History Group
Kalamazoo, Michigan
December 2010

Prologue

This is not the typical book on "UFOs." There are no discourses regarding aliens or detailed personal accounts of "UFO" encounters. There are no arguments on whether extraterrestrial civilizations have or have not visited Earth. Nor will there be conclusions drawn as to the origin or cause of "UFOs." This is a historical treatise of a subject that has been maligned by the deniers of the theory of extraterrestrial visitations, as well as those who refuse to consider the merits of serious investigations into this phenomenon. It is a subject where simply the utterance of the word "UFO" brings up thoughts of little green men; where witnesses are ashamed to admit to have seen an unidentified object in the sky, less they be considered irrational and untrustworthy; and where, unfortunately, few have treated it with the historical merit that it is due.

It is appropriate to define some key terminology used in this book to describe this phenomenon. The term "UFO phenomenon" represents a unique experience in human history related not to any single event, but to a continuous string of historical human observations of unidentified flying objects that to the observer are not explainable within his or her knowledge and experience. The original term "U.F.O." means exactly that—an unidentified flying object. It means nothing more and nothing less. The newer definition of UFO will be reflected in quotes and refers to the unfortunate association and misuse of the term to signify an alien spaceship.

For the entirety of our existence, we humans have been experiencing things that seem mysterious to us. Some of these things seem to fly about in the air. Some of them, even many years or centuries, ago, may have been the same phenomena that we today call UFOs. But due to the blurring that comes with centuries of time, and due to the relative paucity of resources and research in those olden times, it is difficult to say with any assurance that the aerial mysteries of the 19th century and earlier were similar to those we experience today. In this book we will consider events for which we have a great deal of documentation, and consequently, a great deal of assurance for their validity. Whether or not one believes in the existence of these unexplained UFO phenomena, they are a real part of human history. This book concerns the "modern" UFO phenomenon and how government has reacted to that phenomenon. This phenomenon is documented by thousands of pages of government releases and thousands more of formal witness testimonies. That mountain of documentation began during World War Two, and that is where we begin.

UFOs and Government

Chapter 1: World War II and the Immediate Post-War Era

During World War Two, in both the European and Pacific theatres-of-war, allied pilots began encountering aerial phenomena that they could not explain. Given the circumstances, it was natural and prudent to assume that these phenomena could be enemy technology.

What were they seeing? There are dozens of known reports and surely not all of them were of the same phenomenon. Some pilots seem to be making understandable human errors, perhaps even firing at the stars or other (friendly) planes or true enemy technology, like balloons. But the bulk of these reports tell a different story. When these reports are read as a group, the anomalous aerial phenomenon appears like this: Balls or spheres of light, sometimes seeming transparent or even metallic. Usually a nocturnal phenomenon. Appearing sometimes as a solitary object, but often in pairs. Colors varying across the spectrum, but mainly in the yellow-to-red. Seeming to pace planes, off wing tips or forward or back. Often changing relative positions within the same incident. Despite the consternation they cause, there is no concrete activity indicative of hostility towards planes. Often making erratic flight maneuvers, leaving the area in a variety of directions, including straight up, or simply switch off or disappear. Like any recurrent phenomenon, they received nicknames: "kraut fireballs" and "foo fighters." Although this phenomenon became a military concern in the European and Asian theatres of war, scattered reports occurred more widely, geographically, as subsequent research has shown. These and other reports following the war indicated that Axis personnel in Eastern Europe had also encountered the phenomenon.[1]

Post-war conversations with veteran pilots have determined that foo-fighter-like encounters occurred throughout the war, but they only became common in late 1944 and 1945. Due to patient and meticulous work by UFO historians Barry Greenwood and Lawrence Fawcett, the first official military records of foo fighter incidents were uncovered in 1992. These records consist of very brief excerpts from mission reports, required of each flight commander upon returning to base. They were entered in the Unit History of the 415th Night Fighter Squadron (in the European Theatre), and began appearing in late 1944. The comments which follow are quoted to give the reader a flavor of the variety of ways the pilots felt that they were encountering the phenomenon. These records are available in the National Archives, in College Park, Maryland.[2]

Another outstanding instance occurred in October. While flying an intruder mission in the Rhine Valley, Capt. Edward Schlueter and Lt. Don Myers experienced contact with the first foo fighters, referred to as such by Lt. Myers for the lack of a better name and because of the eerie feeling it gave the crew. At first these two officers were taunted by their buddies and began to wonder if they had developed combat fatigue. However, other crews began to report seeing foo fighters in the Rhine Valley at night, thus the foo fighters were definitely established as an existing phenomena.

November 27, 1944. A weird excerpt comes from Lt. Schlueter's report of an intruder mission:

> Upon returning to base saw a red light flying through area about 35 miles ENE of Pt. A. Came in to about 2000 feet off starboard and then it disappeared in a long red streak.

December 15, 1944. An excerpt from the Operations Report:

> Saw a brilliant red light at 2000 feet going E at 200 MPH in the vicinity of Ernstein. Due to AI [Air Intercept radar] failure could not pick up contact but followed it by sight until it went out. Could not get close enough to identify object before it went out.

December 22 and 23, 1944.

> Mission 1 – 1705-1850 Put on bogie by Blunder at 1750 hours, had A.I. contact 4 miles range at Q-7372. Overshot and could not pick up contact again. A.I. went out and weather started closing in so returned to base. Observed 2 lights, one of which seemed to be going on and off at Q-2411.

December 23, 1944.

> More Foo-Fighters were in the air last night. The Ops report says: 'In vicinity of Hagenau saw 2 lights coming toward A/C from ground. After reaching the altitude of the A/C they leveled off and flew on tail of Beau [Beaufighter—their aircraft, Ed.] for 2 minutes and then peeled up and turned away. 8th mission—sighted 2 orange lights. One light sighted at 10,000 feet the other climbed until it disappeared.

World War II Beaufighter

December 28, 1944. The Ops Report says:

> 1st patrol saw 2 sets of 3 red and white lights. One appeared on port side, the other on starboard at 1000 to 2000 feet to rear and closing in. Beau peeled off and lights went out. Nothing on GCI scope at the time." And then again: "Observed lights suspended in air, moving slowly in no general direction and then disappeared. Lights were orange, and appeared singly and in pairs. These lights were observed 4 or 5 times throughout the period.

Instances of foo fighters continued into the year 1945.
January 30, 1945.

> Foo-Fighters were at it again last night. This is the operations report: "Halfway between Wissenbourg and Langau sighted amber lights at 2000 feet. One light was 20 to 50 feet above the other and of about 30 seconds duration. Lights were about a foot in diameter, 1000 feet away and following Beaus. Lights disappeared when Beaus turned into them.

February 13 and 14, 1945.

> Mission 2 – 1800-2000 – About 1910, between Rastatt and Bishwiller, encountered lights at 3000 feet, two sets of them, turned into them, one set went out and the other went straight up 2-3000 feet, then went out. Turned back to base and looked back and saw lights in their original position again.

February 14 and 15, 1945.

> Mission 2 – 1940-2140 – String of lights north of Freiburg, (1 red one in center, 4 white ones on each side) blinking on and off.

March 26 and 27, 1945.

> Mission 5 – 2230-0130 – Patrol. Patrol Worms area. Saw an orange ball that came up from ground and disappeared before it reached the Beau.

April 23 and 24, 1945.

1945: Mission 5 – 0105-0320 – P-61 Patrol – Wisenburg-Ludwigsburg Area. At Rhine River, R-9593, observed 4 lights arranged in a square. Lights went out as plane approached.

Despite the Spartan brevity of the extracts above, they serve two useful purposes: they end the discussion as to whether U.S. pilots were seeing and reporting anomalous light "bogies" during World War Two, and the excerpts nicely lay a foundation of credibility for the multitude of post-war interview reports made by pilots, which offer much more detail.

Pilots were reporting anomalous bogies.[3] What was the government's reaction to these sightings? Of course there was concern that some of these incidents constituted evidence of German or Japanese technology. There was a common enough theme in the reports of apparent interest in our planes (pacing, buzzing, monitoring?) to make this an obvious issue of military security. Did the military do anything about it? The answers are: "we don't know" and "yes."

The "we don't know" answer applies to the possibility that the U.S. military created some sort of focus person, desk, or even a project to collect specific reports and attempt some form of analysis (an "Estimate") to determine what they were dealing with. Such a project or collection point may have existed within the U.S. or Allied military structure, but we do not have the documents to prove it.

The "yes" answer applies to the fact that certain individuals were asked to look into these reports and do what they could to find out as much as they could about them. UFO historians have long known that prominent scientists H.P. Robertson of Caltech and Luis Alvarez of California Berkeley were involved.[4] But the extent of whatever they did is not known. We know a great deal more about a third physicist, David Griggs, ultimately of UCLA, who was acknowledged by Robertson and Alvarez to have been closer to the problem.

David Griggs

David Tressel Griggs was born in Columbus, Ohio, in 1911 and educated at Ohio State and Harvard in geophysics. When World War II began, he was one of the legions of bright young scientists drafted into the MIT Radiation Laboratory, primarily tasked to work on radar science and technology. His immediate contribution was to the application of radar to ground-based anti-aircraft fire. At the time Edward Bowles, MIT expert in microwave radar, was chief scientific consultant for Secretary of War Henry Stimson. He needed a sharp, young radar expert to learn and advise on action right at the European front. Griggs was also an amateur pilot of some skill, so he was the man chosen.[5]

Griggs reported to Bowles's office at the Pentagon in 1942 and shortly thereafter headed overseas. He worked under Army Air Force General Henry (Hap) Arnold's authority, and rotated through the commands of Generals Elwood (Pete) Quesada, Jimmy Doolittle, and Carl Spaatz. He was a hands-on guy, flying both training and combat missions, and got the respect of the military personnel with whom he worked. He spent most of the war in the European Theatre, and, after "Victory in Japan" day, was transferred to the Pacific Theatre to aid in the exploitation of Japanese scientific and technological assets.

Edward Bowles

Griggs, therefore, was in a perfect position to pick up anomalous air-encounter stories, which the flyboys thought would be of interest to a scientific expert who was also a pilot. But his information gathering was not just an accident of his being in the right place to hear stories about encounters with foo fighters.

When it became known to the UFO research community that David Griggs had been asked to collect information on foo fighters during the war, he was contacted (in 1969) by fellow physicist, James McDonald, and asked about this. It is from McDonald's interview that we get a little more light on the military interest in these things.[6]

Griggs was quite friendly and open. McDonald's notes from the conversation include these comments:

> Every place he'd go, these things showed up. Gen. Arnold sent a TWX to ask that he check into it. He wrote reports on it, but has no copies, and is not sure where they'd be in Air Force files.

> We had all kinds of troubles [with these things] in Europe. But the phenomena were quite different in Japan—the accounts were different in Japan—they were all one type . . . "red fireballs."

James McDonald

Griggs went on to tell McDonald his musings about jet exhausts being misinterpreted, about dark nights with no background leading to tricks of perception, about war nerves, and all of that. He then related how he and a crew had been temporarily fooled by the Moon rising under just the wrong (or right) conditions. But Griggs did not really believe that such things explained all the foo fighter reports. McDonald: "I asked if he felt all this was mass hysteria. Griggs said: 'No, of course not.'" Griggs ended this part of the story by saying that "he felt there was something real involved, but was not sure what it was." In the cases Griggs collected in Europe he stated, "The air observers reports were all over enemy territory—never over our ground. Anxiety that the enemy might have something we needed to know about kept the checking under way. [And], there were reports of engine disturbances over— [word could be "Reich" as it begins with an R and is 4 or 5 letters in length]."

The key point here is that Griggs knew of aircraft engine interference cases in connection with foo fighters—not just one, but multiple instances. When the war in Europe ended, Griggs took his expertise and his side-task about foo fighters to the Pacific as that phase of the war also wound down.

General Henry (Hap) Arnold   Notwithstanding the fact that Griggs spent far more time in the European Theatre than the Pacific, he thought the reports from the Pacific were more numerous. There was a lot of concern because Allied Intelligence knew that the Japanese were experimenting with electromagnetic rays, and Intelligence wondered whether the enemy had developed some sort of beamed weapon that could produce the red-orange fireballs. When Griggs was transferred to the Pacific Theatre as part of the Compton Scientific Intelligence Committee to examine Japanese military-technology research, he made a special effort to track down the electromagnetic beam experiments and anything else that might explain the foo fighter observations. Griggs did as much checking as he could, but found nothing. He felt that the Japanese were not hiding anything. They found no records of on-ground observations by Japanese personnel or pilots, though he could have missed that, he conceded.

Concerning the "ray" technology, it did exist, but at a rudimentary level. "[Their devices] could stop engines at short range . . . one massive device could kill a rabbit at a [word hard to read, possibly meter]." Griggs and McDonald go on to discuss the size of the device (a ten-meter dish), power

6

("Megawatt-CW"), and effective agency ("not thermal"). The device was shipped to the U.S. and studied here thoroughly (one wonders what resulted from that investigation).

Concerning the Japanese reports, Griggs stated, "They had a lot of data on location. Certain regions were of high frequency in Japan. Southwest of Tokyo [was one such]. There were three such regions [of high report density]." McDonald noted that through all of Griggs' exploration into cases and into Japanese R&D, "he could not find anything in Japanese records to match our Air Force's B-29 crew reports. He felt that he had really looked for it, but found zero." Japanese technology does not seem to have produced the foo fighter reports.

Griggs' research led him to the conclusion that many of the foo fighter reports were real and unexplained by any military technology. Neither the above-mentioned Compton Scientific Intelligence Committee in Japan, nor the many attempts to "rescue" and assess German technologies in Europe, discovered anything that would account for them. And note: they were seriously looking for it. No on-the-ground recovery missions, such as those led by Wright-Patterson AFB's Air Materiel Command (AMC) came up with any explanatory devices.

Foo fighters remained a mystery and an interest. In February of 1952, the intelligence center at Wright-Patterson sent the Director of Air Force Intelligence at the Pentagon a message about the fireballs and possible explanations for it. Under a paragraph titled "fireballs" are these remarks: "These phenomena made their appearance over both Germany and Japan during World War II. They have never been completely explained, and there is no record of aircraft having been damaged by them."

Wright-Patterson then goes on to speculate about flying bombs and rockets, or balloon-supported incendiaries, despite the fact that none of these concepts match the bulk of the reports. But we crave explanations, even in the military. Our military still had some concerns about these things and the intelligence department at Wright-Patterson had some (currently unreleased) source of information about them to which it could refer.

Another example of ongoing interest occurred the following year when Albert Simpson, the chief of the USAF Historical Division (Air University, Maxwell AFB) learned of an anomalous aerial phenomenon report over Japan. This jogged his memory of an old report of a foo fighter incident from the mid-Pacific. He thought this important enough to send it to General John Samford, the Air Force's Chief of Intelligence. It read:

Headquarters VII Bomber Command
Mission Report No. 11-327
Date: 2 May 1945 (GCT)
OBSERVATIONS:
The crews of plane #616 over FALA ISLAND, TRUK ATOLL, at 021802Z observed 2 airborne objects at their 11,000 foot altitude changing from a cherry red to an orange, and to a white light which would die out and then become cherry red again. These objects were out on either wing and not within range of caliber-50 machine guns. Both followed the B-24 thru all types of evasive action. A B-24 took a course for GUAM and one of the pursuers dropped off at 021900Z after accompanying the B-24 for an hour. The other continued to follow, never approaching closer than 1000 yards and speeding up when the B-24 went thru clouds to emerge on the other side ahead of the B-24. In daylight it was seen to be bright silver in color.[7]

At this moment in UFOlogical history, several conclusions are supported by the documentation:
1. Many Allied pilots encountered light spheres or lighted objects in both theatres of WWII;
2. These encounters have never been explained despite some serious attempts at doing so;
3. The military intelligence community remained aware and interested in the phenomenon well after the end of WWII;
4. Despite there being this interest and information about the foo fighter reports, this information

has, at least in part, never been released (known example: the reports Griggs says he wrote, which could have been what Wright-Patterson was referring to in their 1952 report to Air Force Intelligence.)[8]

At the conclusion of the war in Europe, U.S. Military and intelligence teams swarmed across Germany to harvest every bit of technical equipment and information that they could retrieve. Here, Wright-Patterson AFB engineer, and soon-to-be chief of intelligence of Air Materiel Command, Colonel Howard (Mack) McCoy, leads a retrieval operation in a German field. McCoy is bending over the debris in the cloth cap. Such retrievals were shipped back to the base at Dayton, Ohio, where experts attempted to reconstruct the devices, or at least assess the capabilities.[9] Out of all this came the secret technology manuals of the intelligence division's (T-2, AMC) library, as seen below.[10,11] These are the types of references used to attempt to analyze UFO reports, as well.

At the cessation of World War II, the victors, with thinly veiled hostility, stared at one another across what was to become the "Iron Curtain." The Soviets controlled their nation with a philosophy almost completely antithetical to that of the West, and particularly that of the United States. Very few people saw anything but strife and, probably, war between the two giants. But the United States had The Bomb, and so maybe the West was safe after all.

The Big War was over. People were pouring out of the military and going on with their lives. *Let's not worry about the 'backward' Russians. Let's enjoy what we've earned.* Although no one, not even military and intelligence analysts, could blame the average Joe for this attitude, the shrinkage in the strength of the military force was alarming. And it was not only good old G.I. Joe who was leaving. The high-skills people and the brain trust were "retiring" as well.

The government reacted in a variety of ways. One was to increase salaries and incentives to stay in the force. Another was to allow established skilled people to retire from the military and still serve in the same "military" function: that is, people took off their uniforms and still came to work. Special programs and organizations were funded to attract the brain trust (whether to engineering projects or secret consultancies) to remain within the talent pool controlled by the military.

Left: General Carl Spaatz
Right: General Hap Arnold

One of these latter organizations was RAND. The name was almost an acronym (Research and Development) and was the invention of Air Force chief Henry (Hap) Arnold. Arnold was sensing what almost everyone else was: the future of military supremacy was going to come through the air. But how? Some said through jet planes; some said by giant bombers; but most intuited that the *real* "high ground" was going to be a lot higher. Most thought that, sooner or later, the real power, and the real threat, was going to come from space. That meant rockets, and perhaps even rocket planes, driven, maybe, by nuclear engines.

The Navy inspired the idea of the importance of outer space. Yes, the oceans were their domain, but the powers in the Navy saw that military superiority in the context of inter-service rivalry *within* the United States military establishment was going to be much more difficult if they too were not "in the air." And so, surprisingly to many people, the Navy launched its own rockets and space satellite research alongside the Army Air Force. The two rivals met in March of 1946 to discuss combining their brains into a single rocket/satellite project. The negotiating teams thought that this was a good idea. The recommendation was passed up to Air Force chief of research and development, General Curtis LeMay. We do not know what he said, but it amounted to "no." Arnold (and LeMay) immediately created RAND.[12]

Left: General Curtis LeMay
Right: General Roger Ramey

RAND was composed largely of aerotech experts from Douglas, North American, and Northrop facilities in the Santa Monica area. Its chief was Franklin Collbohm. Collbohm got the

9

first task from LeMay: "get me a feasibility estimate on orbiting a space device." Aeronautical missile engineer Jimmy Lipp got the assignment. In two months Lipp helped author the first-ever RAND report: "Preliminary Design of an Experimental World Circling Space Ship." In June, Air Force General Craigie showed the report to the Navy, ending discussions of any joint cooperation.

Within the report, Air Force Scientific Advisor L. N. Ridenour reminded everyone of what they were *really* doing: "There is little difference in design and performance between an intercontinental rocket missile and a satellite. Thus a rocket missile with a free space trajectory of 6,000 miles requires a minimum energy of launching, which corresponds to an initial velocity of 4.4 miles per second, while a satellite requires 5.4. Consequently, the development of a satellite will be directly applicable to the development of an intercontinental rocket missile."[13]

Aeronautical Missile Engineer Jimmy Lipp

So there it was: ICBMs. And to carry what? Need it be said? The nuclear warhead space missile delivery system was feasible, according to RAND. Next, a power plant had to be developed to launch the system. In a combined effort between the Air Force and Oak Ridge National Laboratory, the Nuclear Energy for Propulsion of Aircraft project (NEPA) was formed in 1946 to pursue this "dream."[14]

Although this discussion so far has focused on developments taking place in the U.S. military establishment, none of these possibilities could have been missed by military authorities elsewhere. It was into this environment that sightings of unexplained rocket-like phenomena began to be reported in Scandinavia.[15]

Notes

[1] The best generic treatment of the foo fighters which might be available in a local library is the entry in the major reference work on UFOlogy: Jerome Clark's *The UFO Encyclopedia*, 2nd edition, 2 vols., 1998. The entry "Foo Fighters" appears in Volume One, 416-420. An interesting treatment, involving cases reported by servicemen to UFO researchers after the War, appears in Gordon Lore and Harold Deneault, *Mysteries of the Skies*, 1968 (Chapter 8, 115-134). Another well-researched piece is part of Loren Gross' *Charles Fort, the Fortean Society, and Unidentified Flying Objects*, 1976 (Chapter 5, 50-62). The most well known early article on the mystery was Jo Chamberlain, "The Foo Fighter Mystery," *The American Legion Magazine*, December 1945: 43-47. A more recent and very thorough coverage of the foo fighters is the entire subject of Keith Chester's *Strange Company*, 2007.

[2] Barry Greenwood and Lawrence Fawcett, "First Official Foo-Fighter Records Discovered," *Just Cause* (32), June 1992 and September 1992 (entire bulletins). These bulletins quote incidents of encounters taken directly from the microfilmed history and "War Diary" of the 415th Night Fighter Squadron of the European theatre, as held at the U.S. Air Force Historical Research Center at Maxwell AFB, Alabama.

[3] "Floating Mystery Ball is New Nazi Air Weapon," *New York Times*, 14 December, 1944. No one knows if any alleged photograph of a foo fighter is legitimate.

[4] Frederick C. Durant, *Report of Meetings of Scientific Advisory Panel on Unidentified Flying Objects Convened by Office of Scientific Intelligence, CIA, January 14-18, 1953*, 1953.

[5] Ivan A. Getting and John M. Christi, *A Biographical Memoir of David Tressel Griggs 1911-1974*, 1994.

[6] David T. Griggs, interview with Dr. James E. McDonald, 10 April, 1969. Notes filed in James E. McDonald archival collection, University of Arizona archives, Tucson, Arizona (Box 5, folder "Foo Fighters.") Material from this file is quoted

extensively in Michael D. Swords, "David Griggs and the Foo Fighters," *International UFO Reporter* 31 (1):17-19, 2007.

[7] Albert P. Simpson, Chief, USAF Historical Division, Maxwell AFB, Alabama, to Major General John A. Samford, Director of Intelligence, Headquarters USAF, 22 January 1953, with attachment "Mission Report No. 11-327. Headquarters VII Bomber Command, 2 May 1945."

[8] Joint Message form from Commanding Officer, Air Technical Intelligence Command to Director of Intelligence, Headquarters USAF, Feb. 1952.

[9] Wolfgang W. E. Samuel, *American Raiders—The Race to Capture the Luftwaffe's Secrets*, 2004.

[10] D. L. Putt, *German Developments in the Field of Guided Missiles*, Document #: F-SU-1122-ND, 12 July, 1946.

[11] N. LeBlanc, *German Flying Wings Designed by Horten Brothers*, Document #: F-SU-1110-ND, 5 July, 1946.

[12] R. Cargill Hall, "Early U.S. Satellite Proposals," *Technology and Culture*, IV (4): 412-434, Fall 1963.

[13] R. Cargill Hall, 421.

[14] R. W. Bussard and .D. Delaver, *Fundamentals of Nuclear Flight*, 1965.

[15] For general overviews of the Ghost Rocket mystery, we again recommend the entry in Jerome Clark's *The UFO Encyclopedia*. Loren Gross' volume in his multi-volume *UFO's: A History*, 3rd edition, 1988, is excellent. Because of the value of Loren's chronicle of directly quoted primary sources, we will refer to his work often. For shorthand, these citations will read: "Gross," followed by the date of the chronicle volume or supplemental notes. A few articles also stand out: 1) Jan Aldrich, "Investigating the Ghost Rockets," *International UFO Reporter* 23 (4): 9-14, Winter 1998; 2) Don Berliner, "The Ghost Rockets of Sweden," *Official UFO* 1 (11): 30-31, 60-64, October 1976; 3) Anders Liljegren and Clas Svahn, "The Ghost Rockets" in H. Evans and J. Spencer, *UFOs: 1947-1987*, 1987, 32-38. Further, an electronic book covering these and wider missile-related matters is also recommended. It is an annotated chronicle by Joel Carpenter, *Guided Missiles and UFOs*, findable at the prolific website "Project 1947" (citation http://www.project1947.com/gr/grchron1.htm).

Chapter 2: Ghost Rockets

For seven months during the first year of peace after the Second World War, Sweden, Norway and Finland experienced a scare that brought back memories of German weapons, weapons powerful enough to bring death and destruction from afar. The year 1946 brought sightings of unknown rocket-type devices that would become known as Ghost Rockets.

It is hard to tell when the first report of an unknown "rocket" was made, and at first they were only reported as lights in the sky in early January.[1] In February an air traffic controller in Härnösand decided to turn on the runway lights since several people had heard a persistent sound from an engine from the sky even though the night was dark and a snow storm made all flights impossible. Two weeks later the second bright meteor for the year left a long trail of smoke in the sky when it crossed the heavens in broad daylight on February 21.[2]

The first report of a rocket-like craft was made over Stora Mellösa not far from Örebro on May 21. Two motorists saw what they later reported to the local police as an elongated craft resembling a rocket or zeppelin. One of the witnesses could distinguish two short wings and thought it to be a glider plane. The other witness, who made his observation separately from the first, could not see any wings during the five minutes that he and his family followed the unknown object.[3]

A couple of days later witnesses who talked to the newspaper *Morgon-Tidningen* compared a series of observations of bright meteors in the south of Sweden with the "flying bombs" they remembered to have seen over Sweden during the war and on May 25 *Aftonbladet* used the expression "rocketbomb" in a headline.[4] And it was in *Aftonbladet* that the expression "Spökraket," Ghost Rocket, was used for the first time in a headline, but not in the article itself, a few days later, on May 28.[5]

Thus far the reports of unidentified objects flying over Sweden had not prompted the interest of the Swedish military. At a meeting in early June between the British Air Attaché in Stockholm and General Bengt Nordenskiöld, the Commander-in-Chief of the Swedish Air Force, the Attaché was surprised over the lack of interest from the Swedish military. "He was convinced they were not true and [were] merely imagination, or observations of ordinary meteorites [sic]," the Attaché noted. And at the time the General may have been entitled to this view. The early reports of Ghost Rockets mostly constituted lights in the sky, most probably meteors.

May 25, 1946 Ghost Rocket report in the newspaper Aftonbladet.

But the many reports in the newspapers and also a few reaching the Defense Staff and local police during the early summer puzzled and interested the military. In a special order dated June 26 the Commander of the military district in Morjärv in the very north of Sweden issued instructions on how to report incidents with "certain kind of light phenomena" that could be associated with "tests made by foreign powers with guided weapons."[6] Starting on July 6 and through a series of meetings a special committee was formed with Colonel Bengt Jacobsson from the Royal Air Management as chairman.

July 9 Bolide

The committee issued its final report on December 23.[7]

The committee did get a head start. On the 9th of July hundreds of observations were made from mostly central Sweden. One of them even produced a picture. The picture was taken by a married couple on vacation that had stopped for a rest on a clear and hot summer day. Erik and Åsa Reuterswärd had just taken a swim in a nearby lake at Guldsmedshyttan, located north-northwest of Lindesberg, 200 kilometers west of Stockholm. The time was 2:30 p.m. and the two of them climbed a forest watchtower, situated by an abandoned silver mine, to admire the view. The tower, which during the war years had been used as an aerial reconnaissance tower, offered them a breathtaking view of the landscape. They could see for miles and miles. "I remember the event very well," Reuterswärd said when he met with Clas Svahn years later:

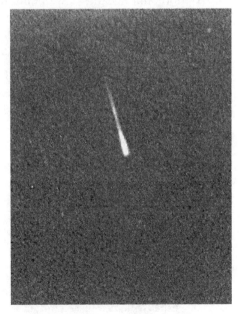

> We were out hiking peacefully and didn't think of any Ghost Rockets. We climbed the tower in order to photograph the view, and we were completely alone except our one-year-old son. At the exact same moment as I pushed the shutter button, there it was! Something mysterious falling from the sky that both me and my wife observed. I'm not able to remember exactly how it looked, but I know that it was a light which passed us. It looked rather special. We were both startled, and for a long time discussed what it could have been.[8]

Enlargement of the meteor

In his report to the Ministry of Defense's Air Defense department, dated on the 11th of July and written on the vicarage at Guldsmedshyttan, Erik Reuterswärd retells the story the following way:

> We observed a sharp, greenish white (neon-colored light) gleam of light in the northwestern direction and at a 45 degree angle, which emerged suddenly and swiftly moved downwards perhaps five moon diameters; after which it disappeared. The disappearance occurred—by my opinion—with a[n] explosion like a burst of flames, and I also thought myself hearing a hissing sound. We got the impression that it was a meteorite, though we have never seen one in daylight. The whole incident was over in a moment.[9]

And Erik Reuterswärd was right. What he had caught on film was a daylight meteor seen by thousands at 2:30 p.m., July 9. The reports came from all over central Sweden where the weather was nice and the visibility good. The many reports coming in from a very large area further indicated that the object spotted must have traveled high in the atmosphere. The picture was handed over to the Ministry of Defense which was swarmed by the press and felt obligated to hand out the picture to *Morgon-Tidningen* in Stockholm.[10]

In spite of all the evidence pointing to a daylight meteor at the time, the picture was a great mystery for the military. In an attempt to find an explanation, Major Nils Dahlgren, who had interrogated Erik Reuterswärd, wrote the head of the shooting range at AB Bofors, a major Swedish manufacturer of weapons. Could it have been a rocket launch by Bofors? The answer was no: No launches had been made at the time of the sighting.[11]

The affair was of a sensitive nature. Major Ahlgren, in his letter to Bofors, demanded the matter be considered classified. Furthermore, he turned to Professor Bertil Lindblad at Stockholm observatory for an explanation. But his answer was ambiguous: "However, judging from the photograph and the visual sightings, one cannot definitely rule out the possibility that what we have here is a meteor." In an attachment to the letter, professor Lindblad presented an idea for a "V-bomb spectrograph," a surveillance camera which could differentiate meteors and rocket bombs by analyzing their spectra.[12]

Even though a picture of a "Ghost Rocket" was a sensation and the photo soon was printed in newspapers in several countries, all Erik and Åsa Reuterswärd earned from it was 50 Swedish Kronor (Seven U.S. dollars).

A more tantalizing documentation of a Ghost Rocket was made on August 22, 1946, when the photographer and owner of a photo business in Gothenburg, Mr. Gösta Skog, was traveling to Stockholm by car together with three friends. After stopping for lunch in Linköping the party passed Norrköping and decided to take a break near the small community of Getå, 100 miles south of Stockholm. Gösta Skog brought out his film camera, a Paillard-Bolex 16 mm loaded with color film, to shoot some views. The camera was put on a tripod and the lenses were rotated so that a middle range lens was put in use for some nice shots around the horizon. But only a few moments after Gösta Skog had started to film he was interrupted by one of his friends who shouted and pointed to the sky right above them. "When I turned my head I saw a cigar-shaped object with fire coming out from the end flying right above me," Gösta Skog told Clas Svahn during one of several interviews. "It was just like an ordinary cigar flying over us, and I turned my camera and switched to the telephoto lens and started to film."[13] The cigar-shaped object came from the South and seemed to be flying at a relatively low altitude, around 3,000 feet. Even though the velocity of the cigar was rather high Gösta Skog says that he was able to keep the object in the lens during the entire observation.

> It appeared from a cloud, out against the blue sky, and into the next cloud, out again and then vanishing to the north. I could not make out any details on the surface but it had a dark color and from the rear exhaust flames were emitted in the same fashion as you could see on American space rockets many years later. But there was no sound at all.

After the rocket had vanished, the four men continued their journey to Stockholm, all very upset and talking about the observation during the remaining 125 miles. Gösta Skog was so excited that he was shaking. The camera had been put into its protective box and after a while the men decided that the best thing to do was to call the Air Staff. "As soon as I came to my hotel in Stockholm I made the call and was asked to go directly to the Air Staff with the film," says Gösta Skog.

According to the only surviving note about the incident in the military archives, Gösta Skog made the call at 7 p.m. At the Air Staff the four men were divided and each subjected to a 30-minute-long interrogation by two military officers. They were asked to come back two hours later when the film had been developed. Seated in a screening room together with several officers, the four friends felt the importance of the occasion. The lights went out and the film started to roll. But it was totally blank. "Then I realized that when I had changed to the telephoto lens the aperture was still on 2.5, so the whole film was overexposed! I had been so excited that I forgot this simple thing," says Gösta Skog, who never got his film back. And the film is still lost, as are the notes from the interrogation of the four men.

The Gösta Skog observation came a little more than a week after one of the most remarkable military sightings during the Ghost Rocket wave. On August 14 Swedish Air Force pilot Lieutenant Gunnar Irholm and his signaler, Corporal Möller, were flying on a training mission between Malingsbo and Krylbo in Dalecarlia. The time was a couple of minutes after ten o'clock in the morning and the visibility was good with a rainstorm coming in from the southeast. The two men were flying a B18A bomber at 650 feet over a forest area 4.3 miles east-northeast of Malingsbo church when Gunnar Irholm suddenly saw an unknown aircraft coming from his left on a southeasterly course in front of their airplane. "Just over the horizon I could see an elongated object without the typical features of an aircraft. It had no tail

Artist Impression of Lt. Gunnar Irholm's encounter with a Ghost Rocket over Dalecarlia.

fin, for example. What we saw was the picture of a cigar, a torpedo. We were close enough to be sure that this was not an aircraft," Gunnar Irholm remembered when interviewed in 1986.[14] His report was filed just minutes after landing in Västerås. There Gunnar Irholm wrote that after spotting the object they lost eye contact for a short period of time, but after adjusting their height it reappeared 20 seconds later. "I immediately put my aircraft on a parallel course and put on full power. The shortest distance we had to the craft was just over 3,000 feet [one kilometer] but I soon realized that we were not able to catch up with the craft whose speed I estimate to between 370 and 430 miles per hour. Two minutes later it had vanished to the South East," Irholm wrote in the official report.[15] The unknown object vanished into the storm cloud.

A full investigation was made and Lieutenant Irholm and Corporal Möller were both summoned to a meeting with one of the prime investigators from the Ghost Rocket committee, Eric Malmberg, eight days later. Eric Malmberg's conclusion was that the object had not been a Swedish aircraft. But what was it? "He must have seen something. I later got to know Gunnar Irholm very well and he was always a very balanced person," said Eric Malmberg later in an interview.[16] And Gunnar Irholm was a pilot with great experience. At the time of the observation he was in charge of a division of B18s and would later the same year fly to Britain in charge of bringing four J28 Vampires back to Sweden. He was later appointed to head the military testing grounds at Malmslätt where new aircraft, missiles and rockets were tested before being used by the armed forces.

To Gunnar Irholm the incident over Dalecarlia was a mystery for all of his life. In one of his telephone conversations with Clas Svahn, he said that no one ever made fun of him or failed to take him seriously when he told them about the strange craft. What it was he never knew: "As I sensed it the object never bothered about us but just kept flying on its course. It was a grey cigar, pointed in both ends, around 50 feet [15 meters] long and just over 3 feet [one meter] in diameter. I had hoped that they should have registered something on radar but I never got any information that it was seen."[17]

Even though Gunnar Irholm's encounter was to be the only contact with a Ghost Rocket made by a Swedish pilot during 1946, there were several other incidents that puzzled the Ghost Rocket committee. During four days in July, the Defense Staff received around 300 reports and when the summer was over, 997 reports had been registered by the Staff. The real number of observations probably far exceeded that.

The objects passed over Sweden in the most varied directions and though many suspected Russia to be the culprit, that suspicion was never confirmed. The Ghost Rocket committee thought that the Russians had continued experimenting with captured German V-weapons and now were trying them out from bases along the coast. On several occasions during the autumn, Swedish reconnaissance aircraft were sent to pick up signals near the Baltic border. Russian fighter aircraft were immediately scrambled against the Swedish pilots.[18] But even though most of the observations were made at night and the bulk of the reports could at the time or later be identified as meteors, the Swedish Defense Staff took the Ghost Rockets seriously, as did the politicians.

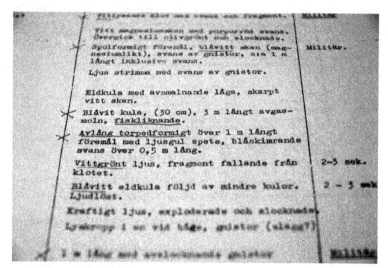

The Swedish military kept lists of Ghost Rocket sightings and investigated many.

The meteor theory was discussed at the time, but in spite of several suspected finds of meteorites that were analyzed by scientists, not one proved to be of meteoritic origin. Several Ghost Rockets were reported to have crashed on Swedish and Norwegian soil, all of them in lakes with huge columns of water rocketing from the surface at the impact. Four of the crashes were reported on the same day, July 19, when a series of observations culminated with the crashes of unknown objects in lakes in Norrbothnia and close to Söderhamn, a town much further south.

Twenty-four hours earlier another object crashed in the 300 meter deep lake Mjøsa in Norway with several witnesses seeing large columns of water coming from the site of impact: "We saw an object coming from the west with great speed before falling into the lake," said Henry Skaug, one of several witnesses. His sister Åse Tandberg recalls the strange sound which made the family look up: "We were out working in the fields when we heard a strong wind and shortly after the water in the lake splashed with a column rising. But it was all over in such a short time that we never got a good look at the object."[19] Theories about the object being a loon or that the water column was the result of a small tornado were being discussed in the press, but neither of these possibilities seemed to cover what was to happen in Sweden the day after.

Friday the 19th of July was one of many hot days during this summer of 1946. In a field below the small village of Bölebyn outside Piteå in the north of Sweden, Leonard Danielsson and his sons Kjell, Dan, and Hans were working out in the fields. It was 11:15 a.m. The oldest brother Börje was not at home, serving as an air force pilot at Ljungbyhed. But his interests had influenced the smaller brothers who liked to build model planes and often looked at the sky for clouds. So also this day. "We had sat down to drink coffee. It was 23–24 degrees Celsius in the shade and just a few clouds were in the sky," remembers Kjell who was 14 years old at the time of the incident.

Kjell Danielsson in the field where he and his young brothers saw the strange object.

Suddenly we discovered something we thought was an aeroplane low at the southwestern horizon. It went right against the wind and rather high up, and sometimes it twinkled as if it had moved, maybe rotated. Sometimes it disappeared for a short while behind a cloud.[20]

What the boys saw they later described as a large metallic canister for milk, a bit thicker at one end. The object traveled from horizon to horizon for at least 20 minutes before it disappeared in the northwest. "We stood looking at the shiny object for rather a long time," the other brother, Dan Danielsson tells, as he remembers what trouble they had convincing their father that they should continue observing the strange "aircraft" instead of going back to work.[21]

The three brothers tried their best to catch some sound from the craft that shone like aluminum in the bright sun, but a noisy haymaking machine in a field close by made it impossible to hear. Kjell asked the farmer to turn off his machine for a while but the farmer refused. Just after 11:30 a.m. the "milk can" disappeared out of sight. And after that things began to fall out of the sky.

To Knut Lindbäck and his maid Beda Persson, this Friday was a day filled with work. They and many others were engaged in haymaking. Knut and Beda were working on one of Lake Kölmjärv's banks. It was 11:45 a.m. and almost lunchtime when they and several others heard a humming sound from the sky. "Since I thought it was an aircraft I looked up," Knut told Clas Svahn 40 years later. "But instead I saw a rocket-like object crashing right into the lake. A high splash rose into the air when the object hit the surface and was soon followed by another cascade as if something had detonated."[22] An ash-grey rocket-like object had not only crashed into the lake but also detonated. On the other side of the lake was Frideborg Tagebo. This 14-year-old girl was cleaning the house as her mother was washing clothes down by the lakeside.

Knut Lindbäck

Suddenly we heard a roaring thunder as from an engine. My mother yelled to me to close the windows. She thought it was a heavy storm coming. Then there was a loud bang as coming from an explosion and I saw a huge splash of water out in the lake. Our dog went mad and ran away. Afterwards there was a total silence and we could see a lot of debris floating on the surface of the lake. The sound was terrible; I have never heard anything like it.[23]

Soon after the crash Knut Lindbäck took a small rowing boat and went out to the site of the impact. The grey "rocket" had crashed a little more than a half a mile away, close to the southwest bank. "When I arrived at the spot I saw seaweed and water lilies that had been torn up with their roots from the bottom and thrown on the bank. The water was muddy with clay and it was impossible to see if there was something on the bottom," Knut related later. "There is no doubt that it was a solid object. It was about two yards [two meters] long, had a stubbed nose while the end was pointed. I thought I saw a pair of small wings on both sides, but I am not absolutely sure. Everything happened so fast."[24]

The incident shook the whole village. Had a bomb exploded out on the lake? Beda Persson walked, as did many others, down to the shore to look at the point of impact. She could see mud thrown up on the banks.[25] Frideborg Tagebo also remembers the effects of the "ghost bomb." "But all we could see was seaweed and water lilies floating on the water."[26] The roots of the water lilies torn off were thick as a wrist. The same evening the police and local home guard posted people around the lake, after a neighbor had phoned the chief of police. The order was to secure the area and guard the point of impact.

On Saturday morning of the 20th of July, Lieutenant Karl-Gösta Bartoll from Boden engineer troops (Ing 3) received a phone call from Colonel Wilhelm Dahlgren and was ordered to leave as quickly as possible for Kölmjärv. In a hastily written order Bartoll was dispatched: "Leave as quickly as possible on motorcycle for Kölmjärv and investigate the possibilities to salvage a 'ghost bomb' that reportedly has fallen down in Kölmjärv," it said. Suddenly things were turning serious.[27] At 2:30 p.m. Lieutenant Bartoll arrived at the spot and six hours later the salvage party, which at this point consisted of seven men, had already searched an area of 430 square yards around the point of impact.

On that same day engineer Roland Rynniger and laboratory technician Torsten Wilner from the Defense Research Department (FOA) also arrived with a portable instrument for detecting radioactivity. It could not be ruled out that the rocket had been carrying radioactive material.[28]

Lieutenant Karl-Gösta Bartoll on Lake Kölmjärv in July 1946.

Karl-Gösta Bartoll's investigation of the lake was very thorough. Not only the bottom of the lake but also its surroundings were searched inch by inch, as the object might have bounced after impact and ended up in the woods. The work usually began shortly before eight o'clock in the morning and was not ended until approximately six o'clock in the evening. Sometimes the work went on even longer, as everybody was keen to find the fallen Ghost Rocket. From the beginning the search was conducted from a small rowing boat, but on the 29th of July the military began building a raft. From there it was possible to see that mud and stones from deeper layers had been forced towards the surface. Everything pointed to an underwater explosion. "They built the raft on the shore," Rune

Lindbäck, the neighbor who first contacted the authorities, relates. "They carefully avoided using nails of metal that could disturb their sensitive equipment." The raft was tied together with ropes.[29] To facilitate the search, the lake was divided into squares. Ropes were tied between the shores and then the equipment was hauled slowly over the bottom. Every square inch was to be searched. At regular intervals samples of the bottom were taken. But in spite of 35,000 samples brought to the surface, no traces of metal were found.

Rynninger and Wilner put forth a theory that the Ghost Rocket had had a nuclear power source onboard. The small size would be proof of that, the two scientists argued. "If the projectile really was so small [around seven feet] it seems hard to explain that with ordinary fuel it had been able to complete the range that could be presumed," they wrote in their report after coming back to Stockholm.[30]

The search in the lake was soon to draw the attention not only from the people living there but also from others. "Already after a few days at the lake our men discovered a couple of mysterious people who stalked the woods," Karl-Gösta Bartoll tells. Soon afterwards Bartoll discovered that the telephone that was used to report to the staff in Boden was out of order. "When we checked the line it was discovered that someone had cut it off with a pair of pliers. It went so far that we finally dared not to use the telephone to report to the staff in case we were tapped. Instead we were forced to send our results by ordnance."[31] In Stockholm the members of the Ghost Rocket committee met to discuss the incident at Kölmjärv just three days after it happened, but there are no indications in the secret documents that the sabotage of the telephone wires was ever discussed.[32] Between the July 15 and December 10, the group held twelve meetings where records were taken, and at several occasions they sent personnel to interview witnesses and investigate the point of impact. Thirty-three pieces of alleged debris from the Ghost Rockets were analyzed, all with natural explanations.

The incident at Kölmjärv was one of several, but probably the one judged to be most important. For a while consideration was given to emptying the entire lake to find the mysterious rocket. The proposal to drain the lake was put forward by Colonel Dahlgren at Ing 3 at Boden and it was discussed in detail in the group. But at a meeting at the Air Staff on the 10th of August, it was agreed that it would be too expensive – at least 3,000 US dollars.[33] Instead hopes were placed in a detector constructed for finding mines. If the object had been made of iron, the instrument would react. But it was not that simple; the deep mud on the bottom of the lake made the search problematic. "We started out with the detector on the raft, but the results were poor," said Karl-Gösta Bartoll. "The lake was two meters deep at the point of impact and it was simply too deep to get a reading."

On the 1st of August specialists from the mine company Boliden came to the lake, bringing with them a new kind of apparatus for spotting ore, the equivalent of the metal detectors of today. With the new instrument Bartoll and his team found a gas apparatus and other objects of iron that had been thrown in the lake during the winter, but no rocket.[34] But the media wanted the Ghost Rocket to be found. Only a week after the crash, the Swedish newspaper *Dagens Nyheter* wrote: "The rocket that some time ago hit Lake Kölmjärv, 15 kilometers [9 miles] north of Överkalix, has been found, according to reliable sources. The message could however not be confirmed Sunday evening due to a fierce thunderstorm that broke the telephone lines to Kölmjärv."[35] The authorities denied the rumors, and in a telegram distributed by Swedish wire service TT they stated that no "ghost bomb" has been found: "The lake is shallow but the bottom has a thick layer of mud that makes it difficult to salvage the projectile. If it can be found. The rumor this Sunday that it had been surfaced is therefore totally unfounded."[36]

It was not only the Swedish media that closely followed the search in Kölmjärv and the ever increasing reports of unknown rockets. As early as July the British Embassy sent some of their staff, privately, to the Finnish Island of Åland to see if any launch facilities could be found that could explain the rocket sightings. But in a short memorandum it was stated that no such facilities, suspected to be of

Russian origin, had been found. Similar actions were taken regarding possible rocket stations at Darlowo and Ustka at the Polish Baltic Sea region.[37] During the summer of 1946 contacts were held between the Swedish Chief of Combined Intelligence Board and the British military attaché to Stockholm. An agreement for complete cooperation between the two countries was made on July 12, and three days later the Swedish Air Force supplied complete analytical reports of all observations to date; they also made a request for radar equipment and other technical requirements. The Swedish requests were immediately sent to the Air Ministry.

The co-operation between Sweden and Britain was working smoothly and had as a goal to make British radar available to the Swedes together with experts running them. Squadron Leader Barrie Heath and Major Malone of the War Office landed in Sweden on July 18 for a stay ending nearly two weeks later to make a first contact. Fleet, a Wing Commander for Britain, was sent as a liaison to spend a week with the Finnish General Staff. In Oslo, British Ambassador Laurence Collier sent regular dispatches regarding the Norwegian approach to the Ghost Rockets to Robin Hankey, head of the Foreign Office's Northern Department, which also included Russia. On August 12 another high ranking officer from the Royal Air Force landed in Sweden, as Wing Commander B. J. Jennings started to scout for possible sites to locate the British radar equipment, and found two potential sites at the island of Gotland not far from the Baltic area. All this was done under the cover of Britain sending experts to get the radar equipment for the newly purchased Vampire aircrafts up and running.[38]

On July 21 the Swedish General Staff decided to reopen a series of radar stations used during the Second World War. Though several echoes were registered, no information that could reveal the source behind the unknowns was found (this could very well be attributed to old and not very reliable radar).

The Swedish military wanted to keep the Swedish-British contacts private. In a telegram from the British Embassy in Stockholm to the Foreign Office in London dated 27 July 1946, the Air Attaché writes that the Swedish Air Staff has requested that "all possible measures" should be taken "to prevent the Americans finding out about Swedish co-operation" with the British. But some information did leak. A top-secret report from the American Naval attaché in London to the Chief of Naval Intelligence stated that Sweden had handed over to the British Air Ministry several pieces of material suspected to have come from the Ghost Rockets. The analysis did not show anything that gave evidence to the theory that the Ghost Rockets were guided missiles.[39]

During these preparations a special group of men and equipment called Task Force 196 had started to assemble in Britain, ready to sail to Sweden on August 22. But just days before Wing Commander Jennings' arrival in Stockholm the British Air Attaché met with the then-acting Chief of the General Staff Colonel Count Thord C:son Bonde, who told him that the British Task Force could not leave at this point due to political considerations. On August 16 an embarrassed Colonel Bonde told the Air Attaché Group Captain Henderson that Swedish Prime Minister Per Albin Hansson, after a meeting with his cabinet, had decided to suspend the Task Force. A definitive decision, after another cabinet meeting, was given to the British Air Attaché on August 21, just hours before Task Force 196 was to have left for Sweden. In a bitter note, scribbled on a handwritten summary over the Prime Minister's decision dated August 30, someone had written: "Mr. Jerram has seen this dispatch and agrees that the Swedish Prime Minister has been both stupid and cowardly."[40]

The events that stirred greatest interest among the British were the Kölmjärv, Vassarajärvi and Kattisträsket crashes—all three in lakes. But the British Military Attaché was not impressed by the Swedish operation: "There has been no progress in the recovery of the missiles at Kalix. In all, three lakes are involved in previous incidents and latest report is of missile falling in the sea nearby, depth of water just over 3 feet (one meter). It must be appreciated that Swedish methods of operation are extremely slow and probably unproductive. Recovery operations are uninspired, radar reports are highly inaccurate."[41]

Interest regarding the Ghost Rockets did not only come from Great Britain but also from the United States. Through their military attachés in Stockholm and elsewhere in Europe, a steady stream of summaries and dispatches was sent back to the Navy, Army, and Air Force. In a French report, translated by the American Naval attaché in Paris and prepared for the French president dated August 13, 1946, it is stated that "a good number of these projectiles are of the V-1 type in the form of a torpedo with two small wings," and a map shows those rockets coming from the Leningrad (St. Petersburg) and the Baltic area. On the same day, several Swedish Air Force officers were interviewed by the Naval attaché in Stockholm and all of them stated clearly that they believed the intrusions to be real and with rockets.[42]

Left: General Edwin K. Wright
Right: General Douglas MacArthur

The United States concern went right to the top. On August 1, Assistant Director of Central Intelligence, Colonel Edwin K. Wright, sent a memorandum to President Truman[43] shown on pages 22 and 23. When General James Doolittle, in his capacity as Vice President of Shell Oil Company, visited Sweden for a couple of days starting August 20, his visit created much speculation. An article in the *New York Times*, quoted in Swedish press,[44] said that the General was to examine the Swedish radar systems used for trying to locate Ghost Rockets. General Doolittle arrived together with another WW2 legend, British Group Captain Douglas Bader, and later the same day, independently from the others, another WW2 celebrity General David Sarnoff. In an interview in the newspaper *Expressen,* Doolittle commented briefly on the Ghost Rockets: "I have only seen a couple of reports about your Ghost Rockets and I have no real idea of what they are. But it would be very interesting to observe one," said the General.[45]

General James Doolittle

General David Sarnoff

But soon a rumor started to spread that General Doolittle's trip to Sweden was a cover up for helping the Swedish military with those investigations. This was denied by the Chief of the Defense Staff, Major Curt Kempff. In a private letter to the Swedish military attaché in Washington, Colonel Arvid Eriksson, Kempff described how the British Military attaché in Stockholm, Major de Salis, had shown him a dispatch from de Salis' colleague in Washington. That dispatch clearly indicated that General Doolittle, during his visit a couple of days earlier, had contacted Major Kempff and forwarded some information regarding the Ghost Rockets. The Major denied this claim as he explained during a telephone call from a Swedish-speaking *Washington Post* journalist and had asserted that he knew that General Doolittle wanted to share some information with the Swedes. Kempff promised to forward this information to Air Force Commander General Bengt Nordenskiöld, who was to have lunch with Doolittle. But Nordenskiöld, who asked Doolittle if he had information to

UNCLASSIFIED

1 August 1946

MEMORANDUM FOR THE PRESIDENT

Subject: "Ghost Rockets" over Scandinavia

1. Since 25 May there have been occasional press reports of "ghost rockets" seen passing over points in Sweden. On 19 July two such "rockets" were reported to have fallen in Norway. The Swedish and Norwegian Governments have now imposed a news blackout with respect to the subject.

2. Official sources, principally the Military Attache at Stockholm, have confirmed these reports and obtained additional, but inconclusive, information. Although ten such missiles have fallen within Sweden, the Swedish General Staff has as yet been unable to reach firm conclusions on the basis of the fragments recovered.

3. From the information presently available, the Director of Intelligence, WDGS, has concluded that:

    a. The missiles are of the jet-propelled V-1 type (rather than rockets).

    b. They contain only small demolition charges (for self-destruction) rather than a warhead.

    c. They outrange the V-1. This result could be achieved by construction from light, non-ferrous materials, and by the substitution of additional fuel for the heavy warhead. It could also be achieved by the use of a turbo-jet engine such as the Germans were developing at the close of the war. German scientists in Soviet employ are capable of completing this development, and the characteristic noiselessness reported supports the supposition of its use.

    d. Their course is apparently controlled, either by radio or pre-set controls. (Turns and circular courses have been indicated).

    e. Their launching from some Soviet-controlled point

 UNCLASSIFIED

in the vicinity of the Gulf of Finland is probable.

4. Since the interior of the U.S.S.R. affords areas suitable for extensive and undetected experimentation, the launching of these missiles over Scandinavia must be a deliberate demonstration for political effect. In this, the Soviet objectives might be:

a. Intimidation of Sweden and Norway, by a demonstration of their vulnerability to attack with such missiles.

b. Intimidation of Great Britain, by demonstration of the vulnerability of the United Kingdom to such attack from continental areas which the Soviets now control or are capable of seizing.

c. Intimidation of the United States by a demonstration of Soviet capabilities for the scientific development of new weapons.

FOR GENERAL VANDENBERG:

E. K. WRIGHT
Colonel, GSC
Executive to the Director.

forward, later reported that Doolittle's answer, "to his surprise," was that he did not have anything to say regarding that matter.[46]

Since then the rumor has been published as a fact in several UFO books[47] and is still widely believed. In 1984 Doolittle answered UFO researcher Barry Greenwood in a letter that he had "no firm knowledge of actual rockets or 'ghost rockets' in Sweden" and referred to press reports as his primary source.[48] Swedish UFO researchers and experts on the Ghost Rocket phenomenon, Anders Liljegren and Clas Svahn, summarized their findings regarding the Doolittle visit in an article in *UFOs 1947–1997*: "Had there been any truth in the rumors about an active exchange of information between Swedish authorities and the two semi-military American generals, both by this time supposedly out of active service, we would have expected to find some indication in the Confidential and Secret Swedish correspondence files we have inspected. We found none."[49]

At Kölmjärv no one was uncertain about what they were seeking, but time was running out. Bartoll led the search for the object until the 12th of August; then the search had to be terminated. After three weeks of hard labor, with rests only on Sundays, the lake had been searched with no tangible results. 2000 square meters a day had been covered in the search for the elusive rocket. The hunt for what once was described by the chief of the Air Force Major Nils Ahlgren as "the safest indication of a crash" had yielded nothing.

While the search at Kölmjärv was drawing towards an end, more "Ghostbombs" were waiting to be rediscovered. Three additional objects had also fallen into lakes on the same 19th of July 1946. At 11:30 a.m., fifteen minutes before the crash at Kölmjärv and just after Bengt Danielsson and his brothers had seen the strange metallic object vanishing behind the tree line in Bölebyn, eleven-year-old Kurt Larsson sat fishing by a stream at the north end of Lake Kattisträsket, 40 miles (50 kilometers) further north from Bölebyn. His father, Börje, and a friend were working 300 meters away. "Suddenly I heard a roaring sound as when a storm is coming," Kurt Larsson stated. "Today I would compare it to a modern jet plane."[50] Kurt looked up to see if the treetops were moving, but everything was calm. Instead a huge column of water rose out of the lake a few hundred yards in front of him. "All I saw was a 15 yard high water column thrown up from the water. It was as if you had detonated a mine." Kurt left his fishing rod on the shore and hurried to his father, while yelling "The devil is in the lake!" convinced that something very bad had happened. Both Kurt and his father were later questioned by military from Boden. But the lake was too muddy for a diver to enter. With the help of a ten-yard-long pole it was decided that whatever had fallen from the sky was embedded in at least five yards of mud.

Within fifteen minutes after the Danielsson family had lost the metallic canister out of sight, two objects had fallen into the lakes of Norrbothnia. And the day had just begun.

At 3:00 p.m. Karl and Tyra Axberg were sitting on the porch of their sporting cabin when they heard a loud noise like a motor coming from above. Visiting were their daughter Ulla and a friend, telephone operator Hildur Frid, who also had a cabin in the vicinity. The powerful sound seemed to come from the west and the party decided to run to the lakeside, where the view was better. But when they arrived, the strange sound had stopped and all was quiet. "Suddenly something gained speed in the reeds not far away and went off to cross the lake," Ulla Axberg relates, the only one of the four who was still living in 1985. "At first I thought it was a bird but the speed was far too high."[51]

In a report written a few days after the incident, Chief of Staff Lieutenant Nils Winstrand, who visited the place and interviewed the witnesses, states: "The projectile seems to have come in on a very low altitude and hit the water in roughly a 30 degrees angle…the object continued 200 yards under water where it seems to have sunk."[52] In his report Lieutenant Winstrand writes that the object had sounded like a flying grenade during its descent and that the speed had been so high that a wind had shaken the bushes closest to the lakeside. Winstrand poked at the bottom with long poles, finding nothing but mud.

In the middle of August, two days after concluding his search at Kölmjärv, Karl-Gösta Bartoll arrived at Vassarajärvi. For eight days he and ten conscripts led by a sergeant searched the part of the lake where the object had been seen sinking. But once again a search for a "ghost bomb" turned out to be fruitless.[53]

The eventful day of July 19 was not over. Forty minutes after the crash at Vassarajärvi, an almost identical incident took place by Lake Marmen 560 miles further south. At 3:40 p.m. Ingrid Hansson, 22, lay sunbathing on a floating jetty in front of a cabin at Sunnanå by the northern end of the lake. Her father, Olov, lay right beside her. "At first I heard a violent roaring over the water like a strong gust of wind was coming but did not see the object until it reached the surface. When I looked up I saw an object bouncing over the surface along the lake. It kind of rolled over the water and stirred up a wake."[54] Ingrid was so frightened by the incident that she ran from the jetty up to the cabin. Since the family did not have a telephone in the cabin, Olav waited a few days before contacting the military. In a report written on the 23rd of July by Captain E. E. Karlström, chief of staff at the regional military headquarters in Gävle, the drama is evident:

> The projectile created a water column 22 yards [20 meters] high. In connection with the impact an explosion was heard after which vapor followed. Following that the projectile moved on, sometimes above the water, sometimes in the water. The water was colored black during the motion of the projectile.[55]

In just a couple of hours, five unidentified objects had been seen from five different locations in Sweden, four of them crashing into lakes. What was the cause? Undoubtedly the majority of the reported "Ghost Rockets" from 1946 were meteors mistaken for something else, especially when they were reported at night. But the events of July 19 did not fit that description.

Surprisingly, one of the best known Swedish astronomers of the time, Knut Lundmark at the observatory in Lund, sided with the view that it was military projectiles since meteors are seldom seen in daylight and rarely observed crashing to the ground. Professor Bertil Lindblad at Saltsjöbaden observatory was of the same opinion. "The great amount of observed phenomena during May and June confirms in my view that these cases cannot be meteors, but that we have here projectiles of some kind," he writes in a letter to the Department of Air Defense at the General Headquarters in Stockholm.[56] But the experts could not agree. The chief of the artillery school at Rosersberg, north of Stockholm, Colonel Sven Ramström, declared that the bombs were nothing but meteors. Whatever it was that crashed into the lakes, it left no tangible traces. A few cut off water lilies, seaweed, and a pit at the bottom were the only material evidence of the extraordinary events.

The July 19 events were strange, especially when compared to one of the Nazi rockets that crashed on Swedish soil during the Second World War, launched from Peenemünde. On June 13, 1944, a V-2 rocket (also called A4 in Germany) crashed near the village of Bäckebo, north of Kalmar in the southeastern part of Sweden. After a thorough search, 2,200 kilograms of debris was collected and pieced together. A detailed report was made by Henry Kjellson and Eric Malmberg, both prominent in the Ghost Rocket investigations two years later. How this, at the time, brand-new technology could produce more than two metric tons of metal fragments in the summer

V-2 Rocket debris found near Bäckebo

of 1944, when the "rockets" of 1946 never left a single scrap of metal, was one of the many unsolved questions that the Ghost Rocket committee discussed.[57]

In a final report to the High Commander, the Ghost Rocket Committee stated that 225 reports had been made in full daylight and that the objects were real. More than 100 of these reports described spool shaped items with or without wings.[58] In the report the committee also notes that about 100 crashes had been reported during 1946. However, that figure does not correspond with actual crashes but to cases where observers had seen something coming down from the sky and therefore assumed to have hit the ground further away. Many of these "crashes" were without doubt night-time meteors.

During the first phase of the Ghost Rocket wave and as late as August, most military sources both in Sweden and abroad, saw the most likely solution to the Ghost Rocket enigma to be found in Russia. The Swedish position, even though not expressed in public, was that the rockets were intended as a political move to intimidate the Swedish politicians and sent over Sweden by the Russian military. In the United States the recently appointed head of the newly formed Central Intelligence Group (which in November 1947 was to be transformed into the CIA), General Hoyt Vandenberg, told President Harry Truman that the Ghost Rockets were likely Soviet missiles launched from Peenemünde.[59]

Even if the Ghost Rockets never were identified, the Swedish Defense establishment never doubted that there really had been intrusions over the Swedish border. In a draft of the report to the Supreme Commander, Karl-Arvid

General Hoyt Vandenberg

Norlin from the Royal Air Material Command suggested the following, writing to Major Frank Cervell: "There is no doubt that foreign experiments with jet propelled or rocket weapons have been going on over Sweden." It was deducted that these weapons belonged to a wholly new generation of military systems. "The projectiles are steerable, either by autopilot, and then with a preset trajectory or steered by radio with radio impulses from a ground station perhaps with television or by a pilot in the projectile."[60]

But the final report, made later in December and containing 987 total reports, was more skeptical: "Despite the quite extensive effort, which has been carried out with the means available, and seven months after the first observations, no actual proof that a test of rocket projectiles has taken place over Sweden has been found."[61] The Swedish investigation committee recognized the problems with eyewitnesses but stressed that even though many of the observations could be attributed to fantasy and misinterpretations, there still were several observers whose reliability could not be put into question. This problem was also discussed by the British, since no hard evidence had materialized in spite of so many reports.

In a secret report made to summarize the activity over Scandinavia prepared by the British Air Ministry for a wide range of branches within the ministry, embassies and several

The Ghost Rocket files were kept secret for 40 years. "Contains Secret Documents" is glued on the

military branches in early September 1946 took the eyewitnesses into consideration. The report stated that it was unlikely that the objects reported during daytime had been total misinterpretations since experience from Britain during the war showed that "very rarely did even untrained observers report seeing non-existent objects in the air during daylight." And if the phenomena observed were of natural origin, "they are unusual; sufficiently unusual to make possible the alternative explanation that at least some are missiles. If this is so, they must be of Russian origin." That being said, the report also concluded that the total of genuine reports of would-be missiles would amount "to but a few."[62]

When 1946 drew to a close, the Ghost Rocket scare was over, but observations of missile-shaped objects passing over Sweden, investigated by the military, continued for decades. A definite answer to the Ghost Rockets was never found.

*The Ghost Rocket files are now
kept at the Swedish War Archives.*

Notes

[1] *Norra Västerbotten*: "Mystiskt ljus över Malmö," 8 January 1946.
[2] E. Rosborg to Kungliga Luftfartsstyrelsens trafikavdelning, report, 9 February 1946; *Umebladet*: "Meteorregn över Västerbotten," 22 February 1946; and several other newspapers.
[3] *Landskansliet i Örebro*, 21 June 1946, C46 A 14-2.
[4] *Morgon-Tidningen*: "Fjärrdirigerade bomber spökar lite varstans," 26 May 1946; *Aftonbladet*: "Nattarbetare sökte skydd för 'raketbomben' i Landskrona," 25 May 1946.
[5] *Aftonbladet*: "Spökraket jagades i bil genom Roslagen," 28 May 1946.

[6] Stabsorder nr. 19, Morjärvs försvarsområde 16/6 1946.

[7] Kungliga flygförvaltningen, Materielavdelningen MEH 412:11, 11 July 1946.

[8] Erik and Åsa Reuterswärd, interviews with the author 14 August and 5 December 1986 and several letters. Eric Reuterswärd passed away 21 February 2002.

[9] Eric Reuterswärd to The General Staff's Air Defense Department 11 July 1946.

[10] Major Nils Ahlgren to Erik Reuterswärd 9 August 1946.

[11] Major Nils Ahlgren to AB Bofors 5 August 1946; Bofors AB to Major Nils Ahlgren 7 August 1946.

[12] Professor Bertil Lindblad to Major Nils Ahlgren 2 August 1946.

[13] Gösta Skog, interviews with Clas Svahn, 11 August 1984, 16 August 1984 and 11 May 1990.

[14] Gunnar Irholm, interviews with the Clas Svahn, 25 April and 20 May 20 1986.

[15] Löjtnant G. Irholm med rapport om flygande projektil to Försvarstabens Luftförsvarsavdelning 14 August 1946.

[16] Eric Malmberg, interview, 13 May 1986.

[17] Interviews with Gunnar Irholm by Clas Svahn, interviews 25 April and 20 May 1986.

[18] "Protokoll från sammanträde i FF den 23/6 1946 betr projektiler över Sverige," Swedish War Archives.

[19] Henry Skaug, telephone interview with the Clas Svahn, 3 February 1987; and Åse Tandberg, telephone interview with the author, 2 February 1987.

[20] Kjell Danielsson, telephone interview with Clas Svahn, 13 June 1984; and a personal visit with Kjell at the observation site on 20 June 1984 and 20 September 1992.

[21] Dan Danielsson, telephone interview with the Clas Svahn, 23 August1997.

[22] Knut Lindbäck, interview at his house by Clas Svahn in Luleå 9 May 1984.

[23] Frideborg Tagebo, telephone interview by Clas Svahn, 13 June 1984.

[24] Knut Lindbäck, interview at his house by Clas Svahn in Luleå 9 May 1984.

[25] Beda Persson (married Johansson), telephone interview by Clas Svahn, 13 May 1984.

[26] Frideborg Tagebo, telephone interview, 13 June 1984 and a visit to Lake Kölmjärv together with her 19 September 1992.

[27] Colonel Dahlgren to Lieutenant Bartoll, handwritten order, still kept by Bartoll.

[28] Roland Rynniger and Torsten Wilner, "Undersökning vid förmodad nedslagsplats för raketprojektil i Kölmjärv," 3 September 1946; now kept at the Swedish War Archives.

[29] Rune Lindbäck, telephone interview, 11 May 1984.

[30] Roland Rynniger and Torsten Wilner, "Undersökning vid förmodad nedslagsplats för raketprojektil i Kölmjärv," 3 September 1946; now kept at the Swedish War Archives.

[31] Karl-Gösta Bartoll, interview at his home 21 September 1992.

[32] Protocols from the meetings of 22 July and 29 July, kept at the Swedish War Archives.

[33] "Protokoll fört vid konferens vid FF beträffande prj över Sverige," 5 August 1946; and "Konferens i FF den 10/8 1946 betr projektiler över Sverige," 10 August 1946. Documents kept at the Swedish War Archives.

[34] Karl-Gösta Bartoll, telephone interview, 21 May 1984 and a personal interview at his house 21 September 1992.

[35] *Dagens Nyheter*: "Rykte i Kalix, bomben funnen i Kölmjärvsjön," 29 July 1946.

[36] *Norrbottens-Kuriren* 30 July 1946 and several other newspapers.

[37] Rocket Projectiles in Scandinavia, N9876/G, all Ghost Rocket files from the Public Records Office could be found in the following files kindly sent to Archives for UFO Research by Dr. David Clarke: FO 371/56988, FO 188/537, FO 371/56951 and FO 188/572.

[38] Public Record Office FO1881537.

[39] "Alleged rockets over Sweden," report from the Naval attaché in London dated April 8, 1947, SC-7301.

[40] Public Record Office FO371156951.

[41] British Embassy in Stockholm to Foreign Office in London, telegram, N9737.

[42] Intelligence Report from the Naval attaché in Paris 13 August 1946, NARA, Serial 39-S-46 and Intelligence Report from the Naval attaché in Stockholm, NARA, Serial 36-S-46. Documents found by Jan Aldrich.

[43] Edwin K. Wright to President Harry Truman, memorandum, subject: "Ghost Rockets over Scandinavia,"1 August 1946, FOIA request to the USAF.

[44] "Doolittle studerar bara bruket av vår ekoradio," *Dagens Nyheter* 14 August 1946.

[45] *Expressen*: "Doolittle skall bara prata bensin – har hört om spökbomber," 21 August 21 1946.

[46] Curt Kempff to Arvid Eriksson, private letter, 30 August 1946, Swedish War Archives, Försvarsstabens Utrikesavdelning BI:1 Vol 1. In a despatch from the British Chargé d'Affaires in Stockholm dated 28 August 1946 he states that when discussing this question with Colonel Kempff the Colonel indicated that he had brought the subject up with Doolittle and Sarnoff and that they both said that they had no knowledge of the subject. General Nordenskiöld is not mentioned in this text. But, as the Chargé d'Affaires notes, there could be some confusion due to Colonel Kempff's "rather tortuous English." Public Record Office FO1881572.

[47] David R. Saunders and R. Roger Harkins, *UFOs? Yes!*, Signet 1968, p. 54, and David Jacobs, *The UFO Controversy in America*, Indiana University Press, p. 36.

[48] *Just Cause*, Number 24, June 1990, p. 8.

[49] Hilary Evans and Dennis Stacy (eds): *UFOs 1947–1997*, Butler and Tanner 1997, pp. 35–42.

[50] Kurt Larsson, telephone interview, 7 October 1984; *Norrbottens-Kuriren*: "Ytterligare en rymdprojektil ner i Norrbottenssjö" 22 July 1946.

[51] Ulla Axberg (Czajkowski), telephone interview, 6 May 1985.

[52] "Rapport över verkställd rekognosering i Gällivare 23/7," Swedish War Archives.

[53] "Dagbok för sökningsarbetena vid Vasaraträsk i trakten av Gällivare tiden 12/8–19/8 1946", Swedish War Archives.

[54] Ingrid Hansson (married Zander), telephone interview, 16 September 1985.

[55] E. E. Karlström, "Rapport angående iakttagen raketliknande projektil," 23 July 1946. Swedish War Archives.

[56] Bertil Lindblad to Department of Air Defense 6 July 1946. Swedish War Archives.

[57] Henry Kjellson and Eric Malmberg , "Beskrivning av brännare eller reaktionsaggregat använt i tysk lufttorped och i tyska reaktionsbomben Hs 293," 9 December 1944; Henry Kjellson and Eric Malmberg , "Redogörelse over den tyska A4-raketen, V2," 7 January 1946. Swedish War Archives.

[58] A Secret draft made by Karl-Arvid Norlin 3 December 1946, now in the Swedish War Archives.

[59] Top Secret Memorandum for the President, 22 August 1946 made by the National Intelligence Authority, kept at National Archives, Washington D.C., Admiral William D. Leahy files.

[60] Karl-Arvid Norlin to Major Frank Cervell,3 December, with a draft of the final report. Swedish War Archives.

[61] VPM beträffande rymdprojektiler över svenskt territorium, December 1946. Swedish War Archives.

[62] "Investigation of Missile Activity over Scandinavia," 9 September 1946, prepared by A.D.I. (Science) and A.I.2. (g). Document found by Don Berliner at Smithsonian Institution's National Air and Space Museum.

Chapter 3: The Flying Disks and the United States

Describing the impact of the UFO phenomenon on the governmental agencies of the United States, and their consequent response, is a difficult and complex task. The task differs from that of the previous chapter due not only to Sweden's relatively small size and clear organization, but also because of the much greater openness of Swedish authorities to researchers seeking historical documents. So, with the United States' situation, we must proceed with greater humility in our analysis, saddled as we are with the confusion of those early days, and the (frankly, still puzzling) lack of cooperation from the government in making those documents available to historians now 60 years later.

Nevertheless, many things can be said which are helpful in understanding what occurred. The primary focus should be the great and common concern of all elements of our security apparatus with the potential of the Soviet Union to create the atomic bomb and some missile system to deliver it. That worry lent urgency to the whole ghost rocket episode. For example, when the great U.S. wave of "disk" sightings occurred in June and early July of 1947, the Wright-Patterson AFB Chief of Intelligence, Howard (Mack) McCoy, immediately asked the Pentagon for their ghost rocket files. He received at least 44 documents, none of which have yet been released to modern investigators.[1]

Howard (Mack) McCoy

Unidentifiable violations of U.S. airspace were potentially matters of the highest importance. Because *all* elements of the security apparatus were concerned with whether unidentified aerial objects were related to the Soviet threat, all elements became involved. Early on, it was not only Army Air Force business, but the Navy considered UFOs its business as well. We can remember that most of our ghost rocket intelligence had come from naval attachés in places like Stockholm. That continued to happen wherever the Navy was the primary agency on the spot. Also, if there were a possible connection to Soviet spy mischief within the United States, the FBI was very anxious to get its agents on the case.

Early in the post-war era our intelligence coordination ranged from primitive to non-existent. People in high places scrambled to correct that fault. President Truman was about to initiate a National Security Act that would, he hoped, create a functioning Central Intelligence Agency (CIA) to replace the inadequate Central Intelligence Group (CIG).[2] "Joint Committees" were established among the military services. One such group, the Joint Committee for Communications Electronics, was tasked to set up the JANAPs (Joint Army Navy Air Force Publications) that would set policy for handling the transfer of information, etc., between the often non-cooperating services. We will address the JANAP system in more detail later. Suffice it to say for now that the information transfer and sharing situation in 1947 was poor, and left much to the personal judgments of authority figures in the different agencies or even at sites (such as regional offices or bases) within a single agency.

The part of the scientific community still involved with military and security matters was equally concerned with Soviet weaponry and its potential. In fact, every memoir and document points to the conclusion that, despite being "scientists," they were much more focused on what their work meant in *security* terms, than on how it advanced some more idealistic vision of "science." There were three primary areas of focus: a) atomic energy, and attention to facilities like Hanford in Washington, Oak Ridge in Tennessee, and a complex of areas in New Mexico; b) aerotechnology and missiles, with attention to Wright Patterson AFB, Muroc AFB, the California aerotech industry, White Sands Proving Ground, and the rocket technology of Patuxent Naval Base in Maryland; c) the lack of an "early warning" detection net (like the later DEW line of radar stations). It was "atomics," "missiles," and "airspace violations."

The list of background factors against which the flying disk wave burst onto the scene could be quite long, but with these next two psychosocial matters, we can stop and get to the phenomenon itself. The first of these might be called the "Aura of the Scientist" in the post War era.

Of the many things that changed after WWII, one subtle but non-trivial change was the collective attitude toward scientists held by ordinary citizens in technologically developed countries. Respect was transformed into awe fretted with fear. The reasons were not a mystery. Scientists made the Bomb, unlocking and releasing the power of the atom on a previously unimaginable scale. They made machines that flew faster and higher and had a seemingly limitless power to destroy. They created devices that seemed to think, solving problems that humans could not. It began to seem as if nothing was beyond their abilities. The Bomb was made in just four years: what would be the next breakthrough, and when would it come?

The image of the scientist was no longer that of a quirky loner working obsessively in a garage or laboratory like a minor Frankenstein. The scientist came to be pictured as a potentially dangerous intellectual stalking the corridors of power in the Pentagon or the Deep Black laboratories of government installations—a genius, perhaps naïve, perhaps uncaring, but frightening when empowered by government money and resources. Was the scientist the driver not only of new technologies but new policies as well? Vannevar Bush, emblematic of the new cadre of technocrats who applied wartime science to military and economic matters, certainly thought so.[3] In the future, only elite scientists would be able to understand the complexities of the world sufficiently to guide ordinary—and ignorant—citizens, politicians, and militarists according to their best interests. *Many* people in government and the military detested that elitist attitude, but they also had a grudging respect for these "egg-heads." If they made the Bomb, after all, what else might they create?

Vannevar Bush

This emotional situation played into military psychology and undoubtedly had a role in how the intelligence community viewed the UFO phenomenon in the war years, but especially in the years just following. When UFO encounters were "new," no one could reasonably be expected to have a good handle on them. They were simply mysteries, and, as far as the actual consequences of their actions were concerned, apparently, benign. As the wave of sightings began in the United States, military intelligence was caught off-balance—its "collections" and "analyses" were still relatively rudimentary. During those first few years following the war, very few government operatives could have known enough to realize, that without a doubt, these things could not be foreign technology. We, today, realize that the reports repeatedly exhibited characteristics far beyond the point our technologies had reached at the time. Back then, this was much harder to see. And, over it all was the new Aura of the Scientists—who could say what "they" had achieved?

As a final "preliminary" observation, we, the American people, are, of course, peculiar ourselves. As far as security matters are concerned, we are, and were, rather obtuse. Barring Pearl Harbor, which occurred a great distance away, America had not had a serious enemy incursion in living memory. We were not exactly careless in 1947, but we had just won the war, and we were the Big Kid on the block. This meant that we had a country in which the citizenry and the security agencies were not always of the same mind. Add to this the radical democratic character of the nation, and the result is a citizenry which thinks it should be able to ask questions of any of its governmental agencies and get "straight" answers, or tell those agencies to "buzz off" unless given an extremely clear reason not to do so. Those attitudes emboldened the American press to ask, even demand, answers to what was, in the minds of security personnel, utterly none of their business. And a speculation: we do not know what the general opinion was (in the agencies) of the emotional stability of the public. Some seemed to think the general populace were so naïve and unhardened enough by the real world as to be ripe for hysteria and panic. What then to say to these people? How does one properly manage the news?

Although June 24 and the famous case of civilian pilot Kenneth Arnold flying near Mt. Rainier is the date set in historians' minds for the beginning of the great wave of unexplained reports in 1947, occasional encounters had been occurring for some time. An example worth mentioning, because it became of interest to the intelligence community, was the Richmond, Virginia, case of April 1, 1947.[4] There were actually several incidents involving the U.S. Weather Bureau station there in the spring of 1947. On at least three occasions, observers from the station, after having released weather balloons and beginning to track them, had seen another object in the sky which they could not explain. These were mentioned by the trackers to co-workers and superiors, but whether any formal notice was made is not known. In April, one of these personnel, Walter Minczewski, saw another of the objects and placed his balloon-tracking theodolite (a very manuverable sighting telescope sometimes equipped with a camera and used to sight balloon and missile launches) on the mystery "whatever-it-was." Minczewski reported what he saw to his superiors and did not pursue the issue any further. The Weather Bureau, some time after the UFO wave began getting national publicity months later, apparently (we do not know the specific transfer of information) dusted off the report and sent it to the Air Force, whereupon it became part of the investigation.

What the Air Force's Project Blue Book files say about the case is this:

Incident No. 79 —— April 1947, Richmond, Virginia.

A weather bureau observer at the Richmond Station observed on three different occasions, during the six-month period prior to April, 1947, a disc-like metal chrome object. All sightings were made through a theodolite while making pibal [pilot balloon] observations.

On the last reported sighting, the balloon was at 15,000 feet altitude, the disc followed for 15 seconds. It was shaped like an ellipse with a flat level bottom and a dome-like top. The altitude and the speed were not estimated, but the object, allegedly through the instrument, appeared larger than the balloon.

Another observer at the same station saw a similar object under corresponding circumstances, with the exception that her balloon was at an altitude of 27,000 feet and possessed a dull-metallic luster. There was good visibility on days of observation. Report of this sighting was not submitted until 22 July 1947.

AMC Opinion: There is no readily apparent explanation. If there were only one such object, it seems amazingly coincidental that it would be seen four times near the pibal of this station only. On the other hand, there would have to be a great number of these objects to rule out coincidence, and as the number of objects increases so do the chances of sightings by other witnesses.

Project Astronomer's Opinion: There is no astronomical explanation for this incident, which, however, deserves considerable attention, because of the experience of the observers and the fact that the observation was made through a theodolite and that comparison could be made with a pibal balloon. The observers had, therefore, a good estimate of altitude, of relative size, and of speed – much more reliable than those given in most reports.

This investigator would like to recommend that these and other pibal observers be quizzed as to other possible, unreported sightings.

This incident (actually a series of incidents) concerned those persons in the Air Force who did not want to believe that some kind of unknown aerial technology was invading U.S. airspace. It is the first recorded instance of a puzzling feature of the flying disk phenomenon in the United States: whatever these things were, they were reported many times approaching balloon project launches, hanging about for a while, and then rapidly leaving the scene. Because the observers were just about the best-trained people to distinguish between known objects in the skies, their testimonies were difficult to discount. The Richmond sightings were brought up several times in official government documents in the next two years.

But Mr. Minczewski and his colleagues were not thinking of flying disks in April of 1947. They, and everyone else, began doing so in late June. The reason was the aforementioned Mt. Rainier case of June 24.[5] Kenneth Arnold, a private pilot flying out of Idaho, was aloft in the vicinity of Mt. Rainier when he witnessed the passage of nine, highly reflective, low-aspect (thin disk-like) objects hurtling at roughly mountaintop elevation towards the southeast. He had time to conduct several simple experiments to assure himself that he was not seeing reflections, that the objects were moving very quickly, and also roughly to judge speed and distance. It was an impressive sighting, especially given that well over a dozen other reports came in from that Washington-Oregon area that same day, and one seems to be very close in time, place, and detail.

Kenneth Arnold

We can only speculate as to why this particular case began an avalanche of reports and press coverage. Part of the answer is Kenneth Arnold himself. He was a deeply concerned patriot. He thought perhaps these things were not our planes, and it was his duty to report all he could about them. He had a strong and likeable personality, and the press responded to his story. But the Air Force did not. For whatever reasons, the governmental agencies were not yet concerned. Arnold himself got so upset about their lackadaisical behavior that he wrote a lengthy letter to the Air Force over a week later pleading with them to pay attention to his and other peoples' observations.[6] We do not know why the government was so slow to react. Perhaps it was just that Arnold, although a pilot, was "just" a civilian. Even Mt. Rainier's general closeness to the Yakima firing range and, to its east, the Hanford Atomic Works, rang no alarms. The main cause of the slow reaction may simply be that our agencies were just very poorly organized and uncoordinated in 1947.

Sometime between June 25 and July 4, the Air Force (until July 26, 1947, called the Army Air Force) began to pay attention. On the 27th of June there was a cluster of seven sightings in New Mexico.[7] Most of these concerned a silver or aluminum "streak" or a flash in the sky. One pilot described a ball of fiery blue, which moved 2000 feet *below* his plane, and then disintegrated. Despite the oddness of that report, the commander at White Sands Proving Grounds announced that all observations were of one or more meteors. The next day brought a report from four Air Force officers at Maxwell Field in Montgomery, Alabama. The following is a reproduction of the document. The original document is difficult to read but is included in the appendix:[8]

SUBJECT: Report of Unusual Celestial Phenomenon

TO: Assistant Chief of Staff, A-2
        Headquarters Tactical Air Command
        Langley Field, Virginia

1. The following report is submitted concerning an unusual occurrence observed by the following AAF Personnel at Maxwell Field, Montgomery, Ala. On the night of 28 June 1947:

      CAPT. WILSON H. KAYKO, 0-38841, Hq, TAC
      CAPT. JOHN H. CANTRELL, 0-255404, Hq, TAC
      1ST LT. THEODORE DEWEY, 0-2094172, Hq, TAC
      CAPT. REDMAN, Randolph Field, Texas

2. At approximately 2120 Central time, a light, with a brilliance slightly greater than a star, appeared from the West. It was first noted above the horizon of a clear moon-light night, traveling in an easterly direction at a high rate of speed. There was no audible sound and it was impossible to determine the altitude, except that it appeared to be at great height. It traveled in a zig zag course with frequent bursts of speed, much like a water bug as it spurts and stops across the surface of water. It continued until it was directly overhead and changed course 90° into the south. After traveling in the above manner for approximately five (5) minutes, it turned southwest and was lost in the brilliancy of the moon. At 2145 Central it was no longer possible to observe it.

3. A call was placed to Maxwell Field operations reference this phenomena and inquiry made if any experimental aircraft were scheduled for a flight in the vicinity. The reply was negative.

4. No plausible explanation is offered for the unusual action of this source of light, which acted contrary to any aerodynamical laws.
This report is submitted upon request, in view of the many recent reports reference unusual [?] aerial objects observed throughout the U.S.

5. Two of the above noted observers are rated pilots and the other two are air intelligence officers. All observers were cold sober.

This case did get the attention of the Pentagon, and was used in later estimates.[9] Perhaps the reason is that it involved their own people.

A day later, three rocket experts employed by the Naval Research Laboratory's Rocket Sonde Section (at White Sands, NM), and one of their wives, saw a round, reflective object moving at great speed but undetermined height. It "simply disappeared" as they watched. The rocket experts felt that it was neither missile, plane, balloon, nor meteor, all of which were familiar to them.[10] Admiral William Blandy, commander of the Atlantic Fleet, gave this puzzling comment of the event: "I have no idea what they might be. I am very curious about them and I do not believe that they exist."[11] An Army Air Force press release said that citizens could be assured that the disks were not enemy secret weapons, Army Air Force (AAF) projects, or "spaceships." The Director of the Naval Research Laboratory (the boss of the rocket experts above) quickly concurred with the AAF statement. As an aside, the AAF stated that no saucer had ever been detected by radar. That was false, at least since July 1.

At this moment a powerful authority figure, who would (several times) be quoted scoffing at the "saucers" as nonsensical figments of our imaginations, entered the drama. Brigadier General Roger Ramey, chief of the 8th Air Force in Fort Worth, Texas, and his chief intelligence officer, Colonel Alfred Kalberer, held a press conference.[12] Referring apparently to Kenneth Arnold's sighting, but making a general comment, Ramey thought people "have been seeing heat waves." (This press conference was occasioned by another burst of reports in Texas. Citizens all across the country were getting concerned and writing to authorities—air bases, the FBI, the Pentagon, even political representatives around this time.) Kalberer said nothing about heat waves, but did label the flying disk business as "Buck Rogers stuff" (i.e. fantasy), and implied that Arnold probably just saw a few ordinary planes. To cast the Air Force's statements into relief, an Oregon minister announced that the disks proclaimed the End of the World. Neither form of emotionalism is, of course, helpful in getting a handle on the problem.

Orson Welles

The next day Kalberer was back at it again with an astronomer (Oscar Monnig) in tow. The astronomer, freely moving outside his area of expertise, said this was merely "an interesting study in human psychology." In fact, he and a Los Angeles colleague had laughed about Kenneth Arnold's report and predicted a wave of hysteria. Kalberer was right behind him, mentioning the Orson Welles *War of the Worlds* hysteria and comparing flying disks to sea serpents.[13] That day, July 1, Hokkaido, Japan, the radar at Chitose AAB "picked up a target at 16 miles, speed in excess of 500. This target split up into two targets, each larger than a P-51." A follow-up report has been reproduced on page 36 for ease of reading.[14]

July 1 allows us to reflect a bit. The "external" (public) comments from the military are already quite different from the "internal." At least some elements of the military are worried and serious, but they do not want the public to be. This Janus-faced dichotomy is natural and understandable. Under the circumstances, one might even call it honorable—people doing their duty as they honestly see it. But it does not make for an *accurate* understanding of the situation for those on the "wrong side of the mirror." This "they do not need to know" philosophy, which is one of the foundational operating principles of the intelligence community, has been extremely successful in clouding the UFO issue up to the present, especially as we have never had (in the U.S.) the type of information releases that our Swedish colleagues have enjoyed.

Extract from 8 August 1947 MEMORANDUM FOR THE COMMANDING GENERAL, ARMY AIR FORCES from Major General George McDonald, Assistant Chief of Air Staff-2 [Intelligence], Subject: Top Supplement to Daily Activity Report - ACAS-2. TS Control # 2-258,

(TS) II. ITEM OF CURRENT INTELLIGENCE INTEREST

The following information from the Far East Command Teletype Conference, 7 August 1947, is supplementary to a previous item of interest. On 1 July 1947 a GCA operator at Chitose AAB, Hokkaido, reported that a target traveling at a speed in excess of 600 mph was observed and further that the target made four turns on the scope. The radius of the turns was one and one-half miles. The target heading when contacted was 100 degrees at range of 16 miles north of Chitose AAB. The target made a 180 degree turn to a heading of 0 (zero) degrees and remained on this heading to a range of 28 miles. At this point the target turned to the left to a heading of 240 degrees and traveled for a distance of 6 miles. It then made a 180 degree turn to a heading of 60 degrees. On this 60 degreee heading the target returned to its original point 28 miles north of the Chitose base to a heading of 0 (zero) degrees and traveled out of range.

(Evaluation: A-1; Completely reliable – Confirmed by other sources.)

A-2 COMMENT: This observation of target maneuvers establishes with certainly that the target is not a weather or other natural phenomenon as we now know natural phenomena. The only objects that could fit the observed facts are aircraft.

Any aircraft traveling at this speed would have to be [?]jet-propelled fighter type since there are no known bombers that could operate at this speed. One type of U.S.S.R. jet fighter has an estimated speed of 525 knots (605 miles per hour).

(Maj Farrier – Ext 71095)

Sometime near the beginning of July, Army Air Force Intelligence's Collections Division in the Pentagon became organized on the flying disk problem. The division's chief, Colonel Robert Taylor, and his main assistant, Lt. Colonel George Garrett, made this a focus issue with Garrett's desk as the collection point. Fairly quickly Garrett, with FBI liaison S.W. Reynolds, was actively receiving and attempting to assess reports.[15]

July 4 produced a flurry of activity on the West Coast, particularly around Portland, Oregon, where one incident, involving five police officers, impressed the Army Air Force once it finally reached them with formal interviews.[16] A commercial aircraft encounter over Emmett, Idaho, also made national news, mainly due to similarities to the Mt. Rainier case.[17] Air patrols were launched to see if any new encroachment could be purposefully confronted. No luck. Two persons claimed to have photographed the things: Yeoman Frank Ryman of the Coast Guard presented a bright spot on his film,[18] and smalltime

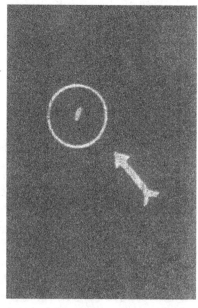

Yeoman Frank Ryman's Photo

engineering consultant, William Rhodes, offered two shots of a black, heel-shaped object.[19] Authorities paid a great deal of attention, ultimately, to the latter. Atomic Energy Commission chief David Lilienthal said the disks had nothing to do with any governmental atomic project. He had no idea what they were but "was anxious to know if any of them had fallen to the ground."[20]

Left: Secretary of State Dean Acheson
Right: AEC Chief David Lilienthal

The wire services that day carried a press release from Wright-Patterson AFB. It said the AAF was on the job and trying to resolve the mystery of the flying disks. It said that Wright-Patterson's engineering division had been specifically asked by Chief of Staff Spaatz to do this. The release added that the AAF had not found anything to confirm that the disks existed and they did not think that the disks were guided missiles. The AAF felt confident as to the latter because it had asked all its captured German technologists about it. The release ended with: "As things stand right now, it appears to be either a phenomenon or the figment of somebody's imagination."[21] The fact that this sentence bordered on nonsense did not seem to bother many people.

Over the next week the two most important aspects to the wave were that cases continued to pour in, and the citizenry began to show greater concern. Both factors put increased pressure on the authorities. There was a series of observations at Muroc AFB and also at the Rogers Dry Lake area, which was used for supersonic test flight work. One sighting was by aerotechnology legend John Paul Stapp who later set high acceleration records riding rocket sleds on the lakebed. Stapp said in his report: "I think it was a man-made object, as evidenced by the outline and functional appearance. Its size was not far from 25 feet with a parachute canopy."[22] [Stapp had said that when he first spotted the object, he thought it was shaped like a canopy. When it lowered and slowed, he described its shape as oval with two projections on the upper surface]. "The path followed by this object appeared as though it might have dropped from a great height."

John Paul Stapp

Another case, which impressed the Pentagon, was the observation of Captain James Burniston and his wife at Fairfield-Suisun AFB in northern California.[23] They described a highly reflective object moving at great speed. It had no wings or noticeable protrusions, but was apparently not a sphere, as it seemed to roll or wobble from side to side as it flew. It is interesting to note that this sighting took place on July 6, but the report did not reach Garrett's desk at the Pentagon until the 23rd of July. This is but one example of the lack of information transfer between different commands at this early stage. The Muroc cases, it appears, took even longer to arrive from California.[24]

The reports of cases had reached such a level (several "old" cases such as the White Sands rocket scientists' observation were just now making the newspapers) that many military personages were being asked about them.[25]

By July 12, the Pentagon's urgency to obtain interviews with the best observers had finally gotten through to the intelligence operatives scattered about the country. On that day, agents questioned both

Captain E. J. Smith (of the Emmett, Idaho case)[26] and Kenneth Arnold in different parts of the Pacific Northwest.[27] They were impressed by both men. One common feature in the interviews was not expected: both Smith and Arnold were already concerned about the ridicule that being a "flying object reporter" brought upon them. Arnold said he probably would not report even if he saw a skyscraper fly past him in the air. All these reports slowly made their way to Lt. Colonel Garrett's desk.

Citizens around the country were increasingly curious, and many were worried.[28] As to why, an example would be an eleven-case burst on July 6 in "Show Me" Missouri (eight cases were essentially simultaneous and by people independent of one another). An hour later, a seventeen-case burst occurred in Alabama. Military bases received calls and letters, as did the FBI. A young congressman from Texas, Lyndon Johnson, was questioned by a constituent, and followed up with a formal request for information from the Pentagon.[29] This started Johnson's long-term curiosity about these unidentified flyovers. Garrett was too busy, apparently, to reply to Johnson, so a Major wrote to him (through Chief of Staff General Spaatz) that:

1. The Army Air Forces is conducting an investigation of the alleged 'flying disks.' Detailed statements of credible witnesses are being carefully reviewed.

2. This investigation to date reveals no indication that the 'flying disks' are new or unusual missiles or aircraft.[30]

This answer was prepared for Johnson on July 21. As we shall soon see, statement "1" was true, and statement "2" was a lie.

It was a lie that was easy to believe, because it was backed by a growing set of comments by the authorities. USAF Research and Development, in the person of General Curtis LeMay, said the disks were nothing to worry about.[31] The top government scientist in the United States, Vannevar Bush, said the descriptions did not fit anything known and so did not deserve to be taken seriously. "They must be illusions." Merle Tuve, the military bigwig scientist who developed the proximity fuse for the atomic bomb, said if there were any developments going on anywhere like this, he'd have heard of them.[32] Therefore, by "logic," they did not exist. In the heart of the Pentagon, Lt. Colonel Garrett felt very differently.

One last case story and then we can peek into Garrett's mind: far western Newfoundland, July 9-11.[33] On three consecutive days, unidentified flying objects were reported in this remote area of Newfoundland dominated by Harmon Field. The reports sandwiching July 10 were viewed as supportive of the middle one, which came from Harmon Field itself. On July 10, three civilian aircraft mechanics were driving to work at the airfield when they spotted a disk tearing a hole in the cloud cover. The object was described as having the proportions of a wagon wheel and as being translucent—the later Air Force report said "silver." The disk emitted a bluish-black smoke trail that remained in the air for some time. As it passed, it cut a swath through the clouds and seemed to push them apart along a path 15 to 20 miles long. It continued on a straight course until out of sight. One of the observers, Robert Leidy, retrieved a camera once they got onto the field and took two pictures of the trail.

The local intelligence officer was quite excited by the case but, once again showing the disorder of the times, did not immediately pass the case on to Garrett at the Pentagon. A brief appeared in a *Weekly Intelligence Digest* on July 16,[34] and Garrett finally got a

General George Schulgen

report about a week later. Some discussion apparently occurred as to how this case had been treated, and around the 28th of July, an urgent order was received by the chief of intelligence of Air Materiel Command at Wright-Patterson.[35] Assistant Pentagon Director of Intelligence General George Schulgen told Howard McCoy to send investigators immediately to Harmon Field and to make a technical report. The investigators were to report directly to the Pentagon afterward, not returning to Wright-Patterson.

We have an unusual document from this very moment. On the orders transmission, McCoy had jotted a variety of notes demonstrating the pressure caused by the urgency of these events. He asked, *"What has Brentnall prepared? What has Clingerman prepared?"* Brentnall was Brigadier General Samuel Brentnall, the chief of the "T-3" top-secret engineering technology division at the base. Clingerman was Colonel William Clingerman, the number two intelligence chief (after McCoy) in the "T-2" division. McCoy expected these two heavy hitters to have ideas about this situation to add to the report-to-come. McCoy also wrote that they must interview a captured German scientist now working

Brigadier General   *Colonel William*
Samuel Brentnall   *Clingerman*

at Goodyear Corporation about Nazi capabilities with blimps or other lighter-than-air machines, possibly acting as "pick-o-back" (piggyback) carryalls for small disk craft on long flights. He also asked about certain jets and the trails they would make. Whatever else went on, in about a day Clingerman and a top assistant, Lt. Colonel E.G. Nabell, were flying to Newfoundland. There they interviewed two of the observers and confiscated Leidy's film.[36]

This report, and the interviews finally coming in from the critical witnesses like Arnold, E. J. Smith, James Burniston, and John Stapp, accumulated on Garrett's desk and motivated him to try to assess the flying disk situation (what the military calls "making an Estimate") and pass the information up the chain of command. (A copy is in this book's appendix.) Around mid-August, Colonel Garrett and FBI liaison S.W. Reynolds, who had been working closely with him, felt they had gotten somewhat of a handle on the matter. But they were extremely puzzled. The cases they were reviewing indicated an

FBI Liaison S. W. Reynolds

unusual aerial technology of at least one type, and, through the first weeks of July there had been intense pressure exerted down the chain of command ("from Topside") to get an explanation. But by late July and into August, that pressure had suddenly evaporated.[37] Why? Garrett and Reynolds felt they needed to know. The only thing they could think of was that some exceptionally secret U.S. technology was doing all this, and the news had finally been passed along to the Big Wheels topside. If so, why were Garrett, Reynolds, and the FBI wasting their time? Garrett prepared a condensed estimate stating his findings and requested that his superior, Colonel Robert Taylor, and Brigadier General Schulgen ask all the services if they knew about any project to explain all this.[38]

Included on the next page is Garrett's estimate as written for Taylor to pass on to Curtis LeMay at Air Force Research and Development. It serves to indicate the state of knowledge at that time.[39]

AFBLR-CO/LC 001 GARRETT

~~RESTRICTED~~

22 August 1947

Flying Saucer Phenomena

Deputy Chief of Air Staff for Research & Development

22 August 1947

AC/AS-2, Air Intelligence Requirements Division
    Collection Branch

Lt Col Garrett/nc/4544

  1. From a detailed study of certain reported observations on the flying saucers, selected for their veracity and reliability, it is apparent that several aspects of their appearance have a common pattern.

  2. Before pursuing its investigation of these objects any further, this Office requests assurance that no research project of the Army Air Forces, at present being test-flown, has the following characteristics and that it may therefore be assumed t   recent flying saucer "mystery" is not of United States origin:

    a. Surface is metallic - indicating a metallic skin, at least.

    b. When a trail is observed, it is a lightly colored blue-brown haze, similar to a rocket engine's exhaust. Contrary to a rocket of the solid type, one observation indicates that the fuel may be throttled, which would indicate a liquid rocket engine.

    c. As to shape, all observations state that the object is circular, or at least elliptical, flat on the bottom and slightly domed on the top.

    d. Size estimates place it somewhere near the size of a C-54 or Constellation as they would appear while flying at 10,000'.

    e. Some reports describe two tabs located at the rear and symmetrical about the axis of flight motion.

    f. Flights have been reported containing from three to nine objects, flying good formation on each other, with speeds always above 300 knots.

    g. The discs oscillate laterally while flying along, which could be snaking.

                    ROBERT TAYLOR 3RD
                    Colonel, Air Corps
                    Chief, Collection Branch
                    Air Intelligence Requirements Division
                    AC/AS-2

          471194 Rocket

~~RESTRICTED~~

LeMay took a week to reply: no such AAF project existed.[40] The other services said likewise. This situation—unusual and unknown aerial technology incursions coupled with the "silence from topside" —remains to this day a completely unexplained behavior.

Whatever his puzzlement, Garrett now felt that he had a technical problem on his hands: metallic disks of aircraft size, often flying in an oscillating manner and occasionally emitting a powered trail. This had become not just an intelligence collections issue but also an engineering analysis one. From this point (and this had begun rather as a matter of course earlier), the Air Force saw that it had a complicated task: a need for technology assessment wizards (that seemed to mean Wright-Patterson) and a need for "security" assessments (which seemed to mean the Analysis Division in the Pentagon). Robert Taylor and George Garrett were Pentagon Collections Division; they no longer met either vital criterion. So, in September, the flying disks problem shifted focus to these two new sites, sites that were rarely "on the same page" as to their goals or behaviors.

Information is incomplete about the personnel in the two locations and how they functioned, but enough is known to draw the outlines of the picture. This is especially true at Wright-Patterson. There, all the senior personnel were aerotechnology engineers.[41] National security was important, yes, but these people wanted to find out what the disks were and how they worked. One engineer who leaped at the chance to join the formative project was top airplane designer, Alfred Loedding.[42] Loedding knew viscerally that the disk-shape was an eminently flyable one if the proper power and stable configuration was obtained. He had, in fact, drawn up a patent for such a device.

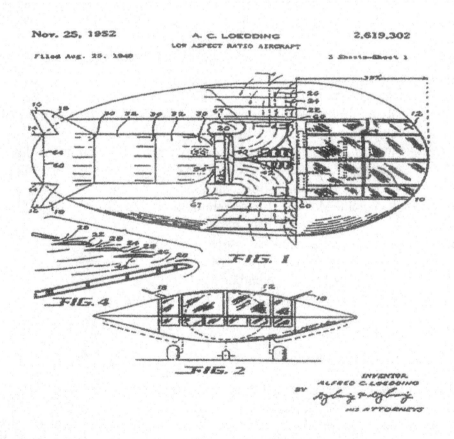

Alfred Loedding's Disk Shape Patent

Although headed by military personnel, the Wright-Patterson group was led by three civilian engineers: Loedding, Albert Deyarmond (a military buddy of Howard McCoy during WWII, recently retired from duty), and Lawrence Truettner, a missiles expert.

At the Pentagon we know less about the details of what was going on, but the attitude towards the disk problem was entirely different.[43] Once the location of the issue moved from the Collections Division to that of Analysis, the Pentagon psychology became almost entirely focused upon its normal business: threat to national security. *Were* these things threats? Were they Soviet? If not Soviet threats, then what were they? Were they what they seemed, or something less: a bogus display of a rudimentary technology meant to rattle the country? Or hoaxes perpetrated by spies or sympathizers? Was this a psychological thing more than a physical one? Was it, somehow, in the end, nothing at all? At the Pentagon some very hardline people adopted a serious and vigilant attitude towards the mystery. Brigadier General Ernest Moore had direct access to the Director of Air Force Intelligence on these matters. Below him, in the Office of Defensive Air analysis, a desk manned by Major Aaron (Jere) Boggs became the alert center for flying disk policymaking. We would like to know more of the mindset of these people at the time. We do not. An example: a very highly placed colonel in the analysis division, Edward Porter, over

Left: Albert Deyarmond
Right: Howard McCoy

the next five years consistently expressed a hostile attitude to the flying disks' mere existence which bordered on raw emotionalism.[44] What was motivating him? We have no idea; but it made a difference in the "corporate atmosphere" as to how the disk problem was discussed.

The formal establishment of a flying disk project at Air Materiel Command did not occur until January of 1948, but it had already happened in every other way by September of 1947.

1. George Garrett had made his first estimate around late August using sixteen or more cases (including Kenneth Arnold, Maxwell Field, White Sands, E.J. Smith, Fairfield-Suisun, Harmon Field, etc.). This estimate was distributed to military technology leaders who vowed that no such U.S. device existed.[45]

2. The Pentagon then decided, in September, to send their information to Air Materiel Command (AMC) to get another expert view. AMC Intelligence chief Howard McCoy convened a sort of think tank of the base experts. McCoy brought together the chiefs of the Engineering Division and several laboratories, plus the Air Institute of Technology, and Colonel Clingerman, his own number two. On September 23 they wrote back to the Pentagon (over General Nathan Twining's signature) that they agreed with everything in Garrett's analysis.[46] They led off with a new assertion, which Garrett may have thought was so obvious that it did not need saying: "The phenomenon reported is something real and not visionary or fictitious." (A copy of this document is available in the appendix.)

General Nathan Twining

3. Showing that plenty of conversation had gone on before sending this famous Twining memo, arrangements were being made the next day for a transfer of files from Garrett's office to Al Loedding at AMC.[47] Also relevant was the coincident Pentagon demand to receive AMC's information on Nazi aero technologists' (the Horten Brothers) experimentation with low-aspect (thin) roughly disk-shaped designs, plus Al Loedding's own disk-shape patent.[48]

Lt. Col. Malcolm Seashore

At the Pentagon, missile expert Dr. Charles Carroll was plotting trajectories of disk flights in an attempt to determine, as had been tried in Scandinavia, the flight origins of these things.[49] We do not have any information directly from his study. At Wright-Patterson, AMC project personnel were tasked with creating a list called "Essential Elements of Information" to be passed on to intelligence operatives worldwide. This "what to look for" EEI was extensive and written with possible ex-Nazi and Soviet technology in mind.[50] A member of McCoy's inner staff, Lt. Colonel Malcolm Seashore, hand-carried the EEI to the European commands. By December, now-Director of Research and Development, Curtis LeMay, wanted to know what was happening.[51] What had we learned? The Directorate of Intelligence responded with a new estimate based on Garrett's and McCoy's earlier ones.[52] (A copy of both the EEI memo to Europe and the Directorate of Intelligence memo are included in the appendix.)

This December 1947 estimate was passed by the eye of Robert Taylor in Collections but, in the new spirit of handling flying disk matters, was written by personnel in the Analysis Division. Still, at this point it agreed with both Garrett and McCoy. The estimate added new cases, especially radar trackings in the area of Japan, and noted that many cases had "several observers [corroborating] separate observations of the same phenomenon at the same time." Thirteen case briefs were given, with the writer particularly impressed by the second radar observation at Fukuoka, Japan:

> On 16 September, 1947, the same NEW radar at Fukuoka, Japan picked up a target at 89 miles and tracked it in to 19 miles, where it faded. Speed was 840 to 900 miles per hour. This observation indicates use of a homing receiver; fading at short range further indicates the possibility of good radar evasion technique. The speed measurement is believed accurate, since it was made by a good crew, through a 70-mile long track.

The memo went on to describe how experts had been quizzed across the board to eliminate balloons, U.S. aircraft, missiles, meteors, or hoaxes from the core data. And it continued to speak darkly of possible Soviet/Nazi technology.

One last thing should be described, as it relates to the problem of how to deal with the rambunctious American public. Dave Johnson was an assistant editor of a prominent Idaho newspaper, the *Boise Idaho Statesman*.[53] He came to know Kenneth Arnold, flew on patrols looking for the disks, and saw one himself on July 9. Obviously he was excited about the things. Johnson pursued flying disk stories as hard as any newsman, so when he heard in mid-November that the *USS Ticonderoga* had seen and tracked two objects by radar, he immediately wrote to General George Stratemeyer at Mitchell Field in New York (Air Defense Command in that era) for information and answers to a lot of rather pointed questions about what was occurring.

Stratemeyer saw this letter as a Pentagon problem, and sent it on. Johnson's questions were partly about the disks, but also partly about procedure. Since this latter had to do with Collections as well as public relations with possible reporters, the Analysis Division ducked and handed the job to their UFO veterans, Garrett and Taylor. On December 11, they wrote a memorandum to the Air Force's Public Relations office outlining the proper answers to such questions as Johnson's.[54]

Johnson asked eight questions. Because the Air Force reply was the first formalized attempt at information management, we can give them a grade on it:

1. Have you come to a conclusion on the source of the disks? *Ans: No.* (True.)

2. Are you convinced such objects are flying above the U.S.? *Ans: No.* (We probably should give them a "false" here as all three military estimates said differently.)

3. Have you investigated reports in the last 2 months? *Ans: Yes.* (True.)

4. Has Army radar ever tracked objects? *Ans: No.* (False.)

5. What is the form of your investigations? *Ans: Interviews of responsible persons.* (Partly true, but recall photos, Carroll's plotting, etc.)

6. Is it possible disks are foreign? *Ans: Yes.* (True, given what they knew.)

7. Could they come from ex-Nazis in Spain (a current rumor)? *Ans: Highly improbable.* (True.)

8. Should people still report? *Ans: Yes.* (True.)

We can give them five full and one half-truth for honesty, and 2½ falses. About 70% in the pursuit of truth. As to doing their jobs, concerning national security and population psychology management, we might give them straight A's.

As 1947 ended, the situation was that almost everyone involved thought the disks were real, and agents were out worldwide looking for more information. The Russian-Nazi "solution" seemed remote, but the only one thinkable. The "spaceships" idea was in peoples' minds but hardly discussable. The theory that this was some type of psychological warfare weapon of the Soviets had some credibility. Far-Eastern radar cases were particularly troublesome.

As a sign-off note: even the Air Force had no concept of the extent of the phenomenon. For 1947, their project knew of less than 100 cases.[55] When UFO researcher Ted Bloecher made a piecemeal survey of regional newspapers, he found approximately 850.[56] When UFO historian Jan Aldrich followed Bloecher's lead years later, that number rose to over 3,000 incidents.[57] And those were just cases reported. Dr. J. Allen Hynek, who was to become Air Force astronomical consultant to the project in 1948, used to ask audiences in his lectures to stand if they had seen a UFO. Many would. Then he would say: all who did *not* report it, please sit down. Over 90% sat. Hynek said this was common. However many cases are read in governmental or news publications, or civilian research files, there are nine times more that are hidden.[58]

Roswell

Because the "Roswell event," the notion that the Army Air Force retrieved a crashed flying disk or parts of one during the summer of 1947, has become so fascinating for everyone interested in UFO phenomena (whether they credit the story or not), we cannot fail to mention it.

There are a few things about the event which no one denies. In the first week of July 1947, the military commander of Roswell Army Air Force base, Colonel William Blanchard, announced to newspapers that the base had "come into the possession of a flying disc." The disk was recovered from "a ranch in the Roswell vicinity" by an intelligence officer, Major Jesse Marcel, who retrieved it after he visited the ranch with a detail from the base. Roswell AAF learned of the object when the ranch caretaker informed the local sheriff, George Wilcox. The sheriff's office notified the airbase. The story flew from local papers onto the national stage: "RAAF captures Flying Saucer on Ranch in Roswell Region" proclaimed the headline.[59]

It is also undeniable that within a few hours, Air Force higher command in the person of General Roger Ramey, commander of the Eighth Air Force in Ft. Worth, Texas, released a second story: the "flying saucer" was just an ordinary weather balloon and radar reflector. This counter-story was punctuated by a press conference featuring an embarrassed Major Marcel posing with an ordinary piece of balloon debris. This time the papers blared: "Ramey Empties Roswell Saucer."[60]

That is how the Roswell incident remained for a long time, an item of folklore forgotten even by the UFO community. Over the years, civilian UFO researchers received a steady trickle of unsupported claims that there had been a crash, usually located in "the late 40's" and "the Southwest desert," most often and more specifically, New Mexico. But few gave the stories credence.

The next undeniable element of the event occurred in the late 1970s. An older and apparently irritated Major Jesse Marcel went public with his side of the story. It is generally agreed that he was indeed the Major Marcel at the base who had been detailed to pick up the debris and called to Ft. Worth to pose with the weather balloon. Marcel had been chewing on this embarrassment for more than forty years and wanted to get it off his chest. His uncorroborated story is different in many details from General Ramey's earlier explanation. His story involved no disk, only debris, but unusual debris with odd characteristics. Marcel said it was easily distinguishable from the sorts of things in ordinary balloons, including the one with which he was forced to pose by Ramey. Essentially Marcel accused the Air Force of covering up the truth, and he was angry at being made a scapegoat.

UFO researchers wondered what, if anything, of Marcel's story was true? The community split into factions that advanced different conclusions. Meanwhile, increasing numbers of people from the Roswell area came forward with tales that mostly supported Marcel.[61] Some additional details came from other military sources. Some were hoaxes or lies; some seemed legitimate. The story became large and complex, difficult to track, with dozens of disparate elements. No author or researcher has presented a single, clear, understandable analysis of all essentials.

As the story evolved into the late 1980s and 1990s, the preponderance of "evidence" was (as usual with UFO reports) in the form of witness testimony. All of it taken together suggested that *something* unusual had left widely scattered debris on a ranch north of Roswell. While dismissed as inconsequential by many persons heavily invested in interpreting this event, that conclusion is not trivial.[62] Regardless of the real nature of the debris, it is significant that there is a consensus the Air Force *did* cover *something* up, created a bogus press conference, and embarrassed the base's leading intelligence officer. So *whatever* happened on the debris field must have been sufficiently serious to require a "Big Lie" to cover it.

Readers may decide for themselves. Was the Roswell event a secret Air Force project, a weapon, a Soviet device, an alien spacecraft—or a big X? To assess the various testimonies is beyond the scope of this book, and more importantly, government documents related to this case are conspicuously absent or of dubious authenticity, and this text is concerned only with a well-documented historical narrative.

Notes

[1] Letter, H .M. McCoy, Colonel, Chief of Intelligence to Chief of Staff, United States Air Force, attention: Lt. Col. George Garrett, 23 January 1948; and reply, Douglass W. Eiseman, Lt. Colonel, Executive, Air Intelligence Requirements Division to Commanding General, Air Materiel Command, attention MICA (sic: should be MCIA for McCoy's chief of Intelligence Analysis, Colonel William Clingerman).

[2] Michael J. Hogan, *A Cross of Iron: Harry S. Truman and the Origins of the National Security State 1945-1954*, 2000.

[3] Vannevar Bush, *Modern Arms and Free Men*, 1949.

[4] *SIGN* microfilm Roll 2; also J. Allen Hynek, "Final Report, Project 364," Appendix B in *Unidentified Flying Objects: Project Grudge* (henceforth "Grudge report;" and James McDonald archives, University of Arizona, Tucson, Arizona.

[5] Blue Book microfilm Roll 1.

[6] Blue Book microfilm Roll 1.

[7] Grudge report; also, Ted Bloecher, *Report on the UFO Wave of 1947*, 1967.

[8] Blue Book microfilm Roll 1.

[9] AFBIR-CO (Pentagon designation of Lt. Col. Garrett), "Flying Disks" (an analysis of 16 cases), 30 July 1947, FOIA request to FBI; also, Robert Taylor (written by Garrett) to Deputy Chief of Air Staff for Research and Development, subject: "Flying Saucer phenomena," 22 August 1947, and George McDonald (written by Lt. Col. Thomas) letter to Director of Research and Development, subject: "Analysis of 'Flying Disc' Reports," 22 December 1947, FOIA request to USAF.

[10] Blue Book microfilm Roll 1.

[11] Newspaper report of 1 July 1947 (*Roswell Morning Dispatch*, Roswell, New Mexico), as quoted in Loren Gross, *UFOs: A History*, supplemental notes for 1947, June 24-July 6, 2000. Because of the value of Loren's chronicle of directly quoted primary sources, we will refer to his work often. For shorthand, these citations will read: "Gross," followed by the date of the chronicle volume or supplemental notes.

[12] Gross, supplemental notes (1947, June 24-July 6), *Matador Texas Tribune*, 3 July 1947.

[13] Hadley Cantril, *The Invasion from Mars*, 1940.

[14] Major General George McDonald memorandum for the Commanding General, Army Air Forces. Subject: Top Secret Supplement to Daily Activity Report – ACAS – 2. TS Control # 2-258. 8 August 1947.

[15] This will be a rather generic reference, but a necessary one. There will be occasions where there are statements made in the text which relate to subtle or complex "organizational" matters, and, sometimes even, "apparent attitudes." Particularly with regard to the Pentagon, there is seldom a simple definitive reference document for things such as this. The understandings expressed in the text come from reading the bulk FOIA releases, and piecing together "who was doing what" and what their tendencies were in handling their parts of the UFO issue. In the case of Taylor, Garrett, and Reynolds at this point in the text, the facts as stated are quite clear from documents obtained from the FBI through the FOIA, as well as reading Taylor's and Garrett's work, passim, in the documents from the Air Force Intelligence Directorate in the Pentagon.

[16] Blue Book microfilm Roll 1.

[17] Blue Book microfilm Roll 1.

[18] Bloecher, Section IV, 3-4.

[19] Blue Book microfilm Roll 1.

[20] Gross 1947, *Denver Colorado Post*, 4 July 1947.

[21] (Newspaper story) Dateline: Wright Field, Ohio, 3 July 1947, *San Francisco Examiner*, 4 July 1947.

[22] Blue Book microfilm Roll 1.

[23] Blue Book microfilm Roll 1.

[24] Blue Book microfilm Roll 1.

[25] Newspaper story: "Disks Discounted: Blandy Wants to See Disks before his Eyes," *New York Times*, 8 July 1947; Newspaper story: "Army says what Disks are NOT," *New York Times*, 8 July 1947.

[26] Blue Book microfilm Roll 1, Frank M. Brown, 4th AF, "Memorandum for the Officer in Charge," 16 July 1947.

[27] SAC San Francisco to D. M. Ladd, office memorandum, subject: "Flying Disks," 28 July 1947, FOIA (FBI).

[28] Grudge, and Bloecher.

[29] Lyndon Johnson to the War Department, 8 July 1947, FOIA (USAF).

[30] Lt. Colonel Douglass W. Eiseman to AGAO, memorandum, subject: "Information Regarding the Flying Disks," 21 July 1947, FOIA (USAF).

[31] Gross 1947, *Chicago Daily Tribune*, 7 July 1947.

[32] Gross 1947 Supplement: July 7 to July 10, *Amarillo Times*, 10 July 1947.

[33] Blue Book microfilm Roll 2.

[34] Blue Book microfilm Roll 2 (In Harmon Field file), extract from Weekly Intelligence Summary, ATC, 16 July 1947, "Flying Objects Reports Summary."

[35] Blue Book microfilm Roll 2 (In Harmon Field file), untitled copy of telegram concerning Harmon Field case upon which Colonel McCoy is noting his immediate action needs in response to the notice.

[36] Blue Book microfilm Roll 2 (In Harmon Field file), W. R. Clingerman and E. G. Nabell, Intelligence Investigation Report, 1 August 1947.

[37] E. G. Fitch to D. M. Ladd, office memorandum, subject: "Flying Discs," 19 August 1947, FOIA (FBI).

[38] General George F. Schulgen to Director, Federal Bureau of Investigation, 5 September 1947, FOIA (FBI).

[39] Lt. Colonel George Garrett, apparent draft summary, "Flying Disks," 30 July 1947, 7 pp., FOIA (FBI); and Robert Taylor to Deputy Chief of Air Staff for Research and Development, memorandum, subject: "Flying Saucer Phenomena," 22 August 1947, FOIA (USAF).

[40] Curtis LeMay to Air Intelligence Requirements Division, note, subject: "Flying Saucer Phenomena," 29 August 1947, FOIA (FBI and USAF).

[41] Blue Book microfilm Rolls 1, 2, et al. passim; plus Ruppelt.

[42] Michael D. Hall and Wendy A. Connors, *Alfred Loedding and the Great Flying Saucer Wave of 1947*, 1998.

[43] FOIA request to the USAF, documents passim; plus Ruppelt; and Michael D. Swords, "Project Sign and the Estimate of the Situation," *Journal of UFO Studies*, N.s. vol. 7, 2000: 27-64.

[44] Edward J. Ruppelt (file of character descriptions of prominent figures that he knew in Air Force intelligence), File #R022 of the Ruppelt archive (currently held for the UFO Research Coalition by Michael D. Swords).

[45] Garrett draft, FOIA (FBI).

[46] Lt. General N. F. Twining (actually written by Colonel McCoy) to Commanding General, Army Air Forces, Washington, DC, memorandum, subject: "AMC Opinion Concerning 'Flying Discs'," 23 September 1947, FOIA (USAF).

[47] Lt. Colonel Douglass W. Eiseman to Commanding General, Air Materiel Command, Wright Field, Dayton, Ohio, memorandum, subject: "Reported Sightings of Flying Discs," 21 September 1947, FOIA (USAF). There are, in fact, a series of sparsely written documents from the beginning of September through the 24th that speak of information exchange, mainly from the Pentagon to AMC.

[48] H. M. McCoy to Commanding General, Army Air Forces, Washington, DC, memorandum, subject: "Flying Disk," 24 September 1947, FOIA (USAF).

[49] H. M. McCoy to Commanding General, USAF, memorandum, 18 November 1947, FOIA (USAF).

[50] Headquarters European Command to Counter Intelligence regions, memorandum, subject: "Essential Elements of Information," 20-28 October 1947, FOIA (USAF).

[51] George C. McDonald to Director of Research and Development, subject: "Analysis of 'Flying Disc' Reports," 22 December 1947, FOIA (USAF).

[52] Gross 1947, 73-74; and supplements, passim.

[53] Dave Johnson to Lt. General George E. Stratemeyer, Air Defense Command, Mitchell Field, New York, telegram transcript or letter, November 18 1947, FOIA (USAF).

[54] Robert Taylor to Director of Public Relations, memorandum, subject: "Flying Discs," 11 December 1947, FOIA (USAF).

[55] Grudge report; Blue Book microfilm Rolls 1 and 2.

[56] Bloecher.

[57] Jan Aldrich personal communication to Michael Swords.

[58] J. Allen Hynek to Michael Swords, personal communication. Note by Michael Swords: "I attended a lecture by Dr. Hynek in which he did this very thing, and he spoke to me about how common this behavior was at later times at the Center for UFO Studies."

[59] *Roswell Daily Record*, 8 July 1947.

[60] *Roswell Daily Record*, 9 July 1947.

[61] Kevin Randle and Donald Schmitt, *UFO Crash at Roswell*, 1991.

[62] Karl T. Pflock, *Roswell: Inconvenient Facts and the Will to Believe*, 2001.

Chapter 4: A Formalized UFO Project

The Status of the Problem

Going into 1948 and the formal working of Project SIGN, quite a bit of "orientation" towards the flying disk problem was established in Air Force intelligence officers' minds, at least in the Pentagon and at Wright-Patterson's Air Materiel Command (AMC). After all, four high-level opinions about flying disks had already been circulated. The first was Lt. Colonel Garrett's estimate in August of 1947. The second was Colonel Howard McCoy's famous Twining memo in September. A third was an update of the Twining memo by McCoy in October. The fourth was a Pentagon response (over Director of Intelligence George McDonald's signature) to General Curtis LeMay in December. This series of four opinions or estimates in five months attests to the fact that these disks were a problem in peoples' minds.

Within the estimates there was a uniformity of detail. *"Flying discs, as reported by widely scattered observers, probably represent something real and tangible."* The only uncertainty regarding the "probably" was that no one had been able to retrieve any piece of the things. Other than that, the widely scattered-ness (by which the estimators meant "independent" and, therefore, objective observations), and the quality of their military, civilian pilot, engineering and science-trained witnesses, put the reality of the phenomenon nearly beyond doubt. The facts of a new formal project plus an ongoing analysis desk (one at AMC and one at the Pentagon) testify that few thought this was nonsense.

As far as the source of the phenomenon was concerned, the Air Force came into 1948 thinking that the core cases were not our own devices, but, given the lack of trust between the services, one could not say for sure. The USSR was a better candidate, but that did not seem too likely either, even though it had to be viewed as the top priority suspect. Other "agencies" verged from the unlikely (an unsuspected and apparently *de novo* natural phenomenon) to the unthinkable (extraterrestrial craft). All these ideas and worse were in the mix early in the UFO game. Because the Soviet theory was primary, many intelligence operations felt that they rightfully should be involved. It is clear that both the Navy and the Central Intelligence Agency saw reason to stay alert to aspects of the phenomenon, and as we will see, did not quite trust the Air Force to do the best job.

Within the Air Force's (formerly the Army Air Corps) intelligence community, the newly declared independent force was trying to sort out its structures. Freedom of Information Act (FOIA) documents with information from this era show a surprisingly frequent change of chains-of-command reporting channels within the Pentagon and also at Wright-Patterson. Consequent alterations of the "alphabet soup" codes for offices and projects make unraveling what was going on difficult for the historian, and had to create at least a bit of confusion in terms of inter-office communications at this time.

The diagrams on the following two pages depict Pentagon and AMC channels of reporting as they appeared during one of the iterations of structure for the time period 1948 through 1949. They are included because they may indicate to some readers how it could be possible that different personnel, allegedly working within the same intelligence community, could end up working in opposition to one another.

At the Pentagon, General Hoyt Vandenberg had taken over from Carl Spaatz as Chief of Staff, and, as is usual, Spaatz' Director of Intelligence (George McDonald) was relieved, being replaced by General Charles Cabell. Just as important for our topic, although the Collections Branch of Intelligence Requirements still received and passed on UFO reports, the center of policy-making activity shifted to

*General Hoyt
Vandenberg*

General Charles Cabell

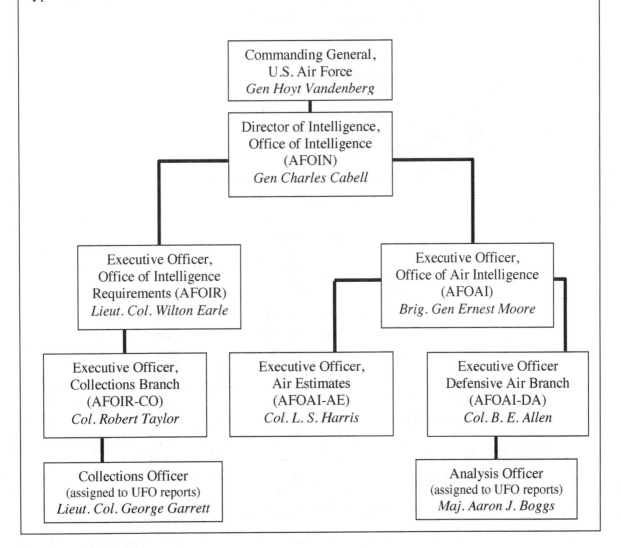

Organizational Chart, USAF Intelligence, ca. 1948

The Pentagon's Directorate of Intelligence was undergoing a reorganization in 1947-1952. Much change also occurred in the executive positions of the Air Force Office of Intelligence (AFOIN), AFOAI and its branches. The chart below is representative of the type of structure and staff as it was in the 1948 Project SIGN period.

Commanding General,
U.S. Air Force
Gen Hoyt Vandenberg

Director of Intelligence,
Office of Intelligence
(AFOIN)
Gen Charles Cabell

Executive Officer,
Office of Intelligence
Requirements (AFOIR)
Lieut. Col. Wilton Earle

Executive Officer,
Office of Air Intelligence
(AFOAI)
Brig. Gen Ernest Moore

Executive Officer,
Collections Branch
(AFOIR-CO)
Col. Robert Taylor

Executive Officer,
Air Estimates
(AFOAI-AE)
Col. L. S. Harris

Executive Officer
Defensive Air Branch
(AFOAI-DA)
Col. B. E. Allen

Collections Officer
(assigned to UFO reports)
Lieut. Col. George Garrett

Analysis Officer
(assigned to UFO reports)
Maj. Aaron J. Boggs

the "other side" of Air Force Intelligence, the Air Force Office of Air Intelligence (AFOAI), the analysis-and-response area.[1] Just as the diagram is split, we know that there was at least a tendency for Pentagon attitudes towards the flying disk phenomenon to be split, as well. Air Force Office of Intelligence Requirements (AFOIR) personnel like Garrett and Taylor had very few doubts about the concrete reality of the objects. They had been talking to and reading first-hand reports of witnesses. AFOAI tended to have more skepticism, perhaps putting more distance between themselves and what might be viewed as subjective elements in the reports. People like Moore and Boggs, and Colonel Porter (who does not appear in the abbreviated diagram) were on that side of things.[2] AFOAI was also the more paranoiac of the intelligence elements vis-à-vis the Soviet threat, as concern for that danger was their main goal.

At AMC, the situation is clearer and, for the most part, simpler. AMC's T-2 (Intelligence) Division had an existing structure into which Project SIGN fitted nicely as a special project. The military chain-of-command stack was in place and all that was needed was to assign an executive officer (Captain

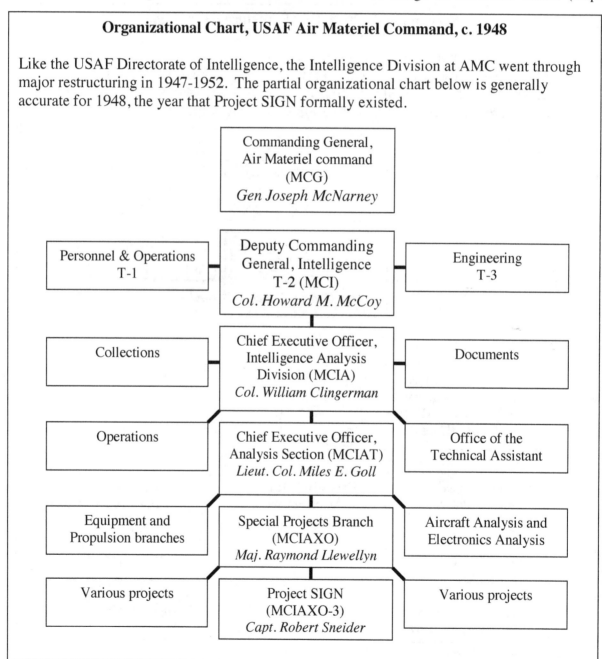

Organizational Chart, USAF Air Materiel Command, c. 1948

Like the USAF Directorate of Intelligence, the Intelligence Division at AMC went through major restructuring in 1947-1952. The partial organizational chart below is generally accurate for 1948, the year that Project SIGN formally existed.

Commanding General,
Air Materiel command
(MCG)
Gen Joseph McNarney

| Personnel & Operations T-1 | Deputy Commanding General, Intelligence T-2 (MCI) *Col. Howard M. McCoy* | Engineering T-3 |

| Collections | Chief Executive Officer, Intelligence Analysis Division (MCIA) *Col. William Clingerman* | Documents |

| Operations | Chief Executive Officer, Analysis Section (MCIAT) *Lieut. Col. Miles E. Goll* | Office of the Technical Assistant |

| Equipment and Propulsion branches | Special Projects Branch (MCIAXO) *Maj. Raymond Llewellyn* | Aircraft Analysis and Electronics Analysis |

| Various projects | Project SIGN (MCIAXO-3) *Capt. Robert Sneider* | Various projects |

Robert Sneider) and a few primary personnel.[3]

After that, the situation was very fluid. Unlike the Pentagon, engineers and technical support people from all over the T-2 division (and occasionally even T-3) could be, and were, utilized as need arose. One might regularly see chiefs of other branches of the division involved in cases and communications, as well as people right up to Clingerman's and McCoy's offices. The AMC situation involved a variety of engineering talent rather enthusiastically scrambling about looking for an engineering solution. It should not be a great surprise that two such groups (AMC T-2 and Pentagon AFOAI) having such different approaches, and consequently, closeness to the phenomenon, would come to dramatically different views.

The early months of 1948

One must begin with the famous Mantell case.[4] Despite an increasingly small possibility that we do not know exactly what happened here (i.e. a heroic pilot making a serious error chasing a top-secret high altitude balloon, and crashing his plane and killing himself), the case not only led off the year (January 7), but for a variety of reasons caused great concern within the military and without.

Thomas Mantell, an experienced and decorated pilot, was flying in a four-plane flight of Kentucky National Guard P-51s, when they were directed to an unidentified object high over the Kentucky-Tennessee border. The three other pilots did not pursue with the same vigor as did Mantell. For whatever reasons, Mantell believed that he could close on the object. He seemed to feel that the thing was at about his level and going at only half his speed. Technical Sgt. Quinton Blackwell was duty officer in the control tower at Godman Field, KY, when the incident occurred. Below are his memories of some of the squawk talk, as he reported them two days later:[5]

Captain Mantell

> Mantell : [sees the object] "ahead and above, I'm still climbing."
>
> Wingman: "What the hell are we looking for?"
>
> Mantell: "The object is directly ahead of and above me now, moving about half my speed."
>
> Mantell: "It appears metallic object of tremendous size."
>
> Mantell: "I'm still climbing; the object is above and ahead of me, moving at about my speed or faster. I'm trying to close for a better look."

Mantell's curiosity and sense-of-duty had gotten the better of him. That was his last transmission, leading analysts to believe that he blacked out and rode his plane down to a deadly crash near the Kentucky and Tennessee border.

Mantell's crash could not help but attract both military and civilian attention. A full air accident investigation took place, as well as a UFO investigation by Alfred Loedding out of the AMC. For our purposes, it was Mantell's third comment ("metallic object . . . tremendous size"), which caused a furor.

In a highly organized world this case could have been solved quickly. But that was not who we were. Neither at the Pentagon nor at AMC was there the facility to simply know of the early USN secret balloon project launches out of Winzen Research in Minnesota and plot the likely path of one particular errant balloon. The "tremendous size" appearance would have supported a balloon explanation, and the metallic sheen might easily have been the sun glinting off the slick polyethylene surface. But no one could put the pieces together. AMC did not know what to make of this and listed the case "unidentified."[6] But the Air Force ultimately put the story out that Mantell "chased" Venus.[7] No one in the project believed that, and calculating Venus's position proved it impossible. This was an early example wherein loose-but-authoritative sounding pronouncements got the Air Force into more difficulties than they solved, and began a growing suspicion of "authority's" opinions that in many circles resulted in complete distrust.

U.S. Navy Skyhook Balloon

Other than the Mantell fiasco, January was relatively calm. Agents in Finland reported some incidents, raising the "ghost rockets" concerns again.[8] Once SIGN was officially operating on January 22, Howard McCoy requested the Pentagon's entire ghost rocket "collection" the next day.[9] Maybe it was because of the Mantell publicity, but the elite Joint Research and Development Board, headed by Vannevar Bush, felt motivated to give its assessment of flying disks as follows:

> A spokesman said the board experts dismiss the flying saucers as a mirage induced by mass self-hypnosis. The scientists declare that the discs were nothing more than optical illusions and say that no evidence ever has been found to show that the saucers were either manmade or products of nature . . . Army and Navy experts on such matters as guided missiles, rockets, and buzz bombs, have closed their books on the flying saucers.[10]

Since we know that a good bit of this "authoritative pronouncement" is not true, a question naturally arises: what was motivating people like this to say such things? These were highly intelligent men, and serious ones (despite the almost complete nonsense of the phrase "a mirage induced by mass self-hypnosis"). Perhaps, because they were all physicists and engineers, we should forgive them their nonsense when they pontificate outside their field. But no. Error is error. But why go to press at all, if it is none of the Joint Research Development Board's business? The answer almost certainly must be: they thought it was their business, and that was the business of national security. By debunking the disks to the American public, even nonsensically, they had to believe that they were doing something useful. We do not know their reasoning. We do not have the necessary documents. The easy guess is that they believed that their opinion would reduce the excitability of the average citizen worrying about mysterious things overhead. Of course, as we have

Joint Research and Development Board
Vannevar Bush closest to camera

been and will be seeing, the people actually studying UFOs at AMC thought completely differently from the R&D Board about the phenomenon.

Whatever the R&D Board may have thought they were doing, it did not seem to work. A growing segment of the population was becoming interested in UFOs, as was shown not only by letters to authorities and newspapers, but also to science fiction magazines. A member of Colonel McCoy's staff showed him such a magazine and he surprisingly noted that people were sending them reports that the Air Force was not getting.[11] He then requested that AMC be apprised of an upcoming article announced in the magazine, and the Pentagon sent an officer (actually a member of the CIA) to quiz the owners of Ziff-Davis Publishing in Chicago—the producers of the classic science fiction magazine *Amazing Stories*. The response that McCoy got from the agent was loaded with sarcasm. The materials in the magazine were useless, and the alleged UFO article had been dropped in favor of a piece

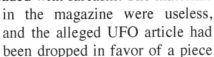

about a big red spider that invades Earth from Mars. All that was correct. Outlets like *Amazing Stories* were useless in solving the flying disk mystery. What they *did* show, however, was what was going on in the minds of some of the public. In that same April 1948 edition was not only the monstrous invasion from Mars, but also a pictorial representation of flying saucers in ancient times from the Angkor Wat temple complex in Southeast Asia, and a story about a wandering prospector coming across a crashed disk in the New Mexico desert.[12] The pictured craft was a nice "lifting body" à la Alfred Loedding or the Horten Brothers. Reacting to the welling up of public interest, the editor of *Amazing Stories* was already in the process of creating *FATE Magazine*, which featured UFOs on its first (Spring 1948) cover, and trumpeted the phenomenon for years thereafter.[13] The American media was getting very interested in the saucers, which gave the Air Force a tricky management problem.

The phenomenon did not help matters by its unwillingness to go away.

1. On January 9 a commercial pilot watched an intensely blue fireball slowly approach, pass by, turn, and blink out. Shades of the foo fighters, albeit the wrong color.[14]

2. From March 5 through March 9, in Bakersfield, California, observers saw repetitions of some sort of light phenomena, which seemed to disintegrate or disappear. Air Force investigators said that it was similar to "star shell" bursts, but no such activities were known to have gone on.[15]

3. The so-called "Rhodes photos" from July of 1947 finally arrived at AMC and were subjected to tests. Colonel James Beam reported very positively on the pictures ("true photographic nature," "image exhibits a 'tail' [that is, a proper photo distortion for the type of camera used]," and the observer's report of seeing a canopy on the disk was within visual acuity of the human eye). The tone of the analysis was that Project SIGN thought that they had a real photo of a somewhat distant, large object, which looked to them, disturbingly, like a thin disk lifting body with a scooped rear section.[16]

Colonel McCoy continued to try to get more help for the project. He requested a news clippings service in the hope of getting better leads. He requested that some, if not all, Air Force bases have stand-by interceptors that could be quickly launched to encounter the objects. Almost everything he asked for was rejected by offices in the Pentagon interested more in penny-pinching than in base requests. If you did not have support from very high up the chain-of-command, you did not get new funding. At least Air Defense Command ordered all bases to send information on unidentified objects to Wright-Patterson.[17]

Early in April, there were reports of a large, "flying wing" object in the Philippines, and a pair of violently maneuvering flattened balls seen by military balloon observers at Holloman AFB in New Mexico.[18] Since unknown "balloons" do not fool professional balloon observers, the Holloman case flummoxed the analysts. Project SIGN felt that this was important enough to make an on-site appearance, so Colonel Beam and Alfred Loedding went to New Mexico.[19] Nothing was resolved on this visit, but later Beam made a second trip, at which time all three observers of the two objects were available for an extended interview. All emphatically denied that the "bogies" were other balloons, despite that being the only imaginable hypothesis. In the untrained writing that is typical of military reporters when writing these documents, Beam wrote:

> All agreed on the following: the object was very high, moved faster than any known aircraft, possessed a rounded, indistinct form, and disappeared suddenly rather than fading away in the distance. It was definitely not a balloon and apparently not manned judging from the violent maneuvers which were performed at a high rate of speed.[20]

Loedding and Beam used the Holloman investigation as an excuse for a side-trip to Phoenix, Arizona, for an interview of William Rhodes, who took the scooped disk photos. They came away from the experience with a good feeling about Rhodes' character and sincerity, despite doubts by earlier agents.[21] For Loedding, these pictures were important indicators that his theories about thin-disk lifting bodies were on the right track. For Beam, perhaps, it was an indication that something like German WWII technology was flying. (In his February memo about the photo analysis to SIGN, he had included a picture of a German model not unlike the Rhodes object).

German Lenticular Model Craft

On April 23, Colonel McCoy, in a letter written by Beam, reported on SIGN's progress to Chief of Staff Vandenberg and Director of Intelligence Charles Cabell.[22] Almost the entirety of the letter speaks of the objects as aerial technology with powered, maneuvered flight, distinct shapes, and high speed to hovering capability, occasional exhausts and sound. The Rhodes photos were featured alongside concerns about Nazi lifting body experiments. The only non-harmonious note was sounded by Dr. Irving Langmuir.

Langmuir was a Nobel Prize-winning physical chemist who worked at General Electric's research laboratories and was a member of the Air Force's Scientific Advisory Board (SAB). Why he was asked to evaluate a topic so far out of his field is unknown, but when one reads available documents it is obvious that much of the military piecework activity was taking place opportunistically and on the cheap. It may be that Alfred Loedding was passing nearby Schenectady, NY, and "dropped in" on his way elsewhere. Whatever happened, Langmuir was the wrong person to ask. Both he and Loedding agreed on the general tenor of this "consultancy": Langmuir listened to the description of what SIGN was doing, looked very briefly at the Rhodes photos, decided they must be blowing pieces of paper, and dismissed the subject. Loedding and Langmuir came away from this encounter at cross-purposes. Here is the formal document's summary:

> Representatives from this Headquarters visited Dr. Irving Langmuir of the Research Laboratories, General Electric Company, Schenectady, NY to discuss Project "SIGN." It was the opinion of this scientist that present available data does not encompass sufficient information to enable a positive identification to be made. Dr. Langmuir was reluctant to consider the so-called "flying discs" as a reality. However, it is believed at this Headquarters that it is possible to construct a low aspect radio aircraft that would duplicate many of the appearance and performance characteristics of reported "flying discs." Experts have agreed that this would be possible through the intelligent application of boundary layer control.[23]

Dr. Irving Langmuir

The summary expressed Langmuir's views mildly. He was one of the earliest of a type of scientist who would be encountered all-too-often throughout the history of this field: brilliant or not, but having a nearly iron-clad boundary between things which were appropriate to be researched and contemplated vs. things which were, "obviously irrational." Langmuir and those around him (Harvard astronomers Harlow Shapley and Donald Menzel, Office of Naval Research nuclear physicist Urner Liddel, and British Astronomer Royal H. Spencer Jones are prominent examples of this mindset.) believed that certain subjects were not only ridiculous but actually dangerous, as they led a gullible public into believing irrational things and rejecting Science. Langmuir nicknamed the pursuit of such subjects "Pathological Science," and the whole treatment of such matters by allegedly objective personalities was, and remains to this day, shockingly emotional.[24] Therefore, both in terms of training in the proper field and intellectual inclination, Langmuir was perhaps the worst "expert" SIGN could have consulted. The chairman of the SAB, Dr. Theodore von Karman, would have been a much better choice: an aero-technical genius who had personally investigated the Coanda Effect to give lift to the disk-shaped bodies.[25] But von Karman was in Southern California and, perhaps, no one was opportunistically heading his way.

Dr. Theodore von Karman

As SIGN moved into May, Langmuir's nay-saying appeared to be having no effect. Despite the "aura of the great scientist" that we have discussed, the project engineers seemed to brush such views aside and to follow their instincts. Feeding these instincts were ongoing reports of unidentified objects.

1. On May 5 there were claims of a series of rocket overflights in Turkey, including a crash at Adapazari with allusions to Soviet experiments in the Mt. Alagos region.[26]
2. Fifty or sixty (estimated) high-altitude objects, shining like bright aluminum, raced across the Memphis, Tennessee, sky on May 7. They traveled mainly in a straight line, but with some zigzagging.[27]

3. On May 28 two USAF officers on a transport plane over Monroe, Michigan, saw disk-like objects of silvery-gold or shiny-brass color. The objects were said to descend through the cloudbank and race away from the C-47.[28]

The second of these sightings has some historical importance. There were three adult civilian witnesses to the multi-object flyover in Memphis and they reported their sighting to a local newspaper, which carried a small story. Personnel at Ft. McPherson Georgia heard of the incident and contacted Wright-Patterson, after their Memphis CIC (counterintelligence) office interviewed the civilians. The three descriptions were consistent. Lt. Colonel Beam was able to get away himself and re-interview everyone a week and a half later. The stories still checked, and the witnesses, trying to find a logical explanation (as do most witnesses), wondered if they could have seen some unusual meteor shower. Lt. Colonel Beam stopped at Cincinnati on his way back to Dayton to query Dr. Paul Herget of the Cincinnati Observatory. Herget seriously doubted that meteors (or an astronomical observation) could have anything to do with the case. Beam had already checked and eliminated balloons, and he knew that there was not an airplane flight explanation. He was running out of options. Herget then suggested that SIGN consult with meteor authority (and often-used Air Force consultant) Dr. Lincoln LaPaz of the University of New Mexico, and a young Ohio State astronomer who had worked in intelligence during the war, J. Allen Hynek.

Dr. Lincoln LaPaz

Neither man could explain the Memphis occurrence, but this outreach to Hynek began the most famous UFO project-scientist relationship in history, one that lasted until the project would finally close in 1969. Something should be said about the relationship here at its beginning. Hynek was a junior faculty member and happy with the opportunity to make some extra money from the Air Force. Consultancies and lucrative projects and facilities were, in those days, a cottage industry among astronomers. Hynek was also quite out-of-touch as to what his job was.[29] To begin with, he would make occasional trips to Dayton and be asked about specific cases, a rather simple task. Not being privy to any airy "politics" involved, he said that he was given the impression that his job was to explain away all the cases he could, even if he had to stretch the possibilities a bit. Hynek was not naïve in two significant ways, however. He knew that scientific consultants needed to "please the boss" to keep their jobs, and he knew that the flying disks were thought to orginate from everywhere from Wright-Patterson itself to outer space. As a thoroughly trained astronomy professional, he began his work with the *a priori* assumption that flying disks could not be extraterrestrial, as no location within our solar system, except Earth, could sustain advanced life, and everywhere else was so impossibly distant as to be unreachable.[30] Hynek's very early interactions with SIGN personnel seem to have been fairly shallow and merely professional. But at the end of the year, he would become more deeply involved and the biases noted above would play an ongoing role, one he later grew to regret.

Dr. J. Allen Hynek

A few other notes are worth consideration before we get to a climactic event in the month of July.

1. Something that was supposedly Top Secret (the high-altitude Spy-on-Russia "Mogul" balloon project) was thoroughly leaked to *Popular Science* magazine, which published it as the answer to the flying saucers.[31]

2. There were rumors that Moscow was interested in the disks.[32] Long after the tensions with the Soviet Union relaxed, we learned that this was true in some fashion at least (details still not explained) in that Stalin had asked his rocketry genius, Sergei Korolev, to look into the matter.[33]

3. Ghost rockets again? A report from Norway of a sighting in December finally made it to the Project in July. AMC's chief of Operations, C.A. Griffith, wrote to the Norwegian staff not just for this case, but any and all which came their way. AMC was becoming aware that this phenomenon was both ongoing and global.[34]

4. In Hecla, South Dakota, on June 30, a husband and wife saw an odd object, like a lighted mass, from their automobile. They stopped to look. Others did, too. After a while, the lighted mass seemed to get larger and then "throw off" three small pieces. These satellites assumed a very regular

Sergei Korolev

isosceles triangle around the larger mass. All objects now appeared silvery, like polished aluminum. The central object then broke apart into an aggregate of many small objects, which seemed to fade away. The satellite triangle moved away, becoming further separated and also dimmer as if going to great altitude, always maintaining the perfect triangle. The project officers who interviewed the witnesses were impressed with their sincerity and meticulous detail. The husband, who was a chemical engineer and an amateur astronomer, said "I am familiar with the new large plastic balloons for weather or cosmic ray observation. It could not have been one." This case, a very early example of what looks to be a geometric display in the sky, proved very difficult to explain.[35] Only much later did Allen Hynek run roughshod over the witnesses' testimony and declare it a cosmic ray balloon, undeterred by either the quality of the observers or the odd circumstance of a rising perfect triangle of objects.[36] This case has been detailed here because it shows that the Project mutated into a haphazard explanation factory late in 1948 and into the 1949-1951 era. The chemical engineer told the project officers: "My convictions at this point (in the observation) were that it could not be anything terrestrial."

Probably the SIGN group, as it went into July, held this same conclusion, too, not only of Hecla but several other cases as well. But there was no critical, compelling piece of evidence. SIGN had given a first interim report in April. If there were some intention of giving regular, perhaps quarterly reports, then July would have been a good month for it. But that did not happen in any formal way. Why? This has to be a deduction, but a guess would be that SIGN personnel felt that they were on the verge of being forced to say something quite astounding about the disks, and they were not ready.

More information from additional cases rattled the analysts.

1. On July 7 impeccable witnesses in West Rindge, New Hampshire, noted curls of smoke rising from a neighbor's property. Small holes and burns were found, plus some metallic debris. The debris was sent to MIT for analysis. Later the FBI got involved. The Project SIGN record card for the case reads, "Fires were apparently caused by metallic fragments similar to the lining of V-2 bombs!"[37]

2. It was the first of July and a Major Hammer of Rapid City, South Dakota AFB was flying over the base when he observed twelve oval-shaped disks.[38] He estimated them as 100 feet in

diameter and described them as having a brilliant yellow-white color. They flew in a tight diamond formation, made a high-speed dive, leveled and made a perfect formation turn, angled upwards at 30° to 40° and accelerated out of sight. Hammer estimated the cruising speed at greater than 500 mph. This case may have been viewed as of high importance. It seems to admit of no commonplace explanation. Analysts in both the Pentagon and at Wright-Patterson were greatly impressed. Project SIGN engineers used it to support their (coming) analysis that the disks were extraterrestrial technology. Even the Pentagon opponents of that analysis used the case to feature the seriousness of the need to find answers to the phenomenon. The oddest part of this (to the current historian) is that the case file has disappeared. And, this file seems to have disappeared very early in project history, having not been given to Allen Hynek for his (alleged) comprehensive evaluations of all project cases, nor a project case number for the microfilm record. Maybe this "loss" is merely incompetence of some kind, but the case is a poor candidate for misplacement, given how the intelligence community viewed it.

3. While on the ground on July 9 in Osborn, Ohio (near Wright-Patterson and Dayton, Ohio), the project officer who flew to investigate the Hecla, South Dakota case, saw his own UFO. It was a self-luminous yellow-white object traveling at an estimated 500-600 mph. It seemed to pulse its light at about three second intervals as it cruised away.[39] It was not as spectacular as the Rapid City case, but it was observed by one of SIGN's own.

4. On July 17 in San Acacia, New Mexico, near Kirtland AFB, members of the base and their families witnessed an overflight of seven round objects with the color of aluminum metal. The flight formation, if it could be called such, varied from a "J" shape to an "L" to a circle. Flashes of light occurred as regular pulses. If the officers were correct in their estimation of altitude (which is practically impossible), then the disks were traveling at 1500 mph.[40]

SIGN teetered on the brink of saying that these things had to be extraterrestrial.

During these early days in July, through the Air Force's Research and Development division, discussion about the possibility that the UFOs might be human-built spaceships resulted in an Air Force formal letter (July 21) authorizing the RAND organization to engage scientists to evaluate the idea.[41] We do not know what RAND did at that time. The action shows, however, that the UFOs were appearing to be very real and of very high performance to the loftiest elements concerned with Air Force technology. Project SIGN made a similar, if not identical, request to RAND in October of that year. Because the thinking must have been roundly discussed within the Air Force community, it would not be at all surprising if the details of this October request, reproduced on the next page and an original copy in the appendix, mimicked the July concept.[42] Given what we know about SIGN's view of the UFO problem, this request had an overt and a covert side. While the Air Force was asking RAND if we humans could create aerial technology to explain some of the most difficult sightings (and SIGN wanted this answer, too), SIGN could view a "no" as ammunition for the conclusion they were moving towards. We can assume from all of this that intelligence and technology elements throughout the Air Force were excited if not alarmed by the unsolved disks.

And then came July 24. Eastern Airlines flight 576 out of Houston was over Montgomery, Alabama at 2:45 in the morning. Most of the passengers were asleep or dozing. At the controls, two of Eastern's best: Captains C. S. Chiles and John B. Whitted.[43] Ahead, and slightly above, they spotted an incoming object. "One of those new jet jobs," they thought. As it came on, it resolved itself into a rocket-shaped thing, sort of like a plane's fuselage with no wings or tail protuberances. It seemed 100 feet long and with a barrel diameter three times that of a B-29. (Chiles was described in the Air Force report as as "a Lt. Colonel pilot, USAF, in a command capacity [during the war], with vast experience in judging and identifying aircraft.") The object passed near their plane to the right and slightly above. Once past, the pilots felt that the flying fuselage gently angled upwards and away. Chiles later said to news reporters:

EXHIBIT "A"

Project Sign Study Requirements

The possibility that some of the unidentified aerial objects that have been reported both in the United States and in foreign lands may have been experimental spaceships, or test vehicles for the purpose of assisting in the development of spaceships, has been given consideration by this Command.

If such craft actually have been sighted, it is believed more likely that they represent the effort of a foreign nation, rather than a product from beyond the Earth.

Present world knowledge, techniques and resources are probably adequate to meet the requirements for spaceship construction, or at least to establish the preliminary experimental foundation for such an accomplishment in the near future.

In any case, the design and performance parameters of the craft would necessarily be in conformance and consistent with the established principles of our sciences.

To assist in the collection of information, relating to unidentified aerial objects that may possibly represent spaceships or spaceship test vehicles, and to assist in the analysis and evaluation of such reported craft, technical information that includes the distinguishing design and performance parameters for spaceships is considered necessary.

While such information is contained outright, or implicitly, in the series of RAND Project reports, it would be of much value to this Command to have a list of the special design and performance characteristics that are believed to distinguish spaceships, together with any further scientific clues that might assist in their detection and identification, prepared by RAND scientific personnel.

"After it passed we must have sat there for five minutes without saying a word."[44] They landed and reported the event to their administrators at Atlanta. Those persons released the report to the press.

The news spread like wildfire. Everyone wanted to interview the pilots. Chiles later said that he got a phone call from the Pentagon telling him that if he said one more word on this in public that he would be called back to active duty.[45] In California, the chief of the Strategic Air Command was cornered by reporters. *"No," he said. "We don't have one of those things. I wish we did. I sure would have liked to see that thing."*[46] Somewhat more seriously, Director of Intelligence Charles Cabell phoned Howard McCoy at Wright-Patterson. The message: get your agents down to Atlanta immediately![47]

By that afternoon, Loedding, Deyarmond, and their boss, Raymond Llewellyn, were on their way to Atlanta. They met Chiles and Whitted at the Henry Grady hotel, split them up, and interviewed them separately. Many details emerged. Both pilots remembered the same shape and dimensions. Both remembered a double row of windows along the side—but their drawings of this are quite different. Both remembered an exhaust out the back but quite a different array of "structure" (Chiles' drawing having much more detail than Whitted's). At this point, one's mind decides to

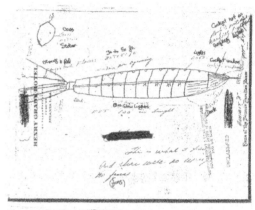

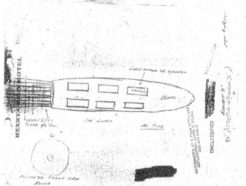

Top: Chiles' drawing
Bottom: Whitted's drawing

become a "lumper" (look how alike they are!) or a "splitter" (look how different!). Loedding and Deyarmond, who conducted the interviews, were lumpers. To say they were impressed would put it mildly. They went back to Dayton convinced that Chiles and Whitted had seen a very advanced, wingless machine, doubtless meant to carry personnel (thus, the windows). Explainers have tried to write this case off as a very unusual near miss with an Earth grazing bolide/fireball. Maybe it was;

2nd from left: Dr. Ludwig Prandtl
3rd from left: Dr. von Karman

Chiles and Whitted did not think so and neither did SIGN.

When Loedding and Deyarmond got back to the Project, all the central figures there thought that they had finally received the critical case. This was a wingless, maneuverable, flying machine shaped like a stumpy projectile. They knew that such a thing was extremely difficult to fly, but not impossible. An esoteric principle, called the Prandtl Theory of Lift and considered foundational in aerodynamic science, indicated that this device could be made.[48] But the problem was power—the power plant must be exceptional. Unfortunately, nothing we had, and nothing that the Soviets could conceivably have had, could power this craft.

And yet it flew. The conclusion that their work had been priming them for had now crystallized in their minds. These things are extraterrestrial.

Alfred Loedding probably greeted this climax with glee, being as he was, a bit of a romantic thinker. Who knows what the others felt. But all the other main players had to have bought into it to proceed with such a risky assessment. Now they had to make a case: an "Estimate."

There has been a long-standing debate among UFO historians as to when this Estimate was written and sent to the Pentagon. It does not matter. Some thought it happened quickly (in August), some more measurably (September, October, or even November). Probably in some senses, everybody is correct. Nobody with any sense in the military is going to drop formally written-up "bombs" on members of the higher chain-of-command. What SIGN was thinking had to be broached to the Pentagon many times before the extraterrestrial bomb formally arrived. What we can say with assurance is that Project personnel began putting together their argument for an extraterrestrial estimate after their assessment of the Chiles-Whitted encounter and before a face-off with their opponents in November.

The Chiles-Whitted sighting seemed to encourage people to report their sightings as well as others to comment. Disks were observed in Washington State, police and airport administrator phone lines were jammed, and planes were sent up to attempt interception.[49] An Oregon astronomer quickly assured everyone that these things were just the planet Venus. Another man was not so sure.

> These aerial objects could be the first reconnaissance flights from another planet. Why not? We know how to build such an escape missile—one that could escape the bounds of gravity and soar off into free space among the planets . . . If we can build such craft, what is to prevent others from doing so, assuming that a similar order of intelligence exists on other planets? You and I may see the day when we will be united with Russia defending this planet against attack from space.[50]

The Air Force wished people would not make statements like this, especially if that person was Moulton B. Taylor, former Navy commander and chief engineer in charge of guided missile development during the war. Taylor may have been making honest and frank comments, but overly exciting the public was not what the intelligence community saw as wise.

Meanwhile, SIGN engineers were hearing of possible ground witness corroboration for the Chiles-Whitted fuselage, and of an identical object over Arnheim, Netherlands on July 20.[51] At the end of the month, a husband and wife observed a "classic saucer" shaped object from their home. This case is carried as an "unidentified" to this day. Sightings were so numerous around government installations in New Mexico that some of the scientists began to organize their own observing groups.[52] On September 23, personnel at Los Alamos Laboratory saw a disk-like object from the lab's airstrip.[53] This is significant as the latest dated case, as stated by former UFO project chief Captain Edward Ruppelt (1951-53 era), to have been included in SIGN's extraterrestrial estimate.[54]

An AMC T-2 meeting in 1948
Colonel McCoy is at the head of table

A reasonable hypothesis of what was going on between SIGN and the Pentagon during the months of August and September was that Colonel McCoy was breaking the news about where SIGN was headed to Lt. Colonel Garrett, Director Charles Cabell, et al. and getting resistant, if not shocked, feedback. If we had the complete documents from the Air Force records, we would not have to guess.

What fragments we do have indicate that in this timeframe offices in the Pentagon, involving at least Major Jere Boggs and the Office of Naval Intelligence, were asked to prepare their own counter-estimate.[55] There was going to be a fight over this.

Early in October a National Guard pilot in Fargo, North Dakota, reported what appeared to multiple observers to be a dogfight-like air dance with a white sphere. SIGN was energized and ordered that the plane be tested for remnant radioactivity.[56] Why? They had decided that the likely power plant needed to fly things like the Chiles-Whitted fuselage was nuclear.

It is almost a certainty that communication between the two Air Force Intelligence Centers over their "difference of opinion" was intense and that Colonel Howard McCoy was caught in the middle. His office once again asked the Navy, the Army, and the CIA whether they were aware of *any* developments that could explain these things.[57] McCoy's assistant director, Colonel Clingerman, then sent the request for analysis on Earth-created spaceships to RAND, which we have mentioned earlier.[58] None of these answers helped the situation. All these organizations were forced to say either "no known technology," or "technology is *possible* but not available." These assessments could have done nothing but strengthen SIGN's confidence that they were on track.

To ensure that things were as complicated and pressure-filled as possible, an interview with Brigadier General Erik H. Nelson (at the time a technical advisor for Scandinavian Air Lines) indicated that Sweden was having overflights by unknown craft again, and that this time they were not just "rockets," but saucer-like disks and round spheres (à la the Fargo case) as well.[59] Jan Aldrich, UFO historian and expert FOIA researcher, was recently allowed to review a formerly Top Secret document which discussed thinking in Sweden at this time.[60] (It is printed on the following page.) Surely opinion about the phenomenon was as split in Sweden as it was in the United States.

Sometime during October SIGN must have been emphatically told that the direction of their thinking was not going to be approved on high. The typical way that this is talked about by historians is that SIGN finally sent a formally written Estimate to Director of Intelligence Cabell.[61] He, for some reason, did not rule on it but passed it up to the chief of staff, Hoyt Vandenberg. Vandenberg, it is said, "batted it back down," with the implication of an aggressive displeasure, almost a "spanking" for SIGN. Perhaps this happened in October, but there is another scenario that provides us at least a bit of documentation for a date.

In the Pentagon the Air Force Intelligence "Office of Defensive Air" was working with the Office of Naval Intelligence to produce a document, which later was formally numbered AIR 100-203-79, and which argued for very different conclusions.[62] On November 3, Director of Intelligence Cabell sent a rather icy letter (in that it went directly to the Commanding General at AMC without the usual "attention" notice to Colonel McCoy or SIGN) which agreed that "the conclusion appears inescapable that some type of flying object has been observed," *but* that (to paraphrase) as far as the Pentagon is concerned these things have *not* been identified (read: *don't* tell us they're extraterrestrial spacecraft).[63] Therefore, increase the efforts to tell us whether these things are *domestic* or *foreign* (read: *don't* tell us that they're extraterrestrial!). This is urgent. And, by the way, we need to decide what we're going to say to the public about this. (The actual letter is displayed on page 64.) SIGN's Albert Deyarmond, Colonel McCoy's friend over all these years, wrote the reply for McCoy's signature five days later.[64] It was basically a defense of SIGN's work to date with a few new projects thrown in to indicate that they were on the ball. The reply repeats the now common estimates of the types of devices SIGN was dealing with (disks, fuselages, spheres, and balls of light). Deyarmond flatly states that there are cases "for which no reasonable everyday explanation is available." He also maintains that all the information

2-5317

TOP SECRET

USAFE 14   TT 1524   TOP SECRET   4 Nov 1948

From OI OB

For some time we have been concerned by the recurring reports on flying saucers. They periodically continue to cop up; during the last week, one was observed hovering over Neubiberg Air Base for about thirty minutes. They have been reported by so many sources and from such a variety of places that we are convinced that they cannot be disregarded and must be explained on some basis which is perhaps slightly beyond the scope of our present intelligence thinking.

When officers of this Directorate recently visited the Swedish Air Intelligence Service. This question was put to the Swedes. Their answer was that some reliable and fully technically qualified people have reached the conclusion that "these phenomena are obviously the result of a high technical skill which cannot be credited to any presently known culture on earth." They are therefore assuming that these objects originate from some previously unknown or unidentified technology, possibly outside the earth.

One of these objects was observed by a Swedish technical expert near his home on the edge of a lake. The object crashed or landed in the lake and he carefully noted its azimuth from his point of observation. Swedish intelligence was sufficiently confident in his observation that a naval salvage team was sent to the lake. Operations were underway during the visit of USAFE officers. Divers had discovered a previosuly uncharted crater on the floor of the lake. No further information is available, but we have been promised knowledge of the results. In their opinion, the observation was reliable, and they believe that the depression on the floor of the lake, which did not appear on current hydrographic charts, was in fact caused by a flying saucer.

Although accepting this theory of the origin of these objects poses a whole new group of questions and puts much of our thinking in a changed light, we are inclined not to discredit entirely this somewhat spectacular theory, meantime keeping an open mind on the subject. What are your reactions?

T O P   S E C R E T

(END OF USAFE ITEM 14)

DECLASSIFIED
Authority NND 863571
By K.C. NARA Date 7/31/—

See TS- 2-3131
for Cover Sheet +
M/R.

AFOIN/Maj Gen Cabell/mcm/5613/2 Nov 48

3 NOV 1948

SUBJECT: Flying Object Incidents in the United States

TO: Commanding General, Air Materiel Command
        Wright-Patterson Air Force Base
        Dayton, Ohio

Classified files

1. By letter dated 30 December 1947 from the Director of
Research and Development, Headquarters USAF, your Headquarters
was required to establish Project "SIGN".

2. The conclusion appears inescapable that some type of
flying object has been observed. Identification and the origin
of these objects is not discernible to this Headquarters. It is
imperative, therefore, that efforts to determine whether these
objects are of domestic or foreign origin must be increased until
conclusive evidence is obtained. The needs of national defense
require such evidence in order that appropriate countermeasures
may be taken.

3. In addition to the imperative need for evidence to permit
countermeasures, is the necessity of informing the public as to
the status of the problem. To date there has been too little data
to present to the public. The press, however, is about to take it
into its own hands and demand to be told what we do or do not know
about the situation. Silence on our part will not long be acceptable.

4. Request immediate information as to your conclusions to
date and your recommendations as to the information to be given
to the press. Your recommendation is requested also as to
whether that information should be offered to the press or withheld until it is actively sought by the press.

BY COMMAND OF THE CHIEF OF STAFF:

/s/ C. P. Cabell
8 to 2 air material command

C. P. CABELL
Major General, USAF
Director of Intelligence, Office of
Deputy Chief of Staff, Operations

Dispatched
11/4 during

Note: C/S + 1, 2, 3 + 4 are TS
in 2-3131, and are filed
in TS control file has a cy of this ltr

available to SIGN indicates that the objects are *not* of domestic origin. Once again SIGN says: such things *could* be made to fly, but not with currently available power plants. Deyarmond says nothing about origins from foreign countries, but that mere omission indicates that no one at SIGN believed that feasible. The memo (included in the appendix of this book) then addresses the extraterrestrial possibility and admits that there is no tangible evidence (meaning pieces of a craft). But, stubbornly, SIGN goes on to say that there is some level of correlation of waves of sightings with approaches of the nearer planets. The Pentagon may have been ordering them to drop the extraterrestrial hypothesis, but Deyarmond and SIGN were not ready to do so without a full-fledged fight.

That fight occurred on November 12, 1948. SIGN was ordered to appear in Washington for a meeting with the relevant intelligence community at a location in the National Bureau of Standards.[65] We do not know all that attended. SIGN sent a "contingent," headed by project officer Captain Robert Sneider, who it is said presented the SIGN position (surely the formally written and fully documented Estimate). The opposition was led by Major Jere Boggs of the Office of Defensive Air and the primary author of the opposing Estimate (AIR-100-203-79). No other name is known with certainty, but the logical candidates from AMC are, of course, Loedding, Deyarmond, Lawrence Truettner, and Colonel McCoy. On the Washington side, representatives from ONI as well as General Cabell and his main advisors almost surely had to be there. Who else? The CIA? Vandenberg himself? The documents and notes of this meeting have never been released.

All we know is that SIGN lost the war. Their humiliation was emphasized by orders that they were in the future required to send copies of all their cases and analyses to Boggs, the ONI, and the Air Force's Scientific Advisory Board.[66] That message was as clear as a woodshed whipping: you are not trusted to do this work without adult supervision. Through all of these stormy affairs difficult cases continued to flow in and to resist explanation.

SIGN was finished. Loedding said that his stock at the Pentagon had never been lower.[67] Deyarmond and Truettner went back to AMC to write up the final SIGN report, notably not including the extraterrestrial hypothesis. SIGN's name was changed to "Grudge" on December 16, 1948, with a bit of malice.[68]

Some of the representatives of the Air Force Advisory Board in 1948. George Valley, nearest to the camera, was assigned to monitor SIGN.

AIR-100-203-79 was formally published on December 10, as the best intelligence statement on flying disks. SIGN's Estimate was ordered destroyed (although this seems to be somewhat of a euphemism as such documents appear to be kept in reference files, regardless).[69] Within a month or two, all of the main contributors to the SIGN project were reassigned to other duties, leaving only the two lowest ranks (a Lieutenant Smith and a civilian, Towles) to maintain a case filing activity under the term Grudge.

Although much, much more could be said (especially concerning cases) about this critical year, we will finish 1948 with just two final points. One is the AIR-100 document. What did *it* have to say?

In the middle 1980s, due to the work of FOIA expert Robert Todd, the government declassified and released this Top Secret document, and we can read it for ourselves. "A.I.R." means Air Intelligence Report, and the rest is just an access number for identification. The title of the report is familiar: "Analysis of Flying Object Incidents in the U.S." The report contained 26 pages plus an index. (This was roughly the size of the rival Estimate as reported by the three persons who we know read that document in the 1952 era.)[70] Both the Air Force and the Navy's intelligence organizations were listed as the preparers. As usual with these things, the report begins with a Summary and Conclusions, and follows with several appendices. The main conclusion is that "some type of flying object has been observed." The idea that U.S. sightings are general hysteria, induced by hearing about Scandinavian ghost rockets is addressed and dismissed. The document properly suggests that not all reports are likely to be of the same sort of thing, and that some cases *may* be advanced technology of U.S. origin, for instance. Therefore one must do a better job assessing the presence of U.S. technology. But the possibility of foreign technology is the real concern. The report maintains that the disks appear in a geographically over-weighted pattern, which features the coasts and the Ohio-Kentucky area. The report says that there are *only two* "reasonable" hypotheses: domestic origin, or foreign (Soviet). Then much is presented to make the Soviet case. In the listing of critical cases appear many of the ones we have already discussed (which were deliberately chosen to give the reader a feeling for the kinds of things which were sticking with the military analysts). The report ends with a discussion of known flying wing research.

The final item that is too important to ignore in this saga seems relatively trivial at first glance. Some magazine writer wanted to write an article about flying saucers. Remember that on November 3, Director of Intelligence Cabell wanted to know what SIGN felt about releasing facts and commentary to the American public.[71] He said that the press was about to take matters into its own hands. In October, SIGN had blasted the commanding officer of the North Dakota National Guard for talking to the press about the Fargo incident. This officer, Major D.C. Jones, wrote SIGN in consternation: What was he supposed to do? Civilians who observed the "dogfight" already knew:

> It was necessary that a press conference be made in order to avoid an exaggerated account being printed and a consequent wild hysteria.[72]

SIGN had handled the press differently when pushed back in Ohio. We're investigating everything, they said:

> The public can be assured there's nothing going on we don't know about . . . Military Intelligence is charged with investigating any reports regarding such as 'flying disks' and the matter is purely routine in nature. If one of these things turned out to be something strange and new, the public will be informed.[73]

The presentation speaks volumes. Within the project, the SIGN engineers were scrambling to test the plane from the Fargo incident for nuclear contamination in pursuit of data for their extraterrestrial theory. Outside, to the public, it was "Ho hum. Nothing, folks, nothing at all." Meanwhile the Pentagon was thinking Soviet. It is well past time that everyone drops the naïve belief that press releases on this topic have been constructed with truth and frankness as their primary qualities. They have not. They have been constructed rather with priority for the security of the public and the nation as the driving goal. One might disagree with the reasoning process which led the intelligence community to do what they thought was best in this regard, but not with their ultimate intention. To achieve that intention, information was not only being withheld, but also occasionally manipulated in some fashion.

So what did SIGN recommend back to Cabell about this general information management problem?

> It is not considered advisable to present to the press information on those objects which we cannot identify or about which we cannot present any reasonable conclusions. In the event that they insist on some kind of statement, it is suggested that they be informed that many of the objects sighted have been identified as weather balloons or astral bodies, and that investigation is being pursued to determine reasonable explanations for the others.[74]

It's as in the popular movie line. The curious public says: I want the Truth (whether it be Soviet, extraterrestrial, or just an "Unknown" hanging over our heads)! And the answer is "You can't handle the truth!"

And along came a rather insistent news writer. Sidney Shallet was a contributor to the *Saturday Evening Post*, a major national magazine. Somehow Shallet got the ear and the approval of Secretary of Defense James Forrestal to enlist the help of the Air Force's UFO project to gather information for a splashy article.[75] This information management problem was about the last thing Cabell and the Pentagon wanted. They would *never* have agreed to this, and they stewed over it in the documents that have been released.[76] But Forrestal was everybody's boss. There was no place to hide.

National Security Council Meeting August 1948
Secretary Defense James Forrestal 4th from right, President Truman 2nd from right

Now it was a matter of damage control. In the convoluted business of military intelligence matters, the Pentagon found itself writing a letter to Secretary Forrestal requesting his approval to "assist" such writers as Shallet in these cases where they insist on writing about UFOs. Cabell's chief of Air Intelligence, Brigadier General Ernest Moore, wrote the letter and attached memorandum to Forrestal.[77] What Moore and Cabell were saying was: look, Mr. Secretary, we've got a problem here. We're investigating every case we can get our hands on, we know that the objects are real, *but that's all*. We cannot make a reasonable identification. All we can do is keep at it. But the press is after us. Since we cannot avoid that, despite us trying to discourage them from publishing such articles, we would like to assist such writers when we have to. (There is no doubt, by the way, that "assist" was a euphemism for "subtly control.") The letter ends: "It is believed that an article of this nature would be less harmful to the national interest if the Directorate of Intelligence assists in its preparation."[78]

Brigadier General Moore

Thus, in late January or early February of 1949, Shallet was taken on a guided tour of the project at AMC and given filtered (unclassified) case information and opinions. More about this later.

1948 ended in continued Air Force confusion. No one knew what they were dealing with, yet they were convinced that it was a real mystery of a technological sort. Project SIGN and its personnel had been crushed, and "Project Grudge" went on with no incentive except housekeeping.[79] And the problem of how to handle the public seemed unsolvable.

Notes

[1] FOIA (USAF). The Pentagon's USAF Directorate of Intelligence structure (particularly the officers occupying each post) has been reconstructed from reading the mass of FOIA documents.

[2] Edward Ruppelt File R022, and FOIA (USAF).

[3] Blue Book microfilm. Similarly the organizational chart of Wright-Patterson's Intelligence division (that went by more than one name across this period; for example, the division is referred to as "T-2," "ATIC," and sometimes simply "AMC") has been deduced from the Blue Book microfilms. There are some charts available from the base, which give snapshots of the community, against which we can check whether we're on the right track for a specific year.

[4] Blue Book microfilm Roll 2.

[5] Blue Book microfilm Roll 2 (Mantell file: "Statement of T. Sgt. Quinton A. Blackwell," 9 January 1948).

[6] O.C. Winzen to James McDonald, 22 October 1968 (James McDonald Archives, University of Arizona, Tucson, AZ, Box 8). Also, former Blue Book chief Edward Ruppelt told UFO investigator Ted Bloecher in 1955 that he had "indications" that there was a skyhook balloon in the area but "I could never find a record of this skyhook flight" in 1952.

[7] See, for example, "Spyglasses Search Through the Southwest Sky But Great What-was-it Keeps Out of Sight" in *Louisville (KY) Courier-Journal*, 9 January 1948, for immediate "Venus" explanation; and see A.B. Deyarmond, note, subject: "Godman Field Air Force Base Sightings," 8 November 1948, wherein Deyarmond states that Venus cannot be the explanation for Mantell's case (Blue Book microfilm Roll 2).

[8] Blue Book microfilm Roll 2; and McCoy to Chief of Staff, 23 January 1948, and Eiseman to CG, AMC, 2 February 1948 in Ghost Rockets chapter, both FOIA (USAF).

[9] Blue Book microfilm Roll 2, and FOIA (USAF), as in endnote 8.

[10] Quoted in "Flying Discs Book Declared Closed," dateline Washington, DC, 31 January 1948 in *Pendleton (OR) East Oregonian* (from Gross, 1948, supplement).

[11] H. M. McCoy to Lt. Col. George Garrett, memorandum, subject: "Flying Discs," 16 January 1948, FOIA (USAF).

[12] *Amazing Stories* (ed. Raymond Palmer), Vol. 22(4): April 1948.

[13] *Fate* (ed. "Robert N. Webster"), Vol. 1(1): Spring 1948.

[14] Blue Book microfilm Roll 2.

[15] Blue Book microfilm Roll 2.

[16] Blue Book microfilm Roll 1; esp. Lewis C. Gust, memorandum, subject: "Identification of Subject Matter," 19 February 1948.

[17] S. E. Anderson to Director of Intelligence, memorandum, subject: "Flying Discs," 3 March 1948, FOIA (USAF).

[18] Blue Book microfilm Roll 2.

[19] H. M. McCoy (J. C. Beam) to Chief of Staff, USAF, memorandum, subject: "Project 'SIGN'," 23 April 1948, FOIA (USAF).

[20] Blue Book microfilm Roll 2.

[21] Blue Book microfilm Roll 1, Rhodes file.

[22] H. M. McCoy to Chief of Staff, subject: "Project 'SIGN'," 23 April 1948, FOIA (USAF).

[23] Irving Langmuir, "Pathological Science," Technical Information Series #G8-C-035, General Electric Research and Development Center, Schenectady, NY, April 1968; and Alfred Loedding, quoted in "Princeton Engineer Believes Flying Saucers Real Thing," *Trenton (NJ) Sunday Times-Advertiser*, 10 October 1954.

[24] Langmuir, "Pathological Science."

[25] Theodore von Karman (with Lee Edson), *The Wind and Beyond*, 1967.

[26] Blue Book microfilm Roll 2.

[27] Blue Book microfilm Roll 2.

[28] Blue Book microfilm Roll 2.

[29] J. Allen Hynek, *The Hynek UFO Report*, 1997; originally 1977.

[30] Hynek, *Hynek UFO Report*; plus Hynek, Grudge.

[31] Devon Francis, "New Balloons Explore Roof of the Airways," *Popular Science*, May 1948: 98-104.

[32] "The Friend," Moscow, USSR, Note (Serial 38-S-48), 10 June 1948, from USAF files as cited in Gross (1948).

[33] Vadim Orlov, interview with Professor Valery Burdakov (associate of Korolev), in *AURA-Z*, No. 1, March 1993: 11.

[34] C. A. Griffith, Chief Operations Section, Air Technical Intelligence Center, Wright-Patterson AFB, note: "Luminous Object," (MA R-365-47-NAD No. 12199), 29 June 1948 from Blue Book files as cited in Gross (1948).

[35] Blue Book microfilm Roll 2.

[36] Hynek, Grudge.

[37] Blue Book microfilm Roll 2.

[38] Edward Ruppelt, *The Report on Unidentified Flying Objects*, uncorrected draft, Ruppelt files (held for the UFO Research Coalition by Michael Swords, Kalamazoo, MI); and Directorate of Intelligence USAF and Office of Naval Intelligence USN, *Analysis of Flying Object Incidents in the U.S.*, Air Intelligence Report No. 100-203-79, 10 December 1948 (hereafter cited as AIR-100).

[39] Blue Book microfilm Roll 2.

[40] Blue Book microfilm Roll 2.

[41] W. R. Clingerman (AMC/ATIC) to Chief of Staff, USAF, Washington, DC, memorandum, subject: "Request for Study by Rand Project," 22 October 1948 (referencing July memo), FOIA (USAF).

[42] W. R. Clingerman to Chief of Staff , memorandum, "Request for Study by Rand Project," attachment, FOIA (USAF).

[43] Blue Book microfilm Rolls 2 and 3.

[44] Albert Riley, "Atlanta Pilots Report Wingless Sky Monster," *Atlanta (GA) Constitution*, 25 July 1948.

[45] Clarence Chiles interview by James McDonald, McDonald files, University of Arizona archives.

[46] William Key, "Sky Devil-ship Scares Pilots," *Atlanta (GA) Journal*, 25 July 1948.

[47] Blue Book microfilm Roll 2.

[48] Blue Book microfilm Roll 2. The Prandtl Theory of Lift is mentioned in a few documents, all concerning this case directly or indirectly. One such document is contained in a fragmentary form in the microfilm above, numbered "102-122-79," and is considered by some as a preliminary piece to the formal extraterrestrial estimate of SIGN to come.

[49] "New Aerial Mystery," Associated Press Story, dateline: Yakima, Washington, 25 July 1948; cited in Gross (1948, supplement).

[50] "Men of Mars May Replace Flying Saucers," Associated Press Story, dateline: Portland, Oregon, 26 July 1948; cited in Gross (1948, supplement).

[51] Blue Book microfilm Roll 2.

[52] J. F. Kalbach to James McDonald, 1 January 1970, McDonald files, University of Arizona archives.

[53] Kalbach to McDonald.

[54] Edward Ruppelt (draft).

[55] Colonel Brooke Allen to Chief, Air Intelligence Division, memorandum, 11 October 1948 (referenced therein), FOIA (USAF).

[56] Blue Book microfilm Roll 3.

[57] H. M. McCoy to Central Intelligence Agency, subject: "Project 'SIGN'," 7 October 1948, FOIA (USAF).

[58] W. R. Clingerman to Chief of Staff, memorandum, "Request for Study by Rand Project," 22 October 1948, FOIA (USAF).

[59] H. M. McCoy to Chief of Staff, USAF, memorandum, subject: "Interview of Brig Gen Erik N. Nelson," date of memo not readable, FOIA (USAF).

[60] USAFE document: USAFE 14, IT 1524, Top Secret, 4 November 1948.

[61] Edward Ruppelt, *Report on Unidentified Flying Objects*, draft.

[62] AIR-100.

[63] C. P. Cabell to Commanding General AMC, memorandum, subject: "Flying Objects Incidents in the United States," 3 November 1948, FOIA (USAF).

[64] H. M. McCoy to Chief of Staff, USAF, memorandum, subject: [basic letter response to above] "Flying Object Incidents in the United States," 8 November 1948, FOIA (USAF).

[65] Edward Ruppelt, draft, and H. M. McCoy to Chief of Staff, USAF, memorandum, subject: "Transmittal of Project 'SIGN' Incident Summaries," 6 December 1948, FOIA (USAF).

[66] H. M. McCoy, memorandum, subject: "Transmittal of Project 'SIGN' Incident Summaries," 6 December 1948.

[67] L.H. Truettner and A.B. Deyarmond, *Unidentified Aerial Objects: Project "SIGN,"* Technical Intelligence Division, Air Materiel Command, Technical Report No. F-TR-2274-IA, February 1949.

[68] Ruppelt, draft.

[69] Blue Book microfilm Rolls 3 and 4, passim.

[70] AIR-100. Re: Estimate, see Ruppelt, draft; and Major Dewey Fournet to Major Donald Keyhoe, 4 May 1958.

[71] C. P. Cabell to AMC, November 3, "Flying Objects Incidents," 1948, FOIA (USAF).

[72] Gross (1948), citing Blue Book microfilms, file #172.

[73] Gross (1948), citing Associated Press News Story, dateline: Dayton, Ohio, 5 October 1948.

[74] H. M. McCoy to Chief of Staff, "Flying Object Incidents," 8 November 1948, FOIA (USAF)

[75] Edward Ruppelt, draft, and C. P. Cabell to AFOAI, draft of letter and notes, 28 November 1948, and 30 November 1948, FOIA (USAF).

[76] (Authorship "AFOAI," coordinated by General E. Moore), memorandum for record, 24 November 1948, FOIA (USAF).

[77] C. P. Cabell to AFOAI, draft of letter and notes, 28 November 1948 and 30 November, 1948, FOIA (USAF).

[78] H. M. McCoy to Chief of Staff, USAF, memorandum, subject: "Project Status Report on Project 'SIGN'," 9 February 1949, FOIA (USAF).

[79] Edward Ruppelt, draft.

Chapter 5: Grudge

As the problem of the flying disks passed into 1949, the Air Force's ability to handle the issue had actually worsened. The dedicated team at Air Materiel Command had become dispirited and had been dispersed, with analysts Albert Deyarmond and Lawrence Truettner just clearing up the debris and writing the final SIGN report. At the Pentagon, there was no clarity of vision as to what the disks were, nor, therefore, how appropriately to organize an investigation. Probably because of leaks, members of the press and public were beginning to hear that the Soviets were the cause of this phenomenon: something not viewed as at all desirable as a public message. Within the military, officers were puzzled as to what the policy towards these objects really was. Do we take them seriously? Do we investigate? Report? To whom? Anyone hearing rumors of the shootout at the National Bureau of Standards and the embarrassment of the AMC Intelligence community probably thought that saying anything at all about flying disks was a career mistake. The Directorate of Intelligence was slow to realize that it had botched the situation, and, in the following year, things would get worse, not better. Things would have gotten better, of course, if the phenomenon would just stop. Then everyone could let these events fade with memory, and ultimately relax in the conviction that they had never happened.

But, of course, the phenomenon was very far from stopping. Sightings by some of the nation's leading technology and science experts would occur during this year. We will get to them in their place, later in this chapter. However, to whet the appetite, and to demonstrate a point, there are two interesting incidents that occurred early in 1949.

In the early afternoon of January 4 at Hickam Field, Hawaii,[1] an Air Force pilot and a base communications officer saw an unusual object, apparently several miles off the base and slowly circling. It was a disk, bright white on the underside and darker on top. The object possessed no other structures. It proceeded for fifteen minutes to make "rhythmical undulation" maneuvers in a cyclical manner. The "object seemed to maneuver under control at all times—completing 360° turns and 90° turns." The object then "departed climbing at accelerated speed out of sight." The observer received rave compliments for his level-headedness and integrity from the base's investigating officer. Project Grudge asked that the captain fill out a form, asked no more questions, and filed it. Even Allen Hynek, in the thick of his orientation towards trying to debunk every sighting possible, felt that this was a rare case wherein the witness had really seen a flying disk.[2] Trying to find something negative to say about this, months later in the Grudge report, the Grudge analyst at that time groused that the witness should have observed "a greater amount of detail."

On January 27 near Eglin AFB, Florida,[3] an Air Force officer and his wife were the witnesses. He was an engineer and chief of the aircraft branch at the base. He had also recently been part of the intelligence group at AMC, having transferred to Eglin in the fall of 1948. This was a nocturnal sighting, occurring around midnight, and lasting about 25 minutes. The object was similar to that seen in 1947 by Chiles and Whitted: an elongated fat cigar or cucumber-shaped structure with what the observers felt were one or two rows of windows along its length. It seemed to pulse its light, and made many maneuvers before disappearing. The witnesses thought, because of the pulses accompanied by "sparks," that the object was rocket-propelled. The sudden "right-angle" changes of direction were an early case of a class of sightings that involved "impossible" non-inertial motions. One can imagine what excitement this would have caused 6 months earlier during the Chiles-Whitted affair. As it was, no one now was interested. The case received a minimal filing.

As the phenomenon continued doing whatever it was that it was doing, Albert Deyarmond and Lawrence Truettner soldiered onward with the last assignment for Project SIGN: the final report. It was completed in February: "Unidentified Aerial Objects, Project 'SIGN'."[4] The report is marked "Secret" and is 35 pages long (about the same as the fabled "Estimate"). The big wheels of AMC (Clingerman signing for McCoy, and Miles Goll signing for Clingerman) approved it for transmission to the Pentagon. To the UFO historian, the whole document is interesting. But, for our purposes, a summary and a few remarks will suffice.

Deyarmond and Truettner had a problem. They had to compose the report but without the conclusion that they believed everything pointed towards. It was difficult to do that and make the report read as if it made sense. Deyarmond and Truettner accomplished this, as best they could, by adopting the view that it was just possible that all the incidents for which no "reasonable" solution was available were caused by inadequacies in human beings' abilities to perceive details accurately. Thereby they could continue to describe the cases as honestly as possible, and dismiss certain theories as unlikely or not fitting the cases, but fall back in the end on the escape hatch that the observations were poor. This also allowed the AMC analysts to obey "to the letter" General Cabell's flat order that any SIGN report would *not* say that we have identified these mysterious incidents. This then also brought them into line, because they could go right with Cabell's "opinion" that we must maintain serious study of these unknown objects till we get the explanation. We know that Deyarmond and Truettner did *not* believe that all the observations of unidentified objects were poor (they believed them sufficient to eliminate all mundane explanations, as we have seen), but they were forced to rest their assessment upon this fiction. To reiterate, the Pentagon tells the analysts that these objects are to be considered unidentified. By definition, that means the information and the observations are not to be considered sufficient.

The writers' language throughout the text is extremely mild and tentative. It's obvious that everyone has gotten the message. Still, the phenomenon is stated as real, and in the "traditional" forms of expression (disks, fuselages, spheres, and balls of light) that we have seen in the previous estimates. The Soviet threat is mentioned; so, even, is the extraterrestrial hypothesis, though not supportively. Two appendices are intriguing: a thoughtful essay by MIT physicist Dr. George Valley, on the physical and astronomical considerations which might be involved in evaluations of the cases, plus suggestions on better investigation and analyses;[5] and a RAND report by Dr. James Lipp, entirely on the consideration of extraterrestrial civilizations and space travel.[6] Though neither Valley nor Lipp were about to make statements in support of the SIGN/Chiles-Whitted hypothesis for the flying disks, their objective, well-

Dr. George Valley

reasoned essays gave the report a strong extraterrestrial hypothesis (ETH) afterglow. We are not saying that Valley or Lipp bought into the ETH—Lipp is definitely known *not* to have[7]—but their essays have the open-minded flavor that would give the reader pause. Deyarmond and Truettner, taking no encouragement from any of that, ended by recommending that the project should be continued, but at only a minimal level. Their rationale was that once enough cases, examined over a reasonable period of time, indicated no national security issues, then the project should be terminated. It is almost their final defiance: since you (the Pentagon) don't trust us to do this work, just close the project.

Problems continued at the Pentagon. Commands were confused by an equally confused policy and leadership. Cabell's brief remarks in his autobiography attempted to rewrite this history by claiming that he was always encouraging his operatives to aim at proving that the disks were real.[8] That *might* have been true in 1951, but the documents of 1949 show no evidence of Cabell allowing SIGN the freedom to interpret the UFO phenomenon as it saw fit. In fact, it could be said that the Air Force's behavior towards the phenomenon was completely reactionary and disorganized.

A very important example of this is the way the *Saturday Evening Post* writer, Sidney Shalett, was handled. As we have seen, Cabell wanted none of this "flying saucer article," but Secretary Forrestal's approval forced it upon him. The damage control would be accomplished by giving Shalett a guided tour of AMC and a view of limited, low classification cases, plus a few "conservative" opinions by Air Force personnel. This happened in early February. Simultaneously, the Air Force would produce its own counter-document to be released at the same time as the article (in late April).

At the beginning of March, Shalett, as per a previous understanding with the Air Force, sent the Directorate of Intelligence a draft of his article for review.[9] The Directorate disapproved printing it. It listed four problems. There was objection to Shalett stating a formal Air Force position, and claiming that his primary information source was the Air Force (even though it was). The Directorate did not want Irving Langmuir quoted as deprecating the Air Force UFO project, and they wanted no statement that the Air Force and the Navy were not cooperating in these investigations. In the published two-part article, it appears that Shalett revised his draft to accommodate these objections. Although one can identify commentary that seems to lead up to such declarations, these four points are not directly stated by Shalett.[10] Langmuir, a thoroughly irascible character, was violently anti-UFO and "suggested" (to put it mildly) that the Air Force not even bother to look at the phenomenon (a surprising and paradoxically unscientific attitude for one so honored as a scientist), but at least he was not quoted as trashing the Air Force itself. The bigger problem rumbling beneath the surface was a rift between the Air Force and the Navy, of which we will see clear evidence as we continue.

WHAT YOU CAN BELIEVE ABOUT FLYING SAUCERS

By SIDNEY SHALETT

Is there "something funny" about the silence that still envelops the mysterious disks that alarmed us all and lured three military pilots to crash deaths? Were they missiles from Russia? From Mars? Air Intelligence probed 250 reports and here, for the first time, are its findings.

The tenor of the first part of Shalett's article is quite positive towards the mystery, starting with a brief retelling of several classic cases without much in the way of allusion and mockery. The back part of this first piece then begins laying out all the things that are mistaken for aerial anomalies. This first installment was a fairly even-handed introduction to the mystery.[11]

A week later, part two of the piece begins laying down the anti-mystery thunder. The Air Force's biggest names (Vandenberg, Norstad, McCoy, Spaatz, and LeMay) are lined up with one debunking comment or example after another. "Vertigo," "dizziness," "hallucination," and "stupor" leading to "self-hypnosis" are brought in to reduce (generically) the whole mystery to some unfortunate error. The Fargo "dogfight" is singled out for a particularly detailed trashing. Hoaxes and mass hysteria are then added to the list of the stewpot of errors, building up to Dr. Langmuir and his "Forget it!" climax quote

Left to Right: General Vandenberg, General Spaatz, Colonel McCoy, and General LeMay

on UFOs. One wonders what all the pilots, scientists, engineers, and just plain honest folks who had seen UFOs in circumstances not involving dizziness, stupor, and mass hysteria thought about this treatment. This exact issue, the trashing of peoples' reports (and by association, aspects of their character), immediately became another serious problem for the Air Force. People—even within the military—began to refuse to report their sightings to the Air Force.

We do not know whether Shalett himself felt guilty about the tenor of his treatment, but he reversed course at the tail end of the article to write sympathetically about the Chiles-Whitted case, and of the men themselves. He then told the readers that they really should report their cases and gave them hints on how to make good observations.

On the whole the Shalett "problem" had not turned out too badly. But, strangely, it was the Air Force's *own* simultaneous information management press release that got them in hot water.

We have mentioned that the Pentagon feared what Shalett would say and had recommended that it prepare a simultaneous document for damage control. As January and February proceeded, apparently no one took care of this. As Shalett finished his draft there was apparently a need to get something going which could be released to the press alongside it. This is where documents are lacking that could explain what seems to be a major gaff. During March, when the Pentagon was sleeping on this, some persons at AMC Project SIGN/Grudge decided to write the "companion piece."[12] An enigmatic fragment of a released document dated April 6 notifies the Pentagon that this has been completed. It was entitled *The Flying Saucer Story*. Perhaps it was specifically ordered by the Pentagon, believing that a Grudge-like attitude would be evoked. We do not know who wrote it, but the attitude reflected the beliefs of "SIGN." As publication of Shalett's piece became imminent, Major Boggs finally read it and queried Generals Cabell and Moore as to how to handle it.[13] He recommended removing certain speculation from the writing, plus making it only available to persons who would physically present themselves at the Pentagon and read the report there. Otherwise, he felt, many briefs of cases et al. should be allowed to remain in the document since Shalett had viewed similar material and this document might get other reporters off their backs and, more importantly, *not* talking to AMC. Some exchanges and disagreements went on between General Cabell and Public Information Officer Stephen Leo, but we do not know the substance of this interchange.[14] One thing this back-and-forth did was to shove the decision right up onto the *Saturday Evening Post* publishing date. So, on April 27, 1949, (Shalett's date was the 30th), the Air Force released the re-titled Project "Saucer."[15]

The release is quite remarkable, given what the Pentagon thought they were trying to accomplish. The attitude, as noted above, was pure SIGN. Even on the issue of possible extraterrestrial spacecraft the writer risked stating "*almost* a complete impossibility," and followed with a number of solid and dramatic cases, including Arnold, the Portland policemen case, Muroc, Mantell, Chiles-Whitted, and the Fargo dogfight. All were discussed as if unidentified, *including Mantell*. The Air Force release was far more positive than was the article it was meant to dampen! Later in the release the writer included material taken from James Lipp and George Valley on extraterrestrial possibilities and how one might make a spacecraft go. There were hints that although it was unlikely, it was not impossible that not only life but also even intelligent life could live on Mars and Venus. Speculation was included on why such life could now be visiting Earth. The odds of such intelligent life were given as "*at least a thousand to* one"—a long way from "impossible." The writer went on to say that very advanced life in deep space is essentially a certainty, but could it get here? A speculation on converting nuclear fuel is then made and applied to a trip from a nearby suitable star: time of flight estimate = 16 years. More difficulties are admitted, but the odds have reduced to "*highly improbable.*" Then the "foreign" aircraft (read: Soviet) theory is stated and quickly debunked with one sentence. In summary, all the thinking on the possibility of extraterrestrial craft has been "*largely* conjecture"—not flatly conjecture or pure bunk. Whoever was writing this was taking serious liberties with the Pentagon view of not encouraging extraterrestrial thinking at all. The report ends with: *"The saucers are not a joke. Neither are they cause for alarm."*

Major Donald Keyhoe

Once again, Air Force policy and actions regarding the UFO phenomenon were chaotic, contradictory, and all over the map. As this is a study of the government involvement with the phenomenon, we underplay the civilian involvement here, but one break in this orientation deserves to be made (at least in mention) now. This strange, backwards dichotomy of a civilian writer producing an Air Force–aided piece much more negative than the twinned Air Force release alongside it utterly boggled the mind of a civilian writer researching whether there was really a story to UFOs or not. This writer was retired Marine Major Donald Keyhoe.[16] He could not understand how he could be reading what was in the Project "Saucer" release. His only answer was that there must be some big disagreement among authorities in the Air Force (as we have seen, a good guess), and that one group felt that there was much of importance in this (despite the public comments of the big wheels) and that they used this release as a way to get their ideas out there. Keyhoe was right about his first two guesses and may even have been right about the third. What we know for sure is that this publicity gaff turned him into the biggest advocate for the phenomenon's importance, and consequently the biggest thorn in the Air Force's side for the next twenty-odd years.

Even though Keyhoe had yet to get started with his criticisms of the Air Force, they were already having plenty of difficulty managing things without him. As mentioned, in January leaks were already occurring about the Pentagon's concerns, as the AMC liaison officer to the Nuclear Energy for the Propulsion of Aircraft (NEPA) project at Oak Ridge National Laboratories stated to the FBI, at length, his views that the flying disks were human-made nuclear-powered missiles originating in the USSR, views he felt paralleled those of the Pentagon.[17] A couple of months later, famous radio newsman Walter Winchell was booming the same declaration all over the country, to the Air Force's distress.[18] By July, the idea of the Soviet nuclear-powered saucer was featured again, this time by writer Frederick Moorehouse in *Argosy* magazine.[19] The Air Force was harvesting rotten fruit from its allegedly secret conclusions that the flying disks were real but neither our own nor interplanetary. The idea that people would be satisfied with simply "unknown" or "mysterious" flew in the face of human nature.

Walter Winchell

High authorities in the military wanted answers, too, and we know that at the same time as the Shalett affair, the Air Force was getting urgent inquiries from at least the Army.[20] This indicated to General Cabell that he needed to make a presentation to the "Joint Intelligence Committee." (JIC) In order to understand this, we should explain what the JIC was.

The National Security Act of 1947,[21] among other things, created the Joint Chiefs of Staff (JCS). This was a military super committee composed of the chiefs of staff of the three major services (the Marine Corps commandant was sometimes included), plus one super chief, who usually rotated through the services. The reason for the JCS was that modern warfare, cold or hot, required plenty of interservice cooperation to function properly. The real work of the JCS was done by deputies for each chief plus their staffs, and a JCS secretary, of high rank.

Beneath the JCS were mainly three important subcommittees that fed information, analysis, and strategy "upwards."[22] They were the "Joint Strategic Plans Committee," the "Joint Logistics Plans Committee," and the "Joint Intelligence Committee." Cabell not only sat on the JIC but was also its chair. Cabell's decision in April of 1949 to make a presentation on flying disks indicated that he

Left to Right: General Cabell, Colonel Schweizer, Colonel Allen

thought that this was a critical topic at the moment and needed to be brought forward all the way to the JCS.

Thankfully, this is a document that we have. It is eight pages and Top Secret. Written by a major in "Air Estimates," the document amounts to another mini-estimate of the situation for the Joint Chiefs. It was vetted by the chief of Air Estimates, Colonel B.E. Allen, and Cabell's executive officer, Colonel John Schweizer. The main points were these:

1. Because of difficulties inherent in these type of reports, "positive identification" is extremely difficult;
2. The objects are mainly spherical in shape or elliptical; secondly, disk-like; thirdly, cylindrical;
3. Many incidents may be attributable to human error or the sighting of known technology or astronomical objects;
4. An analysis of the spacecraft concept by the RAND Corporation concluded that there are no reports "which would go against a rational explanation;"
5. In New Mexico, there has been a "repeated occurrence of green fireball phenomena," causing considerable concern. Current thinking is that there is some sort of upper atmospheric phenomenon;
6. The creditable unexplained incidents that might involve the use of atomic powered craft should be studied by the AEC and top aerodynamicists as a concern of the defense intelligence agencies;
7. There are numerous reports from reliable and competent observers for which a conclusive explanation has not been made. Some of these involve descriptions that would place them in the category of new manifestations of probable natural phenomena, but others involve configurations and described performance that might conceivably represent an advanced aerodynamic development. A few unexplained incidents surpass these limits of credibility.[23]

There is much in Cabell's JIC estimate. It is certainly an attitudinal opposite to the manufactured debunking statements that the Air Force big wheels gave to Shalett to quote in his articles. So again, it is the understandable Janus face: serious, on-the-alert concern on the "Inside," relaxed, calming dissembling for the public "Outside." Looking more specifically, the JIC estimate is a natural evolution from the early estimates of 1947 and the AIR-100 document. Added to those is "new" knowledge, such as the RAND opinion, and new concerns, such as the "green fireballs" of New Mexico (we will address that mystery, later). One thing relating to RAND should be mentioned. It appears to be true that it is in the dealing with RAND that the term "reasonable" begins to get replaced with "rational."[24] This may seem a small matter, and perhaps it is. But, as we know, "reasonable" and "rational" do not quite have the same tone. This is especially true when one uses them in the negative. "Irrational" is a term that persons such as Irving Langmuir use to type those things which are so a priori unthinkable that they are simply foolish and insane. The flying disk reality was *not* so considered in the intelligence community in the years we are discussing (by anyone who drove opinion and policy, anyway). Even the extraterrestrial possibilities were not so painted (as we've seen via Lipp and Valley). Such possibilities were highly unlikely and improbable, but not irrational. This is raised now, because, as years of investigation pass, the label of irrational (that is, foolish and insane) begins to be applied to the UFO phenomenon and those who are interested in it. Cabell himself did not view any of this as irrational despite using the "rational" allusion in his estimate. It is likely that it snuck in there due to the military conservatism of using the exact words of a reference document wherever they can in composing their own. The most striking thing within the estimate is, of course, the main summary paragraph: *"there are reliable, competent observers, who report unknowns. Some of these look like advances in aerodynamics. Some surpass even that."*

The green fireballs of New Mexico are a complicated business. Were they part of the flying disk mystery, or a coincidental sideshow? Were they more, or less, likely to be Soviet mischief? Who was investigating them? Who should have been? Whatever was going on here in late 1948 and into 1949, it thoroughly alarmed some of the authorities. However we now choose to look at this episode, it became entwined with all the UFO concerns, puzzlements, and incompetence that we have been discussing.

One can, if one wishes, see the green fireball mystery as a so-called "mini-flap" of incidents (a group of sightings fairly concentrated in time and spatial circumstances). The period: December 1948 to January 1949. The location: New Mexico, particularly near atomic laboratory installations (especially Los Alamos and Sandia). There were other times and places of incidents, but it was this "flap" that awakened concern.[25]

In the following narrative, we will parallel the outstanding write-up of the beginning of our concern about the green fireball phenomenon in Jerome Clark's foundational *UFO Encyclopedia* (which we recommend to readers for many topical subjects within the UFO field). Clark, an esteemed colleague in UFO history, wrote a masterful essay on the fireballs, based upon research entirely from the Project Blue Book documents regarding these original incidents. The readers may consider reading his more artful telling of these occurrences which we will merely outline below.

The first of anything is always debatable, but for our purposes 9:05 p.m. on December 5, 1948 will do. At that time, an Air Force pilot and co-pilot, flying near Las Vegas, New Mexico, saw a bright green aerial flash. Near Albuquerque, N.M., another green light flashed through the air. The officers contacted Kirtland AFB air traffic control. Kirtland then began questioning flight officers, both military and civilian, as to whether they had contacted unusual lights during flights.

By December 6, Kirtland's commander of the Air Force Office of Special Investigations (AFOSI), Lt. Colonel Doyle Rees, was already concerned that the green lights might be products of Soviet technology. Two of his chief operatives, Captains Neef and Stahl, began interviewing governmental organizations as to whether anything that they were doing might relate to flying green flares. Just as in 1947, when Colonel George Garrett and General George Shulgen of the Pentagon were asking similar questions about flying disks, all inquiries came back: not ours.

Neef and Stahl decided upon an aerial reconnaissance of the airspaces within which green flare lights had been seen. After they reached 5000 feet, they got their own dose of the mystery. The Blue Book documents describe their encounter.

Lt. Colonel Doyle Rees

At an estimated altitude of 2,000 feet higher than the airplane . . . a brilliant green light
was observed coming toward the airplane at a rapid rate of speed from approximately

30 degrees to the left of course, from 60 degrees ENE, to 240 degrees WSW. The object was similar in appearance to a burning green flare of common use in the Air Force. However, the light was much more intense and the object appeared to be considerably larger than a normal flare. No estimate can be made of the distance or the size of the object since no other object was visible upon which to base a comparison. The object was definitely larger and more brilliant than a shooting star, meteor, or flare. The trajectory of the object when first sighted was almost flat and parallel to the earth. The phenomenon lasted approximately two seconds at the end of which the object seemed to burn out. The trajectory then dropped off rapidly and a trail of glowing fragments reddish orange in color was observed falling toward the ground. The fragments were visible less than a second before disappearing. The phenomenon was of such intensity as to be visible from the very moment it ignited and was observed a split second later.[26]

Sightings such as these, and others that began coming in on a daily basis, seemed to be showing a pattern of too much familiarity with the big atomic laboratories. Fortunately, Colonel Rees knew that he had, locally, one of the nation's leading experts in the study of meteors, Dr. Lincoln LaPaz. LaPaz had often been an Air Force and Army consultant on atmospheric phenomena. LaPaz was extremely interested and had, in fact, already been collecting some information on the fireballs. He agreed to make an investigation on December 9.[27] At a multi-agency meeting called by Colonel Rees on the 11th, everyone said that nothing they were involved with produced this sort of phenomenon.[28] So, on the 12th, LaPaz went on the hunt.

Dr. Lincoln LaPaz

LaPaz and two Kirtland officers were driving on a desert road near Bernal, N.M. There in the sky was a green fireball flying above the horizon. LaPaz timed the trajectory at 2.2 seconds and thought that it was essentially horizontal. "Horizontal trajectory" meant "Not meteoric" to LaPaz. Because a second simultaneous sighting of this object was reported, a triangulation was possible. The plot indicated a twenty-five mile path flying directly away from Los Alamos. LaPaz was convinced that this could not have been a meteor. LaPaz:

none of the green fireballs has a train of sparks or a dust cloud. . . . This contrasts sharply with the behavior noted in cases of meteoritic fireballs—particularly those that penetrate to the very low levels where the green fireball of December 12 was observed. . . . On the basis of the various differences . . . the writer remains of the opinion that the fireball . . . was definitely non-meteoric and that in all probability the same is true of most, if not all, the other bright green fireballs. . . .[29]

LaPaz and the Atomic Energy Security Service felt that a possible threat was realistic enough that a patrol using "fast" astronomical quality cameras was authorized. They had no luck initially. But just as the patrol was getting ready to quit on the night of December 20, another green fireball appeared. This was also sighted in two places and the resultant triangulation indicated an almost opposite path to the fireball of the 12th. This fireball's path seemed directly *towards* Los Alamos.

By the end of December, Rees and LaPaz felt that they had, at a minimum, ten well-observed cases of the unusual, slow-moving fireballs.[30] LaPaz was careful to point out that the color of these things was wrong. Green does appear in fireball displays, but it is in the deep green and blue-green end of that color's spectrum. These objects were producing light at the "light green" and "yellow green" end, something that LaPaz said he had never observed in the Geminid meteor showers which dominated that time of the year. Rees was very concerned that they had some kind of enemy missile, possibly involved in targeting the atomic sites, on their hands. And (shades of the ghost rockets!), these things seemed to disintegrate, leaving no trace to pick up and test. Colonel Rees was already using his authority to get other OSI offices around the country to send him any similar-sounding incidents in their areas, and a few came in from Idaho, Oregon, and Arizona.

By January of 1949, the 4th Army Command was so alarmed that they asked the Pentagon for help.[31] This was something "in the air" so the Army handed it to the Air Force. Remembering what was happening with the Air Force and SIGN, this could not have come at a worse time. SIGN was crushed, humiliated, discredited, and disintegrating. The Air Force did not want to go that route. Luckily,

Dr. Joseph Kaplan

a member of the Scientific Advisory Board, Dr. Joseph Kaplan, an atmospheric physics expert from UCLA, was visiting LaPaz, and was brought up on the problem. Kaplan received this information and

Theodore von Karman

a preliminary report from an anxious LaPaz, who was absolutely convinced that the fireballs were technology. This happened on February 8. Kaplan went on to Washington and met with SAB chairman Theodore von Karman.[32] Von Karman, though a UFO skeptic, was impressed by this matter. He communicated to Pentagon Intelligence that this looked like a serious issue, which needed to be addressed.[33] (A copy of von Karman's letter is included in the appendix.) Von Karman did not know it, but this opinion was not welcome at the time with the current "Grudge" attitude.

Meanwhile, Rees and LaPaz were taking matters into their own hands. They organized a conference of Los Alamos scientific luminaries. These included Norris Bradbury, Marshall Holloway, Frederick Reines, and Edward Teller, father of the hydrogen bomb. Also included were LaPaz, two Air Force witnesses, and a Sandia representative.[34] Rees sent his investigator/aide, Captain M.E. Neef, to introduce the problem and give background on Air Force UFO

investigations. LaPaz detailed the cases so far, including his own observation. He said that there were ten incidents that strongly fit the pattern and 20 more that might do so. Teller thought that the phenomenon must be "electro-optical" (i.e. more of a "light" nature than "mass") due to the lack of sound. Bradbury was not ready to agree with him, feeling that this was a problem no matter which way one looked at it. The scientists took some heart in the fact that, if Teller was right, these observations were not of massive objects like missiles.

Left: Norris Bradbury   *Right: Dr. Edward Teller*

Everyone agreed that they should be concerned and alert about these things and do more to explain them. Back at the Pentagon, however, Major Boggs was writing a Grudge-oriented opinion that none of this was likely to be of significance, and that analyses such as those pursued by Allen Hynek for Grudge would, in time, prove that.[35]

Boggs and Hynek were not on the same page. Hynek, a friend of LaPaz, received the green fireball facts and assessment from him and wrote:

Dr. Allen Hynek

> Dr. Lincoln LaPaz has summarized thoroughly the nature of these incidents and, particularly, has noted the reasons why the objects concerned cannot be dismissed as ordinary meteoric phenomena. Dr. LaPaz is an extremely able man in the field of meteoritics and an enthusiastic, almost to the point of extravagance, investigator and worker. On the basis of the description on hand, I concur in his conclusions: Dr. LaPaz, who is "on location" and has observed at least one of these objects at first hand, should be fully supported in a continued investigation. Apart from the unusual appearance of the objects, the pattern of incidents is particularly striking. It would be exceedingly unlikely that so many meteors would appear in that small sector of the Southwest and nowhere else; if they did, they would not have consistently horizontal paths and head in a consistent direction. These points alone are sufficient to dismiss the meteoric hypothesis. It is entirely possible that, among the many incidents reported, one or two of the objects may have been fireballs, thus serving to confuse the issue, but a blanket explanation of that sort is improbable.

> I would suggest that Dr. Jack Workman, Director of the New Mexico School of Mines, be contacted. He is conducting highly classified experiments in very high velocity projectiles and may be in a position to offer a worthwhile opinion. High velocity experiments, probably in connection with preliminary trials in the production of artificial meteors or artificial satellites, may prove to be the explanation of these incidents. Such experiments would not be conducted at any of the recognized air bases so far contacted.[36]

Note that Hynek introduced some inside information about top-secret "artificial meteor-launching" experiments that he, somehow, knew about. This is reminiscent of other such high velocity launches accomplished by Dr. Fritz Zwicky a few years earlier in the region.[37] LaPaz was involved in those experiments and should have known about intermediate and current projects. Plus, he knew that the Navy was doing something involving "meteor photography" at White Sands, but could not get their cooperation on information sharing. LaPaz' and perhaps Hynek's views were moving towards "artificial meteors" which burn up with a distinctive color but, for the moment, were not *our* artificial meteors.

Rees became more and more upset with the Pentagon's and AMC's inactivity. AMC was ordered to send someone down, finally. The meeting, on February 24, was hostile.[38] After some angry exchanges about whose business this was and what should be done about it, the attendees finally agreed that there should be an organized observation and patrol project, manned by Air Force personnel, and looking for ground fragments and spectrum pictures.

Two months passed, with no action from AMC or the Pentagon. Rees sent another report. Then a letter: was AMC going to act or not? Pushed by concerns from the Atomic Energy commission, General Cabell decided that it was time, but not for Grudge (they were to be left out of it). Cabell sent

Kaplan to New Mexico on April 27, bringing news that a network of observation posts and a project to attempt to sample the air after a green fireball overflight was approved and to be implemented immediately.[39] The only AMC role was to organize troops for the task of night patrol observations. Somewhat oddly, as this latter was Rees' idea, the Pentagon batted this idea around for the entire month of June, the analysis being again in the hands of Major Boggs, and he denied it.[40] Boggs had, once more, given a "Grudge" opinion that there probably was not anything to this anyway, so why should AMC be burdened with an extra duty.

On June 24, a fireball flyover resulted in an apparently successful air sampling.[41] The analysis was, in LaPaz' mind, flatly abnormal. It showed copper. And copper "burned" green. Meteors, LaPaz reminded, have almost no copper—ever. This cinched, in his mind, that the things were human-made missiles of some kind. Late in the summer, reports like the above and continued communications-of-concern by the bases and the AEC, brought Kaplan and Air Force Research and Development to call for a summit meeting of top experts on the problem. The Pentagon, with its usual glacial pace, took another month before it ordered General Chidlaw, the new commanding officer at AMC, to make an evaluation of the data so far.[42] Chidlaw was not to assign this to Project Grudge, but rather to the Cambridge Research Laboratories of the Directorate for Geophysical Research. A meeting was arranged at Los Alamos on October 14.[43]

Most of the previous players attended (LaPaz, Neef, Rees, Kaplan, Bradbury, Reines, and Teller). FBI agents were present. So was atmospheric physics expert Stanislaw Ulam. Cambridge Research Station was represented by Major F. C. E. Oder, not only of the Air Force, but also of the CIA. No one could agree on an explanation, but all admitted that the concentration of the events around Los Alamos and Sandia did not sound like a natural phenomenon, and was a bit ominous. They proposed that a field project be run out of Oder's lab, with LaPaz' help. Kaplan pushed for the project and, perhaps aided by another letter of concern by the AEC in November, the Air Force's Research and Development Board approved it. The independent-of-Grudge project was initiated in February of 1950 as "Project Twinkle."[44] But, albeit still muddled in the confusion over all this, we will now return to 1949 before picking up the last of this story, in the next chapter.

Whether or not green fireballs were part of the UFO phenomenon in 1949, there were several spectacular cases that were. Right in the middle of the shenanigans in the New Mexican desert, our greatest observational astronomer saw a UFO. At his Las Cruces home, on a summer night of spectacular transparency, Clyde Tombaugh, discoverer of Pluto and leader of many nocturnal missile-launch observation teams for the White Sands Proving Grounds, was relaxing with his wife and mother, enjoying the heavens' display. Then something appeared. Tombaugh's own words are best. A copy of the original letter is shown on the next page.[45] Tombaugh did not run to the papers with this story, nor formally report it to AMC. But he talked with his friends and colleagues who worked out of White Sands. Many of them had already seen unusual objects in the sky. Tombaugh himself had seen two other "unknowns" and three green fireballs. He felt that these objects "defied any explanation of known phenomena, such as Venus, atmospheric optics, meteors, or planes."[46]

Clyde Tombaugh

AN UNUSUAL AERIAL PHENOMENON
by
Clyde W. Tombaugh

I saw the object about eleven o'clock one night in August, 1949 from the backyard of my home in Las Cruces, New Mexico. I happened to be looking at zenith, admiring the beautiful transparent sky of stars, when suddenly I spied a geometrical group of faint bluish-green rectangles of light similar to the "Lubbock lights". My wife and her mother were sitting in the yard with me and they saw them also. The group moved south-southeasterly, the individual rectangles became foreshortened, their space of formation smaller, (at first about one degree across) and the intensity duller, fading from view at about 35 degrees above the horizon. Total time of visibility was about three seconds. I was too flabbergasted to count the number of rectangles of light, or to note some other features I wondered about later. There was no sound. I have done thousands of hours of night sky watching, but never saw a sight so strange as this. The rectangles of light were of low luminosity; had there been a full moon in the sky, I am sure they would not have been visible.

Clyde W. Tombaugh
August 7, 1957

July 1949, Longview, Washington: An air show was in progress as part of local 4th of July celebrations (this event was on the 3rd). Over 200 people were in attendance. At the microphone was local aero-technology legend, retired commander Moulton Taylor. Military and civilian pilots speckled the crowd. As an air performer engaged in a skywriting demonstration, Taylor noticed something else in the sky—something not on the program. Taylor used the public address system to direct attention to the "visitor." The object, in binoculars, looked like a discus, with a metal-like reflective top surface and a darker bottom. As people were ordered into silence, no sound was heard. The object had "an undulating motion with its thwart ship axis rocking approximately thirty degrees above and below level" (that is, through 60° in all). It moved slowly, then undulated more rapidly as it accelerated. There was no shock wave. Especially amazing to Taylor was the object's ability to make abrupt "seemingly right angle corners." Referring to his wartime work as Officer-in-Charge of Guided Missile Research under Admiral Delmar Fahrney (the Navy's program) he said:

> It was in that capacity that we had extensive experience in the actual handling of guided missiles and pilot less aircraft by means of Radio Control . . . We flew the first jet and rocket-powered controlled missiles ever successfully launched in this country, and of course accumulated many hours of flying of aircraft of various types by remote control. We believe that this experience somewhat qualifies us for the remote observation of aircraft and flight phenomena.[47]

The phenomenon had thereby been witnessed by one of the best-qualified technologists that the U.S. could offer. What did he think that it was? Writing in 1957, Taylor said this:

> The sighting was definitely of some flying object unlike anything then or even presently known ... Many of the other observers at that time are still in the area and we have discussed this particular incident whenever UFOs are mentioned. Everyone still agrees that it was not an airplane or any other reasonably well explained object. I have spent many hours looking for other such objects, but have never been successful since. I only wish one would land and that I could be there to interview them. Ha.[48]

May 1949, Rogue River, Oregon:[49] A group of people were taking a vacation, getting away to nature and doing some fishing. Five adults were in a boat. It was still daylight, about 5 p.m. A round object manifested itself, like a brilliant mirror standing on edge. The witnesses had binoculars and passed them around. Two of the group worked for the National Advisory Committee for Aeronautics (NACA, the predecessor of NASA). One worked with the Moffett Field (CA) Supersonic Wind Tunnel, and the other as a drafter (thereby being familiar with fine details of aerodynamic designs). So, we have two more unusually qualified observers. The device was flat on the bottom and judged to have a diameter of 25-30 feet. There was an edge (somewhat like the edge of a thick coin), perhaps a foot high. The top was gently convex, and there was a thick "fin" which began about mid-ship and rose slowly but still was only a modest elevation at the rear. We can thank the unusual situation that this sighting featured an observer who could draw. A copy of that drawing is shown on page 84.

As usual, there was no noise, nor evidence of a jet stream. The object seemed to fly at normal jet plane speed. Both NACA employees were impressed that the object made a turn without needing to tilt or bank to accomplish it. The reader may wonder how a hostile (i.e. Project Grudge) Air Force dealt with reports like this. On the project record card is typed: *"No data presented to indicate object could NOT have been an aircraft. Conclusion: AIRCRAFT."* One wonders what the NACA men would have said if they had been informed of the Air Force's solution.

September 1949, Lexington, Nebraska:[50] Six members of a farming enterprise were threshing wheat when they saw three objects coming from the general direction of the sun (southwest at about 6:30 p.m.). As the objects proceeded they gave off a dazzling brilliance. They maintained a level flight with two of the objects changing positions as they flew. The power of the illumination remained constant throughout the incident (i.e. no pulses or flashes). Once the objects reached a direction northwest of the observers, they made a smooth 90 degree turn straight upwards and climbed rapidly out of sight. One of the farmers was a recent graduate of a two-year course in aeronautical design and thought the objects looked like a domed-disk when viewed face-forward, but were actually like a stubby, wingless, tailless

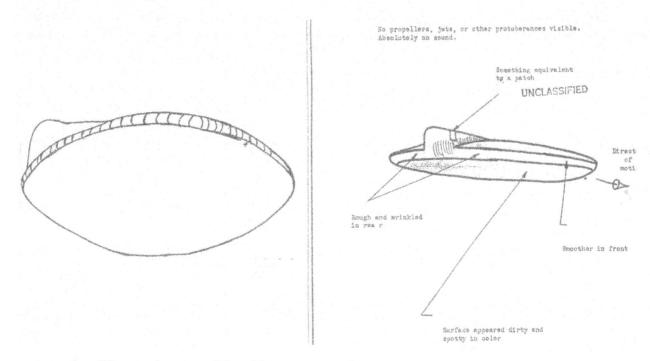

Witness drawing of the object seen near Rogue River, Oregon in May 1949.

fuselage when seen from the side. About five miles away, four other persons saw what they felt were two fast-moving objects flying in the distance at level flight before abruptly turning straight up and flying away from the Earth. This group of people did not know their distant "neighbors." How did Grudge handle this case? They apparently "lost" it. The only record seems to be the local Offutt Air Force Base investigation found in the files of Air Force consultant J. Allen Hynek. The project microfilms simply note: "Case missing." The case (six adult witnesses, four independent corroborative witnesses, abnormal aircraft structure and striking flight plan—disappearing straight upwards) can stand on its own as one worth remembering, but it is mentioned here to illustrate the incompetent neglect that characterized the Grudge period.

April 1949, Arrey, New Mexico:[51] In the midst of extreme Pentagon confusion over Sidney Shalett, the Project "Saucer" release fiasco, and trying to decide what to do about Green Fireballs, a sighting occurred which in many military and intelligence community minds became the poster child for unidentified objects. The reason for this status was not the spectacular quality of the phenomenon, but the spectacular quality of the witnesses.

The witnesses formed the Navy's top Secret balloon-launching Project Team, a group of the best-trained and experienced object-trackers in the world, and scientists who had "seen it all." The prestige and discipline of Dr. Charles Moore's team was such that even Grudge caved in and admitted that this was an "unidentified." As said, the case hardly wows one if taken apart from the circumstances. The team was launching a mid-

Dr. Charles Moore

morning balloon and tracking it with a theodolite. Looking visually, the team members initially thought they had picked up their balloon, but then realized it was something else. It was moving rapidly to the east, a white ellipsoid with a light yellow band on one side as if a shadow. The object altered to a northerly direction (none of this being in the same direction that the wind was taking their own balloon). The new object seemed to be rising all the way until it disappeared in the distance. The balloon experts' flat statement: "the object was not a balloon." But, given size, speed, and shape, what *else* could it be? Moore made what he felt were some reasonable assumptions based upon observations, experience, and knowledge of the current conditions. He guessed that the object was at about 300,000 feet when over their launch station. If true, it would have been about 100 feet in diameter. Once again, we must remember as the Air Force did, Moore and his team knew all about the big polyethylene balloons manufactured at General Mills and flown under Project Mogul et al. They were, after all, the ones who were flying them. Moore, later in the year, concluded:

> We did see an object under almost ideal observational conditions, which we cannot explain nor rationalize, but we do not claim that it was necessarily a flying disk or space ship.[52]

Upon hearing how the Air Force had tried to debunk his team's case, and several other such high-quality observations, Moore had one other insightful thing to say:

> It appears from reading the report analysis that the Air Forces have been more interested in disproving or casting doubt on all unidentified object observations rather than any attempt to evaluate or explore them. It is believed that should some object, extra-terrestrial in origin, actually be observed, this group would spend more time disproving its existence than investigating it.[53]

The Arrey-Moore sighting was just one of a surprising (to say the least) number of incidents involving our Top Secret balloon projects. We will say more about this later, but suffice it to say for now that there was a specific request for General Mills teams to log every incident.[54] Arrey was also just one of a set of sightings involving personnel from White Sands Proving Grounds. More about this later also, as we address the affair with Commander Robert McLaughlin's publication of these facts (much to the distress of the Air Force). These cases involving Naval personnel or projects seem to have created a real rift between the Navy and the Air Force on this subject.

All this activity in New Mexico stimulated the formation at both White Sands and Los Alamos of informal groups of scientists who became interested in the mystery, and spent some of their time in watch groups or otherwise trying to study it. We do not know much about the White Sands people, but a little more about the "Los Alamos Birdwatchers Association."[55]

The Birdwatchers was not their original nickname. As a member of the group attested, they were

> ...a group of our physicists (who) set up watches to observe and record the mysterious green fireballs.[56]
> As watching progressed, we armed ourselves with a camera and grating to try to photograph the spectrum of the light. We set up a Doppler meteor detector . . . and a low frequency electromagnetic listening and recording device.

Though obviously serious and talented, the group was unable to get a correlation between an overflight and a reading on one of those instruments. Later on, that changed.

The group was composed of ten physicists, several of whom were Los Alamos heavyweights (one of whom, Harold Agnew, became the lab's scientific director later in his career).[57] Some of them had seen unidentified phenomena themselves. Upon leaving his lab one evening, Fred Kalbach saw a green object, so brilliant that he could "read a newspaper" by it, fly over the location, apparently soundlessly, abruptly change direction without slowing, and rapidly disappear over the Jemez mountains. The wife of a second member, herself an explosives expert, was in a remote canyon destroying outdated charges, when she witnessed the same thing. "The sightings were so numerous that a group of us staff members produced a reporting form and encouraged those who saw these events to fill out the check list. Over a period of say three months, we collected possibly 50 reports."[58]

Harold Agnew holding part of the A-Bomb core device.

The group announced its desire to the Air Force, the FBI, (and doubtless, by procedure, the CIA) to participate in aiding the Air Force's attempt to solve the mystery. The Air Force approved. The group felt that they already had several observations within the first week. They hoped to prove or disprove two hypotheses: the things are a natural phenomenon (i.e. something like meteors or auroras); and the things are human-made.[59] Fred Kalbach said later: "I have personally attempted to follow up on some of the reports of others only to conclude that there are many things which competent observers have seen which cannot be explained in terms of our present knowledge."[60]

Meanwhile, something taking place at another scientific establishment would concern both the Birdwatchers and the Air Force project. Many persons interested in science know that for many years the world's most prestigious telescope was the great 200-inch reflector at Mt. Palomar, California. What most do not know is that Palomar was also the site of other scientific experiments. One of these was a cosmic-ray measuring project run by the Naval Electronic Laboratory (NEL). This project involved radiation counting equipment housed in the Observatory's powerhouse, located about 800 feet from the dome. The chart recorders were checked regularly by personnel attached to the observatory and, less frequently, by NEL members who had to travel to get there. On at least two occasions in 1949, interesting coincidences occurred: there was a fly-by of an unidentified object, and the cosmic ray counters surged.[61] We do not know much about the two (or more) sightings other than they somehow involved Dr. Ben Traxler of the Observatory and Dr. William Carter, who was completing his doctorate from Cal Tech at the time, and would soon be heading to Los Alamos. We *do* know one incident in a great deal of detail, however, that being the one by the observatory's weather bureau observer.

October 1949, Mt. Palomar, California:[62] Harley Marshall had finished his work at the dome and was driving over to the powerhouse to check on both the permanent weather instruments and the NEL Geiger counter. To his left and above he noticed a light reflection and motion. He looked closely: nine highly reflective objects were moving swiftly in a geometric pattern (a "V" of "V's": imagine three triangles in formation to create a larger one). The objects were "circular" with no wings nor projections, and moved, despite their great speed, without sound or jet trail. They disappeared while never breaking their geometric formation. Mr. Marshall said that he was quite excited as he drove up to the powerhouse to complete his work. Once inside, he saw that the radiation counter had risen to a rapid peak and then tailed off in a slower decline. Wondering if there could be a connection, he called Traxler, who came over, viewed the counter and was impressed. They then immediately called NEL. The Navy technicians arrived within two hours, making jokes until they saw the chart recorder. Also quite excited, they suddenly became serious and said that no one should talk about this until higher authorities were brought in. Sometime later, a Naval officer arrived and told everyone not to discuss the event. Some information, though not apparently an actual report, got to the Air Force eventually, but it appears that the Navy largely withheld the information from the Air Force. Dr. Carter took his information to the Los Alamos labs where the "Birdwatchers" heard about it. And somehow, by means not known, the information ultimately leaked to the hi-tech aero industry engineers of the area within the following two years.[63] So, attempts at secrecy were not like a sieve, but things did tend sooner or later to escape into the wider domain.

By the end of 1949, the Air Force had accomplished essentially nothing on any front except to destroy the only enthusiastic (admittedly, maybe too enthusiastic) group that they had working on the UFO subject. The public was confused by contrary signals. Highly qualified people—some of the best imaginable like Tombaugh, Taylor, and Moore—had seen extremely strange objects, and yet were hearing, both from public statements and through their more "insider" channels of information, that the subject was considered to be bunkum. Inside the intelligence community everything was at least that confused. Not only did the Air Force not know what they were dealing with, they had not figured out any method for properly dealing with the UFO phenomenon, nor even any method for properly dealing with public information. Compounding the Air Force's problems, the Navy seemed already to question Air Force competence (note the number of critical events already which involved Naval personnel and projects). Plus, it was almost impossible to get anyone to take the phenomenon seriously if they a) did not think that the objects might be Soviet, or b) had not seen one themselves (or had a close colleague who had), or c) both.

The Air Force made their next "brilliant" move at solving their problem by announcing to everyone, both within the services and to the public, that their project was now closed, since there was nothing to be concerned with in the phenomenon anyway. The Grudge report was finished on December 30.[64] In the midst of almost nothing but negativity in its pages was one ominous note: a recommendation that this situation be checked for psychological warfare implications.[65]

Notes

[1] Blue Book microfilm Roll 4.

[2] Hynek, Grudge Report.

[3] Blue Book microfilm Roll 4.

[4] Project SIGN.

[5] George Valley, "Some Considerations Affecting the Interpretation of Reports of Unidentified Flying Objects," Grudge Report, Appendix D.

[6] James Lipp, "Space Ship Considerations," Grudge Report, Appendix E-2.

[7] Robert Wood, personal communication (James Lipp was Dr. Robert Wood's uncle).

[8] Charles P. Cabell, A Man of Intelligence (edited by Charles P. Cabell, Jr.), 1997.

[9] Major de La Vigne for Brigadier General Moore, memorandum for record, 2 March 1949 and Major de La Vigne for Brigadier General Moore, memorandum, subject: "Proposed Magazine Article by Sidney Shalett," 22 March 1949, FOIA (USAF).

[10] Sidney Shalett, "What You Can Believe About Flying Saucers (Part 1)," Saturday Evening Post, 30 April 1949: 20-21, 136-139, and Part 2, 7 May 1949: 36, 184-186.

[11] Ruppelt, draft, 61-63.

[12] Nuckols to Colonel Smith, 6 April 1949. ("Smith" is Colonel Sony Smith, Director, Air Information Division, Directorate of Public Relations); and Stephen F. Leo to Director of Intelligence, memorandum, subject: "Flying Saucer Story," (day unreadable) April 1949, FOIA (USAF).

[13] Major Boggs for General Moore, memorandum for record (re: "Flying Saucer Story" release), 25 April 1949, FOIA (USAF).

[14] Cover sheet for correspondence: General Cabell's note to AFOAI on redraft of response, 21 April 1949, FOIA (USAF).

[15] Anonymous author(s), Project "Saucer," 27 April 1949.

[16] Donald Keyhoe, The Flying Saucers are Real, 1950; and see Clark's Encyclopedia, entry: "Keyhoe, Donald Edward."

[17] C. C. McSwain to J. Edgar Hoover, memorandum, subject: "Flying Saucers Observed over Oak Ridge Area," 10 January 1949, FOIA (FBI).

[18] AFOAI for General Moore, memorandum for record, subject: to prepare response to Walter Winchell's comments of 3 April 1949, 4 April 1949, FOIA (USAF).

[19] Frederick Moorehouse, "The Case of the Flying Saucers," *Argosy*, July 1949: 26ff.

[20] Inquiries at this time by the Army were mainly concerned with the problem of "green fireball" overflights of New Mexico bases, and what the Air Force was going to do about them. See that story later in the chapter.

[21] *The National Security Act of 1947*, title 1, Sec 101[U.S.C.402].

[22] Cabell (biography).

[23] Air Brief Special Study: General Cabell to DCS/O Staff meeting, subject: "Unidentified Aerial Objects," 27 April 1949, FOIA (USAF).

[24] Lt. H. W. Smith and Mr. G. W. Towles, *Unidentified Flying Objects: Project "Grudge" (Project No. XS-304)*, Technical Report 102-AC 49/15-100, Air Materiel Command, Dayton, Ohio, August 1949.

[25] The Green Fireballs mystery has been addressed in a variety of ways. Much documentation has been received via USAF FOIAs of the 1949 era. The most extensive FOIA'd document available is the following: "Conference on Aerial Phenomena," a 24-page report of a 16 February 1949 meeting held at Los Alamos with a cover letter by Commander Richard Mandelkorn, USN, reporting for Sandia base. Many other FOIA documents exist for this topic.

[26] Clark, *Encyclopedia*, entry: "Green Fireballs and Other Southwestern Lights," vol. 1, 454-461.

[27] Blue Book files, "Enclosure No. 1 to Investigative Report #24-8, 17th District OSI files."

[28] Gross (1948) 81-2 lists six documents wherein USAF authorities asked various laboratories in the air and airbases for information potentially relating to the fireballs.

[29] Clark, "Green Fireballs."

[30] Blue Book files, "Interoffice memo slip, Headquarters, Fourth Army, 29 December 1948, Major Godsoe to A c/s G-2 Army Intelligence."

[31] Office of the AC of S, G-2, Headquarters, Fourth Army, memorandum (Summary of Information), subject: Unconventional Aircraft, 13 January 1949, FOIA (USAF).

[32] Richard Mandelkorn, USN, Sandia, transcript of "Conference on Aerial Phenomena," 16 February 1949, 11-12, FOIA (USAF); hereafter: Mandelkorn, transcript.

[33] Theodore von Karman to C.P. Cabell, 11 February 1949, FOIA (USAF).

[34] Mandelkorn, transcript.

[35] Hynek, Grudge Report.

[36] Hynek, Grudge Report.

[37] "Artificial Meteors," *Army Ordnance*, July/August 1947: 157-163; and Stephen M. Maurer, "Idea Man," *Beamline*, Winter 2001: 21-27.

[38] Gross' Supplement p. 11.

[39] Doyle Rees, Lt. Col. USAF to Director of Special Investigations, Office of the Inspector General, USAF, Washington, DC, memorandum and letter, subject: "Unknown (aerial phenomena)," 12 May 1949, FOIA (USAF).

[40] Major Aaron J. Boggs for Col. Schweizer (and Cabell), memorandum for record, 16 June 1949, FOIA (USAF), (another followed 28 June 1949, coordinated by Boggs and Colonels Allen and Walsh); J. Kaplan to Major General C. P. Cabell, 13 July 1949, FOIA (USAF).

[41] Lincoln LaPaz to Colonel Doyle Rees, subject: "Anomalous Luminous Phenomena, Sixth Report," 17 August 1949, FOIA (USAF).

[42] Colonel John Schweizer to Director of Intelligence, United States Army, memorandum: draft letter, United States Army, 19 August 1949, FOIA (USAF).

[43] Blue Book files, Lt. Colonel Doyle Rees, memorandum/letter, subject: "Special Inquiry," 27 October 1949; and Major Frederic Oder, letter to Commanding General, AMC, 7 November 1949.

[44] L. Elterman, *Project Twinkle: Final Report*, USAF Research and Development, Washington, DC, 11 December 1951.

[45] C. Tombaugh, an open letter to UFO researchers, "An Unusual Aerial Phenomenon," 7 August 1957, NICAP files; and J. E. McDonald, letter to Richard Hall, 24 October 1966, NICAP files.

[46] L. Stringfield (quoting letter from Tombaugh) to Ted Bloecher, 20 March 1956, CUFOS files.

[47] M. Taylor to Donald Keyhoe, 28 January 1957, NICAP files.

[48] Taylor to Keyhoe, 28 January 1957.

[49] Blue Book files Roll 5.

[50] Blue Book files "case missing," but materials from files found in J. Allen Hynek case files/CUFOS.

[51] Blue Book files Roll 5.

[52] C. B. Moore to Adie Suehsdorf, *This Week Magazine*, 31 December 1949, NICAP files.

[53] C. B. Moore to Adie Suehsdorf, 23 January 1950, NICAP files.

[54] Ruppelt, draft.

[55] Ruppelt, draft.

[56] Sidney Newburger, Security Operations Branch, USAF OSI to Carroll L. Tyler, memorandum, subject: "Aerial Phenomena," 30 November 1949, FOIA (USAF).

[57] Newburger to Tyler, memorandum, "Aerial Phenomena," FOIA (USAF).

[58] J. F. Kalbach to James McDonald, 1 January 1970, McDonald files, University of Arizona archives.

[59] Kalbach to McDonald, 1 January 1970.

[60] Kalbach to McDonald, 1 January 1970.

[61] Blue Book files (T. C. Thomas, ONR Los Angeles to chief of Naval Research, Washington, D.C., 23 November 1949); Ruppelt draft; and Harley B. Marshall to James McDonald, 15 January 1970, McDonald files, University of Arizona archives.

[62] Clark, *Encyclopedia*, entry "Civilian Saucer Investigation."

[63] Ruppelt, draft; Donald Keyhoe, *Flying Saucers are Real*, 1950, 149.

[64] Lt. H. W. Smith and Mr. G. W. Towles, *Unidentified Flying Objects: Project "Grudge."*

[65] Smith and Towles, *"Project Grudge,"* 10.

Chapter 6: Duck and Cover

The onset of the Korean War pushed UFOs off the newspapers during the second half of 1950. This gave the Air Force a respite, for the months of March through June caused the Pentagon some of its roughest challenges related to information management. The Pentagon weathered these challenges, barely, but its handling of the situation left a legacy of distrust by elements of the public, disgust by many witnesses, and more confusion within the services.

Despite Donald Keyhoe's best-selling article in *True* magazine at the beginning of the year,[1] there were few spectacular UFO incidents in the first two months. Students of the subject (even in these early times) have speculated that abundant concentrations of UFO observations and reports are mainly a psychosocial phenomenon, based upon high profile publicity stories stimulating excitable or nervous minds. But, considering the reality of UFO incident frequency, the number of reports rarely responds to publicity in this fashion, and the first months of 1950 ran true in this regard. Though moribund at Air Materiel Command, Project Grudge received eleven reports in January and fourteen in February—statistically "ordinary" in a non-flap year.[2] One of the few incidents that both puzzled the military and was leaked to the public was the Davis-Monthan AFB, Arizona case on the first day of February.

Because of our interest in governmental response to UFO reports, and because of our findings of a great deal of disorganization in those responses, the following incident is worth mentioning. Early in February, the Army, Air Force, CIA, FBI, and Department of State received an intelligence analysis from the Navy.[3] This is a mild surprise to modern historians because, although it has been known that the Navy was getting copies of Air Force reports at least since late 1948, the existence of a formalized method of UFO case analysis by Naval Intelligence has been only suspected. Nevertheless, in February of 1950, was proffered an analysis from "Intelligence Division, Office of the Chief of Naval Operations." The code for the analyzing group was OP322F2, which represented the Naval Intelligence Technical Unit. The contents of the document clearly show a naval intelligence analysis of a very high level.

The subject matter related to reports of unknown objects in the vicinity of Kodiak Island, Alaska, on January 22 and 23, 1950. Although we do not have the important data enclosures that were originally attached to this document, the situation described is still powerful. A naval patrol plane pilot reported a radar contact 20 miles north of the naval air station in Kodiak. Eight minutes later, another contact occurred ten miles southeast of the station. Traffic control indicated that no traffic should be there. Intermittent interference with radar was occurring throughout this period. Meanwhile, watchmen on the *USS Tillamock* witnessed a red light (like an exhaust) come from the southeast, move in a clockwise circle, and fly back on approximately the same course. The light made no noise and had the appearance of a small ball of fire.

About two hours later, the pilot making the original report again received a radar return on an object apparently five miles away and saw it visually. All crewmembers were alerted and witnessed it as well. The object passed directly overhead while indicating a rough airspeed of 1800 mph. The pilot climbed to attempt intercept but "the object was too maneuverable." The pilot tried to chase and close, but the object kept ahead, then abruptly turned left and back and "came up on Smith's quarter" (we assume that this means that it was pacing the patrol plane). The pilot considered this a threatening situation and turned off all lights on his aircraft. The two flew together for about four minutes; then the object left and disappeared to the southeast.

The incidents were viewed as problematical and possibly dangerous. This was not a balloon as none were launched in the affected timeframe, and a balloon would not have matched the observations very well anyway. Meteors were also mentioned in the report but could not be taken seriously. The analysis contended that, whatever this was, "the exact nature of (the phenomenon) could not be determined by this office." Here are the words of two of the analysts:

The opinion of OP322V2C, the Naval Deputy Director of the Air Intelligence Divisions:

> The *possibility* exists that incidents covered by para.2.a, b, & d might be jet aircraft; however, there is insufficient intelligence to definitely identify the unidentified objects as aircraft. Several reports of similar radar interference have been received from DIO/17ND. It is possible that this is interference from another radar in the vicinity, malfunctioning of components within the radar set, or both.

The opinion of F2:

> Many of the previous reports of radar interference tend to indicate local interference (generated within the aircraft). This looks more like external interference from sources outside the aircraft than previous reports, though it is far from conclusive. These reports are always of interest.[4]

Our interests here are two-fold: first, this exercise was well documented and unsolved by military authorities. It described some sort of object of great speed and maneuverability, as well as a conscious intent to turn and pace the patrol plane; second, the Navy's handling of the report indicates an interest in analyzing UFO reports outside the Air Force system. This may be due to the Air Force's confusing messages to the intelligence community generally, or it may even be that they (USN) lacked confidence in the Air Force's approach to the subject. There is further support for this latter view in the documents, and we will return to this Air Force/Navy awkwardness towards the subject as this study proceeds.

One day later, two Air Force pilots were flying from Pope AFB, North Carolina to Bolling AFB, D.C.[5] The object that they sighted was just above their altitude (and the cloud layer, as were they) and seemed to be moving back and forth between two slightly higher cloudbanks. It looked like a hemisphere, rounded on top, but could have been a spheroid, as black smoke seemed to obscure the bottom. Some dark projection seemed to hang below the unknown. The object would move linearly, horizontally, between cloudbanks, then stop and reverse with no tilting or other motion. The pilots pursued in their Beech C-45 but could not close on the object as it moved at a constant pace ahead of them. Then it increased speed and left them behind. A minute and a half later it returned and took up station directly in front of them (distance estimate unstated), and then accelerated and disappeared directly away. Agents from the Air Force Office of Special Investigations debriefed the pilots and their passenger, who was also a witness. One of the questions the airmen were asked was whether they had read Keyhoe's article. They said that they had not. One wonders whether the Air Force really believed that their experienced pilots (both were Captains) could be so influenced by reading a flying saucer article—that their ability to observe and evaluate was so hindered—that they could report something as unexplainable as this. This conjecture is possibly accurate, as an article by Dr. Paul Fitts of AMC's Aero-Medical Laboratory in *Air Force Magazine* of February 1950 attempted to debunk UFO reports on a variety of psychosocial and physiological grounds (just as had been done in the Project Grudge final report).[6]

The Air Force was in full rejection mode at this time. The Pentagon had created a directive, dated 8 February 1950, labeled AFCSI letter #85. Following closely on the heels of its announcement that Project Grudge was discontinued, this directive stated:

> Spot Intelligence Reports concerning sightings of unidentified aerial objects need not be forwarded by TWX unless considered to be of priority Counterintelligence interest to this (Air Force OSI, The Inspector General) headquarters.[7]

What this meant was that if a base command had fielded a UFO report it was no longer required that a report be sent on to either the Pentagon or AMC. It was that command's judgment call as to whether it was important enough. In reality, what this meant to savvy officers was that the subject was being downplayed, and often, as mentioned by future Air Force project officer Edward Ruppelt, no investigation or paperwork need be done at all. Not everyone agreed with this seemingly unconcerned attitude. Brooks AFB, Texas and the Atomic Energy Commission (concerned about the green fireball phenomenon) wrote the Pentagon expressing their disapproval of eliminating the Air Force project.[8]

In February, the UFO phenomenon began in earnest, but south of the U.S. border in Mexico. Both citizens and the military were slow to take notice. But they did notice something else which was to become the real spark of a publicity wildfire in the following months. This is a story-within-our-story worth telling in some detail.

Robert McLaughlin was an engineering graduate of the Naval Academy and an expert on anti-aircraft gunnery. He migrated into guided missiles work and worked on a primitive beginning of what we would call an "intelligent" missile, able to alter flight on its own to destroy evasive targets. McLaughlin was active in the Pacific Theatre during the war, and in 1946 was assigned to White Sands Proving Grounds in charge of naval research units at the base.[9]

As we have seen, there was a great deal of UFO activity in the vicinity of White Sands, and Commander McLaughlin heard about it. He was one of the first to hear from Charles Moore's group about the theodolite observation of an object during their balloon launch of April 24, 1949. In early May 1949, McLaughlin himself saw a UFO during a WAC-B rocket launch at the Proving Grounds. These were not the only incidents he had heard about and on May 12, 1949, he wrote his friend, the legendary atmospheric physicist Dr. James Van Allen, about the phenomenon.[10]

McLaughlin was more than intrigued; all this excited him. His collection of reports indicated to him that these objects could accelerate.

Robert McLaughlin

This meant they were powered, and, therefore, were technology, and that the acceleration and maneuvering characteristics precluded them being manned. He had already talked to Clyde Tombaugh

Dr. James Van Allen

prior to writing Van Allen. Both McLaughlin and Tombaugh thought that the technology perhaps came from Mars. (Tombaugh had seen an unusual, anomalous "flash" light up an area of the Martian surface in his telescope in 1941 and other rare flashes had been seen by Tsuneo Saheki of Japan; plus Mars was in one of its closer positions to Earth when the U.S. set off its first atomic bomb. Both McLaughlin and Tombaugh wondered whether a Martian race had been alerted by that event to come take a closer look). McLaughlin admitted to Van Allen that all of this gave him a bit of a crazy feeling, but the observational facts were at least facts.

On June 14, 1949, another "unidentified" was observed by base personnel, and this series of events, plus the fact that the Charles Moore ground observation had received national press, caused the Public Information Office of the Pentagon to send an officer personally to interview McLaughlin and the other USN research project personnel.[11] When the PIO officer ultimately met with McLaughlin in the Commander's office, McLaughlin began freely unloading all the details of the incidents as he knew them. The third party in the room, a veteran U.S. Army intelligence officer, sternly reminded McLaughlin that he should *not* be freely speaking of these classified matters, and that approval for such talk must come from higher authority in the Pentagon. McLaughlin waved the Army officer off, said that the information was commonly known, and went on over the objections (the Army officer later complained loudly about these indiscretions during an investigation by the Air Force's Office of Special Investigations later in the year).[12] The Army intelligence officer's warning is not what one would expect considering the Air Force's recent termination of Projects SIGN and Grudge and the Pentagon directive that reduced priorities on UFOs.

On August 23, 1949, McLaughlin heard of yet another incident. This occurred just before the Navy invited a group of reporters to watch a Viking rocket launch, be escorted around the base facilities, and talk to U.S. Navy personnel. During this visit, McLaughlin talked to the reporters. One writer, Marvin Miles of the *Los Angeles Times*, returned to his office and penned "U.S. Officers Report Seeing Flying Disks," in the August 30, 1949, edition.[13] He reported speaking to witnesses of three different events, and specifically cited McLaughlin. McLaughlin said that in Moore's case the device was moving at greater than 10,000 miles per hour. The reasoning behind McLaughlin's estimate cannot be established. There were no background objects or any mechanisms whereby the real distance or size of the UFO could be estimated. It is not known how McLaughlin arrived at his estimate, but it is almost certainly an error, which appeared both in the *Los Angeles Times* and in the follow-up *True* magazine article.

When the story broke, the public badgered the Army Commander of White Sands, Brigadier General Philip Blackmore, to comment. He said: "So far as I know these reports are simply untrue."[14] General Blackmore was doing his duty. He had already been told of the Charles Moore sighting earlier.[15] But, not believing that an officer would stand in front of the American press and tell a flat lie, the press and public seemed generally to accept the comment without rebuttal.

But the Pentagon was not happy with such publicity breaks and sent OSI investigators to White Sands to see how this could have happened.[16] The aforementioned Army officer, Captain Edward Detchmendy, was happy to finger McLaughlin as a main source of the problem, but also indicated that the Navy personnel generally were quite casual regarding talking about unidentified flying object cases (even to non-military persons) and considered such incidents common enough so as not to be unusual.

Brig. General Blackmore

We do not know what inter-service communication occurred once the OSI report got back to the Pentagon. We do know that it in no way discouraged McLaughlin. Either in late 1949 or early 1950, he contacted *True* magazine about writing an article on these Navy mysteries (which he regarded as simple, astonishing truths) and his own speculations about them.[17] The Navy itself could not have been too concerned about Air Force feelings, and they approved the release of his story to *True*. By approximately mid-February the contents of McLaughlin's *True* article (scheduled for a March 1950 publication) had been leaked to the press, and national papers like the *Christian Science Monitor* were carrying the United Press story in detail.[18] Around that time the Navy got enough pressure from somewhere and removed McLaughlin from White Sands, sending him literally to sea aboard a destroyer.

We previously mentioned the Air Force's project officer for UFO investigations at AMC in 1951-53, Captain Edward Ruppelt. When he became project chief in late 1951, Ruppelt went about attempting not only to understand the subject matter and the Air Force organizational approach to it, but the history of Air Force attitudes as well. He discovered that McLaughlin's *True* article had caused considerable trouble. According to Ed Ruppelt:[19]

After a quiet January, *True* again clobbered the reading public. This time it was a story in the March 1950 issue and it was entitled, "How Scientists Tracked Flying Saucers." It was written by none other than the man who was at that time in charge of a team of Navy scientists at the super hush-hush guided missile test and development area, White Sands Proving Ground, New Mexico. He was Commander R. B. McLaughlin, an Annapolis graduate and a Regular Navy officer. His story had been cleared by the military and was in absolute, 180-degree, direct contradiction to every press release that had been made by the military in the past two years. Not only did the commander believe that he had proved that UFO's were real but that he knew what they were. "I am convinced," he wrote in the *True* article, "that it," referring to a UFO he had seen at White Sands, "was a flying saucer, and further, that these disks are spaceships from another planet, operated by animate, intelligent beings."

Edward Ruppelt

On several occasions during 1948 and 1949, McLaughlin or his crew at the White Sands Proving Ground had made good UFO sightings. The best one was made on April 24, 1949, when the commander's crew of engineers, scientists, and technicians were getting ready to launch one of the huge 100-foot-diameter skyhook balloons. It was 10:30 A.M. on an absolutely clear Sunday morning. Prior to the launching, the crew had sent up a small weather balloon to check the winds at lower levels. One man was watching the balloon through a theodolite, an instrument similar to a surveyor's transit built around a 25-power telescope, one man was holding a stop watch, and a third had a clipboard to record the measured data. The crew had tracked the balloon to about 10,000 feet when one of them suddenly shouted and pointed off to the left. The whole crew looked at the part of the sky where the man was excitedly pointing, and there was a UFO. "It didn't appear to be large," one of the scientists later said, "but it was plainly visible. It was easy to see that it was elliptical in shape and had a 'whitish-silver color.'" After taking a split second to realize what they were looking at, one of the men swung the theodolite around to pick up the object, and the timer reset his stop watch. For sixty seconds they tracked the UFO as it moved toward the east. In about fifty-five seconds it had dropped from an angle of elevation of 45 degrees to 25 degrees, then it zoomed upward and in a few seconds it was out of sight. The crew heard no sound and the New Mexico desert was so calm that day that they could have heard "a whisper a mile away."

This wasn't the only UFO sighting made by White Sands scientists. On April 5, 1948, another team watched a UFO for several minutes as it streaked across the afternoon sky in a series of violent maneuvers. The disk-shaped object was about a fifth the size of a full moon.

On another occasion the crew of a C-47 that was tracking a skyhook balloon saw two similar UFO's come loping in from just above the horizon, circle the balloon, which was flying at just under 90,000 feet, and rapidly leave. When the balloon was recovered it was ripped.

I knew the two pilots of the C-47; both of them now believe in flying saucers. And they aren't alone; so do the people of the Aeronautical Division of General Mills who launch and track the big skyhook balloons. These scientists and engineers all have seen UFO's and they aren't their own balloons. I was almost tossed out of the General Mills offices into a cold January Minneapolis snowstorm for suggesting such a thing-but that comes later in our history of the UFO . . .

When the March issue of *True* magazine carrying Commander McLaughlin's story about how the White Sands scientists had tracked UFO's reached the public, it stirred up a hornets' nest. Donald Keyhoe's article in the January *True* had converted many people but there were still a few heathens. The fact that government scientists had seen UFO's, and were admitting it, took care of a large percentage of these heathens. More and more people were believing in flying saucers.

The Navy had no comment to make about the sightings, but they did comment on McLaughlin. It seems that several months before, at the suggestion of a group of scientists at White Sands, McLaughlin had carefully written up the details of the sightings and forwarded them to Washington. The report contained no personal opinions, just facts. The comments on McLaughlin's report had been wired back to White Sands from Washington and they were, "What are you drinking out there?" A very intelligent answer—and it came from an admiral in the Navy's guided missile program.

By the time his story was published, McLaughlin was no longer at White Sands; he was at sea on the destroyer Bristol. Maybe he answered the admiral's wire.

Dr. Moore buttressed Commander McLaughlin's claims by speaking freely to the press about his own case.[20] Those stories appeared on March 8. The Air Force did not have many options in the face of the Navy's balloon and missile scientists. They chose to duck and cover, and silently let it blow over.

Due to this rise in public interest and the beginnings of the impact of the hoax about a crashed saucer in 1948 New Mexico (this incident became the basis for a popular book, *Behind the Flying Saucers* by Frank Scully),[21] the FBI in the person of J. Edgar Hoover wanted some answers from the Air Force.[22] FBI liaison, agent S. W. Reynolds, went to the Analysis division and, as usual, was directed to Major Jere Boggs.[23] Boggs' superior, Lt. Colonel J. V. Hearn, also attended. The two Air Force officers told Reynolds not to worry. The Air Force was so unconcerned that it had discontinued Project Grudge and did not consider this to be a subject of any interest whatsoever; the incident would simply be handled at the local base level. All the current excitement was due merely to magazine articles. Boggs and Hearn also reminded Reynolds that the FBI had asked out of the UFO investigation business 'way back in October of 1947. The latter, rather blunt, remark was typical of the Air Force's crude handling of its relations with other important intelligence groups and organizations.

The Air Force's attempts to control publicity and emotions about this subject were about to unravel even further. The duck-and-cover behavior might have worked if the UFO phenomenon would have just quit manifesting, but it did not. In March there were events at Selfridge AFB (03-03-1950); Dayton, Ohio (03-08-1950); the Pennsylvania/West Virginia border (3-15-1950); Dallas, Texas (03-16-1950); El Moro Bay, California, and Pensacola, Florida (both 03-23-1950 and both military); near Washington, DC (03-26-1950); and Okinawa (03-27-1950).[24] There was even another sighting in the Sandia and Los Alamos area on the 21st of March, just to keep the top secret bomb bases on alert.[25] All of these events in one form or another were known to the Air Force or other intelligence operatives, and often known to the public as well through news stories. To pick one prominent example of the sort of things that were happening, we will pause for a moment on March 20, 1950.[26]

It was about 9:30 p.m. when Chicago and Southern Airlines Flight 53 passed over Hazen, Arkansas on its way from Memphis to Little Rock. Captain Jack Adams was the pilot; G.W. Anderson was First Officer. They were low (2000 feet) and in the middle of a dark, clear night. Ahead of them to the south, and moving in their direction, was something that bore "a bright white [light] flashing intermittently from the top of the thing. . . it was the strongest blue-white light we'd ever seen."[27] This light flashed every three seconds as it came forward. Adams and Anderson flashed the plane's own landing lights as a signal to whatever it was, but got no response. The object kept coming, at an estimated 1000 feet higher than their plane and at perhaps 600 mph or more. As the unknown flew in its straight-line course, it passed more or less over their plane, obscuring the top flashing light, but revealing a circular display of eight to ten large "spots" or ports of soft purplish fluorescent light. The pilots thought that these spots looked like windows. The sky was too dark to see the body of the object accurately, but the circular pattern of the "ports," and the eclipsing of the top beacon as it passed over, convinced Adams and Anderson that they were looking at a solid, round aerial device having no obvious method of propulsion (i.e. like jet exhausts).

What did they think they'd seen? Both Adams and Anderson admitted that they had been flying saucer skeptics—but were so no longer. Then *what* was it? Both of them believed that they had encountered a secret device from the military. Adams had his doubts, though. Five years after the hullabaloo died down, he was asked what he thought then. The interviewer caught Adams on the airport tarmac standing next to his own plane.

> I'm sure it was some type of aircraft and it was under control. I do not know what it was. It wasn't anything like this (pointing to his plane). People talk about our not being able to fly to the Moon, but we're going to get there someday. And if we can get that far, who knows but what somebody from somewhere else hasn't already figured out how to make such long trips?[28]

Adams was voicing what a lot of people were thinking, something too exciting to be in line with the Air Force's concerns over an overly excitable public. One factor, however, worked in the Air Force's favor. The publicity was intense and tiresome. The pilots were on radio and television nationally, and hounded by the press. Adams said that if he saw another unknown object in the sky, he would not tell anyone about it. Many persons, especially airline pilots, came to see that non-reporting was an easier path to take. And, whether or not it was a good thing for Air Force policy, Adams' and Anderson's published guess that it was a secret U.S. military device gained momentum. In the midst of all the Hazen, Arkansas, hoopla, the Air Force, while telling J. Edgar Hoover and everyone else that UFOs were nothing to be at all concerned about, approved a $20,000 project to use Askania tracking telescopes in the New Mexico desert to get photographic data, if possible, on the phenomenon.[29]

Regarding public discussion of this "non-problem": back on March 15, an Air Force Captain, flying in Guatemala, heard from other pilots at La Aurora field that saucers—large, extremely fast, and highly maneuverable—had flown directly over the runway. Hall (the captain's name) was obviously out-of-touch with Air Force views, and spoke freely to the press about this (the stories had already been written at length in the Guatemala City newspaper, which even included a photo). Hall returned to the States at the end of March to an air station in Mobile, Alabama. The officers decided to have a seminar on the flying saucer topic and asked Hall to lead it off. However, an intelligence officer heard of this and called Hall in. He was interrogated about the La Aurora incident and noted that others had already confirmed his information from that area. Then, the Major doing the interview ended the meeting with these words: "Listen, there is no such thing as a flying saucer. *You won't discuss them.*"[30]

The Air Force was still trying to settle upon a coherent and effective position to take, at least publicly, towards the UFO incidents. Drew Pearson was a very well-known and influential news columnist at the time. Often he received personal interviewing opportunities from governmental and military figures that other newsmen did not receive. Pearson was a useful media contact since—at least on the topic of flying saucers—he was willing to go along with the position and tone of the person whom he had just interviewed. On March 31 he published a nationally distributed column entitled: "Worried about Flying Saucers?"[31] In it Pearson reported that all this was a great burden to the Air Force which

*Left: President Harry S. Truman
Right: Drew Pearson*

96

was being uselessly harassed by having to reply to all this groundless public excitement. He had been assured that as regards flying saucers, *"there ain't no such animal"* (a quote from his authority contact). This down-home phrasing of the Air Force position struck a chord among several news writers, who repeated it, sometimes believingly, sometimes not. And, it had the value of being a clear, flat, unmistakable denial of UFO reality, which was the position-of-choice at the moment for the Pentagon. Then along came Henry Taylor.

Henry Taylor was just as well known at the time for his nationally broadcast radio show as Pearson was for his column writing. Speaking as if he had received insider information, Taylor stated on his April 3 broadcast that the flying saucers were not only real, but when the military decides that the time is right to release the whole story, it will be the best of news. Taylor stated that the flying saucers were one of our own top-secret new weapons. Getting many details wrong, he went on to speak of several UFO incidents with the tone that they were undeniably real events showing technological advancements far beyond known aircraft.

> The flying saucers are a part of a big and expanding experimental project which has been progressing in the United States for nearly three years. I know what these so-called 'flying saucers' are used for. But they are an important military secret.[32]

Taylor left no impression whatsoever that he didn't know what he was talking about. The Air Force's digestive tract curdled further when, almost simultaneously, *U.S. News and World Report* dedicated three pages in the magazine to say the same thing as had Taylor.[33] In the article, it was "revealed" that the disks were, in all probability, a Navy project. Several pictures of disk-like model technologies and one of the infamous technical failures, the Navy's "flying flapjack," were appended to make the point that all of this was ours.

This double-punch to the standard line was sensational, and everyone was badgered into commenting upon it. These comments began right at the top. President Truman and his staff knew that he was going to be asked about this. We, of course, do not know how the internal conversations went, but we do know what the President's press secretary said the next day, April 4.[34] Charles Ross stated that Truman had conferred with his two top military advisors, Rear Admiral Robert Dennison and Brigadier General Robert Landry, and that their information continued to indicate that the United States military had no such projects.

Charles Ross addresses the Press

Furthermore, the Air Force study of the alleged phenomenon concluded that there were no such things as flying saucers.

Right after this press conference came a statement from highly regarded scientist and chairman of the Air Force's Guided Missile Committee, Clark Millikan of California Tech: "If anyone should know about such a project, I should know—and I know of no such development in the aircraft or guided missile field."[35]

Back in Washington, then Secretary of Defense Louis Johnson trotted out both the Secretary of the Navy and the Chief of Naval Operations to deny that the Navy was engaged in any such project. Johnson mocked the concept and said that it was the Air Force who really could use that sort of help.[36]

On April 5 the topic was the subject of an exchange on the floor of congress.[37] The Chairman of the House Appropriations subcommittee for military expenditures stated that flying saucers did not exist and the United States certainly did not fund research on them. But another member of the same committee soured the impact of this by replying that he had seen such an object himself. Because of this personal experience, Congressman Engel of Michigan said that the theory being recently publicized (that the saucers were ours) was probably true. He did not think that the Soviets were in any way capable of this.

On April 6 the matter of the saucers arose on the floor of the Senate. Senate Armed Services Committee member Richard Russell of Georgia said:

> I am completely baffled by Flying Saucer stories. It seems inconceivable that so many pilots would have hallucinations or be fooled by cloud or atmospheric formations.
>
> From their testimony, it seems they do exist. But our Air Force says they do not. I just can't understand it. No, I don't think it is in the stage for a Senatorial investigation as yet.[38]

Left: President Truman
Right: Sec. Defense Johnson

That last remark certainly shook the Air Force. A Senate investigation was the absolute last thing that they wanted. GOP floor leader Kenneth Wherry of Nebraska said that the statements about flying saucers are "like our foreign policy. It is in a state of confusion and no one seems to know what it is all about."[39] While this intuitive remark was probably exactly correct, it did not describe a state-of-mind that the Air Force wanted Senators or anyone else to ponder and comment upon. The powerful Armed Services Committee Chairman, Millard Tydings of Delaware, said that they had not discussed the flying disks with military officials or anyone else, and had assumed that all this was "our own experiments in embryo stage."[40]

One baffled Senator wondering about investigations, one sarcastic Senator commenting on non-understandable confusion, and one Senator thinking that they are our devices: *none* of these was the mindset desired by the Air Force. Nevertheless, the Air Force persevered. A Pentagon Public Relations

Left to Right: Senators Kenneth Wherry, Richard Russell, and Millard Tydings

Officer, Major DeWitt Searles, now met with the press to assure them that there was nothing to the saucer claims at all, and that the final report of the now defunct saucer study (i.e. Project Grudge) was "The Death of Saucers." He repeated the Grudge conclusion that all cases were the result of misinterpretations, mass hysteria, and hoaxes. Calling himself the office in charge of "clay pigeons," he read to the reporters what he said was his standard spiel on the telephone:

> No, no, a thousand times no. As far as the Air Force goes, there's no such thing as a flying saucer. Further, there are no such things as flying chromium hub caps, flying dimes, flying teardrops, flying gas lights, flying ice cream cones or flying pie plates. Thank you and good-by.[41]

He left the reporters with a comedic picture of himself at his desk and phone: hands raised, pleading for relief from the nonsense.

We have to admire the Air Force at this stage for putting forward such strong action. Major Searles' performance for the press left very little room for interpretation. As a result, the Air Force had crudely insulted numerous people from scientists to commercial pilots to their own

Major DeWitt Searles

officers, but they must have felt that it was worth it. Perhaps they were correct, as, in the end, they *were* successful in getting the majority of the citizenry and politicians not only to disbelieve in the reality of the flying disks, but to view UFOs generally as a joke. They paid for this approach by causing anger in many of the observers and a growing distrust of military authorities by the citizenry, who felt that this was a clear case of their being lied to. A good example is Edward Ruppelt's comments about the difficulties he had in getting both pilots and the General Mills balloon experts even to talk to him.[42] This distrust not only encouraged the formation of civilian investigating groups, which began popping up in 1951, but may have had the more subtle, but much more important, impact of evolving a general distrust of government handling of information and the "truth."

In the media, legendary newsman Edward R. Murrow produced the first extended television commentary on the subject.[43] It aired at the end of the first week in April and was called "The Case of the Flying Saucer." The program was surprisingly well balanced. Murrow began with Kenneth Arnold, spoke of early cases such as Muroc AFB and the Mantell accident, and had a Major General who gave an extremely negative trashing of the subject, using Grudge-like words. However, Murrow came back with quotes supporting UFOs from *True* magazine, countered by the entry of the "great debunker," Donald Menzel, astronomer of Harvard, into the field. A lengthy description of a close encounter by a doctor was balanced by a Lockheed executive saying he did not believe UFOs

Edward R. Murrow

existed. Henry Taylor's views that the phenomenon was a Navy project was aired, and then that theory was debunked by the designer of the "Flying Flapjack," engineer Charles Zimmerman. Truman's press secretary came on to reiterate that the President believed that there was no substance to the concept of the disks. Finally, Murrow took to the street and got every conceivable opinion one could imagine, before signing off saying that he could find no pattern in this, and so was skeptical. It was an honest taking of the American pulse on the enigma. A couple of days later, almost as if the Universe were delighting in mischief, the Japanese astronomer, Saheki, saw another intense flash of light on the surface of Mars.[44]

This policy of strong public debunking worked well as a tool for keeping the general public in line, but it did not work well with the UFO observers. When the Air Force characterized all UFO sightings as misinterpretations of common things (planes, stars, balloons, et al.), or hysterical emotionalism, or deliberate lying, it was the same as characterizing the witnesses as liars, hysterics, or, at the best, incompetents. Worse, it projected an attitude of utter disregard to observers *inside* the services, whose reports the intelligence officers still wanted to see. Added to the problems caused by the policy was the fact that it was essentially a lie, and responsible people saw through the lie and questioned the Air Force approach and message in its entirety.

Moderate analysis of most historical complexities would caution any scholar from labeling such matters so strongly as "the Air Force lied." But there is no room to allow a more polite evaluation. We have seen that the Air Force's analysts certainly knew that almost none of the unidentified cases reaching them were due to either hysteria or hoaxes. The third explanation (misinterpretations) was the only one with any potential for intellectual honesty, if one stretched it to its limits. Even there, we have seen that none of the many "Estimates" of what this phenomenon was could be utilized to support the categoric statement that misinterpretation of planes, stars, bolides, balloons, birds, auroras, etc. could explain the multitude of strong cases.

Eddie Rickenbacker

Living with a Lie, especially a blunt one, would be easier if the stimulus that called up the Lie would simply go away. It did not. There were more incidents at Los Alamos (April 19), White Sands (April 25 and May 29), thirty-five civilian airline pilot encounters between April and the end of June,[45] and enough sightings in Texas for Secretary of the Air Force Stuart Symington to feel compelled to state that there was "nothing to it at all."[46] On May 19, professional astronomer Dr. Seymour Hess reported a UFO at Flagstaff, Arizona.[47] Eddie Rickenbacker, legendary flying ace and chief executive of Eastern Airlines, had naturally been hearing of many pilot encounters. He told the press:

> There must be something to them (UFO's) for too many reliable persons have made reports on them. I am duty bound not to say what I know about them—or what I don't know about them. However, if they do exist, you can rest assured that they are ours.[48]

Those in the Pentagon wished that people like Rickenbacker would just shut up. Referring specifically to his quote, a Pentagon document said that such things only serve to "maintain the chain reaction of such reports."[49]

Living with a Lie is also easier if you don't really have to care much about the people to whom you are lying. While that may have been the case as far as civilians were concerned, many authorities in the Air Force did not believe that it was acceptable to discourage or confuse their own people about reporting unidentified airspace violations. As we have mentioned, Air Force letter AFSCI #85 had done just that. Combined with the blunt language of the announcement of the elimination of Project Grudge, and the even blunter condemnations of flying saucers by Air Force authority figures, base commands were confused if not thoroughly antipathetic about investigating and transmitting reports. While the Korean War did much to push UFOs out of the American press beginning in June of 1950, it also made unidentified airspace violations over Korea a major issue. This concern went right to the top of Air Force Intelligence. On June 1 Commanding General Earle E. Partridge of the 5th Air Force, responsible

General Earle Partridge

General George Stratemeyer

for the Korean Theatre, wrote to Commanding General George Stratemeyer, of the Far Eastern Air Force, asking for analysis of a number of such cases.[50] From this high place, Chief of Intelligence General Charles Cabell once again assessed his organization's stand on handling the UFO problem, and, once again, decided that they had not gotten it right. And so, during June and July of 1950, Cabell and his aides began to repair their mistakes, and to communicate better to the rest of the military and intelligence community what they wanted done.[51]

Cabell et al. came to the realization that they had several things to undo:

1. It had been a mistake to cancel the UFO Analysis Project, and to announce to the services and agencies that they had done so;
2. It had been a mistake to give the personnel at AMC (including the new intelligence chief, Colonel Harold Watson) the impression that UFOs were considered so unimportant that they could ignore them entirely, with or without a formal project;
3. It had been a mistake to adopt such a crude and uncivilized tone in their public statements about the phenomenon, a tone to which Watson himself was particularly prone.

The focal point for the worst of these three mistakes was Air Materiel Command at Wright-Patterson AFB with its defunct UFO project and its irascible chief intelligence officer. So, Cabell addressed himself directly to Watson as regards policy.

In July of 1950 Cabell, via his aide Colonel Barber, sent a notice to Watson telling him that the UFO project at AMC was to re-open, and to do so with a serious intelligence analysis basis.[52] Cabell reminded Watson that despite the official closing of Project Grudge, the Air Force had never wavered in its desire to receive UFO reports and to take them seriously. He noted that Watson, and everyone else, possessed a letter dated January 12, 1950, titled "Reporting of Information on Unconventional Aircraft," to this effect. (See the appendix for a copy.) Now, in this July letter, Watson was told how it would be. Here are the key paragraphs:

General Charles Cabell

c. Gen Cabell's views are that we should reinstitute, if it has been abandoned, a continuing analysis of reports received and he expects AMC to do this as part of their obligation to produce air technical intelligence. He specifically desires that the project, as it existed before, be *not* fully re-implemented with special technical teams traveling around the country interviewing observers, etc., and he is particularly desirous that there be no fanfare or publicity over the fact that the USAF is still interested in "flying saucers."

d. Gen Cabell desires that we place ourselves in a position that, if circumstances require an all-out effort in this regard at some future time, we will be able to announce that we have continued quietly our analysis of reports without interruption.

e. Under this philosophy then, we will continue to receive from USAF sources reports of "flying saucers" and we will immediately transmit these reports to AMC. You will be at liberty to query, through AFOIC-CC normal channels, the USAF reporting source for more information. We will also be scanning State, CIA, Army, and Navy incoming reports for pertinent information which will be relayed to AMC. You may also address queries regarding specific reports of this nature to AFOIC-CC in the normal manner.

f. Ordinary newspaper reports should be analyzed without initiating specific inquiry. Information received direct from non-USAF individuals may be acknowledged and interrogated through correspondence. Where geographically convenient, specific sightings may be investigated quietly, at your discretion, by AMC depot personnel, and requests for investigation may be filed with your local CSI office.

g. Queries from news agencies as to whether USAF is still interested in "flying saucers" may be given a general answer to the effect that AMC is interested in any information that will enable it to produce air technical intelligence—and just as much interested in "flying saucer" information as it would be in any other significant information. Work in the "flying saucer" field is not receiving "special" emphasis because emphasis is being placed upon all technical intelligence fields.

The memo tells Watson how the USAF will handle military encounters—as serious, normal intelligence functions, particularly at AMC as a focal point. And it tells how the USAF will handle civilian encounters—an unemotional statement of general interest and quiet, unpublicized targeted investigations. A last comment indicated that the Pentagon was a bit miffed at Watson, saying essentially "if you don't understand any of this, call us and we'll explain it to you again."

Watson tucked his tail and got into line, although at AMC itself the two officers in charge of the re-instituted Project Grudge knew that the boss was derogatory on UFOs and were doing little or nothing at the job.[53] Still, Watson worried about striking the proper public pose—if this was the new UFO attitude in the Pentagon (formalized by a new letter, September 8, 1950,[54] with the same title as the aforementioned January memo), then what was he supposed to say, precisely, when the press came calling for information on an incident?[55]

General Harold Watson

The Pentagon came right back to Watson with a policy. (A copy is available in the appendix.) Cabell aide, Brigadier General Ernest Moore, wrote:[56]

2. In a recent telephone conversation between Colonel Watson, Hq AMC and Colonel Harris, this headquarters, Colonel Watson requested guidance in the matter of releasing results of investigation, analysis, and evaluation of incidents brought to his attention. This headquarters believes that release of details of analysis and evaluation of incidents is inadvisable, and desires that, in lieu thereof, releases conform to the policy and spirit of the following:

"We have investigated and evaluated _____ incident and have found nothing of value and nothing which would change our previous estimates on this subject."

3. Results of analysis and evaluation of incidents possessing any intelligence value will be forwarded to this headquarters for information and for any action relative to possible press releases.

The policy is significant. It says that the only statement that the public will get (regardless of the actual nature of the incident) is one of robotic, non-embellished negative conclusions.

Cabell wanted *quiet*—quiet analysis of military and civilian reports (with the military well-informed that the Air Force and AMC were interested, while the public only vaguely so). He wanted quiet fieldwork—invisible if possible—on civilian cases. And he wanted an emotionless and non-insulting denial that anything of military or technical interest had been found in any new investigation, should the public make inquiries about such. Beyond that, Cabell wanted AMC to be *serious* about its job, which he suspected, and Edward Ruppelt later confirmed,[57] was no longer true.

Unfortunately for Cabell, "quiet" was not on the agenda. The latter part of 1950 saw the publication of the first two full-length books about the subject. One, *Behind the Flying Saucers* by Frank Scully, appeared in September, and sensationally claimed truth for a government-collected crashed saucer with several dead pilots.[58] Another, *Flying Saucers Are Real* by Donald Keyhoe,[59] appeared in October and had far greater and lasting impact, bringing many interested civilians and military people to believe in UFO reality, government withholding of information, and the extraterrestrial hypothesis.[60] But an even

Movie Poster

better indicator of the size of the Air Force's information-and-attitude manipulation problem occurred when the popular grammar school publication *My Weekly Reader* offered an article claiming that flying saucers were real and that they were Air Force devices. When the editors were queried as to why they had written such a story, they said that they had been "deluged" by letters from school children excited by thought of saucers landing and mini-pilots from other worlds being inside. This indicated a "widespread hysteria" building among children of this age, and the editors thought it their educational duty to nip those ideas.[61] Whether the Air Force thought that this was a wise fabrication by the editors, we do not know. Certainly it was not their public position. There are two other powerful instances of public relations problems. First: the publication of the Scully book was condemned as contributing to mass hysteria in the public during these times of war. This charge came from a Congressman, Edward Jenison of Illinois.[62] The Air Force's Public Information Officer, Clare Welch, guessed that 3 to 4 million people had gotten "into contact" with the idea of flying saucers due to the book[63] and the FBI wondered ominously if Scully had a political purpose of undermining public morale with it.[64] Second: Air Force documents revealed a strong negative attitude toward a more obviously fictional project, a Hollywood motion picture film. Well-known movie director Howard Hawks arranged for the making of *The Thing*, a UFO horror story about a crashed saucer discovered in the Arctic, and petitioned the Air Force for help in using military locations, personnel, and equipment during the shooting. The Air Force reply, from Pentagon Intelligence to the local base commander, is what we would expect now that we have delved into this policy morass:

Reference is made to proposed Winchester Pictures Corporation proposed motion picture to be entitled 'The Thing.' It is understood you have been approached to extend cooperation to the producer and writers as pertains to filming location and to endorsement of the film. The Air Force has maintained for a considerable period of time that the 'flying saucer' is a myth and it is our policy not to participate in any proposal that will perpetuate this hoax. Therefore, the Air Force has refused cooperation on this production. Further, the Air Force is objecting to any mentioning or pictorial display of Air Force personnel or equipment in the film. In view of the above, it is requested that you consider disapproving their request to you for cooperation.[65]

No encouragement to the public. Period.

During the final third of the year, public cases of astonishing character were much less frequent than were such cases inside the military and intelligence community. These reports were, as we have seen, particularly bothersome, since the credentials of the witnesses and, often, the strangeness of the details reported, placed the cases well outside the misinterpretation /hysteria/ hoax mantra of blanket dismissal. A few examples are appropriate:

As was mentioned earlier in this book, during World War II there were two major scientific and engineering efforts taking place in the United States: The Manhattan Project to create the atomic bomb, and the Radiation Lab to improve the function of radar technology. Both efforts continued in their different ways during the Cold War. The Manhattan Project goals were continued at Oak Ridge, Tennessee, and Hanford, Washington, as well as at several locations (especially Los Alamos and Sandia Labs) in New Mexico. UFO incidents occurred at all these locations. The Radiation Lab had been focused at MIT and Harvard in the Cambridge/Boston, Massachusetts area. The main concern was that the continental U.S. had a very poor radar detection system, both in terms of coverage and ability to analyze the targets detected. Fear of Soviet air incursions by missiles or jets was the primary worry, but the mysterious flying disk incidents were not helping anyone relax.[66] It is interesting that on September 21, an MIT research plane with radar technologists aboard had a UFO encounter. The research group was flying in the vicinity of Provincetown, Massachusetts, when they picked up an object on their equipment making very abrupt high-speed turns and showing straight line-of-flight velocity of 1200 miles per hour. The researchers were flabbergasted but felt that this incident needed to be reported to higher authorities. They reasoned that this must be some U.S. secret project, and therefore *not* to be discussed, but what if it was not? The team leader's own words convey the peculiar atmosphere of the event:

> The whole thing doesn't seem to make sense as you will discover when you reflect a moment about it. It was very evidently an interception of some sort on our flight, but what? The turn was utterly fantastic, I don't think the human frame could absorb it, but if the object was radio controlled, it had no particular business flying on such courses as planes occupied on legitimate business. A few rough calculations concerning control surfaces, angles, etc., only adds to the puzzle that this object must have been entirely unconventional in many and basic respects. Perhaps the thing that bothers me the most is that it gave a very good radar echo, which implies irregular surfaces and comparatively large size, large enough so the pilots might have had a good chance to see it.

> It seems highly probable that I may be poking into something that is none of my business, but on the other hand, it may be something that the Air Force would like to know about if it doesn't already. I wish you would take the matter up with your intelligence officer or C.O. and get their reactions. The whole thing has got us going nuts here and we don't know whether to talk about it or keep our mouths shut. Until I hear from you, we will do the latter.

> Perhaps we could run another mission for the purpose of luring it out again and this time track it, or at least get your pilots close enough for a look—they'd never catch it I'm sure . . .[67]

Yes sir, exactly. "The whole thing *doesn't* seem to make sense," as long as we are forced to think about it in conventional terms. We do not know how the scientists' questions were resolved by Air Force intelligence, or whether they tried another mission to "lure it out."

Meanwhile, the other half of the high-tech world of government technologists was getting plenty of action, especially in New Mexico and at Oakridge.

In September, Project Twinkle, the project to attempt to explain the green fireballs (especially in the vicinity of Los Alamos) had, as was inevitable, become involved with typical UFO reports. The main event here was the photographing of an object viewed by one of the missile-and-balloon-tracking cameras, the cinetheodolites.[68] These appearances of uninvited objects during missile launches allegedly occurred several times (as, similarly, the General Mills balloon launchers also testified for their flights).[69] The images were

Army photo by
White Sands Proving Ground

On top of Station "C" in the flat desert, the Askania theodolite is waiting also to visually follow and record on film the journey of the Martin Viking.

ZERO HOUR! Viking No. 12 is off toward the ionosphere. "She's a good missile!" cries out the Flight Safety Control man through the loudspeakers.

Cinetheodolite at White Sands Proving Grounds

apparently like mere elliptical smudges on the film, but these, when joined to the scientists' testimonies, seemed to assure that something unexplained, and probably unwelcome, had occurred. Holloman AFB housed the local interceptor squadron and became involved, as it was their charge to defend that region's airspace. Project Twinkle personnel and Holloman officers conferred to discuss what should be done.[70] Holloman was happy to do its duty, but it wanted one crucial piece of approval. Would higher Air Force authorities allow Holloman pilots to fire live ammunition at the bogies? This is, on minimal reflection, *not* the request of people believing in hoaxes, hysteria, and misinterpretations. It is *exactly* the inquiry of people worried about unknown technological violations of sensitive airspace. The FBI was similarly serious about the New Mexico situation, having been involved since the earlier meetings called by Colonel Rees and Lincoln LaPaz. Doubtless partially informed about the latest developments with Project Twinkle, the Bureau asked for an update on the findings.[71]

The Air Force once again brushed the concerns aside, and said that Wright-Patterson analysts were on top of the situation and that no patterns of any kind existed in the reports, let alone was there any reason to believe that there were any objects from the Soviets or other planets responsible for those reports.[72] However, in early October at the Los Alamos laboratory of Dr. William Carter, radiation counters went on unexplained "excursions," that is they detected abnormally high radiation on four instances coincidental with UFO reports gathered by the volunteer scientific watchdog group at the laboratory.[73] We do not know to whom the "Los Alamos Birdwatchers" reported these radiation detections. It was not to AMC. Probably the incidents were reported to the Air Force's Cambridge

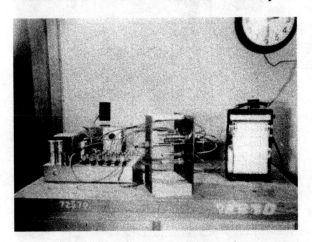

Research Lab (as executive for Project Twinkle), and it was only a year or two later that Captain Ruppelt received a general report at AMC's Project Blue Book which was to be the new name, in 1952, for Grudge.[74] Ruppelt commented that the fact that Blue Book did not have any investigative files for the UFO incidents which were concurrent with these radiation readings did not surprise him, because the two "responsible" AMC officers at the time (James Rodgers and Roy James) were so incredulous about UFOs, and so lax about their duties, that they actually threw files away.[75] This is mentioned to convey, in another way, the mess that was made of all this, "officially."

Dr. William Carter's radiation detector

This leads us now to Oak Ridge. We have very poor documentation for what happened around the nation's nuclear laboratory for the first two thirds of 1950. But *something* was happening. In July there had been enough sightings and interest that a laboratory officer and a Vanderbilt University professor decided to try to correlate radiation detector "excursions" (à la Mt. Palomar and Los Alamos) with UFO incidents.[76] It is believed that they did not find such a correlation at the time. With the beginning of October much more documentation becomes available to us, as U.S. Army and FBI records come together to paint a picture of a month loaded with activity. The events which are known are mainly of two types: cases of the Knoxville airport picking up radar bogies in the laboratory area (Oct. 12, 16, 24 twice), and personnel associated with the lab reporting visual sightings of unknowns (Oct. 13, 14, 20, 23, 24 twice).[77] Whether any of these visual sightings strongly correlate with radar returns is not known; the radar pick-ups were the occasion for several interceptor scrambles, none of which saw anything. There were certainly more incidents than these. On October 12 the Oak Ridge Atomic Energy Commission placed a request in the newspaper for anyone seeing flying saucers over the lab to report to them.[78]

The FBI knew all about this flurry, too. By mid-October Bureau personnel were on the hunt checking the backgrounds of all the UFO witnesses they could find in the area, in search of information that might point to them being communist sympathizers or otherwise a danger to the nation's interest. Their report found none of that. And, in fact, they found no explanations of any kind.

> . . . The most reliable sources available were utilized in the compilation of this report. The employment records and the Federal Bureau of Investigation reports concerning the witnesses were inspected to ascertain their reliability, integrity, and loyalty to the United States Government.
>
> The opinions of the officials of the Security Division, AED, Oak Ridge; AEC Security Patrol, Oak Ridge; FBI, Knoxville; Air Force Radar and Fighter Squadrons, Knoxville; and the OSI, Knoxville, Tennessee, fail to evolve an adequate explanation . . . the possibilities of practical jokers, mass hysteria, balloons of any description, flights of birds (with or without cobwebs or other objects attached), falling kites, objects thrown from the ground, windblown objects, insanity, and many other natural happenings have been rejected because of the detailed, similar descriptions of the objects seen by different persons; and because of impossibility.[79]

One gets used to the awkward phraseology used by some of these intelligence community writers. That last sentence bangs on the ear, and we honestly cannot tell what the writer meant by it. The overall report attempts to say that, when one accepts the descriptions given by the witnesses as generally accurate, none of the mundane explanations cited are even possible explanations for what was seen. This is the general truth of UFOlogy; if one accepts the witnesses' testimonies as being close to true reporting, then one must throw up their hands and admit that they are dealing with a major mystery.

The Air Force, of course, was not going to admit anything like that, even to the FBI. So, when the FBI sent one of its agents to inquire about these matters, and the general state of incident investigations, to General Joseph Carroll (chief of the AFOSI), the General downplayed any mystery involved. Carroll did say one important thing: as part of General Cabell's renovation of intelligence community attitudes about the seriousness of reporting UFOs, Carroll told the FBI that the Air Force had resuscitated Project Grudge at AMC and was once more particularly focused on

General Joseph Carroll

this issue.[80] One wonders how this mixed message of a "nothing-to-it" phenomenon with a revitalized intelligence project to study it really played in the minds of the other agencies and areas of the military.

The quotes listed earlier were taken *verbatim* from an Army document given to the FBI in response to their inquiry about what happened. That document also listed the three hypotheses that were going through peoples' minds:

> The trend of opinion seems to follow three patterns of thought. The first is that the objects are a physical phenomenon, which have a scientific explanation; the second is that the objects are experimental objects from an undetermined source guided by electronics; and the third is similar to the second except that an intended demoralization or harassment is involved. The fantastic is generally rejected.[81]

Again, the language is not optimized for our understanding, but to give another opinion and to re-phrase: the writer seems to be saying that the experts believe that this concentration of cases is explicable by some natural phenomenon, but not as yet recognized; some technological development, probably remotely controlled (and by the United States); or some technological development, employed by parties not having U.S. interests at heart (i.e. Soviets), and aiming to harass and demoralize the nation (the psychological warfare theory). The final statement about rejecting the "fantastic" almost certainly means extraterrestrials. As such, this is the perfect political statement, beginning with the most acceptable idea (an elaborate way of saying "nothing to it") and progressing through the next two vaguely acceptable concepts in order of their desirability.

In November, AMC project monitor James Rodgers was handed the Oak Ridge UFO problem to analyze. He did so in a classic Grudge manner.[82] The letter, written for Colonel Harold Watson's signature (actually signed by the person who would replace him, Colonel Frank Dunn, a much more open-minded officer) was polite but said curtly that all this sounded like errors in the radar system's detection of air inversions and the like. The visual cases were dismissed as weather balloons, aircraft, or odd cloud formations. Shortly after receiving Rodgers' explanations, the lab had a UFO report and had a coincident radiation excursion on detectors in the laboratory.[83]

Army and AEC authorities obviously did not take Rodgers' easy write-off as some definitive statement. On the 1st and 2nd of December, military authorities met in the Oak Ridge area to discuss the problem of the Knoxville radar signals and oddly, even a Tennessee Senator attended.[84] Their conclusion was to set up additional radar to attempt multiple set detections should cases occur again. Oak Ridge engineer Lt. Colonel John R. Hood, along with others at the lab, dispersed radiation counters around the lab's restricted area.[85] Hood wanted to map the presence of any unusual radiation, but also to set up a source of very radioactive material to see if its presence had an effect on the air above it. If the air was affected, perhaps by ionization, could that be the cause of the anomalous radar returns over the lab? If such home-made aerial anomalies were not the cause of the radar reports, perhaps the testing could give a hint about possible effects of a flyover of a nuclear-powered aircraft. Hood also mentioned using a magnetometer array. It was good "outside-of-the-box" engineering thinking, and we have no information whether anything came of it.

Despite all of this activity at the country's most secret national laboratories, and despite General Cabell's desire to change at least the *inside* atmosphere regarding UFO reporting, Colonel Watson at AMC had not changed one iota, emotionally, about the subject. Watson brought in famous news columnist Bob Considine for an in-depth interview on flying saucers. The tone of the resulting piece was just what Cabell wanted to avoid.[86]

> I've seen lots of flying saucers . . . and every single saucer turned out to be the sun shining off the wing or body of a distant DC-4, or a jet, or a weather balloon, or it was a reflection off a water-tank or

something else that is readily explainable. I don't know what it takes to convince the public, but there are no such things as flying saucers. They don't exist. They just don't exist!

Watson went on to characterize saucer reporting as "mass illusion" and "seasonal hallucination," always sparked by publicity. Then he went far over the line. He characterized witnesses: *At the end of nearly every flying-saucer report that can be tracked down stands a crackpot, a religious fanatic, a publicity hound, or a malicious practical joker.* Considine asked him about commercial airline pilot reports. Watson accused them of being fooled by fatigue-caused "optical tricks, plus the "power of suggestion." He went on to mock the extraterrestrial hypothesis sarcastically.

Even if we grant Colonel Watson some space for his opinion that the extraterrestrial hypothesis was unthinkable, the rest of his characterization of the UFO phenomenon was off-base, and certainly was not shared by military personnel at places like Los Alamos, Oak Ridge, et al., let alone the many pilot and technical witnesses, or just simply good people who had honestly reported what they had seen. What motivated Watson? He was not even in line with current thinking at the top of Air Force Intelligence.

Ed Ruppelt, who became AMC UFO project officer just as Watson left for assignment overseas in 1951, said this about Watson in unpublished notes from Ruppelt's manuscript files (writing in about 1954-6):

> Colonel Watson, now a Brigadier General and once again chief of ATIC [the renaming of AMC's T-2 intelligence division], was chief of ATIC when I arrived. (He later went to Europe for three years). He was violently anti-saucer but he crossed himself up too many times trying to grab publicity. He was the one who made the famous remark about all UFO observers being nuts or fatigued airline pilots. He continually hauled in writers who would plug him and debunk the UFOs. I've overheard him tell how he completely snowed Bob Considine.[87]

Even with Ruppelt's frank observations, we still do not know what was really going on in Watson's head. But as chief of intelligence at Wright-Patterson, his opinions mattered, both inside his own intelligence organization and when his views were aired in public. We know from Ruppelt that Watson's belittling comments about UFO witnesses angered many people that Ruppelt came across during his tenure as UFO officer. Watson's actions demonstrated how little control General Cabell exerted even over his own people.

Notes

[1] Donald Keyhoe, "Flying Saucers Are Real," *True*, January 1950: 11-13, 83-87.

[2] Edward Ruppelt files.

[3] Office of Chief of Naval Operations, Navy Department, intelligence report, subject: Unidentified Phenomena, 10 February 1950 (coversheet plus 5 page report), FOIA (FBI).

[4] Office of Chief of Naval Operations, intelligence report, subject: Unidentified Phenomena, 10 February 1950, FOIA (FBI); Blue Book microfilm (OSI records).

[5] Blue Book microfilm (OSI records).

[6] Anonymous (but either Dr. Paul Fitts or a paraphrase of his work), "Psychoanalyzing the Flying Saucers," *Air Force*, February 1950: 15-19.

[7] Blue Book microfilm (OSI records). There is some confusion as to whether this document properly dates to 30 January 1950 or to 8 February 1950.

[8] Lindsey J. Sanford to AMC, subject: "Request for reports," 10 March 1950, FOIA (USAF). Brooks AFB asks for information and is concerned about "change in attitude toward security;" memorandum by Major J. Boggs, subject: AEC request for Grudge files, 24 May 1950 (original request 14 March 1050). Later we will cite concerns from Far Eastern Command.

[9] Robert McLaughlin, "How Scientists Tracked a Flying Saucer," True, March 1950: 25-27, 96-99.

[10] Robert McLaughlin to Dr. James Van Allen, 12 May 1949, NICAP files.

[11] Blue Book microfilm (OSI files) [frankly written 25 October 1949, Report of OSI investigation of press leakages.], cited as "Detchmendy file," below.

[12] Detchmendy file.

[13] Marvin Miles, "U.S. Officers Report Seeing Flying Disks," Los Angeles Times, 30 August 1949, 1.

[14] Miles, "U.S. Officers Report Seeing Flying Disks," 1.

[15] Detchmendy file.

[16] Detchmendy file.

[17] McLaughlin/True.

[18] United Press, "Missiles Expert 'Convinced' Flying Saucers from Planets," Christian Science Monitor, 23 February 1950.

[19] Ruppelt, draft, 70-72.

[20] Paul Ellis, "Those Flying Saucers Are Here Again," U. P. release (NY), 8 March 1950.

[21] Frank Scully, Behind the Flying Saucers, 1950.

[22] C. E. Hennrick to A. H. Belmont, memorandum, subject: Frank Scully—security matter, 20 October 1950, and A. H. Belmont to Mr. Ladd, memorandum, subject: Flying Saucers, 19 October 1950, FOIA (FBI).

[23] ---- (illegible) to Director, FBI, memorandum, 22 March 1950; D. M. Ladd to The Director, memorandum, subject: Flying Saucers, 26 March 1950.

[24] Most of these cases have at least some investigation or at least notice in Blue Book microfilm Roll 7; also see Gross, monographs and supplements for 1950.

[25] Blue Book microfilm (OSI files), 27 March 1950.

[26] The "Hazen, AR" case was widely known, and so published at the time. The best-detailed coverage is in Gross, monographs and supplements for 1950. Blue Book microfilm is relatively scant despite the impact of the case.

[27] Gross, monographs and supplements for 1950.

[28] Anonymous news writer, "Arkansas Has Its Share; Pilot Sticks to His Story," (Little Rock) Arkansas Gazette, 24 July 1955.

[29] Air Force Technical Directive #55 (not seen by the authors; referenced in Gross, monographs and supplements, ref. 24).

[30] Blue Book microfilm ("Request for Information," Lt. Colonel DeWitt Searles, Office of Public Information, Washington, D.C., 21 February 1952).

[31] Drew Pearson, "Worried About Flying Saucers?" syndicated column, Washington, DC, 31 March 1950.

[32] Henry Taylor, "The Flying Saucer," Your Land and Mine radio program, Dallas, Texas, 27 March 1950. This radio broadcast was distributed as a pamphlet over the following days.

[33] Anonymous, "Flying Saucers—The Real Story," U.S. News and World Report, 7 April 1950: 13-15.

[34] Associated Press, "White House Pooh-poohs 'Secret Weapon' Saucers," dateline: Key West, FL, 4 April 1950.

[35] Associated Press, "White House Pooh-poohs 'Secret Weapon' Saucers;" "CalTech Weapons Expert Also Denies Weapons Story," additional story linked to preceding in some papers, for example: Long Beach Press-Telegram, 5 April 1950.

[36] Several 4 April 1950 newspaper citations in Gross, 1950.

[37] United Press News Release, "I Saw Flying Disc, Rep. Engel Asserts," dateline: Washington, DC, 5 April 1950.

[38] Several International News Service quotations for 6 April 1950 in Gross, 1950.

[39] International News Service quotations for 6 April 1950 in Gross, 1950.

[40] International News Service quotations for 6 April in Gross, 1950.

[41] Douglas Larsen, "U.S. Air Force Has Flying Disc Debunker," NEA news release, dateline: Washington, DC, 4 April 1950.

[42] Ruppelt, Report on Unidentified Flying Objects.

[43] Edward R. Murrow, "The Case of the Flying Saucer," CBS television documentary, 7 April 1950.

[44] Associated Press news release, "Mars Acts Up: Strange Formations Seen on Planet," dateline: Osaka, Japan, 10 April 1950.

[45] Ruppelt, Report.

[46] News story quotation cited in Gross (1950).

[47] United Press news release, "Flying Disc-Astronomer Views Sky Visitor," dateline: Flagstaff, AZ, 23 May 1950. Hess' case is covered widely in the UFO literature, and correspondence exists (for example: James McDonald files; CUFOS files) wherein he maintains his sighting over the decades.

[48] Associated Press news release, "Rickenbacker Says Saucers Not From Mars," dateline: Indianapolis, IN, 12 June 1950.

[49] FOIA (FBI), document not seen by authors; reported by Bruce Maccabee, "UFO Related Information from FBI Files: Part 7," *MUFON UFO Journal*, November-December 1978: 12.

[50] Colonel Rogers, Deputy for Intelligence for the Commanding General (FEAF) to Director of Intelligence USAF, memorandum, subject: Unidentified Object, 8 June 1950; and ---- (author not legible) for General C. P. Cabell, memorandum for record, subject: to prepare response to FEAF, 31 July 1950, FOIA (USAF).

[51] Brigadier General E. Moore to Chief Evaluation Division; Chief: Air Targets Division; Chief: Estimates Division, memorandum, subject: Unidentified Objects, 1 July 1950; Colonel H. J. Kieling to Commanding General (FEAF), draft letter, 31 July 1950, FOIA (USAF).

[52] Colonel Barber to Colonel H. E. Watson, memorandum for Colonel H. E. Watson, AMC (hand-carried to "save the bother of an officially coordinated directive"), memorandum, 7 July 1950, FOIA (USAF).

[53] Ruppelt, *Report*.

[54] Lt. Col. C.J. Stattler to AFOIC (The Pentagon's "Collections [of Information] Division"), memorandum, subject: Special Instruction, for preparing a letter to all major commands, 29 August 1950, FOIA (USAF), (and several related FOIA documents of same date); and Lt. Colonel Earnest, to higher officers, memorandum: Notice that letter to Commands has been prepared, 8 September 1950 (plus memorandum this same date noting that letter was to be sent to Army, Navy, Coast Guard, Department of State, FBI, and CIA), and actual letter referred to above over General Cabell's signature (same date).

[55] Colonel Harris (to higher officers), memorandum, subject: to reply to Colonel Watson regarding "proper procedure for handling unidentified aerial object reports," 12 October 1950, FOIA (USAF).

[56] Brigadier General E. Moore to AMC, attn. Chief, Intelligence Department, subject (restricted): Releasing Results of Analysis and Evaluation of Unidentified Aerial Objects Reports, ---- (illegible; looks to be "18") October 1950, FOIA (USAF).

[57] Ruppelt, *Report*.

[58] Frank Scully, *Behind the Flying Saucers*, 1950.

[59] Donald Keyhoe, *Flying Saucers Are Real*, 1950.

[60] Clark, *Encyclopedia*.

[61] Associated Press news release, original document not seen by authors; referenced in Gross, 1950 Aug-Dec.

[62] *Appendix to the Congressional Record*, Vol. 96, part 17, 20 September 1950: A6711.

[63] Colonel Clare Welch (AMC) to Brigadier General E. Moore, 1 November 1950, FOIA (USAF).

[64] C. E. Hennrick to A. H. Belmont, memorandum, subject: Frank Scully, Security Matter, 20 October 1950, FOIA (FBI).

[65] Blue Book microfilm, "Department of the Air Force Staff Message," 13 September 1950.

[66] Ruppelt, *Report* (Ruppelt mentions his interactions with the Cambridge/MIT group of scientists working on radar, called the Beacon Hill Group. They were so concerned about the airspace violation problem that they wanted to take over analysis of the UFO problem).

[67] Blue Book microfilm Roll 7.

[68] Blue Book microfilm Roll 7. Ruppelt also mentions incidents of theodolite and gun-camera films, and his inability to track them down.

[69] Ruppelt, Report; and Tom Tulien, *UFO Oral History Video Project*, Video, "J. J. Kaliszewski" (General Mills balloon testing engineer, late 1940s-early 1950s.)

[70] Blue Book microfilm, Holloman AFB HQ to Commanding General, AMC, October 1950.

[71] A. H. Belmont to Mr. Ladd, memorandum, subject: "Flying Saucers," 19 October 1950, FOIA (FBI).

[72] Belmont to Ladd, memorandum, "Flying Saucers," 19 October 1950, FOIA (FBI).

[73] Blue Book microfilm. Edward Ruppelt writes a memorandum of "Trip to Los Alamos on 23 October 1952," wherein he verifies the sketchy information which had reached AMC about these events. Other relevant items exist in the microfilm, including a letter from Ruppelt to "Birdwatcher" Homer Gittings, and a picture of Carter's device.

[74] Ruppelt, memorandum "Trip to Los Alamos," and Ruppelt, *Report*.

[75] Ruppelt, *Report*.

[76] Blue Book microfilm, untitled document, July 1950.

[77] Gross, 1950, Aug/Dec, has outstanding coverage of the October 1950 Oak Ridge series, based wholly on the primary documents (primarily Blue Book microfilm, OSI files).

[78] Robert B. Allen, "AEC Wants Info On Flying Saucers Seen Near A-Plants," *The Oak Ridger*, (Oak Ridge), TN, 12 October 1950.

[79] J. Allen Hynek, *The Hynek UFO Report*, 1977, 142-3. Hynek, USAF Project Grudge/Blue Book scientific advisor, quotes the relevant Blue Book microfilm document in his coverage of the Oak Ridge incidents.

[80] A. H. Belmont to Mr. Ladd, memorandum, subject: "Flying Saucers," 19 October 1950, FOIA (FBI).

[81] U.S. Army Intelligence, 111th CIC Detachment, Knoxville, TN, "Summary of Information," 21 October 1950 (original document not seen by authors; quoted in detail in Gross, 1950, Aug-Dec).

[82] Harold E. Watson (signed Frank L. Dunn; written James J. Rodgers) to Assistant for Atomic Energy, memorandum, subject: "Unconventional Aircraft," 15 November 1950, FOIA (USAF).

[83] U.S. Army Intelligence, 111th CIC Detachment, Knoxville, TN, ("Summary of Information," 2 January 1952 but referring to November 1950 event).

[84] Blue Book microfilm, memorandum of 4 December 1950.

[85] Blue Book microfilm, OSI files, 5 December 1950.

[86] Bob Considine, "Air Force Insists Imagination, Reflections Have Tricked Public," International News Service column, dateline: New York, 16 November 1950.

[87] Edward Ruppelt, Ruppelt archive file, unpublished commentaries on military and scientific figures that he met during his tenure as UFO Project Blue Book chief. (This archive currently held for the Coalition for UFO Research by Michael Swords, professor emeritus, Western Michigan University, Kalamazoo, Michigan).

Chapter 7: Transition

Let us catch our breath and begin the story of the year 1951 by summarizing what the Pentagon's General Charles Cabell thought was the status quo and how he tried to fine tune it. The general deserves some sympathy. He attempted to walk the nearly impossible line of privately stating, "*We* take these incidents seriously" while publicly saying, "There is no need for *you* to take these incidents seriously." He was burdened with a need to create an atmosphere generally disrespectful of the phenomenon, while maintaining respect for the phenomenon's reporters—all this plagued by the circumstances that no one knew exactly what they were dealing with, how to understand it, and, consequently, how to assess its national security implications.

Cabell decided to try to "split the audience" regarding the seriousness with which one should take UFO incidents. To the public, the message would be "don't worry about it, but do report it just in case;" and, "for the most part, there's nothing to any of this." To the military community, the message would be "we take this very seriously; *quietly* look into all reasonable cases and report them to our project." If the world were strongly compartmentalized, this dichotomy might have worked, but there were too many feedback loops between the public and the military. Additionally, Cabell wanted to stop the mocking of witnesses, citizens or military. This also was nearly impossible inasmuch as the subtext of a statement like "the perceived object was a star, but the witness said it was a craft," is that the witness is a fool.

As for learning what really was going on, Cabell tended to treat each incident as precisely that, an incident, one after another but with no relationship between them, as he would do in normal intelligence function analysis. The purpose of a focused project (SIGN/Grudge/soon-to-be Blue Book) was to see if any useful pattern arose; if not, serious single incident analysis was the least they could do. Cabell thought that his late 1950 directives had established the right tone within the military and that other services and other airbases understood that Air Materiel Command was back on the job and Grudge seriously at work. Colonel Watson at AMC thought that all of this was nonsense (as we have seen), but alleged that, yes, Project Grudge was doing its job. Captain Ruppelt, soon to show up in the AMC intelligence division at a desk next to that of Project Grudge, reports to us that all of Watson's claims to Cabell about project function were lies, and cases sometimes were thrown away, not even filed, after a cursory reading by Project officers James Rodgers and Roy James.[1] Like the difficulties of all parenting, it is difficult to guide staff through the complexities they will face, but it is impossible if both parents are "not on the same page" in their message. Cabell and Watson certainly were not. And other top officers within Air Force HQ Intelligence did not see things Cabell's way either (people like Jere Boggs, who, as we have seen earlier, wrote most of the policy opinion drafts on the UFO issue between 1948 and 1950, and Colonel Edward Porter,[2] Boggs' boss two levels up, and, seemingly, Brigadier General E. Moore, who was, at times, chief of the analysis division).[3] By the end of 1951 Watson, Rodgers, James, Boggs, Porter, and Moore would no longer be playing prominent roles in forming policy on this topic. But, even with a wholesale change of atmosphere, little could be done to resolve the problem of how to deal with UFOs.

Thomas Finletter, Secretary of the Air Force

An example of policy and publicity problems occurred at the beginning of 1951. In January, Secretary of the Air Force Thomas Finletter received a letter from the President of the Aero Club of New England, Robert Sibley. The Secretary passed this on to the Director of Intelligence, General Cabell, for a reply.[4] Why did Finletter bother to do this? The Aero Club of New England was no trifling organization—it was and is the oldest aeronautical club (read: private citizens dedicated to the advancement of the science of flight) in the Americas, and thoroughly connected with the Who's Who of the aviation community. The Club would shortly (in 1952) begin giving out what was and is still considered an extremely prestigious honor, The Cabot Award. Early recipients of this award included Generals Jimmy Doolittle and Curtis LeMay. The Aero Club was a group that could command some attention.

So what bothered Cabell's group about the response they had to write to Finletter? Lt. Colonel Willis, who got the job of drafting a reply, tells us that the Aero Club disagreed thoroughly with the current attitude of the Air Force towards UFOs. The Willis memorandum on the Aero Club letter summarized that letter's position thus:

> . . . further inquiry into the sightings of unknown aircraft should be made. It was the impression of the Aero Club that no notice was being taken of the many reports concerning unidentified flying objects. The letter requests the Air Force to resume its inquiry and consider the possibility that some of the unidentified aircraft sighted by reliable witnesses may have been vehicles from a planet other than the Earth.[5]

This letter had to be disturbing to Cabell, as it indicated that open-minded curiosity, bordering on enthusiasm, for the UFO phenomenon was penetrating the established aeronautical community.

We do not have Cabell/Willis' letter of reply; only Willis' memorandum of January 29, 1951. Judging by other memorandum-to-letter correlations, however, we can be fairly certain of the letter's contents. Willis said that the Aero Club was sent a copy of the Air Force's press memorandum of April 4, 1950, "a clear cut statement of present Air Force policy." Regardless of the press release's exact wording, it was buried beneath the turmoil surrounding Henry Taylor's claim that the saucers were ours and the flurry of countering statements that went right up to the White House. The content of the press release must have been pure "Grudge" (and from the hand of Jere Boggs), as that was the policy at the time and what they told the Navy on, essentially, the same day.[6] In an attempt to get more in line with Cabell's new approach, Willis went on to include two statements to pacify the Aero Club: the Air Force still investigates incidents and sends them on to AMC if deemed necessary; and an officer at the Pentagon (Willis himself) is assigned the task of monitoring all cases of UFOs. In other words: "Fear not, we are on the job." Project Grudge was stated as being eliminated, even though it was not. As an aside to his superiors, Willis said that "there have been several incidents, during the last six months, which cannot be explained and further investigation may be necessary," and "to date, there has been no physical evidence of any flying object having caused injury or damage."[7] Willis seems to have included his own summary remarks since this was apparently his first major UFO analysis task, having recently replaced the great saucer antagonist, Jere Boggs.[8]

Another publicity problem occurred that same month. After a very skeptical four-part article series by Bob Considine was published in national newspapers during November 1950, the most destructive version of his interview with Harold Watson appeared soon after. Entitled "The Disgraceful Flying Saucer Hoax," it appeared in the January 1951 edition of *Cosmopolitan*[9] and offended people so badly that Edward Ruppelt said that many pilots forever after refused to report cases to the Air Force.[10] Nicholas Mariana, a UFO witness mentioned by name in the article, threatened to sue the Air Force for defamation of character and loss of business at his baseball park.[11] The AMC public relations officer, Colonel Clare Welch, helped organize Watson's meeting with Considine and publication with

Cosmopolitan.[12] Years later, in 1967, Welch was still blissfully unaware of how out-of-tune all this was with what Cabell tried to create. From his point of view, AMC was being deluged with hundreds of reports, many of them hoaxes by people who "would go all over the country to carry out a hoax," and that the AMC engineers were totally disinterested in the task because they had better things to do. Welch seemed to believe that the problem was caused by people such as Donald Keyhoe, and that his and Watson's Considine project was aimed at defusing Keyhoe's influence.[13]

Welch's memories of those times were clearly inaccurate vis-à-vis Keyhoe's influence—that came later—and how much hoaxing anyone did, especially on a cross-country scale. But what probably *was* accurate is this: Welch remembered most vividly the atmosphere surrounding the subject with his boss, Watson, and the project engineers, Rodgers and James. That attitude was that this was a) nonsense, b) a pain in the butt, and c) a con game.[14] It is astonishing how persons sitting in slightly different information streams can come to such widely divergent mindsets as Welch's mildly irritated nonsense vs. DeWitt Searles' "tell me what to say and I'll say it" vs. Al Chop's (Chop replaced Welch) enthusiastic support for flying saucer information release and ongoing investigations. All three men were Air Force public information officers directly involved with UFO press releases at the time.

Of course, the UFOs themselves did nothing to help out General Cabell. Particularly uncomfortable was the continuance of incidents around Oak Ridge and various installations in New Mexico. Such cases were not happening daily (New Mexico cases dropped off sharply in 1951), but they were problematical nevertheless.

January 16, Artesia, New Mexico:[15] General Mills project engineers launched a secret Skyhook balloon. The appearance of this balloon during its later flight is known to have triggered a number of UFO reports, and the event was used as an example of misidentification, a handy category for debunking UFO cases generally. In the complexity that characterizes this subject, it was never mentioned that after the General Mills personnel launched their balloon, it was apparently "visited" by two UFOs. Two engineers saw a roundish, dull white object approach their balloon, and then fly away. The object was larger than the balloon. The object was an estimated 150 feet in diameter or more. The balloon's altitude was about 110,000 feet. Slightly later, at the Artesia airport, the engineers again, now in the company of four civilian pilots, spotted interlopers near their balloon. This time two seemingly identical objects moved towards the balloon. The objects made a nearly complete circle around the balloon, and left at high speed. They looked like disks. The General Mills people, almost certainly because they were aware of how their colleagues had been insulted by pejorative Air Force explanations and comments, did not report this incident.[16] (We will speak more about how this case emerged later.)

January 21, Holloman AFB, New Mexico:[17] Project engineers had launched a secret Project Gopher balloon and Air Force personnel were following it, ground and air. The pilots tracking the balloon saw what first appeared to be a smallish (star-like) light near their device. The light seemed to be pacing the balloon. As it neared the balloon, the light resolved itself into a round structure, clearly outlined, about ¼ to ½ the balloon's size. The unknown then broke away and proceeded to the west at very high speed. Just before it disappeared it emitted a series of brilliant flashes. General Mills engineers on the ground were later informed of the details of the encounter. By that time, the engineers would probably have been surprised if they had not had one.

The two pilots in the above case were on temporary assignment at Holloman, and soon thereafter returned to their home base, which was, somewhat ironically, Wright-Patterson.[18] Once there, they apparently talked freely about their story. They appear to have been unaware of Air Force policy (probably because of they had just come from New Mexico where people like McLaughlin, General Mills people, and even personnel from Los Alamos and Holloman seemed to be freely blabbing about these occurrences all the time), because they consented to an interview with the local newspaper, in which they told the details of their encounter. They described the object as a milky silver object shaped like a disk, "a dime," at between 50,000 and 60,000 feet, hovering and then flying away at great speed. *"I saw something I never saw before,"* said Captain E.W. Spradley of the Aerial Photographic Laboratory. Naturally, the press wanted to know what AMC thought about this. AMC's answer: "Air Materiel Command officials said Thursday they had received no official reports from the two officers and 'do not take it too seriously'."[19] There is much to ponder in that remark. We know that the pilots did give a report to AMC, and, given the predispositions of Watson, Rodgers, and James, we can be certain that AMC did not take it seriously. But how could one not take it seriously? What sort of mindset allows one to dump immediately into the analytical trash bin incidents witnessed by the Air Force's best technologists and its own pilots? There is something about this subject, some barrier to its believability, some challenge of an emotional kind, which produces the most inexplicable responses by otherwise reasonable, highly functional, people.

March 14, Holloman AFB, New Mexico:[20] The Air Force was hosting a test of a secret aircraft manufactured by Bell Aircraft. For that time period, it was cutting-edge technology. Bell's engineers were in a B-50 flying at 15,000 feet when they spotted a group of objects they could not identify, flying in a confusing "swirl," then breaking into a "V," then back to a swirl and a "V" again. The objects were slightly higher than the engineers' plane and seemed to be moving at a high velocity. Perhaps the Bell people got it wrong. Birds, such as high-flying geese, can travel at well over 15,000 feet. But the Bell engineers said that what they saw were not birds.

July 14, White Sands Proving Grounds, New Mexico:[21] During a guided missile launch, personnel saw two unidentified objects in the vicinity of the missile and a B-29 aircraft. One of the phototheodolite trackers watched one of the UFOs near the B-29 and took pictures. Two radar operators confirmed the presence of the object, reporting its speed as comparable to that of a jet plane. Development of the film revealed an oval object, which, as usual, either lacked detail or was too far away to show it.

While these events were occurring, Project Twinkle, the Green Fireballs project, attempted to catch the fireball phenomenon on film using dedicated Askania phototheodolites. As mentioned previously, this project was destined for confusion. It was given to the Air Force's Cambridge Research Laboratory instead of AMC, on the presupposition that the fireballs were distinctly separate from flying disks—and perhaps they were—but Twinkle personnel encountered reports of both. (It is important to note the irony in AMC's efforts to separate these events. While on the one hand the Air Force claimed that UFOs did not exist, on the other

Artist conception of a Green Fireball

hand they felt they were able to distinguish them from green fireballs. Barry Greenwood delves into this issue more deeply in a sidebar at the end of this chapter). Also, Cambridge was far from New Mexico, which created a situation rife for misunderstanding. As long as one had a Cambridge "boss" sympathetic to the reality and importance of the study, that was acceptable. Dr. Anthony Mirarchi, the first Project leader, was of that temperament. He felt that the evidence pointed towards artificial, not natural, phenomena, and consequently, to the possibility of dangerous Soviet mischief.[22] Mirarchi would soon retire from the Air Force, and his replacement, Dr. Louis Elterman, thought the whole business was bunk. During

Dr. Anthony Mirarchi

Elterman's tenure, with the theodolite surveillance up and running, green fireballs suddenly stopped appearing. From Elterman's point of view this meant that the phenomenon was transitory and that continuing the Project was a waste of time.[23] Dr. Mirarchi viewed the curious cessation with more suspicion, wondering whether Air Force surveillance plans could have been leaked to enemy agents who then altered their activities.[24] Elterman declared the Project a failure, recommended closing it down (it did, essentially, by the Fall of 1951, and formally at the end of the year), and wrote the final report. In that report, using terms like "no information was gained" Elterman laid the issue to rest, at least in his own mind. This approach and phrasing by Elterman seem to point to another difference in the ways various people respond to phenomena that are not easily categorized. Consider Elterman's words in the final report:

> Some photographic activity occurred on 27 April and 24 May, but simultaneous sightings by both cameras were not made, so that no information was gained. On 30 August 1950, during a Bell aircraft missile launching, aerial phenomena were observed over Holloman Air Force Base by several individuals; however, neither Land-Air nor Project personnel were notified and, therefore, no results were acquired. On 31 August 1950, the phenomena were again observed after a V-2 launching. Although much film was expended, proper triangulation was not effected, so that again no information was acquired.[25]

Most of us would probably not consider sightings by qualified observers, even if only one camera verified a sighting, as constituting "no information." One might admit that triangulation would help with some parts of the information, but to wave the phenomenon off because we only have multiple witnesses who were technical experts and just one source of photographic supporting evidence seems strange and risky when national security is an issue, especially if the objects were Soviet. Nevertheless, for those of similar persuasion, Elterman's report killed the issue.

In 1951 Oak Ridge continued to have activity related to unidentified objects in the sky. In January, employees of the NEPA (nuclear aircraft) division reported a brilliant object hovering over restricted airspace.[26] A check showed no aircraft or balloons airborne at that time. As mentioned in the last chapter, AMC, in the person of Project Grudge's James Rodgers, had prepared a debunking explanation for the perplexing radar reports that were occurring in the Oak Ridge region. The explanation was the usual one: atmospheric conditions, for example, ice-laden clouds. This apparently did not sit well with someone involved, for in January the Pentagon sent the military command at Oak Ridge a memorandum stating that they had analyzed the reports of the previous October 12 and 13 and found that weather conditions were *not* conducive to spurious echoes on the Knoxville radar.[27]

As mentioned in the previous chapter, Oak Ridge's Colonel Hood had decided to spread out an array of radiation detectors to search for a radiation signature of any sort when a UFO was around. Hood was inspired to do this by numerous rumors that the disks might be nuclear powered. Los Alamos, by the way, had another couple of instances of possible "coincidences" of such Geiger counter excursions with UFO sightings,[28] and in mid-1951 the Air Force Cambridge Laboratory believed there was some evidence that this might be true.

In July, Colonel Hood thought that he might have found strong evidence of a UFO's passage. The Oak Ridge personnel, participating mainly as a voluntary "saucer watch" in the region around the laboratories, reported visual observation of a UFO supported by a radar observation as well. It was found that the radiation counters had recorded a significant rise in some kind of emissions. This understandably excited Hood, and he wanted to pursue the possibility of hard data by not only increased diligence at the base, but by adding new approaches, such as a dust-catcher-equipped pursuit plane which (à la the similar procedure used to detect copper dust from a green fireball event in New Mexico) might capture enough detritus from the passing UFO to allow determination of what the stuff might be that had caused the radiation.[29] As far as we know, none of this was allowed to proceed, or at least it did not proceed even with an excited and determined officer wanting to pursue it. If the plans did not go forward, why not? If Los Alamos could catch fireball dust, why not Oak Ridge? One would not think that UFO incursions over Oak Ridge would be taken so lightly that a well-known detection technology, which worked, would be ignored. It would be nice to know what discussions occurred among higher authorities that led to this course of inaction.

So, these are some examples of what was going on phenomenologically in the Secret world. We will look at some other important cases later. Now we should examine the Air Force's public policy problems again, because they were surely having them.

Just as Henry Taylor had caused a terrible wrong-toned message problem for the Air Force in 1950, a scientist working for the Navy caused a similar one in 1951. Taylor had said that we should be relaxed because the saucers are our aircraft. Urner Liddel said that we should relax because they are *our balloons*. The Liddel story is curious. One can easily see how a newsman like Henry Taylor could end up believing his sources that flying disks were secret U.S. aircraft. It stretches the imagination to understand how a scientist working at the nuclear desk of the Office of Naval Research could not only decide that UFOs were Top Secret Navy balloon projects, but go public with it. In fact, Liddel's opinion is far odder than even that makes it sound.

Dr. Urner Liddel

Dr. Urner Liddel was a credible and respected scientist. His primary area of expertise was atomic and molecular spectroscopy. He was also known in scientific societies such as the Institute of Radio Engineers, the Optical Society, and the IEEE. Liddel had served with the Navy during the war, and stayed on afterwards as a civilian physicist at the Office of Naval Research. He was there in late 1948, when the Project SIGN team created their chaos in the Pentagon with their "Extraterrestrial" Estimate of the Situation. One of the fallouts of that fiasco occurred when the Office of Naval Intelligence insisted on being informed of cases and analyses coming into and out of Project Grudge. At about that time Urner Liddel, sitting at his Chief of Nuclear Physics desk at the Office of Naval Research, began collecting UFO case information out of this flow, apparently informally (that is, it seems to have been his own idea and not a formal Navy watchdog project).[30]

Because this was at the ONR, it is a very small assumption that Liddel had to be aware that many of the most enigmatic cases were from naval personnel or scientific personnel engaged in secret Navy projects. Somehow that blunt fact did not prevent Liddel from writing up an unofficial report of his "study," which concluded that essentially every puzzling UFO report could be attributed to naval balloons.[31]

The Office of Naval Research published Liddel's report in the *Research Reviews* of March 1951. The review was titled "Bogies at Angels 100." ("Bogies" means the unknown objects; "Angels" are one thousand foot altitude units in the jargon of the time). In the brief piece (about four pages of print), Liddel said that he had studied hundreds of sightings in detail (the one which he reports in a little specificity sounds like he was, indeed, reading the Project Grudge case files). The review is incredibly shallow and is largely a bit of braggadocio about cosmic ray studies via the balloons. Liddel admits that some of the balloon scientists themselves have reported UFOs, but waves them off with insulting statements about their not being aware of things like mirages and "internal reflections" in optical devices.

The public presentation of this was worse. Liddel's release of his pamphlet review alerted both the newspapers and the larger media to this "authoritative" new idea, and Richard Wilson of *Look* magazine gave him a lengthy interview.[32] The result of this was "A Nuclear Physicist Exposes Flying Saucers," in the February 27 issue. Once again Liddel used an article as a vehicle to brag about the importance of the Skyhook balloon research. Directly relating his private study to the Office of Naval Research, "Dr. Liddel *and his associates* arrived at their findings on these baffling stories by studying about 2000 reports of flying saucer observations of every kind and description [emphases added]." The historian finds no evidence anywhere that Liddel worked with anyone else on this and he, much later, wrote to Edward Condon that the work was his own,[33] and the number "2000" would be pushing it for any known available set of case files, let alone the belief that Liddel studied them all carefully. Nevertheless, Wilson believed it, as did many readers (including some important ones, as we will see). Among these "2000" case reports, Liddel is quoted as saying, "There is not a single reliable report of an observation which is not attributable to the cosmic balloons."[34] One wonders what Charles Moore,

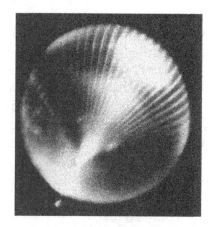

Inflated Skyhook Balloon

Commander McLaughlin, Clyde Tombaugh, etc. thought of such a preposterous remark. Nevertheless, this became the signature quote from the *Look* article to spread around the country via newspaper stories. Interviews with J.J. Kaliszewski of the General Mills launching team at the time indicated that all the engineers were aware of what Liddel had published, and none of them could fathom how out-of-touch he was.[35] (As a note for purists: Liddel's initial run to the press seems to have been to Associate Press science writer Alton Blakeslee, who included some of Liddel's views in an article earlier in February.[36] Some people noticed this but the impact came more with the *Look* story.)

Because, as is the case with many magazines, *Look* actually came out earlier than the printed publishing date, newspaper notices of Liddel's opinions were often published alongside those of William Webster, chairman of the Research and Development Board of the Department of Defense. Webster gave a "Grudge" oriented opinion:

> As far as I know, there is nothing to flying saucers. Careful studies have been made and to the best of my knowledge I've never seen anyone, who, having had an opportunity to look into the situation, believes there are flying saucers as such.[37]

Webster said that these reports, which he characterized as "rumors," arise from people seeing clouds or airplanes under unusual viewing conditions. For all we know, Webster may have been making an honest statement. What we can say, as we have seen, is that it was simplistic and almost entirely false. Nevertheless, this was the Chair of the Pentagon's R&D Board, and it would be natural to assume that he must know what he was talking about.

So, without some special experience or knowledge, what was John Q. Public to think? Some people saw Liddel's and Webster's comments as supportive of one another and affirming the concept that, in one sense, there were no such things as flying saucers, and, in another, there *were*, but they were Navy balloons. A great many publications jumped on this bandwagon, including overseas media, and seemed happy to lay UFOs to rest with the comfortable assumption that they were not Soviet devices of any sort. Still, Air Force Intelligence did not really like the Navy solution, as some

William Webster

commentators were blaming them for being so obtuse that they should have figured this out long ago. Plus, the Air Force knew that Liddel's theory was wrong. *Aviation Week* blasted everyone, especially the Navy, for not eliminating a dangerous nonsense concept (flying disks, UFOs) far earlier.[38] It went on to trumpet an elimination of such secrecy generally and an enhancement, thereby, of the free press. The Air Force might have smiled at the Navy getting the brunt of the criticism, but not at the implication the President was involved in this fiasco or the "solution" that the military would freely talk about secret projects.

Liddel's views did not stand unchallenged for long, but the challenge came in one of the worst forms that the Air Force could have conceived: one of its own former scientists went loudly public that Liddel was not only wrong but he was dangerously wrong, because the flying saucers were indeed Soviet technology. You can almost hear General Cabell groaning as you read the old newspaper quotations.[39]

The scientist was none other than Dr. Anthony Mirarchi, the original Project Twinkle scientific leader and former chief scientist at the Air Force's Cambridge Research Laboratory. Here was, then, an authority even more centrally involved with the UFO mystery than either Liddel or Webster. Because of the cases he reviewed while leading Twinkle, and doubtless because of the very strong views of Dr. Lincoln LaPaz, Mirarchi became convinced that the Green Fireball phenomenon was a) real, b) human-made, and c) Soviet.[40] Liddel would have agreed with the first two of these; Webster, really, with none of them. The Air Force was simply puzzled by all three elements, though its policy depended upon operating as if all three were true, but publicly communicating as if none of them were. As usual, the Air Force would have much preferred that both Liddel and Mirarchi had shut up.

Freely commenting about his credentials and past UFO-study involvement, Mirarchi criticized Liddel's views as not in the best interest of the country. "The Navy report is erroneous. It lulls people into a false sense of security."[41] Some few reports could have been due to mistaken viewing of naval balloon projects, but the important cases in the Green Fireball phenomenon appeared consistent with "a missile programmed in advance." He reminded the nation of the critical nature of the installations in New Mexico, including Los Alamos, and argued that they were the targets for some form of reconnaissance. *"If they were launched by a foreign power, then they could lead to a worse Pearl Harbor than we have ever experienced."*[42] Calling on Congress to appropriate funds for serious radar, sky watching, and photographic data-collection on the UFO topic in general, Mirarchi blasted the government for a policy amounting to "suicide by secrecy" and for its interference in scientific research.[43] Astoundingly loose-lipped, he gave many details from cases (including LaPaz' project capturing copper dust after a fly-by,) and speculated that the fireballs stopped coming because enemy spies had tipped their superiors off that photo-tracking cameras were in place.

Well, wow. From Air Force Intelligence's point of view that was about as bad as it could get. Enemy spies. Enemy devices. A new and worse Pearl Harbor. A Pentagon Suicide by Secrecy. The Air Force *had* to respond, of course. What came was a plain vanilla dismissal: "In over 500 investigations we have made so far, we have yet to find one concrete bit of evidence to back up these reports of flying saucers."[44] Although moving much more slowly, behind the scenes the Air Force contemplated a stronger response. Apparently instigated by the FBI, a round of communications began taking place within Air Force Intelligence as to whether Mirarchi should be prosecuted. The grounds for prosecution were that Mirarchi's loose comments specifically violated Air Force regulations (AFR205-1, written March 14, 1949) prohibiting the release of classified information to unauthorized individuals. Lt. Colonel Frederic Oder, Mirarchi's one-time colleague at Cambridge Labs, wanted prosecution:

> . . . in [Oder's] opinion, the information released by Mirarchi to the *Quincy Patriot Ledger* could cause serious harm to the internal security of the country, pointing out that if this information were to fall into unfriendly hands, it would definitely be prejudicial to the defense effort of this country, both from the point of view of the prestige of our Government and the point of view of revealing our interest in certain classified projects.[45]

Admittedly, Mirarchi could be charged with violating AFR 205-1 and of being astonishingly unhelpful with his remarks, but Oder's views seem to be a bit over the top as well, bordering on paranoia. Air Force higher-ups felt that way, too, and told the FBI that they did not believe that the intensity of Oder's remarks or a prosecution of Mirarchi was warranted. Still, it is informative that a highly ranked Air Force scientific officer could have felt this strongly about security violations related to UFO data. That concentration of focus on "unfriendly hands" and the "prestige of the Government" is indicative of the obsessions of the times. Perhaps mentioning that Oder was also undercover CIA is explanation enough.[46]

Ace Pilot, Ruppelt before joining AMC

Just after all the February uproar caused by Liddel and Mirarchi, and perhaps because it left the whole UFO business once again in confusion, *Life* magazine wanted to do a story on UFOs and to visit Wright-Patterson to prepare it. We do not know how *Life* obtained permission to do this; possibly due to its importance as a national magazine; possibly that Air Force authorities felt that Mirarchi had caused things to get out of hand and a major article showing the Air Force "On the Job" would be helpful. General Cabell at that time had been informed that Grudge was back doing its work and all was well. Still, the Pentagon inquired of Watson and Rodgers if such was the case.[47] Captain Ruppelt, who would take over the Project later in the year and who was analyzing Soviet jet technology in the same offices at the time, reports this about that awkward moment:

Back went a snappy reply: Everything is under control; each new report is being thoroughly analyzed by our experts; our vast files of reports are in tiptop shape; and in general things are hunky-dunky. All UFO reports are hoaxes, hallucinations, and the misidentification of known objects.

Another wire from Washington: Fine, Mr. Bob Ginna of *Life* is leaving for Dayton. He wants to check some reports.

Bedlam in the raw.[48]

In order to bail themselves out on their lies to Cabell, and to save face in front of Bob Ginna, one of *Life*'s best, the personnel at AMC attempted to brazen it out. In his private notes, Captain Ruppelt tells us this:

The "legitimate press" first showed renewed interest in UFOs in early 1951 when Bob Ginna of Life Magazine came out to ATIC. He met Al Chop at the AMC PIO office and came over. He was

AMC in 1951. Center: General Benjamin Chidlaw
2nd from right: Colonel Harold Watson
2nd from left: Intelligence Operative John Honaker

introduced to Red Honneker [Honaker] and Jim Rogers [Rodgers]. They gave him the pitch about thoroughly investigating everything and having this top notch project. Actually nothing was being done and they couldn't even find the files on the sightings he asked about. They attempted to "snow" him but I found later they hadn't done it. All it did was to make him suspicious as hell. This visit scared ATIC.[49]

It would be several months before Ginna and his co-writer, H. B. Darrach, finished their countrywide research and published their article,[50] but actions at ATIC/AMC began much more quickly. Air Defense Command had just issued a letter to all of its widespread organizational elements encouraging them, in line with Cabell's and Pentagon thinking, to be concerned and to report unconventional aircraft sightings in a timely manner.[51] The ever-unrepentant Harold Watson at ATIC/AMC seems to have taken this as an excuse to lobby Cabell to get his organization out of the UFO business and leave it to the Air Defense Command (ADC). A lengthy reproduction of Watson's views is, for the reader's benefit, warranted:

> This Command [AMC] has investigated thousands of reports on unidentified flying objects over the past several years. The project was originally initiated at Air Materiel Command several years ago as a result of numerous incidents occurring throughout the country where people indicated that they had seen unidentified flying objects, or so-called flying saucers. Extensive investigations of many incidents were made and conclusions were drawn on each incident and insofar as the facts available would permit, it was concluded that the objects did not represent a development of any foreign power.
>
> Many of the incidents cannot be fully explained because of the lack of facts upon which to base a technical investigation. However, a great number of the incidents were found to be the result of unusual cloud formations, balloons, meteors, sunlight reflecting from aircraft, etc. In August 1949 a report was prepared entitled "Unidentified Flying Objects Project Grudge," and the project was cancelled.
>
> In October 1950 the project was reinitiated at the request of your headquarters. Since that time hundreds of reports have been received and investigated. The conclusions which have been drawn since the re-initiation of the project are for all practical purposes identical to those drawn in the earlier investigations.
>
> In view of the above, it appears that the project as it exists has been carried on to such an extent that it has been established that there are little if any results being obtained which are significant from the standpoint of technical intelligence, other than to conclude that so-called unidentified aircraft are not considered to be air weapons of a foreign power. Notwithstanding this conclusion, it is considered that it would be impracticable in connection with Air Force responsibilities to say that we are no longer interested in any incidents of the aforementioned nature.
>
> Accordingly, it is felt that the project requirements should be revised to assure that all unidentified aircraft are reported without delay and by expeditious means to the Air Defense Command. In the event that any of these incidents require technical interpretation or analysis, AMC could be called on to carry out this work as required by ADC provided that sufficient significant technical details are supplied to furnish a basis for such a study.[52]

In other words: if you have something that is actually important, send it on to us. Otherwise, let ADC do it.

For several months the Pentagon did not formally reply. But change was in the wind. Watson was apparently notified that his assignment would change by the end of the year, and his replacement, a much more open-minded and less outspoken colonel named Frank Dunn, was onsite and learning his way into the job. James Rodgers was reassigned within AMC in May, and another much more open-minded Lieutenant named Jerry Cummings got the UFO desk. Informally, "Grudge" was supposed to be back in serious operation, although Ruppelt reports that Rodgers and Roy James would still intercept incoming cases and never bother passing them on to Cummings.[53]

Cummings had not only these difficulties of clearing unwanted old hands out of the way, but also trying to get some semblance of order into things generally. A later staff report contains this:

In July 1951, this project was reorganized. A review of the data available at that time showed that the first three assumptions made in the 1949 report [mass hysteria, hoaxes, psychopathological persons] probably were not valid. The basis for this was the fact that although publicity had been at a low ebb, or nearly non-existent, between 1949 and 1951, reports from good sources continued to come in to ATIC.

These reports were mainly from military personnel, and could be classed as good reports.

To us, a good report is one in which several people were involved and the motives of these people in making the report cannot be questioned. They have made comparatively careful observations and have reported everything that they observed.[54]

In mid-1951, it seems, the Air Force project began to reside in more thoughtful hands.

Air Defense Command had spread the word to bases all over. AMC/ATIC personnel seemed to be going towards a reasonable transition. Was Cabell finally getting it right? In September, he accomplished his penultimate impact on the subject: the Air Force issued JANAP 146(B).[55] To make sense of the significance of this action, it is appropriate now to take a short step back in time to reflect upon how the military communicated vital information between its structures.

During WWII there existed an "Order" which went by the acronym CIRES (Communications Instructions for Reporting Emergency Sightings). This told pilots and other personnel what they must do in all cases of "sightings" which involved everything from enemy aircraft to our own planes or civilians in trouble.

After the war it was apparent that the United States' structure of three distinct military organizations was too disorganized, and "Joint Committees" of the Armed Forces were initiated to deal with this problem. On the issue of communicating vital intelligence of the CIRES type, a Joint Communications-Electronics committee was established. The committee initiated the JANAPs (Joint Army Navy Air Force Publications) that would apply to all three services, regardless of which service was the "lead agency" in the particular concern. CIRES was revised and became JANAP 146-CIRMIS (Communication Instructions for Reporting Military Intelligence Sightings). It was from JANAP 146 that military bases took their orders whenever a UFO incident occurred.[56]

This revision took place in the summer of 1948, but its implementation was delayed by some concerns about civilian pilots involved in non-U.S. airspace accidents. (JANAP 146 did not apply to UFO incidents only). There was also a desire, coming surprisingly from *outside* the Air Force, that JANAP 146 be utilized, as one point of emphasis, to ensure that civilian pilots having UFO encounters report those encounters according to military chains of command. This interest was inspired in major part by the then-famous July 1948 Eastern Airlines near-miss encounter with an apparent UFO. (The Chiles-Whitted case, which we have described earlier and which was reported as very rocket or missile-like.) The Air Force's chief of intelligence at the Pentagon, General Charles Cabell, agreed with this use of JANAP 146, and it was distributed to all Air Force bases during December of 1948. Note, therefore, that reporting channels for UFO incidents prior to that time were not clearly established. As with all orders, confusion occurred anyway. When the initial SIGN/Grudge UFO analysis project was established in early 1948, most Air Force organizations had been told in a less universal, piecemeal, fashion to report UFO incidents to Air Materiel Command at Wright-Patterson AFB. Some did, while others sent their reports to the Pentagon. Some, because the concept of a UFO was not clearly interpretable, did not send certain reports at all. Whatever came in allegedly got to Project SIGN. It is certain that reports containing particularly sensitive information did not. Apparently, actionable judgments were being made.

The confusion was not helped when the Pentagon announced in 1949 that the UFO Project was closed. Although that announcement was aimed at the public, the policy *within* the Air Force wallowed in total confusion. At Wright-Patterson, the chief of technical intelligence, Colonel Harold Watson, was more than happy to reduce his effort to a disorganized, station-keeping, report-filing, two-man operation.[57] At the Pentagon, General Cabell thought that Wright-Patterson was still doing the work, though now as a normal, serious, intelligence function. External commands, such as the Far East Air Force (FEAC) and the Continental Air Command (ConAC), did not know what to think. Where should their cases go, if anywhere?

Partly as a response to his growing awareness of this confusion, Cabell revisited JANAP 146 and the Joint Committee approved JANAP 146A: CIRVIS in September 1950. CIRVIS is "Communications Instructions for Reporting Vital Intelligence Sightings." CIRVIS stated that all vital intelligence sightings would be reported in two ways: to the Air Defense Command (ADC), and to the Office of the Secretary of Defense. Once again, as far as UFO reports were concerned, Cabell's office failed to alleviate the confusion. Neither ADC nor the Secretary of Defense is Wright-Patterson, which handled Air Force UFO Intelligence analysis. Nevertheless the new order went out in December of 1950. The policy would not be clarified completely until 1953.[58]

The apparent dichotomy of orders in JANAP 146A (send vital communications to ADC or the Department of Defense) and the Air Force's "new" reinforced policy (to send them to ATIC/AMC at Wright-Patterson) continued to cause trouble. Cabell tried again in 1951 to clear things up. On September 6, JANAP 146B was issued with the signature of the Joint Chiefs of Staff. It was titled: "Communications Instructions for Reporting Vital Intelligence Sightings from Aircraft."[59] JANAP 146B may be considered an improvement only if one assumes that the Air Force had sharpened up its activities internally (*i.e.* beyond the literal words of the document). The September 1951 JANAP stated three things of particular interest:

1. Unidentified Flying Objects were specifically singled out as the subject for serious consideration in CIRVIS reporting;
2. The (usual) strong reminder was issued that all CIRVIS reports are of "vital importance to the security of the United States" and that such communications are governed by espionage laws; consequently, the transmission of information contained in these reports to any unauthorized person is prohibited by these laws;
3. All CIRVIS reports will be forwarded in three ways: a) to the Commanding General of Air Defense Command; b) to the Secretary of Defense's office in Washington, D.C.; and c) to the nearest U.S. military command.

The first two of these points served to emphasize the seriousness of the reports in the mind of Air Force Intelligence. Not as clear is what the third point accomplished. It seems to be a recognition that UFO reports are probably caused by a wide variety of events. Some of these might well be of immediate interest to Air Defense, and some might well be of immediate interest to the local military authority. Both departments should get the timely report. Other cases could have broader intelligence concerns. Thus, reports should also go to Washington, where the Department of Defense will transmit them to both the CIA and Air Force Intelligence at a minimum. So far, we have still not seen how AMC/ATIC would be involved. At this point, though not specifically laid out by JANAP 146B, Air Force Intelligence would transmit the reports to other elements within its organization, as appropriate. Translation: they would go to Wright-Patterson. If, as JANAP 146B insisted, those reports were "delivered immediately" and "by the most expeditious means available" to the Pentagon, then Wright-Patterson could still receive the information relatively quickly. The solution to the communications "chain" was to send reports to Washington D.C. and to make the exchange rapid. Making this all slightly more orderly was the fact that Air Force Intelligence had decided in the Summer of 1951 that the Intelligence Division at Wright-Patterson (symbolically called "T-2") would be designated the "Air Technical Intelligence Center" (ATIC) and become an operation more closely allied to the Pentagon than to the other functions of Air Materiel Command (it would report directly to it in about another year).

Getting back to what was really going on at Wright-Patterson, *i.e.* ATIC, we had mentioned how Watson had been regularly politicking the Pentagon to dump UFOs and stick ADC with the job. Even with the new JANAP, it was obvious that Watson would need another direct communication. Such a letter ultimately came his way, following an explosive meeting at the Pentagon in mid-September. The story of the Ft. Monmouth sighting and consequent events represented a "catastrophe turning point" in this labored transition, which the Air Force made in its policies.

September 10, 1951, 11:10 a.m. military radar at Ft. Monmouth picked up an unknown following the coastline and moving at high velocity.[60] The radar return was sharp and strong, more so even than a return from a large aircraft. The radar operator said that it was more equivalent to a radar return from an ocean vessel, but obviously moving far too fast for that. At about 11:35 a.m. an Air Force pilot on a training mission, along with a major who was in the plane with him, observed a lenticular disk about 40 feet in diameter. It flew much below their altitude of 20,000 feet; they estimated it at approximately 5000-8000 feet. The object was over Sandy Hook, New Jersey. The pilot banked and descended towards the object, but it made a banking 90° turn and rapidly left the area, disappearing out to sea. The Air Force officers felt that its speed was amazing.

The crew of the plane had been talking to the ground over a "public" frequency during their encounter, and a civilian on the ground picked up the transmission. The contents of that military conversation rapidly spread among the local civilian population. Later, the pilots were in a public place and were overheard by a newsman discussing it. He queried them on it and got part of the story. (Note that this violates JANAP 146B.) The story hit the news and all the big East Coast papers wanted more information from the local base. Pandemonium ensued, only to be met by a flat refusal from the base to speak about it. The base Commander and Public Information Officer apparently *did* know what the policy was.[61]

Meanwhile a report was sent to Air Defense Command. ADC considered the incident significant and seems to have sent the report on to the Pentagon *and* directly to Wright Patterson. At the Pentagon, two issues were clear to General Cabell: the Ft. Monmouth/ADC report and that a big news leak had happened over it. We will see his response shortly. At ATIC (at Wright Patterson), something helpful to our understanding of how botch-ups can happen in serious matters took place. We know this almost blow-by-blow because Edward Ruppelt, a primary witness to some of it, and a close secondary witness to the rest, left the details in Ruppelt's files.

For full understanding of what happened, an outline of ATIC's command structure at the time is presented (see the chart on page 125.) The commanding officer at ATIC headquarters, Colonel Watson, was in and out during the summer and early fall, as his replacement, Colonel Frank Dunn, began to get the feeling for the job. Watson had several offices and three Technical Divisions under him. The main one, and the one we are interested in, was the Technical Analysis Division. This is where issues involving current or projected air technology problems, particularly as concerned enemy or unknown technology, were analyzed. The chief of this division was Colonel Brunow Feiling, a veteran intelligence man and an engineer. Among those immediately working for him was Albert Deyarmond, the former Project SIGN engineer, who had been around since the beginnings of the flying disk problem and had suffered, and survived, the winds of change.[62]

Beneath the Technical Analysis Division headquarters office were twelve areas called sections or branches. These were category areas, broken down according to the nature of the technological threat that a given report, set of reports, or retrieved hardware, identified. The titles are explanatory enough: "Aircraft and Propulsion," "Performance and Characteristics," "Nuclear Energy," "Armament," etc. The chief of the Performance and Characteristics Branch was Lt. Colonel Nathan Rosengarten. The other section chiefs knew and worked constantly with one another, and all this was housed in the same building.

Transition

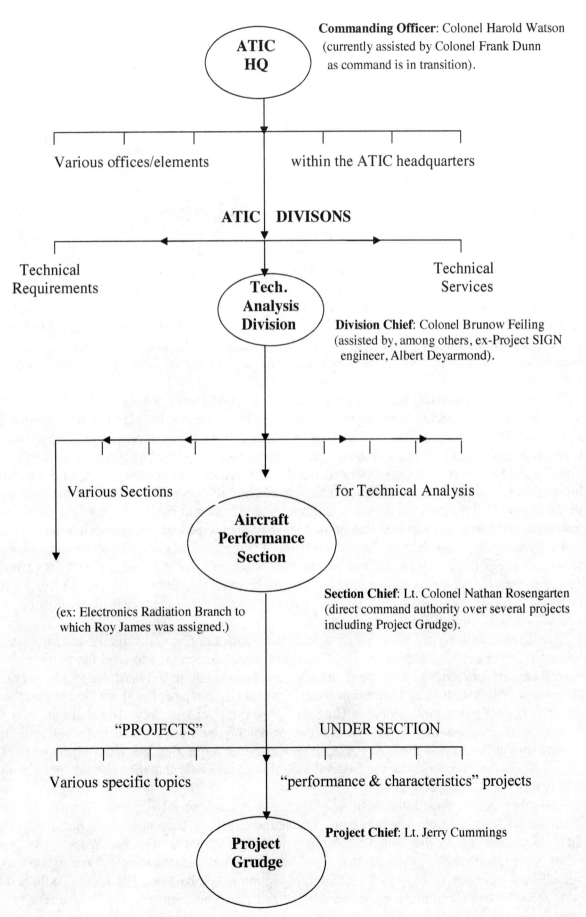

ATIC HQ

Commanding Officer: Colonel Harold Watson
(currently assisted by Colonel Frank Dunn
as command is in transition).

Various offices/elements   within the ATIC headquarters

ATIC   DIVISONS

Technical
Requirements

Tech.
Analysis
Division

Technical
Services

Division Chief: Colonel Brunow Feiling
(assisted by, among others, ex-Project SIGN
engineer, Albert Deyarmond).

Various Sections   for Technical Analysis

Aircraft
Performance
Section

(ex: Electronics Radiation Branch to
which Roy James was assigned.)

Section Chief: Lt. Colonel Nathan Rosengarten
(direct command authority over several projects
including Project Grudge).

"PROJECTS"   UNDER SECTION

Various specific topics   "performance & characteristics" projects

Project
Grudge

Project Chief: Lt. Jerry Cummings

Under Rosengarten's command were several projects, often composed of one or a very small number of officers, the "desks" of which were often side by side in the same room. Lieutenant Jerry Cummings occupied the Grudge "desk," now that James Rodgers was assigned elsewhere in the sections structures. Near Cummings' project desk was Lieutenant Edward Ruppelt, then involved with a project on the performance characteristics of the Soviet MIG aircraft. A person such as Roy James was in an entirely different branch and project, involving "Electronics" (i.e., Radar). Into this apparently orderly situation dropped the ADC report of the Ft. Monmouth incident. ATIC headquarters received it and sent it down to

Pilot, Major Nathan Rosengarten

Brunow Feiling. He read it and, since a radar return was involved, chose to send it not to Rosengarten's branch, but to "Electronics" and Roy James. Why Feiling made this error we do not know. The case was an obvious unidentified *object* incident since it had visual confirmation by airborne military witnesses.

The material from ADC had an urgent tone about it, and James got his old buddy James Rodgers to read the report and decide how urgently to dismiss it. Somehow Lt. Colonel Rosengarten heard that James and Rodgers were inappropriately handling an unidentified flying object report and informed Cummings about it. Cummings, Rosengarten, Feiling, and Rodgers all gathered in Feiling's office for a jurisdictional shoot-out. Rodgers claimed that he had taken this over because Cummings was slow in his analyses, and the Pentagon wanted a fast response. "Rodgers' solution," that the "whole outfit [at Ft. Monmouth] were a bunch of young impressionable kids and the T-33 crew had seen a reflection," was something Rodgers claimed that he had already discussed and cleared with Watson. Rosengarten and Cummings both disliked not only the territorial usurpation of Cummings' assignment, but also the seeming severe mismatch of the report and the "solution." All this—from ADC wire reception, to "solution", and confrontational meeting—occurred in about three hours. Given a meeting with Watson in between those events, Rodgers and James were being very efficient indeed. It helps one's speed, of course, when the investigation is bypassed.[63]

A wire then arrived in Feiling's office from the Pentagon. General Cabell's office wanted to know what ATIC planned to do about the Ft. Monmouth case. Rodgers was to send the "solution" to them to "get them off our backs" (all these details and quotes are in Edward Ruppelt's notes from his discussion of this with Jerry Cummings later). Someone (perhaps Feiling) decided to call the Pentagon directly. Cabell's assistant (probably Colonel Schweizer) was on duty. The assistant was astonished that any debate was taking place "as to whether or not anyone would go out and investigate the report." Feiling then lied and said that, of course, there was never a question that they would go to investigate. Cabell's assistant then said that the General took this so seriously that they should "get him out of bed" if they were not getting cooperation.

Therefore debate ended and both Rosengarten and Cummings were on their way to New Jersey. Their actual investigation was less than spectacular. Military personnel were not always trusting of them, doubtless due to the fouled atmosphere over UFOs that people like Watson had created. The pilots were absolutely convinced that they had seen an unconventional "intelligently controlled" vehicle and were put off by ATIC's attempt to explain it as a balloon. The radar people had kept very poor records, and Cummings wondered whether all they had seen was the T-33 aircraft (despite the time differential). Nevertheless, the fieldwork now done, Cummings and Rosengarten were allowed to charter a plane at Pentagon expense (very unusual, by the way) to see General Cabell as soon as possible.

The meeting is famous in UFO history. Cabell, of course, was there himself. Many Pentagon officers, plus a few civilian aircraft technologists, attended. While Cummings and Rosengarten were in New Jersey, Cabell had personally phoned ATIC to ask what was going on. Watson or Feiling handed the call to James Rodgers. Rodgers' inability to give Cabell what he considered to be proper answers made the General suspicious that what he thought to be true about Project Grudge was in fact not true at all. Therefore, when Cummings and Rosengarten finished their statements about Ft. Monmouth, Cabell turned to Cummings and asked him for a frank assessment of the project. Rosengarten nodded to Cummings to go ahead and let fly.[64]

Cummings, about to leave the service anyway for an engineering job at Cal Tech, did. Both Watson and Rodgers were fingered for bias, which resulted in various forms of incompetence, including neglect (some cases lost or thrown away) and inappropriate analysis (such as simply trying to think up new and original explanations that had not been sent to Washington before). Everything had been treated as a joke.

This meeting was recorded on the old form of "wire" recording, as Rosengarten and Cummings wanted the people back at ATIC to hear the General in full voice. Edward Ruppelt was one person who heard it before it was ordered destroyed. It made quite an impression on him as, doubtless, it did on everyone else. These are some of the quotes Ruppelt remembered from General Cabell. They are probably not precise, but in all likelihood suggest the tone accurately. (A copy of Ruppelt's notes are included in the appendix.)

Cabell, hearing about Watson's and the Project's absolute antithetical bias: "I want an open mind. In fact, I *order* an open mind. Anyone that does not keep an open mind can get out, now. As long as there is any element of doubt [about what this phenomenon is], the Project will continue."[65]

After one of his staff suggested that perhaps the civilian aero-engineers did not need to hear this, Cabell said he did not care how embarrassing it was, and he was not ashamed to give people hell as long as they deserved it. He was especially miffed by the description as to how his personal orders were just disregarded.

As to answers: *"What do I have to do to stir up the action? Anyone can see that we do not have a satisfactory answer to the saucer question."*

Cabell then turned to face the Pentagon officers. A long silence issued (Ruppelt says "45 seconds"). Then: *"I've been lied to, and lied to, and lied to. I want it to stop. I want the answer to the saucers and I want a good answer."*[66]

One of the most intransigent of the Pentagon officers, Colonel Edward Porter (one of Major Boggs' main bosses), said that he thought the whole Project was a waste of time. Cabell confronted him with a statement that he did not see *himself* as some sort of crackpot, and that he had a great deal of doubt in his mind about the current [Grudge] stance that the saucers were all "hoaxes, hallucinations, or the misinterpretation of known objects." The Grudge report, he said, was the "most poorly written, inconclusive piece of unscientific tripe" he had ever read.[67]

Colonel Edward Porter

After that withering experience, things changed in many ways, some by accident, some by design. Watson was out and Dunn was in as head of ATIC. Cummings got enough cooperation to begin organizing the Project before leaving it to Ed Ruppelt. Even Brunow Feiling was reassigned. His replacement was Colonel S. H. Kirkland. At the Pentagon, the "UFO desk," already vacated by Boggs, was in the hands of a station-keeper, but soon to be occupied by the very sympathetic Major Dewey Fournet. Although Colonel Porter was still around, Fournet would be insulated from him by two layers of colonels (Weldon Smith and William Adams) whose views ranged from sympathetic neutrality to positive bias on the subject.[68] Porter himself was sandwiched both above and below his rank in the intelligence chain when General Cabell himself left to be replaced by General John Samford. Samford's primary assistant, Brigadier General William Garland, had seen a UFO himself. The "corporate atmosphere" on flying object reports and analysis was in total change. We will see what the results of that shift were in the following chapter. Before we move on, however, it

Colonel Frank Dunn

is worth reinforcing the attitude of Cabell towards the reality of the problem by visiting a few more of the cases themselves.

July 9, Dearing, Georgia:[69]

> Object sighted by 1/Lt. George H. Kinmon, Jr., 160 Tac Recon Sq. Lawson AFB, Ga., at 1340, 9 July 51 until about 1350, same date. Object described as flat on the bottom and appearing from a front view to have rounded edges and slightly beveled. From front view as object dived from top of plane was completely round and spinning in a clockwise direction. From front view as object dived observer noted small spots on the object which he described as being similar to craters observed on the moon through a high powered telescope. Object did not appear to be aluminum. Only one object observed. Color white. No vapor trails or exhaust or visible system of propulsion. Described as traveling at tremendous speed. Object appeared near Dearing, Ga., 25 miles West of Augusta, Ga., while pilot was on a routine flight from Lawson AFB, Ga. Pilot had leveled off at 8,500 feet altitude on a course of 247 degrees. As he leveled off, object dived from the sun in front and under the plane and continued to barrel roll around the plane for a period of ten minutes, when it disappeared under the plane. Pilot states object was 300 to 400 feet from plane and appeared to be 10 to 15 feet in diameter. Pilot states he felt disturbance in the air described as 'bump' when object passed under plane. Object left the plane a few miles South of Milledgeville, Ga., and 15 to 20 miles from Macon, Ga. Pilot was flying a F-51 at 270 miles per hour when object was sighted. Weather conditions .6 to .8 broken clouds. Wind 2 to 7 miles per hour.

October 10, St. Croix, Wisconsin:[70] This is another report from the General Mills balloon team. A test launch supervisor, J. Kaliszewski, and colleague, J. Donohue, were following their balloon in a chase plane, when another object came down from above and approached the balloon. The unknown was featureless with a soft glow. In approximately two minutes of total observation, the object leveled its flight, crossed behind the balloon, made an abrupt turn, and then accelerated up at a 50° angle at very high speed until lost to vision at height. Kaliszewski said: "From past experience I know that this object was not a balloon, jet, conventional aircraft, or celestial star." The very next day, flying with a different colleague, Richard Reilly, Kaliszewski again observed an unidentifiable object. Just north of Minneapolis, again monitoring a balloon from the air, they saw a brightly glowing object, which, for a change, had not rendezvoused with one of their balloons.

> This object was peculiar in that it had what can be described as a halo around it with a dark undersurface. It crossed rapidly and then slowed down and started to climb in lazy circles slowly. The pattern it made was like a falling oak leaf inverted. It went through these gyrations for a couple of

minutes and then with a very rapid acceleration disappeared to the east. This object, Dick and I watched for approximately five minutes.

I don't know how to describe its size, because at the time I didn't have the balloon in sight for a comparison.

Shortly after this we saw another one, but this one didn't hang around. It approached from the west and disappeared to the east, neither one leaving any trace of a vapor trail.

When I saw the second one I called our tracking station at the U. of M. Airport and the observers there on the theodolite managed to get glimpses of a number of them, but couldn't keep the theodolite going fast enough to keep them in the field of their instruments, both Doug Smith and Dick Dorian caught glimpses of these objects in the theodolite after I notified them of their presence by radio.

The ground observers corroborated the air report of the last objects, as follows:

The object was visible in the theodolite for little under two seconds and appeared to be smoky gray (no halo or glow was noticed), cigar shaped, left no vapor trail and gave off no reflection such as sun reflected by metal . . . [and] that during their period of visual observation they saw two more like objects which finally formed in straight pattern after the first and all departed at same time.[71]

As mentioned earlier, the General Mills technologists were so irritated by what they considered to be incompetent and insulting handling of incidents like these that they rarely were motivated to report them to the Air Force.[72]

October 9, Indiana and Illinois:[73] In an apparent independently witnessed event, a Civilian Aviation Authority (CAA) employee at an airport in Terre Haute, Indiana, observed a silvery disk or flattened ball-shaped object approach the airport and fly directly overhead at high speed. It had a very shiny metallic sheen and was apparently quite large: "the size of a 50-cent piece held at arm's length." Shortly after, a civilian pilot, flying in the vicinity of Paris, Illinois, saw a large, metallic (shiny) object, looking like a flattened ball and hovering in the sky. The pilot banked his plane and flew towards it. The UFO then accelerated away and disappeared at distance. Ed Ruppelt checked this case himself and concluded that the witnesses' reports coincided exactly. All the rest of his checking (balloons, aircraft, meteors, even the witness backgrounds) left him without any explanations. The policy for such things was to simply write "Unknown" or "Unidentified" on the Project record card, and go on to the next case. This is mentioned to reinforce the frustration that people who want answers face in dealing with UFOs.

Flying Saucers May Be Real Space Ships, Rotary Told

It is probable there really are such things as "flying saucers," and they could be space ships from elsewhere in the universe, John L. Cramer told Minneapolis Rotarians Friday.

Cramer, director of balloon research for General Mills, spoke at a luncheon meeting in Pick-Nicollet hotel.

He bases his flying saucer supposition, Cramer said, on these bits of scientific theory:

THE UNIVERSE probably contains other solar systems similar to the earth's. There is little reason to believe only the earth can support life.

IT IS ESTIMATED the earth will be able to send manned expeditions to the moon by 1970, to Venus by 1975 or 1980, to Mars by 1980 or 1985 and all over the universe by 2000.

"Someone in the universe may have solved the problems of flying through space and may be visiting us."

Manned balloons, added Cramer, can accomplish much in outer space in such fields as sun photograph cosmic rays, measurement fallout and "other classifi fields still too new to ta about."

John Cramer, Director of Research at General Mills

They do not get them. For those with a low tolerance for ambiguity, this is, in some sense, an unacceptable situation. Many persons who have been involved with such matters end up losing their objectivity and yearn to "come to a conclusion." This seems to have happened to Air Force personnel all the time during these years, and, of course, to civilians as well. Edward Ruppelt was not one of those types of personalities. He seems to have been able to accept a very large "gray basket" of Unknowns and continue to do his job.

December 12, Hastings, Minnesota:[74] An Air Force captain was piloting his F-51 on a test flight. The skies were exceptionally clear, except for a strange-looking object off to the left. The white "thing," which at a larger distance looked a bit like a kite (the pilot realized that kites at 10,000 feet altitude were unlikely), resolved itself upon approach as a spinning, roundish blur. It was changing speeds and seemed to maneuver. Getting very close now, the object looked like two small two-foot diameter disks only one foot apart and moving in tandem. They then accelerated to about 400 mph and disappeared at distance. This encounter is mentioned because the pilot was Donald K. [Deke] Slayton, who would become one of the original American astronauts.

Left to Right: Donald Slayton, Alan Shepard, and Jim Lovell

November 24, Selfridge Air Force Base, Michigan, and surrounding environs:[75] This case is not included here because it is a probable unknown, but because it says something to us about the state of reporting and Air Force publicity attitudes. Between 6:20 and 6:25 in the evening, in at least four locations in Michigan, persons witnessed and reported a bright, white roundish object flying (generally as stated) to the southwest. These people included three Air Force personnel, with one Tower operator and one civilian airline crew. Due presumably to the civilians, the incident was reported to newspapers, whereupon the Air Intelligence Technical Center found out about the sighting. It was not reported to ATIC by Selfridge AFB where two of the witnesses viewed the object. When the newspaper contacted ATIC and Ed Ruppelt about the case, ATIC knew nothing and was, undoubtedly, not happy about it. Once again, JANAP 146B had not penetrated sufficiently into every command. An immediate reply was requested. Whether that happened is not known, but by late December Ruppelt was still seeking information. He even composed a letter to appear in newspapers around southern Michigan to appeal to citizens to report what they may have seen of the incident (Ruppelt was very interested as to whether the object flew a straight track). Ruppelt had a creative idea there but was obviously naïve as to the Pentagon's position on exciting the public interest by overt demonstrations of the Air Force's own interest. He got word from his commanding officer, at this time Colonel Dunn, that they were *not* going to advertise in the newspapers.

Late August through early September, Lubbock, Texas:[76] The famous "Lubbock Lights." This puzzling business was so prominent that it needs at least a mention. It is, unfortunately, so complicated that any brief treatment cannot do it justice. However, the interested reader can always get more information.

Sometime during the last two weeks of August, citizens of Lubbock, Texas, were puzzled by greenish-white, glowing, objects, often in groups, flitting about their skies. Because the phenomenon repeated over about a two-week period, many people began night sky watching for the lights. What particularly interested Project Grudge was a report that four Texas Tech college professors had seen the objects. Ed Ruppelt was intrigued by the fact that the professors had seen their formation of lights at a time very close to when an employee of Sandia base and his wife saw a huge metallic "flying wing-shaped" craft with pairs of lights along the wings. A high-speed object could easily travel the distance between Albuquerque and Lubbock in a brief time. There was also a radar report from Washington State which calculated a velocity of a bogey there at something in the neighborhood of 900 mph. Ruppelt noted that at such speed, given the times that people were reporting, one object could have accounted for all three events. He knew that this was only guesswork, but it is what a good intelligence analyst begins with. Several days later in Lubbock, an amateur photographer out looking for the lights produced four photos of what seemed to be an array which either maintained rigid formation, or which was attached to an undeterminable structure very much like a flying wing. Carl Hart's photos have been the source of unrelenting controversy.

To tease this complexity apart, we can state the following:

1. The flying wing case reported by the Sandia couple has never been explained;
2. When shown Carl Hart's photos by the Air Force, the couple immediately felt that this is what they saw;
3. Hart's ability to get the clarity that he achieved in two of the photos, with a hand-held camera at night, was doubted by Air Force photo analysts;
4. Ruppelt's giving the Washington state radar case to Roy James resulted in an old-style Grudge opinion that the returns were caused by weather conditions. Additionally, when Ruppelt conveyed the opinion to the people in Washington by a phone call, their response was less than polite. As Ruppelt said: *the long distance wires between Dayton and Washington melted.*[77]

Although the above shows that nothing was settled, we will leave those issues alone, and say a little more about the observations made by the professors.

These people were all scientifically and technologically trained: a geologist, a chemical engineer, a petroleum engineer, and a physicist. One evening, they saw a semi-circular formation fly overhead. It was fast and difficult to see accurately. There were so many lights that they could not even make a good estimate ("fifteen to thirty"). One hour later, a similar group, but not in any formation, flew over. The professors decided to meet on consecutive nights and sky watch. They made twelve more sightings over the next few weeks. The objects always traveled north to south, and once appeared three times in the same evening. So, why wasn't the obvious interpretation migrating birds? Some people thought they were. Some said some were, but other cases were not: they had seen both and could, in their minds, clearly distinguish. Some said that it was obvious that the main incidents were not things like ducks or geese, as one could neither hear their incessant honking, nor see wings flapping when sky conditions and "object brightness" would ensure that those features would be evident.

For a long while, the Texas Tech professors were in the latter camp. They kept records and often communicated with ATIC. They also became better known than they would have liked, which caused them, as members of the academic community, some level of irritation. As time passed, so did the phenomenon, and without resolution. Then one day, Ed Ruppelt received a final communication via a Western Union telegram that is shown on the following page: the professors had figured it out; they were embarrassed and they did not want Ruppelt to tell anyone what they felt they had seen. In his *Report on Unidentified Flying Objects*, Ruppelt honored this request with only "a very commonplace and easily explainable natural phenomena."[78]

What was the professors' solution? They would never tell Ruppelt, or, if they did, he refused to mention it in his files. Whatever it was—birds, moths, some other flying bit of nature—the "ducks" answer tended to stick over the years. Conveniently ignored, as far as this theory is concerned, was something another Texas Tech professor had done. R. S. Underwood was a member of the mathematics faculty at the college. He, like the others, was curious about the lights and kept watch and notes. One evening, he and his wife observed three flights, one of which passed directly overhead. During that same evening, his father-in-law and a neighbor also watched flights. For the third flight, as it happened, both Underwood and his father-in-law had good time information. Being a math professor, and doing

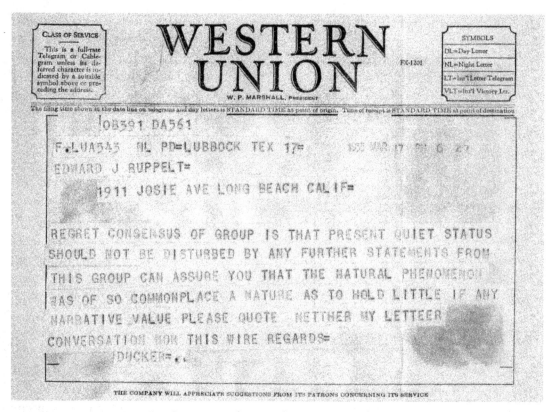

Professor Ducker's telegram to Ruppelt

the trigonometry, Underwood calculated that the group was somewhat but not greatly higher than 2000 feet above ground, which worked out to an approximate 700 miles per hour at a low end estimate. The height is fine for birds; 700 miles per hour is not. Underwood told the original Tech foursome about this but they did not want to accept his conclusions. He then wrote Ruppelt at ATIC, where the letter was placed in a mixed file of correspondence and may never have been read.[79] No mention of it appears in the Project records, and it was only discovered years later. Regardless, Lubbock had burdened people, especially the original professors, too long. They wanted a solution. They wanted to move on.

General Lionel Chassin

A final phenomenological note for 1951: Military pilots in France had a puzzling encounter in June when two French Vampire jets encountered a large metallic craft. That and other incidents seemed to mobilize elements of the French military establishment to take up interest in the subject. By the Fall or earlier, it became known that General Lionel Chassin, chief of staff of the French Air Force, and his assistant, Colonel Clerouin, had become extremely interested in the subject, authoring articles and supporting case investigations.[80]

Ed Ruppelt ended the year attempting to firm up the Project organization by building greater ties to important organizations, such as the Air Defense Command; bringing more technical aid to the general overview of the situation via the Battelle Memorial Institute; and briefing the new powers in the Pentagon. Those new powers were the chief of intelligence John Samford, and his primary aide, William Garland.

132

Green Fireballs

CENSORSHIP: THE KIRTLAND FIREBALL CATALOG[81]

Government censorship has always been a curious thing. The intent is to keep outsiders from knowing certain facts. Sometimes it is done for practical purposes; i.e. to protect legitimate national security concerns. For example, the exact method and materials for making an atomic weapon should not be publicly available; people can be blown up! Sometimes censorship is performed for political purposes, i.e. to hide waste and ineptness by government officials. Such certainly cannot be justified for the greater good, but in our imperfect society it is done nevertheless. Sometimes the censorship backfires and reveals more than it was intended to hide.

Censorship has generally been counterproductive where the UFO topic has been concerned. The government's intent was to hide information and prevent the public from paying undue attention to UFO reports. However, the censorship was often unnecessarily and ineptly applied, leading to public suspicion that great secrets were being suppressed. Maybe there are or are not great secrets still to be discovered, but, either way, the government's handling of censorship on UFOs has contributed to a widespread belief in the existence of extraterrestrial beings visiting the Earth. The following is a little-known example of this.

One of the many documents released through the Freedom of Information Act (FOIA) twenty years ago was a sizeable collection of reported "green fireball" incidents. The reports were part of a 209-case catalog collected by the 17th District, Air Force Office of Special Investigations (OSI) at Kirtland Air Force Base, New Mexico. The cases run from January 1946 through May 1950, with the majority running from mid-1949 to the spring of 1950. The catalog describes the sightings in chart form, giving details of size, shape, color, speed, direction of travel, etc.

A characteristic of many of the reported incidents in the southwestern U.S. during this period was the odd green color of many of the streaking objects, thus giving rise to the term "green fireball."

Also, upon investigation of incidents by OSI, it was determined that some of the objects behaved in an anomalous manner. Speeds greater than aircraft but less than meteors were reported. A persistence of horizontal flight paths suggested that many objects soared rather than fell. But most interestingly, such a concentration of large, green fireballs over one state (New Mexico) is difficult to explain as meteoric activity. Meteors tend to be a random phenomenon, scattered rocks or metal in space sporadically encountering the Earth. The exception to this would be the occurrence of meteor showers—when the Earth passes through the dust paths left by comets in their orbits around or past the Sun. Showers do not last more than a few hours intensely, or a few days for encountering the most scattered members of the comet path. And they certainly don't aim at individual U.S. states over several years' time as the green fireballs seem to have done.

The OSI catalog was released in the late 1970s with minor, but telling, censorship. Two columns on the chart were entirely deleted: "Reliability of Observer" and "Evaluation." The reason? "B5," meaning that under the FOIA, insight into decision making processes could be withheld from public view. This was a way to protect freedom of expression by officials without fear of later being made accountable for decisions that may or may not have ever been implemented.

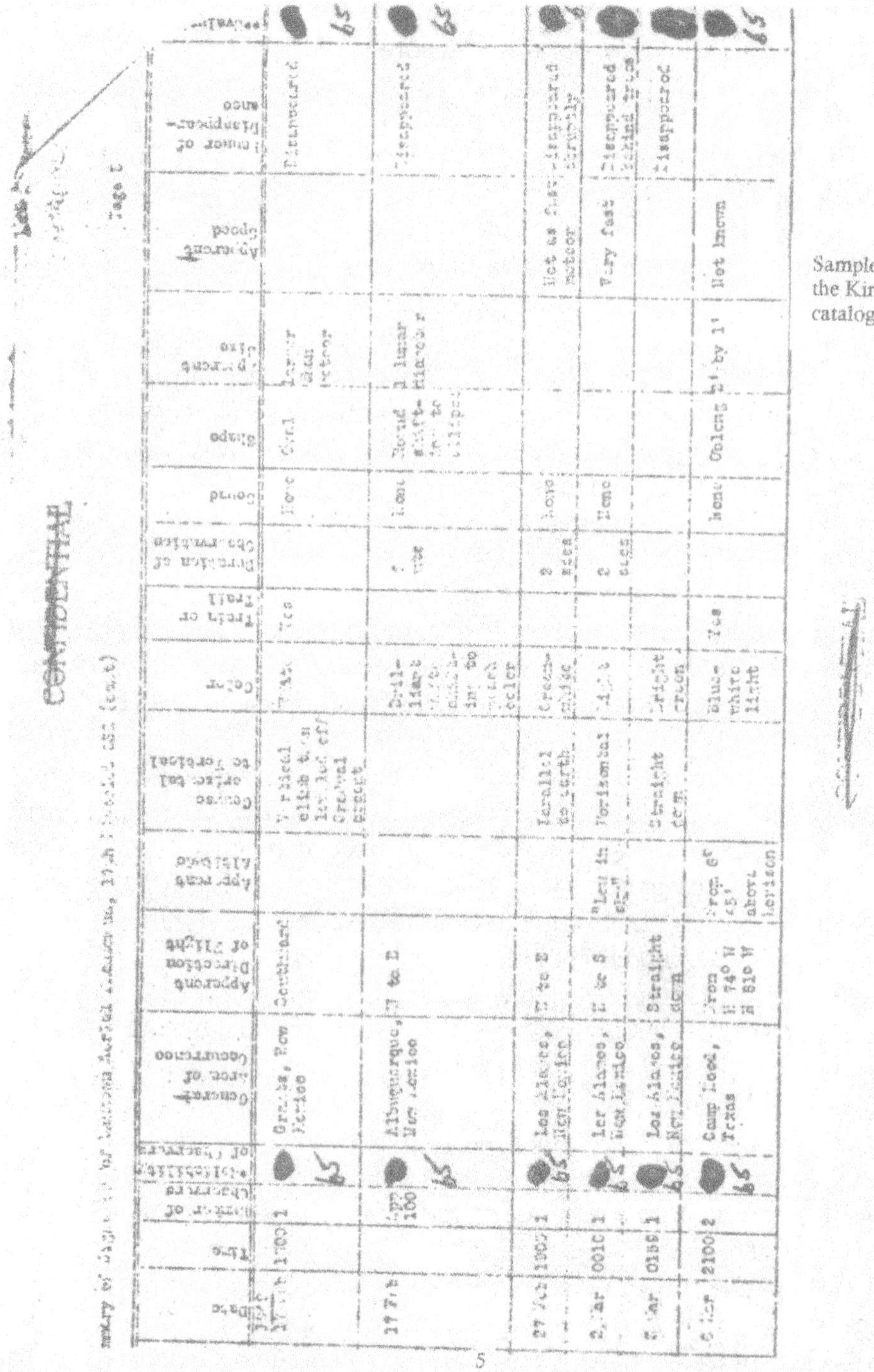

Sample page of
the Kirtland fireball
catalog

"Reliability of Observer" lists codes "VR," "R," and "Unk," meaning "very reliable," "reliable," and "unknown." The censorship appears rather pointless here because while the files that may have accompanied the catalog at one time identified the witnesses, the selected codes in no way cast a witness in a negative light. They were either great witnesses, good witnesses, or little was known about the individual, according to OSI.

Stranger still was the evaluation censorship. The same exemption under FOIA is used as in the reliability column.

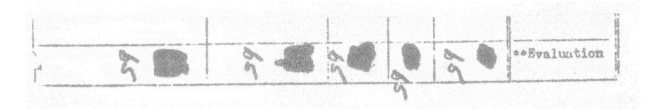

But the selection of conclusions is curious indeed.

LIGHT:
*Reliability of Observers: V2 = Very Reliable   R = Reliable   Unk = Unknown Reliability
**Evaluation: (1) "Green Fireball Phenomena"   (2) "Disk" or Variation   (3) Probable Meteor

"1" is "Green Fireball Phenomena," "2" is "Disk or Variation," and "3" is "Probable Meteor." Distinguishing "1" from "3" is clear in suggesting that the green fireballs were not considered to be normal meteors. Moreover, "2" suggests a flying "Disk," essentially a flying saucer, or variation (whatever that means!) as an explanation, meaning that they were not considered as an explanation for the fireballs either. Considering that explanation #2 must have been used for at least one of the cases listed (otherwise it would not be an option at all), it is curious that during the era of Project Grudge—a time when flying disks, or saucers, officially did not exist—such was being used to explain unexplained phenomena by Air Force investigators.

The evaluation deletion in the catalog, while literally justified under the "B5" exemption of the FOIA, did not help the government's case for dismissing the UFO phenomena as non-existent. The deletions were applied in the late 1970s, almost a decade after official investigations were closed down. Revealing those conclusions would certainly have raised uncomfortable questions about why the Air Force was explaining a peculiar aerial phenomenon as either a "Green Fireball Phenomena" or a "Disk or Variation." The scientists studying the green fireballs for the government didn't know what they were, and those studying the disks or variations didn't know what those were. But, based upon this catalog, there was obviously a distinction! That distinction was deemed necessary to veil long after the Air Force was done with UFOs.

The final entry in the Kirtland catalog was on May 1, 1950, a few months after the Air Force initiated "Project Twinkle." "Twinkle" was an effort to catch the green fireballs in the act, using instrumentation to detect any anomalies. The effort failed to detect anything useful and Twinkle was shut down in December 1951. In their final report, Twinkle investigators suggested that "earth may be passing through a region of space of high meteoric population," a suggestion offered as a possible explanation for the abundance of high-flying, streaking objects seen during the UFO wave of 1947.[82]

There are more examples of government officials, more so than UFOlogists, fostering notions that UFOs were more mysterious than official statements would lead one to believe in certain instances. Whether or not it is evidence of extraterrestrials remains debatable. But any historical discussion of the UFO controversy must credit, or blame, the U.S. government for at least an assist to ET belief.

Notes

[1] Ruppelt files.

[2] Ruppelt files.

[3] Memoranda involving Moore, passim, FOIA (USAF).

[4] Lt. Colonel Willis (for record), memorandum for record, subject: "To prepare a non-military letter to Mr. Robert B. Sibley for signature of the DI/USAF," 29 January 1951, FOIA (USAF).

[5] Lt. Colonel Willis, memorandum, subject: letter to Sibley, 29 January 1951.

[6] Op-322F2-Weekly Briefing Topic, Office of Naval Intelligence, 4 April 1950, FOIA (USN); see Gross, April-July 1950 supplement, 9-10.

[7] Lt. Colonel Willis, memorandum, subject: letter to Sibley, 29 January 1951, FOIA (USAF).

[8] Ruppelt files.

[9] Bob Considine, "The Disgraceful Flying Saucer Hoax," *Cosmopolitan*, January 1951: 31, 110-112.

[10] Ruppelt, *Report*.

[11] David Saunders and Roger Harkins, *UFOs? Yes!*, 1968.

[12] James McDonald to Robert Low and Richard Hall, 14 March 1967.

[13] McDonald to Low and Hall, 14 March 1967.

[14] This agrees precisely with what Edward Ruppelt says about the attitudes at the time (Ruppelt files).

[15] Air Technical Intelligence Center, *Project Blue Book Report No. 6*, 30 April 1952.

[16] Ruppelt, *Report*.

[17] Blue Book files microfilm Roll 8.

[18] Newspaper article quoted in toto by Gross, 1951 supplement, 15-16, *Dayton* (OH) *Journal-Herald*, 15 February 1951; and Blue Book files, microfilm Roll 8.

[19] Article quoted by Gross, 1951 supplement, 15-16, *Journal-Herald*, 15 February 1951; and Blue Book files, microfilm Roll 8.

[20] Blue Book files microfilm Roll 8.

[21] Blue Book files microfilm Roll 8.

[22] AP news story, "Flying Saucers Not Just Balloons, Says Scientist," 26 February 1951.

[23] Louis Elterman, *Project Twinkle Final Report*, 27 November 1951.

[24] Anthony Mirarchi, interview, *Quincy* (ME) *Patriot Ledger*, 27 February 1951.

[25] Elterman, *Project Twinkle Final Report*.

[26] Blue Book files (OSI files).

[27] Colonel H. J. Kieling (Lt. Colonel Willis) to 1009th Special Weapons Squadron, subject: Unconventional Aircraft, 5 January 1951, FOIA (USAF).

[28] Ruppelt, *Report* (Note: Ruppelt may have gotten his date on this wrong. Radiation excursions are recorded, in Blue Book files, for 1950 and 1952).

[29] Ruppelt, *Report*.

[30] Urner Liddel to Edward Condon, 30 November 1966.

[31] Urner Liddel, "Bogies at Angels 100," *Research Reviews*, March 1951.

[32] Richard Wilson, "A Nuclear Physicist Exposes Flying Saucers," *Look Magazine*, 27 February 1951.

[33] Liddel to Condon, 30 November 1966.

[34] Wilson, *Look Magazine*, 27 February 1951.

[35] Ruppelt, *Report*, and J. J. Kaliszewski, "Oral History Video Interview," (Tom Tulien, interviewer for the UFO Oral History Project).

[36] Alton Blakeslee, "Flying Saucers Are Explained," Associated Press news story, 13 February 1951.

[37] Webster quoted in Gross, 1951, from *San Jose* (CA) *Mercury*, 14 February 1951.

[38] Robert H. Wood, "Saucers, Secrecy, & Security," *Aviation Week*, 19 February 1951.

[39] United Press news story, dateline: Scituate, MA, 26 February 1951, "Flying Saucer Radar, Spotter, Posts Are Urged," and Associated Press news story, dateline: Scituate, MA, 25 February 1951, "Scientist Raps Saucer Report: AMC Here Continues Study."

[40] Fred Pillsbury, "Soviet Saucers Spied on Atom Tests, Expert Says," *Quincy* (ME) *Patriot Ledger*, 27 February 1951.

[41] U.P. /A.P. stories, above.

[42] U.P. /A.P. stories, above.

[43] Pillsbury, "Saucers Spied," 27 February 1951.

[44] Quoted in Gross, 1951, from *San Jose* (CA) *Mercury*, 26 February 1951.

[45] Colonel Kenneth King, Counter Intelligence Division Office of Special Investigations to Deputy Chief of Staff, Development, memorandum, subject: Dr. Anthony O. Mirarchi, former AFCRL Employee—Violation of AFR 205.1, 2 September 1953, FOIA (USAF). Note: this was the finale of a drawn-out "discussion" between FBI and elements of the Air Force that began April-May 1951, FBI involvement beginning at least by October 1951, and ended here by General Garland in September 1953.

[46] See Robertson (CIA) Panel discussion, later. Oder attended as a CIA engineer.

[47] Ruppelt, *Report*.

[48] Ruppelt, *Report*.

[49] Ruppelt files.

[50] H. B. [Darrach] and Robert E. Ginna, "Have We Visitors from Space?" *Life Magazine*, 7 April 1952: 80-96.

[51] Air Defense Command, Letter 200-1, subject: "Unconventional Aircraft," 11 April 1951, FOIA (USAF).

[52] Colonel Harold E. Watson to Director of Intelligence, 23 April 1951, FOIA (USAF).

[53] Ruppelt files.

[54] Colonel John O'Mara, *Project Blue Book Staff Study* (these are usually referred to as *Project Blue Book Reports*), 2 July 1952 (in the Blue Book files microfilms).

[55] Joint Chiefs of Staff (Joint and Allied Communications Publications, *JANAP 146B*, "Communications Instructions for Reporting Vital Intelligence Sightings from Aircraft (CIRVIS)," 6 September 1951.

[56] FOIA (USAF). There is no single history of the development of the JANAP regulations towards which to send the reader. The context of the development of JANAP/CIRMIS, CIRVIS/MERINT is well known, and the reader can consult any of the many resources on the post-WW2 need for military intelligence coordination, which led to the National Security Act, the establishment of the Joint Chiefs of Staff, and the beginnings of formalized Joint Intelligence Committees for the bigger picture. The precise creation and utilization of the first JANAP documents can be read from the USAF FOIA documents. Unfortunately for citation purposes, these come in one-page-at-a-time doses, and would require listing several dozen documents at a minimum, including JANAP 146A through JANAP 146E. It is sufficient for current purposes to simply remark that these USAF FOIAs are mainly 1948 vintage extending up to 1952, and either directed to General Cabell's office from the USAF Director of Communications or are internally generated by USAF intelligence itself.

[57] Ruppelt files.

[58] Colonel Glover, memorandum for record, subject: "Reporting of information on unidentified flying objects," 15 October 1951, and Lt. Colonel Eugene Cook to Air Coordinating Committee, Dept. of Commerce, 26 December 1950, FOIA (USAF).

[59] Joint Chiefs of Staff (Joint and Allied Communications Publications, *JANAP 146B*, "Communications Instructions for Reporting Vital Intelligence Sightings from Aircraft (CIRVIS)," 6 September 1951.

[60] Blue Book files (OSI files).

[61] The Ft. Monmouth story and its details have three sources: 1. The Blue Book microfilm (OSI files) as just cited; 2. Edward Ruppelt's published book (Ruppelt, *Report*); and most importantly 3. The Ruppelt files, which contain a lengthy retelling of this whole business based upon Ruppelt's direct observation and his talk with Jerry Cummings about it.

[62] Our understanding of ATIC command structure comes from diagrams of that structure given to UFO historian Michael Hall, while visiting Wright-Patterson AFB. Reading the Blue Book microfilms and Edward Ruppelt's materials confirm their accuracy. The diagram in the text is congruent with the 1951 diagram obtained by Hall.

[63] See note 62, as regards these and details above and below.

[64] See note 62.

[65] See note 62, especially Ruppelt's file notes.

[66] See note 62, especially Ruppelt's file notes.

[67] See note 62, especially Ruppelt's file notes.

[68] Similarly to the above referencing on Ft. Monmouth et al., these Pentagon-based matters rely on a variety of sources: 1. the USAF FOIA documents, showing the changes in persons authoring UFO policy letters and memoranda; 2. Ruppelt's *Report*; and 3. Ruppelt's files, wherein he comments on the UFO leanings of officers like Porter, Smith, Adams and Fournet.

[69] Blue Book files (OSI files).

[70] Blue Book files Roll 8.

[71] Blue Book files Roll 8.

[72] Ruppelt, *Report*, and J. J. Kaliszewski, "Oral History Video Interview," (Tom Tulien, interviewer for the UFO Oral History Project).

[73] Ruppelt, *Report*.

[74] Blue Book files Roll 9.

[75] Blue Book files (OSI files).

[76] The Lubbock Lights case engaged Captain Ruppelt extensively and he has much to say about it in both his *Report* and a folder in his files. Blue Book microfilm also contains extensive material (especially in OSI files). For the reader seeking a well-written extended essay on the enigma, see Clark's *Encyclopedia*, Volume 2, article: "Lubbock Lights."

[77] Ruppelt, *Report*, and Ruppelt files.

[78] Dr. Ducker to Edward Ruppelt, telegram and letter, Ruppelt files.

[79] R. S. Underwood to Air Technical Intelligence Center, 1 June 1952. Note: the reason that it is suspected that this letter may never have been read is that it (and much other apparently undealt-with correspondence) was recovered from an unsorted pile of letters dating from this era. The "rescue" occurred much later in time when a PhD student was asked whether he wished to take the materials, rather than have Wright-Patterson just destroy them, as they were being cleaned out. The other side of this issue, why Ruppelt et al. never got to this and other letters, seems to be due to the huge upswing of incoming cases that the Project was faced with in the summer of 1952. Ruppelt admitted that he was swamped and months behind.

[80] The information comes from French UFOlogists, Jimmy Guieu (*Flying Saucers Come From Another World*, 1956) and Jacques Vallee (*Anatomy of a Phenomenon*, 1965). General Chassin served on the board of at least one civilian UFO research organization.

[81] Barry Greenwood, ed., *U.F.O. Historical Revue*, #8 (February 2001): 4-7; cf. www.cufon.org/uhr/uhrndx.htm. Reprinted with permission by The Computer UFO Network.

[82] Barry Greenwood, ed., *U.F.O. Historical Revue*, #4 (April 1999): 4-7; cf. www.cufon.org/uhr/uhrndx.htm. Reprinted with permission by The Computer UFO Network.

Chapter 8: Tacking Against the Wind

The year 1952 was a "flap" year with hundreds upon hundreds of reports of unidentified flying objects. Media coverage was exceptional with an explosion of news reports. Working only with Air Force records, one historian estimated that 30,000 different news stories concerning UFOs appeared between April and September of 1952.[1] The phenomenon expressed itself dramatically with two extended occurrences over Washington, D.C., in July. These incidents involved not only the Air Force, but the CIA and President Truman as well.

This chapter will describe the changes that occurred in the Pentagon and at ATIC at this time, and how they affected policy. It will focus on the worrisome incidents that occurred in the Korean military theatre and the fallout from those concerns. It will look at the gathering storm of UFO reports that climaxed over Washington, and the profound shaking of Pentagon thinking that this caused. It will mention the serious entry of the CIA into these matters, as well as an alternative UFO study pursued by the Navy. And, a smattering of particularly significant cases will be presented.

Let us begin with the situation within Air Force Intelligence. Early in the game, retired Marine Major and civilian writer Donald Keyhoe had surmised from rumors and conflicting Air Force behavior that a severe split in opinion existed in the Pentagon over what the saucers were and what to do about them.[2] Documents from the Air Force and from Edward Ruppelt confirm that Keyhoe's intuition was correct.[3] But things were much more fractured than Keyhoe ever thought. To say that there were "two schools of thought" regarding the UFO phenomenon widely misses the complexity of the issue.

Dr. J. Allen Hynek

One school of thought rested with those who believed there was no such thing as a flying disk. One could conceptualize a faction within this group which felt that there are no "flying disks," most of these reports are misidentifications, and there seem to be hints of a new natural phenomenon involved in a cluster of them. These people would find "UFOs" non-threatening but intriguing and worthy of pursuit for scientific reasons. The professionals of the intelligence community paid no "practical" attention to this view whatsoever— no resources were to be put into UFO investigation for reasons of science or curiosity. Only the scientific advisors, people like Hynek and Kaplan, would speak in support of this position.

A second faction within the "there's no such thing" group believed that all of this was caused by human errors. The false reports were due either to the witness' lack of knowledge, the limits of visual perception, hoaxes, or even drunkenness. These reports and the UFO phenomenon itself elicited various types of reactions by people with this viewpoint. People such as Colonel Porter and, apparently, Brigadier General Moore in the Pentagon, and Harold Watson, Roy James, and James Rodgers at AMC/ATIC were needlessly derisive and outspokenly negative about the issue. At a minimum, they believed that this business was a waste of time and resources and made the Air Force look foolish. Other persons were not as scornful of witnesses, even though they believed the subject was bunk. At AMC, the Grudge report and its authors, George Towles and Lt. Howard Smith, were in this camp and, for the most part, this was the stance of the early Pentagon UFO-desk operative Jere Boggs and the arch-debunker,

Donald Menzel, although Menzel could not always contain his emotions in public. These people simply said: no flying disks, only understandable misidentifications. Due to possible psychological warfare issues, it was appropriate to deflate "saucers" not only to save time and resources, but to maximize national security.

The other school of thought consisted of the people who believed that flying disk technology was probably real. Within this group there were three theories: the technology was American; it was Soviet; it was extraterrestrial. After an initial analysis, almost no one believed that these sightings were caused by U.S. technology. Occasionally someone outside of Air Force intelligence, such as Urner Liddel with his balloons or Henry Taylor quoting his unnamed sources, would float this idea, which Air Force insiders knew was preposterous. That left the Soviets and ET. It was possible to hypothesize with either or both

Center: Lieutenant Howard Smith

possibilities. Early in the game the Collections Area in the Pentagon (George Garrett and Robert Taylor) went forward in such an open-minded way, as did Colonel Howard McCoy at AMC. Malcolm Seashore carried a "look for Soviet influence" document to Europe in the fall of 1947, and most of Jere Boggs' policy writing, including the famous "AIR-100" study, is written with concern that the sightings could be of Soviet origin. Almost everyone involved in the Green Fireballs study (Mirarchi, LaPaz, Rees et al.) were concerned about Soviet mischief, and the Far-Eastern Air Force prodded the Pentagon more than once about their encounters.

Lastly within the "flying saucers are real" group were persons who appear to have believed fairly strongly that the disks were extraterrestrial (ET). This faction included not only the famous SIGN engineers, but highly-placed Pentagon personnel such as Weldon Smith, William Adams, Dewey Fournet, and possibly General William Garland.[4]

The operational gap between "it's all a waste of time/get rid of it!" vs. "stay very vigilant, it might be Soviet!" is about as wide as one can get. Throw in the confusion of "UFOs = ET" as a possibility with its own range of possible responses, and the Air Force has a complex issue to address. Viewed in this way, the correct stance should have been "Stay vigilant with an open mind, and pursue no agenda except national security." That is precisely the stance that General Cabell ultimately took. It is the behavior indicated by Colonel Frank Dunn, Lt. Jerry Cummings, and, in the end, new chief of intelligence, General John Samford. Edward Ruppelt's behavior also fits the mode of, "whatever I believe isn't important…I have a job to do."

At the end of 1951 and into 1952, the atmosphere in the Pentagon and at the ATIC was not of this objective, down-the-centerline style. The Pentagon and ATIC both leaned towards the ET hypothesis. General Cabell's replacement, General Samford, was like him, open-minded and concerned with national security. But Samford's main aide, General Garland, had seen a UFO himself, and unlike Cabell aides like John Schweizer, was UFO enthusiastic. Fournet had replaced Boggs; an almost 180° turn of opinion in favor of the ET hypothesis (ETH). Fournet's bosses, Adams and Smith, both felt that the ETH was a real possibility. Porter, who was derisive towards the entire subject, was essentially silenced. Another key Samford advisor, Stefan Possony of Georgetown (who worked right out of Samford's office), initially was concerned that UFOs were Soviet devices. By mid-year, he became an open-minded prober of the ETH.[5] Even the Public Information Officer changed to the E.T.-enthusiastic Al Chop. At Wright-Patterson, Watson was out, replaced by Dunn and then Garland himself. Rodgers and James were shunted to the side for Cummings and then Ruppelt. This was a massive change in the philosophical approach by the major figures involved with UFO investigation and policy. Shown is the array of officers who changed from late in the Grudge Project to early Blue Book. The changes in command move vertically from top to bottom. Below the names are the roles occupied by those individuals.

General Cabell	Colonel Schweizer	Major Boggs	Colonel Watson	Captain James
↓	↓	↓	↓	↓
General Samford	General Garland	Major Fournet	Colonel Dunn	Captain Ruppelt
Directors of Intelligence	Primary Advisors	Pentagon UFO Desk	AMC/ATIC Director	AMC/ATIC Investigator

The main ingredient of change in all this had to be General Samford's chief aide, General William Garland. Whether Garland thought that there was any chance that UFOs were of an extraterrestrial origin is not known. What Garland brought to this new environment was that he thought the UFO issue was important—very important. As stated earlier, Garland had seen a UFO himself. As far as he was concerned, the debate about their *reality* was over. His logical deduction was that they were Soviet and very dangerous. He seems to have been quite fixated by this, and on January 3, 1952, wrote a stunningly strong and clear memorandum to Samford that laid down the investigative shortcomings of the Grudge Project and suggested investigative policies and agendas for the immediate future.[6] Since Garland and Samford had to be communicating with each other all the time, this memo likely reflected information that Garland had presented to Samford at a much earlier time. The memorandum is so illustrative of the concerns at that moment in time by the Air Force Intelligence leaders that it needs to be printed here in text so that the reader can appreciate it. The memorandum is displayed on the next two pages.

3

DECLASSIFIED PER EXECUTIVE ORDER 12356, Section 3.3, NND 841508
By *W G Lewis*   MARS, Date   *Jan 29, 1985*   SECRET —
Auth CS, USAF

SECRET

DEPARTMENT OF THE AIR FORCE
HEADQUARTERS UNITED STATES AIR FORCE
WASHINGTON 25, D. C.

2 JAN 1952

3 JAN 1952

AFOIN-A

MEMORANDUM FOR GENERAL SAMFORD

SUBJECT: (SECRET) Contemplated Action to Determine the Nature and
Origin of the Phenomena Connected with the Reports of Unusual Flying Objects

1.   The continued reports of unusual flying objects requires
positive action to determine the nature and origin of this phenomena.
The action taken thus far has been designed to track down and evaluate
reports from casual observers throughout the country. Thus far, this
action has produced results of doubtful value and the inconsistencies
inherent in the nature of the reports has given neither positive nor
negative proof of the claims.

2.   It is logical to relate the reported sightings to the
known development of aircraft, jet propulsion, rockets and range
extension capabilities in Germany and the U.S.S.R. In this connection, it is to be noted that certain developments by the Germans,
particularly the Horton wing, jet propulsion, and refueling, combined with their extensive employment of V-1 and V-2 weapons during
World War II, lend credence to the possibility that the flying objects
may be of German and Russian origin. The developments mentioned
above were completed and operational between 1941 and 1944 and subsequently fell into the hands of the Soviets at the end of the war.
There is evidence that the Germans were working on these projects
as far back as 1931 to 1938. Therefore, it may be assumed that the
Germans had at least a 7 to 10 year lead over the United States in
the development of rockets, jet engines, and aircraft of the Horton-
wing design. The Air Corps developed refueling experimentally as
early as 1928, but did not develop operational capability until 1948.

3.   In view of the above facts and the persistent reports of
unusual flying objects over parts of the United States, particularly
the east and west coast and in the vicinity of the atomic energy production and testing facilities, it is apparent that positive action
must be taken to determine the nature of the objects and, if possible,
their origin. Since it is known fact that the Soviets did not detonate
an atomic bomb prior to 1949, it is believed possible that the Soviets
may have developed the German aircraft designs at an accelerated rate
in order to have a suitable carrier for the delivery of weapons of mass
destruction. In other words, the Soviets may have a carrier without the
weapons required while we have relatively superior weapons with relatively

COUPON DESIGNATION MADE _____

X-322.7-ATIC

13 Feb 52

To: File,
Edwin Bishop Jr
Lt Colonel, USAF
A-...

SECRET
SECURITY INFORMATION

4

SECRET

inferior carriers available. If the Soviets should get the carrier and the weapon, combined with adequate defensive aircraft, they might surpass us technologically for a sufficient period of time to permit them to execute a decisive air campaign against the United States and her allies. The basic philosophy of the Soviets has been to surpass the western powers technologically and the Germans have given them the opportunity.

4. In view of the facts outlined above, it is considered mandatory that the Air Force take positive action at once to definitely determine the nature and, if possible, the origin of the reported unusual flying objects. The following action is now contemplated:

a. to require ATIC to provide at least three teams to be matched up with an equal number of teams from ADC for the purpose of taking radar scope photographs and visual photographs of the phenomena;

b. to select sites for these teams, based on the concentrations of already reported sightings over the United States; (these areas are, generally, the Seattle area, the Albuquerque area, and the New York-Philadelphia area) and

c. to take the initial steps in this project during early January 1952.

1 Incl
   Tech. Rept #76-45

W. M. Garland
Brigadier General, USAF
Assistant for Production
Directorate of Intelligence

Shortly after this memo, Edward Ruppelt was asked to come to Washington to brief the Pentagon on UFOs. He and his colleagues at ATIC had been busy. They had created master maps of sightings that would illustrate areas of UFO concentration. They found plenty. Ruppelt reported that the data showed incidents concentrated around White Sands and Los Alamos/Sandia in New Mexico, Camp Hood in Texas (an area with many reports of green fireballs), Oak Ridge National Laboratory in Tennessee, and two areas of Ohio—one being Dayton, Wright-Patterson's hometown.[7] Ruppelt noted that the maps were made with crude data, but

Wright-Patterson AFB. Left to Right: Capt. Edward Ruppelt, Lt. Robert Olsson, Lt. Kerry Rothstein

regardless, the areas listed as concentration zones could not have done anything but rattle the Pentagon.

Ruppelt returned to ATIC and began composing a Status Report (#3) for the new project Grudge.[8] Shortly thereafter, he was called back to the Pentagon by Garland for another briefing. Since his latest status report was published two days after the briefing of January 29, Ruppelt must have told Garland exactly what was already in the report. Ruppelt reviewed the geographical list of UFO concentrations, stated the project's obstacles, lobbied for new approaches (with which Garland seems to have already agreed), and included a list of 15 incidents reported to ATIC in the month of January. Those cases included UFO sightings that had happened earlier, such as Lubbock, two General Mills cases, an Oak Ridge incident, etc. Ten of the fifteen cases were by General Mills scientists or military personnel, mostly pilots. For only one instance did Ruppelt believe that he had an identification at the time.

Between these insider activities at the end of January and more such briefings and policy debates in March and April, a real publicity problem occurred concerning UFOs in the airspace of Korea during the Korean War. This was, of course, the worst possible choice of an area of the world to have UFOs show up, due to constant media coverage of that War.[9]

Late at night on January 29, in the vicinity of Wonsan, Korea, a B-29 crew observed an object described as both an orange-colored disk and sphere that also projected a bluish tint at times. It was slightly fuzzy-edged. The crew thought that it was quite small, although there was no way for them to estimate that correctly. The object flew parallel to the B-29, then closed in, and then departed. Shortly thereafter, another B-29 crew observed the same or a similar object. Both sightings were at just over 22,000 feet. The witnesses were all military veterans and the B-29s were from different squadrons. The two crews were interrogated separately.

As per policy, the Far Eastern Air Force (FEAF) command sent the reports to Pentagon Intelligence. The reports were passed on promptly to Ruppelt at ATIC as well. The case was creating a stir in the Pentagon, and Dewey Fournet received word that General Garland would soon quiz him on the incident. He wrote to Ruppelt on February 8, asking for ATIC's help. Ruppelt was already involved in the case and had requested details from FEAF about a week earlier. When these interrogations arrived, he brought in an expert from Wright-Patterson's Engineering Division, Peter A. Stranges of the Propulsion Branch Power Plant Group, to help with the analysis. Here are the conclusions:[10]

The times that the object or objects followed the B-29s indicate that the objects were propelled by some means, which eliminated the possibility of an unguided ground-to-air missile, drop missiles, etc. . . . The color and shape of the flame could have been the exhaust of a conventional jet engine with or without an afterburner, a pulse-jet, ram-jet, or rocket engine. None of these possibilities were considered to be applicable.

The report is somewhat similar to the reports of "fireball-fighters," a type of phenomena observed in Europe during World War II. The exact nature of this phenomena was never determined but bomber crews reported large fiery balls, similar to the sun, passing through or near their formations. There is no documented evidence or data available on this phenomena, and all the information that has been obtained is verbal from WW II bomber crewmen, consequently, few actual facts are available.

This is the information that Ruppelt would have passed on to Fournet and Garland. Ruppelt passed the B-29 report on immediately. This guess is based upon the urgency from Fournet and the fact that we *do* have a formal ATIC memorandum by Ruppelt from the 18th of February that referred to all of this. The importance of the timing is that the next day someone in the Pentagon decided to violate all past policy on UFO case information and leak this incident to the public.

How and why this happened is mysterious. The information came apparently anonymously via what was described in a Pentagon document as a press release.[11] Dewey Fournet tended not to support public information releases on the subject, so the release of information came from someone above him. Someone in the Pentagon itself thought that releasing this story was a good idea. Was it Garland himself? With his fear of Soviet mischief, did he attempt to increase pressure to make this subject be taken more seriously? We will probably never know the answer to that. FEAF officials, when asked by the press about the incidents, replied that they had no comment since such matters were classified. At least *they* understood the policy.

The result of this press release was that the Pentagon public information desk and Edward Ruppelt at ATIC were swamped by requests for more information. Ruppelt said that, for a while, he was badgered daily by Washington big-wigs.[12] The chairman of the Senate Committee on Armed Services, Richard Russell of Georgia, immediately wrote the Secretary of the Air Force, Thomas Finletter, about the reports. Colonels J. G. Eriksen and H. J. Kieling took the next two weeks to prepare a proper reply.[13] Kieling-Eriksen tried to ease concerns by referring to jet exhausts and searchlights (neither of which had been concluded as feasible by ATIC—a fact not mentioned to the Senator). Although the occasional news writer praised the Air Force for its movement towards opening up the information to the public, all the coverage was not that complimentary. An example of something that may have been problematical was a column by a pair of very famous and politically involved writers, Joseph and Stewart Alsop.

The Alsops' column, "Problems of Scientific Development," was extremely detailed on the facts of the two incidents. They then wrote: "when queried about them, the highest sources in the Air Force have replied that 'there is no doubt about the facts but the Air Force still does not believe in flying disks.'"[14] The Alsops then got to the point of their article:

Left to Right: General LeMay, Richard Russell, Roger Ramey

Whether as hoax, or as illusion, or as intimation of something unpleasant to come, the facts nonetheless seem worth recording to these reporters, simply because they are symbols of the opening of the Pandora's box of science. Here is a tale, in source at least not laughable but close to laughable in substance, which is not being laughed off. In fact, it is the subject of anxious enquiry at high levels.

The plain truth is that this now-opened Pandora's box of science may contain almost any kind of disagreeable surprise; and thus the experts can no longer say with assurance, "This is silly, that makes sense." The further truth is that the Korean experience has convinced American experts of our earlier folly in underestimating Soviet technical capabilities.

Much more solid evidence than the two queer intelligence reports from the B-29 crews continues to pile up. More recently, for example, information has come in of Russian production of a genuinely supersonic jet fighter, the MIG-19. The raised estimates of a Soviet atomic output are in the same category.

The Alsops were part of a group of Washington-based intelligence and media figures that might be described as hyper-patriots. They believed that it was justified to use (read: manipulate) the press in the service of national security.[15] Joseph was a member of the WWII Office of Strategic Service (OSS), a precursor to the CIA, and he cooperated with CIA missions later. It could be that emphasizing the possibility of Soviet-German technology in the Korean War Zone was viewed as of some value vis-à-vis public concerns and consequent congressional funding. The closeness of the Air Force to the CIA in those early years is very well known. Air Force Chief of Staff Vandenberg was a former director of the CIA's predecessor, the Central Intelligence Group. Charles Cabell became the Deputy CIA Director and had hand-in-glove interactions on all the spy balloons, spy planes, and soon-to-be spy satellite projects. What actually happened here with the Korean case release is unknown. It was out of the norm, in direct opposition to written policy, and perhaps explainable by either political or funding agendas. It caused the Air Force some publicity problems, and it hinted at a complex intelligence community that operated in a variety of different directions, which makes our understanding of their handling of the UFO phenomenon more difficult.

The Korean case press release did not cause an upturn in instances reported to the ATIC, but did serve as a catalyst for a consistent build-up of press interest and coverage for several months.[16] Because of the Korean incidents, and several others, Pentagon authorities wanted to remove all the negative stigma from the UFO project and insisted that the name "Grudge" be changed. The project was re-named "Blue Book" after the blank-paged examination booklets that Edward Ruppelt used in his college days at Iowa State University. An open-minded examination: that's what Cabell had wanted, and now Garland after him.

Open-minded, yes. Open book, no. A query came to Major Fournet's desk that requested liberalizing the policy of information release in the form of declassifying and making available Eltermen's final report on Twinkle and the Green Fireballs. The report was wholly negative towards the phenomenon being a type of technology. One can understand that its release would be viewed as relaxing the public, who might easily connect fireballs over Korea with fireballs over Los Alamos and Oak Ridge. However, Fournet said no, and the report remained classified. This was in mid-March.[17]

By the end of March, the combination of increased public badgering, increased public coverage and, most importantly, positive pressure from the Pentagon to increase information gathering and analysis, took its toll. ATIC Chief Frank Dunn wrote Garland that it would help greatly if they could declassify the entire project.[18] This would help him and Ruppelt more easily to engage non-military personnel such as civilian pilots in the gathering of data. By keeping case investigations of that sort "open," Dunn felt that more could be accomplished. That was a little too much openness even for Garland's view, and a compromise was made. The project was not declassified and thrown open, but certain case investigations were to be classified at the relatively low level of "Restricted," which made interaction between investigators and civilian observers more free-flowing.

The Korean news release, the visits of *Life* and *Look* correspondents to ATIC, and the softening attitude towards the release of UFO information, gave news writers and citizens alike the idea that they could just write the Pentagon and ATIC about anything they wanted and expect to get an answer.

Allegedly, some in the Pentagon such as Colonels Smith and Adams thought that this was a good final goal. Others severely differed. In mid-April, Major Fournet got an elaborate letter from a writer of the *Baltimore Evening Sun*, asking all manner of questions. Colonel Adams wanted Fournet to respond to all of them. The writer wanted to know everything: cases, concentrations, procedures, chain-of-command, relation to atomic energy, and so on.[19]

Fournet answered the letter as ordered—two and a half single-spaced pages, as vague as he could be on some questions, while still attempting to be convincing. He gave a flat "no" to atomic power and extraterrestrials. He reminded the civilian that much of the requested information regarding procedure and specific detail was classified. He said that hoaxes occasionally occur, such as bogus photographs, and that nothing they had ever found pointed to any "startling possibilities." At least he ended the letter with an elaborate and generally truthful statement of Air Force philosophy:[20]

> Present USAF philosophy on this subject is essentially as follows:
> On incidents which have not been reasonably explained as known objects, Headquarters USAF does *not* speculate as to what they may be. In many "unexplained" cases there is probably a logical explanation which USAF Intelligence has not been able to reach because of insufficient basic data. Obviously the percentage of incidents in this category is indeterminate, and it is therefore impossible to say whether they could account for a large proportion of the unexplained cases. The policy of the USAF in revealing information on this subject to the public is to avoid completely the insertion of a "scare element" based on speculation. This is accomplished by announcing only facts and factual analysis. Since, over the course of the past five years, nothing detrimental to our national security has materialized from these incidents, the only reasonable conclusion is that they cannot yet be considered as direct threats to the U.S. or its citizens. It is also desired that the American public be aware of USAF attitude in this matter, viz., it is not considered a joke or something which can be brushed off lightly as readily explainable, but rather it is considered to be something which warrants constant vigilance and thorough Intelligence analysis in an attempt to provide a satisfactory solution. In this connection it is to be noted that the USAF does not allow itself to be stampeded into finding satisfactory explanations. Only after all available facts have been determined through thorough investigation and these facts are carefully analyzed to the point of establishing an identification beyond any reasonable doubt is an explanation arrived at and announced.

Fournet is to be applauded for this description of the Air Force's service. He leaves out only its unsatisfactory past record and the very high level of tension some of this had produced. He projects a fine level of concern along with competence and security. On the other hand, Edward Ruppelt was not doing so well with his public tone. While he was basically an honest, open man, Ruppelt's interactions with the press were felt to be a little too newsy for Pentagon nerves. According to Ruppelt, the Pentagon advised him to shut up, or at least to be more selective with his commentary.[21]

Although the growing flood of news articles increased the rate of requests for information, the Project did not notice any relationship with the number of UFO reports that it received. Reports in April *were* up dramatically, but they were almost entirely from within the military.[22] As 1952 moved towards the summer, the bothersome trend of unidentified encounters near bases and critical facilities continued. Here are a few of them.

May 2, George AFB, California:[23] The director of personnel for the 146th Fighter-Bomber Wing watched five circular white objects fly over the base. They did not seem to be metallic because there was no reflection from the Sun, and they moved silently with no exhaust. The objects' diameter seemed to be about the length of a P51 aircraft, and their velocity was about twice that of a jet. They were highly maneuverable, made quick movements ending in a sudden right turn, and moved rapidly away. The colonel was stunned by this and checked weather (there was almost no wind aloft), balloon launches (none known, but with no wind they could not have had the reported speed anyway), and active aircraft (there was one small plane in the entire area). He immediately reported to the Pentagon, which called ATIC in to investigate. Ruppelt left for George AFB and interviewed the colonel and rechecked everything. He flew back to Dayton and filed "unidentified" on the record sheet.[24]

As soon as Ruppelt returned to his office, Colonel Dunn told him to cancel his date with his wife, whom he had barely seen in two weeks, and fly to Washington, DC. There, he interviewed a high-ranking CIA member, who, with several other prominent people, had witnessed a UFO at a garden party there. This somewhat mysterious incident is described in Ruppelt's book.[25] It is mentioned because it demonstrates the heavy workload that Ruppelt handled. Public reports of UFOs were widespread and included witnesses in the CIA.

May 10, Savannah River Atomic Plant near Ellenton, South Carolina:[26] Four employees of DuPont Corporation saw four objects described as small disks flying over the plant to the north. They seemed to be yellow-gold, silent, and they moved at high altitude and high velocity. Shortly thereafter, two similar objects crossed the sky in generally the same path. Then, one object passed silently over the plant at a much lower altitude (only "tank high"), but moving southwest instead of to the north. Finally, another single object flew over to the north, once again at high altitude. This was reported to officials and investigated by the FBI. The FBI sent their report on to the Pentagon and the Atomic Energy Commission. Needless to say, no one could explain what the four employees had seen, and, given the location, the authorities were concerned. The same day, at another restricted area, Kirtland AFB, near Albuquerque and Los Alamos, an Air Force colonel and his wife observed and reported two silvery disks flying over the area, and flipping (turning on their axes) as they did.[27]

May 29, Edwards AFB, California:[28] Two silvery metallic disks flew in close formation and moved in an arc past the base. They made no exhaust, nor sound. The four witnesses were all high technology people: a mechanical engineer who worked in aeronautics, an Air Force test mechanic, an aeronautical instrumentation engineer, and a Caltech laboratory employee. The quality of the witnesses attracted the Air Force investigators' attention. Three days later on June 1, engineers working at a Hughes Aircraft Radar Instrumentation facility noticed an odd radar blip that indicated an object traveling at 180 mph at about 11,000 feet. Radar showed the object's speed triple to about 550 mph as it accelerated straight upwards. The object then leveled off at a great height and plunged downwards at a great speed. It leveled off again at 55,000 feet and flew horizontally until out of radar range.

The engineers contacted Edwards AFB since it was the only place in the vicinity that could conceivably fly anything like this, and they were told that nothing they had was in the air at the time. ATIC and Ruppelt got involved. The Hughes engineers had checked their equipment and considered the possibility of strange atmospheric effects—no explanations in either area. If Edwards AFB had nothing flying that day that could perform this way, then Blue Book was left with another unknown. Ruppelt said he then checked his card file for "High-Speed Climb" and found that there must have been at least a hundred cards of different incidents.

Because of incidents such as the above, Project Blue Book had grown to include Ruppelt plus four Lieutenants, two airmen, and two civilians, one of whom was probably Dr. J. Allen Hynek as an astronomical consultant.[29] Ruppelt received so many requests for press briefings that not only did it interfere with his job, but his responses resulted in too many gaffs and caused certain colonels in the Pentagon to call Frank Dunn and ask "why did he say that?!" The solution? Ruppelt was to direct such inquiries to Al Chop's press desk at the Pentagon, to everyone's relief. Such cases were also grounds for the growth of ideas in the Pentagon such as

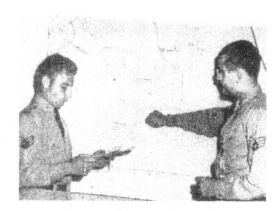

Project Blue Book 1952
Left to right: Airmen First Class Max
Futch and Ronald Castellaw

stripping down jets to act as interceptors at bases all around the States. Ruppelt said that no one was laughing. The plan was not enacted due to its expense and the need for so many planes for adequate coverage.[30]

July 2, Tremonton, Utah:[31] A Navy photography specialist and his wife saw what seemed to be a "fleet" or a "flock" of fast-moving objects. Chief Petty Officer Delbert Newhouse quickly readied his camera and began filming. He obtained a few dozen feet of motion picture photography of these objects in their odd, seemingly rapid, milling movements. He thought that the objects were clearly disks, not birds. And around that hypothesis began quite a controversy. This is one of the many instances where the witnesses say that their eyes saw better than the camera, but the camera is, unfortunately, all that the rest of us have. The film

Delbert Newhouse and Tremonton photo
Note how objects move in pairs

ultimately made its way to the Photographic Interpretation Center (PIC), which at that time was in its last year under U.S. Navy control (called NAVPIC), before NAVPIC was handed to the CIA. NAVPIC was our highest quality photo analysis institution; later transforming from PIC to NPIC (National Photo Interpretation Center); it did satellite reconnaissance work and helped Kennedy play his hand properly in the Cuban Missile Crisis. Were the analysts at NAVPIC/PIC/NPIC always at the top of their game? Who knows. What we *do* know is that two NAVPIC specialists spent hundreds of hours with this film. Their conclusions: birds, no; disks, yes. There is much more to this story and we will probe into some of it later.

July 5, Hanford Atomic Plant, Washington:[32] Four commercial pilots flying in the area of the Hanford plant encountered a bizarre object that spewed huge quantities of smoke. The object seemed to be round at first and hovered beneath a 10,000 foot cloud deck. Its shape seemed to change towards a flatter form, colored similarly to the clouds but with an opaque (dark?) center. The object flattened out, accelerated, and moved away quickly. Three of the four pilots were military veterans. Alarmed that such a thing should be hovering over the Hanford facility, they made a report to Air Traffic Control in Denver from which the story apparently leaked out. By the time the pilots returned to their homes in Miami, Florida, the story had spread all over the country. By the morning of the 6th, Ruppelt was bombarded by press questions, particularly about flying saucers and atomic facilities. He stonewalled them. Ruppelt asked his immediate chief, Colonel Donald Bower, for advice. Bower said: Stall them. Say, "No comment."[33] And if they persist, tell them to see me. This Hanford case demonstrated how awkward it was for ATIC and the Air Force when an incident was not reported to them before it hit the public news.

July 14, over Chesapeake Bay, Virginia/Maryland:[34] This is a classic case that attracted relatively little attention initially but built into a major enigma and a defender/debunker battleground over the years. Called by most students of this subject the "Nash/Fortenberry Case" (after the pilots, William Nash and William Fortenberry, who reported it), it was another instance of something that got more attention through civilian channels than military. The reason for this is that Ruppelt and Blue Book were, by mid-July, overwhelmed with work. As an example, Ruppelt had been publishing a monthly Status Report until May, and then just gave up—the next one not appearing until December. The Nash/Fortenberry case *should* have received a more thorough investigation, as we will see.

The pilots were flying a commercial Pan Am DC-4 en route to Miami at 8000 feet. As they approached Norfolk, Virginia, they noticed a red-orange brilliance coming in their direction. As it grew nearer, it resolved into six fiery-colored disks that flew in a stepped-up echelon line, just below their plane's altitude. The objects were clearly disks, not fireballs, due to their sharp edges. Then, when almost below the plane, they did something completely inexplicable and difficult to describe. They abruptly stopped and the entire line rolled on its edge. This change in formation revealed the objects to be lighted on top but apparently not on bottom, and to be coin shaped. The disks then shuffled past one another back-to-front so that the echelon was facing the opposite direction. This weird

Left: Pilot William Fortenberry
Right: Pilot William Nash

maneuver had left the echelon pointing at an angle perhaps 30° to the right of its approach angle. Once reconfigured, the assembly raced away on its new trajectory. As it did so, two more apparently identical objects emerged from below the Pan Am plane and rapidly chased the formation. Once they caught the leader disk, they formed a line of eight disks, and the formation raced away. Nash and Fortenberry radioed the encounter in and were called the next morning by the Air Force.[35] Air Force personnel questioned them promptly, but the case report just died under the July avalanche of work. Even Ruppelt showed only a minimal awareness of the quality of the case, especially of the level of strangeness in the objects' behavior, and barely mentioned it in his book. He later said that they disregarded this event because it was known that some aircraft were in the air in the general vicinity.[36] (That is plainly preposterous, of course, and at the Pentagon, Major Fournet viewed the case as the most detailed report they had so far.) Unfortunately, several independent ground witnesses were never interviewed and documented.[37]

As time has passed, most analysts tend to agree with Fournet. This fact has made the Nash/Fortenberry Case a target for persons who would prefer if there were no unsolved UFO accounts, even if their proposed explanations are not viable. Some have accused the pilots of smoking and seeing reflections of their own cigarettes, of misidentifying a series of stars, and there was even a theory that lightning bugs were trapped inside the DC-4's windshield.[38] These types of wild guesses usually enraged Captain Nash, who spent a good part of the rest of his life collecting UFO encounters from fellow airline pilots in hopes of understanding what he and Fortenberry had seen on July 14, 1952.

Although not well documented, there are just enough fragments of information to make it legitimate at least to mention another Pentagon figure and his activities across this period. This man was Stefan Possony, and he ran a small "Special Study Group" right inside General Samford's office. This group was quite involved with UFOs. What was this all about? How could a special study be going on in the highest office of Air Force Intelligence?[39]

Here is what we know: Stefan Possony was born in Vienna in 1913. He received a PhD in political science in 1935 and was a lecturer and an editor of an anti-Nazi, pro-nationalist magazine when Hitler began his aggressions. Possony fled to France where he continued radio broadcasting for Free Austria, and somehow became an Air Ministry consultant. He was apparently good at this and became respected on the topics of Air Power and Psychological Warfare. He came to the U.S. in 1941 to the Institute for Advanced Study at Princeton, while

Dr. Stefan Possony

150

simultaneously serving the Office of Naval Intelligence's psychological warfare desk. After the war he moved on to the graduate faculty at Georgetown University and became an intelligence advisor to the Air Force. He wrote a widely read book, *Strategic Air Power*, in 1949.

In 1951 Possony was regularly involved at very high levels of the intelligence community. Late in that year, he was in General Samford's office as the brain trust behind something called the Special Study Group. The exact purpose of the group is not known for certain, but it may have been exactly as stated in a *Memorandum for Record* (anonymously written perhaps by Possony or Lt. Col. E. Sterling, the military chief) of April 29, 1952. This is an astounding memorandum of 5½ pages entirely about Special Study Group thinking and why Sterling and Possony should go to Europe to assess certain possible threats to national security.

The memo states that the Air Force is pursuing technology at an accelerating pace and the Soviets will be doing so as well. The main area of unpredictability is not the weapons themselves but the types and effectiveness of their delivery systems. Because of the pace of advances, we cannot be sure of where the Soviets are. Then it says this:

> The Special Study Group has undertaken a comprehensive study of Russian capabilities in the field of advanced aerial delivery systems, their strategic implications, and probable timetables as to development and operational availability. As an important side product, it is hoped that some much needed light can be shed on the vexing 'flying saucer' problem.[40]

The text goes on to enumerate the technologies that Sterling and Possony would investigate. The list included "flying saucers," and it addressed them specifically:

> In connection with flying saucers, the Group is attempting to develop a proper framework for fruitful analysis. The Air Force cannot assume that flying saucers are of non-terrestrial origin, and hence, they could be Soviet.

The rest of the memorandum was an extended set of reasons why the working hypothesis that the saucers were a nascent Soviet delivery system must not be ignored. In the narrative, one case example was utilized to make the argument that, whereas the behavior of the objects was beyond U.S. capability, it was not beyond theoretical capability, and therefore could have been an advanced terrestrially produced device. This argument was based on the sighting reported to Commander McLaughlin by Charles Moore and the General Mills balloon team. Possony used this case study with explicit faith in the reality of its details, including the velocity estimate of slightly greater than gravitational escape velocity, which he found significant. Possony and Sterling believed such sources were not from outer space, based on the testimony of astronomers that indicated that the astronomers would have seen the objects coming.

Charles Moore

Possony and Sterling's concerns sound exactly like Garland's. They all felt that they "knew" UFOs were real craft, but they could not believe that they were extraterrestrial; they all greatly feared a novel Soviet delivery system in the making. Elsewhere along the Pentagon's UFO beat, Colonels Smith and Adams, and Major Fournet, thought the disks were real *and* extraterrestrial.

Possony and Sterling returned from Europe in about five weeks and had become convinced that the disks were *not* Soviet, after all.[41] Possony, however, remained interested in the phenomenon. He, according to Ruppelt, attended many relevant Pentagon meetings and always severely challenged persons dismissive of the reality of the incidents. He asked his civilian assistant, Les Rosenweig, to bring together materials for desktop studies on topics such as the possible propulsion systems used by the disks, and potential methods to contact them. Possony often put ideas in Major Fournet's ear and may have played a role in his "motions study" of flying disk maneuverability, from which Fournet concluded that the flight capabilities of the UFOs were well beyond terrestrial technology. Fournet said that he was inspired to look into this by his direct bosses, Colonels Smith and Adams, but it matters little, as all these people communicated together, and all seemed drawn to the conclusion of UFO technological reality.[42] One of the crucial cases for all these men (certainly for Fournet) was the Tremonton, Utah, film. The NAVPIC analysts, Woo and Neasham, were convinced that they had determined that the objects in the film were disks and that they moved *not* in a random milling fashion, but in an overlapped set of revolving motions, quite impossible (Fournet believed, and Woo later agreed) for terrestrial craft.

Left to Right: Dewey Fournet, Al Chop, and Edward Ruppelt

It is useful to mention one other incident in which Possony played a role.[43] The astronomer-debunker, Donald Menzel of Harvard, visited Air Force Intelligence at the Pentagon with two express interests: to get Air Force endorsement for his views that all difficult-to-explain UFO cases were caused by strange optical effects or atmospheric plasmas; and to get funding to produce data and demonstrations which could convince the public of this. This was in late April or May before Possony left for Europe, and they met in his office. Ruppelt and Dunn were in town and they attended. So did General Garland and Les Rosenweig. Because everyone else in the office knew that Menzel's ideas explained very few UFO cases, he did not get the reception that he had desired. In fact, General Garland exploded at him, Possony challenged his thinking, and then Menzel exploded himself. There was no funding and no endorsement, yet Menzel went ahead and published articles implying that the Air Force *did* approve of his theories. Menzel's optical and atmospheric explanations received eye-rolling if not exasperated disbelief by Pentagon experts. Both Possony's personal scientific advisor, Francis J. Heyden, a Georgetown astronomer, and USAF atmospheric physics advisor Joseph Kaplan thought Menzel's ideas were amateurish. Heyden compared them to high school experiments. The weakness of Menzel's arguments was also captured in an Air Force status report that stated:

Dr. Donald Menzel

> The papers of Menzel and Liddel, though differing somewhat in content, were identical in spirit. Both papers were characterized by the fact that numerous explanations for unexplained sightings were given without a single reference to a specific sighting in the files of the Air Technical Intelligence Center.[44]

Still, the community of academic scientists soon accepted Menzel's opinions, at least in their public statements. The academic response to UFO opinion began to emerge strongly in 1952 with Menzel following on the views of Liddel. The military students of UFOs knew that Liddel's views were nonsense and Menzel's views largely nonsense.[45] However, Menzel's view of the UFO phenomenon had some value to the intelligence community because it reduced over-enthusiasm and hysteria. There is no convincing evidence that persons such as Liddel or Menzel operated as partners with the intelligence community, by the way. All that we know of them points to the hypothesis that they were highly self-assured individuals who believed that they were extinguishing unthinkable (unscientific) irrationality.[46] Another example of this academic arrogance in the same time period was the statement by Iowa University astronomer C.C. Wylie, who dismissed UFOs because astronomers had not seen them.[47] Wylie failed to mention that the field of vision of a large telescope is so small that such an event would be unlikely, and astronomers do not often look directly through those telescopes anyway. If Wylie meant instead that astronomers *personally* never see UFOs, then he was incorrect. Dr. Hynek surveyed astronomers for a Blue Book study and found that many astronomers had seen UFOs—they just would not admit it in public.[48] One wonders what Clyde Tombaugh and Seymour Hess thought of Wylie's remarks? Still, such claims went unchallenged because there was no academic-related advantage to do so.

We are now approaching a climactic event in UFO history. UFOs manifested themselves during two weekends in July over the nation's capital and, in doing so, incited a chain of responses that would finally set the policy of government's approach to the UFO phenomenon.

According to a 1967 interview, there occurred, just prior to the UFO sightings over the nation's capital, the first claim of a military order to fire upon UFOs. Jay Nogle, a Boeing engineer, recalled his experience as an Army radar specialist in an audio recording made by Roy Craig, of the famed Colorado Project which was funded by the USAF in 1967 to study UFOs. The time was May or June of 1952. At a distance of 130 miles to the northeast of the capital, Jay Nogle's M33 radar along with two to three other Army radar units had detected an unknown at 18,000 feet. The object's signal was strong, and it remained stationary on radar for 30 minutes before it began to move. By the time the object had reached the edge of their radar scopes, it was traveling at over 1000 mph. Nogle's own words best describe the military reaction:

> We didn't think too much of it ourselves that night. But the next morning the Battalion commander, a light colonel, came into our radar area and wanted to know what happened and all the back ground. Apparently this report went all the way to the Pentagon that night and the order came back that if another one came in then we were to fire on it . . . After that first night, we had orders to fire on them and we loaded our guns (90mm anti-aircraft), which was an unusual thing to do in a populated area. We also scrambled fighters off McGuire AFB. About the time the F-94 fighters would take off, these objects would leave.[49]

Nogle went on to describe how these unknowns were picked up on radar during most of the nights of May to June of 1952. He vividly recalls the last time that these objects showed up on his radar, in July. Twelve F-94 Star Fighters were scrambled from McGuire AFB. The lead F-94 fighter locked onto the unknown with his fire control radar and indicated over the radio that he was closing in for the kill. Before he could fire, the unidentified objects moved rapidly out of range.

In mid-July there were a couple of incidents near Washington, D.C., which presaged the pair of experiences that have come to be called the "Washington Merry-Go-Round." Of more intrigue than these preliminary cases is a remark made by Edward Ruppelt in his book. There he says that, while in Washington on another UFO matter, a member of an intelligence agency told him that they had been plotting and tracking UFO events. Their analysis pointed to an increase in East Coast activity, leading to some sort of climax, probably in Washington.[50] Even without knowing anything more about this mysterious prediction, it is, to say the least, interesting because it came true. It also is of some direct interest to the subject of this book, as it indicates that people other than the Air Force had monitored

UFO activity and had attempted to pattern and predict it. Whatever agency it was, someone else was actively involved in UFO data gathering.

On July 18, the day before the first half of the Merry-Go-Round, Ruppelt was in front of the press and talked too much again. Some of his remarks:

> . . . ground radar had tracked some aerial objects at speeds ranging between 1500 and 2000 miles per hour.

> . . . jet fighters equipped with the very latest radar have been sent aloft to 'make contact' with the phantom objects, but all efforts to catch up with them have failed.

> . . . we are convinced that persons making these reports actually see something in the sky, but what they are is another question.[51]

This does not quite match the tone of the stated policy of being respectful but not encouraging.

On July 19, the press interviewed Lincoln LaPaz, who never failed to have something astonishing to say about the phenomenon. LaPaz stated "By whatever name you call them (flying saucers, guided missiles, discs, space ships), they all act strangely." LaPaz then listed their outstanding characteristics:

> They can reverse directions and cruise back and forth; they travel at high speeds in wide sweeping circles. They are spherical or disc-shaped and for the most part give off a steady yellow light; they travel at high altitudes and can be followed as long as 3½ minutes.[52]

The bottom line of this message: real technology.

Twenty minutes before midnight, July 19: Edward Nugent, Air Traffic Controller at Washington National Airport, saw seven blips, not moving in established flight paths, to the southwest. He called ATC crew chief Harry Barnes over. Barnes stated:

> We knew immediately that a very strange situation existed. . . . their movements were completely radical compared to those of ordinary aircraft. They followed no set course . . . were not in any formation, and we only seemed to be able to track them for about three minutes at a time. The individual pip would seem to disappear from the scope at intervals. Later I realized that if these objects made any sudden burst of extremely high speed, that would account for them disappearing from the scope temporarily.[53]

At this time, most (but not all) of these returns were weak. Barnes set two other controllers to checking the equipment. It seemed to be working properly.

Washington National had a second radar facility using somewhat different equipment. Barnes called Howard Cocklin there. They had noted the phenomenon, too, and one controller had stepped outside and seen something visually. The objects appeared to move to the area of the White House and the Capitol Building. More alarmed now, Barnes called Andrews AFB. This was at midnight. Two personnel from the Air Force Base then saw objects visually. In each of these first three sightings, the objects were described as orange colored balls of light. Even with Washington National and Andrews AFB both tracking unknowns on radar, records do not speak of many visual reports.

[A personal aside to additional visual sightings of this event is warranted. The Washington sightings are the most complicated and harried cases, perhaps, of all time. The Air Force was completely overwhelmed by the task of sorting things out and did a poor and very fragmentary job of doing so—concentrating nearly exclusively on the radar returns. As to both complexity and visual witnesses: once, at a meeting in Washington in the 1980s, a gentleman came over to one of the authors of this book, Michael Swords, and presented his card. He was the owner of an East Coast real estate business and wanted to talk. In 1952, the man had been stationed at Andrews as a low ranking officer with some intelligence duties, during these two Merry-Go-Round encounters. He was on duty on one of those two evenings, and, when Washington National notified Andrews, he and several other Army and Air Force personnel were told to go outside and look for the objects. They had binoculars for visual aid. He said, "We all saw them. Not just radar returns." He described what they saw as moving balls of light, "stacked up," making sharp turns, and lasting long periods of time on the radar scopes. He described the speeds as impossibly fast.[54] The point of this second-hand anecdote is that this businessman wrote up his report at the time, as did many others, and it never made its way into Blue Book files. How many dozens of others were never spoken to and their stories just lost to the record? Dr. Swords' experience with this gentleman is common among UFO historians, and particularly with enormous cases such as the one in Washington.]

Meanwhile, between midnight and 1 a.m. there were several sightings recorded by Blue Book and the media up and down the East Coast. Around one o'clock, Washington National told a Capital Airlines pilot that radar indicated objects ahead. Vectored towards the objects, Captain Pierman described them as bright blue balls-of-light, six in number, hovering sometimes and rapidly moving at others. Back at National, Barnes' radar saw both them and Capt. Pierman's plane. The other National radar tracked a different object during this period. One of these tracks was good enough that the controllers thought that they could reasonably estimate speed: 7,100 mph.

Between 2 a.m. and 3 a.m., personnel at Andrews were tracking some unidentified objects and occasionally seeing them. There were also mistakes made visually, as excited airmen sometimes misinterpreted stars low to the horizon as unknown objects. One instance that was unlikely to be a mistake was an unidentified simultaneously detected on radar by Washington National, Andrews and Bolling AFB. The radar blip suddenly vanished from all three installations' radars regardless of where it was. Soon thereafter, two Air Force interceptors flew into the area. We do not know what the Air Force thought about the coincidence, but it bothered ATC Harry Barnes. Once the interceptors left, the phenomenon returned sporadically until 5:30 a.m., when it finally ceased. Barnes, probably much to the Pentagon's distress, had no qualms about talking to the newspapers:

> The only recognizable behavior pattern which occurred to me from watching the objects was that they acted like a bunch of small kids out playing. It was helter skelter, as if directed by some innate curiosity. At times they moved as a group or cluster, at other times as individuals over widely scattered areas.
>
> I could safely declare that they could make right angle turns and completely reverse their flight.
>
> I'm positive they were guided by some intelligence. If no planes were in the air, the things would fly over the most likely points of interest—Andrews Field, the aircraft plant at Riverdale, the (Washington) Monument, or the Capitol. One or two circled our radio beacons. But as soon as an airliner took off, several would dart across and start to follow, as if to look it over.[55]

With that we wrap up a very bare bones retelling of the first half of the Washington sighting. That morning, Edward Ruppelt was informed that President Truman was personally concerned and had asked his military adviser, General Landry, to look into this matter. Ruppelt met immediately with his direct boss, Colonel Bower, and Dewey Fournet at the Pentagon, but the situation was far too confused to create even an official release. Al Chop, at the Pentagon press desk, was authorized only to say "no comment."

By the 23rd, Ruppelt and his confreres decided to make a statement that included three points:

1. They could not prove nor disprove flying saucers;
2. Reports always rise when there is a lot of publicity;
3. Very few reports cannot be explained.

As we have seen, number one was true, especially using a rigorous physical evidence definition of the concept of "proof;" number two was false, as Ruppelt had noticed earlier in the same year; and number three was at least debatable, as Ruppelt was finding the unexplained rate to be over 20%.[56] Still, the goal of these releases was to calm people, not to make science statements.

People were not yet calm. A reporter accosted the attaché at the Soviet embassy to accuse the Kremlin of violating U.S. airspace. Of course this was denied. A spokesman of the Civil Aeronautics Administration gave an opinion that the Washington sightings could have been

Left: General Landry
Right: President Truman

"weather." Barnes et al. disagreed with this severely, and for years afterwards. The Air Force then denied to the press that Andrews AFB had ever tracked the unknowns, again lying in the interests of national security. Inside the Air Force, Mitchell AFB, New York, complained about having to deal with too many UFO reports while McGuire AFB, New Jersey, publicly encouraged people to report any sightings. Television coverage of the Democratic National Convention was actually interrupted to report on UFO sightings.[57] Lastly, on the Friday of that frenetic week, the *Washington Post* stated:

> Until now, the strongest argument against the objective reality of the flying saucers has been the absence of any support by radar observation. At last, however, that argument has been removed . . . [T]he best advice at this point would be to keep your mind open—and your fingers crossed.[58]

Everyone who paid attention was on edge. And so, that weekend, "they" came again.

At 8:15 p.m. on the evening of the 26th, Captain Berkow of National Airlines saw several objects that approached him from an altitude higher than his plane. He, and one of the stewardesses, saw several burning orange-red objects sail directly overhead. At 8:22 p.m. both Washington National and Andrews AFB had about twelve unknown objects on their radarscopes. These were tracked intermittently with occasional visual sightings almost to 9:00 p.m. Between 9:15 p.m. and 9:30 p.m. a B-25, which was coincidentally in the air, was vectored to look for the unidentified objects. It was the B-25 crew's opinion that the radars must have picked up reflections of some sort from ground objects, as they saw nothing.

Somehow, the press was already alerted. Bob Ginna, the now-famous UFO-writer from *Life Magazine*, called Edward Ruppelt in Dayton to tell him that things were breaking loose in Washington again, *and* that *Life*, and several other media outlets, had reporters right in the National Air Traffic Control Tower watching the action as it happened. Ruppelt immediately phoned Fournet, who rounded up a Navy radar expert named Holcomb, and left for the tower. Public Information Officer Al Chop was already there. This must have been a surrealistic moment for the Pentagon. Their policy was, in part, management of public information with an emphasis on never encouraging overexcitement about the reality of unexplained phenomena. Yet here were national

Al Chop

media reporters, in the presence of radar experts and even Air Force personnel, watching activities over the nation's capital in real time. It would seem to be an unsolvable news management problem. But, as we shall see, one cannot overestimate the human mind's ability to become thoroughly confused, and "let it go." But first: what went on that night?

Once again, the amount of action taking place was hard to get one's mind (or one's radars) around. We, surprisingly, have some portions of transmission transcripts between Washington National and Andrews, and, to give some of the flavor, here is a piece:

> Washington Tower: Andrews Tower, do you read? Did you have an airplane in sight west-northwest or east of your airport east-bound?
>
> Andrews: No, but we just got a call from the Center. We're looking for it.
>
> Washington Tower: We've got a big target showing up on our scope. He's just coming in on the west edge of your airport—the northwest edge of it eastbound.
>
> Andrews: What happened to your target now?
>
> Washington Tower: He's still eastbound. He went directly over Andrews Field and is now five miles east.
>
> Andrews: Where did he come from?
>
> Washington Tower: We picked him up ourselves at about seven miles east, slightly southeast, and we have been tracking him ever since then. The Center has been tracking him farther than that.
>
> Andrews: Was he waving in his course?
>
> Washington Tower: Holding steady, due east heading.
>
> Andrews: This is Andrews. Our radar tracking says he's got a big fat target out there northeast of Andrews. He says he's got two more south of the field.
>
> Washington Tower: Yes, well the Center has about four or five around the Andrews Range Station. The Center is working a National Airliner—the Center is working him and vectoring him around his target. He went around Andrews. He saw one of them—looks like a meteor (garbled) . . . went by him . . . or something. He said he's got one about three miles off the right wing right now. There are so many targets around here it is hard to tell as they are not moving very fast.
>
> Andrews: What about his altitude?
>
> Washington Tower: Well, must be over 8,000 feet as we don't have him on radar any more.[59]

USAF pilots that scrambled during the Washington sightings

Between 10 p.m. and 11 p.m. there were many radar incidents, often of multiple returns. Andrews got some visuals. At 10:30 p.m., a chaplain of the Edgewood Arsenal in nearby Annapolis, Maryland saw a flyover. He described it as like a bolide (red-orange ball-of-fire traveling at jet-speed in a straight line). At 10:46 p.m., a CAA flight instructor saw five orange balls-of-light. At 10:52 p.m. all radar returns simply vanished. At this point, with code-based communications passing between pilots and towers, the press was asked to leave. Al Chop also, belatedly, thought that this was too big a deal to have the press witness everything as it occurred. At 11:22 p.m., the blips were back on the radar. The two jets were still in the vicinity and Lt. W.L. Patterson was directed to return. He saw four bright lights ahead. What happened next is not found in the Project Blue Book files. So that the reader knows (since this is rather astounding), our information comes from a taped interview with Al Chop, the Air Force's Public Information Officer who was in the Tower at the time.[60] Chop said that Patterson was pushing his plane,

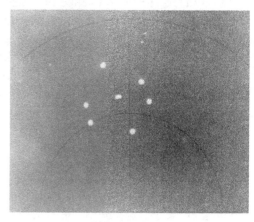

Radar simulation of UFOs surrounding AF plane

attempting, unsuccessfully, to close on the objects, when suddenly they approached and surrounded his position. The radar operators saw this, too. This situation, understandably, scared Patterson quite badly, and he radioed the Tower for advice on what he should do. No one had any ideas. After some frightening moments of silence, the objects (always appearing as balls-of-light) moved away and left him behind.

When Dewey Fournet and Lt. Holcomb arrived at Washington National at about midnight, blips from the unknowns still frequented the radar screens. Holcomb checked the sets and the returns and pronounced at least seven of the blips as "solid." He called for weather data, and although he noted a small temperature inversion at about 1000 feet, he said this could not produce these effects due to "false echoes." Holcomb, Fournet, and everyone else in the Tower agreed that these returns were *not* like weather-influenced illusions, and strongly resembled those coming from solid metallic objects. Fournet noted that there *were* weather-related returns elsewhere on the scopes and that they were noticeably different, and that no one paid any attention to them. Here are two formal quotes given to Fournet by the two groups of controllers to put into his report:

1. Washington National:

> ARTC crew commented that, as compared with unidentified targets picked up in the early hours of 20 July 52, these returns appeared to be haphazard in their actions, i.e. they did not follow a/c around nor did they cross the scope consistently on the same general heading. Some commented that the returns appeared to be from objects 'capable of dropping out of the pattern at will.' Also that returns had a 'creeping appearance.' One just 'disappeared from the scope' shortly after the F-94 started pursuing. All crew members were emphatic that most unidentified returns were 'solid.' Finally, it was mentioned that unidentified returns had been picked up from time to time over the past few months but never before had they appeared in such quantities over such a prolonged period and with such definition as the experiences on the nights of 19/20 and 26/27 July 52.

2. Andrews AFB:

> We observed and noted a great many targets, some of which later were identified as aircraft (conventional). We continued to maintain sharp lookout and observed targets following very erratic courses, sometimes appearing to stop, then reverse course, accelerating momentarily, and then slowing down. Target sightings were all coordinated with Washington ARTC and verified, using radar facilities.

Another peculiarity noted was the sudden disappearance of targets then suddenly reappearing 8-10 miles further along the same course.[61]

The Washington sightings produced two of the most significant occurrences in UFO history: one, internal to the intelligence community, was the direct involvement of the Central Intelligence Agency in an attempt to get this problem under control; two, in the realm of the public, was a major press conference featuring Air Force Director of Intelligence John Samford himself.

For the first of the developments, the formal entrance of the CIA, we will leave the details to the following chapter. Suffice it for now to mention that President Truman on July 28 asked the National Security Council (chaired by CIA director, General Walter Bedell Smith) to do something about UFOs. Smith set the Agency to work on it the next day. The CIA probe culminated in a watershed event: a panel to evaluate the potential threats to national security as related to unidentified flying objects. This panel/workshop took place over four days in January 1953, and may be said to have set general policy on the subject until the present day. It is nicknamed the "Robertson Panel" after its chairman, Dr. Howard P. Robertson, Caltech physicist and CIA scientific consultant. We will describe how this evolved in the next chapter.

The second of these developments, what has become known as the "Samford Press Conference," we will deal with now.[62] After the UFO incidents of the post-midnight hours of the 27th, there arose a flurry of concern (as mentioned by Truman and his aide, General Landry) at the highest levels of the Pentagon. Assistant Chief of Staff Nathan Twining told General Samford that he must have a press conference, quickly. Meanwhile there was a media circus. Famous newsman Drew Pearson said his sources informed him that the phenomenon over Washington was due to solid objects, that Wright-Patterson was seriously charting and plotting the courses of objects, that camera tracking posts were set up in the southwest, and that no one should pooh-pooh the possibility that these were extraterrestrial since our own research into nuclear-powered aircraft could result in ourselves traveling between planets.[63] All of this had been on peoples' minds for some time, but the "solid" objects over Washington were beginning to sound like an admission of truth.

General Nathan Twining

Various press releases and comments added to the excitement and confusion. The Air Defense Command allegedly admitted that it had interceptors poised to scramble after UFOs anywhere in the country.[64] But, because no hard patterns could be found, the Air Force doubted that there was a reasoning intelligence behind the phenomenon. The latest flurry, including Washington D.C., was deemed similar to things in the past and showed no threat to the United States. The military argued that people should relax because every "report is being given a most careful and complete analysis."[65] Edward Ruppelt would have laughed at that last claim, because the July flurry of reports had swamped him so badly his team could not even keep up with the filing, let alone any "analysis."

On the other side of the publicity page, Lt. Colonel Moncel Monts, an Air Force public information officer, told the press: "The jet pilots are and have been under orders to investigate unidentified objects and to shoot them down, if they can't talk them down."[66] Such commentary could scarcely be easily reconciled with the other Air Force claims that the UFOs were nothing to worry about. Into this media maelstrom strode General Samford and his array of Air Force UFO experts.

We are fortunate to have the complete transcript of this press conference from which the quotations on the following several pages are taken. There are even some runs of motion picture film of the press conference in some of the media archives. We also have the commentaries of Edward Ruppelt, who represented the Air Force side, and Donald Keyhoe, on the side of the press.

Samford's show of force consisted of himself, Air Force Director of Operations Major General Roger Ramey, Edward Ruppelt and his direct boss, Colonel Bower, plus two Wright-Patterson radar experts, the oft-mentioned Roy James and a civilian electronic expert, B. L. Griffing. At 4 p.m. on the 29th, Samford began his attempt to defuse the press community's concerns. He began with a brief introduction and then took questions. In the introduction he assured everyone that the Air Force was responsibly at work on all its jobs, including this one. He bemoaned the lack of

Standing, left to right: Bower, Ruppelt, Roy James, and B.L. Griffing Seated: Generals Ramey and Samford

scientific data available to allow them to make adequate progress. Edward Ruppelt, on his copy of this transcript, underlined two paragraphs in red.

Paragraph 1:

> However, there have remained a percentage of this total, in the order of twenty per cent of the reports, that have come from credible observers of relatively incredible things. And because of those things not being possible for us to move along and associate with the kind of things that we've found can be associated with the bulk of these reports, we keep on being concerned about them.

Both sentences are interesting in very different ways. Sentence number one is the closest thing to an admission to the public that there was a major mystery to be solved. It is refreshing in that it is based on the facts as Ruppelt and the Air Force knew them, rather than being some crude, manipulative remark. The *"credible observers of relatively incredible things"* is a phrase of the ages, and could even be because Samford had his close friend and advisor, General Garland, in mind.

Sentence number two is also interesting. It is difficult to read and is awkward as it meanders in the point that it attempts to make. Sentences like this, and worse, became the hallmark of this conference. They staggered questioners and amused Don Keyhoe.

Paragraph(s) 2:

> The difficult part of it, as far as advancing the program is concerned, is that our ability to measure doesn't seem to have advanced in any way as well as our opportunity to observe and the greater recurrence of more disturbing things of this sort that are actually in existence from man-made air participation that we know about.

> So our present course of action is to continue on this problem with the best of our ability, giving to it the attention that we feel it very definitely warrants in terms of identifying adequately the growing or possible or disappearing, if it turns out to be that, menace to the United States to give it adequate attention but not frantic attention.

Ruppelt liked the allusion to maintaining a serious, adequate project; Keyhoe marveled at Samford's ability to make the mind swim a bit even on the simplest of topics.

Early on Samford was asked about how much money was being invested to track down the reports. His answer (with just his somewhat irrelevant-to-the-question mention of the percentages of civilians, etc. reporting) produced this mind-numbing phrasing:

> Well, the energy that's going into it at the present time is outside of anything except the normal reporting procedures. And the effort to further analyze them and profit in going after that in a big way is going to have in some way to be related to a standard measurement that makes this material for workmen to work on.

Perhaps Samford did not hear the question. He certainly did not answer it. What exactly he *did* answer, readers can decide for themselves.

The press tried to get Samford specifically to describe the Washington National and Andrews sightings. He said:

> Major General Samford: Well, I could discuss possibilities. The radar screen has been picking up things for many years that, well, birds, a flock of ducks. I know there's been one instance in which a flock of ducks was picked up and was intercepted and flown through as being an unidentified phenomenon.
>
> The Press: Where was that, General?
>
> Major General Samford: I don't recall where it was. I think it might have been in Japan but I don't recall.

And Samford went on to speak of other odd things that happen with radar. The press tried to bring him back to Washington. He expressed ignorance as to whether there were military radar sightings, airborne. General Ramey said two pilots were just looking at each other. (Ruppelt notes: NO!, but obviously he did not say so at the press conference since he represented the Air Force.) Samford then admitted that the blips were not things like thunder clouds, but "good returns." Sensing news, the press then suggested that he meant returns similar to *aircraft* (which is what Air Traffic Control Crew Chief Harry Barnes had said).

> The Press: Which would indicate that these were solid objects similar to aircraft?
>
> Major General Samford: No, not necessarily. We get good returns from birds.
>
> The Press: Well, you wouldn't get as large a blip from a bird as a --
>
> Major General Samford: No; unless it was close.

One almost gets the impression that Samford was playing with them. Once he sensed what Samford was doing, Keyhoe stopped taking notes and just sat back and admired the performance.

Roy James was allowed to try to explain false echoes, temperature inversions, et al. and, by underestimating the press corps, did not do a particularly good job of it. Plus, James was not nearly as good as Samford in fogging up the specifics of the cases. Finally Samford broke in and took the microphone over again. He

General John Samford

was asked if these objects could have been missiles or a similar technology.

> Well, if you could select out of this mass any particular one or two and start working on them and say, "What is the possibility of them being these things?" Then you come to the point and say this one is reported to have done things which require for it to do those things either one of two conditions, absolute maximum power or no mass. If this is a thing in terms of a guided missile, it does these things that have been measured and reported. It can do those things if there is theoretically no limit to the power involved and there is theoretically no mass involved. That's one of the conditions that would say well, if someone solved one of those problems, this could then be explained as one of those things. You find another one and it has—it just develops into no other purpose or no other pattern that could be associated with them, a missile. Those which we might identify as being missiles will be tracked. They'll have a track to develop something that people can put a measurement to. I don't know whether that answers the question. It satisfies some of it, but maybe not all of it.

After a couple more equally mysterious and useless exchanges, an apparently exasperated newsman asked Samford if he had *any tentative* conclusion or "even a trend towards a belief" of what the blips were. The general's response was broken up, twice, by uncontrolled laughter—so much so that it is noted in the transcript—of the press corps attempting to maintain some tenuous contact with reality. Even Samford seemed to sense that he had gone too far, and he tried to get Roy James to bail him out with more concrete and concise answers.

Finally Samford's approach seemed to work. The primary thought that bubbled up through the linguistic morass was that the Air Force did not take these occurrences too seriously because radar anomalies and misidentifications had taken place continuously ever since the first use of radar. But Samford made the mistake of relaxing, and he handed the problem back to Roy James. Cleverly, the press guided James back to Washington National and the radars, and the fact that Major Fournet and naval radar expert Holcomb were on-site and verified the radar blips were not due to a weather inversion. The press asked James flat out: what was Fournet and Holcomb's opinion? Samford cut James off before he could speak.

> May I try to make another answer and ask for support or negation, on the quality of the radar operator. I personally don't feel that is necessarily associated with quality of radar operators because radar operators of great quality are going to be confused by the things which now appear and which may appear in a radar. The ability to use the radar for the thing it was designed for is, I believe, dependent upon the thing that they see doing a normal act. If it does a normal act, then it becomes identified as the thing that they thought it was and then it pulls itself along through this mass of indication and they say, "That one has normal processes." I think that a description of a GCA landing has some bearing on that in which to get associated with the GCA you have to make a certain number of queries and do a certain number of things and then you become identified through the fact that you obey. Other things that are in there don't obey. If you obey, then you have an identity and you can then be followed with precision. So I wouldn't like to say that this is a function of inadequate radar operations. I think it's a thing that can happen to any radar operator. If he sees something in there and says, "That one is neither behaving nor any other normal pattern." What is it? Curiosity stimulus, any other kind of stimulus can result in overemphasis at any particular time on any radarscope. These recently appear to have been much more solid returns than are ordinarily classifiable by the arguments that I have just given.

Bizarrely, Samford then told press members to address themselves to what *he* just said. A canny newsman said: what do these experts think? "*That* was the question." Outmaneuvered, Samford said that in their opinion there were "good returns" and "they should be followed up." Asked point-blank what he thought, Samford said that he felt that they were little or poorly understood scientific phenomena.

162

An arcane argument then ensued over what could be classed as "simultaneous." At the point when the press thought that they had achieved an unavoidable precise question, Samford said he would take a question from someone else instead. The new question was about sightings clustered around atomic installations, which we have seen was part of the briefings to Garland and Samford earlier in the year. Samford denied that there had been UFO sightings around atomic installations, but then made the mistake of asking Ruppelt, who said "yes." Ruppelt then tried to retract his statement by saying that it is perhaps because people at atomic installations might be more nervous about such things. Ruppelt then did a generally honest job on succeeding questions, obviously aware that he was standing next to his commanding officer. Many more questions arose. One series backed Samford into a corner so that he said that the answer was probably temperature inversion. This would, of course, be the main storyline that the press took away.

To maintain the tone of unreality that surrounded things whenever Samford took the floor, we will conclude with one last Samford remark that occurred very late in the hour and a half session. The press was suspicious of the claim that temperature inversions and false echoes were responsible for UFOs in the cases where airline pilots were directed to locations and reported seeing balls-of-light. They wanted to know how Samford could explain that. Samford said he could not. A newsman said, "Have you investigated that phase (the vectoring) of this thing." Samford delivered this in response:

> You can investigate, but the technique of investigating a process of mind-reading, for example, or the technique of investigating the process of mesmerism. You can say will you investigate those things? I think probably we know no more about mind-reading than the technique of investigating that or the technique of investigating evidences of spiritualism than we do about these fields but for many years the field of spiritualism had these same things in it in which completely competent credible observers reported incredible things. I don't mean to say that this is that sort of thing, but it's an explanation of an inability to explain and that is with us.

One can almost feel the world of common experience melting away.

When the conference ended, Donald Keyhoe had easily seen through what Samford had tried to do, but Samford's ruse was successful with most of the reporters. The flying saucers and any threat that might accompany them seemed unreal. Keyhoe even wrote admiringly that the Air Force officers had gone through the stress of the press conference and "obviously they had acted for the good of the country." Ruppelt was a bit more terse and pragmatic, saying that it "got the press off our back."

After the press conference, Donald Keyhoe began to receive unlikely cooperation from persons high up in the Pentagon, through his contact, Al Chop, at the press desk. This support, which included the release of high quality selective case reports directly from Project Blue Book, could almost be called deliberate leaks. It is not known exactly who the Pentagon higher-ups were who authorized this, whether it was official, or if so what their agenda was. The leaks were going on precisely while the CIA was intensely seeking UFO information from the Air Force authorities. Keyhoe even received a magazine draft on the subject of extraterrestrial migration to other planets such as Earth, by a Pentagon officer, Colonel O'dell.[67]

Donald Keyhoe

During the latter part of 1952, worrisome incidents with unidentified objects continued. There was an in-air encounter with a UFO by the assistant of the Secretary of the Air Force;[68] more information on possible radiation detection after UFO flyovers;[69] an encounter near the Hanford, Washington, atomic works;[70] and an incident in the North Sea during the combined NATO air forces' Operation Mainbrace.[71] Also in this period were two very strange reports: a close encounter with physical injury in Florida on August 19,[72] and an encounter with what seemed to be a giant robot in Flatwoods, West Virginia, on September 12.[73] These two stories had such spectacular elements that no one wished to take them seriously. *But the Air Force did.* They are mentioned here to demonstrate something most people would not suspect: once a person is immersed in enough strong and puzzling case reports which have come from people that person would normally unquestionably trust, the mind has only a few choices: close down and walk away, or open up. Ruppelt, ATIC, Fournet, and the 1952 Pentagon opened up. They were willing to hear reports about a scoutmaster in a Florida palmetto grove, who claimed to have been zapped by a landed disk, and not throw the report in the garbage can. When they heard that the scoutmaster was known as a teller of tales, they *still* did not throw the case away, because there were effects on the plants at the alleged landing site which could not be explained, except perhaps by a large electromagnetic source beaming something like microwaves into the soil and charring the plant roots below ground, but not plant parts above. The physical evidence bothered Ruppelt well after he left the scene, and he used the case when he briefed base "UFO officers" about the variety of things an investigator might come across. Scientists at the RAND Corporation were privy to the case. They challenged Ruppelt about it and whether the evidence pointed to an unknown high technology. When he hedged, they said in exasperation: how much evidence do you need?

The Flatwoods case was even more strange with its seven-foot-tall robot, but the witnesses were multiple and of better reputation. The Air Force took this case seriously, too, and Dewey Fournet is known to have inquired about whether samples taken from the site had commonalities with the Florida incident.[74] It is not necessary to "believe" in the reality of either case. It is important to recognize that the 1952 Air Force experts on these matters were far, far beyond the cool, assured mocking of James Rodgers and Roy James of Grudge or the irritation and even anger of Harold Watson or Colonel E. J. Porter. No one was laughing off or assuming anything. The world that *they* were living in could readily accept some very "world-expanding" possibilities. What they simply wanted to know was this: what is the evidence? Ruppelt said that many in the Pentagon felt that "extraterrestrial" was the only viable answer. An FBI memo dated October 27 said that the Pentagon officers with whom the FBI liaised were saying the same thing.[75]

We can leave this crucial 1952 year with a mention of something alluded to much earlier in this chapter: that the U.S. Navy pursued its own UFO investigation for, perhaps, the majority of this year if not well beyond. This study, and the Navy's role in general, are not well understood as we have only fragments of primary documentation released by that service. But we know enough to create part of an outline to describe the Navy's investigations.[76]

We have mentioned that in 1948 the Navy's Office of Naval Intelligence (ONI) co-authored a major document that opposed the famous "extraterrestrial" Estimate of the Situation written by Project SIGN. During and after that confrontation in the intelligence community, Project SIGN/Grudge was directed to send all its case analyses not only to the Pentagon, but to the ONI as well. Apparently ONI passed these on to the Office of Naval Research (ONR), as we know that at least one person, Urner Liddel, reviewed them there in the 1949-1952 era. On a different front, there were complaints among the Navy's secret balloon-project scientists that outstanding case reports from their personnel were not being treated with the seriousness that they deserved. In fact, as we have seen, after a while those scientist-engineers did not bother to send in reports. Possibly associated with this lack of respect for the Air Force's behavior, the Naval authorities in the Pentagon had to approve Commander McLaughlin's article on these same sorts of cases for publication in *True* magazine, thus delivering a very "pro-technological reality" message dramatically in opposition to how the Air Force wanted to handle public opinion.

Into this rough-edged environment between the two services (remember also that Generals LeMay, Craigie, and the RAND corporation were rebuffing the Navy from anything having to do with space missiles and satellite platforms research at the same time), there came a UFO encounter.

Sometime during March of 1952, the Secretary of the Navy, Dan Kimball, and the Chief of Staff, Admiral Arthur Radford, made a trip in separate planes to Hawaii, Guam, Hong Kong, and Taiwan. Somewhere between their stops at Pearl Harbor and Taiwan (we do not have the exact date; sometime in the March 20 period, probably), the aircraft were "buzzed" by a UFO. A couple of weeks later, back in the States, Kimball talked to an audience of air cadets and naval officers. He told them that his and Radford's planes had a UFO fly-by, whereupon he was told that his plane's pilot and co-pilot had seen a "flying saucer" race up to their aircraft, fly abreast for a moment, and then shoot past and upwards. The crew radioed Radford's plane that was behind them and was told that crew had seen a similar performance.

Left: Secretary of the Navy Dan Kimball
Right: Admiral Arthur Radford

The public knowledge of this incident came from news writers that attended Kimball's event. Additional evidence of this encounter came from Donald Keyhoe, a retired Marine Corps Major. He had graduated in the same Naval Academy class with Admiral Calvin Bolster, Chief of Naval Research, and Admiral Delmar Fahrney, Chief of Missile Development. Both Admiral Bolster and Secretary Kimball himself told Keyhoe of the UFO fly-by. Then in the 1960s, Admiral Fahrney and the Chief of the photographic interpretation center, Art Lundahl, related the same information to Dr. James McDonald. What Keyhoe and McDonald were told was this: Kimball and

Left: Admiral Delmar Fahrney
Right: Admiral Calvin Bolster

Radford had returned to the U.S. curious and concerned about the fly-by incident. They went to the Air Force with their concern and someone in the Air Force made the mistake of brushing off Kimball's aide on some technicality about not sharing case analyses details with witnesses, or some such blunder. Kimball was sufficiently irritated by this Air Force posture that he immediately ordered an independent Navy probe into UFOs to report back to him.

The officer who received the job was Fred Lowell Thomas (either a Lieutenant Commander or a Captain), of the Office of Naval Research. The project was set up similarly to the original SIGN group as a "Special Study." Part of Thomas' responsibility seems to have included the collection of particularly good incidents associated with Naval personnel and Naval research projects. Shortly after Thomas got started, for instance, the primary witnesses in a year-old balloon technology case were visited and a report taken. This was

Arthur Lundahl

Dr. James McDonald

one of the "General Mills" type cases from Artesia, New Mexico, that went unreported due to the negative attitudes of Grudge in early 1951.[77] This case consisted of two objects that "visited" the research balloon, maneuvered, and then left on a direct course at very high speed. The event was witnessed by six persons at a small airport and is one of those early "bullet-proof" cases that ended many experts' inner debates regarding the reality of the UFO phenomenon. The new Navy probe apparently shared this report with the Air Force about a week and a half after they received it, as Ruppelt acknowledged the general details of the case in one of his status reports.[78] Because of the year's delay in the case being reported, Ruppelt initially had the date wrong but later noted the correct date.

What happened to the Navy study? We do not know. The Artesia incident showed that they cooperated in some information sharing with the Air Force. Whether regular reports or briefings were produced, we do not know. Art Lundahl told James McDonald that he attended the final session in the old ONR building, and the whole study was summarized. The Air Force was invited. There is one note that the final session was in 1955, but that seems unlikely as the main driving force (Kimball) was long gone from the scene. Whatever is true, the phrase "final session" would seem to admit of several briefing sessions.[79]

Because of the quality of many of the Navy cases, it would be informative to know a great deal more about this. Heavyweight Navy figures, such as Fahrney and the initial CIA chief, Admiral Roscoe Hillenkoetter, were strongly outspoken regarding the reality of the UFO phenomenon. Other Navy figures, such as Moulton Taylor, Commander McLaughlin, and all the balloon experts were insistent upon UFO reality. Those involved in the Navy, with the exception of Urner Liddel, seem almost entirely "convinced" of a technological presence of some sort, but it remains poorly documented (relative to the Air Force) and, thereby, more mysterious.

Admiral Roscoe Hillenkoetter

Notes

[1] Herbert Strentz, *A Survey of Press Coverage of Unidentified Flying Objects*, 1970. Estimates based on Air Force microfilm.

[2] Donald Keyhoe, *Flying Saucers Are Real*, and *Flying Saucers from Outer Space*.

[3] Edward Ruppelt, *Report*, and Ruppelt files.

[4] Ruppelt files.

[5] (authors, apparently: Lt. Colonel Sterling and Stefan Possony for signature by Colonel Kieling and Colonel Garland), memorandum for record, subject: temporary duty travel to Europe, 29 April, 1952, FOIA (USAF); and Ruppelt files.

[6] W. M. Garland for General Samford, memorandum, subject: (Secret) Contemplated Action to Determine the Nature and Origin of the Phenomena Connected with Reports of Unusual Flying Objects, 3 January 1952, FOIA (USAF).

[7] (Edward Ruppelt), *Status Report Project Grudge—Report #3*, 31 January 1952.

[8] (Edward Ruppelt), *Status Report Project Grudge—Report #3*, 31 January 1952.

[9] The material on the Wonsan incidents comes mainly from Air Force documents in the Blue Book microfilm files of February 1952. There are more than a half dozen references there. Supplementary to these are the news articles (c. February 19) originating from the anonymous release. An example of the latter is: Dean Dittmer, United Press news release, "See Flying Spheres," 19 February 1952.

[10] (Edward Ruppelt), *Status Report Project Grudge—Report #4*, 29 February 1952.

[11] Colonel J. G. Erickson to General Samford, memorandum, Evaluation of News Articles Concerning Observation of Flying Saucers, 4 March 1952, FOIA (USAF).

[12] Ruppelt, *Report*.

[13] Richard B. Russell to Secretary of the Air Force Thomas K. Finletter, 21 February 1952, FOIA (USAF); and (Major Turk) General Nathan F. Twining, Vice Chief of Staff, for Secretary Finletter, memorandum, subject: Evaluation of Observation of Unidentified Object in the Far East, undated FOIA (the following memo indicates memo was sent March 8 or later).

[14] Joseph and Stewart Alsop, "Problems of Scientific Developments," dateline: Washington, D.C., 20 February 1952.

[15] Thumbnail biographies for the Alsops are readily available on the internet from sources such as Wikipedia and the *NY Times*. The more controversial material on CIA and public media manipulation comes from sources such as Carl Bernstein, "The CIA and the Media," *Rolling Stone*, 20 October 1977 (available on the internet), and a thumbnail biography of "Frank Gardiner Wisner" on the Arlington National Cemetery Website (www.arlingtoncemetery.net) with allusions to corroborating CIA documents on "Project Mockingbird" (documents from CIA not seen by this writer).

[16] Ruppelt, *Report*.

[17] (Dewey Fournet for) Colonel Harry J. Kieling to Directorate of Research and Development, subject: (Unclassified) Project Twinkle, 4 March 1952, FOIA (USAF).

[18] (Ray W. Taylor for) Colonel Frank L. Dunn to AFOIN-A, attn. Brig, Gen. Garland, memorandum, subject (Unclassified) Declassification of Project BLUE BOOK Material, 31 March 1952, FOIA (USAF).

[19] W. D. Blair, Jr., *Evening Sun Baltimore*, letter attached to memorandum from Major Edwin G. Jane, AF Press Desk to Directorate of Intelligence, Technical Capabilities Branch, 9 April 1952, FOIA (USAF).

[20] (Dewey Fournet for) Colonel William A. Adams to Office of Public Information, memorandum, subject: Inquiry from *Baltimore Evening Sun*, 17 April 1952, FOIA (USAF).

[21] Ruppelt, *Report*.

[22] Ruppelt, *Report*.

[23] Blue Book files microfilm Roll 9.

[24] Ruppelt, *Report*.

[25] Ruppelt, *Report*.

[26] Blue Book files microfilm, OSI files.

[27] Blue Book files microfilm Roll 10.

[28] Blue Book files microfilm Roll 10.

[29] Ruppelt, *Report*.

[30] Ruppelt, *Report*.

[31] Ruppelt, *Report*, and Blue Book files microfilm Roll 11.

[32] Blue Book files microfilm Roll 11, and United Press news story, Ellensburg Washington, as quoted in Gross 1952, June-July 20.

[33] Blue Book files microfilm Roll 11.

[34] Blue Book files are minimal on this classic case, as is the Ruppelt book. A better resource is Clark's *UFO Encyclopedia*, "Nash-Fortenberry Sighting," and the pilots' own public report: "We Flew Above Flying Saucers," *True*, October 1952: 65, 110-112.

[35] Clark's *Encyclopedia;* and *True*, October 1952.

[36] Ruppelt, *Report*.

[37] Gross 1952, June-July 20, and Richard Hall, *The UFO Evidence*, 1964.

[38] Donald Menzel and Lyle Boyd, *The World of Flying Saucers*, 1963.

[39] Stefan Possony is a somewhat shadowy figure. Information from this section comes from a) Ruppelt files; b) Lt. Col Sterling for approval of Colonel Harry J. Kieling and Brigadier General Garland, memorandum for record, 2 April 1952, FOIA (USAF); c) Donald Menzel files, American Philosophical Society Archives, Philadelphia, PA; and d) archival material from the Stefan Possony file at Georgetown University, Washington DC. The Georgetown file provides vita-like

information and suggestions of Possony's hawk-like conservatism as a cold-warrior. The USAF FOIA provides information of his and Sterling's Special Study Group. Ruppelt provides insight to Possony, the Special Study Group, and the meeting with Menzel. Menzel also has information on the latter. One could also read his militaristic classic on *Strategic Airpower*, published in 1949.

[40] Memorandum cited above.

[41] Ruppelt files.

[42] Dewey Fournet to Michael Swords, 30 June 1998.

[43] Ruppelt files, but generally corroborated by Menzel's own files.

[44] Air Force Status Report Summaries declassified in 1960, *Report #9*, 31 January 1953. Roy Craig files related to the Condon Report and held at Cushing Library Archives, Texas A&M University.

[45] Comments on the inadequacy of Menzel's views occurred widely in remarks by UFO "insiders" all the way from Ruppelt (see especially Ruppelt files "private" comments on Menzel) to the AF-sponsored University of Colorado study in 1966-68 (see Robert Low's address at California Institute of Technology, October 1967, audiotape, Center for UFO Studies files).

[46] David Menzel, unpublished autobiography, Menzel files.

[47] C.C. Wylie, "Saucers Not Seen by Astronomers," news story, dateline: Iowa City, IA, 4 June 1952.

[48] J. Allen Hynek, *Special Report on Conferences with Astronomers on Unidentified Flying Objects*, 6 August 1952.

[49] Roy Craig audiotape interview of Jay Nogle, location of interview at Malmstrom AFB, Montana, 19 Oct. 1967, Roy Craig files at Cushing Archival Library, Texas A&M University.

[50] Ruppelt, *Report*.

[51] Ruppelt extensively quoted in "15% of Saucer Reports Are Labeled Mystery," United Press news story, dateline: Dayton, OH, 18 July 1952.

[52] Associated Press news story, dateline: Albuquerque, NM, 19 July 1952, as quoted in Gross, 1952, June-July 20.

[53] The Washington DC sightings are *very* widely discussed. The best simplified overview is in Clark's *UFO Encyclopedia*. Edward Ruppelt gives an extensive description as he lived it in his *Report*. Loren Gross' June-July 20, 1952 and July 21-July 31, 1952 is extremely valuable for all this but especially the quotes from Air Traffic Controllers. Blue Book microfilm has, of course, much primary documentation (see microfilm Rolls 11 and 12).

[54] Personal communication with Fred L. Preyer, 1966 (Dr. Michael D. Swords).

[55] Quoted in Gross.

[56] Ruppelt reported almost 27% unknowns in his *Report*.

[57] This, and the previous information, are all from news articles quoted by Gross, June-July 20, 1952, and July 21-July 31, 1952.

[58] Gross, June-July 20, 1952, and July 21-July 31, 1952.

[59] Blue Book files microfilm Roll 12.

[60] Al Chop, taped interview, c. 1960-63 era, NICAP files (quoted in Hall, *The UFO Evidence*, and Gross, June-July 20, 1952, and July 21-July 31, 1952).

[61] Blue Book files microfilm Roll 12.

[62] For the Samford press conference, the most relevant materials are Donald Keyhoe, *Flying Saucers from Outer Space*, and Department of Defense Minutes of Press Conference Held by General John A. Samford, Director of Intelligence, U.S. Air Force, 29 July 1952 (copy in Ruppelt files).

[63] Drew Pearson, "Washington Merry-Go-Round" for 28 July 1952, as quoted in Gross July 21-31, 1952.

[64] INS news story, 28 July 1952.

[65] Ruppelt, *Report*.

[66] INS news story, 28 July 1952.

[67] Donald Keyhoe, *Flying Saucers From Outer Space*, and Keyhoe's extensive notes from his reading of O'dell's manuscript, NICAP files, held by Center for UFO Studies, Chicago, Illinois.

[68] Blue Book files microfilm Roll 15.

[69] Ruppelt, *Report*; and Blue Book files microfilm Roll 16.

[70] Blue Book files microfilm Roll 16.

[71] Operation Mainbrace's report is less readily documented than most "high profile" cases, perhaps because it was not primarily an American case. Edward Ruppelt (*Report*) describes it, as does the fine French UFO researcher, Aimé Michel, in his book *The Truth About Flying Saucers*, 1956. News stories with quotes from flyers exist from the times, and there is a small handful of FOIA fragments released by the USAF.

[72] Ruppelt, *Report*, and Blue Book files microfilm Roll 14.

[73] Ruppelt, *Report*, and Blue Book files microfilm Roll 15.

[74] Blue Book files microfilm Roll 89 (OSI files).

[75] A. H. Belmont to V. P. Keay, memorandum, 27 October 1952, FOIA (FBI).

[76] The story of the USN involvement during 1952 is documented by the following set of references. For the original incident of Secretary of the Navy Kimball, there is the news story of Kimball revealing it to Naval personnel (in Gross January-May 1952; plus Donald Keyhoe's books: *Flying Saucers from Outer Space*, and *Flying Saucers, Top Secret*, 1960); and there is the "insider" information on Kimball's ordering of the USN study as found in Keyhoe (as above), and in the McDonald archives held at the University of Arizona (Box 8, notes on September 1967 trip).

[77] Blue Book files microfilm Roll 8, and (Ruppelt) *Status Report #6 Project Blue Book*, 30 April 1952.

[78] Comments (by J. J. Kaliszewski) as reported in United Press news story, dateline: Minneapolis, MN, 12 April 1952.

[79] McDonald archives.

Chapter 9: The CIA Solution

In the middle of January 1953, a panel of scientists operating under the jurisdiction of the Central Intelligence Agency played a crucial role in setting a policy towards unidentified flying objects that dominated the field for many years. This panel, "The Robertson Panel," is an unusually important part of the history of UFOlogy and deserves a focused retelling in this book. To do that best, we will step just slightly backwards into 1952 to describe how the CIA became involved.

Almost all aspects of CIA involvement in UFOlogy are controversial and inadequately documented. This statement includes the events prior to the January 1953 meeting, though, thankfully, *not* the meeting itself, which is extremely well recorded. The CIA had at least occasional interest in the subject ever since the phenomenon expressed itself over U.S. airspace. In the spring of 1952, there were indications of what might be called the beginning of an unusual interest. Frederick Durant, an officer in the CIA's Office of Scientific Intelligence, befriended Pentagon UFO chief Dewey Fournet and Project Blue Book chief Edward Ruppelt, and gathered information about how the Air Force was handling the subject.[1] This was well before the big summer 1952 "flap," so the increase in sightings does not explain this. What, then, motivated Durant? The following is a speculation. The date of Durant's (CIA's) special interest coincides with the time when the Secretary of the Navy was upset with the Air Force due to what the Secretary viewed as an improper investigation of his and Admiral Radford's encounter. This incident was discussed in the previous chapter. In the subsequent Navy

Frederick Durant

UFO investigations, a case field investigation at Artesia, New Mexico, was done by a CIA agent for the independent Navy project.[2] The CIA would have known that some sort of conflict had arisen between the Office of Naval Intelligence and the Air Force Directorate of Intelligence over the handling of UFO cases. The CIA would have viewed clashes between services and prior communications about invasions of U.S. airspace as a national security issue, and of course would be interested.

Walter Bedell Smith

We do not know how much information Durant collected. But when President Truman requested that the CIA get involved after the Washington D.C. sightings in late July, the CIA was ready with recommendations about agency action the next day.[3] As detailed in the previous chapter, the Washington events of the last two weekends in July were not treated cavalierly. The President and his chief military advisor (Landry) were alerted as soon as anyone had courage enough to wake them up and tell them about it. Truman instructed the top intelligence and security organization in the land, the National Security Council, to get answers on how to proceed on the UFO problem.[4] The chairman of the NSC, CIA director and former Army general and ambassador to Russia, Walter Bedell Smith, immediately notified the CIA's Office of Scientific Intelligence that they had the job.

Let us ground ourselves by taking a partial look at the CIA's structure at this time.

The CIA

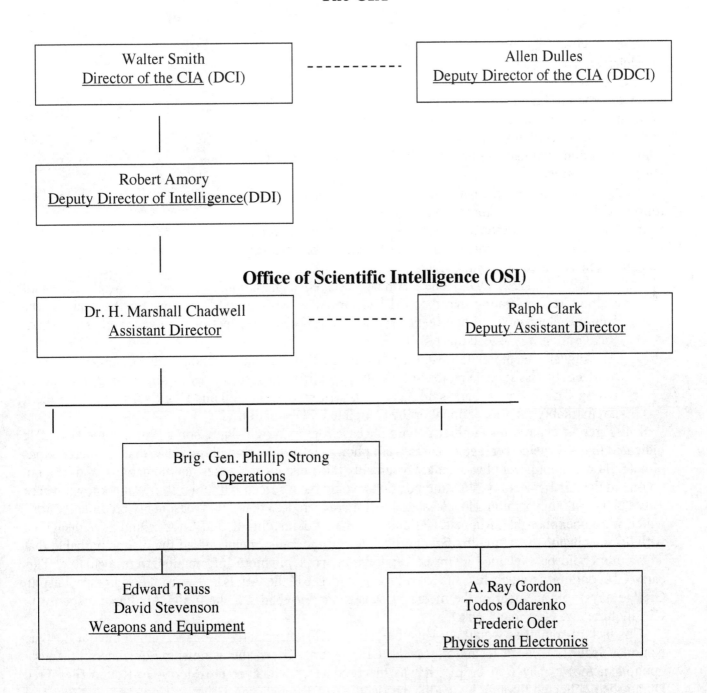

As mentioned, the head of the agency was General Walter B. Smith, Director of Central Intelligence, and his Deputy Director at this time was the famous Allen Dulles.[5] The main civilian professional in the organization, Robert Amory, reported directly to Smith. Amory's title was Deputy Director for Intelligence ("DDI" to Smith's "DCI", and Dulles' "DDCI"). The CIA, still relatively young, was evolving a working structure. Under Amory were several offices, including the Office of Scientific Intelligence (OSI), headed by a civilian "Assistant Director," Dr. H. Marshall Chadwell.

Chadwell's deputy was Ralph Clark. Under the OSI were several other offices, including "Operations" under Phillip Strong, a Marine Brigadier General. Beneath Operations were other areas of specialization such as "Weapons and Equipment" (Edward Tauss and David Stevenson), and "Physics and Electronics" (A. Ray Gordon, Todos Odarenko, and Project Twinkle Engineer and physicist Frederic Oder). All of these men were mentioned in the handful of documents released by the CIA, which allows us to piece together a fragmented outline of their work on the UFO problem.[6] As an example of the piecemeal nature of all this, we do not know with certainty which office (and consequently under whose direction) the main information-gatherer in this story, Fred Durant, was assigned.

Assistant CIA Director, Dr. H. Marshall Chadwell

As best we can reconstruct, the pattern of events went as follows. The basic sequence is derived from an article by Gerald K. Haines, a CIA and National Reconnaissance Office historian, writing about the agency's role in the UFO problem from primary documents he received in the mid-1990s.[7]

1. On July 29, 1952, DDI Robert Amory received a memorandum from Chadwell's assistant Ralph Clark indicating that the OSI had created a "special study group" for the study of the UFO problem as an ad hoc branch within the Physics and Electronics division of the OSI. A. Ray Gordon was to lead this effort.[8]

2. An August 1 memorandum went from Edward Tauss of the Weapons and Equipment division to "Deputy Assistant Director/SI" (Haines identifies this person as Phillip Strong, but this is wrong. This is Ralph Clark's title). Tauss is writing to Chadwell and Clark's office to give them a remarkably early assessment of the complete UFO situation.[9]

Tauss' report evinced his familiarity with the case files at Wright-Patterson's Project Blue Book. He indicated that a large percentage of cases were phony, defined as something other than misperceptions of natural or technological phenomena. Presumably this must mean hoaxes, hallucinations, and lies, but no one in the Air Force's investigating positions would have agreed with this, so it is not known where Tauss picked up this opinion. He also stated that there were less than 100 "reasonably credible reports" which were unexplainable. Ruppelt, Garland, Fournet, Adams, Smith, and Chop would have disagreed with his conclusion. Speaking in "Grudge-like" terms, the Tauss memo stated that it was probable that all reports could be explained as misperceptions, or worse, if more information were available. This early CIA opinion is much like the view one would get if the Air Force were talking (especially in Grudge days) to a member of the media. It causes one to wonder if the initial Air Force response to CIA inquiries was less than frank.

This lack of frankness would not have been impossible, especially prior to Truman's request to the National Security Council to investigate the UFO reports. Given the astonishing quickness of Tauss' opinion memo, it may well be that it was the product of whatever pre-Merry-Go-Round files Fred Durant had collected through his earlier befriending of Ruppelt and Fournet. However, that "lack of frankness" would change very quickly. Tauss mentioned at the memo's end that a "thorough and comprehensive briefing" from ATIC personnel at Wright-Patterson had been arranged for August 8.

3. On August 11, two memos were written which we have been permitted to read.[10] One of these was made available to Gerald Haines, the Agency Historian at the CIA. The memo seems to have been referenced in the August 8 meeting (mentioning "Air Force briefers"), and stated that the Air Force rejected theories that the UFOs were U.S., Soviet, or "Men from Mars" technologies. The other memo was the product of the newly formed special study group, headed

by Ray Gordon of the Physics and Electronics Division. It reported on a meeting of eight OSI operatives and its words betray an unexpected naiveté about the subject—much greater ignorance than one would have predicted from earlier memos (and Fredrick Durant's involvement), almost as if Durant's and Chadwell's own information had not been passed on to Gordon's group and they had begun from scratch. At the end of a series of elementary questions and assignments was an enigmatic reference to "Mr. S. Possony who may be a special officer . . ." It was obvious that this special study group was starting from point zero.

Major Dewey Fournet

Meanwhile other Air Force personnel were having more intense interactions with Frederick Durant. Major Dewey Fournet of the UFO desk remembered Durant in those days very well:

> I knew that he had been given authority to see me and was told that I could tell everything that I possibly could about the UFO project, from Day One. I do know that he was on the CIA payroll. I assumed he was just one of the project managers, and, there again, you don't go asking questions like that of those people. He told me what his objective was, which was to take the stuff up in the CIA and they would determine whether any further recommendations should be made to the Air Force or to the President.[11]

That Durant's name is not among the listed members of the "special study group" in Physics and Electronics indicates that the Agency was pursuing the UFO problem on two parallel paths, the latter being an OSI main office study involving Durant, Phillip Strong, and H. Marshall Chadwell himself.

4. August 14, a memorandum from Phillip Strong of the Operations Office indicated that the higher level CIA study had already interviewed "a representative of the Special Air Force Special Study Group" (almost certainly Possony, but perhaps Colonel Sterling). The CIA also went to Wright-Patterson to interview Blue Book officers.[12] Next, they had consultancies with several CIA-associated scientists. One of the latter was Dr. Walter Whitman, chairman of the Research and Development Board. Through all these inquiries, Strong reported that the phenomenon seemed almost certainly neither U.S. nor U.S.S.R technology, and that no shred of evidence supports an extraterrestrial theory. The consensus seemed to be that the cases would be explained by misperceptions, and some sort of "as yet little understood" natural phenomena.

Dr. Walter Whitman

5. An August 15 document which appears to be a transcript of a briefing by a CIA official was released discussing the difficulties in explaining and trusting UFO reports from a human frailties standpoint ("personal elements" and "psychological and physiological factors").[13] Although striving to provide a sensible context for doubting the reports, the speaker admitted that "we are still left with numbers of incredible reports from credible observers."

6. Middle of August: a notation at the bottom of a military case report sent to Blue Book indicated that the Air Force was sending certain cases directly to the CIA for their own uses, probably vis-à-vis the exact investigation under discussion here.[14]

7. An unsigned August 19 memo of a briefing session indicated that a study of the Soviet press had been made finding "not one report or comment" on the subject of UFOs.[15] This alarmed the analyst as it smacked of official censorship. One reason for such censorship could be a fear of what publicity might cause among the citizenry, and another reason was the possible use of the UFO idea as a psychological tool against the U.S. Psychological Warfare concerns within the U.S. were then addressed, and focused largely on one prominent (unnamed) UFO organization that was being monitored by the U.S. Air Force. Though unnamed, this almost surely had to be the hi-technology aero-engineering group known as the Civilian Saucer Investigation of Los Angeles (CSI-LA), which Ruppelt visited. Coral Lorenzen's Aerial Phenomena Research Organization (APRO) group had, as yet, no prominence and no funding, and Donald Keyhoe's National Investigations Committee on Aerial Phenomena (NICAP) did not yet exist. The only other (low probability) groups that come to mind are the fledgling New York group of Eliot Rockmore which morphed into the influential CSI-NY later and cultish West Coast organizations such as the Borderland Sciences Research Organization, which believed in trance-channeled UFO entities and messages of peace, brotherhood, and economic ideas which sounded suspiciously like communism.[16] A popular UFO group like CSI-LA could, the analyst reasoned, "touch off mass hysteria and panic."

A second warning from the analyst is particularly germane to this monograph and the spirit of the times:

Of even greater moment is the second danger. Our air warning system will undoubtedly always depend upon a combination of radar scanning and visual observation. We give Russia the capability of delivering an air attack against us . . . At the moment of the attack, how will we, on an instant basis, distinguish hardware from phantom . . . until far greater knowledge is achieved of the causes back of the sightings . . . we will run increasing risk of false alerts and even greater danger of tabbing the real as false. This is primarily an operational research problem, but as long as it exists it will have intelligence implications because of its bearing on air vulnerability.[17]

The document signs off with the information that the CIA study team had received an offer from MIT to assist the Air Force in the study of UFOs.

8. A later memo indicates that on the 20th of August, the Office of Scientific Intelligence felt that it knew enough to brief the Director, Walter B. Smith.[18] General Smith expressed concern over whether the Air Force project was sufficiently large and well-funded to solve the problem, and even if the phenomenon did not constitute a national security threat, it was the CIA's job to eliminate even the smallest possibility. He also wanted to know the extent that the phenomenon could be used by the United States in psychological warfare.

The reason for all of these maneuvers in August of 1952 is unclear. Gerald Haines, the Agency Historian at the CIA, seems to think that the CIA's special study group headed by Ray Gordon was an important player. This is probably wrong. Unless Haines has more documents than he cites, Gordon's group comes across as a secondary effort that operated not only more slowly than Durant, Chadwell, and Strong, but digested poorer quality information. Few of the documents released are from Gordon's group, whose presence essentially disappears as the CIA evolves across the Fall months. A "last" document by Gordon (c. August 22 or later), reports on a briefing he has received from the CIA on "The Air Force Stand on 'Flying Saucers.'"[19] The document looks like something that Gordon had gathered for his group for the file that they are charged to maintain on UFOs. The next significant appearance of this group (whose file has never been released by the Agency) was a couple of years later when the chief of the Physics and Electronics Division asked if his personnel could please stop doing this.[20]

The CIA's serious effort in pushing this examination of UFOs forward was directly the effort of Chadwell, Ralph Clark, Phillip Strong, and Fred Durant. Given the high level of the people applying the pressure for answers (Truman, Landry, Walter B. Smith), the timely handling of this by the highest OSI officers is not surprising. Part of this push by Chadwell was one or more meetings with the influential MIT physicist and government consultant, Julius Stratton. In an August meeting, Stratton told Chadwell that he and other personnel at MIT and in the Boston area would like to be part of a scientific study of the UFO phenomenon.[21] This is, at first glance, rather amazing. Their interest becomes clear, however, when one realizes who these people were and what worried them. The MIT scientists were part of "The Lincoln Lab." This was a secret government project, a holdover from the famous "Radiation Lab" of WWII days.[22] Lincoln Lab was greatly concerned about U.S. airspace vulnerability and possible radar technologies and networks to eliminate that vulnerability. UFOs, especially cases like the D.C.

Dr. Julius Stratton

Merry-Go-Round, and the violations near Los Alamos, Oak Ridge, etc. were part of the problem.

Stratton and the Lincoln Lab people were quite serious and wanted to take on the UFO study. Stratton suggested that Project leader Alfred Hill should organize the study. Although unnamed, it would be highly likely that George Valley, Air Force Scientific Advisory Board member and contributor to the Project SIGN final report and a Lincoln Lab mainstay, was involved. It is also known that Lincoln Lab personnel met with Edward Ruppelt (he called them the "The Beacon Hill group" in his book) to discuss the status of the UFO investigation.[23] This sense of urgency from Stratton seems to have had at least one important impact on Chadwell: he became alarmed at the dangers potentially associated with the phenomenon. Across September, his memos took on an aura of "Red Alert."

Indicative of this heightened concern is an extensive briefing memo sent by Chadwell to CIA Director Smith on September 7 or 17 (the date is disputed).[24] It is a remarkable document in many ways, but its main attraction for the historian is that it seems to be a completely frank and intelligent assessment of the UFO situation at the time. It contains many items of interest to this book and so is included it in its entirety. The original document is difficult to read and is in the appendix. A recreated version of the original document is displayed on pages 177 through 181. The reader's attention is drawn to a summarization of several points that were expressed in the memo.

1. The CIA analysts viewed the Air Force handling of the UFO problem as honest but inadequate. The Air Force was criticized for creating a poorly supported effort in terms of funding and personnel, as well as a wrong-headed philosophy of trying merely to find satisfactory (i.e. conventional) explanations on a case-by-case isolated basis, rather than making a serious effort to reveal the nature of the reality behind the reports. As an aside, in August, plans were made by the Air Force to transfer their highest-ranking intelligence expert, other than General Samford himself, to become chief of intelligence at ATIC. Since this man, General Garland, was also the major cog in the Air Force's interest in solving the UFO problem, it is unlikely that this transfer was merely coincidence.[25]

2. The CIA's research indicated that the phenomenon was frequent and worldwide, and that the Air Force's reporting network was set up to handle such a distribution. Twenty percent of the reports were judged "unexplained." (From the point of view of the UFO historian it is astonishing that, given the attitude of finding satisfactory explanations almost regardless of how well they matched the actual words of the witnesses, there were still twenty percent that survived such analysis. It is possible that the CIA put this two and two together as well.)

3. The OSI noted that the field was charged with partisanship. One can read the remarks as related solely to the civilian groups, or more broadly, as a critique of the Air Force as well. Oversimplification could easily be a charge leveled at the Air Force, perhaps more so than at the civilian groups such as CSI-LA or APRO.

4. After consulting with three scientists, Chadwell stated their opinion that the solution to the UFO mystery would be found "just beyond the frontiers of our present knowledge." Therefore, new discoveries in atmospheric science, electrical and plasma phenomena, and extraterrestrial (meaning in this context things analogous to rare bolides, ice comets, etc.) novelties were, in their view, hidden within the reports. The idea that unexpected side-effects from the concentrated depositing of radioactive waste could play a role is intriguing, which in all probability means that they were aware of the series of events at Oak Ridge that incited similar speculations. Of special interest to the UFO historian is the awareness that, once again, the examination of the UFO reports ended not in doubt that something real and mysterious was going on, but in the perception that something was interesting and worthy of serious investigation. All this indicated to the consultants and Chadwell that a serious scientific study should be made, for without such, the UFO problem and its security implications would not be solved. At that point, Stratton's offer to do just that was mentioned.

5. The conclusions were lengthy, specific, and delivered with a "no nonsense" air. Psychological warfare concerns were one of two prominent worries. The American public was viewed as containing a large group of people primed for hysterical panic. Because the risk was so serious, a national policy on what the public should be told was recommended as a protocol to minimize the risk of panic.

The second big concern was air vulnerability. Chadwell emphasized that the armed forces could not distinguish hardware from phantom. Erring in one direction created false alerts. Erring in the other brought catastrophe. This was, of course, the Beacon Hill/Lincoln Lab concern.

Several large undertakings were recommended: something to distinguish accurately hardware from phantom and whether that hardware was friend or foe; traditional CIA information gathering as to Soviet capabilities and intentions and studies of how the phenomenon could be used in psychological warfare both for and against the United States. Since the problem was so big and important, its solution transcended any individual department of government. All of this would certainly have alarmed many offices in the Air Force for a variety of reasons. Curtis LeMay's Air Force Research and Development would have been particularly irritated. They viewed the radar net schemes of Lincoln Lab as "budget busters" which would severely constrict R&D dollars for LeMay's hoped-for long-range

General Curtis Lemay

nuclear-carrying bomber fleets.[26] It had been rumored that LeMay had initiated an in-house study of UFOs himself in that general timeframe. If true, it could have been to make the argument that UFOs were *not* a serious concern, and therefore not to be used in support of Lincoln Lab's air vulnerability arguments.

The September document was a blockbuster. It contained, *four months in advance*, all the concerns that were featured at the famous Robertson Panel. A mystery, useful to the historian if solved, is the identity of the CIA service consultants who firmed up Chadwell's reasoning on the UFO phenomenon. Other than Julius Stratton, documents indicate Chadwell conferred with Stratton's colleague, Jerrold Zacharias, and well-known intelligence consultant and scientific giant, Lloyd Berkner. The ultimate chair of the Robertson Panel, Howard P. Robertson of Cal Tech, was former chief science consultant

MEMORANDUM FOR: Director of Central Intelligence   7 Sept 1952

THRU   : Deputy Director (Intelligence)

SUBJECT   : Flying Saucers

1.   PROBLEM

   To determine:

   a. Whether there are national security implications in the problem of "unidentified flying objects" i.e. flying saucers;

   b. Whether adequate study and research is currently being directed to this problem in its relation to such national security implications; and

   c. What further investigation and research should be instituted, by whom, and under what aegis.

2.   FACTS BEARING ON THE PROBLEM

   a. OSI has investigated the work currently being performed on flying saucers and has found that:

      (1) The only unit of government currently studying the problem is the Directorate of Intelligence, USAF, which has charged the Air Technical Intelligence Center (ATIC) with responsibility for investigating the reports of sightings.

      (2) At ATIC there is a small group consisting of a reserve Captain, two Lieutenants and two secretaries to which come all reports of sightings through official channels, and which conducts investigation of the reports either itself or through consultation with other Air Force officers or with civilian technical consultants.

      (3) A world-wide reporting system has been instituted and major Air Force bases have been ordered to make interceptions of unidentified flying objects.

      (4) The research being carried on is strictly on a case basis and appears to be designed solely to attempt a satisfactory explanation of each individual sighting as it occurs.

      (5) ATIC has concluded an arrangement with Battelle Memorial Institute for the latter to establish a machine indexing system for official reports of sightings.

(6) Since 1947, ATIC has received approximately 1500 <u>official</u> reports of sightings plus an enormous volume of letters, phone calls and press reports. During the month of July 1952 alone, <u>official</u> reports totaled 250. Of the 1500 reports, Air Force carries 20% as <u>unexplained</u> and of those received January through July 1952 it carries 2[----unreadable, ed.] <u>unexplained</u>.

3.   DISCUSSION

a.   OSI entered into its inquiry fully aware that it was coming into a field already charged with partisanship, one in which objectivity had been overridden by numerous sensational writers, and one in which there are pressures for extravagant explanations as well as for oversimplification. The OSI Team consulted with a representative of Air Force Special Studies Group; discussed the problem with those in charge of the Air Force Project at Wright field; reviewed a considerable volume of intelligence reports; checked the Soviet press and broadcast indices; and conferred with three OSI consultants, all leaders in their scientific fields, who were chosen because of their broad knowledge of the technical areas concerned.

b.   OSI found that the ATIC study is probably valid if the purpose is limited to a case-by-case explanation. However, the study makes no attempt to solve the more fundamental aspect of the problem which is to determine definitely the nature of the various phenomena which are causing these sightings, or to discover means by which these causes and their visual or electronic effects may be immediately identified. Our consultant panel stated that these solutions would probably be found on the margins or just beyond the frontiers of our present knowledge in the fields of atmospheric, ionospheric, and extraterrestrial phenomena, with the added possibility that our present dispersal of nuclear waste projects might also be a factor. They recommended that a study group be formed to perform three functions:

(1)   Analyze and systematize the factors of information which form the fundamental problem;

(2)   Determine the fields of fundamental science which must be investigated in order to reach an understanding of the phenomena involved; and

(3)   Make recommendations for the initiation of appropriate research.

Dr. Julius A. Stratton, Vice President of the Massachusetts Institute Of Technology, has indicated to OSI that such a group could be constituted at that Institute. Similarly, Project Lincoln, the Air Force air defense project at MIT, could be charged with these responsibilities.

4.   CONCLUSIONS

   a.   The flying saucer situation contains two elements of danger which, in a situation of international tension, have national security implications. These are:

      (1)   Psychological – With world-wide sightings reported, it was found that, up to the time of our investigation, there had been in the Russian press no report or comment, even satirical, on flying saucers, though Andre Gromyko had made one humorous mention of the subject. With a State-controlled press, this could result only from an official policy decision. The question, there-fore, arises as to whether or not these sightings:

         (a)   Could be controlled,

         (b)   Could be predicted, and

         (c)   Could be used from a psychological warfare point of view either offensively or defensively.

The public concern with the phenomena, which is reflected in the United States press and in pressure of inquiry upon the Air Force, indicates that there is a fair proportion of our population which is mentally conditioned to the acceptance of the incredible. In this fact lies the potential for the touching-off of mass hysteria and panic.

      (2)   Air Vulnerability – The United States Air Warning System will undoubtedly always depend upon a continuation of radar screen-ing and visual observation. We give Russia the present capability of delivering an air attack against us, yet at any given moment now, there may be current a dozen *official* unidentified sightings plus many unofficial. At any moment of attack, we are now in a position where we cannot, on an instant basis, distinguish hard-ware from phantom, and as tension mounts we will run the increasing risk of false alerts and the even greater danger of falsely identi-fying the real as phantom.

   b.   Both of these problems are primarily operational in nature but each contains readily apparent intelligence factors. From an opera-tional point of view, three actions are required:

      (1)   Immediate steps should be taken to improve identification of both visual and electronic phantom so that in the event of an attack, instant and positive identification of enemy planes or missiles can be made.

(2)   A study should be instituted to determine what, if any, utilization could be made of these phenomena by United States psychological warfare planners, and what, if any, defenses should be planned in anticipation of Soviet attempts to utilize them.

(3)   A national policy should be established as to what should be told the public regarding the phenomena, in order to minimize risk of panic.

c.   Intelligence problems include:

(1)   The present level of Russian knowledge regarding these phenomena.

(2)   Possible Soviet intentions and capabilities to utilize these phenomena to the detriment of US security interests.

(3)   The reasons for silence in the Soviet Press regarding flying saucers.

d.   Intelligence responsibilities in this field as regards both collection and analysis can be discharged with maximum effectiveness only after much more is known regarding the exact nature of these phenomena.

e.   The problem transcends the level of individual departmental responsibilities, and is of such importance as to merit cognizance and action by the National Security Council.

f.   Additional research, differing in character and emphasis from that presently being performed by Air Force, will be required to meet the specific needs of both operations and intelligence.

5.   RECOMMENDATIONS

It is recommended that:

a.   The Director of Central Intelligence advise the National Security Council of the security implications inherent in the flying saucer problem with the request that, under his statutory coordinating authority, the Director of Central Intelligence be empowered to initiate through the appropriate agencies, either within or without the Government, the investigation and research necessary to solve the problem of instant positive identification of "unidentified flying objects."

b.   CIA, under its assigned responsibilities, and in cooperation with the Psychological Strategy board, immediately investigate possible offensive or defensive utilization of the phenomena for psychological warfare weapons both for and against the United States, advising these agencies charged with U.S. internal security of any pertinent findings affecting their areas of responsibility.

c.   On the basis of these programs of research, CIA develop and recommend for adoption by the National Security Council a policy of public information which will minimize the risk of panic.

H. MARSHALL CHADWELL
Assistant Director
Scientific Intelligence

OSI PG Strong: (11 September 1952)

Orig. & 4 – Addressee
        1 – Ad/SI
        1 – Daily Reading
        1 – Subject
        1 - Chrono

for the CIA, and a member of the on-call payroll for 1952-1954.[27] It is not known how early Robertson became involved with the CIA. Although the general concerns of the September document reflect the discussions of the Robertson panel, the specific conclusions regarding scientific study do not. *That* emphasis changed between September and January. (Another CIA release, of September 24, appears to be a formal copy, Chadwell to Walter Smith, of the material which we have been discussing, so there is no need to comment further about it here.)[28]

During October and into November, Chadwell's office was apparently busy getting clearer information from the likes of Ruppelt, Fournet, and others in pursuit of a better understanding of what their formal recommendations should be.

By the end of November, Chadwell's OSI group had settled on the establishment of a UFO research project aimed at determining exactly what UFOs were.[29] Their reasons were that it was obvious that *something* was going on and needed immediate attention; and this was particularly serious because many of the unexplained credible sightings took place at high altitude, and others were over important defense installations. In order to establish the project, the CIA determined to write an "NSCID" for approval by the National Security Council. An "NSCID" was a "National Security Council Intelligence Directive," which, when agreed upon, immediately became U.S. policy in the intelligence community. *But* there was more going on than just this. To understand this moment in time, we need to digress and examine the relationship between the CIA and the military services. This intelligence community "sociology" apparently played a major role in what was going on here.[30]

When the concept of centralized (i.e. coordinated) intelligence arose after WWII, the initial Director was merely the chairman of the National Security Council, with an "office" at his disposal. It was immediately obvious that such a director could not do much. President Truman was a particular supporter of the concept of central intelligence and a strong director who could come to him in person with coordinated intelligence analyses that he could trust. He endorsed the concept of a full-fledged "agency" as a powerful tool for the Director. Thus the CIA emerged, a large and aggressive organization. The military services and the Department of State were suspicious and nervous about this new power.

The National Security Council, with the CIA Director as its chair, reported directly to the President. As stated earlier, the NSC made policy by agreeing to NSCIDs. Such directives could arise for discussion and approval from any of the members (Army, Navy, Air Force, State, Atomic Energy Commission, or CIA). But the NSC itself was largely a meeting of giants, actual chiefs of staff or directors, and not a proper working body. Because of that, the CIA established, under its agency structure, the Intelligence Advisory Committee (IAC), composed of working intelligence officers from the groups represented in the NSC, still chaired by the CIA director, and viewed as "advisory" *to the CIA*. It was within this group that the CIA Director could, if talented enough, manipulate the intelligence community and create the powerful NSCIDs for NSC approval.

The military did not like this arrangement and pushed to make the IAC a working group advisory to the NSC, not under the CIA. Truman and a CIA Director that he particularly liked, Walter Bedell Smith, fought off that pressure and the IAC stayed under the CIA.

In addition, the CIA established its Office of Scientific Intelligence (OSI) in 1948 and immediately began building a scientific empire. In 1949, the CIA Director persuaded the IAC to

Left: CIA Director Walter Smith
Right: President Harry Truman

accept the idea of another advisory committee, even deeper inside the Agency, under OSI. This was the "Scientific Intelligence Committee" (SIC) and would be chaired by the Deputy CIA Director of OSI. The following table shows the relationships between these organizations.

The President
↓
NSC
↓
CIA → IAC
↓
OSI → SIC
↓
_____
↓ ↓ ↓ ↓ ↓
Various scientific and technical divisions

The actions of the Scientific Intelligence Committee, and the expansion of the OSI science and technology "empire," pushed the military services to the point of full rebellion and then all-out war. The beginnings of this war were the initial subcommittees that the SIC established. These were targeted toward biological warfare, chemical warfare, electronics, and even guided missiles. This stunned the services, as these subcommittees and the concomitant expansion of OSI divisions relating to these subjects were clear intrusions onto traditional military turf. In 1950, the SIC even got away with establishing a subcommittee on aircraft and antiaircraft systems. In 1951, all semblance of cooperation ceased when the CSI-OSI tried to establish subcommittees on undersea warfare and army ordnance. It was naïve to create subcommittees to look into not only existing weapons systems of the U.S. and her enemies, but also make recommendations about weapons development. The services went through the roof. By early 1952, they had created their own joint military (no CIA) intelligence subcommittee to look into these topics and refused to countenance the SIC committees and OSI involvement in general.[31]

Left: CIA Director Smith Right: Director Roscoe Hillenkoetter These two officers built up the CIA's OSI arm.

By August 1952, the Army, Navy, and Air Force had won this war. CIA Director Smith retreated and abandoned OSI intrusions in all areas that involved weapons and weapons development. OSI was left only with research on basic sciences, scientific resources, and medicine.

It is significant, then, that when Truman asked Director Smith to get answers to the UFO problem, Smith was presiding over an OSI which had just been denied the right to look into things like "Electronics" or "Weapons and Equipment," considered within the sphere of interest of the services. Upon getting the UFO job, Chadwell immediately assigned some of the people who were formerly in "Electronics" and "Weapons and Equipment" to a UFO study group. Perhaps it was a convenient make-work for scientists and engineers suddenly short of work. Whatever their thinking and however long it took for them to come to a conclusion, Chadwell and Smith ultimately decided to produce an

NSCID that directed the CIA-OSI to create a full-fledged scientific study of UFOs. This, they reasoned, was a basic science research project, and therefore one that they were empowered to do.

On December 4 the IAC, with Robert Amory substituting for Smith in the chair, took up this potential NSCID.[32] Chadwell led the report and made the arguments. The IAC agreed to a scientific review. Air Force Director of Intelligence Samford agreed to cooperate.

Dr. Thornton Page

Thus far, despite our not knowing the details of all the principal parties' motivations, this series of actions is understandable. Truman wanted answers and wanted them from the CIA. The CIA Director wanted to serve Truman and perhaps get something for the Agency at the same time. The current rules seemed to encourage a basic science research project overseen by OSI, and OSI needed basic science projects. The Air Force was in an awkward spot, not having solved the UFO problem to anyone's satisfaction (especially the Navy's), and with some reluctance had to agree. Added to this, OSI Director Chadwell's memos indicated that by October-November, he himself was completely convinced that the subject was of great significance. And, although the following must remain a speculation, it appears there was another huge "carrot" hidden in this undertaking for the OSI. This was all research and development activity involving radar, electronics detection technology development, and airspace vulnerability. Why else were there so many meetings with Julius Stratton and suggestions by him to partner Lincoln Labs with OSI on a giant UFO science review? The Air Force had to be bothered by this, but the science review idea went forward.

Sometime in October or November, Chadwell chose Howard P. Robertson (rather than Lincoln Lab people) to head up this formative science review. Robertson chose Dr. Thornton Page, an astronomer and a military intelligence expert on Operations Research, to join him. Page believed that he was picked because he was handy—he was there at the Pentagon at the right time.[33] Robertson, Page, Chadwell, Durant, Clark, and Strong began discussions to decide what this review would become. Briefings and trips to ATIC followed and then something significant happened.

We know only that in late December it was decided *not* to begin a full scientific review involving organizational elements such as OSI division personnel or Lincoln engineers or any other research program but instead to hold a small review meeting to assess briefly a variety of UFO topics. It is conceivable that this could also be viewed as another step toward the full scientific project rather than a change of direction.

Robertson and Chadwell could not get anyone to agree to serve on this five-day workshop except Page until the end of December.[34] For example, world-renowned and imaginative physicist John Wheeler could not get the Atomic Energy Commission to approve his time commitment. Ultimately, top-level physicists Luis Alvarez and Sam Goudsmit agreed to attend. They apparently did so grudgingly, as indicated by their behavior at the meeting and later exasperated answers to letters. Major government science leader Lloyd Berkner also agreed, but did not even show up for the presentation days that involved UFO evidence. The scientists who did come were ignorant of the matter under discussion (even Robertson and Page were corresponding about an article in the *New Yorker* which they thought gave a good functional background to the subject!),[35] and they were biased against the topic from the start (Donald Menzel reports this about Robertson, who was a friend).[36] The idea that a workshop meeting with such personnel could accomplish anything towards Chadwell's NSCID and its support for a full-fledged investigation of the phenomenon would not be credible to those inside the CIA who watched this materialize. It *would* be understandable to an insider, however, if the workshop were to be phony: a display of brilliant minds signing off on a set of conclusions already arrived at and in concert with the NSCID. But this is not what happened. The brilliant (though uninformed) minds were there and *did* sign off on a predetermined set of conclusions related to national security that one could read in CIA memos from months earlier, but which did *not* support the December NSCID that argued for a more extensive scientific investigation with the possibility of solving the UFO phenomenon .

What happened?

Let us reflect back to the momentous early December meeting of the Intelligence Advisory Committee (IAC). As early as late August, CIA Director Smith had ordered Chadwell to prepare an NSCID to present (ultimately) to the National Security Council on how the CIA would recommend dealing with UFOs. Although differing elements of the intelligence community viewed them as anything from bunk to enemy aero-technology, General Smith was mainly interested in their psychological warfare potential. This might seem an odd emphasis, but we must remember what actually happened to inspire all this: the Washington DC sightings. These sightings acted more like a psychological warfare display than anything else—"here we are right over your capitol—catch us if you can." If the U.S.S.R. could turn such a phenomenon on and off whenever and wherever it wished, it would be a major psychological weapon of war. It would be just as valuable a weapon for the U.S.

Marshall Chadwell prepared himself for his NSCID by gathering information from every Air Force element available. The Research and Development Board people told him that Air Force R&D did not view the subject with undue concern.[37] This is not a surprise, as their leaders, Generals LeMay and Craigie, viewed this whole "invasion of airspace" scare as a possible diversion of funding from LeMay's SAC bombers. Other Pentagon people (Fournet, Garland, Ruppelt, etc.) gave a very different story. Their emphasis was that the concentration of sightings over major nuclear installations made this entire problem exceptionally real and alarming. Lincoln Labs, whether they believed in a LeMay or a Garland interpretation, saw this as reason to push their agenda of systematically identifying all such air intrusions as a national priority. Chadwell began as a LeMay-like doubter but evolved rapidly into a Garland-like Soviet-fearer. His mind, as revealed in his December 2 memo[38] (two days before the IAC meeting to consider an NSCID), apparently settled on two primary beliefs: we will never *really* get anywhere in creating an Intelligence solution to this problem until we understand what it is; and we will never really be able to counteract or utilize this "whatever" as a psychological warfare tool until we understand what it is. Because of the previously stated prohibition of the CIA-OSI from meddling with weapons and new potential weapon technologies, Chadwell had to frame his sought-for study of UFOs as a "basic sciences" study, and, given the difficulty of the problem, a serious and probably lengthy one. This is what Julius Stratton had suggested to him using the Lincoln Labs people and reemphasized in a December 2 meeting. At that meeting was another colleague of Stratton's (and the MIT-Lincoln people), Dr. Max Milliken. Milliken was a former assistant to the Director of the CIA and was currently the director of the Center for International Studies (CENIS). CENIS was, in large part, a secretive Soviet-watching think-tank, which included such intelligence heavyweights as Allen Dulles and Walt Rostow.[39] CENIS assessed such issues as the vulnerability of the Soviet Union to psychological warfare. Milliken and Stratton felt that CENIS could host a study, stacked with top level scientific brainpower from Lincoln Labs, with both basic sciences and psychological warfare potential. Chadwell said that, as a preliminary step, he would proceed to establish a consulting group to review UFOs. The goal would be to "convince the responsible authorities in the [intelligence] community that immediate research and development on this subject must be undertaken." He said CENIS would provide a proper environment for this consulting to take place.

The next day Chadwell wrote another memo that stated much the same but that admitted the Air Force would be suspicious of Project Lincoln involvement; therefore if MIT could not "go," perhaps

Princeton or Caltech would do.[40] Stratton very much wished to be kept in the picture. The politics of all this seemed finally to penetrate Chadwell's thinking on these machinations, and he stated:

> My conclusions from these conversations [which included sessions with Lloyd Berkner and Jerrold Zacharias as well on the 2nd] is that it will probably be necessary to secure the full backing of the DCI [General Smith] in order that a scientific review of the problem may be laid on. Without this backing, it would probably be impossible to secure the Air Force cooperation which would be necessary . . .

Chadwell's words seem highly significant. Chadwell has, even one day prior to the IAC meeting, *not* gotten General Smith up to speed on exactly what he is going to propose. General Smith's level of awareness about territorial touchiness between the CIA and the Military Services was, doubtless, at a far greater level of sensitivity than Chadwell's.

In an undated memorandum (but, from content, probably the same day, December 3), Chadwell described his proposal and sent it up the CIA chain.[41] The project was labeled "External Research Project Concerned with Unidentified Flying Objects." Note that the project is an external (i.e. not within CIA) project, and it was to be administered by Milliken at CENIS. It was, as a first step, to be an "ad hoc panel of top-level scientists." This step would be relatively brief and inexpensive. It was presumed that the panel would recommend further action to be taken toward a solution of the problem. Given the previous two memos, it reflected Chadwell's belief that a preliminary consultancy would lead to a larger Stratton-Lincoln-like study.

The IAC meeting was held the next day.[42] General Smith did not attend. He sent his Acting Deputy Director, Robert Amory, to handle the chairmanship. Smith, however, *did* direct the attendees that this was to be a *limited* discussion. It was to be aimed at a preliminary panel, and only to informally discuss the larger study of the NSCID. The military sent some big guns. General John Samford himself was there. The Navy sent Rear Admiral Carl Espe, director of Naval Intelligence. The

Left to Right: General John Samford, Rear Admiral Carl Espe, General John Willems

Army sent General John Willems, acting for the Assistant Chief of Staff. Other powerful operatives, like W. Park Armstrong of the Department of State and Walter F. Colby of the AEC, attended. The Joint Chiefs of Staff sent a very interesting person to carry their views: Colonel Edward H. Porter, who—along with Jere Boggs—was one of the Pentagon's original "saucer killers." Chadwell presented his case for the preliminary panel and the main study of the NSCID. We believe we know what he said to the committee, because an undated draft memorandum has been released which reads precisely like a draft that Chadwell would have had "in his pocket" for IAC approval once the discussion was complete.[43] The draft assumes that the IAC had approved the included remarks and that this was their recommendation, in Chadwell's words, to be sent up to the Secretary of Defense and/or the NSC. In the memo Chadwell says:

> It is my view and that of the IAC that this situation has possible implications for our national security with respect to the vulnerability of the U.S. to air attack. Intelligence, however, cannot discharge its responsibilities with regard to estimating the capabilities of an enemy to create and use such

phenomena against the U.S. unless we first determine through scientific research whether or not such phenomena can in fact be generated and controlled by humans.

Note that this paragraph frames the problem in CIA-OSI-friendly terms: the need for basic scientific research. Chadwell then goes on:

It is therefore recommended, that the Department of Defense undertake an expanded scientific research program to reveal the nature of the various phenomena which are causing these sightings and means by which these phenomena may be identified immediately. It is also recommended that in such a project there be close cooperation between those conducting the research and scientific and technical intelligence research. The IAC agencies are prepared to do their part in such a project.

Here Chadwell demonstrated the tact that was needed in this time of military suspicion of the CIA: the *Department of Defense* needs to expand into a scientific research program, but other agencies should be involved and the IAC (read: CIA-OSI) is prepared to do its part. All this would have made Ed Ruppelt (expanded project) and Allen Hynek (scientific approach) extremely happy had they known (it is possible that this attitude towards future UFO studies leaked through the grapevine to them at ATIC and was the source of their naïve optimism going into the January "preliminary" meeting to come).

In the cover letter to his draft, Chadwell made his intention very clear: the letter is "recommending the initiation of fundamental scientific research with respect to the nature and causes of unidentified flying objects (Flying Saucers)." Chadwell then went on to emphasize that this could only succeed through cooperation and coordination among the various agencies. It also suggested that the NSC's (CIA-directed) Soviet Watch Committee (a very high level coordinated council with the task of monitoring all-things-Soviet in order to avoid "surprise developments") be tasked to

. . . give close attention to indications which may reflect Russian actions are being taken with respect to or on the basis of cognizance of Flying Saucers or with respect to the state of United States public opinion in respect of Flying Saucers.

Once again it is psychological warfare that is on their minds.

At the IAC, Chadwell did *not* get what he apparently expected. The IAC admitted that there seemed to be a problem, but decided that the problem would be best approached not generally but in relation to *specific* intelligence and defense issues. That sounds like a mild refutation of an open-ended basic science research program. Because ATIC had the best evidence and reporting channels, Chadwell pointed out that Air Force cooperation was necessary. Samford said he would fully cooperate on this report-sharing requirement. Then the concept of the preliminary scientific panel was approved and recommended to go forward immediately. *But*, and this was the fatal and perhaps inevitable change, the NSCID and its larger scientific research requirements were to be dependent upon what the panel said if they were to go forward at all. The NSCID was no longer on a procedural highway to approval, but instead would face a go/no-go decision moment.

By this time, someone in the CIA had already decided who some of the panel would be (Howard Robertson and Thornton Page) and it would *not* be Lincoln Labs, CENIS, et al. Perhaps Chadwell wanted to save them for the bigger IAC-OSI component to come (a different preliminary group from the final science operatives would in fact make sense). Chadwell believed that the panel should have experts that covered the fields of astrophysics, nuclear energy, electronics, etc. These fields made sense if one had seriously read the case reports and was concerned about a composite of topics such as *de novo* natural phenomena, nuclear propulsions, a statistically significant number of sightings over nuclear facilities, radar reports and anomalies, and the Lincoln problem of radar detection. Cases were gathered en masse, and a handful or so continued to grab the CIA's attention. Some of these were obvious candidates (two motion films of alleged UFOs). Some were not (the "Florida Scoutmaster" case wherein a male claimed to be attacked by a beam from a UFO, and the Presque Isle/Limestone ME radar case which was later explained as errors). The selection of such cases may have played some role in the Panel's ultimate conclusions.

The panel itself consisted only of Robertson and Page right up to the beginning of January. Perhaps the CIA wanted a completely naïve set of scientists for some reason not stated in the documents. As we have mentioned, Luis Alvarez and Samuel Goudsmit very reluctantly agreed to serve.[44] Lloyd Berkner, who thought that UFOs were probably some natural phenomenon, also agreed to participate but would not even show up until after the conclusions had been decided. Page himself later admitted that he knew nothing about the subject except for some briefings and the *New Yorker* article.

Left: R. V. Jones
Right: CIA Director Woolsey

Charles Fort

Robertson, however, was different. His friend Donald Menzel said that he had gone into the panel meeting with the thought that the whole subject was preposterous.[45] Between the IAC and the January panel, Robertson contacted a colleague in British intelligence, R. V. Jones, who reinforced this by telling Robertson that their British investigations had indicated that the "mysteries" were due to ignorant and inadequate observations and that there was nothing to the subject.[46] Robertson viewed supporters of the mysteriousness of UFOs in derisive terms. He called them "Forteans," as if they were disciples of the early twentieth century collector of anomalies, Charles Fort.[47] Fort, by focusing on odd, poorly understood aspects of peoples' reports of unusual things, was a critic of conservative (he believed, closed-minded) science. Robertson assessed such behavior as irrational and impractical, and lumped Fort and UFO study encouragers into one pile. With four scientists ignorant of the phenomenon and one extremely biased panel administrator, the panel, in January, was complete.

The panel met for the first time on January 14. It would help the historian to know what the major players were thinking at the time. We do not. We have no information that would document whether the panel had any freedom to come up with its own genuine conclusions or whether higher authorities had already negotiated with one another and decided what policy would emerge. We know that the UFO "sympathetics" (Ruppelt, Fournet, the Navy Photo analysts, Allen Hynek—the people that Robertson would have labeled "Forteans") knew nothing about how this game would be played. But what did Robertson, Chadwell, or even General Garland know coming in? On the outside, did CIA Director Smith and Air Force Intelligence Director Samford already have their plan?

It is not the function of this book to engage in much undocumented speculation, but this panel's resulting directives were *very* important to the handling of the UFO subject and some "buyer beware" statements are justified. The theory that the course of decisions had changed and were already set cannot be proven. However, it can be defended by the following facts from the panel's own record:[48]

1. Although the Air Force had approximately 1500 case reports in its files, 20% of which were "unknowns," the scientific panel looked at a mere handful;

2. The attitude of the panel was to dismiss things authoritatively without discussion. Allen Hynek said that he was stunned by this;[49]

3. With the possible exception of two movie films, the most critical cases for analysis (those involving Los Alamos, Sandia, White Sands, Oak Ridge, and Hanford) were barely addressed or not at all. Considering that this is the featured concern in Chadwell's December 2nd memo, this remains a great mystery;[50]

4. All attempts by UFO analysts to introduce their studies of patterns in the phenomenon were quickly dismissed.[51] Earlier a large study by Battelle Memorial Institute (for ATIC) was noted to be partially completed, yet the CIA panel was scheduled so as not to wait for it;[52]

5. Lloyd Berkner arrived two and a half days (5 sessions) late and missed the entire presentation of evidence yet had no qualms about signing the finished report the next day;

6. Robertson was tasked to write the final report after dinnertime on the 16th. By 9 a.m. the next day it was completed, had already been read by Berkner, and was already in General Samford's office. *Mild* revisions, not surprisingly, followed;

7. After returning to Caltech, Robertson immediately wrote to Chadwell. He began his letter: "Und sssooo! Perhaps that'll take care of the Forteans for a while."[53] He then mentioned that he had spoken to General Samford following the meeting (the panel ended Saturday; he met with Samford on Monday), and that the General was not unhappy.

The previous seven points may be viewed as deriving from a scenario in which the major players had already decided the outcome of this panel (and the NSCID), and that Howard Robertson was well aware as to how this surface drama was to be played out. Possibly Berkner was aware as well. Whether Chadwell was, no one knows. He was, in his October and November attitude, one of those very "Forteans" (he believed that there was an important mystery here) that Robertson derided. In fact, it is difficult, having no more information on behind-the-scenes decision-making, to explain the seven points listed in any other way. We know that what the panel was doing could *not* be labeled as a scientific analysis, which is what the IAC's intention. The other scientist in the room, Allen Hynek, remarked over and over in later years that it was obvious that science "was not on the agenda."[54]

Some formal retelling of the panel meeting is appropriate.[55] On the morning of January 14, 1953, the panel convened in the OSI conference room. The panel consisted of Dr. Howard P. (Bob) Robertson, 49, mathematical physicist from Caltech, and former head scientific consultant for the CIA; Dr. Thornton Page, 39, astrophysicist from the University of Chicago, and researcher from the Naval Ordnance Lab during the war, winning the Legion of Merit Award in 1945; Dr. Samuel Goudsmit, 50, atomic physicist from Brookhaven National Labs, where he was chief scientist; and Dr. Luis Alvarez, 41, radiation physicist from the University of California at Berkeley, who had worked on both big projects (MIT Rad-Lab, and the nuclear bomb) during the war. Expected but not present was Dr. Lloyd Berkner, 47, atmospheric physicist from the Carnegie Institution, former director of the electronic materials branch of the Navy's Bureau of Aeronautics, and currently Assistant to the Secretary of State.

The Robertson Panel
Left to Right: Drs. Howard Robertson, Lloyd Berkner, Samuel Goudsmit, Luis Alvarez, Thornton Page

The leaders of the CIA's project team—Chadwell, Durant, and Strong—were present, along with Ralph Clark, Frederic Oder, and David Stevenson. Durant took the notes. The people giving testimony (Ruppelt, Hynek, et al.) were told to wait in the hall. There were some preliminary sarcastic remarks made by some of the panel, which were quickly silenced by a severe Bob Robertson, who told them to shut up and take the job seriously. A summary of this meeting is described in the next several pages.[56]

Robertson Panel Auxiliary Figures
Left to Right: Fred Durant, Dewey Fournet, Ed Ruppelt, Allen Hynek, Frederic Oder

Chadwell began the meeting by informing the scientists how the CIA had arrived at this point. He was especially careful to describe the December 4 IAC meeting, what the IAC's legal status was, and what the minutes conveyed as to the job of the panel. The emphasis of the IAC meeting, as presented to the scientists, was that this panel was to assess the possible threats to national security posed by the UFO phenomenon. The concept of a "scientific evaluation" and a further scientific research program was not emphasized, and, in the end, received very little focus in the panel's report. What *was* emphasized, by Phillip Strong, were the dangers to national security. Those dangers were:

1. Enemy induction of mass hysteria in the general population at a critical time;
2. An excessively excited general public clogging up communication channels and rendering early warning systems impotent;
3. "Cry Wolf" psychology: creating "bluff" sightings which end up casting doubt in the minds of military watchers et al., so that they are not taken seriously, and might let their guard down in the future.

The problem of psychological warfare usages was stressed, especially as it seemed to be a one-way possibility (i.e. the Soviets might use it on our "open" and nervous population, but we could not do much in their "closed" system). A brief mention was made that Air Defense Command was worried about our radar inadequacies.

Chadwell and Strong then told the scientists what sorts of reports tended to come in, what instrumentation (if any) was involved, and that *no* crashed hardware or debris was available. They then said that natural phenomena was the *Accepted* (their emphasis) explanation, that U.S. technology had nothing to do with this, and that the odds were very high (98 and 99% *against*, respectively) that the Soviets or extraterrestrials were responsible. Britain's R. V. Jones' opinion that the mystery was, essentially, bunk, was mentioned.

At this point in the meeting, the discussion shifted to topics that showed the astounding lack of preparedness of anybody on the panel. Robertson said that they needed a psychologist, such as the author Hadley Cantril, who had written a monograph study of the Orson Welles-inspired *War of the Worlds* panic of 1939. Robertson also wondered whether they should recommend getting "more technical evidence." Goudsmit said the "problem" looked psychological to him.[57] Fred Durant then discussed a statistical breakdown of ATIC cases and month-by-month numbers from the summer wave. The two movie film cases were mentioned before the lunch break. The scientists did not hesitate to get a showing of these films (done against the wall with no proper screen) before they left the room. Somewhere in the latter part of this session, Robertson had a pile of UFO case information placed on the tabletop and told everyone to grab parts of it as evening homework. Again, this illustrates an astounding lack of any preparedness for an important task that had brought in high-level scientists.

Over the next four sessions (the afternoon of the 14th, two sessions on the 15th, and the morning of the 16th), the "outside" experts came into the meeting and gave their presentations. The Photographic Interpretation Center people described their analyses of the motion pictures and why they believed the objects in the film were reflective disks. Ed Ruppelt gave a very extensive presentation on cases and the functions of the ATIC. Hynek spoke about his role in Blue Book and on the Battelle Project. Colonel Oder spoke on Project Twinkle. Dewey Fournet gave a report on selected cases, including the Tremonton Utah film, which he believed demonstrated motion characteristics beyond known aero-technology. Hynek then read a paper, possibly a draft of one soon to be published in *the Journal of the Optical Society of America*, on the possibility that many UFOs are a new physical phenomenon that he labeled "nocturnal meandering lights."[58] One mysterious element in these sessions was a brief appearance by General Garland on Thursday afternoon. It was Garland who had recently reminded everyone that the investigation of the UFO phenomenon was entirely within the province of the U.S. Air Force. Whether he reiterated that at the panel meeting is unknown. What he *did* say, as recorded, was that the Air Force needed to involve more intelligence officers in the field, that ATIC needed some expansion, and that as many reports should be declassified as possible. One assumes that, by this last comment, he meant *explainable* reports (so as to reduce the sense of mystery in the public mind). The other two suggestions, however, were basically saying to the CIA-OSI: we do not need you meddling in our business. Given the tensions of the "internal war" between the CIA and the military over this very issue, and given the desire of CIA Director Smith *not* to inflame the situation, this sort of blunt commentary is entirely in tune with the historical moment.

It may have been true that the panel got that message loud and clear, or it may have been the case that the matter was already settled and Garland need not have bothered. Either way, the concept of an ongoing UFO study involving CIA-OSI or Lincoln Labs never surfaced in the panel's report and recommendations.

What *did* surface had everything to do with national security and the American public as the weak link. The panel report returns over and over to the problems of the nation posed not by the phenomenon, but by a fragile citizenry. Basically all conclusions and recommendations were aimed at changing the public mind on this subject and making sure that policies existed and were followed that ensured that public perception *remained* changed. It is stunning to read the final report, knowing that it is discussing psychological and social manipulation about which none of the panelists had the slightest qualification. None of the CIA people in the room were versed in these matters either, being chemists, electrical engineers, physicists, etc. The one expert on such matters who was in attendance was a very significant name in the field of psychological warfare: Stefan Possony of Samford's Special Study Group. Possony is listed as an interviewee, but the minutes of the meeting are silent on anything he said.

The final report reads like two separate documents: one half abruptly dismisses the phenomenon itself (in opposition to almost every expert witness brought in to testify), and one half worries about how to control the public.

As to the former: Allen Hynek came to the meeting expecting a scientific hearing. His work with ATIC had convinced him that there were, indeed, strange things being reported, and, therefore, there needed to be a scientific study. He had taken the easy road on this and put forward a hypothesis that some new form of "light ball" phenomenon was the cause of many "unknowns." Feeling on safe ground, and amid his own "tribe," he was optimistic going into the panel. He was wrong. In later years, he reflected back upon these days:[59]

> I can remember that day very well . . . I had very mixed feelings being among such a group of highly respected and high-power scientists: Dr. Robertson, Chairman of the panel; Samuel Goudsmit, an associate of Einstein; Louis Alvarez, later to win the Nobel Prize; Thornton Page, astrophysicist; and the distinguished Lloyd Berkner.

> At that time, I was somewhat a newcomer and a junior—an associate member of the Robertson Panel. I guess I was somewhat nervous and apprehensive—but also quite interested in UFOs, having spent some four years, at that time, working with Air Force officials investigating sightings. . . .

> The viewing of the two films is the incident which remains by far the most vivid in my mind, the rather informal attitude at the time. The men had left their austere positions around the conference table and were sort of crouching around and leaning over each other's shoulders watching the films. There was a whole interplay of comments. Not exactly wisecracks, but "Well, it certainly looks like seagulls to me," and, "You can't convince me that that's not birds, it's gotta be birds," and words to that effect. Some people expressed a little dismay at the Tremonton films that they didn't realize that birds could reflect that much and someone would say, "Oh, yes, if the light's right, sun's right," and I believe I mentioned that the change in light was too rapid for it to be birds in flight, but that got nowhere.

And about the attitude and atmosphere of the sessions:

> Certainly, throughout the whole meeting, I did not feel at all like a colleague of the panel, but rather as one of the witnesses brought in for certain evidence or comments, and then dismissed as a witness would be when he's asked to step down from the chair.

> . . . Another way to describe their basic attitude . . . was very clearly an attitude of "Daddy knows best, don't come to me with these silly stories, I know what's good for you and don't argue."

And whether the scientific examination was genuine and earnest:

> If the whole Robertson panel was a put-up job, then one could argue that they deliberately chose high scientific-establishment men, men who were terribly terribly busy, could obviously not spend a lot of time examining things and had no intention of doing their homework, but of simply passing judgment on the basis of their previous scientific experience in, and only in, their present scientific framework. And, it would have been just as difficult to express a different idea as it would have been to convince a physicist in the year 1880 that matter and energy are interchangeable. The law (in 1880) said that matter was conserved, *no matter what*, and that was that! And, you just don't come around with this nonsense about matter being changed into energy. I mean it was that sort of attitude that I sensed all throughout.

Hynek felt that, due to that attitude, convincing the panel that they were mistaken would be difficult.

> Do I have any outstanding evidence to present to the contrary? Well, I thought I might have had, but in the face of that onslaught, I wasn't about to bring it up; and furthermore, the data at that time was not convincing in the sense that a physicist wants something to be convincing . . .

> And when the report finally came out, that is, the recommendations, I was not overly surprised to find the tack they had taken of the general need for debunking.

Hynek's impressions command some respect, even if one does not want to go as far as he does with his suspicion that the panel's mission had to do with national security and *not* at all to do with science, *and* that the principal parties involved knew it. Also, in later years, Thornton Page reflected back upon these matters. Page was the only panel member to speak frankly and relatively openly about this meeting. Here is a particularly telling comment that would have had Allen Hynek nodding his head:

"H. P. Robertson told us in the first private (no outsiders) session that our job was to reduce public concern, and show that UFO reports could be explained by conventional reasoning."[60]

And the "second half" of the report:[61] what of "national security"? As we have seen, and quoted, everyone on the panel side of the meeting seems to have understood that this was why they were there. Even some people who gave testimony, such as Hynek and Ruppelt, later stated that they too understood the importance of that part of what was being assessed. The panel itself briefly dismissed the possibility that the phenomenon itself was a security issue. Their reasons seemed to revolve around a view that UFOs were like the WWII foo fighters. Both Robertson and Alvarez had some occasion to be aware of the foo fighter phenomenon during the war, and they believed that, whatever they were, they caused no damage, nor even any hindrance to the war effort, and, thereby, were no threat. UFOs, to them, seemed at least in this way to be like foo fighters: no physical threat.

But the effect on the public was another matter, and it was emphasized. The Air Force's way of handling UFO reporting, including openly encouraging it at times, was given a good bit of the blame for this. (One wonders, as a historian, who was writing these words in the report, as none of the elite physicists on the panel had any in-depth knowledge or social psychology expertise.) Because the damage had already been done (that is, the concept of a mysterious thing called a flying saucer was thoroughly embedded in the minds of both civilians and military personnel alike), the intelligence community needed to undertake "educational programs" in both areas to moderate the excessive excitement exhibited by persons who had witnessed unusual aerial phenomena.

As far as military personnel were concerned, the report realized that it was vital that personnel who witnessed unusual, and thereby potentially dangerous, objects be alert to those observations and faithfully document and report them for analysis. However, the panel also stated that the vast majority of reports already obtained were of very poor quality, lacking needed details, and mostly a waste of everyone's time. The key here should be to create in the minds of the military effective methods of rapidly eliminating sightings and making better judgments on whether a report was worth following up at all.

> It was felt that there will always be sightings, for which complete data is lacking, that can only be explained with disproportionate effort and with a long time delay, if at all. The long delay in explaining a sighting tends to eliminate any intelligence value. The educational or training program should have as a major purpose the elimination of popular feeling that every sighting, no matter how poor the data, must be explained in detail.

Thornton Page was specifically quoted as saying that "more complete screening or filtering . . . is required; and that this can best be accomplished by an educational program."

While an educational program within the military could be formal and overt, "educating" the American citizenry was a subtler problem. Four full pages of the document were dedicated to the ideas and opinions about how to handle this. This section began with:

EDUCATIONAL PROGRAM

> The Panel's concept of a broad educational program integrating efforts of all concerned agencies was that it should have two major aims: training and "debunking."

The training aim is hardly controversial. That concept was to extend training of military personnel to civilian helpers, such as Ground Watch Observers, Air Traffic Controllers, civilian radar operators, and airline pilots. The training would be to recognize better the things commonly responsible for bogus UFO reports. The "debunking" program was entirely a different matter. These suggestions were, as the reader will see, quite remarkable, especially to the naïve citizen. The "debunking" program amounted to a very extensive and specific set of actions aimed at manipulating the public's mind and emotions. Since this sort of governmental behavior is not what many of us would prefer to believe, an extensive quoting of the Robertson document is appropriate:[62]

> The "debunking" aim would result in reduction in public interest in "flying saucers" which today evokes a strong psychological reaction. This education could be accomplished by mass media such as television, motion pictures, and popular articles. Basis of such education would be actual case histories which had been puzzling at first but later explained. As in the case of conjuring tricks, there is much less stimulation if the "secret" is known. Such a program should tend to reduce the gullibility of the public and consequently their susceptibility to clever hostile propaganda. The Panel noted that the general absence of Russian propaganda based on a subject with so many obvious possibilities for exploitation might indicate a possible official Russian policy.

Members of the Panel had various suggestions related to the planning of such an educational program. It was felt strongly that psychologists familiar with mass psychology should advise on the nature and extent of the program. In this connection Dr. Hadley Cantril (Princeton University) Cantril authored "Invasion from Mars," (a study in the psychology of panic, written about the famous Orson Welles radio broadcast in 1938) and has since performed advanced laboratory studies in the field of perception. The names of Don Marquis (University of Michigan) and Leo Rosten were mentioned as possibly suitable as consultant psychologists. Also, someone familiar with mass communication techniques, perhaps an advertising expert, would be helpful. Arthur Godfrey was mentioned as possibly a valuable channel of communication reaching a mass audience of certain levels. Dr. Berkner suggested the U.S. Navy (ONR) Special Devices Center, Sands Point,

Arthur Godfrey talks with NACA pilot George Cooper and NACA-Ames Director, Smith De France

L.I. [Long Island], as a potentially valuable organization to assist in such an educational program. The teaching techniques used by this agency for aircraft identification during the past war was cited as an example of a similar educational task. The Jam Handy Co. which made World War II training films (motion picture and slide strips) was also suggested, as well as Walt Disney, Inc. animated cartoons. Dr. Hynek suggested that the amateur astronomers in the U.S. might be a potential source of enthusiastic talent "to spread the gospel." It was believed that business clubs, high schools, colleges, and television stations would all be pleased to cooperate in the showing of documentary type motion pictures if prepared in an interesting manner. The use of true cases showing first the "mystery" and then the "explanation" would be forceful.

Walt Disney with Dr. Wernher von Braun

To plan and execute such a program, the Panel believed was no mean task. The current investigatory group at ATIC would, of necessity, have to be closely integrated for support with respect to not only the historical cases but the current ones. Recent cases are probably much more susceptible to explanation than older ones; first, because of ATIC's experience and, secondly, their knowledge of most plausible explanations. The Panel believed that some expansion of the ATIC effort would certainly be required to support such a program. It was believed inappropriate to state exactly how large a Table of Organization would be required.

After agreeing that the task would probably require some expansion at ATIC to help with the training and debunking, the report continued:

> This proposal met with generally favorable comment. The Panel believed that, with ATIC's support, the educational program of "training and debunking" outlined above might be required for a minimum of one and one-half to two years. At the end of this time, the dangers related to "flying saucers" should have been greatly reduced if not eliminated. Cooperation from other military services and agencies concerned (e.g., Federal Civil Defense Administration) would be a necessity. In investigating significant cases (such as the Tremonton, Utah, sighting) controlled experiments might be required. An example would be the photographing of "pillow balloons" at different distances under similar weather conditions at the site.

> The help of one or two psychologists and writers and a subcontractor to produce training films would be necessary in addition. The Panel considered that ATIC's efforts, temporarily expanded as necessary, could be most useful in implementing any action taken as a result of its recommendations. Experience and records in ATIC would be of value in both the public educational and service training program envisaged. Dr. Robertson at least was of the opinion that after public gullibility lessened and the service organizations, such as ADC, had been trained to sift out more readily explained spurious sightings, there would still be a role for a very modest-sized ATIC section to cope with the residuum of items of possible scientific intelligence value. This section should concentrate on energetically following up (perhaps on the advice of qualified Air Force Scientific Advisory Board members) those cases which seemed to indicate the evidence of unconventional enemy artifacts. Reports of such artifacts would be expected to arise mainly from Western outposts in far closer proximity to the Iron Curtain than Lubbock, Texas!

Note the sarcasm that had crept into the "serious deliberations" as evidenced in the final sentence. All thoughts of mysteries and overflights in the Los Alamos/Sandia/White Sands area (all quite near Lubbock, Texas) had been banished as if they had never occurred. At this point it was acceptable, apparently, to reduce the entire U.S. UFO experience to a joke.

Somewhat more ominous than a sarcastic joke was the final panel recommendation: keep certain citizen UFO groups under surveillance.

UNOFFICAL INVESTIGATING GROUPS

> The Panel took cognizance of the existence of such groups as the "Civilian Flying Saucer Investigators" (Los Angeles) and the "Aerial Phenomena Research Organization (Wisconsin)." It was believed that such organizations should be watched because of their potentially great influence on mass thinking if widespread sightings should occur. The apparent irresponsibility and the possible use of such groups for subversive purposes should be kept in mind.

Once again, one wonders who was writing on such matters for a panel who could not have known anything of significance of a Wisconsin housewife (Coral Lorenzen) operating a fledgling UFO club (Aerial Phenomena Research Organization/APRO).

It seems preposterous that these five physicists would elaborate such an "educational"/debunking program for the public, and, as most of us cannot remember anti-UFO programs by Walt Disney or Arthur Godfrey, it might be reasonable to assume that none of this was carried out. But it was. In the middle-1960s, UFO sightings had exploded across America and caused the Air Force quite a problem with public opinion. Walter Cronkite decided to host a major "documentary" on the subject on television.[63] The show, an edition of *CBS Reports*, aired on May 10, 1966. It was well produced and convincing. It portrayed the topic, in the end, as the product of human errors and foibles. A devastatingly embarrassing analysis of a UFO filmstrip flaunted by a British ufologist was a climactic piece of evidence. After the showing, Thornton Page, of the Robertson Panel, wrote to Fred Durant, who had written the report thirteen years earlier. In his private letter, Page informed Durant that *he* had been technical consultant on Cronkite's special and had structured the documentary "along Robertson lines."[64] The sledgehammer case of the bogus filmstrip was handled word for word just as the original panel report had suggested. One wonders if Cronkite had any idea that this had been done; the American viewing public certainly did not.

One cannot make the claim, without further documentation, that such Robertsonian meddling continued over the years. The Cronkite-Page case is mentioned because we

Walter Cronkite with President Johnson at about the time of the documentary

have the evidence, and that should at least make the hypothesis entertainable that other such actions occurred. Regarding the Panel recommendation that the civilian UFO groups be under surveillance, we also know that this occurred, even in a timely manner, and in both cases (CSI-LA and APRO) by ATIC personnel, which will be discussed shortly. As will be covered in Chapter 11, there is evidence that other agencies (specifically the FBI) kept watch as well. The point of these concrete instances is to give evidence that the Panel was far from ignored.

The first appendix to the panel report (TAB A) includes two passages worth mentioning:

> The Panel further concludes:
> That the continued emphasis on the reporting of these phenomena does, in these parlous times, result in a threat to the orderly functioning of the protective organs of the body politic.

And that, among other undesirable things, such excessive reporting contributes to:

> . . . the cultivation of a morbid national psychology in which skillful hostile propaganda could induce hysterical behavior and harmful distrust of duly constituted authority.

That "harmful distrust" would become automatic if, now that the Air Force had established a record of lies about these things already, a truly transparent policy on UFOs should ever be initiated. So, the intelligence community would be bound to this approach for years to come.

The Panel completed its business on January 17, and the scientists went back to their respective occupations. The Panel's recommendations were already in the hands of General Samford and CIA Director Smith. Eisenhower was replacing Truman as President, so the original source of these procedures was no longer in office. Nevertheless, the Panel's conclusions seem to have had an immediate impact and, following on, a lasting one. The list that follows describes some of the ufologically-relevant occurrences in the post-Panel years. Documentation almost never exists in these instances to establish a link between the Panel and its possible results, but the readers can determine for themselves whether there is a likely connection.

1. General Garland was shortly replaced at ATIC by the saucer-hating Harold Watson, now in his second term as executive officer of that intelligence department.[65]

2. Edward Ruppelt was instructed to bring Air Defense Command up to speed on UFO case investigation as Blue Book would be taking on responsibility for reports "in the field" (rather than ATIC, which would normally serve as a collecting center).[66] Some of Ruppelt's phraseology was word for word like the Robertson panel language.

3. Ruppelt had planned to retire anyway, and did so, along with Dewey Fournet and Al Chop. Their replacements were nowhere nearly as sympathetic to the UFO subject. After Ruppelt's assistant, Lt. Bob Olsson, filled in briefly, Captain Charles Hardin was named as chief of Blue Book. Ruppelt knew him. Here is what he said: (In the quote, Ruppelt refers to the "4602nd." That was an element of ADC, which took over UFO field reports.)

General Harold Watson

Chuck Hardin is running Project Bluebook at the present time. Since the operation of the project has changed and the 4602nd has taken over the leg work, he doesn't have much to do. By his own admission, he has a good deal at ATIC and he is playing it for all it is worth. General Watson doesn't like UFO's so Hardin is keeping things just as quiet as possible and staying out from under everyone's feet. In other words, being a regular Air Force, he is just doing as little as possible because he knows how controversial the subject is and his philosophy is that if you don't do anything you won't get hurt.

He definitely doesn't believe in UFO's, in fact he thinks that anyone who is even interested is crazy. They bore him.

He has been the one big bottleneck in my getting anything from the Air Force because he is afraid that my book will stir things up too much.[67]

In the last sentence, Ruppelt is of course, referring to his valuable book, *The Report on Unidentified Flying Objects*, which he was writing at the time (c. 1955-1956). ATIC was *not* helpful to him in this endeavor, and he got most of his post-retirement Air Force information from other friends in the Air Force intelligence community.

4. Coral Lorenzen (APRO) was visited by the Air Force (Bob Olsson and Allen Hynek) in June 1953.[68] They tried to convince her that it was in the best interest of the nation if she would help reduce the excitement around UFO cases, particularly by publishing the ways in which observational errors are made, and known things are misidentified due to ignorance.

5. Dr. Walther Riedel, the most famous aero-technology member of the CSI-LA, was under regular FBI surveillance at talks he gave in the Los Angeles area as early as February 1953.[69] Professional colleagues suggested to him to remove himself from CSI-LA.

6. CSI-LA disbanded in July 1953.[70]

7. Ruppelt was interviewed for a newspaper feature in March 1953. His public conclusion was precisely Robertsonian as stated: "They [ATIC] have never seen a saucer that couldn't be explained away as natural phenomena."[71]

8. The Tremonton, Utah movie film analyzed by the Photographic Interpretation Center (as "not birds, etc.") and dismissed by the panel (via a few showings on the conference room wall as "yes, birds") was scheduled by Air Force personnel for declassification and public release. This was cancelled.[72]

9. No further evidence exists for the CIA-OSI NSCID to create a scientific study of UFOs, nor is there further evidence of any involvement by Lincoln Labs or MIT personnel. NSCIDs of any kind are rare during the next few years and relate only marginally to anything associated with the UFO problem.[73]

Lincoln Labs in mid-1950s

10. Coverage of the subject changed from the "relatively open to wide possibilities" of the previous couple of years to a return to Grudge-like flat negativity, often colored with derision. Authority figures began to take a more consistent line, such as the simple debunking statements by President Eisenhower at a press conference in 1954.[74] *The New York Times* engaged in heavily negative statements and could with justification be called the leading source of such commentary for the next several years.[75] An example, which occurred at the same time Eisenhower was replying to concerns about a UFO flap that had passed across most of Europe in late 1954, is this:

> The sightings range from sober reports of real flying objects that prove to be something else besides saucers—mostly weather balloons—to fantastically weird stories, some of them obviously from troubled minds.[76]

The writers could not resist mentioning that a "young woman from the Netherlands" wanted to come see the U.S. Air Force, so that her brother (in Heaven) could materialize and return in a golden saucer, which then would explain everything. One finds that there are very few subjects that would be deemed worthy of two columns in the *Times*, yet would be treated with this type of winking mockery, and accepted as good reporting. But one sees this over and over, and it became a standard burden carried by the subject.

Eisenhower sharing a moment with Von Braun to his left and Keith Glennon, head of NASA, on his right

11. As a last item in what could be a much longer list, the military decided to change the major document, which governed UFO reporting, JANAP 146B. This change was connected to an Air Force regulation (AFR 200-2),[77] which was empowered in August of 1953. Dr. James McDonald studied the Air Force's history of dealing with UFO reports, particularly as they passed through Project Blue Book, and said the following vis-à-vis the effect of the Robertson Panel recommendations:

> This CIA request, made in January 1953, was followed by the promulgation, in August, 1953, of Air Force Regulation 200-2, which produced a sharp drop-off in public reporting of Air Force UFO sightings, by forbidding release at air-base level, of any information on sightings of unidentified aerial phenomena. All sighting reports were to be funneled through Project Bluebook, where they have been largely categorized as conventional objects with little attention to scientific considerations. The strictures implicit in APR 200-2 were made binding with promulgation of JANAP-146, which

made any such public release of UFO information at air-base or local-command level (by any of the military services and, under certain circumstances, commercial airlines) a crime punishable with fines up to $10,000 and imprisonment up to 10 years. These regulations have not only cut off almost all useful reports from military pilots, tower operators, and ground crews, but even more serious from a scientific viewpoint has been their drastic effect on non-availability of military radar data on UFOs. Prior to 1953, many significant UFO radar sightings were disclosed. Since then, military radar sightings have been scientifically compromised by confusing denials and allusions to "weather inversions" or "electronic malfunctions" whenever word of radar observations accidentally leaked out in the midst of a UFO episode. Air Force Regulation 200-2 contained the specific admonishment that "Air Force activities must reduce the percentage of unidentifieds to the minimum." This has been achieved.[78]

Many items in the above list might be judged as coincidental rather than causal (as related to the Robertson Panel). As to "retirements" of some of the participants, agreed. As to the other, more essential, items, it seems unlikely that they just happened to occur then.

This chapter has concentrated upon what many students of UFOlogy believe was the most important sociological moment in UFO history. Because of that focus, and the fact that CIA actions overlapped the previous chapter's information, this chapter has almost neglected the phenomenon itself. To rectify that neglect, we can look at how one frazzled UFO officer at a famous Air Force base grappled with a case just two weeks after the Robertson Panel concluded.

January 28, 1953: Mitchell AFB, New York:[79] Major Geyer had taken on the task of following up on UFO reports at the base. He was quite interested in this and for at least two plus years was an active investigator. He even convinced a group of amateur astronomers in the area to send him reports of any unknown objects seen in the sky. One evening he received at least three local reports (one from the base and two separately from Long Island) of what seemed to be the same object at the same time. The Blue Book document on this sighting is somewhat difficult to read and incomplete. It does indicate that there is an observation of an oval object glowing with different colors and with a tail or projection.

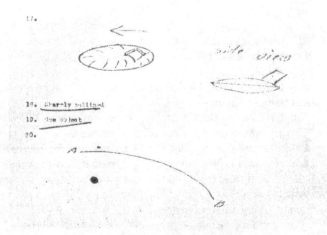

Drawings of the "meteor"

Geyer interviewed two non-commissioned officers at the base who had witnessed the object, and may have talked to several more witnesses, as he told the female citizen witness in Long Island that *seven* other people had reported what she had seen. The case was written up for ATIC, and the conclusion given: meteor.

This brings us to the female witness, Marie Armstrong Essipoff of Long Island. She was an elderly lady married to an ex-WWI flying officer. She had read Keyhoe's *Flying Saucers Are Real* and had just received his second book from a friend. That inspired her to write to Keyhoe, congratulating him on his writing and telling the story of Major Geyer visiting her earlier in the year.[80]

Mrs. Essipoff admired Geyer, working so hard to do his job properly, and was amused at how he tried to hold consistently to what she called his "prepared statement." After recounting her experience, Geyer said in an emphatic voice: "What you saw was a meteor." Mrs. Essipoff said that this assertion and the following rehearsed statements about how people make mistakes was "making me feel a little silly," but being a good hostess, and a military wife, she offered him some "Christmas whiskey." They had several and the Major "mellowed perceptibly." During the drinks and small talk, she said that one thing that still puzzled her was that her "meteor" (she was not buying this) "bobbled" (wobbled side-to-side as it flew) and as it did you could occasionally, during the rotation, see a turret on top or some such structure. Geyer suddenly became very interested. He asked her to draw it. She did. He asked her if she had ever seen a pilot-training device called a Link Trainer. She said no. Geyer paused:

> "Yes . . . and here's the funny thing. You have drawn an outline of a Link Trainer, and the men who saw it from Mitchell Field compared it in shape definitely to a Link Trainer."

> She said: "And it is still a meteor?"

> Geyer, firmly: "Still a meteor."

Dr. Robertson would have been proud of Major Geyer.

Notes

[1] "CIA releases documents—GSW prevails in FOIA lawsuit," *Just Cause* 1 (7): 1-2, January 1979. The CIA document cited in the article has not been viewed. However, the timing for CIA interest fits the circumstances perfectly, so it is cited here, secondhand.

[2] Ray Stiles to James McDonald, telephone notes transcript of communication, McDonald archives, Box 1 ("Artesia, NM"), University of Arizona.

[3] Ralph I. Clark to Robert Amory, Jr., memorandum, 29 July 1952, FOIA (CIA).

[4] Exactly how fast all this occurred cannot be known, but it was *very* fast. The CIA was already acting on Truman's request in a day or two, as is evident by CIA releases for July 29 and August 1. That Truman had Landry *directly* contact CIA Director Smith is also unknown but extremely likely (rather than, for example, some sort of memo), as Truman and Walter Bedell Smith were close and talked personally, because Truman liked the eye-to-eye contact.

[5] Allen Dulles, *The Craft of Intelligence*, 1963. There is no evidence that Dulles played any role in any of the UFO-related matters. Many other references for CIA structure exist and will be cited later.

[6] For a mainly accurate overview see Gerald K. Haines, "CIA's Role in the Study of UFOs, 1947-90," *Studies in Intelligence* 1: 67-83, 1997. Also available at https://www.cia.gov/library/center-for-the-study-of-intelligence/csi-publications/csi-studies/studies/97unclass/ufo.html and in Gross, especially 1952 volumes passim.

[7] Haines, "CIA's Role in the Study of UFOs, 1947-90." The following numbered block quotes summarize Haines' major points.

[8] Ralph Clark to Amory, memorandum, 29 July 1952, FOIA (CIA).

[9] Edward Tauss to Deputy Assistant Director/SI, memorandum, subject, "Flying Saucers," 1 August 1952, FOIA (CIA).

[10] See Haines' reference 19, and Minutes of Branch Chief's Meeting of 11 August 1952 (unsigned), FOIA (CIA).

[11] Antonio Huneeus, "Inside the Early Days of Project Blue Book: an exclusive interview with Major Dewey Fournet," *UFO Universe*, November 1988: 14-17. This is not a scientifically based magazine, but Huneeus is known to the UFO community and does respectable interviews, so Fournet's quotes are included here.

[12] See Haines, reference 21 (extensively quoted in Gross, August 1952, 42-43.

[13] Philip Klass, *UFOs: the Public Deceived*, 1983, 18-19, where the FOIA (CIA) document is quoted extensively.

[14] Blue Book microfilm Roll 14 (Travis AFB, CA).

[15] Haines, reference 21, and Klass, pages 20-21. A companion reference to Soviet press activity is George C. Carey to Deputy Director (Intelligence), memorandum, subject: USSR and Satellite Mention of Flying Saucers, 22 August 1952, FOIA (CIA).

[16] Borderland Sciences Research Organization's connections to UFO topics are covered by many citations in Clark, *Encyclopedia*. Rockmore was an early newspaper clippings collector who published a rapidly and widely spreading

mimeographed newsletter, that he called *Flying Saucer Review* (prior to the famous British journal). Borderland sent Rockmore information, and when FSR associates Isabel Davis, Ted Bloecher, and Lex Mebane, split off to form Civilian Saucer Intelligence of New York (CSI-NY), their organization ultimately received the files of CSI-LA when it collapsed. Any of these groups and any of their connections could have been seen at least as suspicious by the FBI or CIA.

[17] Haines, reference 21, and Klass, 20-21.

[18] H. Marshall Chadwell to Director of Central Intelligence, memorandum, subject: "Unidentified Flying Objects," 2 December 1952, FOIA (CIA). Haines refers to General Walter Bedell Smith's focus on the psychological warfare implications at this time. Document: CIA, Deputy Chief Requirements Staff to Deputy Director Plans, memorandum, subject: "Flying Saucers," 20 August 1952.

[19] A. Ray Gordon, memorandum, "The Air Force Stand on Flying Saucers—as stated by CIA, in a briefing on August 22, 1952," date otherwise unlisted, FOIA (CIA).

[20] Todos Odarenko to Director Scientific Intelligence, memorandum, subject: "Unidentified Flying Objects," 8 August 1955, FOIA (CIA).

[21] H. Marshall Chadwell, memorandum for record, subject, "Flying Saucers," 3 December 1952, FOIA (CIA).

[22] William P. Delaney and William W. Ward, "Radar Development at Lincoln Laboratory," *Lincoln Laboratory Journal* 12 (2): 147-166, 2000.

[23] Ruppelt, *Report*.

[24] H. Marshall Chadwell to Director of Central Intelligence, memorandum, subject, "Flying Saucers," September 17, 1952, FOIA (CIA). The 17th is the probable date as is cited by Haines. Confusion has arisen due to prior photocopying of the original, it would seem.

[25] Although ATIC personnel respected Colonel Frank Dunn, people like Ruppelt welcomed the transfer of Garland as they felt it signified a greater status for UFO investigations, which Garland believed were solely the province of the Air Force. See Ruppelt, *Report*.

[26] Loren E. Gross, "A New Look at the Robertson Panel," *FOCUS* 3(4): 1, 3-5, April, 1988; and David F. Winkler, *Searching the Skies*, 1997.

[27] Howard P. Robertson files, California Institute of Technology archives, Pasadena, CA.

[28] H. Marshall Chadwell to Director of Central Intelligence, memorandum, subject: "Flying Saucers," 24 September 1952, FOIA (CIA).

[29] See the very concrete evidence of conviction about the reality and possible threat of the phenomenon in the October memos: H. Marshall Chadwell to Director of Central Intelligence, subject: "Flying Saucers," 2 October 1952, FOIA (CIA); and James Q. Reber to Deputy Director (Intelligence), subject: "Flying Saucers," 13 October 1952; and the reflections on November proceedings in: H. Marshall Chadwell to Director of Central Intelligence, subject: "Unidentified Flying Objects," 2 December 1952.

[30] Ludwell Lee Montague, *General Walter Bedell Smith as Director of Central Intelligence*, 1992. The authors would also like to thank Robert A. Lieser for his unpublished work: *The Troubled Background of CIA's UFO Venture* (copy in MDS files), wherein he points at many of the connections between Montague's monograph and the material we have considered here.

[31] Montague, *General Walter Bedell Smith*.

[32] Richard D. Drain, Minutes of the Intelligence Advisory Committee, 4 December 1952, FOIA (CIA).

[33] Thornton Page to James L. Klotz, 3 October 1992; and Page's notes on his talk to the Society for Scientific Exploration, 30 May 1987, originally sent to UFOlogist Bill Pitts (copies in MDS files).

[34] John A. Wheeler to Frederick C. Durant, cc: to H. P. Robertson, 30 December 1952; notes of expenses of phone calls to Luis Alvarez and Samuel Goudsmit made by Robertson in late December and early January, Robertson files, Caltech archives.

[35] Thornton Page to H. P. Robertson, 12 December 1952, Donald Menzel files, American Philosophical Library; and Daniel Lang, "A Reporter at Large: Something in the Sky," *New Yorker*, September 6, 1952: 64, 66-82.

[36] Donald Menzel to Lyle Boyd, memorandum, 13 June 1961, Menzel files, APL.

[37] H. Marshall Chadwell to Director of Central Intelligence, memorandum, 2 December 1952, FOIA (CIA).

[38] H. Marshall Chadwell to Director of Central Intelligence, memorandum, 2 December 1952, FOIA (CIA).

[39] Christopher Simpson, *The Science of Coercion, Communication Research, and Psychological Warfare*, 1994, especially 79-85.

[40] H. Marshall Chadwell, memorandum for record, subject: "Flying Saucers," 3 December 1952, FOIA (CIA).

[41] H. Marshall Chadwell to Deputy Director (Intelligence), memorandum, subject: "Approval in Principle—External Research Project Concerned with Unidentified Flying Objects," no date, FOIA (CIA).

[42] Richard D. Drain, Minutes of the Intelligence Advisory Committee, 4 December 1952, FOIA (CIA).

[43] [H. Marshall Chadwell] to Secretary of Defense, memorandum, subject: "Unidentified Flying Objects (Flying Saucers)," no date, FOIA (CIA).

[44] The reluctance of persons like Alvarez and Goudsmit is documented by the Ruppelt files; and subsequent replies by them to later UFO researchers (for example in 1965 letters to NICAP associate Julian Hennessey, Alvarez said, "UFOs weren't important to me in 1953, and they aren't now." Goudsmit said, "In my opinion the subject is a complete waste of time and should be investigated by psychiatrists rather than physicists." Letters in CUFOS files).

[45] Donald Menzel to Lyle Boyd, memorandum, 13 June 1961, Menzel files, APL.

[46] H. Marshall Chadwell, memorandum for record, subject: "British Activity in the Field of UFOs," 18 December 1952, FOIA (CIA).

[47] Charles Fort and his potential relationship to UFO reporting and imagery are discussed in Clark, *Encyclopedia*.

[48] F.C. Durant, *Report of Meetings of Scientific Advisory Board Panel on Unidentified Flying Objects, Convened by Office of Scientific Intelligence, CIA, January 14-18, 1953*. (This was considered, formally, a "Memorandum" for the Assistant Secretary of Scientific Intelligence, and was "published" to appropriate parties in early March 1953). Known as the "Robertson Panel Report." (CUFOS files, and many other UFO archives).

[49] J. Allen Hynek, audiotape, 1974, CUFOS files; Hynek writes similarly, though with less emotion, about the Panel in both of his well-known books: *The UFO Experience*, and *The Hynek UFO Report*.

[50] H. Marshall Chadwell to Director of Central Intelligence, memorandum, 2 December 1952, FOIA (CIA).

[51] Hynek, audiotape; *UFO Experience* and *UFO Report*, as in reference 49.

[52] Hynek, audiotape; *UFO Experience* and *UFO Report*, as in reference 49.

[53] H.P. Robertson to Chad [H.M. Chadwell], 20 January 1953, Robertson files, Caltech Archives, Pasadena, CA.

[54] Hynek, audiotape; *UFO Experience* and *UFO Report*, as in reference 49.

[55] The panel activities are easily resolvable (at some level) due to the detailed report by Durant (*Report of Meetings of Scientific Advisory Board Panel on Unidentified Flying Objects, Convened by Office of Scientific Intelligence, CIA, January 14-18, 1953*), as in reference 48. Ruppelt (*Report*), Hynek (audiotape; *UFO Experience* and *UFO Report*, as in reference 49), and Page (meeting notes of the first sessions: Donald Menzel files, APL archives, and correspondence with James Klotz) add detail.

[56] Thornton Page, meeting notes of the first sessions, and Page to James L. Klotz, 3 October 1992; and Page's notes on his talk to the Society for Scientific Exploration, 30 May 1987, originally sent to UFOlogist Bill Pitts (copies in MDS files).

[57] F.C. Durant, *Report of Meetings of Scientific Advisory Board Panel on Unidentified Flying Objects, Convened by Office of Scientific Intelligence, CIA, January 14-18, 1953*.

[58] J. Allen Hynek, "Unusual Aerial Phenomena," *Journal of the Optical Society of America* 43(4): 311-314, April 1953.

[59] J. Allen Hynek, interview, in Robert Emenegger, *UFOs, Past, Present, and Future*, 1974, Chapter 7, 46-51, passim.

[60] Thornton Page to James L. Klotz, 3 October 1992; and Page's notes on his talk to the Society for Scientific Exploration, 30 May 1987, originally sent to UFOlogist Bill Pitts.

[61] F. C. Durant, *Report of Meetings of Scientific Advisory Board Panel, January 14-18, 1953*.

[62] Durant, *Report of Meetings of Scientific Advisory Board Panel, January 14-18, 1953*.

[63] *CBS Reports*, 10 May 1966, hosted by Walter Cronkite, Title: "UFOs: Friends, Foes or Fantasy."

[64] Thornton Page to Frederick Durant, 8 September 1966 (copy in author MDS' files).

[65] Watson immediately returned the ATIC atmosphere to Grudge days. See Ruppelt files comments on Charles Hardin.

[66] Ruppelt files: *Project Blue Book Special Briefing for Air Defense Command*, March 1953 (held by MDS for UFO Research Coalition).

[67] Ruppelt files: "Chuck Hardin."

[68] James and Coral Lorenzen, *UFOs Over the Americas*, 1968, and *The Great Flying Saucer Hoax*, 1962.

[69] Chief, Contact Division to Assistant for Operations, OSI, office memorandum, subject: "California Committee for Saucer Investigation," FOIA (FBI).

[70] *Civilian Saucer Investigation Quarterly Bulletin* 1(III), July 1953.

[71] Peter Wydem interview with Captain Ruppelt, *St. Louis Post-Dispatch*, 8 March 1953.

[72] Donald Keyhoe, *Flying Saucers from Outer Space*.

[73] See Office of the Historian at history@state.gov for "Foreign Relations of the United States, 1950-1955: the Intelligence Community, documents 256-359" for NSCIDs in the general time period.

[74] Anthony Leviero, "President Discounts 'Saucer' from Space," *New York Times*, 16 December 1954.

[75] Terry Hanson, *The Missing Times*, 2000, and John C. Hickman et al., "Fewer Sightings in the National Press: Content Analysis in *The New York Times*, 1947-1995," *Journal of UFO Studies* n.s. 6: 213-225, 1995-6.

[76] Anthony Leviero, "Air Force Remains Calm while the 'Saucers' Fly," *The New York Times*, 19 December 1954.

[77] Department of the Air Force, *Air Force Regulation No. 200-2, "Intelligence: Unidentified Flying Objects Reporting,"* 26 August 1953.

[78] James McDonald, "The Problem of the Unidentified Flying Objects," summary of a talk given to the District of Columbia Chapter of the American Meteorological Society, 19 October 1966.
[79] BB microfilm Roll 17.
[80] Marie Armstrong Essipoff to Major Donald E. Keyhoe, 17 December 1953 (CUFOS files).

Chapter 10: Intermission

This mini-chapter is a pause for reflection. There is a feeling of significant change in the press between the periods before and after the Robertson Panel. What is different about the coverage is a sort of lessening of the seriousness of the subject. This occurs not due to stories of mockery (although contactee "conventions" provided plenty of raw material for that), but by a decrease in the number and "authority" of major figures in the military and government giving any comment upon the matter of UFOs at all. Essentially gone are the days when a Vannevar Bush, a William Webster, or a David Lilienthal would be quoted on the subject. An Air Force authority might say something (briefly), but the other service leaders were quiet. There were exceptions, of course, but mainly the only authority one heard was the public information office at the Pentagon. Wright-Patterson was ordered silenced, and visits by the press eliminated. This very restrictive information management strategy was ultimately very effective. Although certain officers at other bases either did not get the message clearly, or did not agree with it, this policy of everyone shutting up and channeling all inquiries to the Public Information Officer was working, and reduced the number of public relations incidents to a manageable amount. What the public got, almost uniformly, was an exciting-sounding case, a non-committal response from local military authority, a subsequent debunking response from the Pentagon, and no other authority commenting.

This simple and brilliant approach kept the citizenry confused but relaxed about UFOs. The reason why this system of management was not employed before is that, as said, it's a big military, and if the Pentagon policy makers were not obvious and clear on exactly how the UFO subject was to be dealt with, officers went their own ways. Even regulations such as JANAP 146 were not enough to make it imperative that cases would be handled in this strict way. Whether the Robertson directives were themselves specifically the cause of this attitudinal sea-change, or whether it was a more random spreading of awareness that the high brass *really* did not want this handled casually, the atmosphere about UFOs changed.

As we will see in the coming chapters, all of this would have gone smoothly if no one but the Air Force had anything to say about it. But, unfortunately for the Air Force, a few matters were out of its control. The first of these were the citizens. Some of them were having encounters, becoming curious, asking questions, getting very unsatisfying answers, and, now distrusting the Air Force, looking elsewhere. One result of this was the growth of large civilian research organizations such as NICAP and APRO. APRO went about its business, directed not at the government, but at the phenomenon, and, because the major media was generally lulled to sleep by the Pentagon, APRO did not constitute much of an irritation, let alone a threat. NICAP was completely different. Major Keyhoe and his band of ex-military board members and advisors went directly at the Air Force, demanding full document release. This was, of course, the *exact* opposite of information management, and, therefore the exact opposite of Robertsonian principles on how to handle the UFO problem to avoid national security vulnerability. NICAP and "Robertson" were irreconcilable opposites. There could be no compromise.

In such situations, assuming the attacking side refuses to quit, the only alternative is war. A "Cold War" immediately began between NICAP and the Air Force, and the ground of battle was the U.S. Congress. As a secondary effect of the Air Force policy, citizens in large numbers began to distrust the military's handling of civilian cases and, so, stopped communicating them to the Air Force. That meant that Project Blue Book, which still wanted the good cases to evaluate, received less and less material. This so frustrated Dr. Hynek that he quietly began liaisons with civilian researchers and reading civilian UFO newsletters to uncover additional information on cases. Other members of Blue Book, thought that this was just fine (especially after 1958), and saw in that trend a reason to close the project altogether.

Other than the public, the other element that the Air Force could not control was the phenomenon itself. After the 1952 wave, the phenomenon (in the U.S.) diminished though sightings continued during the 1953-1956 period. In late 1957 it went wild again, causing no end of troubles for the Air Force. This thoroughly re-excited the population and served as a good stimulus for Donald Keyhoe's agenda of pressuring Congress that he had begun a year earlier. Unfortunately for Keyhoe, but a blessing to the Air Force, the U.S. expression of the phenomenon trailed off in 1958 and then saw the quietest period on record, 1947 to the present. That "desert" lasted five years (1959-1963). During that time period, the Air Force won the war with NICAP and Congressional hearings were constantly denied (although private briefings were frequent).

All of the above is obvious from the record, and hopefully will ring true in the following chapters. But, before that, there is another important matter which could benefit from comment now, one that is not as easy to document and "see." That question is this: how could the Air Force simultaneously take the UFO phenomenon so seriously that it would set up an elaborate psychological management program to deal with it, while *not* taking it seriously enough to go all-out to find out what it was? Even if one believed that the stimulus for UFO reports did not have anything to do with the Soviets, it seems wise to know scientifically what, then, it actually was, as that knowledge might solve all of the attendant psychological and security problems. Or, if one went so far as to think that these things might be non-terrestrial technology, would one not want, even more, to learn all one could about them?

The following remarks involve some degree of speculation, though, hopefully, not an excessive amount. They are derived from many hours of reading the documents (with their opinions and, sometimes, emotional outbursts) written by various military figures involved in this saga. The previous paragraph contains two different, albeit related, questions. One: why such seriousness as to require a universal information management system? Two: why not, internally, *really* research the phenomenon?

As to the management of the public: it made absolutely no difference to those concerned with national security whether they believed that UFOs were Soviet mischief, extra-terrestrial technology, or utter nonsense. In the end, all roads led to the conclusion: keep these over-excitable civilians under control so that they do not expose us to psychological warfare vulnerabilities that might clog our communications systems or create raw panic in which they might even harm themselves. The intelligence community had many real-world incidents to support that view (regardless of what we "sophisticated" 21st century denizens might like to believe today). Some examples include:

*Orson Welles' famous
War of the Worlds broadcast*

1. the famous 1938 panic due to Orson Welles' too-realistic broadcast of the *War of the Worlds*;[1]
2. a Chilean rendition of *War of the Worlds* in 1944[2] and an Ecuadorian rendition in 1949[3] resulted in panic in the streets;
3. the communication lines jamming due to the highly publicized July 1952 U.S. flap;[4]
4. in 1957, another *War of the Worlds* broadcast had large numbers of Canadians thinking Sputnik had "landed" and brought hostile Russians nearby;[5]
5. in 1958, the *War of the Worlds* struck again, this time convincing thousands of people that Mars had invaded Lisbon, Portugal;[6]

6. in 1959, hundreds of London TV viewers panicked over a fake newscast broadcast in concert with a Men from Mars play;[7]
7. in 1960, a government-sponsored study (by the Brookings Institution) on the consequences of ET-contact painted a very negative picture, regardless of how "friendly" the aliens might be.[8]

This is a small list; it could easily be made larger. Dozens of incidents are on record where the first thing that the citizen witness does is go for his gun (and in several cases, fires it). There is much real-world evidence that, when confronted with an unknown of this magnitude, many of us either would respond with violence or lose control altogether. Giving the national security operatives the benefit of the doubt, they probably did not want individual citizens either shooting one another or having heart attacks. But, we can be absolutely certain that they did not want these same citizens to constitute a manipulable threat to the State. Minimizing "scared rabbit" behavior had to be a priority.

But what of the concurrent *low* level of interest in finding out what the UFOs really were? Despite public press releases, nothing is more obvious from reading the "insider" documents, and the interviews with military personnel later in their lives, that a very large number of them believed (and felt that they had very good reasons to believe) that UFOs were a real, substantive, and technological phenomenon operating in our atmosphere, and that no mundane terrestrial explanation came close to providing a convincing explanation. So why no serious research? That question has several answers:

1. The Soviets have the A-bomb;
2. The Soviets have the H-bomb;
3. The Soviets launched Sputnik;
4. The Soviets have a heavy-lifting rocket expert (Korolev);
5. One can make an H-bomb small enough to fit into an ICBM.

The overriding concern was clear. The Soviet bomb and its intercontinental missile weaponry systems were the real world. They were obsessively nerve-wracking. We *had* to be able somehow to oppose these concrete threats. Many officers, particularly Air Force leaders like Curtis LeMay, Harold Watson, and all the missile development people (each with his own idea on how best to do this), felt that technology and weapon-system development was the *only* thing to which every person (and every dollar) should be dedicated. Any officer and any dollar not directed to opposing the Soviet threat was not only wasted, but, in their minds, indefensible foolishness.

To this rather emotional frame of mind add this: for several years (at least counting from 1947), these "things" had been flying about and acting more like irresponsible teen-age hot-rodders than anything else. Irritating, yes. Dangerous? Apparently *not*. That is the peculiar wild card in this story. It appears (and here we are making a deduction beyond the documentation) that military officers began, sooner or later, to drop their concern (vis-à-vis security) in regards to UFOs: "They are there." "They are real." "They are irrelevant" (at least so far). As the years progress, all manner of military persons might maintain even an intense interest in the phenomenon. But the "worry" about it went away. A military research project to try to nail down the physical details of the phenomenon was believed to require a huge upgrading of manpower and expense—"criminal" expense, LeMay would have said. And there was no guarantee of any success anyway. Leave it alone. Military-UFO encounters rarely elicited any panic, but civilian encounters (even make-believe ones) often did. On the "inside," the thought was just leave it alone. On the "outside," it was do not give the public fuel for their fire.

Once the Robertson policies spread throughout the Air Force and beyond, the atmosphere described here would prevail, year after

General Curtis LeMay

year, until the formal project Blue Book was finally cancelled at the end of the 1960s. This cancellation was the only logical conclusion to the policy. Blue Book's mere existence was a contradiction to the message of "no problem/no concern" that the security community wished to present to the citizenry. Still, there would be plenty of fights between the Air Force, the media, Congress, and various UFO organizations.

Notes

[1] Hadley Cantril, *The Invasion from Mars*, 1966

[2] Front page of *The New York Times*, 14 November 1944.

[3] Front page of *The New York Times*, 14 February 1949.

[4] See Chapters 8 and 9, this volume.

[5] Associated Press news story, dateline: Kelowna, British Columbia, 10 November 1957.

[6] Dateline: Lisbon, Portugal, *London Daily Telegraph*, 26 June 1958 (quoted in Gross, May-June 1958).

[7] "Londoners Panicked by TV 'Invasion' Play," UPI news story, dateline: London, U.K., 21 February 1959.

[8] Brookings Institution (Donald Michael, project director), *Proposed Studies on the Implications of Peaceful Space Activities for Human Affairs* (prepared for NASA), especially 203-227, 1961. The press immediately "paged past" the "practical" areas of the report and created large headlines about how we were being warned about the dangers of extraterrestrial contact.

Chapter 11: A Cold War

This chapter reviews the immediate Post-Robertson Panel period (1953-1956), during which time the Air Force made strides towards finally addressing the UFO security problem. Simplifying this as much as is reasonable, we can continue with our historical timeline and watch the situation evolve. It would be possible to spend an entire chapter coursing across several years following only Donald Keyhoe and NICAP's striving after Congressional hearings (with the Air Force's counter-strategies to fend this off), but it is the decision here to take the multidimensional complexity as it comes. Hopefully, the interplay between all these things will provide the reader with a deeper understanding of why events went as they did.

In 1953, Eisenhower replaced Truman as President, and Josef Stalin died. Change of any kind always brings some anxiety. There was plenty of that and plenty of reason for it. The U.S. received reliable intelligence that the Soviets had a long-range rocket;[1] von Braun launched a Redstone rocket from Cape Canaveral,[2] and North American Aviation developed a 50,000 lb. thrust rocket engine at Edwards AFB.[3] The ICBM missile race had just launched. Worse than all of that, a committee chaired by John von Neumann, called by many of his colleagues the world's most intelligent mind, proved (on paper) that one could structure the mechanisms of the H-bomb so as to fit into the nose section of an ICBM.[4] The Air Force and the missile developers began to receive the lion's share of defense funding. LeMay's SAC bombers were way up; the Army's budget was way down.[5] Within the Air Force, LeMay (long-range bombers) and General Bernard Schriever (long-range missiles) were at war between themselves. Ike did not want to go

John von Neumann

for the ICBMs, but the military-industrial complex, backed by the horrible revelation of the von Neumann Committee, practically demanded that he do so.[6] With all that, how important were UFOs?

The Robertson Panel Report stated that UFOs were still important and that the potential security consequences of citizen interest in them needed to be taken seriously. Plus, there was that annoying habit UFOs had of "visiting" areas associated with the nation's nuclear and missile launch facilities. In the Green Fireball era, 1948-1950, more than 200 "events" were logged, the great majority of which were in the vicinity of Albuquerque, White Sands, and western Texas military bases;[7] and, in a different set of data, Blue Book "UFO" files showed almost 80 cases of UFOs at nuclear sites.[8] Ed Ruppelt thought this significant enough that he went "map-in-hand" to his 1952-3 briefings, including to the Robertson Panel itself, to make this point. So, it was not yet time to disregard UFOs completely, no matter how terrorized we were by the Soviets.

The most important thing that the Air Force did in response to the new philosophy was to close Wright-Patterson (and Blue Book) to inquisitive reporters.[9] All inquiries were to be directed to the Public Information desk at the Pentagon. At the Pentagon, the information sent out was to include no substantive case materials, and, generally, only orchestrated non-commital or debunking remarks. The old guard from the Garland era was not happy with this. Two colonels, high in the Air Intelligence Analysis chain-of-command above the UFO desk and the Public Information Office desk, were the remaining decision-makers whom the CIA attitudinal takeover would have chafed the most. We have no documents that reference the actions taken by Colonel William A. Adams or Colonel Weldon H. Smith, but we do have a fairly strong indication of their feelings. After the Panel's report had swept through Air Force offices in the Pentagon, it was clear that civilians should be shut off from UFO information. But one civilian, the most dangerous civilian, was not. As a last hurrah, more than a month after the Panel's recommendations were "out," PIO desk chief Al Chop gave Donald Keyhoe at least ten official case reports which Keyhoe used in his book.[10] Chop did not clear this action with his superiors. That clearance had to come from the levels of Adams and Smith.[11] Chop was on his way out of the service and, thereby, "safe."

When Chop left Air Intelligence, Captain Robert White replaced him. White was more of a gentleman than the continually-insulting Lawrence

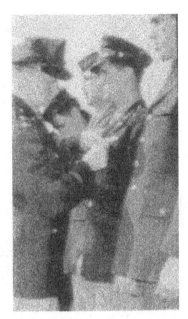

Colonel William Adams decorated by Gen. Spaatz

Tacker who followed him, and he created fewer public relations gaffs. But he did his job—no more case releases to people like Keyhoe. Of course, it is different when one is dealing with friends, and just-retiring Edward Ruppelt was a friend. A couple of years later, White would quietly clear as much as he could get for Ruppelt who was writing his book *The Report on Unidentified Flying Objects*.[12] During that time a person from Colorado, who had obviously read Keyhoe, wrote to the Pentagon and wanted answers. White's letter to the citizen was calm and civilized, although it was filled with (apparently deliberate) misleading comments. It was a nice dance between truth and fiction. Some of White's remarks are worth review here. Our comments are shown in brackets.[13]

Right: Al Chop interviews Nicholas Mariana of Great Falls, MT case

Concerning Dewey Fournet's "UFO motions" study that he presented to the Robertson Panel:

The report prepared by Major Dewey Fourney [sic] was simply a report of his own personal views [False]. They were not concurred in by members of the staff. [False. Colonels Adams and Smith *initiated* the idea, according to Ruppelt. But, it's cleverly worded. "By all members of the staff" would have been true.] If his report had been made public it would have been construed as the official views of the Air Force [True], which it was not [Also true]. I believe he is now a civilian and he may publish his personal views to any extent he so desires. [Yes and no. Fournet was not allowed to take his report with him, nor copies of the case files he used.]

Concerning the ET hypothesis:

You ask why we do not make a true statement about the UFO's. I'm sure that we're being as honest and forthright about them as it is possible to be. [False.] Thousands of "saucer" fans want us to say that they come from outer space, manned by people from Mars, Venus, and planets not yet discovered. Unfortunately, our investigations simply do not support such a contention. [This depends upon what one accepts as "support." Fournet felt that the "investigations" supported this hypothesis quite nicely, although they did not *prove* it.] We don't rule out the possibility; we can't so long as there remains a percentage which can't be explained. However, we do feel, quite honestly, that the probability of unidentified flying objects being space craft is extremely remote. Quite often our disagreement is labeled dishonesty. [This is generally well-said. The estimate of "probability," however, would vary greatly with the AF officer speaking.]

White goes on to recommend to the citizen three magazine articles which he says were written by authors who made a "thorough and honest investigation." The articles are not gushingly enthusiastic about UFOs, but they are not grindingly negative, either.

Then comes the climax message paragraph:

In closing, I would like to make one point which does not seem clear to many people. The Air Force does not care whether people believe that flying saucers are from outer space or not, [False. The Air Force knows perfectly well that belief in "invasions from Mars" causes people to freak out.] and we don't attempt to influence their beliefs aside from announcing what we know to be factual. [Very false. Captain White can be forgiven for doing his job, but he gets a zero on the truth scale for this one.] Our primary concern is to assure that there is nothing on our skies which could represent a threat to security of the United States. [Complete honesty.] We are far less concerned whether an unidentified flying object is from outer space than if it is an enemy missile or aircraft. [Complete honesty.] For that reason, we continue to immediately investigate every worthwhile report. [False.]

Captain White's letter was one of the best that the PIO desk produced during these years. It was as non-confrontational as possible, while appropriately mixing truths, lies, and misleading half-truths into a professional-sounding "we're doing our best for you" response. Others were not so good at this.

The new "nothing positive" policy required the spokespersons to go back to a "Grudge"-like position, but without the insults to the witnesses. Many of them tried loyally to do this. In early March, Captain Ruppelt, fairly fresh from the Robertson Panel, gave an interview in which he made light of all his travels in Blue Book fieldwork, and said that he had never seen a report "that couldn't be explained away by natural phenomena."[14] He *knew* that was untrue (unless he crossed his fingers behind his back and silently added "by Donald Menzel"). He also said that he did not know why he bothered to carry a Geiger counter. But he knew *perfectly* well why he did so: he was, after all, the one who tracked down the Geiger counter "excursions" phenomena at Palomar, Los Alamos, and Oak Ridge and reported on them to the Robertson Panel. Ruppelt (irrespective of what he, personally, may have believed UFOs were) simply lied to the press on certain matters of fact. He did so as chief officer of the Air Force's UFO investigating project. He did so in clear concert with the concerns of the Panel.

Very unusually, Director of Intelligence John Samford chipped in with an interview for one of the small popular magazines of the day, *SEE*.[15] Samford gave a series of very straightforward, factual answers to the lead-in questions asked by the magazine about the Air Force program, when saucer sightings originated, and the inadequacy of Menzel's theories. Samford and *SEE* established a very grounded feeling to the interview. Admitting that 20% of reports were unexplained, Samford simply said that the Air Force was working on them. Speaking reasonably and non-authoritatively, Samford reflected upon the possibilities of visitors from space but reiterated that the Air Force had no evidence for them. Consistently and calmly, he reassured *SEE* that the Air Force had found no danger from UFOs and no sign of a Soviet threat. And, of course, he had to do some lying:

(*SEE*): Are you or is the Air Force keeping anything secret from *SEE*'s readers regarding this 'Project Saucer'?

(Samford): No, we have withheld only two things: the names of those who report sightings to us (this at their own request) and the methods used by Intelligence men to investigate and evaluate these reports.

SEE asked about Communist meddling (in a psy-warfare mode). Samford said that this was under investigation. *SEE* ended by asking what his personal views were.

My view is that of the Air Force—that many credible people have seen incredible things, some of which have later been satisfactorily explained, while others so far have defied explanation. However, we believe that all of this will eventually be understood by the human mind, and that, for the time being, it is our job to hasten this understanding.

It was a masterful statement and the magazine applauded: "(the) candor of Maj. Gen. Samford on saucers impressed *SEE*'s correspondent." It was beginning to look like the Air Force was finally getting a handle on how to do this job. It helped, of course, to have good, well-balanced people who had a clear policy goal— like White, Ruppelt, and Samford—to do the talking.

Ruppelt's assistant on the project, Lt. Bob Olsson, took over for him for a while in 1953, and gave another calm, courteous, and somewhat humble overview of the UFO issue to the press in early August of that year.[16] The impression was exactly what was wanted: a hard-working, open-minded Air Force, laboring to solve the (now) 14% of reports which were unknowns. Once again, the right sort of man for the job was on the job. Ruppelt himself left the service in the fall and moved to California to take a position in the aircraft industry. Immediately, the press jumped on him. Never shy about talking, he did.[17] Ruppelt was, at that freshly-retired moment, still the Air Force loyalist (in this he never changed) and gave a fine set of Grudge-like comments. Some of this was

Left: Ed Ruppelt; Center: Bob Olsson; Right: Kerry Rothstein

because Donald Keyhoe had just published his book *Flying Saucers from Outer Space*,[18] which was very critical of the Air Force's project and, by implication, Ruppelt himself. While he referred to Keyhoe's accusations as "nonsense", the rest of the interview was in harmony with the tone we have been describing. This all was, in some ways, an ideal situation for the Air Force. But it could not go on: Donald Keyhoe, and the phenomenon itself, would not let it.

On the other hand, not all current and former personnel toed the line. Al Chop was also in California when the press found him in October. His comments were nearly at perfect opposition to a Robertsonian approach.[19] Chop strongly defended Keyhoe. He strongly defended the Washington, DC, radar tower operators and observers in general. He criticized flimsy Blue Book "explanations." Asked for his general take on the phenomenon, he was forthright:

There is too much unexplained. Granting the reliability of the observers, one draws the conclusion that they are faster than anything on earth, are controlled, can hover, can go from hover to thousands of miles per hour in a split second. Where they come from we don't know. But they are here, have been since one was first seen over Sweden in 1945, and probably are from somewhere else. With no earthly explanation, what else is there to think, if I believe in the creditability of the persons reporting?

Happily for the Air Force, this story got only local publication.

Blue Book soldiered on much as before, but the old process was gradually shutting down. Air Defense Command's 4602nd Air Intelligence Service Squadron (AISS), which had personnel at many major air bases in the continental United States, would provide UFOB (Unidentified Flying Object) officers to do the actual field investigations and interview witnesses.[20] The UFOB officers would send reports to ADC headquarters at Ent AFB in Colorado Springs. Other times the reports were apparently so worthless that they were not sent at all. Then a decision would be made as to whether the case was solved or not. If solved, the case might never reach Blue Book. This mechanism was theoretically meant to increase efficiency (minimizing long-distance travel), and to reduce the burden on Blue Book (less personnel needed, and fewer cases to closely scrutinize). The theory in some ways made sense.

The practice was more mixed. UFOB officers varied in skill and commitment, and any sort of thorough training program for them was economically out of the question. Incentive to be a UFOB officer (unless one had a personal interest in the phenomenon) was also poor. This was not a prized assignment. Because many persons were involved in case judgements (the UFOB officer, his base command, the ADC UFOB coordinator, ADC higher command itself) *before* Blue Book even became aware of a case, Blue Book slowly became more and more irrelevant. The level of irrelevance altered with the moment, however. There were times when the word was out to rush case reports to Blue Book. These rush orders tended to be coincident with how worried the Pentagon people were as to whether Donald Keyhoe could use the cases against them in the war for Congress.[21] Sometimes the cases were just too big to ignore, or to delay a response. But sometimes, as Allen Hynek later said, some of the best cases never made it past ADC at all.[22] Much, much later in the game, the final Blue Book chief told James McDonald (in 1966) that in his tenure (then 1963-1966) he had *never* gotten a case from ADC![23]

That is what the humans were doing. What was the phenomenon doing? In January of 1953, while the Robertson Panel was doing its covert best to "remove the aura of mystery surrounding the UFO phenomenon," the UFOs were doing their quasi-overt best to enhance that aura. The month had seven "official" unknowns and at least three more that rivaled them:

January 1, Craig, Montana:[24] A witness had a close encounter (about 200-300 feet away at nearest) with a silver disk. Conditions were such that he felt confident of the distance to the object across its course of flight. That allowed him to estimate a speed of greater than 3000 miles per hour. (Blue Book: Unidentified).

January 8, Moses Lake, Washington:[25] Sixty members of the 82nd Fighter-Interceptor Squadron of Larson AFB observed a green disk soundlessly wobbling and swerving as it moved along a southwesterly path for 51 minutes. It moved against the wind. (BB: Unidentified).

January 10, Sonoma, California:[26] Two credible witnesses (one was a retired Air Force colonel) witnessed a very astounding feat of flying by a flattened disk-like object. The disk produced three rapid 360-degree loops, completing each in 3 seconds or less; it flew two 90-degree (right angle) turns (one left, then one right to return to its original direction); it then slowed to a hovering stop, and rapidly accelerated, and showed this maneuver twice; lastly it rapidly disappeared upwards. Hynek said that he and the others were severely stretched by this case.[27] But, in time, they, as always, "let it go." (BB: Unidentified).

January 17, northern Japan:[28] this date refers to when the case exploded in bold headlines in several major U.S. newspapers. Exactly how the leak occurred is not known, but, once again, air operations in the Japan-Korea area *did* leak and caused trouble for Pentagon management. The actual observations took place (mainly) on December 29, and appear under the designations of "Chitose AFB" and "Misawra," Japan. The phenomenon was described as like a "circular, ferris-wheel disc-type with rotational red, green, and white lights." Five military witnesses watched the lights from Chitose. They viewed the phenomenon through binoculars, as well. Operations at Misawra had called Chitose to report that they had a radar contact heading their way, but whether what was seen at Chitose and the radar were the same, cannot be said. Because this object barely moved (and was small), not much can be claimed for it. But what made it particularly interesting was that crew members in five in-air flights also claimed to see something. And, one of the pilots was one of the most decorated airmen of WWII, Colonel Donald Blakeslee. Blakeslee said: "the object appeared to be a cluster of lights rotating slowly in a counterclockwise direction or from E to W. The object was unusual in its color effects. Its body, whose shape can only be assumed to be circular, gave off three, red-white-green . . . ." Colonel Blakeslee went on to describe three beams that projected some distance from the parent body. What is missing in the case is a precise statement of whether the object's disappearance to the west was faster than a typical astronomical body "rotating on the celestial sphere." One detail eliminated the possibility of an astronomical object with unusual optical effects. Blakeslee said that when he first saw the object, he was flying below its altitude. He then began a rapid climb and was able to achieve the same altitude as the unknown. Whether all that was explainable or not, the U.S. papers thought it was sensational and screamed out "Mystery Flying Discs Sighted over No. Japan."[29] Blue Book was less enthusiastic. It first wrote the case off as "Jupiter," then scratched that out and substituted "Venus." One thing is certain: the Air Force wished its heroes would stop seeing UFOs and then talking about them.

Colonel Donald Blakeslee

January 17, Guatemala City, Guatemala:[30] The witness saw a brilliant greenish-gold flattened sphere sail along horizontally, come to a hover point and rise straight up, stop again, and then resume horizontal flight at the new altitude with the same direction and speed. This geometric flying baffled Blue Book and the case was classed: Unknown.

January 28, Point Mugu Naval Air Missile Center, California;[31] and in air over Malibu, California;[32] and in air over Albany, Georgia:[33] Over Point Mugu, witnesses to a missile launch saw, shortly thereafter, a flat, white disk flying higher than a jet plane in the area, then overtake and pass that plane at much greater speed. (BB: Unidentified). Over Malibu, Northrop test pilot Rex Hardy and two crewmen saw four aluminum-colored circular objects travelling in a flight pattern. The test pilot estimated their size as similar to a B-36 bomber and their speed to be in excess of 1000 miles per hour. Over Albany, a jet fighter on a training mission encountered a brilliant light that took on a triangular formation and then split in two with one triangle above the other. On the ground, Moody AFB had both the fighter and the "impossible" object on radar.

Things did not stay so busy and irritating to Blue Book as the year went on, of course. Still, incidents were reported over Los Alamos, Oak Ridge, Hanford, the Savannah River Nuclear Plant,[34] and several times at Holloman AFB in New Mexico.[35] Several photographic cases came in to Blue Book. In five of those cases, after looking at the photos, they either lost or could not locate them. Included in those five were *both* photos they considered "unidentified."[36] We may make anything we want out of this information (carelessness, incompetency, conspiracy, theft), but none of it sounds like a professional and disciplined pursuit of the truth.

One film that they managed to retain was 30 feet of gun-camera footage taken by Captain Roderick Thompson. Three jets out of Luke AFB, Arizona, witnessed the object and its contrail, and one of the F-84s attempted to get nearer.[37] At closest approach the pilot reported that the object looked like a very thin sharp-nosed craft, possibly ejecting twin vapor trails. The gun-camera film could not distinguish the object itself. This event was on March 3. Ed Ruppelt was still at Blue Book, and he and Olsson looked fairly hard at the case. The check on other flights showed nothing, and the object had to be at 50,000 feet or higher. It seemed unlikely that some advanced spook plane had wandered all the way over from Edwards AFB in California. No other explanation fit. Ruppelt

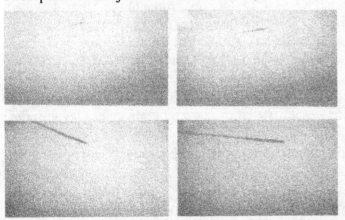

Luke A.F.B. Film

et al. initially marked the case "Unknown." Later, someone re-did the records and "explained" it as "a vapor trail formed by two unknown aircraft." The change to the records and the basis of this explanation were inappropriate, as the pilot reported only one craft, and it would require two aircraft, one placed perfectly behind the other at all times during the sighting, to create the twin trails with a needle-nosed leading edge. And the distinction between an "Unknown" and "two unknown aircraft" is naively creative and demonstrates the measures they were willing to take to eliminate the concept that an aerial object's identification could simply be "unknown."

March 14, off Honshu, Sea of Japan:[38] A ten-man crew of a Navy P2V-5 patrol plane was witness to a particularly strange and seemingly inexplicable experience. Captain Robert Wooten was ordering his gunnery personnel to stand down and secure their turrets, when

> Immediately, the copilot began tapping my leg and pointing aghast at something off the port bow. I looked and saw nothing immediately, but in a matter of about 10 seconds, I too, saw what was causing his amazement. At what appeared to be very close aboard, there was an electrifying display of colored lights. They were in groups of from 4 to 6, lasting only about 3 seconds, and would reappear in about 10 seconds. Sometimes they would be in two groups appearing simultaneously. Each group and the succeeding group had no marked relative motion as if it were flying near the same speed as we were, and maintaining a relative position. They did, however, move aft along the port side and disappear when just off the wing after a period I estimate to be about 5 minutes.

> When I first saw the display, I countered my order to secure the turrets, alerted the gun crews, had all personnel not otherwise occupied to man lookout posts, and had radar concentrate in the area.

> The radar operator first reported a target about 45 degrees off the port bow at 7 miles. This, he reported had every appearance of an aircraft and had very little relative motion. I had him repeat bearings and they coincided with the appearance of the lights as they slowly moved aft. At one point he reported that they appeared to be two targets which then merged.

> It is estimated that approximately 20 groups appeared making a total of from 90 to 100 separate lights. Without regard to distance, they appeared to be the size of an orange and to be about a foot apart. When two groups appeared, one would be about two feet above the other and the top group slightly aft the bottom.

Blue Book admitted it was an "Unidentified." Was this 'The Mother of all Foo Fighter cases,' or flashing lights on an otherwise invisible craft?

April 12, Sweetwater, Nevada:[39] The crew of a flight out of Stead AFB observed ten flat, round, metallic objects that flew in a loose formation and at moderate-to-fast speeds. Allen Hynek, back at Blue Book, got extremely excited about this case and wrote to Lt. Olsson: "I like to see Menzel explain this one!" Apparently, someone did. It was written off in Blue Book records as "aircraft." Menzel's book (*Flying Saucers*)[40] was achieving quite a bit of favorable publicity in the science-oriented press, as popularizers like Patrick Moore said that "the recent book by Dr. D. H. Menzel has pricked the bubble once and for all. Flying saucers are neither spaceships nor terrestrial aircraft. They are natural phenomena."[41] Simultaneously, Project Blue Book and Air Force Scientific Advisory Board member Joseph Kaplan consigned a proposal by Menzel to explain all UFO cases by high-school level optical demonstrations to the trash bin.[42]

In late September of 1953, another of Menzel's claims (astronomers never see UFOs, because they are smart enough not to be fooled by them) came, once again, unglued. Well-known Baltimore, Maryland, astronomer Dr. James Bartlett was doing a bit of recreational sky-gazing (with binoculars) from his home. He saw four large lights. "They came from the noses of two enormous craft which more than filled the binoculars." There were cabins in the noses and portholes along the sides of the hulls. Believing that they must be some kind of U.S. weapon, Bartlett did not report the sighting either to the military or to the press. Later, after the next great wave in 1957, Dr. Bartlett told a group of astronomers what he had seen. And on the other side of the country, the Air Force was having its own experience of an unknown detected both by radar and visually over Palmdale, California, at essentially the same time (September 28).[43]

August 5, Ellsworth AFB, South Dakota, and Bismarck, North Dakota:[44] This became one of the busiest cases in the record, and one of the messiest investigations and analyses. Initially, a UFO was reported to Ellsworth by Ground Observer Corps (GOC) observers. Air Traffic Control received a puzzling radar return, and airmen arrived and saw a rapidly moving light, which then left the area. Next, the GOC said that the light was back again. Once again, airmen spotted it. A plane was vectored in, but the pilot did not see the light. However, ground radar achieved good tracks for both plane and UFO (now moving away to the northwest). The pilot finally picked it up visually and gave chase, seeing it as a silver object. Unable to catch up, he then returned to base. GOC meanwhile had spotted both plane and object. A second F-84 took off and got a visual, but not a radar contact. Ground radar showed both going north. The pilot could not close, and he turned back. Ellsworth/Blackhawk then alerted Bismarck that the north-flying UFO was headed their way. Bismarck then spotted the unknown visually.

This event was right at the end of Ruppelt's career, and he wanted one last field trip, so off he went. He seems to have talked to most of the people on the Ellsworth/Blackhawk (i.e. the South Dakota) end of the experience. He came away so impressed that he not only put it down as an unknown, but said it was "the best" in his later book. Sometime afterwards, for unknown reasons, Allen Hynek took a trip to this area, going to the North Dakota end (Bismarck) instead. There, he interviewed several persons and wrote that the case was a) bunk and b) an embarrassment and a security nightmare because the Air Force had three hours of continual sighting and could not identify what was up there cruising around.[45] Hynek's second point is easy to agree to. His first point is not anywhere near so, due to his failure to interview several of the most important witnesses. Donald Menzel reviewed the case in his second book, *The World of Flying Saucers*, and used only Ruppelt's facts. He proceeded to explain the rapid, sky-crossing object as the star Capella.[46] Hynek later did his own "Menzel" by denying that anyone had the object on radar, despite not having talked to the South Dakota operators.[47] Years later, the Colorado "Scientific Study" looked at the case. They somehow read only Hynek's write-up and not Ruppelt's report, and ended up saying that the case was multiple misidentifications of Arcturus, Capella, and also Jupiter and Betelgeuse.[48] One wonders what Ruppelt would have said about his "best case." A final small point about all this: whoever was in charge of making up the records lists for the project labeled the case "Bismarck, South Dakota," just one more piece of data that illustrates the quality of the people and their concern for this job.

At the opposite end of the spectrum were the aviation design geniuses and test pilots of Lockheed Aircraft Corporation. In more than one instance in 1953, they sighted unknowns during flights.[49] One of the cases was pictured in the company newsletter. Another involved arguably Lockheed's greatest designer, Kelly Johnson, creator of the U-2 spyplane. Johnson maintained his fascination with UFOs throughout his life, later taking part in a quiet "private" study of the subject for President Lyndon Johnson.[50]

Left: Kelly Johnson Right: Pilot Gary Powers

MYSTERY OBJECT — By super enlarging, Lockheed's photo department salvaged this picture from tiny movie camera print. Film was taken from T-33 at extremely high altitude, but object was too distant for good picture.

Despite all of those incidents, things were quiet for the Air Force, since most of the incidents were within the military-industrial complex and had minimal publicity (particularly *national* publicity). The one person who could change that was Donald Keyhoe. His article in *Look* magazine[51] was sensational. It was composed of extracts from his soon-to-be-in-stores book, *Flying Saucers from Outer Space*, and featured all the Air Force-released cases. *Look*, sensing its sensationalism, sent page proofs to the Pentagon in mid-September. The powers were not pleased. Ruppelt was chewed out (unjustly) by a Pentagon colonel for releasing those cases (he did not).[52] Then Al Chop (whose hands the releases formally passed through) was visited and given an earful. The actual individuals who authorized the release of cases were high in the Pentagon, as we have seen.

When *Look* went to press in October, its editors added a few Air Force-friendly statements at the beginning, which included an assurance that the U.S. was not being invaded from outer space. When Keyhoe's book arrived shortly thereafter, it made an even greater impact in some quarters, particularly because Al Chop wrote a very strong letter (printed on the book's back cover, and reproduced in the appendix of this book), that all of the Air Force cases that Keyhoe cited were legitimate and released to Keyhoe as official project files according to a policy allegedly in practice at that time.[53] It was a very "silent" policy, however, and was clearly in favor of, and aimed at, facilitating Keyhoe. This book had worldwide impact, and we know that key figures in the UFO investigations of at least two countries (Australia[54] and Brazil[55]) were influenced by it. The CIA's Chief of Operations, OSI, General Philip Strong, was tasked with reading and evaluating the book. He wrote to Marshall Chadwell that the book was readable but greatly misleading.[56]

Donald Keyhoe

General Strong fingered Chop as a serious element in the problem, which was (mainly) criticism of the Air Force policy of concealing information. (One wonders how Strong could have written that this was "misleading" with a straight face, having participated in the Robertson Panel himself.) All references to

Howard Robertson

the CIA were noted, with a bit of relief that nothing major seemed to have leaked. Strong suggested that the CIA not worry any more about it. However, a second CIA memo, in late December, said that any Air Force policy that allowed the release of case file information was asking for trouble, just like they had received from the Keyhoe book.[57] The document quotes an interesting remark by Lt. Colonel Harry Johnson (Chief of CIA-OSI's Electronics Branch and the officer who had quizzed the Air Force as to the current status): "if it turns out that these things (UFOBs) are space things or long-range aircraft from another country, ADC is the (Air Force) Command that would have to take action." So, both the *big* concerns were still very much alive.

One last matter concerning the CIA: a puzzle not answered. After the Robertson Panel (at which none of the panelists showed any interest in any of the actual sightings other than wanting to watch the two films), Howard Robertson himself requested that

Blue Book send to him at Cal Tech their best cases as they came up.[58] This actually went on for several months in 1953, and we do not know what Robertson did with, or said about, them. But why? Why did this man who stated that there was nothing in the phenomenon (only in the public reaction to it) want to see the best reports? Despite everything, the phenomenon itself had *some* sort of interest to him.

Captain Walter Karig

Near the end of the year, the Navy, or at least one of its officers, Captain Walter Karig, fired another salvo across the Air Force's bow. This was an article, "Operation UFO, The Official Truth about Flying Saucers," published in the well-read newspaper insert, *The American Weekly*.[59] In the article, Karig spoke of Secretary of the Navy Kimball's sighting and the Office of Naval Research UFO probe. Washington D.C.'s "Merry-go-round" was not written off as weather phenomena but was said to be unexplained. A strong "glass half-full" tone was presented, emphasizing the 20% unexplained remaining even after study. Even the possibility of "men from Mars" was broached. Though not grossly pointed out, the piece could be read as a statement of flat opposition to the Air Force's public view.

The next three years were extensions of the transition that took place in 1953. The frequency of spectacular cases was down in the United States though up in the rest of the world. In the real world of

Los Alamos Nuclear Rocket Program

intelligence concerns, the Soviets had activated a multistage rocket project ("USSR-1," 1954),[60] NACA conceived the design characteristics of an X-15 type spy plane,[61] and defense analysts calculated that ICBMs would have an approximate 20-mile targeting error, but with the H-bomb that would be "no problem."[62] In 1955, the Air Force and the Army took their own "war" over missile development before Congress.[63] Ike suggested an ICBM ban to the U.S.S.R. (summarily rejected),[64] Los Alamos produced a secret report claiming the feasibility of nuclear-powered missiles,[65] and von Braun's satellite group claimed that they could launch a satellite almost any time.[66] In 1956, the U-2 spyplane began actual flights under CIA project control,[67] von Braun launched a three-stage Redstone rocket to 700 miles,[68] Bell Aviation's X-2 flew to 126,000 feet at a speed of 2094 mph,[69] and USSR-1 was ready.[70] The following year, Sputnik was launched into orbit.

Meanwhile, at Project Blue Book, case reports slowly rose (486 in 1954; 541 in 1955; 667 in 1956), and "unknowns" went the opposite way (46; 25; 15).[71] One would have to make an extensive study of the nature and quality of incoming files (for example, to see if the quality of observers, pilots et al., changed) and the reasonableness of the explanations assigned to cases to try to give an honest characterization of what was going on here. But, at the moment, it seems justifiable to say that upon reading a variety of cases in the files, the use of certain explanatory solutions seems to get "liberal," to say the least.

August 12, 1954, Maxwell AFB, Alabama:[72] The ATC tower observed an initially stationary object which then accelerated to a high velocity across the sky. It then returned along its path and reassumed its original hovering position. The object then slowly dimmed out. Blue Book wrote: "Mars, astronomical." One cannot imagine what the witnesses (both ground and air) would think if they were told this.

August 14, 1955, Minnesota:[73] Two adults reported a shiny aluminum-colored object, shaped like a balloon, which had been compressed or flattened at top and bottom, that silently moved against the wind, and then climbed rapidly out of sight. The object was marked with a V-shaped coloration on the bottom, and had a row of what looked like dark "Pullman" windows around its middle horizontal axis. Blue Book wrote: "Star."

May 6, 1956, Oklahoma City, Oklahoma:[74] Several adults, the primary ones were an Air Force engineer and a MIT graduate, reported an intensely bright, orange-colored object, shaped like a tea-cup (no handle) oriented on its side (roughly like a half-moon is drawn). The rim of the "cup" was filled with many flashing lights. The object hovered, then moved rapidly, as it darted and zig-zagged around the sky, and finally disappeared to the west. The object was the apparent size of a dime held at arm's length. Blue Book wrote: the star Capella.

July 23, 1956, England, Arkansas:[75] Multiple witnesses, one with binoculars, reported an object which seemed to change shape (initially oval, then flat, then to a diamond configuration). The object had a red light at the bottom. When the object would move, it left a trail of white smoke approximately six times its length. Observers guessed its speed at 70-100 knots. Blue Book wrote: the star Spica.

August 24, 1956, Westerville, Ohio:[76] One witness, a civilian, reported a round object of red coloration and large apparent size (that of a basketball at arm's length). The object appeared stationary, but shrunk in place to the size of a softball. Blue Book wrote: color suggests that this was Mars.

December 9, 1956, Woodstock, Minnesota:[77] One witness, a civilian, reported that an object which was shaped like a half-sphere (flat side on top) and colored fiery orange-red, rested in the sky, then tipped slowly and moved northwest. It was quite large (the witness said larger than the apparent size of a baseball held at arm's length). Blue Book wrote: Mars.

Anyone reading these evaluations with a fresh and open mind would be amazed by, and suspicious of, these types of explanations. Dr. James McDonald, when he went through Blue Book files in the later 1960s, went well-past doubt to actual anger about these so-called evaluations.[78] But, letting the emotions go, how could such absurdities get into the record? How could someone even come up with such ideas, which in some cases, almost completely ignored the witness testimony? Dr. Hynek said that, as chief astronomical consultant, it was his job to come up with astronomical "solutions," even if they were "stretched." Sometimes, he said, he stretched too far.[79] But the absurdities listed above probably were not those of an overly-imaginative Hynek. Later on, Hynek would occasionally come across such an obviously erroneous solution, or be confronted by someone regarding one, and say: that was not *my* evaluation. This could easily happen because, particularly in the mid-1950s, there was a desire to get all the cases solved regardless; and Hynek was not available as much (he was preparing to be part of the Smithsonian Astrophysical Observatory's Moonwatch Project to plot the upcoming satellite orbits, courtesy of the Soviets).[80] Someone else at Wright-Patterson was "doing a Menzel"—that is, checking the "star charts," seeing if anything bright was in the appropriate direction, assuming sky conditions will create spectacular mirages, and writing things off. This method of using what Hynek later called a tool-box of explanations made Blue Book analysis much easier.[81] A new addition to the tool-box that began to be exploited at this time was ball lightning, even though the phenomenon was very poorly understood scientifically, and many scientists were not sure it even existed.[82]

With all of that, it is a real miracle that any cases avoided the tool-box and emerged as "unidentifieds" at all. Few did. Blue Book bragged that by the end of 1956, their pace of explaining cases was at 98%.[83]

Charles Hardin

218

With Captain Charles Hardin running the Project with a forced normalcy (of result, anyway), *that* end of the problem of UFOs was solved. The 4602nd continued its mixed quality case investigations, Wright-Patterson continued to be closed to reporters, and attempts were made to address sources of trouble. (for example, the Ground Observer Corps was a massive UFO "leak", since it was composed mainly of civilians. Questions of whether to forbid GOC personnel from talking came early.)[84] Generally, citizens were viewed as unhelpful actors in the narrative, "unreliable," and in one case, sarcastically laughed off as drunk.[85] Blue Book complained about the citizens all the way up the intelligence ladder to General Millard Lewis, who would succeed John Samford as Director of Intelligence in 1956.[86] The FBI continued to monitor specific individuals, such as "contactees" like George Adamski,[87] who had a "no war/no bomb/utopian commune economy" message, and civilian UFO researchers like Coral Lorenzen and Robert Gribble.[88] In one heavy-handed instance, the Lorenzens were told that

General Millard Lewis

their appearance on a national TV program was "indefinitely postponed out of consideration for the Air Force."[89] Of course, at the Pentagon, no longer were any actual case materials cleared for news reporters or writers. As far as the atmosphere at Blue Book was concerned, Allen Hynek later said, in his usual civilized way:

> The term of office of each of the directors of Project Blue Book was never very long; turnover was frequent. The rank of the officers was relatively low—a further indication of the low level of priority given the project.
>
> With each new director there came some new viewpoint and methodology. But in the Air Force, or the military in general, one takes orders, and the unspoken orders from the Pentagon, stemming from the recommendation of the Robertson Panel, seemed clearly to be to "hold the fort," to "play down the UFO subject," and not to "rock the boat." And these directors were all, in turn, good officers: they knew what the orders were and they followed them well—perhaps too well.[90]

On the other side of the mirror, there was, of course, one civilian who was undaunted in causing trouble: Don Keyhoe. It is a little surprising that a single book (*Flying Saucers from Outer Space*) should cause so much concern. But it did. In March, a Pentagon spokesman told *American Aviation* that: "The Pentagon definitely attributes the latest rush of saucer reports to Major Keyhoe's book."[91]

Simultaneously, the Air Force's congressional liaison, General Joe Kelly, told Senator Francis Case that despite Keyhoe's claims: "All information on sightings of aerial phenomena, including our conclusions, is unclassified and available to the public."[92]

Keyhoe was astounded at the nerve of the lie. However, he decided to proceed as if it were true. Keyhoe went to Public Information Officer Lieutenant Robert White at the Pentagon and asked for the last three months' reports, since Kelly had just told the Senator that such information was open to the public. White said "no." Why? White stated: "There's no change in policy. General Kelly made an error." Keyhoe rebutted that the Pentagon should retract General's statement. The Lieutenant asked Keyhoe to keep him out of that argument. Kelly never directly admitted to any errors in his comments to Case, but a

General Joe W. Kelly

letter to the Senator mentioned something vague about policies being in a state of flux.[93] This "game" that the Air Force had gotten themselves into was difficult, just as any game based upon the necessity of manipulating and hiding information would be. With a junkyard dog like Keyhoe hounding them, it was especially difficult. As for Kelly, he ultimately contradicted himself in letters to congressmen and to Keyhoe's NICAP organization so completely and publicly that Keyhoe was able to publish that fact, without fear of contradiction, in one of NICAP's first bulletins (January 1958).[94] Kelly was not heard from on the subject thereafter, and a new Pentagon spokesman took over.

Whether Keyhoe had anything to do with what followed or not, the Air Force issued a revision of JANAP 146 (C) in March 1954.[95] It specifically ordered that civilian pilot reports of unidentified flying objects be reported through the CIRVIS procedure, which in practical terms meant report the incident, put the report through to ADC, and do not talk about it. As a possible case in point, three civilian air crews saw something streak across the sky over Pennsylvania on September 27, 1954. Keyhoe learned the name of one of the pilots and contacted him. The pilot refused to talk, specifically citing the JANAP restriction.[96]

Also in March, the Pentagon, in response to a talk before the Greater Miami Aviation Association by prominent UFO witness and airline pilot William Nash, not only denied what Nash said but complained about the "rash of magazine and newspaper articles, radio and television shows, and a couple of books on flying saucers." The Pentagon blamed those articles and shows for the increase in UFO sightings.[97] At almost the same time, Battelle Memorial Institute finally completed "Blue Book Special Report #14,"[98] their statistical evaluation of hundreds of project reports, and the Air Force began wondering how best to use it. When it was released about a year later, an Air Force memorandum said that it was done in accordance with the attitude on information release recommended by the "Scientific Panel" (i.e. the Robertson Panel).[99] The Air Force had high hopes that this would be the bomb necessary to flatten civilian interest and objectors like Keyhoe.

Keyhoe met the retired Edward Ruppelt in April of 1954, and that began a series of exchanges of information (mostly Keyhoe asking Ruppelt for information and support). Ruppelt told Keyhoe of some cases he had not heard about and gave him his standard opinion (when he was not talking as an officer) on the subject: that he was not a "believer" like Fournet was, but if there *were* actual flying disks, then they must be from another planet. For Ruppelt, whether we were dealing with "disks" (i.e. technological craft) was never proven.[100] Keyhoe accepted their difference of opinion and maintained the relationship. Ruppelt published a fairly conservative article in *TRUE* magazine in May,[101] which still displeased certain persons in the Air Force despite its conservatism.[102] Nevertheless, as he got further from his duty days, Ruppelt's published views became less, as he said, "in the Air Force line," and more a sort of middle-of-the-road "here are the facts as I know them; you decide." Ruppelt made a visit to Blue Book in July to gather information for his upcoming book (as an ex-officer he was allowed access). He was told that all publicity on the subject was controlled by a Lieutenant Colonel from the Pentagon. Ruppelt said this about the Blue Book evaluations: "They claim to have gotten the unknowns down to about 10% but from what I saw this was just due to a more skeptical attitude. The reports are just as good as the ones we got and their analysis procedures are a hell of a lot worse."[103]

Near the end of 1954, people within the Air Force were beginning to receive notice of the huge upswing of cases being reported from Europe (and later, from South America). The phenomenon was about to engage in its most active and widespread flap ever, and, for a change, the United States was not at the focus. The Air Force decided that it was still Keyhoe's fault.[104] In a memo about the beginnings of the wave, they attributed "the majority of these sightings for two basic reasons." One, "the European press" (apparently regarded by the Air Force as sensationalist); and Two, "Mr. D. Keyhoe's book." In December, a memo reiterated the Keyhoe theory and added that there have been a lot of meteors seen in Europe recently.[105] The fact that the 1954 wave featured cases of landings with entities (reports that Keyhoe and his book absolutely abhorred)[106] just added to the preposterous nature of these "intelligence" reactions. Nevertheless, Keyhoe's book was just one nuisance, and, with proper handling, even it would "go away." And that is what happened the next year. At the end of 1954 Eisenhower himself stepped up to the plate and announced that there were no such things as flying saucers.[107]

FLYING SAUCERS:

AN ANALYSIS OF THE AIR FORCE PROJECT BLUE BOOK SPECIAL REPORT No. 14

In 1955, a slow year, thankfully, from the Air Force's view, the Pentagon and Blue Book spent time preparing themselves for civilian attacks and getting ready to release their ultimate weapon: Blue Book Special Report #14 (hereafter Blue Book 14). The preparations took two main forms: subscribing to, and reading, the civilian newsletters;[108] and creating a card file on the main cases used by Keyhoe[109] in his famous books. When the Australian Air Force inquired as to how the USAF evaluated *Flying Saucers from Outer Space*,[110] the USAF replied that it was misleading and they should not trust it. The Aussies accepted this and decided to send copies of their difficult cases to the Pentagon,[111] rather than establish an

Secretary of the Air Force Donald Quarles

analytical system themselves. In October, Blue Book 14 was released with much fanfare and an accompanying statement by Secretary of the Air Force Donald Quarles.[112] Major media hailed Quarles and the release as a death knell for the saucers.

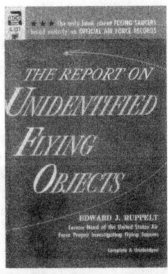

THE REPORT ON UNIDENTIFIED FLYING OBJECTS

EDWARD J. RUPPELT

In 1956 the "UFO Empire" struck back. Ed Ruppelt's watershed insider book, *The Report on Unidentified Flying Objects*, hit the stands.[113] A film company obtained permission from the owners of the Great Falls and Tremonton movie films to use their copies as the anchors of a UFO-sympathetic documentary dramatized around the role of Al Chop and the Washington, D.C., sightings.[114] And Don Keyhoe began to assault Congress in earnest. Despite constantly jumping from one side to the other of the "they're real/they're not" fence, Ruppelt's book was a sensation for many readers who did not know what to believe in all the contradictory information that was being released. Keyhoe's *Flying Saucers from Outer Space* had made its impact due to Al Chop's letter which authenticated it. Now here was the real thing itself: the Air Force's own "man" of the project. Many people read this book and became believers in the phenomenon, despite Ruppelt's style and careful language. One could never judge where the Captain himself stood, but it was very easy to take all he wrote and build a UFO-sympathetic position in one's own mind.[115] Fortunately for the Air Force, with the exception of a few public lectures and TV appearances, Ruppelt did not become a public figure or an ongoing nuisance. It was, really, just his book that was the problem.

Ed Ruppelt

The movie "UFO" had an even smaller impact. Despite claims heard over and over that publicity, like Ruppelt's book and the movie, caused UFO flaps, reports did not go up at all.[116] Still, the Air Force knew the movie was coming and feared a public flare of excitement. The concern began when they were taken completely by surprise by Douglas Aircraft Company. Douglas' Missile Engineering Department had made an analysis of the Great Falls, Montana, film of 1950 incidental to a study of publications dealing with unconventional propulsion schemes.[117] Douglas said that it had received the film from Greene-Rouse Studios, which was producing a movie. The Douglas analysis was done by Dr. Robert M.L. Baker.[118] Baker and Douglas rejected both Air Force (and Robertson) "solutions," saying that the films showed neither jet exhausts/reflections nor birds. This horse had apparently already run far out of

Greene-Rouse Studios meeting. Left to Right: Edward Ruppelt, Clarence Greene, and Air Force radar expert Wendell Swanson

Great Falls frame of two balls of light flying over a building

the barn, and the Air Force could only hope that, since it was "only" a movie, little harm could be done. To be as prepared as possible for any collateral damage, George Gregory (then running Blue Book as Captain Hardin's replacement) asked ATIC photo experts to compare the Air Force's own footage with that shown in the movie;[119] he also asked the ATIC scientific intelligence ace, A. Francis Arcier, to compile a complete file on the cases used in the film,[120] and to collect all movie reviews and even movie posters. Gregory specifically stated his concerns that the movie would set off an uproar "similar to that which the USAF was subjected to in 1952 with regards to UFOs as a result of the unwarranted sensationalism generated by so-called 'UFO experts,' writers, and publishers."[121] This was, of course, the concern of the Robertson Panel. Note also, however, the emotionalism that had crept in. Keyhoe et al. were the enemy.

The Air Force was very fortunate with the release of the movie, "*UFO*." It was, in the end, "just a movie." As a documentary-style dramatization, it still has great interest for UFOlogists, but as exciting entertainment for the general public, no. Keyhoe himself created far longer and greater concern. Donald Quarles and the presentation of Blue Book 14 as a death-hammer-blow to UFOs riled Keyhoe, and he decided to play on a more serious playing field as well. In April 1956, Keyhoe wrote Senator Harry Byrd of Virginia.[122] Keyhoe resided in Virginia so that beginning was a natural. His long letter blasted everything about Air Force actions that could be tied to secrecy, and took apart Blue Book 14. In the end he asked Byrd to engage in a congressional investigation. Major Keyhoe then said: send this to the Air Force for their response, and—typically aggressive Keyhoe—I will call you Monday. Keyhoe then leaked the entire letter to the press.[123]

Byrd's office did send Keyhoe's letter to the Pentagon, and the Pentagon replied in the form of a letter from General Joe Kelly, about a month later.[124] (This was before Kelly was canned as the Pentagon's PR manager, as mentioned earlier.) Kelly politely dismissed both Keyhoe (a typical "well-meaning" person) and UFOs, citing Blue Book 14, the new hammer. Robertson-like verbiage filled the "conclusion" statements. One month later still, Byrd's office sent Kelly's response to Keyhoe. Keyhoe claimed to be shocked by Kelly's remarks, but that is hard to believe.[125] Still, it was "political" to say so, and to make hay out of the claim that not even a U.S. Senator could get a straight answer from the

Air Force. These actions, both those of Keyhoe and of the Pentagon, were straight applications of power in a face-to-face war. This war lasted until 1961 when the Air Force finally won due to private briefings with key Senators and Congressmen, who ultimately flatly rejected Keyhoe's pressures (one even violently so). The Senator Byrd episode was the war's first salvo, and the Pentagon and Blue Book quickly responded. As the years passed, the Air Force set up a five-man team, meeting regularly, to defeat Keyhoe's Congressional assaults.[126]

But in 1956 the war had just begun. In June, Congressman John Moss wrote the Secretary of the Air Force about UFOs (for reasons unknown, and perhaps having nothing directly to do with Keyhoe).[127] Colonel John Eriksen, an ATIC heavyweight and formerly high in the Pentagon, got the job of writing a response for Donald Quarles' signature. Quarles/Eriksen's reply to Moss was entirely about Blue Book 14, why the Air Force was not printing and handing copies out by the truckload, and that there was no intention of withholding any information (in Blue Book 14) from the American public. That much was true.

Up through 1956, Don Keyhoe could be of only occasional irritation to the Air Force, because he was only one man. He needed help. He needed an organization of people who would push the cause. In 1956, that organization did not exist. What did exist was a somewhat misdirected Washington, D.C., UFO organization named the National Investigation Committee on Aerial Phenomena (NICAP).[128] For various reasons, it was getting nowhere. But in late 1956, things would change. Keyhoe would soon agree to be its leader, and powerful (often ex-military) people would join him. By early 1957, the Air Force's private demon, NICAP/Keyhoe had arrived. But that would be next year and this study's next chapter. For now, we shall end this post-Robertson transition with a look at what the phenomenon itself was doing, and how some people other than the Air Force and Donald Keyhoe were talking about it.

It has been mentioned that 1954 was a boom year worldwide, but a mediocre one in the United States. Blue Book statistics indicate that the drop-off continued into 1955 and 1956. As already indicated, some of that decline was false and clearly attributable to egregiously bad "solutions." But it was true, as far as even worldwide records indicate, that 1955 was a particularly low year for "interesting unknowns." The year 1956 actually showed an up-tick in such cases, despite Blue Book's claims. Even in down years there were interesting incidents, however, and to give the reader a flavor of what was going on, and how the Air Force concluded the cases (if they even got them), a 1954 table sampling the sightings is presented on the next page. In a small number of cases, some textual commentary is important, as well.[129]

The St. Toms River, New Jersey, case has a bit of irony in it. This Blue Book investigation is one of the most thorough in the files and was done by Allen Hynek's graduate assistant, Jennie Zeidman (then Gluck).[130] Jennie is a fieldworker now well-known by many people in UFOlogy, and she is a terrific case investigator. Her report stretches several dozen pages and is replete with careful interviews and on-site measurements. There were 22 witnesses interviewed, only one of whom disagreed in any significant way from the others. With this much input from different sighting positions, the following picture emerged: three bright oval lights (white-to-pale-bluish end of the spectrum) moved about

Major Keyhoe and the current author's old NICAP membership card.

Jennie (Gluck) Zeidman

the sky, sometimes turning sharply and then flying off at tremendous speed. The average time for a witness' observation was 30 seconds to a minute. The lights were large and were estimated at between the apparent size of a baseball and a basketball at arm's length. Some witnesses viewed the objects through binoculars. By mapping all the locations, sighting directions, and elevation angles, a restricted fix on the objects' location in space was possible within a reasonable degree of confidence. This in turn allowed an estimate of size and velocity. Using *minimum* values for all of this, the numbers were still astounding: Altitude = 4 miles; Object diameter = 1500 feet; Velocity as objects broke off slower maneuvering and raced away = 90,000 mph. Doubtless error bars exist, although the witness locations and angle of view should be close. "Apparent size" is usually difficult, as people tend to think things are bigger than they are, and the actual size of something streaking across the sky is difficult to simulate. Still, the estimates point to large objects at about four miles of height, which accelerate extremely rapidly. Blue Book, doing something that it became infamous for, ignored large portions of the testimony, and the analysis concluded: "searchlight" (not even plural).

A Sampler of 1954 Blue Book Cases:

Place	Date	Witnesses	Object	Comments	Blue Book Conclusion
St. Thomas NJ	Jan 1	Military & civilian	3 oval lights	Over 20 witnesses saw objects; investigation excellent/ allowed triangulation (see text).	search light
Las Cruces NM	Jan 25	scientists	oval light	White Sands missile trackers triangulated glowing object (see text).	meteor
Tuscaloosa AL	Feb 1	scientists	5 oval objects	Winzen balloon scientists tracked another "balloon watcher" UFO case; photos taken.	balloon (!)
Puente, CA Marysville OH	Feb 1 Oct 22	multiple civilians	ovals and angel hair	Many people see object pass and air fill with a gossamer, which dissipated on touch (see text).	spider webs
Fresno CA	Mar 24	multi (plus)	metallic	Ruppelt told Keyhoe that Secretary of the Air Force Talbott had an in-air encounter. Case did not go to files.	(no case)
Fl. Coast Dallas, TX	Mar 25 May14	marine pilots	1 round 16 objects	Though both cases were noticed in papers, neither apparently made it to Blue Book.	(no cases)
Pitsfield ME	Apr 23	2 civilians	saucer with dome	Brilliant flashing light; sound like bees; stones moved on ground; flew out of sight.	unidentified
Washington DC	May12	Three Air Police	3 pairs of lights	Pairs of lights in formation passed over and made right angle turns and flew away.	unidentified
nr. Hanford WA	June 6 and 9	civilian police	orange yellow ball	6th: lights merged into large ball.* 9th: light hovered and just faded away.	insuff. data
Estacado TX	Jun 10	military pilots	white light	Light came down from high altitude, slowed, circled plane, blinked, and "went out."	unidentified
Labrador CAN	Jun 30	civilian aircrew	1 large, 6 small objects	Famous BOAC airliner case; objects seemed to change shape, and suddenly disappeared.	Mars (!)
AL/FL line	date unk	AF pilots & civils.	1 shiny object	Wingless object "solid disk" descended from great height; instant acceleration; reported to Air Force.**	(no case found)

* The policeman was told by the Air Force not to discuss the case.
** The pilot was William Coleman, who became the Pentagon PIO officer with the responsibility to debunk UFOs.

Las Cruces, New Mexico:[131] This evaluator fiasco has much the same flavor as the St. Tom's River case, but, in a way worse, since the measurers were White Sands scientists whose job *was* to observe and measure things. At about 10 p.m. the observers had set up their ballistic cameras to monitor a missile launch from White Sands. (There were several observers, and two "stations" play a role in this case.) One observer was located 17 miles northwest of the other. Observer 1 noticed a bright pulsing light to his northeast and immediately called the second person. Observer 2 said that he had it too. Thinking quickly, they decided to note the direction and angle of elevation of the object at each pulse. At one particularly bright pulse, seen and noted by both men, their notations anchored their two sets of data together. Later they were able to make a triangulated estimate of altitude, and, consequently, true rather than apparent velocity. At its brightest pulse, the object calculated to be twelve miles away from Observer 1 (or about nine miles high). Moving from one pulse-point to another, the object's velocity was around 12,000 miles per hour. Observer 1 told Clyde Tombaugh about this (Tombaugh was involved with all these observer teams as a leader), and Tombaugh insisted that he make a formal report. This the witness, reluctantly, did. The Observer was a graduate of Columbia University and was employed by the University of Chicago's Yerkes Observatory (many of the younger faculty and researchers got temporarily "loaned out" and stationed at White Sands et al. for this kind of work). In the report, he said that, "I have observed many thousands of meteors and I can definitely state that this object was not any kind of meteor." Blue Book received the report, sent on by Tombaugh. They wrote on the record sheet: "was a meteor."

Puente, California[132] and Marysville/Jerome, Ohio:[133] These cases are mentioned because they consist of many people seeing a UFO going overhead, and the object emitting or trailing some sort of substance. As the substance drifted down in great volumes, it draped itself over plants, power lines, etc. In both cases, unlike most similar claims in cases elsewhere, someone had the presence of mind not only to pick up some of the material, but to place it in a jar and seal it. Up to this point, this human behavior is perfectly natural, curious, and potentially helpful to the Air Force. In California, the jar-savers were regular citizens; in Ohio, they were grade school teachers. In both cases, it was not just the coincidence of the UFO with the "gossamer" that interested them, but the phenomenon that the wispy stuff just seemed to "disappear," or, perhaps, "sublimate" as a chemist would say. Touching it seemed to make it sublime faster; sealing it in a jar seemed to stop it. In both incidents, multiple persons are on record as witnessing this. All very peculiar, and hard-to-believe, admittedly, but there were the independent testimonies. The Air Force was interested in both cases but wrote them off as "spider webs" (due to the fact that certain spiders produce great globs of webbing within which small spiders take to the air and are thereby ecologically dispersed). There is no analysis (available anyway) of the materials in the jars themselves. Spontaneous dissipation of spider web protein does not ring true, in any event. What was this really about? Later, an Air Force engineer, then working for Battelle Memorial Institute, said they received a jarred specimen from the Jerome event for some "midnight" analysis. He did not know what the analyst found, but the material ultimately just disappeared.[134]

The year 1955 was definitely a time of fewer UFO sightings, but the phenomenon is so robust that even in sparse years there are many incidents worth noting. (A table with a sample of cases in shown on the next page.) One such sighting occurred off the coast of Newfoundland on July 5.[135] The encounter involved multiple pilots, other Air Force personnel, and radar. In the Blue Book files at least six airmen in different airplanes provided testimony. The event happened during an airborne refueling exercise, which explains why so many planes were available as witnesses. Ground radar picked up several objects. Some were in a distant cluster "flying" erratically, while a lone target seemed, initially, to hover. One pilot noticed this first, and thought that it was Venus. As more pilots became involved, however, this explanation faltered for a variety of simple reasons: the object was below one plane at first; the object was at large different horizon angles from different planes; at different times in the subsequent "chase," the UFO (looking like a bright light) moved at very high velocities, and it reversed

A Sampler of 1955 Blue Book Cases:[136]

Place	Date	Witnesses	Object	Comments	Blue Book Conclusion
Cochise NM	Jan 1	2 military	metallic disk	Object maneuvered near plane, paced it, then disappeared.	unidentified
Winterset IA	Jan 29	2 military	round light	Regularly flashing white light engaged in dogfight-like passes with aircraft.	possible aircraft
Miramar CA	Feb 2	1 military	polished sphere	Shiny white object descended & hovered, changed color, instantly accelerated w. trail.	unidentified
Hillcrest Hts, MD	Jun 26	4 civilian and military	yellow sphere	Brilliant object with trail; searchlights & lighting in National Airport went off as passed.*	balloon (!)
off New-foundland	July 5	multiple military	multi objects	One main and several secondary objects were seen visually & by radar (see text).	Venus plus weather
Long Island NY	Jul 29	multiple civilians	bright light	Group of astronomers watched light seem to circle objects deliberately (see text).	no case
Edmore MI	Sep 1	4 civilians	silver disk	GOC observers saw large disk pass which was followed by a fall of big pieces of "ash."	no case
Trans-caucasus	Mid Oct	2 civilians 2 military	triangle of lights	This is the ultra-hushed up Senator Richard Russell affair (see text).	no case
Minneapolis MN	Oct 20/21	Military and civilian	white oval	Observers on ground and in air saw luminous oval make right angle turns; radar track.	meteor plus weather
Williston FL	Oct 30	1 police	"washtub" shape	Policeman got to within (est.) 150 yards of object and got heat & numbing sensations. **	aircraft
Desert Hot Sprgs CA	Nov 14	2 civilian	white globe	2 prominent Banning citizens saw globe in flight which seemingly responded to light flashes.	no case
Lake City TN	Nov 20	6 military	2 oblong objects	Bright orange, semi-transparent objects flying erratically and at tremendous speed.	unidentified

* Blue Book completely ignored the light failures in the case, and the balloon launch used as a solution was in the wrong direction.
** Blue Book refused to address the officer's physiological sensations and looked only at a lights case of the next night!

course, ultimately climbing and fading away; it was seen doing the same motions by different air crews at the same time; and it was detectible by the ground radar in appropriate relation to the planes. The ground radar equipment was checked and found to be working properly, and the weather showed no indication of an "inversion" situation that would cause false images. Blue Book wrote "Venus" and "Weather effects," again caring little for the actual details reported. The CIA was less careless. They wrote:

> Essentially the 'object' was apparently simultaneously observed by a tanker aircraft (KC97) pilot (visually) [actually many others] and by a ground radar (type unknown) site (electronically). While such dual (visual and electronic) sightings of UFOs are reported from time to time, this particular report is somewhat unique in that:
> a. The pilot of Archie 29 maintained visual contacts with object, calling direction changes of object to (radar) site by radio. Direction changes correlated exactly with those painted on scope by controller.
> b. In previous cases the dual (visual and electronic) sightings are mostly of a few minutes duration at most. This was observed by radar, at least, for 49 minutes.[137]

In fact, as we have seen, more complete case information would have impressed the CIA even more.

A second 1955 case worth review took place on Long Island, NY, on the evening of July 29/30.[138] This incident was reported to the same Major Geyer whom we met at the end of Chapter 9, the UFO Officer for Mitchell AFB, NY. Geyer had asked astronomers in the area to report to him any odd observations they might have during their "star parties." In this one, he got a lulu. Five astronomers were setting up telescopes near Lake Ronkonkoma when they spotted an object similar in brightness to a star of 2nd magnitude doing something astronomically interesting but exceedingly strange in their line-of-sight towards the planet Saturn. The object made a precise circle of one degree of separation around the position of the planet. When it completed this display of precision flying, the object made off in the direction of their line-of-sight to the Moon and flew a precise half-circle around it, continuing on through a couple of odd but not obviously astronomical maneuvers, and then it disappeared. The astronomers, two of whom had a great deal of technical training, were stunned by this display, which seemed to be directed at *them*. This hard-to-swallow speculation arises because there is only one narrowly-defined spot from the planet from which observers would be in position to see both the precision circle apparently "around Saturn" followed by the half-circle "around the Moon." Unless Luck was running wild, or some very creative mental gymnastics can be constructed, this light seemed to be "performing" for witnesses at one spot only. The "performance" was astronomical. The audience was astronomers. Major Geyer either never sent this report on, or it got intercepted somewhere along the chain. It does not appear in Blue Book files. We know of it only through a detailed letter of that time to UFO researcher Ted Bloecher of New York. The case, again, does not speak well of Air Force efforts nor organization. It also starts to verge into a "creepy," almost personal, area of the subject, which made nearly everyone uncomfortable.

Our third case elaboration, the Senator Richard Russell affair, makes one uncomfortable in other ways.[139] This event, whatever it was, and the (deliberate?) confusion which attended it, indicate that many forces were at work in government at that time, and their relationship to the handling of the UFO mystery still is not at all understood. First, what we know. The new Chairman of the Senate Committee on Armed Services, Richard Russell of Georgia, was travelling by train in the Soviet Union. With him were his Air Attaché, Lieutenant Colonel E. U. Hathaway; an "aide," Ruben Efron; and a "businessman" (never identified). They were en route between two towns (Atjaty and Adzhijabul) in what used to be called the Transcaucasian Federated Republics, U.S.S.R. On the evening of October 4, Russell, not feeling well, was alone in one compartment, and the other three men were next door. Out of the window of the moving train, Russell saw something and rushed next door to tell his companions. The others caught a glimpse of what Russell saw, and then, perhaps a minute later, they saw another object similar to the first. Days later the group came to Czechoslovakia, where Colonel Hathaway made a report on October 13. The Air Intelligence Information Report, taken by Air Attaché Lieutenant Colonel Thomas Ryan, was sent to the Pentagon the next day. In the report Hathaway described to Ryan that the men had seen a disk with a revolving middle area and a non-revolving top. The disk, bearing two stationary lights, ascended slowly and generally vertically, reached a height of approximately 6000 feet, accelerated sharply, and then moved away. About a minute later, another object seemed to rise low out of the dark fields and repeat the same maneuver. Two searchlights pointed generally skyward in the distance. Sparks or some flame seemed to be emitted from the "craft." Hathaway said to Ryan that as far as he

Senator Richard Russell

was concerned, the travelers had witnessed something "your people" (Air Force Intelligence, supposedly) tell us does not exist: flying disks. Well, strange enough, but, in some ways, straightforward.

The story became convoluted after Russell returned to the U.S. (apparently ahead of his companions). He was immediately interviewed (within a day or two) by the CIA in a TOP SECRET meeting. This story (via Ryan's report) had apparently aroused interest in the entire national security community, and CIA director Allen Dulles called an IAC executive committee meeting for October 18, with the report on the agenda. Dulles stated that Russell told them that he could distinguish no shape for the "plane" that he saw. Later, in a second CIA interview with OSI chief Herbert Scoville, Russell said that he saw a greenish-yellow ball rise rapidly, and that it was followed by a second one. This significantly more vague account diffused concern at the IAC, who decided that the event should be kept in secret so as not to upset the Russians, who might then restrict travel!

Finally, a third party of the group was interviewed (Russell's aide Efron?), and that interview described an elaborate story of the launch of a triangular shaped object by ejecting it and spinning it

Allen Dulles

upwards from the ground. This assisted take-off was shortly followed by another one. How are these discrepancies possible? Three intelligent and highly-placed (presumably *extremely* security-minded) individuals telling three wildly differing stories? One cannot easily fall back on flawed human sense preceptors—Hathaway's and "X's" descriptions are too detailed. Plus, these men had to have talked extensively to one another about what they had seen. At *some* time between the Caucasus and Czechoslovakia there must have been a far greater consensus than what we read. Is there any solution to this? With our level of documentation, no. Hathaway's early report seems clear, detailed, and fresh; the sort of report one would expect after a puzzling encounter. Both Russell's and "X's" accounts occurred after someone in Washington could have "talked" to them. Why would Russell "dumb down" his report? As Chair of the Armed Services Committee, one of the Senator's subcommittees had just derided President Eisenhower's defense policies as being responsible for an air-power gap with the Soviets.[140] Was Russell "playing cute" by making the incident seem more like a plane than a flying saucer—a more credible possibility to be disturbed about? Was LeMay with his ferocious anti-saucer position lurking behind all this? We do not know. All we know is that when the story leaked to the press a few months later, Russell said that the affected agencies of government had told him not to discuss the matter.[141] And what of "Mr. X's" ejection-assisted vertical take-off triangles? One of these two people (Hathaway or X) had to be lying, and not to the public (which is the norm, as we have seen), but to elements of the intelligence community. What then is *that* about? Whatever was going on, it was going on far above the "heads" of the UFO documents we have been allowed to see.

Filled with the mysteries of the phenomenon in 1955, we move on to 1956. The Air Force said that the UFOs were down even further than in 1955, but a better look at the case files shows that statement to be erroneous. Interesting and unsolved UFOs cases were (despite Blue Book statistics) up across the country. Neither year would be anything like the following (1957), but there were things of note. (A sample of 1956 cases is shown on the next page.)[142]

As one year drifted into the next, the quality of work at Blue Book deteriorated even further. This is particularly noticeable in the number of excellent and interesting cases which do not even enter the Blue Book record. Part of that was due to the policy of pooh-poohing the subject, of course; who would want to report to someone who was going to make you feel foolish, if you did not have to? But some of

A Sampler of 1956 Blue Book Cases:

Place	Date	Witnesses	Object	Comments	Blue Book Conclusion
Pasadena CA	Jan 3	2 civ. ex. mil.	3 circular	Craft approached plane at 4000', circled one and half times; 50' diameter; 1200 mph.*	no case
Henderson NC	Apr 6	2 civ. (1 FBI)	bright round	Low-flying spinning obj. flew directly over car; witness called one of FBI's best employees.**	no case
Schnect-ady NY	Apr 8	multi civil. pilots	bright light	Light seemed to hover, speed up, make right angle turn, slow, speed away, seen by air and ground.	Venus!
White Sands NM	Start May	multi milit.	metallic ball	Vice Commander of Pacific Missile Range + 200 others saw object motionless after missile malfunction.	no case
Marinette WI	May 4	2 civil.	25 orange blobs	Objects passed in groups of 5-2-9-1-6-1-1 seemingly in organized flight (see text).	insufficient
Lakewood CA	May 12	3 civil.	bright round object	A round extremely bright red object hovered, spun like pinwheel, temporarily blinded witness.	no case
Monroe LA	May 22	2 milit.	elliptical object	2 pilots in T-33 jet were buzzed by 30-40 foot domed object; which raced away and returned at great speed.	Unknown
Banning CA	Jun 6	1 civil.	domed disk	Silvery metallic disk came within 100 yards of observer, hovered, and disappeared instantly.	Unknown
Laken-heath, UK	Aug 13/14	multi milit. & radar	2 white balls	Multiple observations in air and ground and radar in famous case. Blue Book wrote it off absurdly, but even Colorado Project said: UFO.	weather effects
Modesto, CA	Oct 7	multi milit. & radar	like dome	Pilots and ground personnel saw object over long period. BB bail out (see text).	insufficient info
Mobile Al	Nov 14	civil. air crew	brilliant light	The famous "Captain Hull" (commercial airliner) display (see text).***	no case!
Guam	Dec 31	1 milit.	round white object	Jet pilot was approached, passed, and circled by object with blinking lights.	Unknown

* A letter was sent but ignored.
** The FBI said that it passed the case on to the Air Force, but it was not investigated by the Air Force.
*** This was a *very* public case by a pilot. It would be nearly impossible that it would not be investigated by Blue Book.

the "loss" of case material for the record was from a lack of basic investigation on the part of the Air Force. One can simply note the number of "no case" entries in the "Blue Book Conclusion" columns of the three previous sample tables for sightings from 1954-1956. A couple of these were understandable due to the elevated status of the witnesses, but most have no obvious reasons for being missed or ignored. In fact, most were written up in newspapers and some even communicated to the authorities. The other element of shoddy performance has been mentioned and illustrated earlier: preposterous write-off "solutions," which require either not reading the actual reports or deliberately ignoring the "higher strangeness" aspects of them. The following cases illustrate some of this behavior.

May 4, 1956, Marinette, Wisconsin:[143] A Protestant minister (and amateur astronomer) was stargazing one evening, when five "orange blobs" flying in a U-shaped formation passed East-to-West at high speeds. Three minutes later two more "blobs" sailed over, and again, *nine* more. The amazed observer called to his family, and his son joined him. One more object passed (all these more or less on the same flight path), and then a group of six. One more passed by, and then one more again. The last few flights were quite bright and glowing. Upon receiving the report, Blue Book, without even consulting their "astronomical consultant" (Allen Hynek), wrote "meteors" as the solution. Hynek, upon seeing this, pointedly informed them that the explanation could *not* be meteors. The two sides of the argument wrote up multi-point defenses of their views: Major Ray Jones defending "meteors"; Dr. Hynek defending "absolutely not meteors." Blue Book's resolution was not to acquiesce to an "unidentified," but it dispensed with the problem by "insufficient information." Flights of luminous objects in formation and that followed repetitive flight paths would, however, seem to have been enough information, given a lifetime astronomer as an observer.

The second case is another one marked "insufficient information." October 7, 1956, near Modesto, California and Castle AFB:[144] Civilian sightings reached the air base and a lighted object was seen by the tower. Planes were directed to the object. There was a narrow overcast layer and the UFO would duck under and over the layer. The pilots decided to fly one above and one below so they could catch where the object was either way. It seemed to be a fat disk (dome-shaped when viewed from the side). Ground radar could pick up the planes, but never the UFO. One pilot decided to return, but upon breaking off, saw that the UFO had altered its flight and was now chasing his buddy's plane. He ascended towards the object, which then broke off and flew away. Upon landing both pilots were given an extended debriefing by Air Force officers from a different base. The witnesses were, according to policy, reminded that they were not to speak of this event. Only a small news article appeared. It suggested that citizens may have seen migratory birds with phosphorescent glows. Years later, both pilots were located. Their stories still matched. Both men were still amazed at how fast the unknown object accelerated. But all this was not enough for Blue Book: "insufficient information." Did they even read the case?

Lastly, we have a case of a commercial airliner whose pilot witnessed an awe-inspiring display.[145] Shortly after the event, the captain of the flight, W. J. (Joe) Hull, wrote of the experience to John DuBarry, who was then president of the CSI-NY civilian UFO investigation group, and a person Hull knew, and disagreed with on UFOs (until this case). Hull's letter is well-written and gives a special "being there" flavor to the case, so we shall quote the Captain at length:

> On the night of November 14, 1956 I was flying a Viscount at high altitude from New York to Mobile, Alabama. We were above a layer of clouds which were occasionally broken, giving us a glimpse of the ground now and then. At 10:10 p.m. E.S.T., when only about 60 miles from Mobile, my co-pilot Peter MacIntosh and I saw what we thought was a brilliant meteor. We were flying south-southwest and it fell across our path from left to right, first becoming visible at the top of the windshield. (The Viscount has wonderful visibility upward.) It decelerated rapidly, just as any meteor does when entering our denser layers of the earth's lower atmosphere, and we expected to see it burn out with the customary flash, which pilots often see, but which people on the ground are often denied.

> Imagine our consternation when this brilliant light did not burn out, but abruptly halted directly in front of us! It was an intense blue-white light, approximately 7 or 8 times as bright as Venus when this planet is at its brightest magnitude. Pete shouted "What the hell is it, a jet?" His first thought, of course, was that the object was a diving jet fighter which had turned sharply away from us and in departing, was giving us a view right up its glowing tailpipe. Instantly I knew this could not possibly be an airplane. I have seen the glow of too many jet pipes at night not to recognize one when I saw it. It was not the right color; it did not diminish in size, as a departing jet fighter's exhaust should have; and it remained motionless directly ahead of us, how far I cannot say, but it must have been quite a few miles.

> I quickly grabbed my microphone and called the Mobile Control Tower. "Bates Tower, this is Capital 77! Look out toward the north and east and see if you can see a strange white light hovering in the sky."
> "Capital 77, this is Mobile Bates Tower. We are unable to see much of the sky because of a thick cloud cover. Do you think the object is in our vicinity?"

"Affirmative. It looks like a brilliant white light bulb, about one tenth the size of the moon. It is directly ahead of us and at about our altitude, or slightly higher. We are right over Jackson, Alabama and have descended to 10,000 feet. Please initiate a call to Brookley Field Tower (Air Force Field 20 miles southeast of Bates Field) and ask the controller if he can see it on their big radar scope." (We did not have the military frequency crystals in our transmitter to work Brookley Tower.)

Just after this exchange, the object began to maneuver. It darted hither and yon, rising and falling in undulating flight, making sharper turns than any known aircraft, sometimes changing direction 90 degrees in an instant. All the while the color remained constant, a brilliant blue-white, and the object did not grow or lessen in size. MacIntosh and I sat there completely flabbergasted at this unnerving exhibition. I thought of calling the passengers over the public address system, but the object was dead ahead of us and putting on its performance in an area whose arc was not large enough to enable anybody in the cabin to get a view of it out the side windows. After a half minute or so of this dancing, unorthodox flight the object suddenly became motionless again and hovered dead still. We were simply confounded by this.

Bates Tower called back. "Capital 77, we are trying to raise the Brookley Tower."

Right at this moment the strange light began another series of crazy gyrations, lazy 8's, square chandelles, all the while weaving through the air with a sort of rythmic [sic], undulating cadence, the likes of which neither Pete nor I had ever seen. Then, apparently content at the consternation which it had wrought, the object shot out over the Gulf of Mexico, rising at the most breathtaking angle and at such a fantastic speed that it diminished rapidly to a pinpoint and was swallowed up in the night.

This unearthly exhibition probably went on for at least two minutes, according to our best judgment. I glanced at the clock and noted it read 10:12.

The most puzzling thing about the whole occurrence, aside from the dancing flight, was that the object, whatever it was, had remained at the same distance from us throughout the performance. How do we know this? It never increased in size, and yet we were bearing down on it at more than 5 miles a minute in the Viscount. If it was in view two minutes and performing in one area we should have been at least ten miles closer to it. Now, any object that flies certainly looks different when viewed at such a great variance in distance. So this UFO must have managed to remain at the same distance from us throughout the entire display.

If you know southern Alabama you know that it is pretty desolate country, with few inhabitants and only a few small hamlets between Mobile and Montgomery up in the middle of the state. We were above the clouds, precluding any reflections of searchlights from below. I have seen hundreds of advertising searchlights playing on clouds, and this was nothing remotely related. Likewise I am summarily ruling out aircraft (at least the ones we know), balloons, missiles, or any other earth-launched device within my ken. The one thing which I can't get over is the fact that when it came, *it came steeply downward*; when it departed after its amazing exhibition, *it went steeply upward*! Now I ask you, John, is this machine based on the earth?

There is a splendid irony in this, in that Captain Hull, three years earlier, had written a severely debunking article on UFOs for *The Airline Pilot* magazine.[146] This case became well-known, but the Air Force never bothered with it. Why not? Decisions like that certainly help one's statistics but not one's reputation. Years later, the Colorado "Scientific Study" (sponsored by the Air Force) looked again at the Mobile case and pronounced it "unidentified."[147]

Going into 1957, ideas about UFOs formed a mighty and confusing stew. Unless one had seen a UFO oneself, it was very difficult to know what to believe. The Air Force was now consistently saying that UFO sightings occurred through errors and that the phenomenon was largely a product of the imagination. Yet, in a surprisingly constant trickle of contrary opinion, "authority figures" such as Dr. Hermann Oberth, called the "Father of Modern Rocketry" (and Wernher von Braun's teacher), were saying that UFOs were obviously real and most probably from outer space.[148] Oberth was not alone. Jet designer William Lear said essentially the same thing.[149] So did British Air Marshall Hugh Dowding.[150] And French aviation pioneer Eugene Farnier testified to a high-speed close encounter.[151] The Air Force said that cases were down, while the Military Air Transport Service reported that cases were up.[152] Dewey Fournet, now retired, wrote to UFO researcher Max Miller that current Air Force policy (of debunking and down-playing UFOs, regardless of what was going on) was a misconceived policy and not good for national security.[153] Some scientists and "authorities" continued to spread nonsense. Old

Center: Dr. Hermann Oberth
Left: Dr. Ernest Stuhlinger
Far Left: General Holger Toftoy
Right: Wernher von Braun
Far Right: Dr. Robert Lusser

Left: Queen Elizabeth
Center: King George VI
Right: Sir Hugh Dowding

falsities like the Avro disk craft[154] and General Mills balloons[155] were re-entered into the discussion as if they had great relevance. Even science popularizier Willy Ley threw his weight behind the nonsense,[156] though, to his credit, Arthur C. Clarke did not.[157] The Navy continued to be unhelpful to the Air Force by inviting to Hawaii a large group of news reporters, whose conversations with Navy pilots turned to saucers, but not by design. The pilots were not at all reluctant to speak of all manner of "pro-UFO" things including permission they had received to shoot down a saucer should it be necessary.[158] Thus ended 1956.

Notes

[1] Eugene M. Emme (ed.), "The History of Rocket Technology," a special dedicated magazine edition of *Technology and Culture*, Fall 1963; specifically, Robert L. Perry, "The Atlas, Thor, and Titan": 466-77.

[2] Emme (ed.), specifically Wernher von Braun, "The Redstone, Jupiter, and Juno": 452-65.

[3] Welmena Shrader, *Fifty Years of Flight*, 1953.

[4] Jack Manno, *Arming the Heavens*, 1984.

[5] Manno, 1984.

[6] Manno, 1984.

[7] An extensive listing of cases called the "LaPaz List" has been extracted from Blue Book and AFOSI files from the 1949-50 era.

[8] This list has been created by simply counting listings in the Blue Book microfilm.

[9] Air Force release (not seen). Quoted from newspaper stories by Curtis Fuller in *FATE*, May 1954: 18-19. Despite the weakness of the source here, the stated policy was clearly as such, as inquiries became routinely passed to the Pentagon.

[10] Al Chop to Donald Keyhoe (complete list can be read at http://www.nicap.org/chop.htm).

[11] Al Chop to Michael Hall, 11 September 1999. (Chop tells Hall that all his action vis-à-vis UFO work came down from Dewey Fournet's desk, and he did not know the colonels above Fournet, and, therefore, who approved passing on the case reports.)

[12] Ruppelt files (esp. White to Ruppelt, 1 February 1955, file RO24).

[13] Robert White to C. H. Marck, date approximate, early April 1955, reproduced in a letter from C. H. Marck to Harold Fulton, 22 April 1955.

[14] Peter Wydem, *St. Louis (MO) Post-Dispatch*, 8 March 1953.

[15] General John A. Samford, interview, "Flying Saucers—the last word," *SEE*, March 1953.

[16] Lowell Bridwell, "Aerial Experts Still Mystified by Stories of 'Flying Saucers'," *New York World-Telegram*, 3 August 1953.

[17] James Phelan, "U.S. Saucer Expert Debunks 'Em," *Long Beach (CA) Independent*, 9 October 1953.

[18] Keyhoe, *Flying Saucers from Outer Space*.

[19] Dick Sweeney, "Air Force Uncertain About Flying Disks, Says Santa Monican," *Santa Monica (CA) Evening Outlook*, 13 October 1953.

[20] FOIA (USAF). A large number of document pages concerning 4602nd history have been released, much in relation to the UFOB program. A valuable example of these is: Captain J. Cybulski, "Unidentified Flying Objects (UFOB)," 3rd Commander's Conference, Ent AFB, CO (date not on document, but c. November 1954).

[21] See Chapter 13.

[22] Hynek alludes to this here and there in his *Hynek UFO Report* and in some of his speeches, but clearly said (with exasperation) that the "best material he was able to get he read out of Flying Saucer Review," and he was sure that the best Air Force cases weren't getting to Blue Book from ADC (personal communication, MDS).

[23] Notes from a trip to Wright-Patterson AFB, June 1966, McDonald archives, University of Arizona.

[24] Blue Book microfilm Roll 17.

[25] Blue Book microfilm Roll 17.

[26] Blue Book microfilm Roll 17.

[27] *Hynek UFO Report*.

[28] Blue Book microfilm Roll 17.

[29] Associated Press, "Mystery 'Flying Discs' Sighted Over No. Japan," dateline: Northern Japan, *San Francisco (CA) Call*, 21 January 1953.

[30] Blue Book microfilm Roll 17.

[31] Blue Book microfilm Roll 17.

[32] Blue Book microfilm Roll 17; and Gross, January-February 1953.

[33] Blue Book microfilm Roll 17; and Gross, January-February 1953.

[34] All cited in Gross, 1953 volumes.

[35] Gross, 1953 volumes; but also Coral Lorenzen of APRO would move shortly to the Holloman area and was to work (along with her husband) at the base. Officers often dropped by to tell her (on the quiet) of another anomalous object they had seen. (This move occurred in 1954, but the nature of the times of the mid-'50s seemed to be that UFO overflights were an unusually frequent occurrence there.) Mentions of these events appear in several of Gross' histories and in the *APRO Bulletin*, passim.

[36] Blue Book microfilm "Statistics for the Year 1953."

[37] Blue Book microfilm Roll 17; and the "Statistics for the Year 1953."

[38] Blue Book microfilm Roll 17.

[39] Blue Book microfilm Roll 18.

[40] Donald Menzel, *Flying Saucers*, 1953.

[41] Patrick Moore, *Guide to the Planets*, 1955.

[42] BB microfilm: Lt. Robert Olsson to J. Allen Hynek, 26 March 1953; and Ruppelt files (Menzel meeting).

[43] (NICAP) *UFO Investigator* 1 (5), August-September 1958 (for Bartlett); and Blue Book microfilm Roll 19 (for Palmdale).

[44] Blue Book microfilm Roll 19; and Ruppelt (*Report*); and (Ruppelt) *Blue Book Special Report #12*, 30 September 1953.

[45] J. Allen Hynek, "Preliminary Draft of Recommendations on the UFO Project," undated (probably late 1953 or 1954); Blue Book microfilm, and CUFOS files.

[46] Donald Menzel and Lyle Boyd, *The World of Flying Saucers*, 1963.

[47] J. Allen Hynek to Zan Overall, 19 October 1965.

[48] Daniel S. Gillmor (ed.), *Scientific Study of Unidentified Flying Objects*, 1969.

[49] Joel Carpenter, "The Lockheed UFO Case, 1953," *International UFO Reporter*, Fall 2001: 3-9, 33-34; and, "Mystery Object Sighted by Pilots over Victorville," *The Lockheed Star* 20 (6): 1, 5, 19 March 1953.

[50] John Timmerman of the Center for UFO Studies received, in the early 2000s, a series of letters and then draft manuscripts from Hubert Humphrey's former advisor on military and NASA affairs, Frank Rand. These materials described in detail a "private" UFO study done for President Lyndon Johnson by Rand, Kelly Johnson, and several other prestigious scientists in the late 1960s. Kelly Johnson is described by Rand as one of the two group members absolutely convinced of UFO reality as technological devices (materials all seen and read by current writer [MDS]).

[51] Donald Keyhoe, "Flying Saucers from Outer Space," *Look*, 20 October 1953.

[52] Donald Keyhoe, *Flying Saucer Conspiracy*, 1955.

[53] Donald Keyhoe, *Flying Saucers from Outer Space*. The letter is reproduced at the end of this chapter, just before the endnotes section.

[54] Australian researcher Bill Chalker has been very successful in getting Australian Air Force officials to make their files public. He reports on the Harry Turner UFO Intelligence report, and the Keyhoe references in his *The Oz Files*, 1966, 64-9.

[55] Guillermo Troconis, "Brazilian Air Force Affirms Existence of Flying Saucers," translation of a South American news story by Alexander Mebane of CSI-NY (NICAP files), 20 December 1954. Although this is (appropriately) viewable as a flimsy source, the very pro-UFO views of Brazilian Air Colonel Oliviera are documented in many places. The relevance here is that this source specifically indicates that Oliviera had read Keyhoe and was influenced by him.

[56] P. G. Strong to Assistant Director, Scientific Intelligence, memorandum, subject: "Report on Book Entitled 'Flying Saucers from Outer Space'," 8 December 1953, FOIA (CIA).

[57] Todos Odarenko to Assistant Director, Scientific Intelligence, memorandum, subject: "Current Status of Unidentified Flying Object (UFOs) Project," 17 December 1953, FOIA (CIA).

[58] Blue Book microfilm files. J. Allen Hynek ultimately hoped that Robertson would perhaps continue this interest and give opinions on what Hynek called the "pinchbottle" (hard to explain) cases. Robertson, however shortly went to Europe to do intelligence work there.

[59] (Captain) Walter Karig, Special Deputy to Chief of Information, U.S. Navy, "Operation UFO," *The American Weekly*, 22 November 1953: 4-5.

[60] G. A. Tokaty, "Soviet Rocket Technology," 515-28, in Emme, "The History of Rocket Technology," a special dedicated magazine edition of *Technology and Culture*, Fall 1963.

[61] Kenneth Kleinknecht, entry in Eugene Emme (ed.), *The History of Rocket Technology*, 1964.

[62] Manno, *Arming the Heavens*.

[63] Manno, *Arming the Heavens*.

[64] Manno, *Arming the Heavens*.

[65] David Baker, *The Rocket*, 1978.

[66] Emme, "The History of Rocket Technology," a special dedicated magazine edition of *Technology and Culture*, Fall 1963 (von Braun).

[67] Manno, *Arming the Heavens*.

[68] Emme, "The History of Rocket Technology," a special dedicated magazine edition of *Technology and Culture*, Fall 1963 (von Braun).

[69] Kenneth Kleinknecht, entry in Eugene Emme (ed.), *The History of Rocket Technology*, 1964.

[70] G. A. Tokaty, "Soviet Rocket Technology," 515-28, in Emme, "The History of Rocket Technology," a special dedicated magazine edition of *Technology and Culture*, Fall 1963.

[71] Blue Book microfilm statistical annual summaries.

[72] Blue Book microfilm Roll 21.

[73] Blue Book microfilm Roll 23.

[74] Blue Book microfilm Roll 25.

[75] Blue Book microfilm Roll 25.

[76] Blue Book microfilm Roll 26.

[77] Blue Book microfilm Roll 27.

[78] McDonald files, University of Arizona. Files passim, but particularly correspondence with Richard Hall (late 1960s).

[79] *Hynek UFO Report*.

[80] J. Allen Hynek files, Center for UFO Studies, Chicago, Ill.

[81] *Hynek UFO Report*.

[82] "Ball Lightning" shows up on Blue Book explanation lists at least three years before the big "auto-stopping" flap in 1957; a good deal of discussion of it went on at Blue Book in connection with the 1957 flap, for which it was the explanation-of-choice. Blue Book microfilm Rolls 29 and 30.

[83] Blue Book statistics.

[84] "100 Mystery Flying Objects Spotted Here," *Wilmington Morning News*, 9 July 1954 (apparent publicity flap due to release of GOC logs): Keyhoe, *Flying Saucer Conspiracy* (wherein Keyhoe notes that GOC logs shortly became "closed," and Brad Williams, "Scribe Finds Tracking 'Saucer' Confusing Job," *Portland (OR) Journal*, 5 March 1955 (wherein a newsman runs into a GOC observer told to shut up, a local data filter spokesman who referred him on to Washington, and a Major there who told him there was nothing to it—all apparently part of new tightened policy).

[85] Blue Book microfilm Roll 23. The case involved multiple military and civilian witnesses, yet the "analyst" wrote "unreliable observer" as an explanation. Even Allen Hynek got angry about that one. ATIC's Colonel Spencer Wheelon went on national television (*Armstrong Theatre of the Air*) to essentially call an entire family "drunk" for reporting an entity case in Kentucky. (This was unusually crude behavior for the Air Force, which was trying to get away from such belittling activity.) Reference: Ted Bloecher and Isabel Davis, *Close Encounter at Kelly*, 1978.

[86] Blue Book microfilm (quoted in Gross, Sept-Oct. 1956).

[87] Memorandum for Director, FBI, subject, "Detroit Flying Saucer Club, Espionage-X," undated (about Adamski's talk), FOIA (FBI).

[88] Lt. Col. Leon F. Bugh to Director, Special Investigations, memorandum, 23 May 1955, FOIA (CIA). (Gribble was essentially no more than a news clipping collector and newsletter printer at the time.)

[89] Coral Lorenzen to NICAP, 9 October 1956.

[90] *Hynek UFO Report*.

[91] Quoted by Keyhoe in *Flying Saucer Conspiracy*.

[92] Keyhoe, *Flying Saucer Conspiracy*.

[93] Quoted by Keyhoe in *Flying Saucer Conspiracy*.

[94] "Air Force General Admits UFO Sightings Kept from Public," *The UFO Investigator* 1 (3): 1, 3, January 1958.

[95] Joint Chiefs of Staff, *JANAP 146 (C): Communicating Instructions for Reporting Vital Intelligence Sightings from Airborne and Waterborne Sources*, Joint Communications-Electronics Committee: Washington, DC, March 1954. News stories of the February meeting between Military Air Transport Service (MATS) and civilian airline reps also carried the "gag rule." For example: Jim G. Lucas, Scripps-Howard, dateline: Washington, February 12, 1954, "5 to 10 'Saucers' Reported Nightly by Airline Pilots," *Rocky Mountain News*, Denver, CO.

[96] Keyhoe, *Flying Saucer Conspiracy*.

[97] Associated Press, "Air Force Denies It Hides Hunks of Flying Saucers," dateline: Washington DC, 23 March 1954.

[98] Project Blue Book, *Special Report No. 14*, Air Technical Intelligence Center, Wright-Patterson AFB, OH, 5 May 1955.

[99] Blue Book microfilm Roll 87.

[100] Ruppelt, *Report*.

[101] Edward Ruppelt, "What Our Air Force Found Out About Flying Saucers," *TRUE*, May 1954: 19-20, 22, 24, 26, 30, 124-34.

[102] Edward Ruppelt to Donald Keyhoe, 3 August 1954; printed in *The UFO Investigator II* (2): 6, October 1961 (after Edward Ruppelt's death).

[103] Edward Ruppelt to Donald Keyhoe, 3 August 1954; as printed in *The UFO Investigator II*.

[104] Blue Book microfilm (no date, apparently c. October 1954). Printed in Gross, September 1954.

[105] Blue Book microfilm, "Foreign sightings," 7 December 1954. Printed in Gross, Nov-Dec. 1954.

[106] For the 1954 wave, see Clark, *Encyclopedia*; the same for Keyhoe and his hyper-conservative attitudes about entity cases.

[107] Anthony Leviero, "President Discounts 'Saucer' from Space," *New York Times*, 16 December 1954; see Chapter 9, ref. 74.

[108] Gross (July/September 1955, and passim); also Blue Book microfilm (wherein, increasingly, would appear papers from such newsletters with a file, but a designation "no case," meaning no AF investigation).

[109] Gross (July/September 1955, and passim); also Blue Book microfilm.

[110] (signature illegible), Wing Commander, RAAF Intelligence to Director of Air Force Intelligence, 19 October 1955, subject: Flying Saucers.

[111] (signature illegible), Group Captain, D. Ops, memorandum to D.A.F.I. [Department of Air Force Intelligence}, 15 February 1956.

[112] See, as prominent example, coverage in *TIME*: "Saucer Blue Book," November 7, 1955.

[113] Ruppelt, *Report*.

[114] Clarence Greene and Russell Rouse, *Unidentified Flying Objects*, United Artists, 91 minutes, 1956.

[115] It has been the experience of the current writer (MDS) that a high percentage of "life-time" UFO researchers in the United States from the post-war generation were heavily influenced by Ruppelt's book, more so even than by Keyhoe's.

[116] Blue Book microfilm, Statistics 1956.

[117] A. M. Rochlen to Brig. General Harold E. Watson, 16 April 1956 (reprinted in Gross, Jan-April 1956); and Blue Book microfilm, Watson to Rochlen, 4 May 1956.

[118] Robert M. L. Baker, "Photogrammatic Analysis of the 'Montana' Film Tracking Two UFOs," *Douglas Aircraft*, March 1956; and "Observational Evidence of Anomalistic Phenomena," *Journal of the Astronautical Sciences XV* (1): 31-36, Jan-Feb. 1968. (Baker did a concurrent analysis of the 'Utah' film, and also refuted AF conclusions.)

[119] Blue Book microfilm, as quoted and discussed in David Jacobs' excellent history *The UFO Controversy in America*, 1975; and also, Colonel John G. Eriksen to Lt. Colonel T. R. Johnson, Director of Intelligence office, memorandum, subject: UFO movie, 1 June 1956 (this latter details the words that the Pentagon Press Desk is to use when inquiries come regarding the movie, and the two films within it).

[120] Jacobs, *The UFO Controversy in America*, 1975.

[121] Quoted in Jacobs, *The UFO Controversy in America*, 1975.

[122] Donald Keyhoe to Senator Harry F. Byrd, 3 April 1956 (printed in its entirety in Max Miller, *Flying Saucers*, 1957).

[123] Example: Sam Gordon, "Flying Saucer Probe is Asked," *Washington (DC) Daily News*, 4 April 1956.

[124] Max Miller, *Flying Saucers*.

[125] Max Miller, *Flying Saucers*.

[126] For details of this strategy, see Chapter 13.

[127] Blue Book microfilm, John G. Eriksen (writing for Donald Quarles), memorandum, subject: proposed reply by the Secretary of the Air Force to the letter from the Honorable John E. Moss (undated, but polished draft for Quarles was 25 June 1956).

[128] For formation of NICAP, see entry in Clark, *Encyclopedia*.

[129] Cases for 1954 appear in date order in Blue Book microfilm Rolls 20-22; also, references to many of them are in Gross for 1954. The latter particularly applies to the "no case" designators.

[130] J. R. Gluck, "Report to Bluebook," 8 pp. in files.

[131] Blue Book microfilm Rolls 20-22; and Gross for 1954, plus specifically note: J. R. Gluck, "Report to Bluebook," 8 pp. in files; plus Michael Swords, "Fun and Games in the Desert near Las Cruces," *International UFO Reporter 30* (3): 20-21, 2006.

[132] Blue Book microfilm Rolls 20-22; and Gross for 1954, plus specifically note: J. R. Gluck, "Report to Bluebook," 8 pp. in files; Michael Swords, "Fun and Games in the Desert near Las Cruces," *International UFO Reporter 30* (3): 20-21, 2006; plus Lt. Colonel James McNamara, "Angel's Hair," *Pageant*, November 1954: 52-56; and Mrs. W. J. Daly to Coral Lorenzen, 2 March 1955 (taken from the APRO files).

[133] Blue Book microfilm Rolls 20-22; and Gross for 1954, plus specifically note: J. R. Gluck, "Report to Bluebook," 8 pp. in files; Michael Swords, "Fun and Games in the Desert near Las Cruces," *International UFO Reporter 30* (3): 20-21, 2006; plus Lt. Colonel James McNamara, "Angel's Hair," *Pageant*, November 1954: 52-56; and Mrs. W. J. Daly to Coral Lorenzen, 2 March 1955 (taken from the APRO files); plus "Jerome Teachers, Students Watch Strange Occurrence in the Sky," *Marysville (OH) Evening Journal-Tribune*, 25 October 1954, and James McDonald files, University of Arizona archives.

[134] Jack Pickering (ex-AF and, then, Battelle) interview with William Jones (audiotape), 1977, CUFOS files.

[135] Blue Book microfilm Roll 23.

[136] Cases for 1955 appear in date order in Blue Book microfilm Rolls 22-24. Also, references to many of them are in Gross for 1955. This applies to most "no case" designators. For "Long Island," see #137 below.

[137] Todos M. Odarenko, memorandum for Acting Asst. Director for Scientific Intelligence, subject" "Unusual UFOB Report," 12 July 1955, FOIA (CIA).

[138] Lionel Day to Ted Bloecher, 5 October 1955, CSI-NY/NICAP files.

[139] Gross, Sept-Dec 1955 references the entire story as we have it. Primary source documents are reproduced there. Most significant are a) Lt. Col. Thomas S. Ryan, *Air Intelligence Information Report*, subject: "Observations of a Traveler in USSR," 14 Oct. 1955; b) A. Belmont to L. Boardman, memorandum, subject: "Flying Saucers," 18 Oct. 1955, FOIA (FBI); c) A. Belmont to L. Boardman, memorandum, subject, "Flying Saucers," 4 Nov. 1955, FOIA (FBI); d) Herbert Scoville, memorandum, subject: "Interview with [deleted]," 27 October 1955.

[140] This refers to the Armed Forces subcommittee chaired by Stuart Symington in 1955.

[141] Richard Russell to Tom Towers, January 20, 1956.

[142] Cases for 1956 appear in date order in Blue Book microfilm Rolls 24-27. Also, most cases are referenced in Gross for 1956. Case #4 (White Sands, NM) is from McDonald files, University of Arizona archives. Case #1 (Pasadena, CA) is, briefly, in Blue Book, but also *Flying Saucer Review 2* (2), Mar-Apr 1956. Lakenheath is widely covered.

[143] Blue Book microfilm Roll 25; see especially the "dueling letters" of Jones 23 May 1959, and Hynek, undated.

[144] Blue Book microfilm Roll 26.

[145] W. J. Hull to John DuBarry, June 5, 1957, CSI-NY/NICAP files.

[146] Joe Hull, "Men in Motion: Obituary of the Flying Saucers," *AIR LINE PILOT* 22: 13-14, September 1953.

[147] Gillmor (ed.), *Scientific Study of Unidentified Flying Objects* [Colorado Study].

[148] Hermann Oberth, "Flying Saucers Come From a Distant World," *The American Weekly*, 24 October 1954.

[149] "Flying Saucers Are Real, Lear Says," AP news story, dateline: Bogota, Columbia, *Grand Rapids Herald*, 2 February 1955.

[150] Lord Dowding, "I Believe in Flying Saucers," *London Sunday-Dispatch*, 11 July 1954.

[151] "It Keeps Up," *Le Courier de l'Ouest*, 19 October 1954 (translated news story, CSI-NY files).

[152] Jim G. Lucas, Scripps-Howard Staff Writer, "Flying Saucer Sightings Increase," dateline, Washington, DC, 13 February 1954.

[153] Dewey Fournet, letter, produced in Max Miller, *Flying Saucers*.

[154] For example, David Lawrence, "Flying Saucer 'Mystery' Solved Officially At Last," *New York Herald Tribune*, 2 Nov. 1955. (A rather astonishingly wrong article by a so-called science and technology writer.)

[155] For example, "Flying Saucer Scare Solved, Gen. Mills Chief in L.A. Tells Research," *Los Angeles Herald Express*, 4 October 1954. (Another incredible set of comments by the Chairman of the Board of Directors of General Mills, whose balloon launchers were the very people seeing the UFOs.)

[156] "Expert Debunks 'Saucer' Stories," *Chicago American*, 31 January 1956. Ley wrote the "few unexplained reports" off to "simple electrical phenomena," of which he could not possibly have known what he was talking about. These references are included because they are evidence of an irrational sociology which accreted to the discussion, in which people could utter any imaginable nonsense (as long as it was *negative* nonsense) without dissent.

[157] Arthur C. Clarke, book review [Ruppelt's], *Journal of the British Interplanetary Society* 15 (5): 289-90, Sept-Oct. 1956. Clarke waffled on UFOs (mainly negative) for years, finally coming down safely on the debunking position in the 1980s.

[158] "Shoot to Kill: Pacific Navy Fliers Ordered to Engage Saucers," *Fullerton (CA) News-Tribune*, 26 July 1956.

Chapter 12: Something Closer This Way Comes

In the American Experience, the UFO Phenomenon had displayed itself almost entirely as a mystery of the air, of flight, and seemingly, of technology. It remained at a "proper" distance. There were very few claims of landings. There were very few claims of "entities," other than those by the non-believable "contactees." There were very few of what we call today "close encounters" of any kind. In Europe and in Latin America, that had been different, especially in 1954. But that was far away and one could, even if one were in the military, say that these stories were merely stories. For the United States, the UFO Phenomenon was just something in the air, something *possibly* threatening, but until now "no threat to national security." Although citizens saw and reported UFOs, they did so at-a-distance, and so, despite the UFO writers and organizations, were only distantly involved. Unidentified flying objects were military business. Citizens just sometimes accidentally saw UFOs because they were (distantly) there. If one ignored the world experience (and an assessment of Project Blue Book files shows that, with the exception of cases by U.S. military personnel in areas like Korea, American intelligence practically did), then one could sit in the Pentagon and rationalize that, whatever this was, it was far away and harmless. Not all intelligence operatives felt so relaxed about the issue, but it made one's life simpler, thinking about defense and the Soviets, if one did. Without the Close Encounters it was a lot easier to push the UFO bugaboo away. In 1957, the phenomenon would change that. Fortunately for the intelligence community, the change would only be temporary.

Nineteen hundred and fifty seven was the year of ICBM launches and, finally, Sputnik.[1] No one in the public really believed that the Soviets were ahead of us in military technology until then—a dangerous situation, yes, but ahead, no. With Sputnik orbiting and our "response," Vanguard, flopping in plain sight on the launching pads, the public was nervous in the extreme. But Sputnik I was only a little metal ball, the commentators said. In November, the Soviets launched Sputnik II: one thousand pounds of metal and a dog inside. The citizenry was on the edge of panic. Coincident to that panic, in early November the UFOs engaged the country in a series of close encounters never yet seen in the United States, providing another major stress that the military did not need. The small band of UFO debunkers at Wright-Patterson and the Pentagon would have to handle that matter on their own; the Big American War Machine had Sputniks and ICBMs on their minds. To cope, Eisenhower asked for a monster of a Department of Defense budget. Far from Ike's having to fight for the budget, Congress increased it even more. While politicians and strategists sweated, Texas, Oklahoma, Missouri, Washington, and California got rich. Quietly, the technology and intelligence communities created the Advanced Research Projects Agency (ARPA, later DARPA) inspired in 1957 by Sputnik, and formed in 1958, to secretly produce the advanced weapons systems of the later century and to "prevent technological surprise." UFOs did not qualify as a "technological surprise," although Sputniks, Soviet ICBMs, and, if they should occur, *Soviet* flying disks would. It was an interesting psychology: the thing we knew but could not be, versus the thing that was not, but we feared *could* be. But Sputnik and its ICBM dwarfed them both.

Perhaps the terrible realities associated with Soviet technology simply made anything else an irritating distraction best handled by ignoring it. The practical military certainly seemed to cope with UFOs that way. Only if it could be shown that there was some serious threat present would any action, any expense or application of manpower, be even evaluated, let alone approved.[2] As it was, the UFO phenomenon presented only two such defensible threats: it could still contribute to, or be simulated to create, dangerous panic;[3] and the manipulation of flying saucers "nuts," scam-artists, and cultists could be used to spread anti-American, pro-Communism, and unhelpful anti-war, anti-bomb messages throughout the public.[4]

These were threats that the intelligence community understood, and the militarist war-makers could leave them to it, and hopefully be bothered no more by it. The "hysteria" problem remained Blue Book's and a small part of the Pentagon's job. The "propaganda and spy" problem was the FBI's and the CIA's. A few people like Allen Hynek naively thought that UFOs were a neat scientific puzzle to be solved. Hynek never got it. Much later, near the end of Blue Book, then chief officer Colonel Hector Quintanilla exasperatedly told an interviewer that Hynek would casually drop by, engage in small talk for hours, and waste military time while there was work to be done.[5] Far from *not* being serious about UFOs, Blue Book was deadly serious about preventing dangerous excitement and enthusiasm about the subject. It just was not the kind of seriousness certain portions of the citizenry wanted.

We shall begin with a problem mentioned in the last chapter that was left on the Air Force doorstep by Congressman John Moss, when he wrote to Secretary of the Air Force Donald Quarles. Moss asked why the ballyhooed Blue Book 14 report was so hard to access. Was the Air Force, as some charged, hiding something? This question put the Air Force in an immediate bind from which it took more than a year to extricate itself. The Air Force could not afford to be accused of a cover-up (they knew that NICAP was ready to leap at that), and they had no money to publish a mass printing. The original report by Battelle was about 300 pages. They

Lt to Rt: Under Sec. AF Douglas, Sec. AF Quarles, Chair of Joint Chief of Staff Gen. Twining, AF Chief Staff White

distilled this to less than 100 pages when they printed the formal document in 1955. Conversation between ATIC and the Pentagon concluded that there was no solution except to fund a large reprinting of Blue Book 14, tell Secretary Quarles about it, and draft a letter for him to send to Congressman Moss.[6] That was more expensive than they liked, but at least it solved the immediate problem. The longer range issue was: should the Blue Book 14 report be reproduced as is, or should some addendum be attached (with textual polishing) to make the report as useful as possible? That addendum and polishing took another year.

The available documents say many things of interest, especially when read in the context in which they were created.[7] They present a Project Blue Book entirely fixated on problems resident in the public rather than those resident in the phenomenon. It was as if, for Blue Book, the phenomenon had disappeared.

To accomplish the upgraded publication of Blue Book 14, a special coordination group was set up between ATIC and the Pentagon. The main individual on the Pentagon side was Major James F. Byrne, who would serve as contact point for whatever the Pentagon "Press Desk" released to the public and also provide a link in the chain of information to specific congressional offices. On ATIC's end, Captain George Gregory, then-chief officer of Blue Book, would be a focus-point, but as a scientific advisor, A. Francis Arcier played a large role as well. As the months went on, these three men plus two others, Colonel James Boland and Major Lawrence Tacker, would crystallize into a regularly meeting "fire suppressant" anti-Keyhoe group. For the moment, however, Byrne, Gregory, and Arcier were only worried about Blue Book 14's required publicly-accessible release. Initially, Byrne and an associate, Mr. L. A. Sanderson, were invited to ATIC so that, as Arcier said it, Captain Gregory could "conduct this indoctrination."[8]

Byrne seemed happy with the resultant plan. In May 1957 he wrote to Pentagon higher-ups that publication of Blue Book 14 alongside an updated Air Force Regulation 200-2 (reworded to eliminate language that might provoke suspicion or misinterpretation by the public), "should do much toward the relief of [Air Force Intelligence] AFOIN in the UFO Program . . . In every instance where by inference the Air Force might appear critical of, or attempt to deceive the public, the text has been removed or altered."[9] Byrne also noted that "The subject of U.S. persons using the UFO hysteria for personal gain has been informally brought to the attention of the FBI. Documented cases where illicit or deceptive devices or methods are used by individuals to arouse public interest in UFOs should be made available to the FBI."

By July, the polishing of the original Blue Book 14 and the writing of the new addendum were well along. In the rewritten "Preface," Captain Gregory said that its goals were to make the subject more understandable, to inform the reader discreetly that the Air Force is well aware that there have been detractors of the Air Force and the Report, and to "leave the impression of 'good faith' towards the public."[10] All of that can be viewed as completely appropriate, but, given what we have seen of the attitude of the times, there is a hint of less-than-frank-openness in these words.

The wording of the draft document for the new preface shows very careful consideration. The specter of Keyhoe and the rest of the UFO community, ready to pounce at any hint of cover-up or information manipulation, haunts the language used. Gregory, in his margins, explains his strategies to head off these expected attacks and predicts UFO organization attacks if certain phrases are not included. At one point Gregory notes that the confession of an Air Force error (in the statistical use of the Chi Square method) will make them look good.[11]

The second, and longer, addition to the new Blue Book 14 report consisted of material bringing the subject up-to-date (from mid-1955 to 1957). The big message was: reports are up but unknowns are down. This was because of "improvement in reporting, investigating, and analytical techniques." The inaccuracy in this wording is striking. The rise in reports was said to be due to publicity (particularly certain books) and organizations, clubs, and societies. That claim was a half-truth. Early on, students of the field realized that publicity (particularly of impressive *cases*) stimulated people to report *old* sightings about which they had been reluctant to speak. But publicity did *not* typically produce new case claims. *When* people told others (about having seen the phenomenon), it *did* have a social component. Ed Ruppelt had noted this in 1952 as we have seen.[12] The Air Force of 1957, however, did not see an advantage in mentioning this distinction. Instead, Gregory and Arcier composed both a page of writing and a highly debatable, if not meaningless, chart of UFO reports (with about two dozen peaks and dates of four magazine articles and two instances of press publication) that attempted to correlate publicity to sightings. The magazine articles, one would assume, would have spawned bursts of UFO claims. There is no graphical evidence that they did. The press coverage, by definition, must come *after* the sightings it is covering—a point seemingly opaque to the ATIC people, who had a viewpoint to sell. This is not to say that one *could not* make a study of publicity (of the proper type, like Keyhoe or Ruppelt books, or the movie *UFO*), then do the difficult job of plotting post-publication (i.e. new) reports vs. a background level (i.e. of ordinary publicity) of reports, and then see if such a hypothesis were true, but Gregory and Arcier did nothing of the sort. In an otherwise good strategic effort, it was a surprisingly sloppy blot on their work.

The argument that UFO publicity caused more UFO sightings allowed Gregory and Arcier to complain about the growth of the civilian organizations and their newsletters. They also complained that civilian organizations pulled in cases to themselves and away from the Air Force, and, having described such cases "with occasional lack of restraint," then the Air Force was badgered by inquiries on these too-old-to-investigate cases, and was unjustly criticized for having no answers. Indeed, it is a sad and unfair picture painted by Gregory. The Air Force is doing the best it can but, due to the "personal impressions and interpretations" inserted into reports by the witnesses, the lack of controlled conditions, and the consequent low quality of the reports, "it is doubtful that the number of 'unknowns' will ever be reduced to zero."

Nevertheless, the Air Force had the full backing of the scientific community, established by an addendum in testimony before the House Appropriations Committee on February 19, 1957. Authorities Dr. Hugh L. Dryden and Dr. James H. Doolittle, Director and Chairman of NACA, "flatly denied the existence of such space vehicles." Asked why, then, did such eminent persons like themselves not speak out more frequently to deny and refute the UFO commentators, they said: "we would have no time to do anything else. We cannot compete with the science-fiction people."[13]

Dr. Hugh Dryden

This was well-played. What better authority could there be than the leaders of the National Advisory Committee for Aeronautics? Donald Keyhoe, however, was not asleep. Keyhoe had heard of Dryden's flat denial before Congress, and immediately challenged him to back his declaration with facts that would make a flat denial appropriate. In fact, Keyhoe said that he would disband NICAP if Dryden could do so.[14] The press now turned to Dryden: what evidence did he have to support his position? His quote: "I was only expressing my personal opinion. I have nothing to support it."[15] It *was*, however, left in the Blue Book 14 addendum. All in all, the new Blue Book 14 was a success. Only intense students of UFO data could see through its words and analyze the numbers in order to draw a different conclusion. When all the smoke and mirrors were cleared away, there were many UFO reports that resisted all explanations. That was the conclusion one would reach if focused on the exploration of scientific mysteries. If one were focused on national security, an explanation for all the unknown cases was not as important.

Donald Keyhoe

It is not as easy to say what the Air Force's opponent, NICAP/Keyhoe, was focused upon. Certainly many members wanted to know what UFOs were, and, at least, to have the authorities acknowledge that they were real. Perhaps underneath his crusty outer shell, that is all Donald Keyhoe wanted in the end. But if it were all about mystery, romance, and exploration on the inside, it did not show on the outside. There the public battle was an exchange of escalating challenges and pointed accusations. These challenges were augmented by the raw power of experts, like Dryden and Doolittle on the Air Force side, while much to the surprise of the Air Force, Keyhoe and NICAP also rolled out their own Big Guns. The first "gun" was a former Naval Academy classmate of Keyhoe's: Delmar Fahrney, an Admiral and, worse, the former chief of the Navy's Guided Missile Program. Fahrney's name was not as well known as Dryden's, but his

Admiral Delmar Fahrney

241

credentials about leading-edge aerial technology were just as sound. Unlike Dryden, Fahrney could stand on the fact that he had actually been interested in UFO cases and could discuss *why* he had the opinions that he held. NICAP's press conference for the new Chairman of the Board (Fahrney) was held in mid-January of 1957 and made national news.[16] At that conference, the Admiral tried to be non-accusatory of the Air Force, while still emphasizing how important that he thought flying disks were. The Associated Press coverage was blunt: "there are objects coming into our atmosphere at very high speeds."[17] The United States cannot match them; neither can the Soviets. Their maneuvering shows that they are under intelligent control. Fahrney was questioned after his opening remarks: Why is NICAP in existence if the Air Force is already studying these reports? Fahrney was diplomatic, but easy to read: "NICAP will share what data it receives with the public, in contrast to the Air Force's policy."[18] Keyhoe was delighted with the coverage, which swept across the nation. Often it was accompanied and supported by an interview with Clyde Tombaugh, the discoverer of Pluto. Tombaugh once again stated his beliefs in the phenomenon's obvious reality and its probable extraterrestrial nature.[19] All this was unwelcome at Blue Book and the Pentagon.

The problem was what to do about it. A pattern in Air Force behavior when faced with a difficult public relations situation (such as a prestigious commentator like Fahrney) was to do the least possible immediately, then mop up the mess behind the scenes or, later, issue a stronger statement. In this case, since attacking Fahrney was out of the question, the Air Force issued an almost robotic repetition of their non-findings about UFOs over the years, and then went silent.[20] Fahrney's message contained a call for information from citizen sources. It also produced a rush of citizens volunteering to help NICAP with the investigation.[21] The Air Force could not do anything about the latter, but hopefully servicemen would not also leak information to NICAP. Theoretically, this was already policy through JANAP 146 and AFR 200-2, but many military did not take the regulations seriously, especially when (they rationalized) the basics of the case were already known to the public. The intensity of ATIC's desire for verbal restraint did not always translate to what a given officer in the field felt about the matter. It was an ongoing predicament: how seriously did everybody take the problem, and why?

The atmosphere at ATIC and the Pentagon at that time was probably the most violently anti-UFO that it ever was, past or future. We could guess this just by behavior, but we do not need to. Allen Hynek was slowly becoming aware just how far removed this thing that he was involved with was from an investigative study of a phenomenon, and how hotly political and sociological it was, instead. Concerning NICAP, Hynek remembers how his own feelings were formed in those days.

> Oh, well, my impression of NICAP was completely soured and prejudiced, perhaps because I never had any direct contact with them; all I knew about NICAP was through Blue Book and they were painted to me as a bunch of crackpots; Keyhoe was presented as a scoundrel and a mountebank, and all I remember was that, time after time, when Keyhoe seemed to be getting a little ascendency and calling for congressional investigations, suddenly there was a big flurry at Blue Book, so there was a real counter-offensive mounted . . . and after . . . I wasn't sharp enough to see that this was a highly political move. I really thought then that NICAP was a bunch of nuts.[22]

Blue Book was obsessed with Keyhoe. On a case field study report, as far back as 1954, in the margins of the report near an underlined detail of the case were the words: "Keyhoe would like this."[23]

In preparation for whatever Keyhoe and Fahrney would do next, the Air Force, as we have mentioned, formed a team (Gregory, Arcier, Byrne, and shortly later, Boland, and Tacker) to deal with them on a day-by-day basis. Everyone else at ATIC and the UFO-related elements of the Pentagon (including Hynek and all the PIO officers) was supposed to support this activity. The disconnection between researching cases and what they were actually spending their time on finally penetrated Hynek:

When it became clear to me and others with the project (as a result of personal conversations with officers of colonel rank and higher) that the official Pentagon policy was to debunk UFO sightings, intelligence analysts and investigators alike (myself included, since at that time I felt the lack of 'hard' evidence justified the practical 'it just can't be' attitude) did their best to come up with 'commonsense' explanations for each new UFO report. I stress the word 'each,' for there was no attempt to look for patterns in the reports; each report was regarded as though it were the only UFO report in the world. This made it easier to find some individual explanation, even though it was sometimes far-fetched.

The Air Force was very cooperative with the media when a case was easy to explain but if it was puzzling the military would stall the media with a 'no-comment.'

The public was, in fact, placed in the role of 'the enemy,' against whom 'counterespionage' tactics must be employed. From my personal experience, I frequently felt that those in charge did indeed consider people who reported UFOs or who took a serious interest in them and wanted information about them, as enemies.[24]

The big enemy, NICAP, shortly escalated the conflict with another admiral. This one was even more impressive, even more unassailable, than Admiral Fahrney. Roscoe Hillenkoetter had been director of the early CIA.[25] This was, for the Air Force, almost a catastrophe. Applying Hillenkoetter to the UFO information-release talk guaranteed an audience from the media, but, more importantly, an audience in Congress. No longer could anyone lightly disregard NICAP and its stated positions. A man like Hillenkoetter could not be ignored. Although it is not central to the theme of this book, we do not know why Hillenkoetter joined. It cannot be simply because he, too, was an old Naval Academy classmate of Keyhoe's.

Admiral Roscoe Hillenkoetter

Hillenkoetter had probably heard of the many powerhouse UFO cases involving Navy personnel and research projects. Perhaps he had discussed it all with Fahrney, who knew them well. Hillenkoetter seemed to be unaware of the details and conclusions of the Robertson Panel (the substance of which was driving this policy that NICAP was fighting). Perhaps Hillenkoetter just had a different view of what America and the Service were all about. He told Keyhoe, disapprovingly, that "the Air Force has constantly misled the American public about UFOs."[26]

Congressman William Ayres

Using the prestige of the Admiral and the energy of their citizen members, NICAP began to make inquiries, and even more pointed requests, to specific congressmen. The politicians were, in a way, just like the public. Some were already interested; some were not. Some became interested; some thought it all the most inane nonsense. But every time a congressman or senator said that, yes, there seemed to be something in this and maybe "we" should look into it, a fire alarm rang for the anti-Keyhoe team. Much of 1957 was an exploratory year in Congress for NICAP, but the big pressures would build in 1958 and 1960. ATIC and the Pentagon were able to keep things quiet by employing the simple tactic that they had used with Congressman Moss in late 1956—a private briefing for him and his subcommittee. This method continued in 1957 and beyond. Congressman William Ayres of the Veterans Affairs Committee told a constituent:

Congressional investigations have been held and are still being held on the problem of unidentified flying objects and the problem is one in which there is quite a bit of interest.

Since most of the material presented to the Committees is classified, the hearings are never printed. When conclusions are reached, they will be released if possible.[27]

One such 1957 briefing did have an apparent long-term effect of some significance. In mid-November, Edward Ruppelt, though now a civilian, was called from California to Washington to testify in what had to be a major briefing.[28] Ruppelt had already been informed that the Air Force was "angry" about his book.[29] The briefing seems to have stunned Ruppelt. After returning, Ruppelt came to feel that his interest in UFOs had gotten completely out of hand, to the point where it was taking up the time of senators and congressmen who had much more important things to concentrate upon. Ruppelt later told Keyhoe that he was not going to contribute to this.[30]

Although significant inroads into Congress were not obvious, Keyhoe himself, unmoved by concerns such as Ruppelt's, had many inroads into the media. The broadest-based opportunity was an appearance on the national television show, *Night Beat* (Sept. 26). The Air Force knew that Keyhoe would be on, and, of course, knew what his main agenda would be (attacking a policy of secrecy). They armed the host with a document to be read (in Keyhoe's face) at the beginning of the program.[31] In it, the Air Force charged Keyhoe and NICAP with flat lies and claimed that they had been given all UFO information in the hands of the Air Force. It was a very strong bluff to play, meant to take Keyhoe by surprise. It did not work that way. Keyhoe had outguessed and out prepared the Air Force. In the face of the blunt charges, he produced his own document. The *Night Beat* host, now forced to cooperate, let the camera focus on the paper. It was a request from NICAP to Secretary of the Air Force Douglas to review those Air Force case files. Douglas' reply said: "We must decline your offer to review and publish the Air Force's reports on this subject." The host, reduced to a stunned and emotional naïf, said: "You mean the Air Force *lied* to *Night Beat*?"

Let us take a break from that unpleasantness to see what the phenomenon itself was doing during the first two-thirds of 1957, prior to the big flare-up in November.

January 16, northwest of Ft. Worth, Texas:[32] Lt. Col. Howard Wright was resting while his co-pilot flew their B-25 home to Reese AFB, Lubbock, Texas, the first of a flight of three B-25s returning from Birmingham, Alabama. Wright's crew and the B-25 following 25 minutes behind them flew a straight-line "dark" route (without constant radio beacons), while the third B-25, with a less-experienced pilot, took the longer way. About 90 miles from Sweetwater, Texas, Wright saw a bright light source and alerted his co-pilot to a possible aircraft. The source had an apparent size smaller than the full moon and was a round, soft light. The Colonel immediately noticed that his plane's radio compass was pointing directly at the object. A radio compass is not a common compass that points towards a magnetic field, but is, rather, a radio beacon detector. Its function is to allow pilots to locate the radio beacons of a distant landing field (in this case, the B-25's compass was pointing towards and "seeking" Lubbock), and to keep a straight flight path. This new object, however, had overpowered the Lubbock signal, and therefore was a radio source of some power.

Shortly, the object came swiftly down from above the plane and ahead of it to a position more or less level and off the right wing. At this time the light seemed smaller, thus a bit more distant. Then the entire object began blinking on and off. Wright gathered himself and, using a flashlight, tried to blink a signal back in Morse code. There was no obvious response, but the thing kept blinking away for an hour in its 3 o'clock position. One of the crew, thinking that maybe this was some kind of code, took four pages of notes. During this hour, the object would occasionally speed up and fall back, (rarely) move up and down, and sometimes come a little nearer. Always the radio compass needle followed it. At the object's closest approach, it had a markedly larger size, but what this amounted to is not possible to determine from the words used in the interview. The term was "as big as a basketball" in apparent size, but whether Wright meant "at arm's length" (which is the normal way of relating this) or at some greater distance (such as the tip of the wing), we cannot say. Either way, Wright and his crew felt that the object had some significant size. Through much of this time, the crew tried to get into contact with ground stations but was unable to do so. Once in range of Lubbock, the object broke away and flew off on a straight-line course in about twelve seconds.

Upon landing, Wright and the crew demanded to talk immediately to the base intelligence officers and make their report. While they were doing so, the trailing B-25 landed, and its excited crew rushed in, asking, "Did you see what we saw?" Wright said that the second crew seemed to have been followed by an identical, blinking light source, but that it was probably a second object. Reports plus the code notes were taken all around, and a B-25 was refueled, outfitted with some of the same crews and intelligence agents, and went up to look for the object or objects. Four hours later, having found nothing, the airmen returned. All this is interesting enough. What Blue Book did with the case adds a little bitter flavor. They evaluated the case as "insufficient data." The only material in their file was a bare-bones telegraphic description—no full interviews, no pages of code, no mention of the radio compass effects! Where did all this material go? Was it stopped at Air Defense Command (ADC) headquarters? Was it lost at Blue Book? However one views it, the adequacy of the UFO project looks worse and worse. The details that *are* available come from the fortunate circumstance that things like this became very puzzling and interesting to Colonel Wright, and when he had the opportunity he told Donald Keyhoe and later had even more extensive interviews with Dr. James McDonald. One wonders what could have been learned, even in terms of physical forces, about the phenomenon if people had been paying attention.

March 9, in the Atlantic Ocean North/South commercial flight lane:[33] As usual, commercial airliners were strung out all along the route between New York City and Miami. At about 4:30 a.m. one of the Pan-Am flights saw an object ahead, which had a greenish-blue perimeter and a bright white center. The light seemed to be at their level and coming directly forward. Then the thing seemed to veer, pass by to starboard while descending, and then "go out." A piece of the object, red in color, seemed to fall off before the light went out.

The next plane was another Pan-Am, piloted by Captain M. Van Winkle, and flying well to the rear of the first airliner. This time the initial observation was of something orange. It, too, seemed to be moving very fast and on a collision course with Van Winkle's plane. As the object neared, it took on the appearance of a brilliant greenish-white spotlight. The object seemed sharp-edged and well defined. Instinctively, Van Winkle roughly yanked the plane upwards and to the left. The light raced by to the right and slightly below. The flight engineer said that it then just "went out." In the back, passengers and stewardesses had been thrown all over the place. Van Winkle immediately reported the "near miss" to ground control. Another 150 miles behind, a third pilot saw an unusual brightly flashing, greenish tinged light moving rapidly in the distance (though not at an angle that it could be the same object as Van Winkle's).

Because four persons were hospitalized, this event became a major affair. Van Winkle was on the hot seat, but, since other pilots testified to seeing similar objects that night, his story was credible. The Air Force immediately denied having any missiles or experimental traffic in the area.

The Department of the Defense could not identify today the flaming object that almost collided with an aircraft of Pan American Airways at great altitude over the Atlantic.

A spokesman said that the Department had not received any information regarding the incident. It refused to state if a runaway guided missile could have been the flaming object. There have been considerable controversies in the last few years over similar incidents where flying saucers are seen. The

Air Force said in October, 1955, that after a study of over eight years they could say that such objects could not exist.

Retired Rear Admiral Delmar S. Fahrney, expert in all that refers to guided missiles, said at the beginning of this year certain unidentified objects, guided it seems by certain intelligences, are penetrating the earth's atmosphere. He also says that these rare objects acquire such velocity that neither the United States nor Russia could duplicate.[34]

The Blue Book records marked the case "meteor" but also "classified."

March 22/23, Oxnard, California:[35] The wife of an Air Force officer along with her 17-year-old daughter saw a series of unusual lights. First they saw a large, soundless, and pulsing light, with something like a pole on top, making fast and erratic motions. Later, they saw a green object accompanied by two smaller red lights—whether these sightings were related is difficult to tease out of the text. She called a military friend and then Oxnard AFB. The officer inquired about radar and was told that radar was detecting something there. The woman said that the two red objects had moved lower and seemed to be approaching. The sheriff's office was contacted and they sent a patrol car. The patrol officer confirmed the woman's report to Oxnard, with the exception that by that time there were five red objects flying well below the green one. Somehow, between the time of this report to the Air Base and the later Air Force investigation by the 4602nd, these red objects were changed, on the report, to stars and the Moon above. This happened despite the witness stating that the red lights were below the hills on the horizon. To deal with that, the Air Force added the theory that a temperature inversion had caused light to bend the images of the stars, or, alternatively, the witness saw lights on a barn. The woman herself was judged hysterical due to her pregnancy. The Air Force's explanation was completed without anyone bothering to interview the teen-age daughter or taking anything associated with the airbase into account (for example, the radar returns).

The press knew all about the case due to the fact that others in the area were reporting things at the same time. Three Ventura County deputies and two Port Hueneme police spotted *single* red objects, and other sightings are recorded. None of this made it into the Blue Book record. Still, Blue Book was worried. This case was in the news; they knew that Keyhoe would be on the hunt, and they needed to head him off. Their message to ADC about Oxnard said: "in reference to sighting by Mrs. [deleted], Oxnard, CA, In view of possible publicity, numerous witnesses, and police and sheriff brought in on case, request preliminary investigation, request brief summary of findings by tt [teletype] message."[36] Under special instructions, the message read: "Answer?" The answer given was both "stars" and "lights on barn."

When the requested summary came back with almost no detail, ATIC was incensed. Another message went to ADC. It said:

No details concerning this case received as yet; only comment in your UFO summary with statement was astronomical. This incident recognized by this center as potentially dangerous in that it could give Air Force unfavorable publicity, if exploited by fanatic or die-hard 'flying saucer' proponents. This now definite possibility, with receipt of letter from National Investigations Committee of UFOs (NICAP) demanding full details and answers to certain aspects of Oxnard incident not supported by information in file.

Officially, this incident does not warrant action required, but [name deleted, but obviously "Keyhoe's"] ability to slant material and create unwarranted trouble for Air Force, his stock and trade for almost ten years.[37]

This was an unusually emotional Blue Book communication. What were they talking about? The case report *was* shoddily done. Even the sexist solution of blaming everything on a pregnant woman falls apart immediately given that no other witness' testimony was taken into account. The explanation that all this could be "stars" was later admitted by the astronomical consultant (Allen Hynek) to be impossible. And NICAP had found an Air Traffic Controller who was willing to sign a document stating that his tower *had* picked the objects up on radar. Keyhoe asked an Air Traffic authority if the controller could get in trouble, even though no JANAP 146/CIRVIS report had been turned in, and, therefore, talking about the case violated no law. "Would he still be in hot water?" asked Keyhoe. "Scalding. Tell him to shut up."[38]

The friction over this case lasted all year. In October, when NICAP published its newsletter, *The UFO Investigator*, Blue Book was reading it. George Gregory wrote the Pentagon in a fury:

> Reference is made to a recent briefing given to the office of the Assistant Secretary of Defense [who, with his family had a UFO case themselves earlier in the year] in which the serious nature of NICAP as a cleverly organized instrument of rabble rousing and agitation, was presented in some detail.[39]

Gregory then blasted NICAP's version of Oxnard as "deliberately false," paradoxically citing that the Air Base radar men are on record saying there was no radar return, even if a CAA radar man says that his tower *did* detect a UFO. Then Gregory says that even if the CAA story is true, then it is a violation of government information policy (i.e. CIRVIS) and the operator should be reported to proper authorities. Let the reader judge: where is the logic and where is the hysteria in this case?

May 3, Edwards AFB, California:[40] It was the morning of a tracking day at Edwards, and the two-man crews were out at their stations where the permanent Askania theodolites were being stocked with film and readied. At one station, about 1½ miles from the Edwards perimeter, veteran civilian operators Jack Gettys and James Bittick were prepared for their part of the first test. But there in the sky, a different object awaited them. It was distant, but obviously a shiny domed disk. Gettys and Bittick called to the base operation controller, Frank Baker, and asked for permission to shoot some of their film at the object. Base operations took three or four minutes to decide while the theodolite crew watched the disk, sometimes through the small tracking telescope mounted on the Askania. Base then said: "go ahead." Gettys and Bittick shot 200 to 300 feet of film at 30 frames per second, as the object moved away. The two men took the film canister to base and made

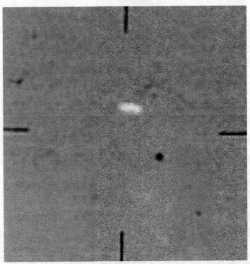

Edwards AFB Film of UFO

their report. The film was developed on base and everyone involved got a look at it, including team leader Baker. These men were veteran "object spotters" and had seen all manner of plane, missile, balloon, bombing run, object drop, and parachute, right up to the U-2 spy plane. All of them knew that what they saw on this film was none of those things. The visual reports agreed on a shiny-as-if-metallic domed disk, and the film, if viewed with a magnifying glass, supported that conclusion, according to Baker. Both Bittick and Baker thought that there was a series of black dots near the dome, which might have been portholes. Gettys did not remember seeing that. Nevertheless, here was a domed disk on film seen by highly credible observers at our nation's top air technology base.

The next morning, the intelligence boys were at Edwards to grill Gettys and Bittick. In an interview much later in time, Bittick remembers their interrogators as FBI, but that is unlikely. The agents were probably plainclothes but part of Air Force intelligence, or even, as occasionally happened in the continental U.S., CIA. Either way, the grilling was insulting. Gettys and Bittick were derided with statements like: you know what it is like when you have stayed out too late at night (they had not), or too long in the sun (it was the start of their 8 a.m. shift), and the desert sun will do funny things to you. Bittick got so angry that he got up and barked: "Do I have to listen to this ---- [deleted]!?" Unsuccessful in getting the trackers to admit that they were mistaken in their report, the questioners told the two to "go home and keep your mouth shut, you understand?" Recalling those moments, Bittick said: "It's a funny thing how they try to cover up what they know and use a stupid answer for it."[41]

The "stupid answer" was that Gettys and Bittick had seen and filmed a balloon. This is not *obviously* stupid, even in the face of the witnesses saying that it looked like no balloon and moved faster than any balloon and they had seen many, many balloons in their spotting scopes, and this was not one. Still, a balloon *had* been launched at 7:40 a.m. from Edwards, so . . . No one from Blue Book, ADC, or from wherever the interrogators had originated bothered actually to look into the possibility of a balloon misidentification. Fortunately, there was in this case a conscientious Deputy Chief of Staff for Operations at Edwards AFB who did so. Lt. Colonel Raymond Klein checked on the balloon launch and obtained the data on it (it was being followed and recorded at ten-minute intervals). Klein knew exactly where that balloon was throughout the theodolite filming experience, and wrote ATIC with his analysis: "Based on the above track made and the location of the observers at the time of sighting, the weather balloon released at Edwards could not have been the unidentified object reported."[42]

Back at Blue Book such information made no difference. The case solution to this day reads "Confirmed balloon." Incidents such as this one at Edwards AFB are stunning examples of what depths Blue Book had reached. It *was* doing something. But that something had nothing to do with the nature of UFOs.

July 17, over Louisiana and Texas:[43] This event is the most examined radar-and-visual air encounter of all time. The case usually goes by the nickname "RB-47," after the type of plane centrally involved. The RB-47 was the Air Force's state-of-the-art bomber of the 1950s, was equipped with the best available radar systems, and was the backbone of the Strategic Air Command's nuclear strike force. The case was studied by James McDonald, the Colorado Project, Brad Sparks, and many other individual researchers, each in their own way. It is a very complex affair that involved our leading-edge radar detection equipment, a long duration plane pacing and chasing, a visual observation throughout most of the incident, radar detection from both ground and air, and a

Air Force RB-47 Bomber

corroboration of cross-talk between pilots and radar personnel. To do this case complete justice would require much space and a detailed highly technical discussion, so we will refer the reader to a good, solid analysis elsewhere.[44] Suffice it for our purposes to say that this experience was like an expanded and thoroughly documented version of the January 16 encounter of Colonel Wright that was described earlier. Here, there are more witnesses, longer observations, higher level technology detection capabilities, and stronger corroboration. Both experiences involve the long-term pacing of military aircraft by luminous objects that are strong radio signal emitters. The fact that these radio emissions could overpower our best radio-sensing technology should have been of the greatest concern to the military. In the "RB-47" case, the reality of the experience was clinched when pilots (visually), plane radar operators, and ground radar operators, all simultaneously saw the object "blink out" at the same moment. The extreme anomalousness of *that* instantly eliminated conventional explanations using any but the most contrived coincidences.

This case was, of course, reported extensively by the crew at landing. At this point in our general story, it should not come as a surprise that many of these reports were lost; their whereabouts are still a mystery. Even then, what made it to Blue Book convinced an electronics (i.e. radar) expert there that the detected signals were hard to explain on any grounds other than an unknown: "there is such a mass of evidence which tends to tie in together to indicate the presence of a physical object or UFO."[45]

Despite everything, when Blue Book heard that there was a commercial airliner in the general area, they seized upon the idea that somehow a "near miss" had occurred, and that all their military technologies and trained personnel had made a colossal misidentification. Such preposterous claims frequently have been thrown up in the history of this field, as we have seen. Sometimes, interested parties have time to refute them; often, not. In this case, since by coincidence the commercial plane *had* been involved in a *different* near-miss (including injuries to passengers), a good record of its flight was kept and it was located nowhere near the area of the RB-47 encounter. Since all this was knowable at the time, one would expect that to be reflected in the record. The Blue Book file says: "Aircraft," to this day. This case would have never risen to any prominence except that the captain of the RB-47 flight happened to be at the Colorado Project's briefing of a group of Air Force personnel in the late 1960s. He asked about his encounter, naturally thinking it would be a good one. When the Colorado Project scientists asked the Air Force for the Blue Book file on the RB-47 case, the file could not be found. Ultimately, the case was put together by better file searching at Blue Book, James McDonald's success at locating several crew members and interviewing them, and FOIA searches that located more of the lost documents. Particularly in the "George Gregory" years at ATIC, this sort of rejection of the need to clarify almost any significant aspect of a UFO case was constant. If we did not know, from our earlier information, what Captain Gregory understood to be his duty as chief of Blue Book, we would label this as reckless and incompetent.

July 24, somewhere between Las Cruces, New Mexico, and El Paso, Texas:[46] A woman first spotted a large and very fast object, moving high in the sky and on a straight path. She pointed it out to her husband and the rest of their family. They watched it for about thirty seconds until it disappeared. Compared to most cases, this was not much. But the husband thought that it was an unknown, and he was Nathan Wagner, the chief of Missile Flight Safety of White Sands Proving Grounds (and, today, a member of the WSPG Hall-of-Fame). Wagner, who knew about many safety-related airliner incidents and, apparently, many UFO incidents as well, stated to the newspapers that he felt that these unknowns could have something to do with the near-miss airline incidents recently reported.[47]

Nathan Wagner

In the latter part of 1957, due to the International Geophysical Year and the launchings of the Soviet satellites, a program was initiated that drove many people outdoors, looking at the sky. The program was called Operation Moonwatch. Moonwatch was mainly composed of amateurs under the supervision of the Smithsonian Astrophysical Observatory (SAO), directed by Harvard meteor expert, Dr. Fred Whipple, and assisted by J. Allen Hynek. Moonwatch's goal was the accurate plotting of Soviet and U.S. satellite orbits.[48] The program was supported by some excellently-designed tracking telescopes, the "Baker-Nunn" cameras. People were excited about the human race breaking into space, and many persons volunteered.

As far as UFOs were concerned, this project put many trained and semi-trained observers into place to scan the heavens. From most viewpoints this was a good thing, but not necessarily to the Air Force. They did not want more UFO stories coming in from a government program. In practice, things should have been fairly well controlled. Project Director Whipple was Donald Menzel's closest friend on the Harvard Astronomy Staff and a consultant to Blue Book. What could be a better-controlled situation? As it turned out, the situation could have been much better for the Air Force. Citizens talked, and Allen Hynek began to let his curiosity get the better of himself. Hynek began to think that, at a minimum, there were things in the UFO observations that pointed to at least one new natural phenomenon, if not several. Whereas some higher personnel in the SAO Moonwatch organization did not want citizen observers to log "unidentifieds" even if they obviously were not satellites, Hynek wanted the cases and he was not alone.[49] One of his assistants, Bud Ledwith, was very interested; so was a young apprentice named Walter Webb. Both went on to do research on UFOs beyond Moonwatch, and Webb made a lifetime of it. So signals to the citizen observers were mixed. Many logs of unidentified "non-satellites" were received. Doubtless more were never logged. Hynek gathered additional information by "personal communication." But these observations *were* generally kept very quiet. Only in later years would anybody outside the SAO, Hynek, Webb, et al., have any inkling of the numbers. It is a story still untold. But we *will* tell a little of that story in the next chapter. Suffice it to say for now that in those times the science media used Moonwatch as an argument against UFOs: with so many trained observers looking, surely Moonwatch would have seen unidentified objects if there were any; and, of course, they have not.[50] It was just one more peculiar untruth in what seems to be an endless continuous stream of disinformation.

Sputnik went up in early October and so did UFO reports. Some commentators say that those reports were Soviet hysteria; some say it was just because people were outside looking for Sputnik. In October, reports were about twice what the earlier months averaged, but when the 1957 flap occurred in early November, the cases shot up to ten times the earlier rate.[51] The flap is much too dense and powerful to describe thoroughly in a few pages here. Instead, our coverage of the flap will concentrate upon two main topics: how the phenomenon, for the first time in the United States, "came closer," manifesting itself with "close encounters" involving physical effects on both technology and people; and how the government dealt with these issues to keep the country from becoming too excited or frightened.

Table 1, on page 251, shows what the Air Force had to deal with as the number of cases exploded.[52] It represents what UFOlogists would call a concentrated national "flap." The year 1957 was proceeding fairly quietly until the very end of October. Then case reports rocketed off the chart, spiking on the 5th and 6th of November. The rate of incidents was far beyond the capability of the Air Force to properly investigate. And this flap was distinctively different. Hidden within the sheath of old-fashioned UFO reports was the sharp blade of a new (for the United States) phenomenology: close encounters. These close encounters mainly bore a distinct characteristic: the failures of automobile engines (and often other devices, such as lights and radios) that were coincident with the presence of an unidentified object, and felt by the witness to be due to that object. Also embedded in the flap, in lesser, but still interesting, amounts, were several cases in which the witnesses seemed to have received a mild "burn" from the light, heat, or other radiation from the offending object. Both of these UFO-related or UFO-coincident phenomena were very rare in previous American records. Both of these were much more personal and potentially threatening than what military and civilians had typically dealt with before. How would the citizenry react? How would the military?

Table 2, on page 252, is also worth a short commentary. It graphs the numbers of close encounter "vehicle interference" cases year-by-year.[53] The year 1957 is broken down into quarters to show the concentration in the 4th quarter of the year. As is easily seen, it was completely out-of-the-norm for any previous U.S. experience. It remains the highest peak of such phenomenology ever. In the mid-to-late

1960s, when UFOs sightings increased all around America, "close encounter vehicle interference" cases came back. But during those years they were sprinkled across the months and never concentrated again as in November of 1957. The graph ends in 1979, the year before Dr. Mark Rodeghier published his catalogue of these events, but, as he and others have kept track over the succeeding years, such cases have essentially vanished from the reports.

All of this is part of the mystery: each era is partly distinctive, partly the same. The sameness would lead students towards linking the phenomenology, the differences to tearing the phenomenology apart. It was always this latter element—that the phenomenon would *not* present a tight, predictable pattern—that had been the strongest Air Force tool for arguing against it, and the argument that was featured in Blue Book 14. But sometimes intensity will overcome everything else, and this was an intense flap with spectacular aspects. How would it play out?

Dr. Mark Rodeghier

Earlier in the year (August 22, near Cecil Naval Air Station, Florida),[54] Blue Book had become aware of an isolated case of a vehicle stoppage and had written it off as the sighting of a helicopter (ignoring the car engine problem). Earlier still, several radar-interference cases caused some to think that UFOs could generate electromagnetic radiation, perhaps even as directional pulses.[55] Of course, no one was yet thinking

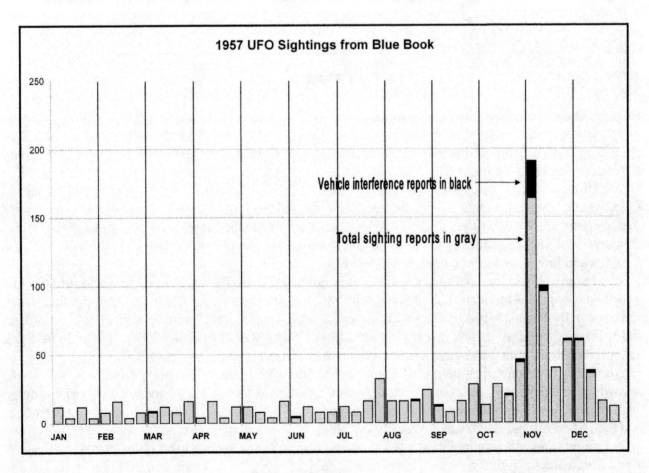

TABLE 1

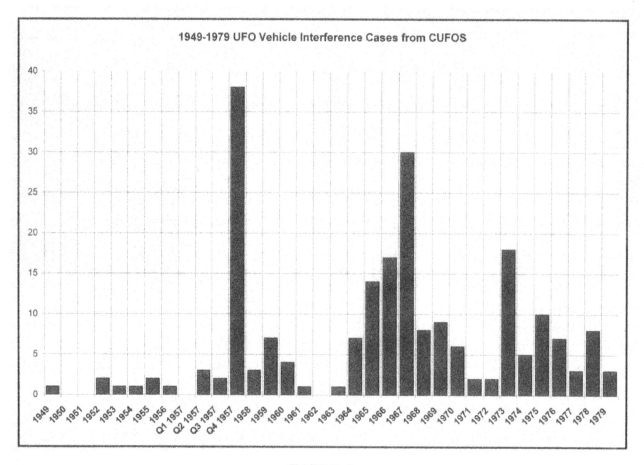

TABLE 2

about UFO electromagnetic pulses stopping automobile engines, but, as time went on, UFO researchers would wonder about this and government labs (such as Los Alamos and Sandia) would initiate research programs on such things as a non-lethal battlefield tool.[56] All of this gained a feeling of concrete reality in Western Texas on the night of November 2 and 3.

All UFO case type categories ("Distant Objects," "Radar-Visuals," "Close Encounters of the 1st Kind," etc.) have representative incidents which the students of the field evaluate as particularly characteristic and difficult to explain. These incidents are the anchor cases. The anchor case for "Close Encounters of the 2nd Kind, type: Vehicle Interference" is Levelland, Texas (Nov 2/3).[57] Again, a complex and long case must be briefly summarized:

Just before 11 p.m. on November 2, the phone rang in the sheriff's office at Levelland. On the line were two Mexican-American truck drivers, who reported that four miles northwest of town their truck had apparently been stopped by the overflight of a rocket-shaped light emitting a great amount of heat and a blast of wind as it flew directly overhead. The thing was big, about 200 feet long. The truck lights failed along with the engine. The deputy on duty did not take the report seriously.

About one hour later, just before midnight, the phone rang again. This time a driver four miles *east* of town reported a very similar occurrence. A blazingly bright sort of egg-shaped object was sitting on the road ahead, when the engine and lights of the witness' car failed. The thing, also estimated at about 200 feet, lifted off and flew away, or just "went out."

A few minutes after midnight, a caller reported his car being stopped ten miles north-northeast of town. This witness' lights went out, too. Here the object was also an estimated 200 feet in length and egg-shaped. It was circling a field by the road. The object stopped and just disappeared. Shortly a fourth caller from the same general area reported the brilliant egg sitting at a crossroads. Once again, the witness' lights and motor died.

This was finally too much for the deputy, and soon the sheriff was roused, and he and several highway patrolmen were on the hunt. Before the hullabaloo settled down, several more encounters ensued. Putting these together, either directly from the phone log that evening, or from people who came in the next day to report, there had been at least eight instances of "vehicle interference" by the marauding egg all across the northern area around Levelland. Added to that, some of the police (including the sheriff) saw a suspicious light at a distance, and the fire marshal saw

Left to Right: Sheriff Weir Clem and Patrolmen Lee Hargrove, Floyd Cavin

a streak of light, whereupon his lights dimmed and his motor almost quit. The image below shows the main incidents that evening.[58]

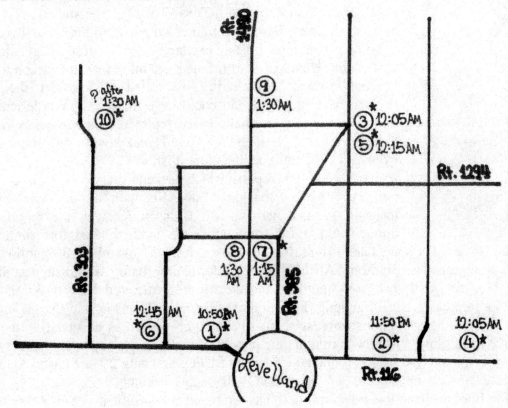

MAP: Events around Levelland, Tx., November 2 and 3, 1957.
Times are those estimated by the witnesses.
★s indicate instances of vehicle interferences.

Even taking the whole experience as likely to have been produced by one object, or at least a few similar objects, the case still frustrates the analyst. That is because, although the descriptions by all witnesses are similar (big, bright, elongated), they do not precisely match. The bottom line, however, is that a rather large number of independent witnesses had their vehicles interfered with somehow. It would stretch credulity past the breaking point to imagine that occurring in that concentrated space and time by *different* causes. So what was the "it" that caused this? That is what the citizens wanted to know (both there and elsewhere, as the story made sensational national headlines); and that is what the Air Force needed to answer.

Levelland occurred early in the UFO wave of 1957, before the Air Force would know what a storm it was facing. The major UFO managers, such as Gregory, Arcier, et al. were busy with Keyhoe and Congress. The case would be handled as just another incident.[59] An Air Force sergeant from Ent AFB was sent to investigate. He arrived about noon on November 5, and spent the afternoon in the area (three hours in Levelland; three hours in Lubbock) interviewing six

Left: Newell Wright. Right: Sheriff Weir Clem

people. Those six people included three from the sheriff's office, none of whom had seen more than a streak of light, and one person whose experience was not involved at all, but occurred almost two days later. The investigation of the eight Levelland incidents, therefore, was limited to interviews of the initial caller, Pedro Saucedo, and a Texas Tech college student, Newell Wright. Sergeant Norman Barth was impressed with Wright, but not with Saucedo. Saucedo was judged to be an excitable fellow whose imagination ran away from him. Handily, Barth failed to interview the second witness in Saucedo's truck, and Barth also failed to consider the remarkable "coincidence" that Saucedo could have imagined an experience that was *later*, with quite a bit of similarity, reported by a witness [Wright] judged to be a a reliable observer. As Allen Hynek always said about such mental gymnastics: "It can't be, therefore it isn't."

Pedro Saucedo

Barth took his report, which lacked interviews with at least seven primary witnesses, back to Ent AFB with a poor assessment of the incident. Lt. Colonel William Brunson received the report, thought it through with Barth, and wrote the Intelligence Information Report for Project Blue Book.[60] For some unknown reason this took him until November 18. Ignoring everything involving the automobiles, Brunson's Air Intelligence Information Report would suggest that Saucedo was unreliable, the sheriff had seen lightning and electrical storms, and Newell Wright must have encountered a rare case of ball lightning. In a moment of candor, Brunson said that he did not really know what the weather conditions were, so the case should be viewed as unsolved. In the meantime, the Air Force had followed its now normal public pattern of issuing a "general comment" type of press release on November 5 (the AF has found no evidence of UFOs and only 2% are unsolved, etc.).[61]

As other events in the flap hit the newsstand, and people became more and more excited and curious, Blue Book realized that it was going to have to comment specifically. Still it delayed. Finally, on November 15, the Pentagon issued a press release. It covered Levelland and four other events. We will confine ourselves to just the Levelland "solution" for the moment.

LEVELLAND, Texas: (Big Light, seen by "dozens," stalled autos)

Investigation on the scene revealed that only three persons, rather than "dozens," could be located who saw the "big light." Preliminary reports have not revealed cause of "stalled" automobiles at this time, although rain and electrical storms at the time of the reported sightings, affecting wet electrical circuits, could be cause. Object visible only few seconds, not sustained visibility as had been implied.

EVALUATION: Weather phenomenon of electrical nature, generally classified as "Ball Lightning" or "St. Elmo's Fire," caused by stormy conditions in the area, including mist, rain, thunderstorms and lightning. [62]

As one can read, the Pentagon wrote this piece based solely upon the incompetent and rushed few hours' "investigation" by Ent AFB. Those aware of what really happened, both during the event and the field study, knew that the language of the press release was so far off target as to be laughable. Beyond that, a simple check of the newspaper or any weather service would have shown that there were no electrical storms, not even rain, in Levelland that evening. Far from being an observer for only a few seconds, Newell Wright, the witness that Brunson said he believed, stated that he watched the "egg" on the road for three to four *minutes*. All the weather elements listed in the "Evaluation" portion of the release as "causes" were non-existent, and the pairing of ball lightning and St. Elmo's Fire indicated an embarrassing lack of scientific knowledge, as the two phenomena are utterly different.

It would have been possible to investigate the Levelland incidents honestly and still try to explain them in conventional terms. In fact, that exact thing has been attempted both within and without the UFO-sympathetic community. The basis of such an investigation would have been interviews of all eight "vehicle-interference" witnesses, with some character checks, and a factual determination of weather conditions that night. That would have been the minimum. Additionally, the various vehicles and their recent functional histories could have been studied. Lastly, some scientific attempt to determine what could possibly stop the engines and shut the lights off would be pursued. Almost none of these things were done by the Air Force, yet they felt no qualms in offering a solution to the nation. As an aside, when Levelland has been analyzed by later skeptics, whether open-mindedly or with debunking in mind, the debate always comes down to ball lightning.[63] Could it have been present under those weather conditions? (Honest answer: extremely unlikely.) Could it last for several minutes before dissociating? (Honest answer: not usually, but possibly.) Could it be 100 to 200 feet large? (Honest answer: there is no record of ball lightning remotely near that size.) Could it stop a car engine from a distance of many feet away? (Honest answer: there is no evidence for this assumption.) To an open mind, Levelland is a very big mystery. Did it involve an ET-spacecraft? One cannot prove anything about *that* hypothesis either, especially taking the case as a stand-alone incident.

But simply saying things from an authoritarian position usually works, almost regardless of what is said. And so it was here. This is and was true because UFO cases ultimately recede from memory and are no longer around to refute the authority. The 1957 wave was powerful enough, however, that the public and the media did not want to forget quite so quickly, and so the Air Force was still under pressure to defend itself throughout the latter half of November. For one thing, near the end of the month, events were proceeding for a major, three-hour TV show covering the flap. Somehow, the Pentagon had been pressured into cooperating with the writers and producers, and the Assistant Secretary of Defense (from whose office this pressure may have been originating) was making (in George Gregory's mind) unreasonable requests that ATIC come up with answers.[64] Even Harold Watson could not stop this media irritation at Blue Book, and Gregory and his crew scrambled to get something so that they could look good. The big card to play, of course, was Science. So some attempt was made to marshal scientific evidence and opinion that the events could be ball lightning, or, more outlandishly, St. Elmo's Fire.

Gregory desperately attempted to put something together under the time pressure. Whatever Gregory told the television crew must have been bunk, because he was still scrambling in early January of 1958 and writing preposterous things[65] (for example, that the weather conditions were fog, rain, mist, and low ceiling although the sergeant's original intelligence reports had listed the ceiling as unlimited). All of Gregory's descriptors for ball lightning were vague, especially omitting size and duration. Despite knowing this, he boldly claimed that the Levelland phenomena had almost exactly these ball lightning characteristics. He even tossed out the speculation that the lightning could so ionize the air as to shut down key parts of the ignition systems—an assertion for which there was no support anywhere. At least he had become aware that he had to drop all allusions to the irrelevant St. Elmo's Fire.

In this Captain Gregory had the backing, astoundingly, of Allen Hynek. Hynek was at his new job tracking Soviet satellites and got a request by phone from Gregory to give an opinion on the case. Hynek apparently listened to Gregory's analysis (we do not know if he even had much in the way of the paper reports to read, and may have read nothing), and then composed his scientific opinion, typed it up and sent it to Blue Book where it was attached to the record.[66] Hynek's half-page opinion reads Gregory's "facts" back to him, but does, as is Hynek's style, include much waffling to protect himself. Still, the feeling is left that Hynek concurred in the explanation, even the speculation that lightning halted the ignition systems.

Much later, when he was well away from his Air Force consultancy, Hynek had several painful "examinations of conscience" on these matters.

> What was needed at the time was swift reaction by Blue Book and a serious, thorough investigation. Captain Gregory, then head of Blue Book, did call me by phone, but at that time, as the person directly responsible for the tracking of the new Russian satellite, I was on a virtual around-the-clock duty and was unable to give it any attention whatever. I am not proud today that I hastily concurred in Captain Gregory's evaluation as "ball lightning" on the basis of information that an electrical storm had been in progress in the Levelland area at the time. That was shown not to be the case. Observers reported overcast and mist but no lightning. Besides, had I given it any thought whatever, I would soon have recognized the absence of any evidence that ball lightning can stop cars and put out headlights.[67]

Hynek's casual actions in this matter supported an effective misrepresentation of this important case.

Levelland was the most spectacular case, but it was far from the only one. Right alongside it were several other West Texas and New Mexico incidents, plus a major claim from a Coast Guard cutter in the Gulf of Mexico. All of these hit the newspapers at about the same time. The Orogrande, New Mexico, or "James Stokes," case, particularly intrigued people.[68] In it, there was not only another claim of multiple car stoppages, but of a mild case of skin burn on top of it. This case was, in the end, only a single witness testimony, and so became controversial not for the UFO but as a referendum on the man. In our context, the case is interesting regardless of how one would finally evaluate it. It contains much that is characteristic of the handling of investigations and the media of the times.

James Stokes was 46 years old and a veteran of about 20 years in the U.S. Navy. He was no longer in active service but was, instead, an electronics technician working at Holloman AFB for a civilian firm. Stokes' skills were largely picked up on the

James Stokes at left during Holloman debriefing

job, but he was evaluated by his bosses as not only qualified, but energetic, conscientious, and even somewhat of a genius at his work. Still he was not a particularly talkative man, unless one engaged him on a favorite subject, like electronics. It was in this way that he came to be known by Jim Lorenzen, the husband of Coral Lorenzen who ran the UFO group APRO.[69] Stokes was mildly interested in UFOs (with all the high profile cases in the area it was hard not to be), but he and Jim talked mainly about electronics and related sciences. Though a quiet man, Stokes had one serious dispute with his Holloman bosses over a ratings evaluation. This did not involve some mundane squabbling over money but was rather a matter of principle and pride, and he quit briefly over it until matters were resolved. When 1957 rolled around, James Stokes was considered a solid technical worker and was viewed with respect. All this is mentioned because the Air Force fell back on insinuations about character issues in order to debunk this report.

Here is what allegedly happened, according to sources available to us. Stokes was driving from his home in Alamogordo to El Paso, Texas, on the afternoon of November 4. About ten miles south of Orogrande, New Mexico, his radio began fading and then went dead. The car engine also died and his automobile rolled to a stop. It was only then that he noticed that what he thought was traffic ahead was actually a group of cars stopped in the same vicinity. Many of the people were out of their cars looking at an object in the sky. The object seemed to be large and egg-shaped, colored like mother-of-pearl. It came from northeast to southwest, then turned sharply and made a pass over the highway, then another sharp turn and pass, then left the way it had come. Stokes was scribbling notes while another man tried to get pictures and a few people were talking to one another. When the object passed overhead, Stokes said that he felt a burst of pressure and a rise in temperature. Once it had left, the people were able to restart their cars without difficulty and drive on. Stokes did not know any of the other people, and he estimated there were about seven cars involved. He thought that the man with the camera was named Baker, and another man he talked to was named Duncan. Stokes had no addresses and only vague locations as to their employment.

Stokes continued on to El Paso, wanting to tell someone about this, but worried about news prohibitions that he had heard about but did not fully understand. So he called his military boss, Major Ralph Everett, and asked him.[70] Major Everett may or may not have had a firm grasp on the policy, but as Stokes was a civilian and off the premises, Everett told him to go ahead and say whatever he wished. The Major himself was impressed with the story and he himself talked it up around the base. By the time that Stokes returned to Alamogordo in early evening, several persons around the base and the town had heard the rumors. Up to this point Stokes had told just the military and was looking to unburden himself with a fuller "get-it-out" session. So he called his

APRO officers: Jim Lorenzen standing, Terry Clarke far right, and Coral Lorenzen second from right

acquaintance Jim Lorenzen, who he knew would be interested and sympathetic.[71] The Lorenzens picked up the phone at 8:55 p.m. and met with Stokes as soon as possible. By 9:30 p.m. the story had been told. Meanwhile, a Holloman employee had heard the rumor and passed it on to a buddy of his at KAIG (the Alamogordo radio station), newscaster Terry Clarke.[72] Clarke called Major Everett at home. Everett identified Stokes. After trying unsuccessfully to reach Stokes, Clarke thought he would try Coral Lorenzen and see if she had heard anything. At that moment, she called him. Stokes was with her and Jim, and they wanted to get the story out.

Clarke was suspicious of Air Force handling of UFO witnesses and he "wanted to get to him before the Air Force did." Plus, he had just gotten a favorable opinion of Stokes from Everett. When Stokes and the Lorenzens arrived at KAIG, his face was reddened "and he seemed to be suffering from a sunburn" (both Clarke and the Lorenzens say this). Stokes was agitated and could not settle down until Clarke gave him some cigarettes. Now somewhat more relaxed, Stokes was able to be interviewed on tape and it made the 10 p.m. news. Clarke then wrote the story for the news services, and it blasted out across the entire country.[73]

By the next morning, the military was awake. Stokes was called in to talk to Base Commander General L. I. Davis and Deputy Commander Colonel Judy.[74] After this briefing, General Davis called KAIG and asked to hear the interview tape. Asked about the incident, Davis said "no comment." Terry Clarke then called the base PIO officers and asked their opinion. Did they believe Stokes? "We have no choice. He's a recognized engineer and a retired Chief Petty Officer with 24 years experience in the Navy. He should know what he sees."

General L. I. Davis

Clarke and the Lorenzens then went about looking for Baker and Duncan, two other potential witnesses, but never found them.

That, of course, did not end the affair. The Air Force now had another situation to control, right on the heels of Levelland. The Lorenzens invited Stokes over Tuesday evening (November 5) to meet other APRO members and discuss the incident. By that time (a little more than a day past the encounter) Stokes' "sunburn" had gone away and he was looking normal. Meanwhile, at Ent AFB, the same Colonel Brunson who had sent the Sergeant to investigate Levelland, sent a Captain to investigate Stokes.[75] Holloman officials had been fairly kind to Stokes, even giving a mildly supportive press release.[76] Ent AFB, ADC, et al. were not. Captain Patrick Shere arrived at Holloman, and Stokes was called in again. We have no transcript of that interview, but it appears from Air Force documents to have been lengthy and more personal. The analysis in the Air Intelligence Information Report emphasizes the personal very strongly.[77] Stokes, a rather private man, did not like this, and later told Jim Lorenzen that if he ever had another sighting "I won't tell a soul. It's just not worth it."[78]

Once back at Ent AFB, Shere and Col. Brunson wrote up their conclusions and published them on November 12. They wrote that Stokes was unreliable and possibly had witnessed some sort of optical illusion or mirage. They also indicated that the remainder of his story must have been due to excitability and misinterpretations. Why did Shere and Brunson think that this was a possible solution? It all depended upon their opinion of Stokes as unreliable. What was their evidence? Shere said that, in his view, Stokes was not a careful observer. Shere's reason for saying that was that Stokes had said that he felt a heat wave as the object passed, which gave him a "severe sunburn" (whether Stokes ever used the word "severe" is unknown). Later, when Shere saw Stokes, there was no evidence of this injury. However, at least three people attested to something similar to mild sunburn, which was gone the next day, 24 hours before Shere arrived. Somehow, such facts were never uncovered by the Captain. The fact that Stokes told Shere that he did *not* have a severe sunburn was taken by Shere as contradictory testimony. Shere criticized Stokes for his willingness to talk to reporters (missing the entire sequence of events which naturally led him to the Lorenzens and KAIG). This seemed suspicious to Shere. Shere and Brunson criticized Stokes because the reporters referred to him as an engineer when he was only a technician, making this charge despite the fact that Major Everett himself referred to Stokes as an engineer[79] (the pettiness of part of this attempt at personality assassination is a little disturbing). They complained that reporters said originally that ten cars were stopped, when in fact there were only

258

seven, this despite the fact that Stokes' diagram clearly showed seven cars, and in his interview with Clarke he had said "several," not "ten." Objections were made to Stokes' estimates of speed versus the length of time he felt he had seen the object. No good case researcher pays any attention to such estimates except under rare circumstances where there is a concrete physical circumstance that might allow some accuracy. Because people continually err in this area, no good researcher condemns them for it either. Finally, Shere and Brunson objected to the fact that they could not find Baker or Duncan. How much effort the Air Force had put into doing that on a one man/one day investigation, we do not know.

Today, all these objections to Stokes' character seem to be shallow, if not irrelevant. Still, to Ent AFB and later to Blue Book, they constituted a sufficient case against Stokes personally to write him off as unreliable, if not publicity-seeking, hallucinatory, or a liar. Holloman did not feel that way, and Stokes went on with his work and was promoted within the year.[80] The later press release of November 15 concluded: "Hoax, presumably suggested by the Levelland, Texas 'reports.'"[81] This was a rather strong defamatory comment for a very poorly done investigation.

Cases continued to pour in, some from the same area of the Stokes encounter. On the early morning of November 3, a routine patrol in the White Sands Proving Ground, near the original A-bomb drop site ("Trinity"), saw a bright object descend and hover about fifty yards above the old bomb test bunkers.[82] It shone with a brilliant red-orange light that, peculiarly, did not seem to illuminate the ground. Then the egg-shaped object completed what seemed to be a controlled landing and the light went out. Despite being on patrol, the men (a corporal and a private first class, both very young) were too scared to go over to the site and phoned in the intrusion instead. Later, the sergeant of the guard went to the site but found nothing. It is worth noting that neither of the patrollers had heard about Levelland. Seventeen hours later, two other patrolmen saw something similar while in the same area: a "blazing egg," about 200 to 300 feet long, hovering over the bunkers and then rising away, its luminosity blinking on and off. The Air Force decided to run two explanations at the same time for this one: the young patrolmen talked this over among themselves and perpetrated a hoax; and it was actually Venus. The first explanation, actually a "charge" as these people were on patrol duty, is difficult to assess because evidence for it (one way or another) is completely lacking. Common sense, if such can ever be applied to UFO matters, would say that the idea of enlisted personnel perpetrating a hoax on senior officers while on patrol duty would be a risky game if played for a laugh. It also leaves to coincidence the unusual descriptive match for the Levelland object that the earlier patrol reported. The second explanation (Venus) is simply preposterous, not only because descriptions do not match but due to the awkward fact that Venus was not visible at either time period.[83] The alternative to Venus (the Moon) was not much better, as few patrolmen would have mistaken the Moon for something that landed or rose rapidly away blinking on and off. The White Sands public information officer gave the radio media a "no mockery" straight report of the patrols' sighting.[84] Unlike the Air Force, White Sands seemed merely curious about what the men had seen.

Left to Right: WSPG patrolmen Richard Oaks, Henry Barlow, and Glenn Toy

November 4, Kirtland AFB, New Mexico:[85] At about 10:45 p.m., Air Traffic controllers saw a small (15-20 feet long) "egg," with a white light at its base, circle one end of the base. The object then made various slow maneuvers as close as twenty or thirty feet off the ground, then rose, as it passed over the nuclear weapons storage area. The thing dropped again, hovered, and then rapidly climbed. Radar tracked it during several of these maneuvers, including its swansong, as it traveled about a half mile behind a C-46, which had just taken off. Whereas places like Levelland, Holloman, and White Sands were leaking UFO news like sieves, this case was better controlled and did not cause as much trouble for the Air Force. At the controls of the case were the same two persons who had evaluated Stokes: Colonel Brunson and Captain Shere. The logic used to analyze this report tells us more than perhaps any other case how things were being done at the ADC level. Brunson wrote:

> The opinion of the preparing officer is that this object may possibly have been an unidentified aircraft, possibly confused by the runways at Kirtland Air Force Base. The reasons for this opinion are: The observers are considered competent and reliable sources and in the opinion of this interviewer actually saw an object they could not identify.
> 1. The object was tracked on a radarscope by a competent operator.
> 2. The object does not meet identification criteria for any other phenomena.[86]

Even Allen Hynek was boggled by this reasoning process, because it said in plain language: both the visual and radar observations were competent, so this event happened.[87] But, because it "does not meet identification criteria for any other phenomena," it must be an airplane. Whoa, said Hynek. It's *real*; it's *unidentified*. That does not mean it's a plane because it's the only thing vaguely like it. If *that* were true, we would never admit to any new discovery. Hardly hidden in the train of logic used by Brunson was: "all UFO reports are identifiable as balloons, meteors, airplanes, unreliable reports, birds . . . etc, each of which have 'identification criteria.' For example, if it is a light in the sky and moves very slow, it must be a star or a planet. If it is a light in the sky and moves very fast, it must be a meteor. And so forth." This case has some of the characteristics, some of the time, of an aircraft, and only an aircraft. Therefore, it *is* an aircraft. ADC and Blue Book were happy to write it off as an unidentified pilot in a private unidentified plane of great power and maneuverability, mistaking the Kirtland AFB for a private airfield and flying for many minutes observed through binoculars but somehow not recognized by veteran ATC controllers, blundering over nuclear weapons areas, then rapidly chasing a military plane out of sight.

The tenor of Brunson's analyses is not that of an unthinking man. It would have been interesting to have interviewed him, and to discover whether he was really comfortable with these write-offs. And, if he *was* comfortable, why was he? Was it just that he believed that things outside the "identification criteria" were impossible? Or did he see it as "doing his job"? This case came up again ten years later when it was revealed to the University of Colorado "Scientific Study."[88] The Study, for reasons explored in a later chapter, was falling apart organizationally, and the radar case analyst was fired. His replacement was burdened with the job at the 11th hour and could give few cases any real time. The Colorado Study, therefore, concurred with the Air Force's completely theoretical explanation. Both Allen Hynek (merely on internal documents grounds)[89] and James McDonald (on that plus interviews with the witnesses)[90] disagreed; McDonald violently so. To him this was one of the Air Force's bigger travesties. But, again, neither Hynek nor McDonald (as scientists) understood what this business of UFO case "investigation" was really, at its deepest, all about. Neither of them, it appears, could take seriously the national security issues.

November 5, Gulf of Mexico:[91] Among the flood of cases, we will mention one more famous one. We are fortunate that not only was the case widely covered in the newspapers, but we have one of the main observers, Thomas Kirk, to edit the minor errors they made.[92] The following is Kirk's rendition of the case as reported:

> Just after 5 AM, the U.S. Coast Guard Cutter Sebago was about 200 miles south of the Mississippi delta. At 5:10 AM the ship board in the combat information center radar suddenly showed an unidentified target at 246 degrees true, moving N to S, range 12,000 yards (almost 7 miles). On duty were Ensign

Wayne Shockley, deck officer, LTJG Donald Schaefer, first class quartermaster Kenneth Smith, radarman James Moore, and radarman Thomas Kirk. Interviewed in New Orleans, Ensign Shockley was asked how good the radar target was.

Shockley: "The ship's combat information center confirmed the sighting. At that point it was reported falling astern rapidly. It was a good pip (target). It was a very strong contact, considered good."

Cmdr. James N. Schrader, USCG spokesman in New Orleans, said that at one point "in two minutes it went 33 miles straight away from the ship." (about 1020 mph).

At 5:14 contact was lost.

At 5:16 contact was regained, object about 22 miles north.

At 5:18 object faded off radar screen, range about 55 miles.

At 5:20 contact regained, object appeared stationary, seven miles due north.

Personnel on deck felt that they saw the object for three to five seconds. It was a brilliant white object. It then entered a cloudbank. A last radar contact may have occurred 17 minutes later, to the north.

The Sebago radioed base (home port Mobile, Alabama) of this incident and was directed to Pensacola Naval Air Station, Florida, for debriefing. That was done by Navy personnel both from the Air Station and from Washington. Once again, the Navy handled the encounter *much* less restrictively than the Air Force. The Navy said nothing to the Coast Guard personnel to prevent them from discussing their sighting in public. Nor did the Navy say anything

U.S. Coast Guard Cutter Sebago

Sebago witnesses

when the Coast Guard reassigned Shockley and Kirk to temporary duty in New York, so that they could appear on the Dave Garroway television show![93] This could easily have been interpreted as against military law, as a "CIRVIS-MERINT" report had been filed, which, under JANAP 146-CIRVIS rules should have prohibited military or civilian personnel from public speaking about UFO incidences. ("MERINT" was the designator for intelligence gained from U.S. or Canadian vessels at sea, about "situations" involving objects in the air. Such intelligence was to be handled/transmitted similarly to land-based JANAP 146-CIRVIS reports by going immediately to land-based military stations, and then on to the Pentagon, where not only the Air Force, but also the Office of Naval Intelligence, monitored the cases.) Many military authorities seemed to pay little attention to these letter-of-the-law prohibitions. The UFO managers in the Air Force had to be very irritated by this. (There are, as mentioned earlier, some documents complaining about this leakage, but it is as if they were hoisted on their own petard; by consistently downplaying and debunking their subject, they had made it difficult for others to take JANAP 146 seriously enough to honor it rigidly and this was particularly true, apparently, if one were not Air Force, but rather Navy, Marine, or Coast Guard.)

From the small amount of information that we have about the case, the Sebago incident owes more to its coincidental timing, alongside Levelland, Stokes, White Sands, etc., than to its quality. Blue Book felt that weather conditions in the Gulf were conducive to spurious weather returns, and perhaps they were. The brief visual sighting could have been a meteor, and it is hard to argue against the "could." A main witness wondered if they had in fact witnessed a secret Navy missile firing (the Regulus program). All this indicates that there was nowhere near the "strangeness" in this case as in the others with which it was associated. Still, the Dave Garroway show was not helping the Air Force. What did save the Air Force, though, was a con-man named Reinhold Schmidt. He provided exactly the distraction they needed.[94] On the afternoon of November 5, with at least the easy opportunity of Levelland and the Stokes' encounter to be echoing in his mind, Schmidt entered a sheriff's office in Kearney, Nebraska, apparently shaken and asking to see a minister. He told of a Stokes- or Levelland-like encounter, with a 100-foot-long object stopping his car. Now, however, Schmidt did them one better. He got out to investigate, was paralyzed by a beam, and was taken aboard the craft. There Schmidt saw human-appearing people who spoke German. Then, after some conversation, he was told to leave. Schmidt took the police officers to the site where they discovered footprints and a greasy substance where he said the UFO had landed. The tale is spectacular but not obviously impossible at this point.

Air Defense Command looked into it. A police check found that Schmidt had been imprisoned for embezzlement 18 years previously—not a good character reference, but still not necessarily relevant to the case. Two psychiatrists thought he was mentally ill and put him in the State Hospital for a few days. This may say more about the psychiatrists than Schmidt, who was released shortly. More telling was ADC's discovery of an empty can of greenish motor oil near the "landing site" and another one in Schmidt's trunk.[95] Asked to take a lie detector test, Schmidt refused. Quickly Schmidt entered the fringe UFO talk circuit and expanded his adventures to saucer rides with people from Saturn.[96] Four years into his new career, he was bilking elderly ladies of thousands of dollars, selling "free energy healing crystals" that he had acquired on board. Tried for grand theft, Schmidt was convicted. As a strange aside, one person that testified against him was a wet-behind-the-ears astronomer: Carl Sagan.[97]

Much of that story was well past our 1957 time frame, but there were already enough reasons not only to doubt Schmidt but (especially given the attitudes of the times) make a mockery of him. This gave the Air Force an opportunity to use the Schmidt story to smear the rest of the events with a broad brush.

They did exactly that. Here is a review of their actions to deal with the flap:

1. On November 5, they released their normal "vanilla" style fact sheet, which directed itself not at all to any specific incident, but referred to the big picture and how there exists no evidence for flying saucers.[98]

2. On November 7, Air Defense Command stated that "it had received 46 reports of unidentified objects," but that only three of them warranted any attention.[99] These three significant reports were the Sebago incident, a meteor-like sighting seen in several southern states, and the Schmidt case. Note that Levelland, Stokes, and White Sands were never mentioned. PIO officer Captain Beasley said that they were most interested in investigating Schmidt.

3. On the same day, Wright-Patterson's Spencer Whedon said "we check them all," and complained that every case cost $10,000; this was particularly problematic because, as Whedon claimed, there were no unknowns, just cases which did not have enough information.[100]

4. Strangely, on the same day, another Air Force spokesman said "we don't investigate all of them."[101]

5. On the November 5, the Air Force gave its conclusions on the five most famous cases:[102]

   a. Levelland was ball lightning or St. Elmo's Fire caused by stormy conditions (false);

   b. the Stokes case was a hoax encouraged by Levelland (possibly true, but no evidence for it);

   c. Schmidt was a hoax (probably true);

d. Sebago was misidentification of aircraft (a weird explanation, since even their own records do not conclude this); and

e. White Sands patrols saw Venus (untrue since the planet was not above the horizon on either occasion).

What a historian or sociologist finds of most interest in this is not that four of the five conclusions contain massive errors, sometimes even contradicting their own document files, but how easily the Air Force got away with it. In these matters there was no effective Court of Accountability whatsoever. And it was not that no important people *tried* to give counter opinions (as we have seen all along in past chapters). Far from joining the train of negative comments, Edward Ruppelt, from his retirement job in California, said that he was "intrigued and fascinated" by the car-stopping reports from Texas and New Mexico, and felt that the Air Force should get more serious and "step up its probe into UFO sightings."[103] He hoped that these new developments would encourage the Air Force into

"reconsidering its current policy of 'playing down' UFOs." Ruppelt then indicated that all the noise about mirage theories, such as that being pushed by Donald Menzel, was looked into by Blue Book during his tenure and found not to hold up. At the time of the Air Force's conclusions, a technology heavyweight, Dr. H. W. Ritchey, director of the Rocket Division at Thiokol Chemical Corporation (working with von Braun at the U.S. missile center at Huntsville, Alabama), weighed in on the matter. Ritchey said that in his view, if the witnesses are reporting reasonably accurately, encounters such as those at Levelland "are hard to explain any other way" than that they are extraterrestrial vehicles.[104] He asked: why would a reasonable person rule out that possibility? Ritchey was particularly interested in that reports seemed to point to some type of anti-gravitational control.

Dr. H. W. Ritchey

Whether a Ruppelt or a Ritchey, a Tombaugh, a Charles Moore, or a Moulton Taylor, a Delmar Fahrney or a Roscoe Hillenkoetter, a Donald Blakeslee, John Stapp, or Deke Slayton . . . on and on and on . . . regardless of who spoke up, it never made any difference. No matter how high their scientific, military, or technological credentials, somehow the sociology of things kept all of these notable persons from forming a critical authoritative mass. Even in the heat of an intense flap, people who *should* have been viewed as authorities (Ruppelt, Ritchey) were nothing but small, non-lingering echoes. Instead, right behind the Air Force, *U.S. News & World Report* (Nov. 15, 1957) published a supportive item titled, "If You're Seeing Things in the Sky."[105] In fact, the article contained no news at all—no commentary on what the recent cases were, no commentary on what a photo used as illustration was all about, nothing but a re-worded generic Air Force press release taking up 2½ pages of the magazine. One wonders why an editor would have approved the piece. Still, something like this worked *for* the "sociology." It fell in line with the "authority" and established it. So, a powerful flap of close encounters rolled across the country (*far* more so than what little could be given here), and within two weeks of the flap's peak, the status quo of non-acceptability had been, almost effortlessly, restored.

Perhaps it was for the best. The Schmidt affair had caused another near-panic in the Nebraska area and an avalanche of phone calls to places like Ent AFB.[106] Other places also seemed like a pot ready to boil. The Portland, Oregon Civil Defense office issued a "Calm Down; Nothing's Going On" message to the citizenry.[107] It seems that some Americans were "crazier" than others thought. But the Air Force was there to provide reassurance that all was well.

On November 7, in the heat of the media action, a story appeared with the title: "Sighting Shakes Scientists."[108] The article stated that "some of the nation's top scientists are pretty shook up about the mysterious flying objects sighted in New Mexico and West Texas skies this week." The source was Charles (Chick) Capen, a major figure at both White Sands and the famous Lowell Observatory. Dr. Capen was internationally known as a leading astronomer in the study of the planet Mars and, later, a force in NASA's Mariner missions. When Levelland and the White Sands' sightings broke, the UFOs were "the principal topic of conversation at the Proving Grounds," but, by the 7th of November were "pretty hushed up." Capen himself hushed up to the reporters and instead talked about missile launches and lunar photography. What if Capen had described in detail what worried the White Sands scientists? What if they all got together (Capen's mentor, Clyde Tombaugh, no doubt in the front row) and held a major news conference statement about this new development in UFOs? What if they went to Washington and gave testimony before Congress? Such things *might* have so shaken common sense thinking that they could have "changed the intellectual landscape" of our age. But if *they* were shaken, how much more so was the citizenry? Capen, Tombaugh

Dr. Charles Capen

and the others did none of those things, and the Air Force was glad of it. The Air Force did not need experiments with the nation's nervous system.

Their silent partner, the CIA, continued its interest in the phenomenon and its management, but at what depth we do not know. Despite much rumor to the contrary, some available documents say that the Agency, by 1957, had markedly backed off from UFOs. CIA historian Gerald Haines identifies a rather messy June 11, 1957, document as a memorandum for Richard M. Bissell from Wallace R.

Richard M. Bissell

Lamphire.[109] Subject: "Unidentified Flying Saucers (UFO)." Bissell had joined the CIA in the early 1950s and by 1954 was in charge of the U-2 "spy plane" project. By 1957, his reach was definitely expanding and he was about to be named Deputy Director for Plans (read: Black Operations) by Allen Dulles. Perhaps because spy planes were allegedly on occasion reported as UFOs, or perhaps because if we were going to overfly the USSR covertly, why shouldn't the Russians do the same to us? Bissell wanted to know the CIA's current role in UFOs. Wallace Lamphire was an operative in Bissell's soon-to-be-office. Lamphire appears from the memo to be wholly ignorant of the UFO situation. In order to find out anything at all, he met with General

Strong (of Robertson Panel days) who told him what he remembered. Strong's five year old memory of this activity was fairly accurate. A comment in the document that the Panel was "extremely thorough" either betrays Strong's own ignorance and naiveté, or he was still playing the fog-production game, even with Lamphire and Bissell. Since that event, the CIA's activity was described as a "watching process," which means an orderly handing off of a UFO report to either the geophysics unit (if it seemed more like a natural phenomenon, à la ball lightning) or to the "former" weapons unit in the Applied Sciences Division, if it seemed more like technology. The "former" is of some interest, as it is a relic of the CIA's loss of the internal war with the services, and the diminution of several of their OSI units to minor functions, if they continued at all. These are the sort of units that would have been engaged with Lincoln Labs in the large "basic sciences" UFO study that Marshall Chadwell had hoped to organize in 1953, before his NSCID was scuttled by the Panel.

Bissell was told that Harold Watson presided over a shrunken Project Blue Book at ATIC, and that little importance was seen in it. As far as CIA cases were concerned, Strong said there were rarely any, and could vaguely remember only the Senator Russell affair (but not even the Senator's name). Lamphire asked if any of this could be Soviet (a question Bissell would want answered), and Strong said: "Conceivably, yes." Strong claimed that no special collection system for UFO reports existed in the CIA, but that a special collection emphasis on radical aeronautical design *did* and was a high priority. Strong knew of nothing in that which pointed to the Soviets developing a flying saucer. Lamphire signed off the memo with a mysterious allusion to a British and Canadian saucer project, which sounded suspiciously like a variant of Avro's project to develop a disk-shaped aircraft, but, at our current level of understanding of that project's lack of development, would seem to have been impossible to take seriously.[110]

In September of 1957 the CIA again became involved with UFOs. In the first of these known instances, Dr. Howard P. Robertson was back in town (from Europe) and now Chairman of the Defense Science Board (DSB). The Defense Science Board was established in the fall of 1956 as a group of elite civilian scientists acting as consultants to the Secretary of Defense and the Joint Chiefs of Staff. There were many early priorities, but one of the greatest concern was the state of missile technology, both in the U.S. and the Soviet Union. When Robertson requested a briefing on UFOs from Air Force Intelligence, however, it was not for the Board's benefit, but was a private briefing for himself and his closest DSB associates.[111] This seems to indicate that Robertson called for this briefing not because it was of DSB business, but because he himself wanted to know how the Air Force was proceeding in implementing the Panel recommendations. Whatever the reason, ATIC jumped. They prepared a relatively thick briefing document, and the contents were delivered by the Pentagon's

Dr. H. P. Robertson

Major James F. Byrne. Why Robertson remained interested in UFOs, we do not know. His remaining papers (at Caltech) are almost devoid of mention of the subject.[112] He did maintain a file containing Blue Book 14, which he may well have received at this briefing. What he did with the 1953 case reports that he had asked Blue Book to send him for evaluation is a mystery. But Robertson wanted to know, and ATIC complied.

Byrne essentially filled in the time period between the Robertson Panel and mid-1957 with large quantities of statistics and other information about how Blue Book was doing its job. "Social" information as to UFO publications, "clubs," and media productions was presented. Bugaboos such as Keyhoe/NICAP and the movie *UFO* were featured. The problem of Congressional hearings was mentioned. Language in the document, perhaps to flatter or appease Robertson, mentioned actions that were being taken "as recommended by the panel." It was clear that the Panel Report was being used at least as a tool to get certain things done. The Ground Observer Corps was cited as an activity that could be the source of information leaks to UFO organizations. Public relations was highlighted as a significant aspect of what they (Blue Book) were now doing, in particular undoing the trouble caused by people writing their congressmen. The usefulness of Blue Book 14 was trumpeted but the reduction of funds was deemed a dire problem if the Air Force were to keep ahead of the problem. At one point, Byrne and ATIC made a very uncharacteristic statement to Robertson, and one wonders why. It was said that the AF "must cooperate with the press and be frank with the public." Robertson knew better than this (his Panel, after all, set the policy of information management, not frankness), so why say this to him? Who knows what angles are created in the minds of the intelligence community; perhaps it was just the precaution of being *too* frank with one another in a document that could be read by someone else. Byrne signed off in the main text by reiterating the dangers posed by uncontrolled citizen behavior in the exact words of the 1953 report.

There were several other things of interest in the appendices of the briefing document. NICAP was again featured with little thumbnail biographical annotations of its key members. The movie *UFO* was broken down by UFOlogical content. Quite a number of recent cases were reviewed and "solved." One of the most interesting things (to the UFO historian) was part of a set of guidelines to the 4602nd UFOB field investigators, telling them in the crudest terms that if a sighting report fits descriptions a, b, c, then, it's a planet . . . or a balloon . . . or an aircraft. When one reads these pages (almost like robotic checklists), one can almost understand how some of the preposterous "conclusions" written on the record cards could occur. Elements of "strangeness" in a UFO report do not, of course, exist on a checklist for a planet, balloon, or airplane. So if one wanted just to do the job in front of them, it would be possible to check off a case without even considering a "strange" element. In fact, on occasion the investigators were encouraged to do so. Under "aircraft," they were told that if other elements match "aircraft" (circular or elliptical was considered a match!), and there were "erratic motions," they should ignore that "because of psychological tendencies of excited people to exaggerate." Another page of relevance was titled "Optical Phenomena." Here the parameters were so broad as to be nearly all-encompassing. Ironically, the main "optical phenomena" UFO write-off, the temperature inversion hypothesis of Menzel and others, would have been eliminated by the mindless list checker, as one line said: no radar. Among the several cases reviewed for Robertson was the Edwards AFB theodolite film that was discussed earlier. Byrne and ATIC misrepresented what it was, while complaining mightily about the base letting the press in on the news. Those checklists constituted in print part of what Hynek called the explanatory "tool box": Brunson's "identification criteria."

Almost at the same time as the briefing, the Air Defense Command had a situation that caused a great deal of concern in many quarters right up to the White House. On September 20:

> as reported by components of the US Air Defense Command, an unidentified flying object (UFO) was tracked by US radars on a relatively straight course from the eastern tip of Long Island to the vicinity of Buffalo. The object was reportedly moving westward at an altitude of 50,000 feet and speed of 2000 kts. 'Jamming' was reported by several radars in this vicinity and westward as far as Chicago.[113]

The case swept through the intelligence community the next day (as shown by the fact that the previous quote was from a CIA memorandum from CIA-OSI chief Herbert Scoville to CIA Acting Director, Charles Cabell). The Intelligence Advisory Committee, containing representatives of all the intelligence agencies, met and considered the implications. It was the CIA's opinion that 1) because they had no evidence of such a development in Soviet technology; and 2) because such an overflight by such technology made no apparent sense (i.e., no one could imagine what they would gain by it); then 3) the offending object must have been something else. The CIA document does not provide a candidate for the "something else," but the FBI agent at the meeting wrote down what someone there had said: there were indications "that the object detected was an atmospheric phenomenon."[114] The Director of Air Force Intelligence, General Millard Lewis, even suggested it could be the

Herbert Scoville

effect of sunspot activity. Again we are struck with Allen Hynek's dictum: it can't be X, so it isn't. Anything we say about it is better than calling it a UFO.

Nineteen hundred and fifty seven was a year with powerful currents, both in the way the phenomenon expressed itself and the way people dealt with that. In the end, however, no matter how much closer the encounters, society as a whole did not accept the phenomenon as any closer to reality. And, in America, the phenomenon was about to enter its longest lull since WWII.

Notes

[1] Jack Manno, *Arming the Heavens*.

[2] Blue Book microfilms, (especially George Gregory, memorandum, "For the Office of the Scientific Advisor," 1 August 1957). This and associated documents indicate that ADC's 4602nd AISS was to cut back seriously on field investigations for Blue Book, due to lack of funding.

[3] At least three instances of panic or near-panic occurred in 1957 alone (Canada, ADC, and Portland). See end of this chapter.

[4] The Soviet Union had begun to accuse the U.S. of using flying saucers as part of a propaganda war against them (reported from *Pravda* in *UFO Investigator 1* (2); 15, August-September 1957), and the U.S. continued to believe that the U.S.S.R. was possibly using UFOs and UFO "cultists" in psychological warfare ways. It is widely known that many UFO figures, both cultists and legitimate researchers, were visited by intelligence operatives early in their careers. Richard Hall, while still a Tulane University student, had his newsletter collected and filed (Blue Book microfilm, see date: 31 May 1957). When NICAP was reformed (under Donald Keyhoe), two CIA experts were ousted. (See Lawrence Fawcett and Barry Greenwood. *Clear Intent*, 1984.) Monitoring of contactees like George Adamski and George Van Tassel must have been even more constant. For an unusual speculative view of this (allegedly based on FOIA'd documents, not seen), see: Nick Redfern, "Operation Espionage," *The Anomalist 12*: pp. 46-73, 2006.

[5] Hector Quintanilla, "Project Blue Book's Last Years," in Hilary Evans and Dennis Stacy (eds.), *UFOs, 1947-1997*, 1997.

[6] Draft letters: Quarles to Congressman Moss: a) Colonel John G. Eriksen for Colonel T.R. Johnson, memorandum discussing detailed contents of letter, 25 June 1956; b) actual letter draft, 5 July 1956; and c) A. Francis Arcier to George Gregory, memorandum, subject: UFO Program (re: creation of standing liaison with Pentagon vis-à-vis Blue Book 14 and AFR 200-2 rewrite publication), 1 February 1957, FOIA (USAF).

[7] A. Francis Arcier to George Gregory, memorandum, subject: UFO Program; FOIA (USAF); plus a) Maj. James F. Byrne to Director AFOIN.4, memorandum, subject: publication of UFO Special Report No. 14, 16 May 1959; and b) George Gregory to Dr. Miley/Mr. Arcier, memorandum, subject: Preface to Project "Blue Book" No. 14, 12 July 1957; and c) Draft of the Preface (undated).

[8] Draft letter: A. Francis Arcier to George Gregory, memorandum, subject: UFO Program (re: creation of standing liaison with Pentagon vis-à-vis Blue Book 14 and AFR 200-2 rewrite publication), 1 February 1957, FOIA (USAF).

[9] Maj. James F. Byrne to Director AFOIN.4, memorandum, subject: publication of UFO Special Report No. 14, 16 May 1959.

[10] George Gregory to Dr. Miley/Mr. Arcier, memorandum, subject: Preface to Project "Blue Book" No. 14, 12 July 1957.

[11] George Gregory to Dr. Miley/Mr. Arcier, memorandum, subject: Preface to Project "Blue Book" No. 14, 12 July 1957 (Blue Book 14 preface Draft).

[12] See chapters 9 and 11 for instances where expected "case creation" did not arise.

[13] Hugh Dryden, *NACA Testimony before the House Appropriations Committee*, 19 February 1957 (quoted in the Blue Book 14 addendum draft).

[14] Donald Keyhoe, *NICAP Special Bulletin*, April 22, 1957.

[15] Frank Edwards, "Guest Editorial," *Flying Saucers (CSI-NE) 5* (2): 1-4, Fourth Quarter 1957. This is a weak source. We include it because we have not seen the original news item, although we have read all the material leading up to the quote. Edwards was a news (radio) reporter and usually seems to have gotten simple quotes right. The editor of *F.S. (CSI-NE)* stated that he was cognizant of the material Edwards was writing about, and, in that spirit, we present the Dryden quote.

[16] United Press, dateline: 19 January 1957, Philadelphia, PA, "AF Stifles Saucer Reports of Civilians, Ex-Admiral Says," *New York World-Telegram*, 19 January 1957.

[17] Associated Press, dateline: 17 January 1957, Washington, DC, "Expert Forms Unit to Study Space Objects," *Washington Post and Times-Herald*, 17 January 1957.

[18] Donald Keyhoe, *Flying Saucers: Top Secret*, quoting Fahrney.

[19] United Press, dateline: 19 January 1957, Philadelphia, PA, "AF Stifles Saucer Reports of Civilians, Ex-Admiral Says," *New York World-Telegram*, 19 January 1957.

[20] Associated Press, dateline: 17 January 1957, Washington, DC, "Expert Forms Unit to Study Space Objects," *Washington Post and Times-Herald*, 17 January 1957.

[21] Donald Keyhoe, *Flying Saucers: Top Secret*.

[22] J. Allen Hynek and Jacques Vallee, *The Edge of Reality*, 1975.

[23] Blue Book microfilm (marginalia written on one of the field reports of the Ellsworth AFB, SD/Bismarck, ND case of 5 August 1953). In that same file, Hynek kids Keyhoe by beginning to write up the case in dramatic "Keyhoe style," beginning with off-stage "Dragnet music" (referring to the popular TV detective show of the time).

[24] J. Allen Hynek, (*Hynek UFO Report*).

[25] Hillenkoetter was announced as a member of NICAP's Board of Governors (with surprisingly little fanfare) in their *UFO Investigator, Vol. 1* (1), July 1957.

[26] Todd Zechel, "NI-CIA-AP or NICAP," *MUFON UFO Journal 133*: 6, January-February 1979. This is considered a weak source, and the current writer has not been able to locate the original material wherein Hillenkoetter says this. It is quoted here because the then-editor of the *MUFON Journal* was Richard Hall, a trustworthy resource and a central figure in NICAP, who would have known about this fact.

[27] William H. Ayres to Melvin V. Knapp, 28 January 1958, CUFOS files.

[28] Ruppelt, *Report* (revised edition: 1960).

[29] Donald Keyhoe, "The Captain Ruppelt Letters," *The UFO Investigator II* (2): 6, October 1961.

[30] Edward Ruppelt to Donald Keyhoe, draft letter, 31 March 1958, and actual letter, 15 April 1958, Ruppelt files. (The actual letter sent is slightly less pointed in its language.) Note that Ruppelt sat on this letter for two weeks. He knew that it was an important moment: the end of his participation in UFO writing or speaking in public.

[31] Donald Keyhoe, *Flying Saucers: Top Secret*.

[32] Blue Book microfilm Roll 27; and James McDonald files, University of Arizona.

[33] Blue Book microfilm Roll 27; and many news sources as listed and quoted in Gross, Jan-March 1957.

[34] United Press, dateline: Washington, DC, 9 March 1957 (quoted in Gross, above).

[35] Blue Book microfilm Roll 27; and many news sources as listed and quoted in Gross, March-May 1957.

[36] Robert E. O'Connor to Commander 4602nd AISS, message form, 27 March 1957, FOIA (USAF).

[37] (Blue Book microfilm). Apparently a quick follow-up message form to the above (reference 36), read by Allen Hynek and quoted in his book, *The Hynek UFO Report*.

[38] Donald Keyhoe, *Flying Saucers: Top Secret*.

[39] George Gregory to Major Byrnes, memorandum, subject: "False Charges by NICAP regarding Air Force Findings in Oxnard and Other Cases," 1 October 1957, FOIA (USAF).

[40] Blue Book microfilm Roll 27; and McDonald files, University of Arizona archives; and James Bittick interview, 28 October 2002, *The UFO Oral History Project*, Thomas Tulien, administrator, Minneapolis, MN; and Frank E. Baker (similar); 20 October 2002.

[41] Quotes are from the Bittick Oral History above.

[42] Blue Book microfilm Roll 27, and McDonald's notes (reference 40, above).

[43] Blue Book microfilm Roll 28; but, more importantly, McDonald files; plus Colorado Project; James McDonald, "The 1957 Gulf Coast RB-47 Incident," *Flying Saucer Review* May-June 1970, pp. 2-6, reproduced from AAAS Symposium papers, Boston, MA, 27 December 1969; and sources in Gross.

[44] An excellent survey of the case by its leading analyst, Brad Sparks, appears in Clark, *Encyclopedia*.

[45] V. D. Bryant, memorandum, 30 October 1957 (issuing from Electronics Branch, ATIC, Wright-Patterson AFB.) This document was not seen by this writer, but is quoted by Sparks in Clark, *Encyclopedia*. The citation is missing.

[46] Blue Book microfilm Roll 28; and *The UFO Investigator 1* (2): 6, August-September 1957 (quoting the *El Paso Times*).

[47] Blue Book microfilm Roll 28; and *The UFO Investigator 1* (2): 6, August-September 1957 (quoting the *El Paso Times*).

[48] W. Patrick McCray, *Keep Watching the Skies! The Story of Operation Moonwatch and the Dawn of the Space Age*, 2008. Most of the material mentioned here, and for the fuller treatment in the next chapter, comes from an extensive file collected by J. Allen Hynek (CUFOS files).

[49] J. Allen Hynek files (CUFOS), as above; and Walter N. Webb, "Allen Hynek as I Knew Him," *International UFO Reporter*, January-February, 1993: pp. 4-10, 23.

[50] Anonymous, "No Evidence for Saucers," *Science News Letter*, 16 November 1957: 307.

[51] Blue Book microfilms, annual statistical lists.

[52] Blue Book microfilms, annual statistics; graph was created by a simple count.

[53] Mark Rodeghier, *UFO Reports Involving Vehicle Interference*, 1981.

[54] Blue Book microfilm Roll 28.

[55] Blue Book microfilm, Johnson W. Ackiss, Air Intelligence Information Report, 5 August 1957 (regarding 3 August 1957 case off N. California coast).

[56] Colonel John Alexander (Sandia Labs); personal communication (MDS).

[57] Blue Book microfilm Roll, 29; plus Antonio Rullan, *The Levelland Sightings of 1957*, 18 October 1999; and Michael D. Swords, document compilation, *The Levelland, Texas, Incidents, November 2-3, 1957, and Coincident Events of the Early November 1957 Wave*, October 1992 (henceforth Swords, *The Levelland, Texas, Incidents*).

[58] This map is redrawn from the original created by Walter Webb for the NICAP case report (included in Swords, *The Levelland, Texas, Incidents*).

[59] Swords, *The Levelland, Texas, Incidents* (the Blue Book documents are included in the CUFOS compilation).

[60] Swords, *The Levelland, Texas, Incidents*.

[61] Department of Defense, Office of Public Information, *News Release*, "Fact sheet: Air Force's 10 year Study of Unidentified Flying Objects," 5 November 1957.

[62] Department of Defense, Office of Public Information, *News Release*, "Fact sheet"; Blue Book and CUFOS compilation above (ref. 57); example press coverage: International News Service wire story, "Air Force Explains Mysteries: Strange Flying Objects Held Hoaxes or Sightings of Natural Phenomena," *Washington Post*, 16 November 1957.

[63] Donald Menzel, *The World of Flying Saucers*, 1963. Menzel originally debunked the Levelland events as some sort of mirage, a guess that he later learned was absurd. In this book, he shifts to the ball lightning theory while rewriting history a bit to blame a newspaper reporter for his error. The generally-skeptical Colorado Project looked at the theory and rejected it. Antonio Rullan has a readable, balanced description of what was and was not known about ball lightning (see Rullan, *The Levelland Sightings of 1957*).

[64] Blue Book microfilm, and Swords, *The Levelland, Texas, Incidents*.

[65] Blue Book microfilm, and Swords, *The Levelland, Texas, Incidents* (see particularly: George T. Gregory, memorandum, "Analyst's Comments or Conclusions: Ball Lightning," 3 January 1958.)

[66] Blue Book microfilm, and Swords, *The Levelland, Texas, Incidents* (J. Allen Hynek, undated letter, but stated by Gregory to be 5 March 1958, to be appended to Gregory's conclusions).

[67] Hynek, *UFO Experience*.

[68] Blue Book microfilm Roll 29; Swords, *The Levelland, Texas, Incidents*; Terry Clarke, "The Day All Roads Led to Alamogordo," *Writer's Digest*, December 1957: 24-5, 27-31; Coral Lorenzen, "The New Mexico Story," *The APRO Bulletin*, November 1957: 1-2, 5; L. J. Lorenzen, "The Stokes Case," *The APRO Bulletin*, January 1958: pp. 2, 6.

[69] L. J. Lorenzen, "The Stokes Case," 1958.

[70] L. J. Lorenzen, "The Stokes Case," 1958.

[71] L. J. Lorenzen, "The Stokes Case," 1958; Coral Lorenzen, "The New Mexico Story," 1957.

[72] Clarke, "The Day All Roads Led to Alamogordo," December 1957.

[73] Clarke, "The Day All Roads Led to Alamogordo," December, 1957. Example of coverage: Associated Press news story, dateline: Lubbock, TX, 4 November 1957, "Missile Aide Tells of Seeing Flying Fireball."

[74] Coral Lorenzen, "The New Mexico Story," 1957; Clarke, "The Day All Roads Led to Alamogordo," December 1957.

[75] Blue Book microfilm Roll 29; Swords, *The Levelland, Texas, Incidents*.

[76] L. J. Lorenzen, "The Stokes Case," 1958.

[77] Blue Book microfilm Roll 29; Swords, *The Levelland, Texas, Incidents*. See particularly, William P. Brunson, *Air Intelligence Information Report*, 12 November 1957, subject: Unidentified Flying Object.

[78] L. J. Lorenzen, "The Stokes Case," 1958.

[79] Clarke, "The Day All Roads Led to Alamogordo," December, 1957; and Holloman press release cited in L. J. Lorenzen, "The Stokes Case," 1958.

[80] Virgil Dominic, Air Force Missile Development Center, Holloman AFB, NM, to Donald Keyhoe, 14 August 1958.

[81] Press release as contained in Swords, *The Levelland, Texas, Incidents*.

[82] Blue Book microfilm Roll 29, and Swords, *The Levelland, Texas, Incidents*.

[83] NICAP, "USAF vs. UFO" (assessment of the Air Force's 15 Nov. 1957 evaluations of the main cases in the November flap), 15 pp. (Study is unsigned; suspected author, Alexander Mebane of CSI-NY. This document is contained in Swords, *The Levelland, Texas, Incidents*.)

[84] Swords, *The Levelland, Texas, Incidents* (and see quotes by the patrols' immediate commanding officer, Lt. Miles Penney, in news stories contained therein).

[85] Blue Book microfilm Roll 29; also, University of Colorado "Scientific Study"; and James McDonald, in Thornton Page and Carl Sagan (eds.), *UFOs: A Scientific Debate*, 1972; and Hynek, *UFO Experience*.

[86] Blue Book microfilm Roll 29.

[87] Hynek, *UFO Experience*.

[88] University of Colorado "Scientific Study."

[89] Hynek, *UFO Experience*.

[90] James McDonald (Thornton Page and Carl Sagan (eds.), *UFOs: A Scientific Debate*; and McDonald files, University of Arizona).

[91] Blue Book microfilm Roll 29; and Swords, *The Levelland, Texas, Incidents*.

[92] See Kirk's testimonies to Francis Ridge at www.nicap.org/cutter2. (The "NICAP" site is often an excellent source of primary documents.)

[93] Kirk's testimonies to Francis Ridge at www.nicap.org/cutter2.

[94] Clark, *Encyclopedia*, is an excellent source for this odd story. See also, Blue Book microfilm Roll 29.

[95] Clark, *Encyclopedia*; Blue Book microfilm Roll 29.

[96] Clark, *Encyclopedia*; plus Reinhold Schmidt, *Edge of Tomorrow: A True Account of Experiences with Visitors from Another Planet*, 1963.

[97] Clark, *Encyclopedia*.

[98] Department of Defense, Office of Public Information, *News Release*, "Fact sheet."

[99] Associated Press news story, dateline: Colorado Springs, CO, 7 November 1957, "Air Force Set to Study 3 of 46 Objects," *Washington Post and Times Herald*, 7 November 1957.

[100] Craig Clifford, "Saucer Sightings Making AF Weary," Scripps-Howard wire story, 7 November 1957, Dayton, OH.

[101] Captain Andy Beasley, ADC public information officer, in Swords, *The Levelland, Texas, Incidents*.

[102] Department of Defense News Release, 15 Nov. 1957 (reprinted in Swords, *The Levelland, Texas, Incidents*).

[103] Bob Wells, "Flying Disks Pure Fantasy to USAF; Ex-Chief of 'Saucer' Survey Urges Inquiry," *Long Beach (CA) Independent*, 7 November 1957.

[104] Marshall Lynam, "Did Space Ship Visit Levelland?" *The Fort Worth (TX) Press*, 17 November 1957.

[105] Anonymous, "If You're seeing Things in the Sky," *U.S. News & World Report*, 15 November 1957: pp. 122, 124, 126.

[106] Gross, Nov. 6.

[107] Gross, Nov. 6.

[108] Anonymous, "Sighting 'Shakes' Scientists," *El Paso Times*, 7 November 1957.

[109] Wallace R. Lamphire to Richard M. Bissell, memorandum, subject: Unidentified Flying Saucers (UFO), 11 June 1957, FOIA (CIA).

[110] Ruppelt files; plus, Daniel C. Murray, "The Avro VZ-9 Experimental Aircraft: Lessons Learned," Paper AIAA 90-3237 at the AIAA/AHS/ASEE Aircraft Design, Systems and Operations Conference, Dayton, OH, 17-19 September 1990; and, see Ben Kociver, "Is this the Real Flying Saucer?" *Look*, 14 June 1955: 44ff. (This design matches the commentary in the memo to Bissell, but proved so inadequate both in power and stability, that one wonders what really was going on with this publicity.)

[111] Air Technical Intelligence Center, *Briefing on the UFO Program for the Chairman of the Defense Science Board*, 16 September 1957.

[112] One of the current authors (MDS) visited the Caltech archives and inspected the Robertson papers there in 1995. There was very little preserved UFO-related material.

[113] R. R. Roach to A. H. Belmont, memorandum, subject: Unidentified Flying Object Reported on September 20, 1957, Intelligence Advisory Committee, Watch Committee, 23 September 1957, FOIA (FBI); (as above): memorandum, 24 September 1957, FOIA (CIA); Herbert Scoville to Acting Director, Central Intelligence, memorandum, subject: Unidentified Flying Object Reported on 20 September, 1957; 21 September 1957; Blue Book microfilm Roll 28.

[114] R. R. Roach to A. H. Belmont, memorandum, subject: Unidentified Flying Object Reported on September 20, 1957, Intelligence Advisory Committee, Watch Committee, 23 September 1957, FOIA (FBI); (as above): memorandum, 24 September 1957, FOIA (CIA); Herbert Scoville to Acting Director, Central Intelligence, memorandum, subject: Unidentified Flying Object Reported on 20 September, 1957; 21 September 1957; Blue Book microfilm Roll 28.

Chapter 13: Battle in the Desert

The wave of 1957 provided public momentum for a change of attitude about UFOs, not in the intelligence community, of course, but in Congress. Therefore, 1958 was a year in which NICAP attacked. In the Air Force's UFO offices, the policy of blocking NICAP and properly managing information remained, but the intensity with which it was done changed. Temple University historian David Jacobs wrote a doctoral thesis (and a fine book) about these matters and these times:

David Jacobs

> Congressional hearings presented a serious threat to the Air Force. They might imply that the UFO phenomenon was vitally significant and that the government was very interested in it. This might lead to another "flying saucer scare," threatening to the national interest. Hearings might force the Air Force to declassify its files, contradicting Air Force claims that its files were open already. Hearings might prompt criticism of the Air Force's UFO program. Therefore, preventing or limiting congressional hearings became a major objective for the Air Force from 1957 to 1964.[1]

NICAP would fight a hard fight, but would lose. Several assaults would be made; glimmers of hope and occasional nods from political figures but, in the end, defeat. Perhaps there never was a real chance, considering what NICAP was up against, but the phenomenon itself did them no favors. After the 1957 wave, national press coverage of UFO activity in the United States, and most areas of the world as well, settled down. It was what UFO historians sometimes call "the Great Silence" or "the Desert" (though more recent surveys of the 1958 period show a higher level of UFO sightings than what was initially apparent). NICAP's assistant director, Richard Hall, reflected back on this time:

> The period of 1958-1963 has to rank as the darkest of UFO 'Dark Ages'. Little or nothing about UFOs was reported by the news media, although scattered (but often significant) sightings were being made. NICAP struggled along trying to survive with little financial support and a staff of one (me). I had a few part-time volunteers as helpers.[2]

Project Blue Book astronomer Allen Hynek saw it the same way from the inside:

> from 1958 through 1963, UFO reports began to diminish in quality as well as quantity, and I felt that perhaps 'the flying saucer era' was on the wane and would soon vanish. But since 1964 there has been a sharp rally in the numbers of puzzling sightings.[3]

This was typical Hynek understatement. The UFO extended wave of 1964-1968 was a worldwide avalanche. But in 1958 matters had not yet come to that, the phenomenon was going quiet, and the Air Force, despite NICAP, had quite good control. The secret formula was to say almost nothing in public, and to defuse Keyhoe's sorties in private sessions behind closed congressional doors. David Jacobs:

> Publicly the Air Force remained silent about its congressional briefings and investigatory problems. It continued to castigate its critics and assure the public that top-level scientists with command of all necessary facilities were conducting a rigorous investigation of UFOs.[4]

The year 1958 began with an embarrassment for the Air Force. Because of all the excitement of the November 1957 wave, and because of Donald Keyhoe's ability to make public noise about it, CBS wanted to present a nationwide special on UFOs under the title of its famous program, *The Armstrong Circle Theater*. CBS wanted it to be a big affair and invited Keyhoe, the Air Force, Kenneth Arnold, Donald Menzel, Edward Ruppelt, and Captain C. S. Chiles of the Chiles-Whitted encounter. Keyhoe accepted avidly. Even the supporting cast was generally to his liking. What he did not know was that the program was *not* going to be any sort of discussion or give-and-take, but rather a scripted set of statements. Plus, with *six* views to be heard, Keyhoe (and presumably everyone else) was told that he would be on-air for only seven minutes. Still, Don Keyhoe was never one to discard an opportunity, and he agreed to present his seven minutes as long as he had final say on its content.[5]

Donald Keyhoe

Edward Ruppelt was in the midst of a serious reassessment of his role in the UFO public debate; his old service was unhappy with him about it. For whatever reasons, after accepting initially, he declined the invitation. Captain Chiles also declined, and it was reported (how true is unknown) that his airline requested that he do so. Kenneth Arnold, more or less at the last minute, decided that this looked to him like an Air Force-rigged program and backed out. Keyhoe, tough in the face of pressure as always, remained "in." CBS informed him that the unfortunate defections would give him more time and he prepared an eleven minute script. This included the constant drumbeat that he used against the Air Force: there were never-released secret documents (such as Project SIGN's ET-favorable Estimate, and Dewey Fournet's ET-favorable Motions study; the latter included in the appendix) that would prove that the Air Force was withholding UFO information from the public, and, occasionally, lying. Of course, the Air Force wanted none of that. What Keyhoe did not realize was that, prior to the program, the Air Force had impressed upon CBS that this subject matter infringed upon classified secrets and security matters, and so the show would have to be "cleared." Keyhoe was aware of none of this. When the Major arrived for the program, he found that all of his favorite bombshells had been stricken from his scripted remarks. From Keyhoe's point of view, this amounted to censorship.[6]

An unhappy, and undoubtedly furious, Donald Keyhoe began reading his emasculated script, then departed from it. He got out three sentences talking about the need for open congressional hearings, when the listener can hear a gruff voice in the background say:[7] "Cut him off." To the television audience, there was the ex-Marine Major silently mouthing something that someone seemed not to want him to say. Keyhoe later apologized to CBS, but he was just being civil. He was deeply angered by the silencing. Later still, CBS admitted to an inquiry by a NICAP member that the Major had been censored because of its security clearance agreement with the Air Force, and that, not knowing where Keyhoe's remarks would lead, had no choice but to cut him off when he deviated from script.[8] Still, here in the 21st century, it seems almost unbelievable that a citizen would be silenced on the air merely for asking for an open discussion in Congress about a subject. The Air Force took some heat for this, both in certain publications and from the occasional congressman who thought this a puzzling, heavy-handed behavior, as well.

Two months later, in March, Keyhoe was invited onto another national program, *The Mike Wallace Interview*.[9] This time Keyhoe was the lone guest, but he was blind-sided nevertheless. The Air Force was monitoring Keyhoe and the media closely, and when Wallace created the program, they were ready. The Assistant Secretary of the Air Force, Richard E. Horner, sent a prepared statement for Wallace to use to bomb Keyhoe at the appropriate moment in the show. It said that none of these secret documents to which Keyhoe referred ever existed, and contrary to Keyhoe's intimations, there were absolutely neither plans, nor a need, for congressional hearings. The first statement, we now know, is a lie. The second statement could be finessed as truth, although closed congressional briefings had already taken place and more were to come. The bombs *were* dropped by Wallace, and Keyhoe, naively, was caught unprepared. All he could say to the second point was that this was not what he had been led to understand.

The real story, from an historical perspective, is that these media affairs indicate a focus upon Don Keyhoe, NICAP, and media management far beyond anything one might suspect today. The Air Force was employing its *Assistant Secretary* as a regular player in counteracting Keyhoe. Horner was also a prime player in the *Armstrong Circle* affair, alongside spokesman Colonel Spencer Whedon. Horner's role was to summarize the information on the program at the end, with no challenges afterwards. Following his roles in these management

Right: Richard Horner with NASA administrators

affairs, he would answer inquiries with the bold remark that he and the Air Force were well aware of their duty to keep the public informed on these matters.[10]

During these first few months of the year, the phenomenon was mostly dormant, but NICAP soldiered on in its attempt to make congressional inroads. Overseas, apparently unnoticed by media in the United States, several big names had made startling statements. The former chief of the Royal Australian Air Force, Air Marshal George Jones, admitted that he had had his own UFO encounter in 1957.[11] The Air Defense Coordinator for Central Europe, NATO, General Lionel M. Chassin, argued for an international program of UFO observation and data collection to determine what the objects were and to avoid misidentification of enemy guided missiles.[12] When asked whether the UFOs could be extraterrestrial technology, the General replied: "Why not?" He remained interested in the phenomenon for the rest of his life, as did U.S. figures Howard McCoy, William Garland, Stefan Possony, Dewey Fournet, et al. Chassin continued to support French civilian UFOlogy thereafter, as did NICAP heavyweights Fahrney and Hillenkoetter. At the same time as Chassin's comments, the

Left to Right: Air Marshal George Jones, Gen. Lionel Chassin, Lt. Col. Petersen, Dr. Hermann Oberth

officer responsible for the Danish UFO investigation, Lt. Colonel H. C. Petersen, spoke out to the press.[13] Petersen was the antithesis of USAF behavior on the subject. In an interview with several reporters that was published in a Danish magazine, he said the most amazing things (for a current military officer involved with UFOs). Examples:

There are only very few single witness accounts. For the most part unidentified objects seen in the air have been observed by several people simultaneously at different places, so one has been able to take thorough bearings . . . in December a space ship was observed from Almind and Sdr. Bjert, bearings showed that it must have been at Pyns Hoved and that it was at least three kilometres in length. Already now I know that no saucers can appear unless in connection with a mother space ship. All accounts seem to coincide. When a space ship appears it will fly around five to ten minutes before anything happens, then it will begin to unload the saucers . . . The wave of saucers we are having now corresponds to that which passed over America in 1951-52. No one can make me believe that the Russians could be so reckless to make experiments over American territory. . . .

Nothing is gained by rejecting all the accounts as phantasy. The official denials the Air Force have issued one could have done without. When ordinary commonplace people can make authenticated observations, it is no good telling them they have been taken in or been subject to optical illusions. Instead the authorities should take the trouble to talk to the eyewitnesses. . . .

When asked, "What happens if a space ship lands near you?" With a smile, Colonel Petersen said:

Stop at 50 metres from the ship and spread the arms out in a friendly manner. It is not necessary to speak, but think seriously in friendly terms. Never attempt to shoot at any object or show war-like intentions . . . I have not the least doubt that I would try and establish contact given the chance, even if my wife forbids me to do so.

Such remarks were far beyond those which any U.S. civilian organization would have made, let alone any military officer. Nevertheless, Petersen followed this up by founding, with five other Danish military jet pilots, the Skandinavisk UFO Information (SUFOI) organization, which remained the leading civilian UFO investigative group in Denmark for decades. SUFOI itself evolved over time to become a much more moderate investigative voice than that of its founder.

As has been mentioned, Wernher von Braun's mentor in rocket technology, Dr. Hermann Oberth, had been outspoken on the non-terrestrial nature of UFOs since 1954.[14] He had just returned to Germany (in 1958) from a tenure with von Braun at the Huntsville, Alabama, rocketry site, and was in the news again with his strongly worded opinions. At Huntsville, Oberth was on his "good behavior" as to UFO comments (perhaps so as not to embarrass his famous pupil), and we know that there were several technologists there who shared his enthusiasm. Years later, two of them showed a civilian UFO researcher the German notes that Oberth had given them for a talk he made in Germany, which expressed his views with a bit more clarity. He said that many reports are misidentifications and some may even be of ball lightning; landing reports are not proven; a crashed disk story from Heligoland was bunk; and persons (such as the American contactees) were not of sound minds. All that said, however, he could not have been more positive about the flying disks.

The appearances are usually described as disks, sometimes as balls or ellipsoids. It sometimes happens that these disks place one upon the other, the largest in the center, the smaller toward the ends, to form an object the shape of a cigar, which then flies away with high speed. Sometimes one already saw such a cigar (UFO) stopping and untie into separate disks. The disks always fly in a manner as if the drive is acting perpendicular to the plane of the disk; when they are suspended over a certain terrain they keep horizontal; when they want to fly very quick, they tilt (tip) and fly with the plane directed forward. In sunlight, which is brighter than their own gleaming, they appear glittering like metal. They are dark orange and cherry red at night, if there is not much power necessary for the particular movement, for instance, when they are suspended calm. Then, they also do not shine very much. If more driving power is necessary, the shining increases (brightens) and they appear yellow, yellow-green, green like a copper flame and in a state of highest speed or acceleration extremely white. Sometimes they suddenly blink or extinguish. Their speed is sometimes very high; 19 km/sec has been measured with wireless measuring instruments (radar). Accelerations are so high that no man could stand it; he would be pressed to the wall and bruised. The accuracy of such measurements has not been doubted. If there would be only 3 or 4 measurements, I would not rely upon them and would wait for further measurements, but there is existing more than 50 such measurements the wireless sets (radar) of the American Air Force and Navy, which are used in all fighters, cannot be so inaccurate that the information obtained with them can be doubted completely. [15]

One wonders who within the United States Air Force and Navy was giving him this radar information.

All these military and scientific heavyweights (Jones, Chassin, Petersen, and Oberth) were "far away" and caused very little rumbling in the typically America-centric press. However, Donald Keyhoe and NICAP were right here and they *did* create a stir. Keyhoe, an action-oriented individual blessed with a complete absence of subtlety, decided to go directly at the Air Force by having them investigated by Congress. NICAP members began badgering their senators, if they were on the famous "McClellan Committee."[16] This was a subcommittee of the Senate's Committee on Government Operations, and was responsible for "Investigations." It had standing linkages to the FBI. The chair was the legendary Arkansas Senator, John L. McClellan, who had already achieved a reputation as a no nonsense straight-shooter by putting down the witch-hunting antics of Joe McCarthy. Keyhoe was shooting high. And the Air Force was paying attention. A meeting was held on January 31, which was not attended by McClellan or any other Senator. The USAF was there in force

Senator John McClellan

(Boland, Byrne, Tacker, and two others) to consult with the subcommittee's FBI liaisons.[17] The meeting was not held in the Senate, but at the office of the Assistant Secretary of the Air Force. The FBI agents were wise. They knew that neither the Air Force nor the McClellan Committee wanted to be bothered by this. They asked: do *you* (the Air Force) *want* a hearing or not? The Air Force said "no," but they would cooperate fully if the committee wanted it. Tacker said he had already sent UFO information and would continue to do so. The idea of a McClellan Committee investigation died right there.

NICAP and Keyhoe did not know this for some time. Basing their hopes upon rumors and occasional encouraging letters from one congressman or another, they kept pushing, opportunistically, trying to find an entry-point for something serious to take place. The Air Force was only slightly less naïve on certain matters concerning Congress. The Director of Information, General Arno Luehman, inquired as to whether the McClellan Committee,[18] "based upon their preliminary informal investigation," would now state that they had "proved that the Air Force is properly conducting its investigation of unidentified flying objects and is not withholding information on this subject from the public." One must suppose that Luehman had no knowledge of the results of the meeting between the two FBI agents and the Air Force. We do not know how Luehman's request was received at the McClellan Committee, but it was ignored. General Joe Kelly's memorandum back to Luehman on this matter seems like deliberate misinformation,[19] stating that they had done "considerable exploratory work" with the committee, which almost has to be untrue, given that the January 31 consultation was the only known

General Arno Luehman

meeting. Even within its own organization, the Air Force may have been doing the least possible while claiming the most.

During this 1957-58 time period, NICAP was informed of one senator who was willing to be quite outspoken on the substantive nature of the UFO issue: Barry Goldwater of Arizona. Goldwater, a Colonel in the Air Force Reserve and a qualified jet pilot, appeared on the front page of NICAP's *UFO Investigator* speaking of his interest.[20] NICAP was never able to exploit Goldwater's energy and position successfully, which says a great deal about the dominant hand that Air Force Intelligence really held in this situation. Despite the constant griping that is apparent in Air Force documents about Keyhoe and other citizens' involvements, not even a powerful senator could make any important headway against the policy. In early 1958 Goldwater wrote to the Secretary of the Air Force concerning the *Armstrong Theater* fiasco.[21] Assistant Secretary Horner replied that cutting off Keyhoe was "an unfortunate

Senator Barry Goldwater

occurrence," but it was entirely his fault and "the Air Force had nothing to do with this intentional fade-out." (One feels impelled to note this shamelessly manipulative use of the language, in a poor imitation of George Orwell.) Most importantly: "The allegations that the Air Force has withheld information on unidentified flying object reports are entirely in error."[22] The boldness of continuing to make such assertions to people like U.S. Senators, in the face of consistently denying such information to citizens, is really stunning. Horner went on to assure Senator Goldwater of his claim by stating, "I am enclosing the Air Force fact sheet dated 5 November 1957 on the subject." And what was someone like Goldwater to do when faced with such a situation as this? He could make a stink about it, or he could let it go. What most people did not realize (maybe even some senators did not realize) was that just being a U.S. Senator did not mean that the intelligence community was going to take one into its confidence. Goldwater, though staying interested in UFOs and remaining a member of NICAP, essentially let matters be.

A much greater challenge for the Air Force came from John Henderson, Congressman from Ohio. Henderson may have been inspired by a constituent (this is not known), but his interest in the UFO phenomenon was genuinely his own. His request for information was written directly to the Secretary of Defense, and it was inspired by his reading of Edward Ruppelt's book.[23] All of Henderson's questions were those of a young, enthusiastic, scientific mind. He even wanted the Air Force to give him a list of their ten best cases. From a member of the public, this complex but specific letter would have been easy to brush off. Major Tacker took about a week and a half to mull this over and decided that a serious letter was necessary. He wrote Arcier and Gregory at Blue Book that he wanted that letter within the week.[24] Tacker said that he would then hand-carry the letter to Henderson immediately. Gregory and Arcier called him back–there was no way they could answer the Congressman's sixteen questions that quickly. The sticking point was Henderson's request for the ten best cases. Gregory and Arcier did not want to honor that, especially since this required the Air Force to prepare a hard-copy document (that would obviously be extremely difficult to "pitch" properly to the Congressman, and, a hard copy could be passed around). The solution was to meet with Henderson personally and discuss cases verbally.

That meeting took place in Henderson's office one month later (June 20, 1958).[25] Attending were Henderson and three other members of Congress plus four staff aides. The Air Force had Tacker, Boland, Byrne, and Arcier to carry the message. The Air Force thought that the briefing would go a full hour; it went the entire morning. Interest was high, and Byrne stated in his summary memo that they had done well in increasing the congressmen's confidence in the Air Force's handling of the UFO program. It is also mentioned that the politicians were made privy to classified portions of the Robertson Panel report.

Henderson's special briefing and showing of classified Robertson Panel material showed that it very much mattered *who* you were. At the same time that the Henderson matter was evolving, the Air Force got another request for information. This time it was from Lyndon Baines Johnson.[26] We do not know the response of the Pentagon when the powerful senator's letter came in, but we suspect that everyone jumped. Johnson's constituent (called the "source" below) was complaining about Air Force handling of some obscure incident in Texas. Nevertheless, the whole relevant apparatus of the Air Force went into action.

> Although source's report was somewhat incomplete and lacking in detail, particularly as to exact locations, four major Air Force agencies immediately went into action to investigate and resolve the alleged sighting: OSI, Keesler AFB, Carswell AFB, and the Air Technical Intelligence Center.

> This will serve to illustrate to Senator Johnson the painstaking efforts and thoroughness with which the Air Force undertakes to resolve UFO sightings, even such as this, where numerous efforts are made to locate the source and obtain the facts because the original report was incomplete.

UFO historian Loren Gross noted, with some amusement, the comparison of four major Air Force command elements chasing down some minor incident, when it had sent a sergeant for part of a day to investigate the Levelland vehicle-interference sightings.[27] But the last person anyone should want to offend was Lyndon Johnson. In a parallel action (the origins for which we have no documentation), the Air Force apparently was able to persuade another congressman, Roland V. Libonati of Illinois, to read into the Congressional Record a nearly unadulterated version of the typical self-congratulating news release that worked so well to defuse concern (and interest).[28] Added to this was the return of the confusing claim (so often debunked both then and with our knowledge today) that saucer-shaped planes were being developed and, just maybe, already tested in prototype.

John McCormack

A further Congressional interaction occurred in 1958, and it constituted what was, perhaps, Keyhoe's best chance at ever achieving a hearing. This challenge to the Air Force came suddenly and was as much a surprise to NICAP as to the authorities. The congressional committee initiating this hearing was the House Select Committee on Astronautics and Space Exploration.[29] Its chairman was John W. McCormack, one of the strongest and most irascible personalities in Congress. The briefing was to be to the Subcommittee on Atmospheric Phenomena, chaired by another prominent politician, William H. Natcher of Kentucky. As far as can be determined from available documents, McCormack and Natcher informed the Secretary of the Air Force that they were going to hold hearings on the subject of UFOs with just two or three days lead time. General W. P. Fisher of the Air Force's Legislative Liaison office wrote, on about August 5, that the subcommittee would begin on August 7, and that the Air Force was expected to be there on August 8.[30] This development and the abruptness of the request had to shock the Air Force UFO-information managers. General Fisher was happy to pass responsibility for the meeting off to Assistant Secretary Horner. We can be sure that Horner immediately got the management team together (Byrne, Tacker, Arcier, and Gregory), plus

William Natcher

the principal "Legislative Project officer" (Major Brower) and geophysicist (Major Best), as they were there with a full-fledged show for the congressmen on the assigned date.[31] The approach was to be based largely on technical materials, with Arcier handling the science and engineering from Wright-Patterson's point of view, and Major William J. Best, the head of the geophysics division of the Air Force Office of Scientific Research, present to unload the heavy upper atmosphere science.

The subcommittee was well-represented. McCormack and Natcher, plus representatives Sisk and McDonaugh of California, Kenneth Keating of New York. and Lee Metcalf of Montana all personally attended. Also present was their chief scientific consultant, Dr. Charles S. Sheldon. McCormack opened the session by stating that the committee did not intend this as an investigation of the Air Force. Rather, he said, they were information-gathering on whatever was going on in "upper space," which could be helpful

General W. P. Fisher

later in their consultancies and support of other agencies of the government. This was, at least, Major Byrne's take on what McCormack said.[32] Frankly, it seems a weak excuse for a hearing. A better guess would be that these people were avidly curious about UFOs. From Byrne's memo, the politicians were treated to lengthy reviews of Project Blue Book's history and activities by Arcier and Gregory, and "Captain Gregory is to be especially commended for his excellent performance." Citizen clubs, books, and organizations were also discussed, as to their effects upon Air Force responsibilities. Shortly after this meeting (within the month of August), Congressman Keating was talking to Bob Barry, news director of the local radio station in Orleans, New York, and a UFO buff.[33] Keating was quite open about the "closed-door" hearing. He said that the Air Force had shown the congressmen motion pictures (plural) of UFOs and many still photos (one would like to know what they chose). The Congressman

Kenneth Keating

said that the committee had not made up its mind yet as to how to proceed. He personally felt that they should hear from groups other than the Air Force to get the full story, but nothing was decided.

Meanwhile, Byrne's memo indicated pleasure with the polite and pleasant reception they had gotten and expressed confidence that the committee would be supportive. Byrnes had to be nervous about something else that he heard, however, and this was the *critical* moment: the committee's comments stated that, while happy with the Air Force's presentation, they would "continue through the week of August 11-15.[34] *Additional witnesses from public life will be called in*" (emphasis added). Who?! Byrne said Menzel, Hugh Dryden, and Ruppelt were mentioned. But he also said: "Keyhoe." It appeared that Keyhoe was going to get to bring his case directly to the Congressional Committee on Atmospheric Phenomena, *without the Air Force in attendance*. Major Byrne must have swallowed hard as he wrote the next sentence: "It is anticipated that AFCIN (Air Force Intelligence) will benefit by the subject hearings." He went on to voice the hope that the fact that all these people would be up for election in November would encourage them to make public statements giving a vote of confidence to the Air Force.

This potential nightmare never happened and, given the attitudes of committee members such as Keating, we do not know why. Whatever happened, happened quickly. Whereas Major Byrne went back to his office to compose the memo just discussed, somewhere else in the system the word was already down that there would be *no* more witnesses and that the hearings were over. Whatever took place, it took place through the person of the committee's science advisor, Charles Sheldon. He told Air Force authorities soon after the Air Force presentation, as reported by General Fisher, that there would be no civilian witnesses and no other hearing dates.[35] This could not have happened during the meeting, as Byrne could have hardly missed that, nor written such a contrary memo to his bosses. Sheldon's comments were behind the scenes. What was going on? Someone higher than the Air Force information management team shut this down. We cannot say by whom. We can say a bit about Charles Sheldon and let readers form their own conclusions.

Charles Sheldon

Sheldon was originally in Naval Intelligence, and he said that, at an early date, he had access to all the USAF's UFO data, if he desired to peruse it.[36] He was quite interested in the subject and spoke positively of it to NICAP's Assistant Director, Richard Hall, in a meeting in the mid-60s. Sheldon had a long record of involvement in space and missile technology, and was considered a top expert on Soviet capabilities. Whether he was CIA or not is not known, but he did work closely with the CIA and once convinced the agency to classify all of an amateur Soviet-watcher's missile research work. Sheldon also spoke of having a close friend "as high in the government as you can get," who was particularly interested in UFOs and especially in the photographic materials. This sounds to the UFO historian very much like another prominent-but-ghostly government "UFO aficionado," the head of the intelligence community's Photographic Interpretation Center, Art Lundahl—a figure who could very easily, as a personal advisor to Presidents, be labeled "as high as you can get." Sheldon ultimately became a NASA expert on the Soviet space program. Although he told Hall in 1967 that plenty of UFO evidence already existed and that the subject needed a proper study, 1958 was not, apparently, the right time. Someone at a higher level informed Sheldon that UFO civilian hearings were not going to happen.

This incident indicates the hopeless nature of what Keyhoe and NICAP were trying to do. Here was an appropriate congressional committee with powerful personnel impervious to intimidation, initiating a hearings agenda with nearly no notice to the Air Force, informing the AF that a whole week of civilian hearings was in the wings. Yet, before the last echoes had died in the committee room, that whole idea was obliterated by higher forces. The lower level Air Force staff (Byrne, Tacker, Arcier et al.) left the room not knowing it. Congressmen such as Keating left the room not knowing it. But very shortly, the congressional investigation was neutralized. With this level of influence working against them, neither Keyhoe and NICAP, nor anyone else, had a chance.

Still, that did not mean that the information management group did not need to stay vigilant. They were getting flack for their clumsy handling of an Ohio housewife's case;[37] they worried over how best to monitor the activities of the civilian groups; they even fretted about beating Keyhoe to the punch on a case involving a witness who was a Catholic nun—sure that they were bound to end up losers if they had to employ their usual tactics against an impeccable witness.[38] Mostly they worried about Admiral Hillenkoetter. How could they get him to quit his defense of the subject and open information sharing? The idea was floated: maybe if we could talk to him personally about the Robertson Panel, he would understand.[39]

Regarding the phenomenon: there are no years which lack incidents of mystery and note, but as we said the years 1958-1963 in the United States seemed unusually sparse. Added to this was the atmosphere surrounding the UFO Project. The orientation of the Project had gotten so skewed towards managing Keyhoe and Congress that, when a scholar looks at the Blue Book records today, one can rarely find cases in which Wright-Patterson took much notice at all. As years have passed, UFO civilian researchers have interacted with dozens of witnesses (many from the military) who will tell of some post-case debriefing and form-filling regarding their sightings, yet no record of it appears in the Blue Book microfilm. Here is one example:

September 8, 1958, Offutt AFB, Omaha, Nebraska:[40] It was 6:40 p.m. at Strategic Air Command Headquarters' airfield, and a large number of Air Force officers were in and about the air traffic control tower. They spotted a brilliant white elongated cylinder hanging in the sky to the west. The brilliance when first sighted was compared to a magnesium flare. This brightness slowly diminished to show the object's shape more clearly, like a long exclamation mark vertically in the sky. Then it turned orange and seemed to have a flurry of small black objects swarming about its lower end. An officer attempted to take still photos, but said they did not appear in the developed film. The exclamation mark began slowly moving away, tilting to the horizontal as it did so. Before vanishing in the western haze, it moved back up to a 45 degree angle, and was gone. At least two dozen Air Force officers witnessed the enigma. None had an explanation. The officer who told the UFO civilian community about the experience five years later was Major Paul Duich, an engineer and a navigator, who later worked on the Space Shuttle program for Rockwell Space Division. It was Duich himself who called in the UFO report to Strategic Air Command Headquarters (military reports went to ADC, were sifted, and then some of them were sent to Blue Book). After giving details on the phone, he was told that he would be contacted by a Blue Book representative for a full report within 48 hours. As he said in 1964: "I am still waiting—5 ½ years later." Perusal of the Blue Book records indicates no notice of the case.

Here is a second example.[41] The reporter in this instance was an airman, not a highly credentialed technologist like Paul Duich, but a man with a good mind, eyes, and intelligence whose story was similar to many others. The witness was part of an air refueling mission that had left Goose Bay in Labrador and was returning to a New Hampshire Air Force Base. The plane was a KC97, and he and another airman were doing grunt duty, acting as "scanners" (visually searching for any other air traffic in the vicinity). The two saw a bright star-like light some distance away, which seemed to be gradually approaching their plane. They notified the commander and everyone on board had a look. By this time the object had about the same apparent size as the Moon and was brightly illuminating the cloud bank behind it with a brilliant blue-white light. On the "face" of the object there seemed to be two dark spots or "holes." The commander was asked whether they should turn towards the object and flash their lights at it or do

Back Right: Paul Duich
Front Left: Dr. Alan Hynek

something else to find out more about it. The airman's memory of his commander's response was rather vivid. The commander laughed at the suggestion and said "No way. I'm not flashing lights at that. They might think that it's a raid or something." So the crew watched their strange companion for a short time, before it rapidly accelerated through the cloud bank out of sight. The airman did not recall making reports and none occur in the Blue Book records.

February 17, 1958, Alcalde, New Mexico:[42] Two women, residents of Albuquerque, were driving south to Santa Fe at 8 p.m. Suddenly a flash lit up the surroundings. The woman in the passenger's seat rolled down the window and was greeted by a second flash of even greater intensity that temporarily blinded her. The light was so engulfing that the driver feared that the car would stray from the road, so she pulled over and stopped. Both women in their different ways (one, distractedly, due to driving, and the other just before the flash and then after the light died down and she could see again) saw a light-orange-colored object, flat on the bottom and rounded on top, perhaps the size of an automobile. The passenger had seen the object just prior to the second engulfing blast, then two minutes later as it moved into the distance.

This case had unusual consequences. The easiest to understand is what happened to the roll of film in the camera in the back seat. The film was entirely fogged. The second was that the passenger was not only temporarily blinded but developed a crashing headache. More difficult to understand was the feeling of "sunburn," followed in the next two days by vomiting, nausea, a heat rash, and diarrhea. One of the women said that she had "never been in such pain and discomfort." Because of these symptoms, which are worrisome in that they mimic radiation exposure, the car's driver talked with a friend, a local science and math teacher, and he brought his Geiger counter over to the women's homes. This was, of course, no scientific test. But the teacher, interviewed thereafter by the *Albuquerque Tribune*, said that the counter registered 25 times the number of counts per minute when measuring the two witnesses as compared to three other women neighbors who served as an ad hoc control group. Particularly high were readings around the neck and hair and at the palm of the passenger's hand. The women went to the famous Lovelace Clinic for professional treatment. This clinic was well-known for work on radiation effects and had strong Air Force ties in the region. The women went there because the passenger's personal physician worked there, and she had medical benefits there due to her job in Civil Defense. Thus began a whole mystery-saga involving several radiation physicians, many casual comments about "high counts" and high body exposure, low white blood cell counts, and skin-reddening, yet the women were never formally told anything about their test results, even by the personal physician. (Both women felt that if the case were publicly widespread and speculated about, the idea that they had gotten close to a nuclear "weapon mistake" would naturally come up.)

One would expect that a case of this magnitude would have initiated a serious Air Force investigation. About a week after the event, an Air Force captain from Kirtland AFB visited the driver. His interview emphasized the characteristics of the object and the resulting medical consequences. He asked if the driver would be willing to be examined at a military hospital, and she said yes. But she heard no more. The passenger had a visit about the same time from a group of military people from the Sandia base. She agreed to take them to the site of the incident, where they scanned the area with Geiger counters. They then went to the mountain cabin, where the women had been previously, and scanned that area as well. Apparently, nothing was found, or at least no information was transmitted to the witness. Other longer-term physiological consequences persisted, and there were extremely puzzling marks or areas of "burn" on their bodies in places that were wholly unexplainable by any commonsense exposure of two women sitting in a car. Those mysteries aside, it is interesting that no report was filed with Blue Book.

One cannot prove anything about the phenomenon from such cases. But their existence (and their number) indicate a certain slackness in the Blue Book system of that era, which showed little real investigative interest in a case unless it was about to become a public problem. If one is not interested in an incident like Alcalde, one cannot easily imagine what *might* be of interest. *Someone* showed interest, true, but the formal UFO investigation project did not. It remains of much concern to UFO historians to learn where, if anywhere, these reports went. And civilian UFOlogists were not the only ones wondering. During this year Donald Keyhoe, using his Navy connections, got an interview with two officers who had connections with the Navy's missile program.[43] (This was probably fairly easy for ex-Navy missile chief Fahrney to arrange.) Keyhoe wanted to talk about rumors of UFO incidents at Cape Canaveral, but neither side wanted to share confidential information. The Navy officers did, however, indicate that they were keeping a report file separate from that of the Air Force. Why, Keyhoe asked, when the Air Force is tasked with this job? The officers replied that they and others were dissatisfied with how the Air Force handled cases. Referring to Project Blue Book as "The Sink," they said:

It's our name for Project Blue Book. We have to give all Navy and Marine Corps sighting reports to the Air Force. Then the lid goes down. If we ask for conclusions, they won't answer. In a few cases, they've even insisted they never heard of certain Navy reports—sightings we reviewed, right in this office.[44]

It is astonishing that the Air Force would not even cooperate with the *Navy* through an open policy of information exchange.

October 7, 1958, Alexandria, Virginia:[45] A bright silvery object was seen hovering in the sky. It began to ascend, and then moved rapidly away. The witness had time to walk about a half-block towards the object as he tried to get a better feeling for its distance and size. It was, however, quite distant, and at one point a commercial airliner flew directly between his line-of-sight and the UFO. This comparison made the witness feel that the object was quite large, "of the order of 600 feet." He drew the object as a globe with a Saturn-ring-like "skirt" about its midline. He said the object was very sharply outlined. This was not an average witness. Dr. John R. Townsend was an expert in chemicals and explosives as well as the corrosive effects of nuclear radiation on materials. He was currently a Special Assistant to the Secretary of Defense, operating as the main consultant on Fuels, Materials, and Ordnance. What would the Blue Book officers tell this man?

It took the Air Force nearly three months to get back to Townsend. Major Tacker wrote the brief letter for General LeBailly's signature (LeBailly was, at the time, "Deputy Director of Information Services").[46] According to the letter, ATIC had gotten to work immediately on the case. The good doctor had seen reflections off ice crystals that were moving towards him as the Sun set, thus giving the illusion of altitude gain and size diminishment. The Air Force claimed this was basically proven by the fact that Townsend said the object was big but that no one else saw it.

But apparently others did. The pilot of a Capitol Airlines flight saw an "unidentified aircraft" just a couple of minutes prior to Townsend's sighting and at the correct location for it to be the same object just prior to its hovering.[47] Someone has attempted to do some geometric analysis combining these two sightings, but the precision necessary to do this is not present in these reports. One thing *is* present, however. The pilot, knowing his own plane's altitude, had reasonably good grounds to assess the UFO's altitude at 3000 feet, which was approximately what Townsend thought it might be. Giving the pilot some credence would mean that Townsend's estimate of an object 500-600 feet across would also be credible. The Air Force pronouncement? "Ice crystals" drifting in an unseen cloud layer in just the right way, with no other witnesses. One wonders what Townsend, a scientist, thought as he read the letter.

At the end of the year, the press was as much at war with the Air Force as the civilian UFOlogists were. A Washington News Bureau chief for several New England newspapers had been researching UFOs all year, and the Air Force made the mistake of thinking that they could influence him. He was briefed by Blue Book officers and shown some documents. Bulkley Griffin, however, was no fool. He saw the intent of the written policy that only cases where the mystery was solved and the object linked to a familiar, known cause were to be passed on to the public.[48] Griffin said, pointedly, "This constitutes pretty effective censorship." He had also gotten to interview the powerful chairman of the House Armed Services Committee, Carl Vinson. Vinson must have felt that Griffin was a friend of the Air Force, as he showed him a somewhat sensitive letter telling Vinson (in eerily Robertsonian terms) that the AF was going to get popular figures like Arthur Godfrey and Dave Garroway "to assist us in our program to put the UFO subject in its proper perspective." In the meantime, they said, "we are attempting to get articles placed in public magazines with large circulation."[49]

It was not a major magazine, but the *Boston Herald,* the major newspaper in New England, under the name of its Washington Bureau correspondent Tom Gerber, published a counter-blast at the end of November that featured materials from interviews by Gerber with unnamed "Air Force Officers." The words were rough and angry:

The Air Force has opened undeclared war on phony organizations that capitalize on the "mystery" of flying saucers. . . . For 12 years now the Air Force has been castigated, abused, criticized, and verbally bludgeoned for hiding something from the public.

More than 30 UFO organizations have been formed dedicated to worshipping . . . [the] unexplained percentage . . . [of UFO sightings].

Top Air Force spokesmen won't acknowledge it publicly, but they are fed up to the teeth with taking abuse and not fighting back.

They have gone through such ordeals as listening for two hours to tape recordings of interviews with persons on Venus. Coincidentally, the alleged persons on Venus spoke English.

The Air Force officers, with a combination of a grimace and a grin, don't hesitate privately to call UFO devotes members of the lunatic fringe.

They have evidence that perhaps as many as 100,000 persons belong to these UFO organizations, reportedly are making a wad of money.

The Air Force normally would have little truck with these outfits. But about 16 percent of the alleged 'sightings' the Air Force has investigated have turned out to be outright hoaxes—originated by members or officials of these organizations.

To Air Force skeptics it's been a time-and-money wasting exercise. Atop the investigating process, the Air Force has had to answer thousands of letters on UFOs.

In addition, the UFO problem has diverted money, personnel, and facilities from the Air Force's mission of defending the nation.

For the past year, Air Force officials quietly have contacted members of Congress, government officials, and influential citizens in the battle against the thirty UFO organizations.[50]

This *was* the language of war. Some statements in the article were crude lies and slanders. The line about 16% of the sightings being hoaxes perpetrated by UFO organization members borders on the outrageous if not the libelous. NICAP would have liked to know where the "wad of money" idea came from, as it was about to go bankrupt. Perhaps the Air Force said none of these things to Gerber, and, for reasons of his own, he made them up—something no reasonable person would believe. This was angry, unreasoning language directed at an enemy.

The only light amid all this heat came from John Lester, a writer for the *Newark (New Jersey) Star-Ledger*. He made the stunning decision to do a little "private" research. Over a month's time, he polled 1000 government radar operators around the nation. Had they seen UFOs? What had they tracked? What did they think? The results were astonishing:

Traveling at fantastic speeds—sometimes thousands of miles per hour—these objects execute perfect 90-degree turns, steep vertical climbs, even abrupt, hovering stops in defiance of all known laws of aerodynamics, the radar men report.

When more than one are involved they fly in a pattern and, when there are many, in a pattern within a pattern. [Many present day UFOlogists are not even aware of the "pattern within a pattern" design of UFO formations.]

In addition, they invariably stay just ahead of Air Force planes sent up to intercept them.

This has led most of these skilled technicians—Civil Aeronautics Authority employees, their official title is Airways Operation Specialist—to conclude that Flying Saucers do exist. At the very least, they say, there is something "out there" that can't be explained in any conventional manner.

Eight out of ten of approximately 1,000 polled during the past month by the *Star-Ledger* are of this opinion.

The others were undecided or noncommittal.

The approximately 1,000 polled, considered a fair cross-section of the 12,000 currently on active duty, were from airfields in New York, Newark, Boston, Miami, Chicago, Los Angeles, Fort Worth, and other major cities throughout the country.

Some were from fields in the Hawaiian Islands.

Each is an expert operator of the super-sensitive electronic 'eye' known as radar. This is the device responsible for precision-safe take-offs and landings of all aircraft and/or a constant search of the sky for unscheduled or unidentified planes—or anything else that might interfere with normal flight plans or endanger national security.

Of the total number whose opinions were tabulated, fully half reported they had seen—'tracked' is their term—unidentified flying objects on their radar screens one or more times and in many instances the objects were observed simultaneously by people in the vicinity—sometimes by thousands.

All are certain the things were not meteors, weather balloons, cloud formations, hallucinations are anything else of this nature.

About 60 per cent—three-out-of-every-five—of the remaining 500 who've never personally tracked a UFO are of the same considered opinion because of their confidence in radar and the knowledge and skill of their co-workers.[51]

At the Pentagon, Major Lawrence Tacker had to respond immediately. The next day he said that all this was probably just natural phenomena ("lightning, meteors, and meteorites") but not flying saucers.[52] Possibly realizing how insufficient that sounded in the face of Lester's 1000-man poll, Tacker said that he would "like to have more detailed information on any reports of CAA watchers who tracked the objects."[53] Going on to talk of how people make mistakes, he almost made his comment sound like a threat. Doubtless, he did not mean it a threat.

Many civilian airline pilots, though, saw it differently. Lester followed his radar bombshell with a quicker poll of fifty commercial pilots.[54] These men were almost unanimous in "blasting as 'bordering on the absolute ridiculous' the Air Force policy of tight censorship, brush-off and denial in regard to unidentified flying objects." One man

Major Lawrence Tacker

said it in the strongest terms: "[The Air Force policy] was a lesson in lying, intrigue and the 'Big Brother' attitude carried to the ultimate extreme." Admittedly Lester had culled out a biased polling group—every one of these pilots had seen *at least* one UFO while flying. All were interrogated by the Air Force, and most of them disgusted by their treatment. "We are usually treated like incompetents and told to keep quiet." One guy said: "Nuts to that. Who needs it?" Not one pilot agreed to have his name used by Lester. Why? Their employers specifically told them no, sometimes mentioning that this was also at Air Force insistence. One pilot specifically cited the updated JANAP 146 regulation with its statement that informants will be liable for a $10,000 fine if they talk about cases in public. As we have seen, this punishment *is* written into CIRVIS-MERINT reports regulations, and is theoretically in effect once an official report has been made.

The Pentagon, and Major Tacker, did not respond directly to Lester this time. One day later, Lester "shot himself in the foot" and relieved them of the need to do so. A "Top (unnamed) Washington official" came to Lester and told him that the Air Force had a crashed flying saucer at Wright-Patterson AFB, maybe two. France had "at least two," England one, Russia one, and Brazil probably another. Saucers were falling from the sky like hailstones.[55] Lester, unaccountably, printed the assertions. Nothing put one in the lunatic fringe faster. Tacker now had a duck-in-a-barrel to shoot, and he blasted Lester's story as "pure rubbish," which doubtlessly registered as true among readers.[56] One would, one suspects, number many NICAP members among them.

As 1959 arrived, the intense, angry George Gregory was replaced by the laid-back, soft-spoken Robert Friend. Major Friend's courteous and professional demeanor has endeared him to UFO proponents, but, in fact, the policy of case management did not change. There was not even a veneer of a change on the Pentagon side. Major Tacker insisted on being the only first contact for any inquiry (civilian or military) regarding UFOs.[57] Neither Wright-Patterson nor *any* base was to be contacted, or, if they were, to say anything. Tacker did not always handle this responsibility as sole mouthpiece well. In response to a media blitz about a civilian airline encounter (the "Captain Peter Killian" case), an unnamed Pentagon spokesman (which according to the policy had to be Tacker or someone reading what Tacker had written) said in response to the clamor connected to this case, "there are always a certain number of cases where they (UFO witnesses) cannot remember a thing when they sober up the next day."[58] Because this remark, which would not have been appropriate under any circumstances, was uttered in the context of a responsible airline pilot's report, Captain Killian was outraged.[59] He protested being called a drunk and angrily noted that such remarks put his job on the line. Tacker never apologized, but his next mention of the case (as an answering letter to a civilian researcher) left out all the derogatory comments and concentrated on a "jet refueling operation" explanation[60] (which was what he should have been talking about in the first place, since it was marginally possible and not demeaning of the pilot and crew).

Major Robert Friend

For whatever reasons there was little momentum for congressional hearings in 1959 and little for the old information management team to do. Early in January, a "leak" stated that a member of the Senate Space Committee was going to ask its chair, Lyndon Johnson, to explore the matter of UFOs.[61] Johnson had a long-standing, if occasional, interest in the topic, so this may have worried the Air Force's UFO group. But there is no evidence that this went anywhere. General Fisher wrote to Senator Harry Byrd the day after the news story and told Byrd that the Air Force bluntly opposed hearings on UFOs. We do not know if Byrd convinced Johnson to forget it. Shortly thereafter, an Air Force fact sheet was released on January 22, 1959, and showed only two unknowns in six months.[62]

Allen Hynek was still on leave of absence from Blue Book while he helped Fred Whipple direct the Smithsonian Observatory's Satellite Tracking Program. He had taken some flack from people about his association with a project that functioned in such an unscientific way, but he knew that he was on his way back to more normal availability as an astronomical consultant. Since Robert Friend represented a changing of the guard, Hynek felt that this might be a moment where something could be done to change the way things were handled. He and Friend therefore called a Blue Book assessment and policy meeting on February 17, 1959.[63] Majors Tacker and Boland were there from the Pentagon, and Majors Friend and Byrne were present; intelligence projects head Colonel L. S. Glaser and his civilian advisor, B. L. Griffing, as well as A. Francis Arcier, attended along with Hynek. Hynek led things off, complaining how Blue Book caused him trouble while at the same time praising the Air Force for how well it did its job. Whether either of these openers were more than a psychological set-up for the rest of the meeting is not clear since the meeting immediately veered into polishing Blue Book's technique for handling sticky cases and sharpening up the UFOB officers who make the initial field contacts. Reading the memorandum of the meeting notes, one finds that every agenda point is aimed at making what the Blue Book/Pentagon Information Desk does easier in terms of convincing the public that there is nothing unusual about UFOs. The meeting was remarkably Robertsonian, emphasizing "Education of the Public" (*only* described in terms of explainable phenomena), faster processing of information to Tacker's office (so that he could defuse the press more quickly), better detail from the field reports (so that the Air Force's conclusions will have more concrete, convincing substance behind them), and a cleverer and more obfuscating way of dispensing with cases in which the mundane explanation was *not* proven. For example: "There is no evidence available to indicate that the object sighted in this case was not a meteor." And: "In view of all the available evidence, the object of this sighting was probably a meteor."[64] The idea here was, apparently, to more "softly" debunk sightings, while sounding more reasonable and not offending the witnesses as bluntly. The meeting went on to describe two further desirable project activities: to review old unknown cases in order to reduce them "from the 'unknown' category and reclassify as a 'probable'," and to write to famous people who have been quoted in support of UFO reality and try to get them to change their minds. The meeting minutes ended with an attachment that was a precise eight-step exposition of the Robertson Panel conclusions and directives. As an aside of some possible psychological force, the Panel was now being described as a Scientific Advisory Panel requested by the Air Force's Director of Intelligence.

The meeting was a reaffirmation of current policies, both the Robertsonian foundations and the need to publicly debunk cases convincingly, and the management of the public, both organizations and prominent individuals. Hynek *was* calling for better fieldwork, but his appeal was couched in phraseology that connected it to better abilities of Blue Book (and Tacker) to get rid of cases rather than to research them openly. Perhaps Hynek was being crafty and knew that better investigation might well uncover the truths behind the anomalies. But there is no legitimate evidence to credit him with such a subtle strategy.

One real change does seem to have been a softening of attitude at Wright-Patterson (not at the Pentagon), although Major Friend was just as tough on allowing "unidentifieds" as George Gregory had been. There may have been some awareness of the more laid-back attitude of Friend's Blue Book leaking out to the larger military community, or it may just have been that 1959 was an exceptionally slack UFO year, but it took the recommendations of the February meeting all year to percolate up to the Pentagon office of Major General Richard J. O'Keefe, the Deputy Inspector General for Security. O'Keefe's office sent a December 24 memorandum to all Air Base Commands in the United States.[65] It reminded commanders of their duties to report all UFO sightings, according to a revised Air Force Regulation 200-2, which specified chains-of-command as related to information transfer and communicating with the public. It reflected the Blue Book meeting's concern for better qualified UFOB officers. Across the top of the memorandum were words that probably took some commands by surprise: "UFOs—Serious Business."

Cases were down but not non-existent but it worth citing a few examples. February 24, 1959, Victorville, California:[66] A young man (seventeen years old) was home babysitting the family pets and his younger brother, when he saw a bright light shining in his bedroom window. The family dogs began to howl and run around. He dressed and went outside. A luminous object like an "elongated egg" was flying on a descending path toward his house. The object went over the front yard at a height of only eight to ten feet. The teenager saw it as it approached and saw its side when it was abreast but, curiously, could not see it from the rear. He took the dogs inside and went back out. The object, in the distance, seemed to be returning. The young man went in to get a gun. The younger brother at this time saw the object's second pass. The older brother went out again and saw the object getting near for a third pass, so he retreated inside. The object passed directly over the house twice, and only on these occasions was a vibration heard and felt. This set of experiences took place between 9 p.m. and 9:15 p.m. The object was roughly estimated by the Air Force officer as a bit larger than an automobile. The thing's color was dull red with "purple waves" in it. When the parents returned home, they found the dogs in a terrified state, whimpering, shaking, and hiding beneath the furniture. The boy said that radio reception turned to intense static when the object was near the home, and neighbors verified that their radio and television reception had been lost. They also admitted to seeing something unusual but would not cooperate further with the officer, and refused to let him put their names on his report. The Air Force officer completed his form with positive statements about the young man's character and consistency. The case went into Blue Book and was thrown out as "Psychological: Unreliable observer" on no grounds whatever, except that the young man was seventeen years old. Later, Allen Hynek, who had nothing to do with this analysis, stated that he was appalled by such explanatory shenanigans.[67]

October 2, 1959, Seattle, Washington:[68] Civilian researchers in the Seattle area reported seeing ball-of-light-type objects over local mountains; there sightings were never reported to the Air Force. The same evening, the Hercules Tracking Radar Site 13 in Seattle picked up a number of objects. The objects moved swiftly and erratically till they were lost at distance. Concurrent visual sightings (not described) went on until the objects were lost in a fog bank. Blue Book was unimpressed by this, but James McDonald resuscitated the case in the late 1960s and declared it an unknown.[69]

August 13, 1959, between Roswell and Corona, New Mexico:[70] A retired member of the Navy, flying his private plane (a Cessna 170), saw that his magnetic compass was beginning to rotate strangely. The electric Magnesyn compass was doing a creepy 360° turn every four to five seconds. A second, standard magnetic compass was gyrating wildly. Then there appeared three "small, gray, slightly fuzzy" ellipses flying in echelon formation. They crossed left to right and then flew around his plane at a distance of only about 500 feet. At this close approach, the Magnesyn compass began to track the ellipses. The objects broke off and disappeared to the rear, and both compasses began behaving normally. Upon reporting to Albuquerque, the pilot was ordered not to land there but to redirect to Kirtland AFB. There he was interrogated by an Air Force officer. He was told not to talk about this case with anyone (even his wife), and if he became ill he should return and a military hospital would take care of it. This latter unusual comment reminds us of the incident of the women and the Lovelace Clinic in this same area. Some of these cases were now entering areas of close encounter and physical impact that investigators had difficulty relating to in standard military or technical models, and often, it seemed, the problem was "solved" by ignoring it. Even when there was a base commander who thought differently, it seems that circumstances conspired to continue the comedy of errors, as the next case illustrates.

November 11, 1958 (and the following Spring of 1959), Topeka, Kansas:[71] Mrs. Kinney was a Lt. Colonel in the Civil Air Patrol and the wife of a prominent local doctor. Her husband was away and she had gone to bed. At 1:35 a.m. her bedroom flooded with light and her three dogs went wild. The light was a copper color, deep amber. Outside, the source—a 25-foot diameter sphere—sat on the walkway in the yard. The object was no more than thirty feet away. Mrs. Kinney put on a robe and went to a room with a porch to go outside. When she opened the door, the sphere zoomed straight upwards and out of sight. The woman turned back to bed and the phone rang. A neighbor, looking at a huge, bright light going toward her house (and with a pair of snarling dogs of her own) was worried that it would set fire to Mrs. Kinney's trees or even her house. Later, at 7:30 a.m., the phone rang again. This time it was the Tower at the Topeka airport, and the controllers, who knew Mrs. Kinney well, were voicing concern about the very bright light that they'd seen. When the next evening fell, she began to notice electrical failure on the east side of the house. Lights would not work. Radios that were on that side would not operate. Even refrigerators were out. In the basement, the woman found the eastside fuses blown. She changed them. Some things responded; some did not. She called the electrician and he called on her the next day. Wiring on the upstairs eastside was burnt out and had to be replaced. So did wiring in two radios. Finally everything was working. Except, that is, for Mrs. Kinney herself. Her eyes developed subconjunctival hemorrhages as well as extreme sensitivity to bright light. She began to wear sunglasses regularly and could not stand the flicker of fluorescent lights. Both male dogs (the ones which watched out the window while the female stayed back behind Mrs. Kinney) developed cataracts. Neither she, her husband, nor the ATC man contacted the Air Force.

Late in December, Mrs. Kinney was at a Civilian Air Patrol meeting and told the liaison officer from the Air Force, a major from McConnell AFB in Wichita about her experience. Although he told her that he did local UFOB investigations, he did not follow up on this for whatever reason. Then, months later, in the Spring of 1959, according to Dr. Kinney's report to Allen Hynek (1974), the nearby Forbes AFB called their home. Mrs. Kinney was ordered to report to the base at once. She got into her CAP uniform and left. Waiting for her were the base commander, the provost marshal, the base operations officer, and some visiting high-ranking officer. The commander was not happy and wanted to know why the woman had not reported the UFO. When the conversation settled a little, he explained that he would have gladly paid for all of the repairs, just to get his hands on the burnt-out stuff to study it. According to the report to Hynek, and who can say how exact it was after all those years, the commander was quoted as saying: "The Air Force has waited for a long time to get their hands on such motors (as in the refrigerators) and things that have reacted to a UFO's approach."[72] One wonders why the Air Force did not provide this level of concern during the huge wave of 1957. Still, perhaps one commander actually cared. No file on the Kinney case appeared in Blue Book records.

March 22, 1959, near Ann Arbor, Michigan:[73] A married couple was driving at 1:30 a.m., when the two saw an intensely lighted object to their southeast. It was hovering and seemed to be about two miles away. If correctly estimated, it was 200 feet high and just south of a main road. The couple guessed it to be twenty to thirty feet in diameter. Very intense shafts of light shown from two oval "ports" at the bottom of the object. As the witnesses approached closer, they could hear no sound and were a little afraid. Now abreast the object, they estimated that it was still 200 feet up at a ground distance of 50 to 75 feet from the road. (This would qualify the sighting, under Dr. Hynek's later typology definitions, as a "Close Encounter of the First Kind": an object within 500 feet of the witness.) The object paralleled their car for a while, then the shafts of light went out, and a circle of eight-to-ten red lights appeared on the bottom. It then rapidly rose and was out of sight in seconds. The press covered this sighting, and it was read by a local radio astronomer who operated a big radio telescope dish near the site, and who was working that very evening. The scientist, Dr. Allen Barrot, decided that the couple had merely seen his radio telescope, which was being rotated into a new position. That, plus an in-line radio station tower, and turning the lights on the radio telescope off solved the mystery. All this ignored the witnesses' statement about the object departing straight upwards, but this sort of thoughtless omission is quite common in such explanations. (The rationale, apparently, is that some elements of witness testimonies are completely in error, while others are correct.)

Barrot was delighted with his solution and wrote to a colleague about it. That colleague was Allen Hynek. Hynek was delighted too, and said he was amused by this witness error and its neat solution. Somehow this was passed on to Donald Menzel, who thought the explanation was fabulous and featured it in his next book, *The World of Flying Saucers*, under the derisive title: Michigan's Flying Bird Cage.[74]

But there was a problem. The Air Force, with Dr. Barrot's solution in hand, visited the couple to make its field report. The checks on air traffic and radar pick-ups were, as usual, negative. The witnesses were seeking no publicity, and the investigator felt they were reliable. In fact, they were upset that someone had told the press about their sighting. The couple was familiar with the area in which they were driving, and knew that, at a minimum, the so-called in-line radio tower had nothing to do with what they saw. But what about the radio telescope dish? Walking through the exact locations of the sighting, the investigator drew everything onto a map. The witnesses were *never looking in the direction of the observatory*.[75] In fact, the object was entirely on the other side of the road on which they were traveling (the object south; the observatory, north). The investigator showed the map to Dr. Barrot who then admitted that his explanation had become "unlikely." Menzel and Hynek, however, went forth in peaceful ignorance, and, of course, Menzel never corrected his error or his derision. Such were the elements of the strange saga of conclusion-jumping, conclusion-inventing, and no accountability that characterized this entire era.

More military and intelligence heavyweights occasionally peeked through this fog and, briefly, uttered completely contradictory opinions to the Air Force and Menzelian cant. In February of 1959, a major operative at Wernher von Braun's missile research area in Huntsville, Alabama, Lt. Colonel Lee B. James, gave a speech to the Detroit Chapter of the Michigan Society of Professional Engineers.[76] James would become one of the top administrators and engineers at NASA during the Apollo Program. The talk was about space flight and exploration, but because there had been a well-publicized UFO incident just previously (the Captain Killian case), he was asked about UFOs. He shocked the *Detroit Times* reporter with these words:

Left: Lt. Colonel Lee James, standing with hands on table

> I know they are not coming from here, and they are not coming from Russia. We in this civilization are not that advanced yet.

Referring to the witnesses on the Killian plane, James said:

> If they (35 passengers and several crew members) saw what they really saw, it would have to come from outer space—a civilization decades ahead of ours.

And when asked about the ability of UFOs to sometimes avoid radar, he replied:

> If that civilization has progressed as far as it might have, it quite possibly also has licked that problem, too.

James was obviously personally interested in the UFO problem and mentioned that Army and Air Force studies have never been able to prove things one way or the other.

At NICAP, Donald Keyhoe was visited by a man identifying himself as Colonel Joseph Bryan III, USAF. Bryan apparently was formally USAF, but what he did not reveal was that he operated as CIA.[77] More than that, and amazingly, he was one of the CIA's highest psychological warfare experts! Later UFO historians have been made uncomfortable by this fact, since Bryan became a member of the NICAP Board of Governors. Was this a CIA Trojan Horse inserted into the main civilian irritant? Nothing would have made more sense. But, surprisingly, there is no evidence of meddling at all. Richard Hall, NICAP's Assistant Director, knew Bryan, and *really* knew how NICAP operated and made decisions. He said that Bryan was strictly hands-off in these matters.[78] Added to that, Bryan was willing to go public with an extremely positive statement about the likely extraterrestrial nature of the devices.[79] (Bryan joined

Colonel Joseph Bryan

NICAP in 1959 and was appointed to the Board in 1962. He made his assertion of "extraterrestriality" much later in the 1960s. His position is inserted here to add to the information that many top military and intelligence people were at odds with the policies that their organizations were following.) Bryan included in his public statement his severe disagreement with the military authorities' policies of secrecy and withholding information.

Rear Admiral Dufek

In March of 1959, Rear Admiral George Dufek was retiring as Commander of the United States' research and exploration program in the Antarctic. Perhaps feeling empowered to speak out by this retirement, he said, vis-à-vis UFOs, that they cannot be discounted, and "I think it is very stupid for human beings to think no one else in the universe is as intelligent as we are."[80] Asked, years later, why he thought that UFOs might be real and extraterrestrial, Dufek said it was because of sightings related to him by people who worked with him on Operation Deepfreeze. He also said that he got no flak for his opinions from the Pentagon.[81]

The year 1959 ended with policy and attitudes firmly in place. The Air Force authorities now had several years of the Robertsonian approach to reflect upon, knew that it worked, and knew why they were doing it. Even the "new" direction of getting better fieldwork done and better Blue Book analysis was not promoted with anything new in mind in terms of public UFO awareness. Such publicly quiet improvements would make Air Force post-hoc handling of case information more effective. What *was* "new," in a minor way, was the growing discomfort with using any money and personnel at all in these matters. Waste of money was a repeated concern. Waste of people was another. In particular, Dr. Charles Sheldon wrote about this to NICAP's Richard Hall. Sheldon:

> So far, the purported UFOs have not given any indication of harming this Nation, while some of the other problems before the committee [Sheldon's House Committee on Science and Astronautics] do involve clear and present dangers, and also courses of future policy action with which we can come to more definite grips.

And,

> You impute to me the view that UFOs are insignificant. Not at all. I think they are extremely interesting; I just think there are other problems to which many of us must devote most of our very limited time.[82]

Sheldon was an intelligent man and was telling Dick Hall exactly what the consensus view was: UFOs are not insignificant, but rather interesting. They *are*, however, *not* a national security threat, and we have plenty of things to address which are. The Congress and the Defense establishment need to spend their energies there.

During 1960, NICAP redoubled its efforts towards congressional hearings, using the reputation of Admiral Hillenkoetter as its ace card. In late February he stated in a NICAP press release:

> Behind the scenes, high-ranking AF officers are soberly concerned about the UFOs. But through official secrecy and ridicule, many citizens are led to believe the unknown flying objects are nonsense. Hundreds of authentic reports by veteran pilots and other technically trained observers have been ridiculed, or explained away as mistakes, delusions or hoaxes. The AF has assumed the right to decide what the American people should or should not know. It is time for the truth to be brought out in open Congressional hearings.[83]

As NICAP, APRO, and other civilian organizations asked members to write their congressmen, occasionally a politician would react and demand responses from the Pentagon. On one day alone (April 19), Major Tacker found himself writing to three Senators (Keating, Magnuson, and Henry Jackson).[84] All these exchanges could be traced back to NICAP.

Hillenkotter, who had previously gone public only in a NICAP publication, now unloaded his views directly to the press. On May 21, 1960, he said:[85]

1. UFOs are guided by intelligence;
2. They are not Russian;
3. We have never properly investigated them;
4. Congress needs to look into this;
5. He would love to find out that they were ours, after all.

News columnist Bulkley Griffin followed Hillenkoetter's statements with a lengthy and well-reasoned news story concerned with the Air Force's unilateral control of information and its national security implications.[86] On June 7, Tacker had heard enough rumblings to write Blue Book that he expected hearings soon, so be ready.[87] The main griping that he was hearing in the congressional winds was about "lack of adequate investigation." Tacker told Friend to come to the Pentagon to discuss this matter. Blue Book had almost one month to prepare. On July 8, Tacker telephoned Friend that Congressional representatives wanted a briefing on the 13th, and to get himself, Arcier, and Hynek there.[88]

The briefing on June 13 turned out to be the first of two.[89] This one was for Senator Stuart French of the Preparedness Committee. He wanted to know how the Air Force evaluated a lot of their more difficult cases. The list of these cases was probably supplied by a NICAP member and included cases like the Levelland vehicle stops and the Washington DC Merry-go-round. Senator French seems to have received satisfactory answers and made no further requests.

The affair on June 15 was larger.[90] Richard Smart (House Armed Forces Committee) and three staff members from the House Science and Astronautics Committee (Spencer Bereford, Richard Hines, Frank Hammill) were there. Two CIA officials (Richard Payne, and Allen Dulles' legislative liaison, John Warner) also attended. *Why* the CIA was there is

Left: John Warner. Right: Gerald Ford

unknown, but in the recent past they had been pressured through Congress to release the Robertson Panel report,[91] and it must have been of *some* interest to them to assess whether the Panel policy was still in effect and working. Throughout this meeting the Air Force had more trouble with the politicians than usual. Richard Smart was particularly skeptical of some of their claims. He requested not only to be kept up to date on Air Force operations but suggested that they needed more people assigned to do the job. Allen Hynek happily agreed that what Blue Book was doing was not adequate. Whether his frankness won the day or not, General Luehman later reported that "all personnel attending the briefing were pleased with the results and the general consensus is that no public hearings will be held in the near future."[92] The Air Force had dodged another bullet.

Despite the strong suggestion from an important congressman, the Air Force did not place any more personnel or funding at Blue Book's disposal—and they did not tell Smart of their refusal to do so. Neither Friend nor his boss at ATIC, Philip Evans, were happy with the burdens that briefings and scrambling about to mollify congressmen were causing them. The problems were all caused by the civilians. In December of that year, Friend and Evans reflected on this in a memorandum to Air Force Intelligence HQ at the Pentagon.[93] Some say the summary was written by Friend and signed by Evans (the usual procedure); some say Evans wrote and signed it. This is mentioned because some UFO historians would like to think that Bob Friend was "nicer" than this memo sounds, but there is evidence that he was just as upset about citizen UFOlogists as anyone. The quintessential paragraph searingly focuses on the dangers of these citizens:

Major Friend at his Blue Book desk

> In the United States there are more than 50 private unidentified flying object (UFO) organizations. Collectively, these organizations boast more than 500,000 members. For the most part, persons belong to those organizations for either financial gain, religious reasons, pure emotional outlet, ignorance, or possibly to use the organization as a "cold war" tool. The principal claims of these organizations are that unidentified flying objects are interplanetary visitors and that the Air Force is withholding information it has concerning them.

Note how brutally the motives of most UFO-interested organization members are cast. Money. Religion. Emotions. Ignorance. And, the worst, psychological warfare-type support for our Cold War enemies! *That does mean* that the Air Force feels that it is "at war" with them. The memo goes on to feature NICAP as the primary bad actor, and notes Hillenkoetter's presence as a problem. One wonders which motive they assigned to *him*.

Future Speaker of the House John McCormack of Massachusetts was the most important politician never to be convinced by the Air Force's briefings and claims. His influence was powerful enough that he was able to direct the House's Committee on Science and Astronautics to look, once again, into the issue.[94] The Committee chair, Overton Brooks of Louisiana, liked the idea. Brooks even went so far as to create a subcommittee which had an august title, which was set up to monitor the UFO problem. The chair of the subcommittee was Joseph Karth of Minnesota. Keyhoe meanwhile was bombarding McCormack and Brooks with his ideas on hearings and what NICAP was prepared to do. He even volunteered to resign and close NICAP if the Air Force could convincingly answer the questions he meant to present.[95] One supposes that this bravado impressed the politicians, and there was momentum for just such a NICAP/AF showdown to be held in early 1962. The Air Force heard about this in mid-1961 and it meant trouble.

Then another unexpected event occurred. Richard Hines, who was a staff member for the subcommittee and who had been in the briefing the previous July, stated that he would go to Wright-Patterson on a fact-finding mission in anticipation of the hearings.[96] ATIC was a little concerned about this, and its Commanding Officer, General A. J. Pierce, took a personal interest in how this would be handled. There was no need for alarm. Hines walked around the Wright-Patterson facilities, with Major Friend as a constant companion who claimed that all of this was employed in the evaluation of UFO cases; Allen Hynek supported Friend's tune. Hines then went back to DC to inform Joseph Karth that there was no problem, the Air Force was doing a fine job, *and* that Keyhoe and NICAP were way off base in their drive to discredit them.[97] Hines wrote Friend back quickly, telling "Bob" that, in line with their wishes, Karth was not going to hold hearings.[98] "For this I am sure both you and I breathe a deep sigh of relief."

General A. J. Pierce

Congressman Karth

Exactly what happened we cannot say. But Hines' report to Karth hit the congressman hard. He wrote to Keyhoe on August 28, 1961, telling him flatly that there would be no hearings.[99] More than that, in barely restrained prose, Karth unloaded angrily on Keyhoe. Stating that he would not allow himself to be part of any process that would facilitate "grandstand acts of a rabble rousing nature," Karth took Keyhoe apart for deficiencies in everything from honesty and forthrightness to fairness and reason. It was not NICAP's best moment. Any momentum for congressional help in releasing UFO information was dead for several years.

The years 1960-1963 were basic station-keeping for Blue Book and the Air Force. NICAP still struggled to stir the pot but, without a great rush of cases, was almost impotent. Inside Blue Book, Friend, now a Lt. Colonel, and Allen Hynek also struggled impotently—to try to get the project either eliminated or passed over to some other element of the Air Force or another institution (e.g. NASA) entirely.[100] All of those other "candidates" were too savvy for that. They recognized a loser when they saw one. Everyone shunned Blue Book as if it carried the plague, and the Air Force, and Friend, and Hynek were forced to carry on. All the old attitudes (towards citizens, excitability and psychological warfare, towards the fear of misidentifying a Soviet attack for a UFO, or vice versa) were still present. But the lack of a big wave of encounters muted everything.

But UFOs were not completely gone, and we should mention some of the incidents from those years including the star case of the year 1960.

March 24, St. Louis, Missouri:[101] Two policemen were in the vicinity of Lambert (Air) Field. One officer was on the north side; one was on the south. A bright light lit up the entire area. Three objects in a "V" formation whisked overhead. They were round, white, and nine feet in diameter. Blue Book said: "It is believed that it might be some form of unusual weather phenomena."

May 19, Dillingham, Alaska:[102] A group of Native Americans saw an object moving towards them. The thing

Lower Right: Dr. Hynek with Robert Friend leaning over him

293

was generally spherical but (apparently from the drawings) more squatty, like a round-ended football. It was metallic like aluminum and had a "something" which whirled in the bottom. When the object ascended, it made a sucking noise and pulled five-gallon cans in the air and tossed them away. Blue Book said: Weather Balloon. Later, Allen Hynek said: What?![103]

July 28, Chicago, Illinois:[104] Robert Johnson, the director of the Adler Planetarium, and two other staff members were viewing the Echo 1 satellite, when a red object flew past the satellite at much greater apparent speed. "I've been dreading the day when I would sight a UFO," he said. University of Chicago astronomer Gerard Kuiper, an absolute skeptic, said to news writers that the Adler astronomers must have been fooled by an airplane. Robert Johnson retorted: "I know an airplane when I see one."

August 25, Grumman Aircraft Engineering Optical Surveillance System, Bethpage, New York:[105] While engaged in satellite tracking, the Grumman Master Station spotted an unknown object of "carrot to straw" color passing east-to-west at about the time Echo 1 would be in the sky. Its orbit was unusual, although its speed was comparable to satellites. Grumman's system, of course, recorded the pass on film. Both Bob Friend and Allen Hynek went to Bethpage to discuss it. Nothing came of this, the "satellite" went unidentified, and the case does not appear in Blue Book records.

Late August, Butte Falls, Oregon:[106] Two men in a car saw a light 100 yards ahead of them in the road. The light was pale white and hovering. After watching for about fifteen minutes, the men decided to drive closer. At that, the light rose to 100 feet and receded a bit. Then it changed to orange. Stopping the car, the men heard no sound. The light then performed geometrical maneuvers in the air, creating rectangle paths and other zig-zags. It then accelerated, changed back to white, and zoomed off. The Air Force did not even receive the case; it went to NICAP. This is an example of a report where the witnesses were afraid to report what they had seen until years later.

September 10, Scituate, Massachusetts,[107] and September 10, Ridgecrest, California:[108] In the Scituate case, which was investigated by NICAP, a married couple saw a trio of brilliant disks parked in a triangle formation in the sky. About twelve degrees to the objects' left was what looked like a huge cylinder, also parked. One witness watched through binoculars, and the brilliance hurt his eyes for two hours. Two more disks seemed to be attached on top of the cylinder. Small domes sprinkled their surface. Several other persons caught glimpses of these things before the big one disappeared too quickly for the eye to follow. NICAP sent an astronomer to take the on-site measurements and testimonies. The Air Force made a phone call. The case does not appear in Air Force files. The Ridgecrest case, on the other hand, does. The four witnesses felt that they had seen rapidly moving objects multiple times that evening. Three of the witnesses thought that the objects were like disks; one felt it was like a boomerang. (Only one object was seen at a time, so all four incidents could have been the same thing.) The objects glowed but dimly. They both hovered and accelerated, and only during the latter activity was any noise heard (a "swishing"). The investigation was sloppy; the report said *two* people saw a boomerang, whereas the witness says otherwise right on the form. Hynek thought that this was a good unknown. Perhaps it was a compromise that the record card reads: "It is quite probable that some natural phenomena was responsible for this sighting . . . Unidentified."

September 14, Lorain, Ohio:[109] The single witness in this case reported to both the Air Force and NICAP. A dispatcher was taking a coffee break from his job at 2:50 a.m. Up in the sky, he thought Echo 1 was headed his way. As he watched (knowing that this was not the right time for Echo), the man saw that there were really *four* objects traveling in a perfectly-spaced line-of-flight. Before the dispatcher was able to resolve the false "Echo" into this string, though, the assembly made a sharp right angle turn, which startled him. After the turn, the objects went on their way, apparently at great height. The Air Force said: probably some natural phenomena.[110] Hynek said: nocturnal meandering light[111] (somehow voiding out in his mind the "line-up" of four). NICAP said: thank you, John, for your report.

Perhaps that is enough to illustrate a little of the times. But, of course, there is still the Star of the Show. August 13 and 14, Red Bluff, California:[112] It was ten minutes before midnight when two California Highway Patrol officers, Charles Carson and Stanley Scott, saw what they thought might be an airplane about to crash. It descended to about 150 feet in altitude, then, shocking the patrolmen, stopped abruptly (almost like an immediate "bounce") and shot back up to 600 feet, where it hovered. The men agreed on its description: like a big football, 150 feet long.

Left: Charles Carson
Right: Stanley Scott

> The object was illuminated by a glow. This glow was emitted by the object, was not a reflection of other lights. The object was solid, definitely not transparent. At no time did we hear any type of sound except radio interference.
>
> The object was capable of moving in any direction, up and down, back and forth. At times the movement was very slow. At times it was completely motionless. It moved at high (extremely) speeds and several times we watched it change directions or reverse itself while moving at unbelievable speeds . . . [113]

The big football-like object had a metallic character beneath the glow, and its most spectacular features were two lights, one at either end, which could project a powerful six-foot diameter sweeping beam. The beams were red and had a peculiar character that was so odd everyone seemed hesitant to mention it. We will save that for the end of this story. Occasionally one or more white lights or patches flashed along the midline.

The officers at one point unholstered their guns and debated whether to fire on the object. Coincidentally, it stopped then moved away. In fact, the patrolmen tried several times to pursue the thing aggressively, and it always moved away.

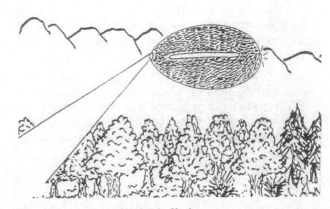

Red Bluff object

Deciding on reverse psychology, the officers would stop motionless, and on two occasions the thing approached more closely. It is difficult to say from the records (which fortunately are many) just how close the object same at its closest, but it was at least as near as 150 yards.

Carson and Scott regularly had trouble getting through to the base dispatcher on their radios, and every time the red searchlight beam swept by, the static was intolerable. Finally, the men got through with two interesting results: a) several people came out of buildings to see the thing in the distance, and b) the local radar operators at an Air Force station in Red Bluff were contacted and said over the phone that they were tracking it there. Before the event was over, six more policemen and at least an equal number of citizens were watching the thing from a distance. Finally, after two-plus-hours-of-meandering, the object moved off to be joined by a similar object high in the sky. Red beams seemed to flash as they hovered, then the two moved over the horizon.

This was a large multi-witnessed affair, so the press covered it immediately.[114] The two primary witnesses were naturally interested in what the radar report showed. Upon the officers' arrival at the facility, commanding officer Major Melden LeRoy told the officers that no such tracking had been done the previous night. Protesting, Carson and Scott asked if they might talk to the on-duty radar men.

LeRoy said that such permission was denied.[115] Two angry highway patrolmen left the facility. Carson said later that he could tell from LeRoy's demeanor, before he said a word, what was about to happen.

Someone from the Air Force briefly talked to the patrolmen later in a way that they thought was not very serious. There may have been a second questioning later still, but it made little impression upon Officer Carson. The patrolmen were interviewed by people associated with NICAP, as well. Allen Hynek was apparently on leave on his satellite-tracking job and does not seem to have handled this case. As suspect a job as he sometimes did, it is doubtful that Hynek would have come up with the Air Force solution.[116] Blue Book said that Carson, Scott, and the others had seen Mars flanked by the stars Aldebaran and Betelgeuse (presumably because all these are red) under amazing atmospheric conditions. NICAP asked a member, astronomer and planetarium assistant director Walter Webb to look into this explanation.

Major Melden LeRoy

The official USAF explanation for the Red Bluff sighting was a refraction of the planet Mars and/or the stars Aldebaran and Betelgeuse. At NICAP's request I checked the positions of the planet and the two stars for the date, time, and place of the observation. It was found that all three objects were below the eastern horizon at the start of the sighting, that Mars did not rise above the horizon until about an hour after the sighting began, that Aldebaran did not rise until 1 a.m., and Betelgeuse not until 3 a.m., an hour after the sighting was over. Atmospheric refraction can elevate celestial objects above the horizon but by no more than 35 minutes of arc (a little more than the apparent diameter of the sun or moon). Refraction can also cause a star or planet near the horizon to appear to shift or wobble slightly. However, the Red Bluff object reportedly performed violent maneuvers over a wide area of the eastern sky before disappearing below the eastern horizon (a celestial object in the east would have continued to rise higher in the sky and eventually set in the west). Further, the object described by highway patrolmen Scott and Carson bore no resemblance at all to a refracted star or planet—a very large, oblong object shaped somewhat like a football with a red light on each end and a row of white lights visible at times between the red lights. According to the officers, the object swept the sky and ground 6 or 7 times with a red beam of light. In my opinion the explanation used by the Air Force is completely without basis and ignores the fundamental facts of the observation.[117]

After hearing of Webb's analysis, and that their two stars were hours below the horizon, Blue Book changed the explanation to Mars and Capella (giving up on stars for *both* ends of the "UFO," and of

Walter Webb

redness for the beam, as Capella is a blue giant). Astronomers then could inform them that, yes, Capella was in the sky but could hardly be placed in a more incorrect direction. By mid-November, when Congressman Smart of the Armed Services Committee wanted to know what the heck was going on here, Bob Friend and Colonel Evans at ATIC "explained" it to him by just using Mars, since no helpful bright stars were anywhere in the vicinity.[118] A great deal of technical "snowing" was used in the memo to Smart, which involved elaborate temperature inversion and mirage phenomena. That plus a certain amount of hysteria was surely the answer. Dr. Menzel of Harvard was likewise interested, as Red Bluff was a tough case to dismiss. He weighed in, in support of the Air Force, with this:

With three brilliant heavenly bodies just above the horizon, on a night of fantastic multiple inversions of temperature and humidity, the only surprising fact is that the number of UFOs reported was not larger.[119]

The good doctor had not done his homework. As we have seen, three of the brilliant objects were *below* the horizon and one other candidate in the wrong direction. What of the "fantastic multiple inversions"? Dr. James McDonald was different from most analysts in that he actually sent away for data upon which to base conclusions. Having read the record, McDonald said this: "I should like to know what radiosonde data Dr. Menzel is citing, since the data I obtained does not fit that description."[120]

As promised earlier, there is one very strange feature of the case. The light beam projected by the object seemed like what would be described today, as a big, fat laser beam. That is, it did not spread out or diffuse "properly." But worse than that, the beam seemed to have an "end" to it. Even Carson, who was much the more verbal of the two officers, did not talk about this in the earlier reports. However, in a 1966 interview with McDonald, he had become comfortable enough that he said: "Its beam seemed to extend out a distance in the air, and then to end in some curious manner that [I] did not understand then or now."[121] McDonald, though a sympathetic interviewer, thought that this was probably impossible and tried to rationalize it on the basis of a limited area of dust in the air. But today there are dozens of other sightings mentioning this peculiar sawed-off light.[122] This feature is mentioned not only because it is part of the report, but also because it illustrates how witnesses will hold back elements of the experience that they believe are too strange for anyone to accept. No one (even leaving the sawed-off light out of the equation) has produced a reasonable explanation for the Red Bluff UFO to this day.

There were a number of 1961 cases (despite the dry year) that featured missile sites, Navy pilots, Air Force bases, as well as "just citizens" and the Mayor of Jacksonville, Florida.[123] None were as spectacularly enigmatic as Red Bluff, though, and we can move on.

This period, as it stretched into the mid-1960s, was speckled with contradictions. From its point of view, the Air Force had finally gotten its policy and its methods right and, as long as it stayed vigilant, it had the UFO problem under control. Yet, the Air Force wanted nothing more than to get out of the UFO business and dump Project Blue Book. No UFO waves occurred, yet in many ways the citizen UFO groups became more sophisticated, with regional investigative organizations arising that often had good relations with local police and media. The national organizations came into greater contact with like-minded individuals and clubs around the world, even though non-U.S. countries saw no flaps, either. Scientists derided UFOs when they bothered to say anything at all, yet this was the age when a new focus-of-discussion arose in the academic community: the Search for Extraterrestrial Intelligence

William Coleman

(SETI), usually envisioned as radiotelescope listening for intelligently constructed signals from deep space.[124] This was another of the strange paradoxes in the field of UFO study: that it is okay to consider the existence of extraterrestrial high-technologists, and listen for them, as long as one does not consider the possibility that ETs have the ability to do something that we cannot . . . interstellar travel.[125] Any extraterrestrials listening to *us* would have concluded that we were an odd group indeed. But UFO flaps or not, exciting cases or not, we had bigger problems on our minds. 1962 was the year of the Cuban missile crisis, the year that some historians believe a nuclear war was at its nearest.

Down at the microscopic level of specific human actions, Major Tacker was replaced as UFO spokesman by the friendlier Major William Coleman. Coleman had to be one of the more conflicted individuals, since he had seen a UFO himself.[126] Tacker did not go quietly, blasting UFOs and UFOlogists both on the major East Coast media giant, WOR,[127] and in a book from which the Air Force was quick to distance itself.[128]

Admiral Hillenkoetter resigned from NICAP, voiding their most powerful trump card.[129] No one knows why he resigned and he has never explained why. Perhaps, as George Gregory had suggested, the Robertson Panel Report and policy were ultimately explained to him and he agreed. In 1963, Allen Hynek showed signs of finally reaching a point of intolerance about embarrassingly bad Blue Book "solutions."[130] Unfortunately for him, at the same time the gentler Robert Friend retired, to be replaced by the iron-willed Major Hector Quintanilla as project head. At NICAP, Richard Hall produced the precursor to a massive piece of work, *The UFO Evidence*,[131] which collected mysterious cases organized by observer quality and behavior of the object (as well as many more significant attributes). The book was the most fully referenced and fiercely condensed encyclopedia of UFO experience to date. NICAP's goal was to use it as a Trojan Horse to create momentum again in Congress. Every congressman was sent an advanced copy[132] but 1962 was the wrong time. A great work effort went by with just a polite and thankful reception, but no action.

Major Hector Quintanilla

There is much to learn by reviewing a few case examples from the last years of the great UFO "desert." To begin with, we can look over the shoulders of the Air Force as they worked the following three cases.

June 7, 1962, Hallett Research Station, Antarctica:[133] The researchers saw a brilliant white light move across the sky, then stop between two mountain peaks for five minutes. In the binoculars the light was round and had a dazzling gold sheen. It then moved out and disappeared behind a mountain.

Hallett Station, Antartica

Blue Book identified this meandering gold sphere as Jupiter before realizing that there was a problem with their proclamation. Jupiter was almost flat to the horizon (five degrees). The researchers specifically stated that the object was much higher (thirty degrees). Blue Book said that the researchers must have made a mistake, and therefore the theory was still correct. Looking at what must have been extremely inadequate maps, Blue Book decided that there were no mountains nearby, so if the object went behind a mountain it must have been very distant and very low. Unfortunately for this theory, almost any photograph of Hallett Station will demonstrate that its buildings are set very close to a small group of mountains which could easily cause one to look up at angles much greater than thirty degrees, let alone five. The case shows the power of theory and attitude over empirical fact.

August 30, 1962, Port-au-Prince, Haiti:[134] Three men were having dinner one evening when a dazzling UFO appeared. It approached and hovered for twenty minutes, during ten of which it was dead still. One of the men was an engineer (the occupations of the other two are unknown, but assumed to be colleagues; their names were deleted on the Air Force report). The engineer had a small theodolite (tracking telescope) available and they set it up and viewed the object. It was a silvery-gray disk, like two rounded hub-caps joined together, and was spinning on its axis. There seemed to be something like an antenna on the top. The "device," for nothing else was easily imaginable, had things like exhaust ports all around its mid-line, and was surrounded by a vaporous jacket or gaseous emission

298

which ran through all the colors of the spectrum. The UFO then flipped into a vertical alignment, turned to show its base flat-on, and then tipped over so that its original topside was now on the bottom. Silently, the object then accelerated and was gone in five seconds. The engineer was well-known to the local Colonel of the USAF Mission to Haiti, and was highly regarded. The case was sent on to Blue Book with high recommendations. Blue Book analysts decided:

> It is concluded that the misidentification of the planet Venus was the cause for the UFO sighting. Atmospheric effects which distorted the planet, the apparent nearness of the star Spica to the planet, and unfamiliarity of the witness with astronomical objects were probably contributing factors.[135]

One hopes that the respected 40-year-old engineer was never told of this "solution."

December 6, 1962, San Mateo, California:[136] This case involved just one witness (a 13-year-old boy at that), so one supposes anything is possible. But the point is not the essential worthiness of the case, but the logic of the solution. The boy saw a low-flying red ball moving at variable speeds (usually quite fast) and at low altitude (football field high or thereabouts). He thought the thing was big, about 100 feet in diameter. The object did hover at one point, and was silent throughout the sighting. The total observation time was two minutes. The Air Force reasoned this way: the object *had* to be an aircraft and the red flame-like ball a jet-afterburner. But because the boy did not hear any sound, which he *had* to be able to do since it was a jet, the Air Force concluded this was an unreliable report. Plus, the amount of time seen, the hovering, and the altitude are all wrong for a *jet*, clinching the report's unreliability. With just one young witness evidentially speaking, it is not a great case. But the Air Force's behavior is astounding.

Now, let us take a look at three sightings which went to NICAP in the same era.

April 24, 1962, Springfield, Pennsylvania:[137] This was a multiple-witness sighting observed by a husband, wife, mother, and several neighbors. The wife and her mother saw the object at its closest, but several others got good looks as well. The UFO was a domed disk, like a flat acorn, with many square "windows" emitting brilliant light as that section revolved. A small green light flashed on the top of the dome. At its closest approach, it was only twenty feet above their heads and was judged to be about thirty feet in diameter. The wife actually encountered the object twice, once in the car at home with her mother, and a second time when returning to her home after dropping off her mother. Both times she rousted her husband out of his basement workshop and he saw the thing as well, though at a greater distance. The man was Colonel Joseph Gasslein, US Army Reserve, and an employee at Boeing Aircraft Corporation (and a specialist on helicopters). Dr. Charles Olivier of the Observatory at the University of Pennsylvania received several other reports that evening (c. 7:45 p.m. to 8:10 p.m.) which supported the close encounter. No sound was ever heard during any of these sightings, even at a fifty-foot distance. NICAP, Dr. James McDonald, and, later, Dr. Allen Hynek judged the case "unknown."[138]

Late April or Early May, 1962 Granby, Connecticut:[139] Four witnesses (three adult women and a ten-year-old son) were driving home. Two bright yellow lights appeared in the sky ahead. The lights crossed the road and disappeared behind clumps of shrubbery. Upon driving nearer, the witnesses saw the pair of objects hovering over a field. Rather than horizontally aligned, the lights were now vertical. Curious, the witnesses stopped the car and watched. The objects then left the hovering position, reoriented horizontally, and came towards the car. Alarmed, the driver restarted the car and accelerated away. The UFOs were right behind, only a few feet from the rear window and matching the car's speed. The two objects were yellow spheres with a reddish patch which rotated around. They were small (only a few feet in diameter), but no less frightening for their size. The UFOs stalked the car for four minutes. Finally the things turned away and were gone, leaving everyone shouting and in panic. One of the better civilian field researchers, astronomer and Hayden planetarium assistant director

Walter Webb did the interviews and other basic inquiries. He could find no mundane explanation. (This case was not reported until about five years later during the middle of the great UFO flap, which induced the famous University of Colorado Study of UFOs, and made the reporting of one's UFO experience less embarrassing.)

The summer of 1962, East Peru, Maine:[140] This report arose because of someone attending one of Walt Webb's planetarium shows in Boston. The contact led him to interview the cousin of the man (an engineer) who had seen the show and wanted Webb to speak to his relative. They did this together. There were five male observers but Webb never could contact the other four; he properly said to the reader "caveat emptor" but felt that the witness was repeating an honest story before him and his relative. The five men were fishing and three orange globes showed up across the pond and began dancing about. For a while this was entertaining—until the globes began to move closer. The men got scared, jumped in their car, and sped away. But, as in the Granby event, the globes were right on them. One globe was in back, and two were close to the side windows. The things seemed to be transparent, orange, three-foot spheres. No matter how the driver changed speeds, the things easily kept pace. Occasionally they would leave their positions and form a kind of three-sphere "joining" with squarish bridges between them. Then they would split and be back pacing the car. The car radio was filled with static. Finally the globes veered off and flew into the woods. One cannot help but wonder what Blue Book would have said about these sightings. Webb and NICAP simply said: unknown.

Generally, the stranger a sighting was, the longer it took for witnesses to risk talking about it. Many unusual reports were suppressed for years, and many have been, undoubtedly, permanently lost. This is an understandable response to a hostile societal atmosphere, an atmosphere that was exactly what the Air Force and the Robertson Panel wanted.

"Close Encounters of the Third Kind" (when it was felt that an entity, a living being, was observed) were the strangest in some ways, and people experiencing them therefore had the greatest reluctance to report them. It is not strictly logical that there should be a *difference* between reporting what seemed to be an advanced piece of technology and reporting a being involved with it, but there is. Nevertheless, some people on rare occasions did see beings—but who could they risk telling about them? One such case may have occurred in August of 1962 in a remote location: Lake Movil, Minnesota.[141] A family was vacationing at a cabin, and some members were away, leaving the wife, her mother, and a younger brother at the site. The brother was asleep. The two women saw an odd object hovering over the boat dock only fifty feet away. The object was a domed disk with large windows in the top. It glowed red. Most shockingly though, silhouetted in the windows were the shapes of three "men." The women sensed that these men were looking at them, and switched off the house lights. The object switched off its own lights. The wife's mother was then overtaken by an urge which she could never explain. She burst out of the cabin and ran toward the object, her hysterical daughter screaming after her. Perhaps fortunately, the UFO lifted and rapidly disappeared. The Lake Movil case was not reported to the UFO community until 1972 by Coral Lorenzen's APRO organization, which had always been the friendliest site for so-called "occupant" cases. As such cases go, this one was mild—just silhouettes in a window—but around this time, there was an incident that would alter how many viewed the phenomena. In 1961, the alleged and now-famous "Betty and Barney Hill UFO Abduction" took place, but it was not generally known until detailed in a book in 1966.[142] The case would change many people's minds as to whether they could accept "Close Encounters of the Third Kind" or not. In any case, the Air Force could safely ignore reports of abductions, and for most people, too, the Hill incident was too much, defeated as even thinkable by its very strangeness. In addition, by 1966 the Air Force was about to be relieved of all responsibilities for UFOs.

But we are not there yet. In 1963, the Air Force recommended to persons asking for UFO information that they read a good book on the topic: Donald Menzel's *World of Flying Saucers*.[143] The Air Force was, if nothing else, by this time, consistent.

Edward Ruppelt

Although it is only marginally important to the topic of this book, an event occurred in 1959 that many UFO historians know well, and remain curious about. Thus we will mention it here in its historical context.

Captain Edward Ruppelt published his famous book in 1956. Many read it, and, although Ruppelt was careful to avoid conclusions, his open-minded, even-handed description of cases, plus the powerful statement of how many unknowns there were, convinced many readers that UFOs were a true mystery, if not extraterrestrial spacecraft. We have also mentioned that Ruppelt ultimately was made aware that the Air Force in late 1957 and 1958 was not happy with the book (after having passing it off as merely "boring" two years earlier), and, probably—and most significantly—he was greatly bothered by the fact that congressional committees were distracted from their work by the subject, and his book was one cause (some congressmen would refer to his report in letters which asked the Air Force for information). Because Keyhoe and NICAP were getting so aggressive about this, and because the attacks were couched in very anti-Air Force terms, Ruppelt felt a great deal of pressure.

Edward J. Ruppelt

At the time, he was making progress towards publishing an updated version of his *Report on Unidentified Flying Objects*.[144] The original edition had 17 chapters. This second edition would add three more. We do not know when in the new writing process Ruppelt made his decision to change utterly and dramatically the nature of the original book, but we do know this. The tone of the 18th chapter matches the tone of the previous 17. The 19th chapter is about the ridiculous and unbelievable "contactees," and is, for the topic, straightforward. Nothing about these two new chapters would change a reader's perception of the first edition. But in the 20th chapter, the book goes radically negative on the nature of UFOs. It is nothing like the rest of the book in tone. The conclusion cannot be massaged: UFOs are bunk, a myth.

Some people want to interpret this as evidence that Ruppelt always believed that UFOs were bunk. Others want to contend that he was forced to say this by the authorities. A third school thinks that Ruppelt was angered by Keyhoe's attacks on his old service and, informed as to how his book was being used in a variety of unhelpful ways, decided on his own to make amends. We do not know the truth, and in this context, it does not matter.

Independent checking of Ruppelt's facts shows them to be generally accurate (if not always precise), and apparently honestly purveyed. When one puts his opinions of individuals into context, his opinions seem to be, typically, shared by others, and he appears to be (if anything) a bit naïve on the "happy" side of interpreting things. We do know that Ed Ruppelt's requests for information to aid in the new edition were looked at very carefully by the Pentagon, and they insisted on a pre-publication review of its contents. The words "edit" and "editing" were, literally, scratched out in the draft letter, but even that reveals the attitude present.[145]

Ruppelt himself may or may not have "believed" in UFOs. There are scenarios that permit either alternative. For our purposes, the question is an intriguing human sidelight to our story.

Notes

[1] David Jacobs, *The UFO Controversy in America,* 1975.

[2] Richard Hall, "Bridging 50 Years of UFO History," in *UFOs 1947-1997,* (eds. Hilary Evans and Dennis Stacy), 1997.

[3] J. Allen Hynek, "Are Flying Saucers Real?" *Saturday Evening Post,* 17 December 1966.

[4] Jacobs, *The UFO Controversy in America.*

[5] Donald Keyhoe, *Flying Saucers: Top Secret,* 1960, and Gross, 1958, Jan.-Feb.

[6] Donald Keyhoe, *Flying Saucers: Top Secret,* 1960, and Gross, 1958, Jan.-Feb.; plus Donald Keyhoe, NICAP Press Release, 28 January 1958.

[7] *Armstrong Circle Theater*: "Enigma of the Skies," 22 January 1958, audiotape, CUFOS files.

[8] *Confidential NICAP Bulletin,* 4 April 1958.

[9] Gross, 1958, Jan.-Feb.

[10] Gross, 1958, Jan.-Feb.

[11] UFO Investigations Center, Sydney, Australia, *UFO Bulletin 1* (4): March 1958. Jones later facilitated a cooperative Australian meta-group, CAPIO.

[12] Aime Michel, *Flying Saucers and the Straight Line Mystery,* 1958.

[13] *BT* (newsmagazine), Denmark, 16 April 1958, as quoted in Gross, 1958 Mar-April.

[14] See Chapter 10.

[15] Hermann Oberth, "Lecture Notes," *Australian UFO Bulletin,* September 1991.

[16] Blue Book Administrative files Roll 89; Colonel Glen W. Clark for Deputy Director of Information Services, memorandum, subject: Congressional Public Hearings—Unidentified Flying Objects, 31 January 1958.

[17] Blue Book Administrative files Roll 89; Colonel Clark for Deputy Director of Information Services, subject: Congressional Public Hearings—Unidentified Flying Objects, 31 January 1958.

[18] Blue Book Administrative files Roll 89; Major General Arno H. Luehman, Memorandum for the Director of Legislative Liaison, subject: McClellan Subcommittee Statement Concerning Air Force Handling of UFO reports, 28 February 1958.

[19] Blue Book Administrative files Roll 89; Major General Arno H. Luehman for the Director of Legislative Liaison, subject: McClellan Subcommittee Statement, 28 February 1958; and Major General Joe W. Kelly, Memorandum for the Director of Information Services, subject: McClellan Subcommittee Statement Concerning Air Force Handling of UFO Reports, 3 March 1958.

[20] "Senator Goldwater Reveals Interest in UFO Problem," *The UFO Investigator 1* (2): August-September 1957.

[21] Richard E. Horner to Senator Barry Goldwater, 19 Feb 1958, CUFOS files.

[22] Richard E. Horner to Senator Barry Goldwater, 19 Feb 1958, CUFOS files.

[23] Blue Book microfilm Roll 89, John E. Henderson to Neil H. McElroy, Secretary of Defense, 8 May 1958.

[24] Blue Book microfilm Roll 89, Lawrence J. Tacker to A. F. Arcier, 20 May 1958.

[25] Blue Book microfilm Roll 89, Major J. Byrne, memorandum for record, subject: Briefing of Representative Henderson and Colleagues on the Air Force Unidentified Flying Object (UFO) Program, 23 June 1958.

[26] Blue Book microfilm Roll 32, Colonel H. K. Gilbert to Major Tacker, memorandum, subject: Results of Investigation requested by Senator Lyndon Johnson, 19 May 1958.

[27] Gross, May-July 1958.

[28] Roland V. Libonati, "Flying Saucers," *Congressional Record-House* Vol. 104, pt. 9, remarks for Wednesday, June 18, 1958.

[29] Blue Book microfilm Roll 89, General W. P. Fisher and Major James Byrne, memoranda, 6 August 1958, 12 August 1958, and undated.

[30] Blue Book microfilm Roll 89, General W. P. Fisher and Major James Byrne, memorandum, 6 August 1958.

[31] Blue Book microfilm Roll 89, General W. P. Fisher and Major James Byrne, memorandum, 12 August 1958.

[32] Blue Book microfilm Roll 89, General W. P. Fisher and Major James Byrne, memorandum, 12 August 1958.

[33] Bob Barry, "12 Years of Flying Saucers," open letter to media outlets, June 24, 1959.

[34] Blue Book microfilm Roll 89, General W. P. Fisher and Major James Byrne, memorandum, 12 August 1958.

[35] Blue Book microfilm Roll 89, General W. P. Fisher and Major James Byrne, memoranda, 6 August 1958, 12 August 1958, undated memo by Fisher.

[36] Richard Hall, file memo, August 22, 1967 (on an exchange of views with Charles Sheldon); also, Stuart Nixon to James McDonald, 2 December 1958, McDonald files, University of Arizona archives.

[37] Blue Book microfilm Roll 34; and Robert J. Durant, *The Fitzgerald Report,* 1958.

[38] Colonel H. K. Gilbert to Commander 1006th Air Intelligence Service Squadron, undated, c. mid-April 1958, FOIA (USAF).

[39] W.E. Lexow, Chief, Applied Science Division, Scientific Intelligence, memorandum for record, subject: Meeting with Air Force Personnel Concerning Scientific Advisory Panel Report on Unidentified Flying Objects, dated 17 January 1953 (Secret), 16 May 1958, FOIA (CIA).

[40] Richard Hall (editor), *The UFO Evidence*, 1964.

[41] John P. Timmerman, witness interview, April 1, 1991, audiotape, CUFOS files.

[42] Witness interviews, James McDonald files; and *APRO Bulletin*, March 1958.

[43] Keyhoe (*Flying Saucers: Top Secret*).

[44] Keyhoe (*Flying Saucers: Top Secret*).

[45] Blue Book microfilm Roll 34.

[46] Blue Book microfilm Roll 34.

[47] Blue Book microfilm Roll 34, plus see thumbnail description in "1958 UFO Chronology" at website: www.nicap.org.

[48] Bulkley Griffin, series of three articles appearing in New England regional newspapers (for example *Worcester Gazette*; *New Bedford Standard-Times*), as reported in Gross, October 1958); and *UFO Investigator 1* (6): December 1958 (article dates: October 7 and following).

[49] Bulkley Griffin, series of three articles, as in reference 48.

[50] Tom Gerber, *Boston Herald*, 30 November 1958 (quoted extensively in Gross, Nov.-Dec.)

[51] John Lester, "Radar Experts Track Mysterious Flying Objects," *Newark (NJ) Star-Ledger*, 19 December 1958.

[52] *Newark (NJ) Star-Ledger*, 21 December 1958.

[53] *Newark (NJ) Star-Ledger*, 21 December 1958.

[54] John Lester, "Pilots Call Air Force Secrecy on Flying Saucers 'Ridiculous'," *Newark (NJ) Star-Ledger*, 22 December 1958.

[55] John Lester, "Flying Saucer Captured, U.S. Aide Claims," *Newark (NJ) Star-Ledger*, 23 December 1958.

[56] *Newark (NJ) Star-Ledger*, 24 December 1958.

[57] Although the general reading of the documents makes this obvious, Major Tacker made the policy pointedly in an exasperated letter to Donald Keyhoe (NICAP/CUFOS files), 23 January 1959.

[58] Ralph Chapman, "Flying Saucer Sightings Still Get Air Force Study," *New York NY) Herald Tribune*, 1 March 1959.

[59] Phone call conversations between a NICAP member and the Killians confirm both the anger and the "silence" order by his company. NICAP files, as reported extensively in Gross, Apr.-June 1959.

[60] Blue Book microfilm Roll 35.

[61] Aaron G. Benesch, dateline: Washington, DC, 19 January 1959 (article quoted extensively in Gross, Jan-March 1959).

[62] Department of Defense: News Release, January 22, 1959.

[63] Blue Book microfilm Roll 87.

[64] Blue Book microfilm Roll 87.

[65] Richard J. O'Keefe, Major General (Deputy Inspector General, USAF), Operations and Training Brief, subject: UFOs—Serious Business, 24 December 1959.

[66] Blue Book microfilm Roll 35, and Hynek, *UFO Report*.

[67] Hynek, *UFO Report*.

[68] Blue Book microfilm Roll 37.

[69] McDonald files, University of Arizona archives.

[70] McDonald files, University of Arizona archives.

[71] Robert Kinney to J. Allen Hynek, 23 August 1974, CUFOS files.

[72] Robert Kinney to J. Allen Hynek, 23 August 1974, CUFOS files.

[73] Blue Book microfilm Roll 35.

[74] Donald Menzel and Lyle Boyd, *The World of Flying Saucers*, 1963.

[75] Robert Kinney to J. Allen Hynek, 23 August 1974, CUFOS files.

[76] Joseph Stair, "Saucers May Be Just That," *Detroit (MI) Times*, 26 February 1959.

[77] NICAP files (personnel), now held at CUFOS; information about Bryan as CIA comes from UFO conspiratorialist, Todd Zechel, but is agreed to by NICAP Assistant Director, Richard Hall: Todd Zechel, "NI-CIA-CAP or NICAP?" *MUFON Journal 133*: 6-9, 1979; Richard Hall, "NICAP: The Bitter Truth," *MUFON Journal 145*: pp. 11-12, 1980.

[78] Richard Hall, personal communication (MDS).

[79] Joseph Bryan III, open letter to NICAP, *The UFO Investigator III* (8): 5, May-June 1966.

[80] Yvonne S. Durfield, "The Eyewitness Report of the Incredible UFO Invasion of Antarctica," *Ideal's UFO Magazine #2*: 44-50, 1978. (Durfield quotes a Reuters correspondent who interviewed Admiral Dufek on 11 March 1959.)

[81] Yvonne S. Durfield, "The Eyewitness Report of the Incredible UFO Invasion of Antarctica," *Ideal's UFO Magazine #2:* 44-50, 1978. (Despite sensational title, reasonably reserved and sensible quoting from military personnel constitutes bulk of article.)

[82] Charles S. Sheldon II to Richard Hall, 13 June 1959, NICAP files.

[83] *UFO Investigator 1* (9): 1, March 1960.

[84] Example: Lawrence J. Tacker for Director, Legislative Liaison, SAFU, memorandum, subject: Reply to Senator Keating on UFO sighting at Redmond, Oregon, 19 April 1960, FOIA (USAF).

[85] "Former CIA Chief Urges UFO Investigation," *Jersey Journal*, Jersey City, NJ, 21 May 1960.

[86] Bulkley Griffin, *Worcester (MA) Evening Gazette*, 1 June 1960.

[87] Blue Book microfilm Roll 87.

[88] Blue Book microfilm Roll 87.

[89] Blue Book microfilm Roll 87 (for all these activities also see, Gross, July-December 1960.

[90] Blue Book microfilm Roll 87.

[91] Memorandum for Record, 16 May 1958, FOIA (USAF).

[92] David Jacobs, *The UFO Controversy in America*.

[93] PGE (initialed; Philip G. Evans), memorandum for HQ, USAF, Chief of Intelligence, "Unidentified Aerial Phenomena, 12-27-(1960). (This memo is due to a request for a summary statement coming from a meeting in Washington, DC on 8 December.), FOIA (USAF).

[94] Donald Keyhoe to Overton Brooks, 11 August 1961, NICAP files.

[95] Donald Keyhoe to Overton Brooks, 11 August 1961, NICAP files.

[96] Blue Book microfilm Roll 87.

[97] Blue Book microfilm Roll 87; and Colonel Edward Wynn to SAFU; memorandum, subject: Congressional Committee Staff Member Visit, 16 August 1961, FOIA (USAF).

[98] Blue Book microfilm Roll 87.

[99] Blue Book microfilm Roll 87. Karth's letter to Keyhoe was also covered (more mildly) in *The UFO Investigator II* (2): 2, October 1961, along with Keyhoe's only marginal success in attempting to patch things up.

[100] Blue Book microfilm Roll 85, and Roll 87; these futile attempts are well chronicled in Gross, years 1961-3.

[101] Blue Book microfilm Roll 38.

[102] Blue Book microfilm Roll 38.

[103] *Hynek UFO Report*.

[104] "Experts Up in Air Over Sky Phantom," *Chicago Tribune*, July 29, 1960.

[105] J. B. Rettaliata to John D. Llewellyn (Rettaliata was Assistant to the President of Grumman Aircraft Engineering Corporation), December 13, 1960; also see Blue Book microfilm document of proposal of Grumman to USAF to study unknown satellite (document is available under case chronology at www.nicap.org).

[106] Caroll Watson, NICAP field report, 1 May 1966, NICAP files/CUFOS.

[107] Steve Putnam and Walt Webb, NICAP field report, 20 May 1961, NICAP files/CUFOS.

[108] Blue Book microfilm Roll 40.

[109] Blue Book microfilm Roll 40; and NICAP case file, NICAP files/CUFOS.

[110] Blue Book microfilm Roll 40.

[111] Blue Book microfilm Roll 40 (Hynek's copy of record card), CUFOS.

[112] Blue Book microfilm Roll 39 (case file is extensive); plus McDonald files, University of Arizona archives; plus APRO field report and NICAP file, CUFOS files.

[113] The officers described the case over and over, and with consistency. The words in the quotes are Carson's, taken from his letter to NICAP's Walt Webb, 14 November 1960, CUFOS files.

[114] Example: "Eight Officers Report Seeing Flying Saucers," *Red Bluff (CA) Daily News*, 15 August 1960.

[115] McDonald files, University of Arizona archives; plus NICAP files.

[116] Blue Book microfilm Roll 39.

[117] Walter N. Webb, Comments upon the Official USAF Explanation (undated), NICAP files.

[118] Colonel Philip G. Evans to Lt. Colonel Tacker, summary, subject: Congressional Request for Summary of UFO Sighting (Mr. Robert Smart, House Armed Services Committee), 18 November 1960, FOIA (USAF).

[119] Menzel and Boyd, *The World of Flying Saucers*.

[120] McDonald files, University of Arizona archives; specifically, his major paper: "UFOs: The Greatest Scientific Problem of Our Time?" personally published and distributed, 22 April 1967.

[121] Carson and Scott vaguely hinted at this to the news reporters, and either did not mention the feature to the Air Force or their questioner did not write it down. The direction (and puzzlement) finally came out in Carson's letter to McDonald and their phone call. McDonald files, University of Arizona archives.

[122] "Sawed-off light" cases are a peculiar feature of a smallish set of "high strangeness" UFO encounters. As these encounters are widely spread across the world, this feature is surprising and difficult to explain on sociological grounds. No attempt at specifically studying this odd phenomenon is known to this writer (MDS) probably due to the small numbers of cases. The author counts 44 cases of so-called "solid light" in his personal files to give the reader one data point on the size of the phenomenon as claimed.

[123] Sally Latham, "Jax Mayor Has Near-Miss With Wednesday's flying Whatsis," *Fort Pierce (FL) News Tribune*, 26 March 1961.

[124] Steven J. Dick, *The Biological Universe,* 1996.

[125] This topic is a book waiting to be written. Dr. Michael Papagiannis of Boston University was a fine contributor to SETI-community work, serving in administrational and editorial roles. SETIans viewed him with suspicion as he pushed the idea of searching the asteroid belt for alien artifacts, possibly including a colony ship. Carl Sagan, in the 1960's, brought fire on his head for suggesting that it was possible that "we" (the Solar System) have been visited 10,000 times in the history of the galaxy. Sagan did not regain his footing until becoming a public crusader against UFOs. His chairman at Cornell told me (MDS) in this regard: "Carl has made some mistakes." And Robert Freitas has always made conservative SETIans nervous with creative ideas like searching the Lagrangian gravity-wells of the Earth-Moon system for artifacts. These ideas bring extraterrestrials too near, and are unwelcome for a great number of reasons.

[126] One of the most personally paradoxical elements of UFO history was having a man paid to do UFO debunking who had seen a UFO himself. William Coleman, adding to the paradox, decided to produce a television series dramatizing real UFO cases. He was interviewed about his own sighting for *TV Guide*, 10 June 1978. While Pentagon spokesman he looked for his formal report, and there was no record of it.

[127] "Meet the Authors," WOR-TV broadcast, 21 October 1962.

[128] Lawrence Tacker, *Flying Saucers and the U.S. Air Force*, 1960.

[129] Roscoe Hillenkoetter to Donald Keyhoe, date unknown: c. February 1962, quoted in Keyhoe's *Aliens from Space*, 1973.

[130] *Hynek UFO Report*.

[131] Richard Hall (ed.), *The UFO Evidence*.

[132] NICAP files, CUFOS.

[133] Blue Book microfilm Roll 45.

[134] Blue Book microfilm Roll 46.

[135] Blue Book microfilm Roll 46 (Project Record Card).

[136] Blue Book microfilm Roll 47.

[137] McDonald files, University of Arizona archives; and "Out of the Past," *International UFO Reporter*, Jan/Feb 1985.

[138] "Out of the Past," *International UFO Reporter*, Jan/Feb 1985; plus interview by John P. Timmerman, CUFOS files.

[139] Walter N. Webb, "UFOs chase car in Connecticut," NICAP field report, NICAP files/CUFOS.

[140] Walter N. Webb, "The Harvey Packard Sightings," NICAP field report, NICAP files/CUFOS.

[141] "The 1962 Occupants Case," *APRO Bulletin* September-October 1972.

[142] John Fuller, *The Interrupted Journey*, 1966.

[143] Menzel, *World of Flying Saucers*. (The Air Force allowed the recommendation to appear on the book's dust jacket.)

[144] Edward J. Ruppelt, *The Report on Unidentified Flying Objects*, 1959 (second edition).

[145] Ruppelt files.

Chapter 14: The Colorado Project

As matters progressed into the middle 1960s, a vast and long-termed UFO wave was about to occur, which would, paradoxically, end the Air Force's formal UFO project. At Blue Book, the intense, serious Major Hector Quintanilla was now in charge. He, too, believed that "UFOs were Serious Business," and that meant that the Air Force policy of keeping information managed and the public relaxed on the subject was not a trifling matter. As mentioned previously, Quintanilla was constantly irritated by Allen Hynek's casual showing up for meetings and spending most of the time drinking coffee and engaging in (what Hynek would have called "civilized") small talk. Quintanilla believed this was a waste of valuable military time. And so were UFOs generally. The best solution to all of this was to get rid of Blue Book entirely, and get back to military work.

Quintanilla seated with Blue Book team

But UFOs were flying again. The spectacular Socorro, New Mexico, incident, in which a patrolman reported a landed saucer, re-energized national interest. Blue Book began to get busy again.

Quintanilla was the perfect officer to create a public relations crisis. Unlike the broad and somewhat open-minded Robert Friend, Quintanilla knew that he had a tough job to do, but a simple one—data collection, no analysis, and consistent negative comment upon the mysteriousness of UFOs. This strategy drove Allen Hynek crazy. In 1965, Hynek took an opportunity to promote to the Pentagon the idea of involving the National Academy of Sciences with UFO analysis. In his letter to Colonel John Spaulding, Hynek suggested a working panel of expert academics, involving themselves over a several month period. They would be physical scientists and also social scientists. Their discoveries should help the USAF solve both its scientific and its social problems. Hynek, of course, volunteered his own services.[1]

At NICAP, the war with the Air Force over Congressional hearings was lost, even though Keyhoe and his colleagues were not completely aware of that yet. Richard Hall continued to try to make headway, whenever he felt there was an opportunity. In early 1965, he was visited by a member of Connecticut Senator Thomas Dodd's staff.[2] This man, a retired Navy Captain, had been tasked by Dodd to visit NICAP and explore what there was to UFOs. Because Dodd was on the Senate committee that dealt with space affairs (Astronautics and Space Science), an important media person and constituent had suggested this. The staff member met with Hall for an hour and a half. Hall tried his hardest to impress the aide, but the only thing that made a dent was the citation of the names of people who supported NICAP, particularly that of Admiral Delmar Fahrney. The aide expressed the Senator's concern that the Committee would be "considered nutty" if they took up the subject. He thought that some type of informal briefing by NICAP might be more feasible. He left the NICAP office saying he "was more confused than ever." Nothing came of this. Dodd's tenure on the Committee was fairly brief and his interests did not lie there. He soon ran into accusations of financial scandal and was out-of-office by the beginning of 1971.

So the pot continued to roil. By the end of 1965 the USAF decided to present the UFO problem to a select group of its Scientific Advisory Board (the "O'Brien Committee"). The meeting, a one-day assessment of Blue Book's problems, occurred in February 1966.[3] The committee recommended strengthening the investigation by contracting with an important university (in an alliance with several other institutions) to do in-depth research on one hundred or so sightings per year. Information and other cooperative links to Blue Book would be maintained. The university's work would be as public as possible and would provide regular briefings to any interested member of Congress. Allen Hynek probably thought that he was finally getting somewhere. And then he played his final fateful role in this process.

Hector Quintanilla's policy of a rapid public disposition of cases was a public relations accident waiting to happen, and in late March 1966, it did. This was the time of the Michigan UFO flap. Quintanilla pushed Hynek to produce a debunking press statement about what the sightings "really" were before people got too excited. The loyal consultant, of course, then made his biggest public blunder: the notorious "swamp gas" suggestion. Quintanilla was happy to have such a ridiculous prosaic explanation, and Hynek did not protect himself with qualifying language. The result was far beyond Hynek's, Quintanilla's, or the USAF's expectations.[4]

Congressman Gerald Ford

People were outraged. They called their congressmen. Congressmen became outraged in front of microphones and in print. Worldwide publicity ensued. Congressman Gerald Ford called for an apology to his constituents and an investigation of Air Force UFO procedures. Hynek became a laughing stock. NICAP made full use of the opportunity to blast the USAF along its usual lines of cover-up and disservice to the public. Dr. James McDonald took courage and began his intense UFO studies, which would lead to his explosive entry into UFO research by the fall of 1966. Hynek, too, finally turned the corner. Feeling betrayed after all his loyal work he said: "This is the last time that I try to pull a chestnut out of the fire for the Air Force."[5]

From that point on, Hynek's relationship with Quintanilla and Blue Book was formal and chilly at best. But the wheels were finally moving to "buy" a university to study UFOs and get rid of the UFO project. Never has so little swamp gas exerted so much motive force.

Within a week of the public furor over the swamp gas explanation, Allen Hynek, Hector Quintanilla, and Secretary of the Air Force Harold Brown were called to testify on these matters by the House Armed Services Committee. The O'Brien Committee recommendations were brought up. Hynek strongly supported them. Brown suggested a study at a major university. The House Armed Services Committee suggested that this was a good coincidence and that they would look forward to Brown's implementing those solutions to this problem-filled situation Blue Book had created[6].

If there had been any doubt about creating and funding a university UFO study before the hearing, it was over. Secretary Brown immediately informed the Air Force Chief of Staff to search for a university. It fell to the Air Force's Directorate of Science and Technology at the Pentagon to recruit a university and monitor its work. Lieutenant Colonel Robert Hippler received the assignment. He organized another panel of experts for help. They suggested that he bring in Dr. H. Guyford Stever, head of the Air Force Scientific Advisory Board, President of Carnegie Tech, formerly of MIT, and (later) Gerald Ford's Science Advisor. Stever, while not the

Sec Air Force Harold Brown

equivalent of Vannevar Bush in the forties, was as much a governmental science insider as one could get.[7]

The panel suggested the University of Dayton, but Stever shot higher: MIT, Harvard, California, and North Carolina, where many previous secret government science projects had taken place. Every institution, however, refused to investigate UFOs despite the bait of a several hundred thousand dollar contract. UFOs were leprosy to academia. Even Allen Hynek's Northwestern University balked at the time at a proposed project for simply placing the Blue Book database on computer cards.[8] Even today, this intensity of concern and emotion in academic communities is striking.

While the Air Force floundered in its search for a university to bail them out,

NACA Special Committee on Space Technology, 1958. Guyford Stever, chairman, fifth from right; Hugh Dryden, head of NACA, to his left; Werner von Braun, closest to camera

the media pitched in to help. We have previously mentioned that CIA Robertson Panel member Thornton Page served as a consultant to the CBS documentary on UFOs at this time.[9] With the "swamp gas" uproar, CBS sensed a good story and produced a lengthy documentary with its major asset, Walter Cronkite, as the moderator. Whether with CBS awareness or not, Page reported to CIA operative and Robertson Panel secretary Frederick Durant that he had maneuvered the documentary into a presentation "along Robertson Panel lines." The program began with an apparently honest give and take but climaxed with a well-presented brutal debunking that left the viewer feeling the subject was unworthy of serious study.

Walter Cronkite

In contrast, once a university was funded to take the heat off the Air Force, University of Arizona atmospheric physicist James McDonald became extremely active and publicly insisted without reservation that the phenomenon was real and must be properly researched. One unknown-to-the-public result of this was that McDonald cajoled President Lyndon Johnson about UFOs. Johnson had always been curious about the subject but did not want to be assaulted continuously by McDonald. So he asked for an informal, internal staff study by top people who would report back to him so he could "get McDonald off his back." Johnson's study involved important people committed to the reality of UFOs, such as Kelly Johnson of the famous aero-engineering "Skunk Works," and Art Lundahl of the National Photographic Interpretation Center. A handful of other scientists was involved, administered by Hubert Humphrey's advisor for aeronautical and aerospace matters.[10] They concluded that UFO phenomena in all

Left: Kelly Johnson. Right: Art Lundahl

likelihood involved advanced technology created off the planet. We have no information to indicate that McDonald, who served as an information-feeder early in the study, saw these conclusions, and the informal study was, of course, never made public. Meanwhile, no public institution wanted to be involved. How could they find a willing university?

Even with the good offices of Guyford Stever, Colonel Hippler could not get the job done. The other office of the Air Force which would be involved as the so-called "buyer" of the project was the Office of Scientific Research. This office would provide the funding and a "project officer" to help monitor and facilitate matters. The officer was Dr. J. Thomas Ratchford. He was soon stuck with the recruitment problem. He started with a long-time Air Force contractor, the National Center for Atmospheric Research (NCAR), and its leader, Dr. Walter Orr Roberts. Roberts had benefited from Air Force monies since the late forties when NCAR was only the High Altitude Observatory and Roberts a fresh PhD from the classroom of Donald Menzel at Harvard. Unlike his famous mentor, Roberts had held a mildly sympathetic closet interest in UFOs for years.

But he still was not convinced. What he *would* do, however, was try to interest NCAR's sister institution, the University of Colorado, by promising NCAR's personnel and moral support. Robert Low, Roberts' long-time executive assistant, was now employed in the Colorado administration. Low would make an effective salesman and organizer. And Robert Low had become friends (even to the point of considering writing a scientific biography) with the perfect head scientist, Dr. Edward U. Condon. At the very end of July, Ratchford personally added the final pressures to Condon to get him to say "yes."[11] By the first of August, Robert Low was already at work. He "officially" lined up NCAR's and the Environmental Science Services Administration's (ESSA) support and made sales pitches to the Colorado administration. It was not all clear sailing. To pull it off, Low found it necessary to write the notorious "Low Memo" on August 9, of which we shall hear more later. Ratchford and his boss, Dr. William T. Price, visited

Robert Low

the campus officially to talk to faculty the next day. Enough interest was shown, enough support marshaled, and enough fears calmed that by mid-August the University of Colorado seemed ready to take the chance. For the next month (mid-August to mid-September) politics and recruitment were still in evidence, but Condon knew that the project would now proceed at least a week and a half before it was informally presented to the Board of Regents. The Air Force also knew. The contract was being prepared. The official Air Force orders were issued that transferred UFOs and Blue Book to Research and Development Command (as Wright-Patterson had requested nearly a decade before). The National Academy of Sciences was lined up to assess the quality of the final report. As an aside to the difficulties in getting anyone to accept the project, Dr. Ratchford thought it prudent to lie to Colorado in the following manner: he told them that, other than their sister institution NCAR, they were the USAF's first choice.[12] Telling the truth about MIT, Harvard, California, North Carolina, Dayton, and who-knows-who-else was impolitic at the time.

Edward Condon

The Air Force contract was for $313,000.[13] It was one of the most peculiar scientific grants of all time. Normally a governmental grant goes to a scientist who has initiated it, or is at least vitally interested and experienced in the field, and, essentially, knows exactly what he is going to do. This grant was to a scientist who was pushed into it, had little interest and apparently no experience, and, despite his brilliance, "didn't have a clue." Because the reports of the UFO phenomenon are so complex and multidimensional, this short-term "backwards grant" was doomed to fail before it was even signed. It did not take project personnel long to realize this, as we shall see. The Air Force surely already realized it. So why did they sponsor such a study? They simply had other goals than an academic study of UFOs.

The recruitment of personnel was easier than expected. The 1966 UFO wave had piqued a lot of interest. Still, it is difficult to make a list of persons who were considered project members. This is because the Colorado Project, as it came to be known, became so disorganized. Scientists came and went out of Boulder, and "consultants" had widely varying degrees of involvement. But we have enough information to make an attempt to say "who was who."

Edward Condon was, of course, chief scientist. It is obligatory to mention that he was a great physicist, a patriot, and a hell-raiser. He was a district head at Los Alamos during the World War II bomb-building era, a National Bureau of Standards head in the late forties, and a target of Richard Nixon for alleged but totally bogus accusations of being a pro-Communist security-risk. Condon was near the end of his science career; he had held presidencies and had been much honored. A strong man, physically and personally, he was proud of ruffling feathers and doing things his way. He was also a hilarious joker. At this stage of his life, UFOs seemed an amusing diversion, as long as he did not have to spend much time on them.[14]

Stuart Cook

The person who would ensure the latter was Robert Low. He had been Walter Roberts' administrator at the High Altitude Observatory for years and consistently had responsibility for keeping the place functioning while Roberts was on never-ending fund-raising trips. Low was a loyal right-hand man. He would do the job which Edward Condon did not want to do and yet be answerable to the grand old man. It was the availability of Robert Low, as much as anything else, which allowed Condon to say yes to the UFO task.

Other persons were named officially as major researchers in early documents: Dr. Stuart Cook of the psychology department (who helped get things going, then backed out and "stayed in touch"), Dr. William Scott of psychology (who never was a factor, and left), Dr. Michael Wertheimer of psychology (who contributed one very important intellectual analysis and then little else so was not a primary member), Dr.

Franklin Roach

David Saunders of psychology (a major player in all ways), and Dr. Franklin Roach, an atmospheric physicist from ESSA (a major element, but a major loss when he left after the summer of 1967).

There was an uproar regarding the preponderance of psychologists; people suspected that a study of "abnormal persons" rather than abnormal aerial phenomena was about to take place. This concern was somewhat alleviated by the additions of Dr. Roy Craig, a physical chemist from Colorado; Dr. Norman Levine, an electrical engineer from the University of Arizona; and Dr. William Hartmann, a planetary astronomer

David Saunders

from Arizona. Although Hartmann stayed in Arizona (Levine came to Boulder), his level of communication and degree of integration qualify him as a full member of the research team. Three members of the support staff also had lengthy in-depth involvement: psychology grad students James Wadsworth and Dan Culberson, and Condon's administrative assistant, whom he loaned to the project, Mary Lou Armstrong.

A hoard of other individuals dipped in and out of the project's business, and it is difficult to know their levels of commitment. Frederick Ayer, a Colorado physicist, deserves notice. He did a few case investigations and wrote a chapter in the report. Although Condon does not cite him, Frederick Hooven of Ford Motors did much consulting for the project, even in Boulder. Gordon Thayer, a physicist and radar expert at ESSA, stepped into the gap and analyzed the major radar cases for the report.

Lastly, Dr. Gerald Rothberg of Stevens Tech spent a whole summer doing field investigations in Pennsylvania. Many others are mentioned in the final report and project documents. Most of these seem to have been bystanders, or disconnected "experts" from whom the Project purchased highly focused but mostly irrelevant studies to bulk up the report.

Another indication of the highly atypical disorganization of the project is the absence of a published list of project staff. This is our best guess of the *dramatis personae*:

A. Primary staff
   Dr. Edward Condon, physicist
   Mr. Robert Low, administrator
   Dr. David Saunders, psychologist
   Dr. Norman Levine, electrical engineer
   Dr. Roy Craig, physical chemist
   Dr. William Hartmann, astronomer
   Dr. Franklin Roach, physicist
   Mrs. Mary Lou Armstrong, administrative assistant
   Mr. James Wadsworth, grad assistant
   Mr. Dan Culberson, grad assistant

B. Secondary staff
   Dr. Stuart Cook, psychologist
   Dr. Michael Wertheimer, psychologist
   Mr. Frederick Hooven, engineer
   Dr. Gerald Rothberg, physicist
   Mr. Gordon Thayer, physicist
   Mr. Frederick Ayer, physicist

Other interesting and talented persons who hung around or were occasionally called upon included Courtney Peterson, Herbert Strentz, Martin Altschuler, William Blumen, John Ahrens, and Joseph Rush. There were late-comers too (Aldora Lee, Paul Julian, Mark Rhine, and Samuel Rosenberg) who contributed to the report but without actively participating in research. Harriet Hunter did outstanding service editing the final report, but did not participate much in investigations. In addition, the Colorado Project was helped in field investigations by many others, including Allen Hynek, William Powers, Raymond Fowler, June Larson, George Kocher, Peter Van Arsdale, and Herb Roth, who did a heroic job organizing the Volunteer Flight Officers Network for reporting satellite decays and other odd aerial phenomena.

Once the "backwards contract was signed and the initial staff marshaled, we can imagine these seven academics (Condon, Low, Roach, and the psychologists Cook, Scott, Saunders, and Wertheimer) sitting in Condon's office staring at one another, wondering what to do.

The group met five times between October 14 and 31, 1966, before the contract officially began.[15] Stuart Cook took an early leading role and tried to organize the initial discussion. The seven agreed on only one thing: they needed a lot of help. From early November through December, there were a number of briefings from Hynek, Jacques Vallee, Keyhoe, Hall, individuals from Wright Patterson AFB, and several others. Through these first three months, the atmosphere in the committee meetings changed from one of lackadaisical verbal jousting between intellectuals to a growing awareness that they had a

Left to Right: Scott, Condon, Low, Cook, and Wertheimer in what represented the first official meeting of project staff.

problem on their hands but with little insight as to whether anything could be done at all, let alone how to do it. Yet decisions had to be made.

A major part of the difficulty was that the seven were there for different reasons. Condon felt that he was doing the Air Force a favor and did not seem to want to be there at all. Bob Low had promised Condon, the University, and probably Walter Roberts that he would administer the project full-time; but Low also seems to have been genuinely intrigued by the mystery of UFOs. Although they had different slants on the subject, three of the psychologists (Cook, Scott, and Wertheimer) were not interested in UFOs. They intended to use spectacular UFO reports to study the psychology of witnesses. Their views on how to spend Air Force money were not central to UFOlogy or even to the interests of the Air Force. The other psychologist, Dave Saunders, and the physicist Franklin Roach wanted to study UFOs, using both old and new cases individually in depth and statistically in bulk. The group had problems even communicating. The three psychologists did not view the work at all in the mode of Saunders and Roach, and vice versa. Bob Low was torn between his natural inclination to go with Saunders and Roach and the overriding drag of Condon's negativity toward studying the older cases.

The briefings did not help to resolve these issues but did push them closer to a decision. The Hynek-Vallee briefing in particular impressed Saunders because of Vallee's views on the potential use of data processing and statistics.[16] The Keyhoe-Hall briefing solidified Roach's and Saunders' feelings that the great old cases were valuable.[17] Bob Low seemed to feel the same. Even Ed Condon reckoned that Dick Hall was a smart cookie and later recommended him to the *Britannica Book of the Year* to author a UFO article.[18] The Air Force briefing was largely spent with Colonel Robert Hippler disparaging the value of looking at old cases. This, in an odd way, reinforced the desire of the psychologists to do experiments on the perception and accuracy of the witnesses.[19]

In early December 1966, two important attempts were made to sway the Colorado Project's methodological direction. A December 7 memorandum from Saunders to the rest of the "seven" outlined his framework for the analysis of UFO data.[20] It was a scheme to place all UFO data into a massive matrix for use in computerized statistical and correlation analysis. It emphasized Vallee's approach and was based on the beliefs of Hynek, Keyhoe, and Hall that there was power in old cases. Saunders wanted new investigative data to go into the matrix as well but perhaps did not see that his suggestion would turn the project into the Dave Saunders Show, feeding his computer and his correlations work. In addition, that strategy depended on lots of cases, but cases not investigated by the

Colorado Project itself. Almost everyone else wanted to emphasize the team's own field investigations at least as much as older "classics."

A second methodology was advanced about the same time. It was a bombshell. Mike Wertheimer had done some deeper thinking about all this. He discussed many ways in which reports might degrade as experiences passed through human sensory and cognitive systems and became narratives. Wertheimer spoke from his strength as a cognitive psychologist and expert in perception. He knew that there was no certainty that UFO reports accurately reflected the stimuli that catalyzed them. That was the pragmatic half of his argument.[21]

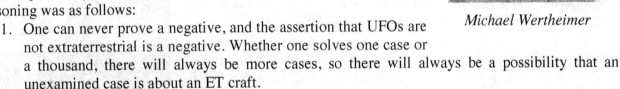

Michael Wertheimer

The more philosophical element addressed the extraterrestrial hypothesis (ETH) for UFOs. Saunders, Roach, Low, and even Condon wanted to make some statement in the final report in support of, or opposition to, the ETH. Wertheimer objected that one could remark *neither* positively nor negatively about it. So why address it? His reasoning was as follows:

1. One can never prove a negative, and the assertion that UFOs are not extraterrestrial is a negative. Whether one solves one case or a thousand, there will always be more cases, so there will always be a possibility that an unexamined case is about an ET craft.

2. Positives cannot be proven either. Unless there is a massive landing in public, any one case or collection of cases can at best be labeled "unknown." Wertheimer invented a nonsense word, framasands, to label anything which was unidentified. Whenever discussion turned to the ETH, he deflected it by talking about framasands and asserted that nothing more could be said. Apparently he did this in a way that was at best unhelpful and at worse obnoxious.

There was no logical argument to rebut the "Wertheimer Hypothesis." Ed Condon said that he was staggered by it, probably an honest statement. Condon had felt that he would be able to make some sort of comment about the ETH in the end (and all indications are that he was sure that his conclusion would be negative). Saunders was also bothered by Wertheimer's logic but considered it more of an irritation difficult to get around. As group discussions spun their wheels, Wertheimer resorted to calling Saunders a "quasi-believer." This was a thinly veiled insult, as the term "believer" had acquired a strong pejorative connotation among academics. Saunders swallowed this for a while.[22]

By the end of December, the seven had met for three months with no agreement on how to proceed. Worse than that, the Wertheimer Hypothesis had made some people doubt that there *was* any way to proceed, at least on certain important questions. And there was already friction: between Saunders and Wertheimer, between Roach and Low (for some undiplomatic remarks Low had made about Roach's skills), and between Scott and people in general (he could not understand why people were not fired up in support of some extremely narrow and nearly irrelevant testing he wanted to do). Meetings in general were tense and unproductive. James Wadsworth, the grad student, was a "fly on the wall." Some of his comments are enlightening:

> Most of the project heads have duties in their departments and are only part-time on this. Thank God that is the case as most of them contribute generously with the axe and have little positive to offer, much less enthusiasm. I feel like each general meeting sets the whole project back. You would not believe the chicken-shit security-notched academic egotism that goes on.

> It's as though the first concern of the group is to protect themselves from getting tainted by the quasi-scientific animal known as UFO. By the time they have succeeded at this, their value as open-minded

scientists has suffered greatly. They are too busy maintaining a role to let loose what little creativity they have.[23]

Bob Low began January 1967, with a sense of urgency. Air Force personnel (Hippler, Ratchford and several scientists) were coming on the 12th to find out how things were going. For Low it must have been a nightmare. His boss was staggered and needed to know what to say. Low gave him a variety of poorly defined works-in-progress to talk about and suggested that he discuss the Wertheimer Hypothesis and the problems it caused them at length.[24]

At the briefing, Condon was definitely in charge. He spoke or interrupted twenty times, more than double the number of anyone else. UFOlogy was not well served as Saunders and Roach spoke only twice each. Even Wertheimer and Cook doubled that output. Condon opened with Low's prepared survey and handed the ball to Wertheimer to explain his hypothesis. Roach ultimately objected but Condon cut him off. Cook, Wertheimer, and Condon then began a disconnected campaign for concentrating the research on those who report seeing UFOs. Dr. Ratchford of the Office of Scientific Research seemed to like this, but Colonel Hippler said *not* to do it—twice. He did not want Colorado and the Air Force taking any more hits for not taking reports seriously and looking at witnesses as if something was wrong with them.[25]

Edward Condon

Saunders made comments about his matrix idea, which, as usual, fell flat. Ratchford briefly referred to it later, saying that finding correlations between old ladies and certain reports might tell someone something. He consistently brought up ideas that were not central to the UFO problem. He advocated work on atmospheric clarity, plasmas and ball lightning, and oddities of the human mind, anything but the core of the mysterious cases and always with no practical research pay-off. The only two positive suggestions from the Air Force side were by Sacramento Peak Observatory director Jack Evans (a former student and colleague of Walter Roberts). Evans suggested that a small amount of scientific (i.e. instrumental and dependable) data was worth tons of unreliable data. Could not a dedicated instrumentation program be set up? This set off a brief pessimistic exchange between Condon and Roach and was dropped. Later, after some typical "just the facts" responses by Colonel Hector Quintanilla of Blue Book, the good observational reliability of pilot reports was admitted. Evans immediately said that what was needed was known cases from reliable observers. Surprisingly Hippler, perhaps letting down his guard at the end of the meeting, agreed. Then he added something odd. He said that when people in the Pentagon who are also pilots talk to him about UFOs, many say that they see unidentifiable things "up there" all the time and that they are getting used to them. Mysteriously, no one followed up on this.

The Colorado Project's main goal in the briefing was to get help with their procedural problems and inability to make decisions. Very little was helping, however. Bob Low, who was more worried about the problem than anyone else, broke in with the statement that the study would not solve UFO mysteries, so what is our role? Ratchford and Hippler were amazingly casual in their response. We want you to just give it a try, they said. You do not need to make any final recommendations that you do not feel strongly about. Condon gave his opinion that if there is a mysterious residue of cases, but no hazard involved, the recommendation should be to ignore the residue. William Blumen, a Colorado geophysicist and secondary staff member, reminded him that ignoring residues is exactly what science should not do. The Air Force representatives, Ratchford and Hippler, each briefly mentioned how much it costs to continue studying this subject. At the end of the meeting one can almost see Condon shrugging his shoulders and saying that while the correct approach is still a mystery the project was way behind on its deadlines.

The meeting did shake some apples out of the tree. Project members were acutely aware that decisions had to be made and that they had better defend their territories. Also, a major private message exchange resulted between Colonel Hippler and Condon and Low (which will be covered later). At least six documents and an unknown number of private conversations were generated in the next week. Low made a strong attempt to define the disparate group as a team, while he laid out a three-pronged investigation (aimed at scientific, political, and educational matters).[26] Since the Project was allegedly only a scientific study, this may have caught some individuals by surprise. The team would perform a variety of activities on the scientific side, aimed mainly at field investigations of new cases and reviews of promising physical hypotheses like decaying cometoids and ball lightning. The educational side involved a manual and a handbook, which could be used to educate the public about UFOs and, most importantly, the many wonders of the natural world which the public sometimes confused with UFOs. Frank Roach, a physicist of the old school, believed that the primary duty of the scientist was public education, and supported Low's approach. The political area was more intriguing, and related to the Project's recommendation for further study (or not) at the end of the research period. Low suggested that he and Condon were concerned about this (and they had just been privately told what the recommendation was to be, as we will discuss later). Low then added to the political area the concern with an Air Force conspiracy to withhold data and the study of the classic old sightings, in case they are "asked about it in a hypothetical Congressional hearing." One wonders if he had thought much about how this division of labor and authority would be accepted by Saunders and Roach. Low ended by saying that this was, however, just a "talking piece."

Roach and Saunders made their feelings known immediately. Roach insisted that their priority should be the unexplained residue of sightings, especially those past ones in Blue Book, NICAP, and APRO files.[27] He argued that the cases should be brought to Boulder, catalogued, computerized, and analyzed under the leadership of Dave Saunders. Saunders also fought for the priority of the statistical database; in addition, he had finally had it with Mike Wertheimer. One day after a "methods shoot-out" meeting on January 20, Saunders blasted Wertheimer's idealistic sophistry as preposterous guidelines for real-world action. Saunders pointed out that *all* science came under the same absolutist criticism, and under the criterion of that philosophy neither science nor any exploration should be bothered with at all. He also strongly hinted that he resented Wertheimer's pot-shots at him, using the term "quasi-believer."[28]

When the dust had settled, Low found himself with a somewhat different-looking organization. Scott had long gone. Cook had just been in it to help in early organizational matters and was essentially gone. Wertheimer went back to full-time teaching and was essentially gone. Roach returned to duties in Hawaii and would do what he could from there. Condon was in rapid retreat into virtual isolation, punctuated by outbreaks of negativity and press gaffs. Low and Saunders stared at one another.

Actually, this situation might have worked out well, if Condon did not have such an understandable influence on Low, and Low and Saunders, despite wide personality differences, could have gotten to understand one another. The deadwood was gone, and left behind were two valuable grad students, James Wadsworth and Dan Culberson. Mary Lou Armstrong was a fine administrative assistant. Fred Ayer, William Blumen, and Joe Rush seemed willing to help open-mindedly

Norman Levine

315

where they could. William Hartmann wrote and volunteered his services from Arizona. Roy Craig and Norm Levine joined the group as active first teamers. Had they been able to keep Roach, this would have made an excellent group to attack the core of the UFO mystery. As it was, what remained was not bad. The only absolute negatives were Condon and a very short time left to complete the project.

The period between late January and late April 1967 is a bit of a mystery. It seems to be characterized by people working seriously and trying to organize the field investigation teams and the communications lines to feed cases to them. Low worked very hard traveling, getting briefings and information, lining up help of all kinds, and thinking about the final report. During this time Dave Saunders

Roy Craig at the Falcon Lake, Manitoba investigation.

began thinking of the project as his own and Bob Low's.[29] Several important briefings were given by CIA picture analyst Art Lundahl, APRO, Donald Menzel, and Ford Motor engineers Frederick Hooven and David Moyers. Dick Hall provided help with the selection of old cases. Ed Condon's activities

Edward Condon

were less helpful. He made an incredible gaff during a talk at Corning (to be discussed later), and did not seem to understand why. He became amused at a psychic prediction of a UFO landing at Bonneville Flats, and sent Jim Wadsworth to investigate, while offering the Governor of Utah and Donald Menzel rides in the saucer when it landed. Condon began studying every weird person and claim at the edges of the phenomenon. And he accepted James Moseley's invitation to attend a public UFO symposium in New York composed almost solely of fringe UFOlogists and kooks.

By the end of this period one assumes that almost everyone in the project had lost all hope for Condon, but that may not have been so (Mary Lou Armstrong seemed to shift the blame onto Robert Low, while Roy Craig never lost confidence in the Grand Old Member of the tribe).[30] Whatever was going through Low's mind, he seemed to be having fun and doing a good job, when he was not cleaning up a Condon mess. By the end of April, Low felt that he had seen enough of the nascent project functions that he could set down the framework for the rest of the study. This was Bob Low's April 21 "Position Paper." It seems quite reasonable, even excellent in many ways. Dave Saunders wrote in the book *UFOs? Yes!* that he was alarmed by it, but one wonders whether that was his feeling early on or late in the project.[31] Either way, Low's paper outlined, with minor modifications, the direction that would be taken and reflected in the final report. Its outline and that of the final report are nearly identical.[32]

The cornerstones of the position paper are the acquiring of data on cases and a set of contracted special topic reviews (optical mirages; radar; plasma, etc.). Low spoke mostly about field investigations on new cases with regard to the former. This may have been part of what alarmed Saunders, who wanted the emphasis on the tough "classics." This new emphasis was probably exaggerated, however, as old cases, and the toughest ones, would continue to play a big role. Low also did not feature the statistical treatment of bulk data in his comments, but he did list it as a special section in his outline. Again, there may have been no problem except one of communication. The impression is that Low knew perfectly well that old classic cases and a statistical treatment were to figure prominently in the report and was taking them as givens. Saunders, however, can be forgiven for a little understandable paranoia. Who would not be paranoid with the way Condon was acting?

The second cornerstone was the contracting of several special reviews. This has been widely viewed in the UFO community as everything from a waste of money to report filler to debunking. As the wheel of time has turned, perhaps all of these concerns became real, but Low's initial decision appears scientifically sound. Low had become clearly aware that the evaluation of many classic cases often came down to irresolvable disagreements *on matters of science* between equally distinguished scientists. Donald Menzel was almost always one side of the disagreement. Lately, James McDonald often was the other. Someone had to be wrong, even probably utterly wrong. But who? Low's solution was, theoretically, brilliant: Get external top-level experts to do review papers on several of these areas of contention, but *don't* ask them to comment on specific UFO cases. Instead, provide relevant, authoritative information from which the Colorado team could apply principles to the puzzling cases, new and old.

Donald Menzel

Whether Low thought of this himself or had some unknown idea-angel (Condon is an unlikely candidate) is unknown. The concept is, in theory, perfectly plausible and doable, given the project's short period of operation. The external experts would not need to dirty their hands with UFOs, just provide a service. Colorado would not have to risk dealing with biases and would make judgments on UFO cases in their own house. It is because the project fell apart due to the infamous "Low Memo" episode, and that the project members did not work diligently enough on the "Case Book" of classic puzzlers (for which all sides should take blame), that these review studies came to reality with nothing to which to apply them and no one to do the work. Thus they sit in the final report as apparent wastes of money, pages, and insight.

Low included several other research directions in his paper, some good; some marginal. He wanted a special section on photo cases, and he fortunately found a special person, William Hartmann, to pursue them energetically.

Robert Low also wanted sections on alleged artifacts, UFO history, the UFO problem outside the United States, the alleged conspiracy of silence, and human problems of perception. Most of this makes sense. Low divided the research question into three tiers. The largest question was, "are there really sightings that cannot be explained?" He felt that the project *must* give some strong answer to this question. He discussed the epistemological and philosophical problems for a while, but then *came down strongly on the side that many reports must be accurate.* Further, he suggested that it is reasonable to conclude that many of these reports will not be explainable. Therefore, the team could almost predict now (April 1967) that the report can say that there really are sightings (something external to the reporter) which cannot be explained, and that, therefore, there is a UFO problem. There should have been little else the UFO-sympathetic community could have desired.

The second tier question for Low then came into play: "are any of these (external stimuli) solid objects?" And the third tier would be: "are any of these objects extraterrestrial spaceships?" Low repeated how difficult it was to determine answers to these questions and suggested that the group needed to discuss their criteria for answering them. He seemed to believe that there might be sufficient evidence to make statements on the probability of solid objects, but the ET-spacecraft question was tougher. Still, he was not opposed to trying. "One can certainly [at that point] say that they are either extraterrestrial spaceships or they are terrestrial phenomena of an as yet unknown source and description."[33]

David Saunders, Allen Hynek, et al., should have taken that conclusion in a minute. What Low was saying was that the direction of the project seemed headed toward an almost certain recommendation in favor of the interesting potential of UFO research (whether ET was involved or not).

Low also laid the Wertheimer Hypothesis to rest with a quote from Richard Feynman: "It is scientific only to say what is more likely and what is less likely, and not proving all the time the possible and the impossible."[34] Therefore, although the team was unlikely to *prove* the ETH for UFOs (barring a captured spaceship), they might be willing to say things like "probably," "perhaps," or "no evidence." Low said that despite a lot of people trying to back him off of the ET-question, he did not want to duck it (if Ed Condon had not been involved with this project as the ultimate authority, this would have been reason enough for UFOlogists to celebrate). Saunders, perhaps because of the benefit of experiencing day-to-day activities and attitudes first hand, reacted to

Richard Feynman

this differently. He viewed the glass as half-empty (we were very unlikely to demonstrate the ETH) rather than half-full (we were very likely to recommend future research on a genuine problem, and could even give a "probably" answer to the ETH). Whatever problems Saunders really saw at the time, he does not seem to have voiced them, and the project began to focus its activities around this schema (which they were already doing anyway): sharpening the field research and early warning systems, contracting reviews, entering statistical data, analyzing photos, and traveling about gathering information. What was falling through the cracks was the "Case Book" on powerful old classics.

According to available documents, it appears that the project moved forward somewhat smoothly between April and June of 1967. This seems to be mainly because Low exercised a very light hand on the steering wheel and people were "doing their own thing." However, there was concern about the efficacy of this procedure, and a Colorado law professor, Courtney Peterson, was hired to do two jobs: (1) look over the team's own shoulders and assess the relationship of their activities to their goals, and (2) create a standardized format and procedure for entering cases into the case book. Oddly, he never did the second task. But he did write a thought provoking piece on the first issue, "Methodology and Purposes of the Colorado UFO Project," June 23, 1967.[35]

From his observations of the team's activities, Peterson judged correctly that the basic points as expressed in Bob Low's April Position Paper were indeed the official methodology of the project. He agreed with Low's assessment of the "three questions": it was certain that some cases were accurately reported and inexplicable, and so it was certain that in some sense a UFO problem existed. In fact, it was likely that the project's work would add to the inexplicability of the phenomenon (by finding more cases, by reversing bad Blue Book diagnoses, and by agreeing with inexplicable diagnoses of formerly unexplained classics). On the second and third questions (Are they solid? Are they ET?), it was equally certain that conclusive evidence was unlikely (especially in the short term of the project), and that the project would be forced to make some sort of statement regarding this inconclusiveness. His view was that a "yes" to question one, followed by an "inconclusive" to questions two and three, would not be "dispositive of public anxiety about the nature of UFOs."

Peterson also suggested that although these are the questions that scientists and the public would like to have answered, they are not really the questions that the project grantor wants answered. The project grantor (the USAF) wants to know what should be done about further UFO study after the Colorado grant ends. Should it be continued or not? If yes, how, at what level of effort, by whom? Peterson believed that the project was not proceeding with these questions in focus. He felt that the project should begin with the premise that some UFO cases were inexplicable and spend its time addressing the "continuance recommendations" question.

The law professor set down a spectrum of recommendations from discontinuance through to maximum effort, and then asked: are your current types of activities heading toward a position on this scale, unthinkingly, by default? Are serious evaluations of the alternatives not being made? He said yes to both questions:

> Simply because an organization as unstructured as this Project staff appears to be tends to develop its own internal structure and objectives, and to do so without much influence of conscious choice even when the final configuration is partly based on compromise.

> Members of an organization cannot readily define their own responsibilities without direction.

Peterson went on to discuss briefly whether the data generated by project activities were sufficient to make valid judgments about specific recommendations of continuance. He featured the "public anxiety" issue, the "potential ET hostility" issue, and the "valuable scientific discovery" issue. He did not attempt to put conclusions or values to these, but merely intended to focus thinking on three of the vital questions that needed to be assessed before making recommendations for continued UFO study and, if so, by whom. He clearly felt that the current activities of the project would be sufficient to make recommendations only with luck, as a sort of by-product to what the participants were actually doing.

Whether Courtney Peterson helped anyone on the project with this analysis is uncertain. He certainly helps the historian by placing another firm data point into the hypothesis that Bob Low was exercising minimal control over day-to-day functions, Ed Condon was exercising no control, and personnel were doing what they found enjoyable to do in the ways they wanted to do it. This seems perfectly in concert with Robert Low's character away from the influence of Ed Condon. It is also not inconsistent with the thinking of persons who would feel that what they were doing was fun, scientific exploration: let's jump in, see what we can see, and make our conclusions about what naturally emerges. All that is fine for a simple ontological question (What are UFOs?), but perhaps not the best way of focusing on development of recommendations. The project's loose way of muddling forward also explains how something as critical as the in-depth analysis of great cases ("the Case Book") could be falling through the cracks: nobody picked it as their favorite thing to do. This is still astounding and Bob Low should take a major share of the blame for this, no matter how loosely he wanted his kinder, gentler management style to be. There is nothing in the copious files to indicate a Low or Condon reaction to Peterson's analysis. David Saunders *may* have had a reaction, but indirectly. All the talk about continuance recommendations and whether the project was staggering toward a pre-ordained conclusion may have gotten him thinking, even in a bit of a paranoid manner, as he was to respond to Low and Condon shortly.

Coincident to Peterson's methods memo, events occurred which marked a change of great significance in Edward Condon. Prior to the end of June, Condon had been relatively mellow, even rollicking, and occasionally tolerant, about this UFO business and the people who studied it. Even his negative media gaffs were mainly in a light joking vein. Although he emphasized the ridiculous, he was at least enjoying himself while doing it. Sometime between the end of June and into July this changed. Exactly what happened is not known. Condon went from an individual who could do things like recommend to Fred Hooven Jacques Vallee's two books (Dec. 27, 1966),[36] recommend to the great WWI physicist Merle Tuve NICAP's *UFO Evidence* (Feb. 9, 1967),[37] and recommend to the *Encyclopedia Britannica* J. Allen Hynek and Richard Hall as excellent persons to write UFO entries (April 28, 1967),[38] to a changed individual beginning to use name-calling pejoratives toward persons like Hynek and Hall who viewed UFO phenomena sympathetically.[39] Condon's "fun with the oddballs" emphasis in his research extended right up to the last week in June when he attended the kook-fringe "Congress of Scientific UFOlogists" in New York City. Then it stopped.

All that can be said by way of explanation is to correlate a few known events from this time period to a weak deduction or two and let the reader judge. As mentioned, Condon attended the Congress of Scientific UFOlogists on June 22-23, 1967. The entire project staff had pleaded with him not to go. He did anyway; the circus atmosphere contributed strongly to negative publicity about UFOs. When Condon returned, he could not have failed to have been greeted by staff disappointment and rejection. This seems evident in the transcript of a project meeting held on June 30. The transcript is fragmentary but very suggestive of the action and interplay, *and* we have polished meeting minutes as well.[40]

The meeting was attended by Condon, Saunders, Levine, Roach (back from Hawaii for a while), Peterson, Mary Lou Armstrong, and visiting journalism graduate student Herbert Strentz. Robert Low was absent for unknown reasons, as was Roy Craig. Condon was unusually ally-less. The meeting concerned the "Case Book" which needed to be gotten off the ground. Condon had listened to Colonel Hippler talk against using old cases and had consistently argued for that position. He took the same position against old cases in this meeting. He may have been surprised at how much Norm Levine and David Saunders stood up to him; in fact Saunders ran the meeting, and Levine did most of the arguing with Condon. It was a pure trialogue with very obvious sides. Saunders and Levine rolled over all of Condon's attempts to sink the old cases research. When the polished minutes came out, it was as if Condon had never been there; they read like a linear mechanical lay-out of how the project was going to pursue the old cases in the "Case Book." Condon's name was listed first on the attendees list, but he had become irrelevant.

This may have stunned Condon. It certainly should have awakened him to how much the internal project was out of his control. When the project met again on July 6, it was to nominate the first set of cases for the Case Book.[41] Condon and Low both attended. Condon refused to nominate a case, but Low happily nominated a lu-lu: the Red Bluff, California, policemen's report of August 1960. This was not only one of the most puzzling cases on record but far outside Condon's desired parameters of limiting the age of cases to a year old at most. Condon must have now realized that even Low was not on the same wavelength as himself. What the psychological effect of this was on the absentee boss is not known. During July, the project met about the Case Book and pursued its regular activities. David Saunders was in the ascendant. Condon retreated. When Low went on a month-long European trip in August, Saunders was alone to run the show.

In the midst of these series of rejections (Condon's insistence on attending the goofy conference vs. the staff not paying attention to his views), something else changed in Edward Condon's mind. He began to view the UFO phenomenon as connected to people with serious mental damage and psychoses. He mentioned this in relation to certain witnesses/contactees during the June 30 meeting. He was thinking of Betty and Barney Hill. Condon accepted the view that UFO stories might add to a person's mental problems, and that the project should consult clinical psychologists about this. He asked Carl Sagan, and received a recommendation to consult Harvard psychologist Lester Grinspoon, which he did on July 24.[42] All of this seems relatively clear in the documents, but here is an added speculation: This may have been the period when Condon decided that the subject of UFOs was dangerous to America's children. As weird as that might seem to some of us, he expressed that opinion several times during the explosive

Betty and Barney Hill

shouting-and-name-calling era that erupted between six months and a year from the summer of 1967.[43]

There seems to be a category of persons including some attracted to science, who conclude that they know what is good for the rest of us. They adopt an authoritarian and somewhat paranoid "thought police" mode. They become convinced that certain irrational concepts do grievous harm to individuals and may even threaten the rational basis of modern western civilization. As mentioned, Irving Langmuir was an earlier version of this class of individuals.[44] (Today we have a whole organization of them, the Committee for Skeptical Inquiry, formerly the Committee for Scientific Investigation of Claims of the Paranormal, CSICOP, proudly reveling in the COP status of their mental policing.) Edward Condon became this sort of person regarding UFOs. He ended up writing that school children should be forbidden to read about UFOs and get credit for writing about them in school. When a columnist suggested that this was policing thought, Condon wrote on the clipping: "School children? You must be out of your mind!"[45] One must remember that this was the man who would ultimately write the recommendations on future UFO studies for the final report.

Condon's biases must have been apparent to almost anyone who was paying attention, but Low's seeming willingness to go with hopeful UFO research directions would have mollified concerns. It was at this same point in time, however, that serious doubts rose about Bob Low's own objectivity. The problems were two: one was an understandable function of Bob Low's early political work in getting the project approved by the Colorado administration; the other was also understandable, an example of bad judgment by Low himself. Taking the second and simpler issue first: Low was leaving for an extended trip to Europe. He had an elaborate itinerary involving much project business. He included several serious things, plus a visit to Loch Ness to satisfy a romantic interest of his in the search for the monster. This would have been at least tolerated by the others had it not been for a major blunder by Low. He scheduled his trip at a time when neither of the Giants of European UFOlogy (Charles Bowen and Aimé Michel) would be available.[46] This the project team considered outrageous. They began to equate the missing of Bowen and Michel with the trip to Loch Ness, and casting the seriousness of the trip in the worst possible light. Low had made a mistake. Every other element in his itinerary should have been secondary to meetings with Bowen and Michel, as they offered the greatest opportunity for the project to learn something about UFOs. It was as if a Soviet UFO investigator had come to America to see Disneyland rather than Hynek and Keyhoe.

The second problem caused far more difficulties in the long run, even though the European flap seemed more emotional at that moment. This was the discovery of the infamous "Low Memo." This memo was written by Robert Low in August 1966, as one of his first attempts to convince the University administration to accept a study of a subject as welcome as leprosy. Low wrote an effective memo to accomplish this task. It was the wording that caused controversy. The offending language should be quoted at length to get the flavor of the concerns:

> Our study would be conducted almost exclusively by nonbelievers who, although they couldn't possibly prove a negative result, could and probably would add an impressive body of evidence that there is no reality to the observations. The trick would be, I think, to describe the project so that, to the public, it would appear a totally objective study but, to the scientific community, would present the image of a group of nonbelievers trying their best to be objective, but having an almost zero expectation of finding a saucer. One way to do this would be to stress investigation, not of the physical phenomena, but rather of the people who do the observing—the psychology and sociology of persons and groups who report seeing UFO's. If the emphasis were put here, rather than on examination of the old question of the physical reality of the saucer, I think the scientific community would quickly get the message. . . . I'm inclined to feel at this early stage that, if we set up the thing right and take pains to get the proper people involved and have success in presenting the image we want to present to the scientific community, we could carry the job off to our benefit.[47]

When one reads the bulk of the documents from the Colorado Project, one gets a different feeling about this memo than the two responses it has normally gotten. The pro-UFO side of the controversy sees the memo as conclusive proof that the project and Robert Low were irrevocably biased against giving UFOs an open hearing from the beginning. The anti-UFO side reads the memo as an innocuous missive using the word "trick" only in the colloquial sense of a clever way of doing something without any prejudice implied. Neither interpretation is correct. The anti-UFO-debunkers are certainly wrong because the flavor of the entire memo argues against a benign use of the word "trick." The purpose of the memo was to persuade a bunch of nervous administrators that they could set aside their fears that this project would smear the good name of the University. Low loaded his language like a used car salesman. He wanted the readers to read the memo exactly as the UFOlogists read it, but with less emotion. Low had a sales job to do. He maximized the slant of his language to make the sale. And he sold it.

So why, then, aren't the pro-UFO people correct? Because Low did not really feel what he expressed. The rest of the project materials support this interpretation. Robert Low seems to be two people: the administrative automaton who does what he is told to do by whatever means necessary to get it done and maintain peaceful coexistence between all parties, and a real person who enjoys shedding his mask and enjoys life, people, and exploring interesting things. Low's actions after the August 1966 memo do not characterize an individual with a negative bias towards UFOs. His January 1967 talking piece, his April 1967 position paper, his willingness to let Saunders, et al; do their things, and his October 1967 talk at Caltech, all show an administrator trying to pursue a difficult mystery with much openness toward its profound mysteriousness. But it is completely understandable that when the "Low Memo" was discovered by Roy Craig in July 1967, and passed around to the rest of the crew, they were shocked and concerned. They read it exactly as he wrote it, albeit for another audience's consumption. Even Ed Condon wrote that the memo was inappropriate.[48]

Rightly or wrongly, these two incidents seriously undermined the confidence that project personnel had in Low. They seem to have brought to a head the concerns with the rogue, off-center behaviors of Condon. (Low was the "door" to communicate with Condon, especially during the long stretches when Condon did not want to be bothered with any of the serious work.) And Low began to be blamed for the lack of organization in several areas of the Project. This latter was a "no win" situation for Low. Without strong, serious direction from the chief scientist, he was left to try to maintain order over a group of strong personalities who considered themselves essentially his peers. David Saunders, in fact, had a right to do so, due to the amount of effort and direction he had contributed. Low and Condon recognized this level of contribution by titling Saunders "Co-Principal Investigator." Low dealt with this situation of being de facto leader without a lot of real authority (he was also neither a PhD nor a scientist), by letting people run their project elements without much interference. Soft non-leadership almost always ends in chaos, no matter how pleasant the management style may be. The chaos of the bumbling Case Book issue and the lack of answers to "where are we going?" were now being laid at Low's feet.

In this environment of rejection of Condon and deteriorating confidence in Low, David Saunders' leadership was rising. In the right hands, this opportunity might have changed UFOlogy's history, but, while a fine individual, David Saunders was not that man. Saunders was taciturn and preferred writing to speaking. He was not the dynamic glad-hander Robert Low or the powerfully present Edward Condon. He lacked the natural characteristics of a leader, yet a leader he was. Had Norman Levine been a more senior man, or Franklin Roach more committed and energetic, either would have been better at the role. Still Saunders did what he could, though probably wishing he was at his computer making data entries and seeking correlations instead.

Saunders meditated on the direction and consequent conclusions of the project. Some of this may have been stimulated by the similarly directed essay by Courtney Peterson discussed earlier. Saunders'

322

concern was different from Peterson's, however. Saunders believed that there was an excellent chance that the final report would support the extraterrestrial hypothesis. At the same time, he felt that this would be a shock, and that he could see no evidence that Condon and Low were worried about that.[49] The paranoia element inherent in all these goings-on made Saunders wonder if the reason that Condon was unconcerned with the consequences of a pro-ETH conclusion was that Condon had already decided not to have one. Because of Low's impending trip to Europe, a summit meeting on this concern had to be put off until September. Just before Low left, Arizona atmospheric physicist James McDonald, the leading scientific exponent of the ETH, returned from a research trip to Australia to brief the Colorado Project. Condon slept through it.[50]

In August Low was away and Condon was in retreat. Saunders ran the project, but not effectively. The Case Book effort again lapsed. Saunders concentrated on what he wanted to do: statistical analysis. Especially compelling to him was the Orthoteny thesis of French researcher Aimé Michel.[51] Michel felt that he had discovered a straight line pattern of UFO landings during the French wave of 1954, which

sequentially seemed to be best interpreted as an intelligent attempt to achieve (exploratory?) coverage of the terrestrial geography. It was a statistical way to indicate probable intelligence and therefore support the ETH—exactly what Saunders wanted. That interpretation subtly pervades an "Alternative Final Report" outline presented to the team on August 27. This was to be the alternative to the outline in Robert Low's position paper of April. Saunders' outline was broken down simply into standardized academic research paper sections (Statement of Hypotheses, Experimental Procedures, Results, etc.), but introduced the device of Technical UFO Reports (TUFORs).[52]

TUFORs were Saunders' solution to most of his current concerns. They were to be reports written by staff members (individually or together) on whatever phase or case of the UFO business they had researched. The TUFORs would be circulated among the staff as a whole for review, *but not veto*. They were the author's own work and would stand as the author's report without censure. The TUFORs would have appropriate disclaimers attached, *and then be issued to the public—*

Aimé Michel's book

long before any final report appeared. Later the project team or its leadership would extrapolate the final report from these TUFORs, as appropriate.

If anyone had bought this idea, Saunders would have had peace of mind on two anxiety-creating fronts. He was concerned that the ideas and results of individual staff members would be ignored by Condon when it came time to issue the final report. And he was worried that the project was doing nothing *inter alia* to release information to the public and prepare them for whatever the final recommendations and conclusions would be. There is no indication in the documents that anyone paid any attention to the TUFOR idea (Condon and Low probably nixed it immediately), and another Saunders suggestion fell flat.

Low returned in September to a tense project with its normal array of function and dysfunction. Field studies flourished and Case Book studies did not. The plasma ball theories for UFOs took a beating from all the experts. Even Bob Low wrote them off as irrelevant. A physics professor named Markowitz wrote a classic example of the type of opinion paper that constantly serves to the detriment of science: a speculative article pointing out a list of impossibilities and deducing, with an amazing air of authority, that all ET-UFOs are therefore a priori impossible. The only astonishing aspect of the paper was that it was happily published by *Science* magazine.[53] Ed Condon, of course, embraced this intellectual soul-mate of Irving Langmuir and himself, and began a correspondence. In a later letter, William Markowitz made the incredible statement that the only reliable UFO report would have to be one made by a *well-known* scientist! Apparently the problem of ridiculous egotism in all this escaped him.[54]

Saunders chose this time to have his summit with Low and Condon. It was a private meeting and the reports of what went on differ. Some of it seems clear, however. Saunders presented his view that if the project did not do any preliminary information release, then it was either a colossal error (because the conclusion was likely to be "probably ETH") or it was a signal that the report had already been decided in the negative. Saunders, not wishing to confront Condon unnecessarily with the "preordained negative" scenario, suggested that they begin a plan of advance releases of information. This suggestion was emphatically rejected.[55] Of that much of the meeting we can be sure. Both Saunders and Condon agree. The tone of the rest of the meeting is not clear. Saunders says that Condon did not understand what he was talking about and said so. Low said he did understand, but that Saunders was in an area that was none of his business. Condon himself claims that he understood what Saunders was saying but did not agree with any of it. Perhaps this is irrelevant, but Saunders did not think so. This whole communications fiasco turned on evidence to support the probability of the ETH and what Condon would do if he had it. Both Saunders and Condon agreed that Condon said that if he had clear evidence about the reality of ET-visitors, he would *not* report it, but instead take it to the President's Science Advisor (Dr. Donald Hornig). Saunders understandably interpreted this as an indication that Condon would permit a negative ET-conclusion in the final report, but not a positive one (that would go to the White House instead). Roy Craig was told separately by Condon that in such a circumstance he would call the Secretary of the Air Force.[56]

Is there another resolution to this exchange? Practically speaking, it may well be that Condon had already fixed his mind to a negative conclusion (many signs, as we have seen, point to that). But this particular exchange with Saunders, in Low's presence, may have a slightly different interpretation. When the two men say "clear evidence in support of the ETH," it is easy to see that they talk two different languages. Condon means something like crashed disks, ET-bodies, super-technology-in-the-lab, maybe a powerfully instrumentally-documented invasion of a high security military facility. No set of puzzling cases, credible witnesses, films and photos will do. For Saunders, those evidences do fine, especially when supported by his statistical work. Saunders believed the case analyses and statistics pointed toward a statement of strong ET-probability. Condon saw the same material as weak at best. Robert Low resided in the middle, just enough to see what both Condon and Saunders were talking about, but siding with his boss that policies regarding opinion-forming (for example advance releases) were none of Saunders' business. Saunders appeared to Condon to accept grudgingly the decision on no releases, but that was just his taciturn manner. Saunders actually left, convinced that Condon had made up his mind in the negative and that any other suggestions would have to be made over his objections. He was correct, possibly for the wrong reasons.

Further evidence of Condon's bias had appeared during a talk at a symposium on atomic spectroscopy held just before the meeting with Saunders. In that symposium Condon was back in his public mode of making the UFO field sound as ridiculous as possible.[57] Several members of the audience were appalled and reported the newest Condon gaffs to McDonald, NICAP, et al. When NICAP passed this information on to the project, Saunders brought the news, and NICAP's reaction, to Bob Low. Low responded with a groan of defeat. Even though this incident is reported only by Saunders, it makes perfect sense.[58] Low had tried to hold this mixture of misfits together and had warded off all the Condon-created crises so far. Now Condon seemed finally to have done him in. At this moment Saunders was not overly sympathetic. The only solution, a statement by Condon that his views did not represent the project's and that project members were now free to express their own views, was again flatly rejected by Condon in a quick follow-up meeting. Condon then went out and gave another press interview which praised Markowitz's "impossibility" article and bad-mouthed NICAP's contributions to the project (1969).[59] Even for someone with the "who gives a damn" reputation of Edward Condon, this is peculiar behavior. This is a person who is supposed to be leading an objective study on an extremely difficult and controversial subject that was over six months from completion and about which he had forbidden anyone else to talk.

The ensuing team meeting took place without Condon, but with Low. Again, because the sources for the meeting's activities were written later by parties with subjective mind-states, it is hard to determine exactly what went on. But it appears as though two things did.[60] One, there was an initial exchange about the "problem" at which Low admitted that he had to support Condon publicly if he ever wanted to return to his administration work at the University of Colorado. This probably really happened because: 1) Low did publicly support Condon; 2) Low did *not* view things (as examples "ridiculousness"; NICAP's quality, etc.) as Condon did; and 3) If Low did not support the boss, he would be in big trouble. The second thing that happened was that Low left the meeting and the rest of the project team discussed all day the problems of Condon particularly, and Low, and what, if anything, to do. Allegedly, most of the staff considered a mass resignation. Roy Craig was, reportedly, the major holdout against this action. Craig, in his memoirs, refused to discuss the incident.[61] The next day, or the day following, the Project team met for a regularly scheduled meeting. On the agenda was Robert Low's report on his European trip. One could have cut the tension with a knife in that room on that day.

The question entering into October 1967 was: could anything worthwhile be salvaged? Condon did not seem to care much, although his attention had turned to the structure of the final report. Low's amazing resilience seems to have allowed him to return to a sort of business-as-usual. Saunders and Levine continued their duties, convinced that something else needed to be prepared as an antidote to how the project was proceeding. They met with outside UFOlogists such as Jim McDonald.[62] The question whether something could be saved from the project turns upon one's assessment of Robert Low and whether he would stand up for what he felt was appropriate in the final report. One cannot say whether Low could have stood up to Condon or at least finessed his extremism in some way, but as to whether Low had a hopeful mindset at this late stage—he did. We know this from a talk that he gave to the Jet Propulsion Lab at Caltech in mid-October.[63]

The contents of the talk are remarkable. It was vintage Bob Low: intelligent, insightful, and serious, but also affable and light-heartedly joking about himself and the project.

Discussing the project's naiveté:

> Imagine yourself in November of 1966 and you suddenly have a contract . . . well, what in the hell do you do?

On evaluating cases:

> Nobody seems to understand what credibility is all about, and if you ask a psychologist it gets much worse.

Commenting on a witness' evaluation:

> My husband and I knew that it was a UFO, because neither my husband nor I could tell what it was.

Throughout the talk, which was entirely upbeat, Low wove interesting and revealing statements. He said that to investigate UFOs properly one must investigate and analyze only the really puzzling cases. He said that all sorts of impressive people, including many scientists, have seen amazing things. He bemoaned the lack of science-quality data, but asserted that the pay-off for getting it would be enormous. He worried about Congress not approving funds but felt that with perseverance (beyond the

Colorado Project) better science could be done. He handled the Betty and Barney Hill case respectfully and fairly positively. He showed the Rex Heflin photos and said that he thought they might be real. Heflin was as solid a character as exists. "I would put him last on my list of persons who would perpetrate such a hoax." And regarding another famous photo: "I believe that McMinnville is even more impressive than this." He was very critical of Blue Book, saying that many so-called explained cases simply are not so, but just vaguely guessed at. Asked about two well-known debunkers, Low hesitated, obviously torn as to what to say. Frankness won out. After a small

McMinnville UFO

verbal dance, he offered that he was not sure that Menzel's books constituted a serious study. As to Philip Klass, the ball-lightning speculator, Low said: "I'm not sure that he has really contributed anything either." Returning to more pleasant topics, he showed a schoolboy's enjoyment in mentioning the Washington, DC, July 1952, radar cases: "that one is my favorite . . . really very strange." He ended the session with a wide statement of praise for NICAP and the quality of their investigations. One almost wonders if Jim McDonald and Bob Low might have changed bodies for a moment.

The state of the project entering the winter of 1967-68 consisted of a group of individuals determined to complete their work despite the emotional traumas which had beset them. Some persons operated almost as if nothing had happened (for example Roy Craig, William Hartmann, Jim Wadsworth); Condon remained in personal charge of planning the final report with the assistance of Bob Low and Harriet Hunter only; and David Saunders and Norm Levine had begun intense contact with outside UFOlogists (Keyhoe, Hall, McDonald, Hynek) to head off a certain catastrophe. The project held together because it was a major event in the history of UFOlogy, and what, really, was the option? Being involved seemed better than not. Something at least could be accomplished, if only in rebuttal.

A November 13 meeting between Condon, Low, and Hunter is informative.[64] Firstly, it was a meeting to plan the structure and contents of the final report, and Condon deliberately excluded all the rest of the senior staff. Secondly, Condon attacked the idea of the Case Book and the inclusion of classic old cases in the report. Thirdly, he insisted on the inclusion of everything in which the Colorado Project participated (even phone call investigations) no matter how ridiculous and insubstantial they might be. Then he unloaded his paranoia: he wanted personally to write a section on UFO publications, emphasizing that the authors were irresponsible and liars: "The harm done via such 'intellectual pornography,' particularly among school children, is immeasurable." Low and Hunter apparently recognized the inappropriate character of this concept (and Condon's emotionality) and tried to talk him into doing a separate article for a teacher's magazine instead.

The meeting ended with a roughed-out list of subject-sections and authors; writing was to be completed by April 1. The significant points from this list are:

1. Condon reserved for himself the Summary (Conclusions) and Methodology sections. In military contracts this is normal for the chief scientist, but in this case almost unethical, given his peculiar off-center involvement and subjectivity. Low also had these sections listed beside his name, supposedly as an aid to Condon. We know, however, that he never wrote anything on

them. Condon, as usual, got his way and even included his "immeasurable damages to school children" paranoia in the Summary.

2. Condon assigned to his administrative assistant, Hunter, the other hot potatoes which he wanted to control: which sort of cases were included (and how they were written up), and whether there was evidence for a U.S. government conspiracy (something which should have obviously been assigned to Low). It appeared that Condon no longer trusted Low to do things exactly as he wished.

3. Low was assigned five topics. In the final report, he wrote none. After May 1968, Bob Low was essentially a non-entity, Roy Craig took over most of the real Project duties, and Low wrote only occasionally about the huge problems that had occurred.

4. Levine and Saunders were assigned three sections (Plasmas and Radar cases for Levine, and Statistics for Saunders). Levine would also have to write up the cases that he investigated in the field. Saunders' role, given the centrality of his involvement, was shockingly small. Still, it illustrates the unfortunate concentration of his efforts on just the single thing that he wanted to do.

Let's compare this November 1967 plan to the final product that emerged by the end of summer 1968. Much of the list survived the intervening months, but many changes occurred. In the final report, these individuals are dropped: Saunders (fired); Levine (fired); Rush, Strentz, and Robert Low. Rush's chapter was a minor one on instrumentation, which he simply may not have gotten around to writing. Strentz was doing PhD work on Press Coverage, and may also have been too busy. But the other three losses are major. If one made a list of the most involved senior staff members on this project, they would be: Roy Craig, William Hartmann, Saunders, Levine, and Low. To have a final report without the contributions of three of the five (and the two *most* central, Saunders and Low) is astounding.[65]

Certain materials also do not show up in the final report: classic old cases (as a special focus Case Book), despite the fact that they were the cornerstone of Low's April 1967 Position Paper; Press coverage (potentially controversial in supporting the idea that citizens do not get a clear picture of the phenomenon); Conspiracy hypothesis (definitely controversial); and Power-outages and UFOs (at least as a chapter; Bob Low wrote a few pages on this which Roy Craig inserted in his section).

Eight authors were added to the final report (Thayer, Roach, Rhine, William Viezee, Vincent Lally, Blumen, Julian, and R. V. Jones). The *subjects* that were added are more indicative of what Condon had tried to accomplish, however. Despite the early insistence of Colonel Hippler not to turn this study into a psychology report, Condon added two more psychology chapters to the previous one by Wertheimer on perception. External reviews on optical mirages and balloons were added to the Stanford Research Institute review of radar, and Altschuler's review of plasmas. All that would have been in accord with Low's April plan, but none of the reviews were applied to the Case Book of exceptional UFO reports, which never appeared. Their presence in the report, therefore, gives the illusion of simple, though unapplied, debunking. Franklin Roach, for some reason (perhaps his own idea), was asked to write a chapter on the alleged astronaut sightings. Roach had been an astronaut debriefer during Project Gemini. Not much can be said about this except that the initial draft reader (Dan Culberson) felt that the write-up was far too lengthy and padded with irrelevancies. He was told to leave all the padding in because they wanted as much bulk as possible in the report.[66] Finally, the former assistant director of intelligence for the British Air Ministry during and after World War II, R. V. Jones, had written a lengthy UFO-debunking article in late 1967 (or early 1968), and Condon wanted very much to include it, even though many other intelligent articles on UFOs had been written. Because it was not part of the project, it was placed in an appendix. Lastly, it should be pointed out that although "Statistics" appears in both November 1967 and the final report, the UFO statistics work of David Saunders is hardly equivalent to the abstract intellectual commentary by Paul Julian that appeared in its place. Between November 1967 and the final report, the report lost significant amounts of its potential punch and added many debunking and negative elements. And, if it could be suggested that this was in some way normal or acceptable, note that the vast majority of project work was completed by November 1967. On what grounds could such major changes of flavor be defended?

What happened? A large part of that answer is "Jim McDonald." When the Arizona atmospheric physicist heard about the state of the Colorado Project, he was very agitated. He wrote to Aimé Michel that Condon was a failure, but maybe the staff might save matters.[67] Still, it was important to plan ahead. McDonald tried to get Congressman Roush of Indiana to hold hearings, but with the Colorado Project still ongoing, there was not much interest. McDonald began to talk with other colleagues and promote in speeches that a NASA-sized effort was necessary. At the same time Condon was quoted, "the whole business is crazy."[68] McDonald, uncharacteristically, bided his time for a while, and then, at the end

James McDonald

of January 1968, blasted Bob Low in a lengthy, heated phone call. He did not mention the notorious "Low Memo," which Levine had given him in mid-December, but he did mention it in a follow-up letter.[69] This was the first time that Low realized that anyone outside the project knew about it.

Low went directly to Condon. Condon blew his stack. Saunders and Levine were called in, and admitted giving McDonald a copy. Condon viewed this as theft, conspiracy, and unforgivable disloyalty. Saunders viewed the memo as a piece of project information in open files (it was) and relevant to the project's true constituents, the American public. Given Condon's absenteeism and Saunders' previous leadership in the project, Dave Saunders felt that he had as much right to make a decision on a thing like this as anyone. Condon fired them both the next day.[70]

Following this cataclysm, there occurred a long sequence of events probably undreamt of in the nightmares of science researchers. A list should suffice to make the point:

1. McDonald threatened Condon with an expose.[71]
2. McDonald wrote and complained to Frederick Seitz of the National Academy of Sciences about the project and the memo.[72]
3. The project's administrative assistant, Mary Lou Armstrong, resigned in protest of Condon's actions.[73]
4. Condon labeled Saunders and Levine "incompetent," then had to retract the charge.[74]
5. Condon stated that Saunders should be "ruined professionally," then had to retract *that charge*.
6. Condon ordered Armstrong to be silent about her views; she would not.[75]
7. In the midst of this, Thornton Page wrote Condon about organizing an American Association for the Advancement of Science symposium on UFOs;[76] this might turn into a showcase for Colorado's problems.
8. An important project member was removed because of marijuana possession.[77]
9. McDonald blasted the Project in talks to professional societies across the nation.[78]
10. A small stream of letters from academic scientists sympathetic to UFO reports trickled into Condon's office.[79]
11. John Fuller and *Look* magazine published the sensational expose of the project: "Flying Saucer Fiasco."[80]
12. Congressman Roush made a concerned speech on the House floor.[81]
13. Several project members were quoted, negative to Condon, in the newspapers.[82]
14. A libel suit was threatened by Saunders and Levine, and reported in the professional literature.[83]

15. Astronomer Frank Drake wrote to Seitz to suggest that the Colorado Study must be discredited.[84]
16. Roush began a GAO investigation of the Project.[85]
17. University deans and the president wanted answers to all this.
18. *Science* magazine published a negative article about the project's problems.[86]
19. A nearly totally pro-UFO symposium took place before the House Committee on Science and Astronautics.[87]
20. A general tide of dissatisfaction about Condon and the project grew on all fronts (UFOlogy, public, media, Congress, some scientists).

Frank Drake

Probably no scientist has had to face so many different types of hammer-blows as Condon faced after he fired Saunders and Levine. As sympathetic to the trials of another human being as one might like to be, it is difficult to feel too sorry for him. Condon did *not* act like a scientist on this job. In fact, he misbehaved egregiously. He sat back in his office and fiddled with irrelevancies while the real work was done by others. He became emotional and paranoid about the subject and allowed that to enter into his actions and writings. He became unjustly autocratic and rejected the input of many of his senior (and junior) staff, who were far more involved. He deliberately, publicly, made the subject of his half million dollar grant appear ridiculous and beneath dignity, even though almost the entire staff did not think so. He consistently opposed the cornerstone of his project administrator's plan (the Case Book), and, despite the opposing feelings of nearly the entire staff, blocked it entirely in the end.

After the debacle, Condon's behaviors were no more admirable. He lost emotional control. He began a series of name-callings and vindictive comments. Saunders and Levine were "incompetent" and deserved to be "ruined professionally." J. Allen Hynek, whom Condon had recommended to write for the *Encyclopedia Britannica*, was now a "kook"; Hynek's crime? He did not agree with Edward Condon. Anyone who knew Allen Hynek knows that he was one of the most polite and civilized individuals one would meet and would never engage in name-calling. Condon constructed an amazing excuse for his troubles: Saunders and Levine had been plotting with NICAP all along to get him and ruin the project. He actually wrote this to Dean Manning in May of 1968.[88] Anyone reading the documents will realize how preposterous this invention is. Condon's own off-center and autocratic behavior pre-dated and forced every attempt by Dave Saunders to inquire what was going on. Condon's mental state did not readily snap back to that of the jovial great scientist that his friends and colleagues remember. Two years later he was still considering black-balling Carl Sagan from membership in the prestigious DC Cosmos Club, because Sagan was too soft on UFOs. Allen Hynek, he said, absolutely should be kept out.[89]

It comes as no surprise that a report written under these conditions would be severely flawed. Actually, the parts of the report not overly influenced by Condon were reasonably objective. William Hartmann's materials on photo analyses are perhaps the model for proper reserve and objectivity. Even here, though, Condon had influence. Hartmann wished to say several things in his conclusions (regarding poorly done Air Force investigations, and that the extraterrestrial hypothesis was at least consistent with the two percent or so puzzling unsolved cases; he also recommended more future research). But Condon wrote "Good God!" on the draft and crossed it all out.[90] (A copy of his commentary is shown on the next page.)

The major offending area of the report (to UFOlogists and, perhaps, to reason itself) was Condon's own "Summary," written unilaterally as we have seen. Again, it is of little surprise that the conclusions and recommendations have so little congruence with other sections of the report. Although it contained statements on his "school children paranoia," most of the Summary is toned down. Either he had a strong editor to inject some strategy into his phrasing of recommendations, or Condon himself had calmed down enough to realize that some subtlety and cleverness was needed. So while Condon

-32-

warranted that some surveillance network might be established and further studies of remaining cases shoudl be carried out, perhaps more directly involving those well-known scientists who have claimed to see in the UFO evidence a tractable problem, and thus substituting their enthusiasm for the neutrality which was consciously designed into the present Colorado committee.

In brief, it is concluded that the UFO problem has been badly handled in the past, by both official and unofficial investigators, that the photographic evidence contains no compelling evidence of hitherto unknown phenomena, that nonetheless there does exist in the small sample studied here some photographic evidence at least consistent with the existence of such phenomena, and thus that some in further modest research would not be unwarranted.

wow!?

Good God!

claimed that he did not wish to block persons from the pursuit of UFO research, he recommended that no funding or ongoing research be facilitated. Although he knew that many of the people who had attempted to look into UFOs believed strongly that the subject was a worthwhile one (for example Hynek, and Condon's own staff), Condon gave the impression that all academics who look into UFOs decide that they are *not* worth researching. He stated that UFOs have not added anything to science and are not likely to in the future, therefore there is no need for the government to sponsor research. He may have known that of the fifteen top staff members listed earlier in the article, at least eleven of them (Saunders, Levine, Hartmann, Roach, Armstrong, Wadsworth, Culberson, Hooven, Rothberg, Thayer, Ayer) definitely disagreed with him. It is probable that Low disagreed as well. If Condon *did not* know of their opposite views, he should have earlier or shortly thereafter, because they were all published externally or written in Condon's own report or drafts. Twelve of fifteen (with three unknowns) seems a pretty big indictment of the appropriateness of Condon's handling of this part of the project.

Condon's summary gives one the impression that few if any UFO cases are puzzling in the slightest way. Again, he wrote from his own bias, which was so great as to ignore even the evidence presented in his own report. It has been pointed out many times, including by knowledgeable, technical academics, how Condon's own report can be used as a strong case for UFOs as an important research area.[91] And, one must remember that it was Condon himself who insisted on eliminating as many unsolved cases as he could from the report, because they were "old." This personal selectivity of data on who-knows-what grounds is certainly a peculiar interpretation of the scientific method.

What really was going on here? Was this just a great old scientist with an unsuspected hang-up and just the right domineering personality to roll over all persons, facts, and mores that would normally moderate such behavior? Well, perhaps. But there was something else going on here, too. Far back in January 1967, after the watershed Air Force briefing at which Bob Low could not get Colonel Hippler to tell him clearly what the project should be doing, Hippler privately responded.[92] His letter, on his Pentagon office stationery, began by saying that his remarks were just his own. Neither Low nor Condon (nor anyone else with common sense) bought that. Hippler then made an argument that the Colorado Project should be able to make an anti-ET conclusion. Low rebutted that in his reply. But more importantly, Hippler stated how seriously the Air Force wanted to get rid of the UFO project at Wright-Patterson. He said that if the project did not have enough time to make a "proper recommendation," an extension could be arranged. That would be far less costly than another ten years of Blue Book. Low thanked him for the clear indication of what the Air Force wanted.[93] Most revealingly, Condon repeated the same ideas in a talk he gave two days after receiving Hippler's inside advice.[94] As far as the final report's conclusion that UFOs show nothing in the reports that would require the Air Force (even in its science branches) to continue studying them, the "fix" was in by January 1967.

Simple logic says that a strong recommendation for the Air Force to get completely out of the UFO business would have a difficult time peacefully co-existing with a conclusion that UFOs are still scientifically interesting. Unless, that is, the project would recommend the Air Force "out," but somebody else "in." This was Bob Low's solution to the problem. In October of 1967, he hinted strongly that another organization should take this on. At the Caltech Jet Propulsion Laboratory he even spelled out N.A.S.A. to the chuckling crowd. Jim McDonald simultaneously suggested his "NASA-like budget." Others like Frank Drake and Bill Hartmann suggested continued research somewhere in a government budget, perhaps at about $1 million per year. Hynek and others chimed in. Condon's state of mind hardly welcomed such thoughts. In Condon's copy of the House UFO Symposium Proceedings, he underlined *every* instance of people talking about grants and funding, even in the few hundred dollar ranges. Equipment, when it was expensive, was also underlined. What explains this obsessive behavior? 1967 was the first of the so-called doldrum years of governmental big-science non-funding. Congress had gone into one of its cyclical penny-pinching moods. Funding for anything would be tougher, yet here was a small furor gaining momentum, in Congress, toward the funding of something Condon considered dangerous.

Emotionality, paranoia, don't tread-on-me anger, orders from the Air Force, fear of failing research funds—how many sources of unscientific behavior do we need? The front-end of the Colorado Report, as written by its director, should stand as one of the worst cases of bias documentable in our recent history. The embarrassment does not stop there, though. Now that the deed was done, the establishment rallied around the honored old member of the tribe. The National Academy of Science reviewed the study (as required in the contract) and quickly and wholly approved it.[95] *Nature*, an outstandingly prejudiced mainstream science magazine on many subjects, happily reviewed the report as "A Sledgehammer for Nuts."[96] Famous Harvard astronomer Fred Whipple praised Condon for doing "a fine job."[97] Smithsonian administrator and former CIA logistics man for the famous Robertson Panel

Most UFO's Explainable, Says Scientist

By DICK OLIVE

CORNING — Unidentified flying objects "are not the business of the Air Force," the man directing a government - sponsored study of the phenomena, Dr. Edward U. Condon, said here Wednesday night.

In an hour - long rundown on the government's interest in the field and the recollection of some baffling and spectacular claims by UFO "observers," Dr. Condon left no doubt as to his personal sentiments on the matter:

"It is my inclination right now to recommend that the government get out of this business. My attitude right now is that there's nothing to it."

With a smile he added, "but I'm not supposed to reach a conclusion for another year."

The University of Colorado professor of physics and astral physics spoke to a full house of members of two local science societies — the Corning Section of the American Chemical Society and the Corning Glass Works Chapter of Sigma XI, a research fraternity — at the East High School auditorium.

Fred Durant pronounced the report the "Gravestone for UFOs."[98] Famous MIT physicist Philip Morrison said that the report would stand forever as a monument to the scientific method.[99] The examples are endless. The only thing that saves these admiring scientists any face at all is that almost certainly they had no idea what had been going on and generally did not know what they were talking about. But are scientists supposed to be making strong comments about things they know nothing about? Face is difficult to save regardless of how it is viewed.

The Air Force got what they wanted out of their money: no more Project Blue Book. This was a great relief in many more ways than saved money. Without Blue Book, the UFO community had no focal point in the government

Philip Morrison

to effectively query and keep interest up when things quieted. This especially affected NICAP, which fed off of governmental leaks, data, and cover-ups. NICAP, which was in something of a decline anyway, rapidly shriveled and essentially died along with Blue Book. A certain type of public interest also died off, and another major UFO presence, APRO, began to fade. This latter development was probably due to bad management (like NICAP, in fact) but without the Air Force, the UFO community had to carry all the weight. But the years immediately following the report were, paradoxically, a Golden Age of UFO research. The Colorado Project had awakened many academics and intellectuals, and they came, at least briefly, out of the closet with their interest. It was a time that saw an AAAS symposium,[100] serious interest within the American Institute for Aeronautics and Astronautics (AIAA),[101] the emergence of Allen Hynek, the so-called "Invisible College," and the Center for UFO Studies.[102] Also, at the grassroots level, the Mutual UFO Network began its powerful rise to become the largest UFO organization in the world. UFOlogy survived the Condon Report, even thrived for a while. This was because anyone who was interested in the subject would so easily see how incomplete and biased the report was. But the report has had one serious lasting negative impact upon the academic community; it demonstrated to them that being sympathetic to UFOs was a very dangerous position if one wished to flourish within the oft-closed corridors and minds of the establishment.

AIAA Subcommittee Panel

Left to Right: Joachim Kuettner, Fred Beckman, David Saunders, Jacques Vallee, Peter Sturrock, and Ted Phillips

Notes

[1] J. Allen Hynek to John F. Spaulding, 30 August 1966, CUFOS files.

[2] Richard Hall, memo (notes on a meeting with Captain John Lawrence Counihan), 19 January 1965, NICAP files.

[3] Harold Steiner, *Special Report of the USAF Scientific Advisory Board Ad Hoc Committee to Review Project Blue Book*, March 1966.

[4] See "Hynek, Josef Allen," in Clark's *Encyclopedia*; and Jacobs, *The UFO Controversy in America*, for excellent coverage of the Michigan flap and the "swamp gas" fiasco.

[5] J. Allen Hynek and Jacques Vallee, *The Edge of Reality*, 1975.

[6] Jacobs, *The UFO Controversy in America*.

[7] Harold Steiner, "Implementing SAB ad hoc Committee on Project Blue Book Recommendations," Blue Book Administrational files, 2 April 1966; and Robert Hippler, "Scientific Panel to Investigate Reported Sightings of Unidentified Flying Objects," Blue Book Administrational files, 22 April 1966.

[8] John A. Cooper to J. Allen Hynek, 4 August 1966, CUFOS files.

[9] See Chapter 9.

[10] Frank Rand, untitled draft manuscript of a book, written c. 1996, and revisions following, CUFOS files.

[11] Edward Condon to Bill Moyers, 23 September 1966, University of Colorado files.

[12] David R. Saunders and R. Roger Harkins, *UFOs? Yes!* 1969, p. 26.

[13] Wesley Brittin, Edward Condon, and Thurston Manning, *A Proposal to Air Force Office of Scientific Research for Support of Scientific Study of Unidentified Flying Objects*, Boulder, CO, 1 November 1966, American Philosophical Library [APL] archives.

[14] "Condon, UFO Agnostic, Should Keep Sparks Flying," *Denver Post*, 19 October 1966; and Grace Spruch, "Reporter Edward Condon," *Saturday Review*, 1 February 1969: pp. 55-8, 62.

[15] Colorado Project memos: a) "First Meeting of the C. U. Investigators"; b) "UFO Project: Members of Meeting of October 17, 1966"; c) "Third Meeting of the C. U. UFO Investigators"; d) "Fourth Meeting of the C. U. UFO Investigators"; e) "Fifth Meeting of the C. U. UFO Investigators"; all memos in the APL archival collection of the Project.

[16] "Briefing: J. Allen Hynek and Jacques Vallee," 11 November 1966, CUFOS files.

[17] "NICAP Briefing Notes (and audiotape)," 28 November 1966, APL archives.

[18] Edward Condon to *Encyclopedia Britannica*, 28 April 1967, APL archives.

[19] "Air Force Briefing," 14 November 196(7) (sic); real date 1966, APL archives.

[20] David Saunders, memorandum: Framework for the Analysis of UFO Data, 7 December 1966, APL archives.

[21] Michael Wertheimer, in "Report of Investigation of 1952 Washington Sightings," 9-11, December 1966, APL archives.

[22] David Saunders and Roger Harkins, *UFOs? Yes!*

[23] James Wadsworth to "Charley," 11 February 1967, CUFOS files.

[24] Robert Low, (untitled) memorandum to Ed Condon (regarding the upcoming USAF briefing of 13 January 1967), APL archives.

[25] "Air Force Advisory Panel Briefing," 12 January 1967, APL archives.

[26] Robert Low, memorandum: "Methods," 19 January 1967, APL archives.

[27] Franklin E. Roach to Edward Condon, 20 January 1967, APL archives.

[28] David Saunders, memorandum: "The Wertheimer-Zeno Paradox," no date on document, APL archives.

[29] Edward Condon, memo to files: "September 18, 1967 meeting," written 2 March 1968, APL archives.

[30] Roy Craig, *UFOs*, 1995.

[31] Saunders and Harkins, *UFOs? Yes!*

[32] Robert Low, unlabelled "informal position paper," 21 April 1967, APL archives.

[33] Robert Low, unlabelled "informal position paper," 21 April 1967, APL archives.

[34] Robert Low, unlabelled "informal position paper," 21 April 1967, APL archives.

[35] Courtney Peterson, "Methodology and Purposes of the Colorado UFO Project," 23 June 1967, APL archives.

[36] Edward Condon to Frederick Hooven, 27 December 1967, APL archives.

[37] Edward Condon to Merle Tuve, 9 February 1967, APL archives.

[38] Edward Condon to *Encyclopedia Britannica*, 28 April 1967, APL archives.

[39] Walter O. Roberts to Edward Condon (Condon marginalia), 15 September 1969, APL archives.

[40] (Colorado Project): a) Notes of Meeting of Friday, 30 June 1967, CUFOS files; and b) unlabelled notes for 30 June 1967 meeting, APL archives.

[41] (Colorado Project), Notes on Internal Meeting of Thursday, 6 July 1967, CUFOS files.

[42] Edward Condon to Lester Grinspoon, 24 July 1967, APL archives.

[43] (Colorado Project), Meeting on 13 November 1967, APL archives.

[44] Irving Langmuir, "Pathological Science."

[45] Henry Pierce, "Professors Threaten Own Free Speech"—(city not listed on clipping from Edward Condon file) *Post Gazette*, 10 May 1969, APL archives.

[46] Saunders and Harkins, *UFOs? Yes!*

[47] Robert Low to E. James Archer and Thurston E. Manning, memo, 9 August 1966, APL archives.

[48] Craig, *UFOs*.

[49] Saunders and Harkins, *UFOs? Yes!*

[50] James McDonald to Robert Low, 31 January 1968, Richard Hall/CUFOS files.

[51] Aimé Michel, *Flying Saucers and the Straight Line Mystery*, 1958.

[52] David Saunders, outline of a possible alternative "Final Report," 27 August 1967, APL archives.

[53] William Markowitz, "The Physics and Metaphysics of Unidentified Flying Objects," *Science 157*: 1274-9, 1967.

[54] William Markowitz to Edward Condon, 31 October 1967, APL archives.

[55] Saunders and Harkins, *UFOs? Yes!;* Edward Condon, Memo to Files on 18 September 1967 meeting, written 2 March 1968, APL archives; Robert Low, memorandum: Recent File Memos by EUC, 8 March 1968, APL archives.

[56] Craig, *UFOs*.

[57] James McDonald to Robert Low, 31 January 1968, Richard Hall files; Donald Keyhoe to Edward Condon, 14 November 1967, CUFOS files.

[58] Saunders and Harkins, *UFOs? Yes!*

[59] James McDonald to Robert Low, 31 January 1968, Richard Hall files; Saunders and Harkins, *UFOs? Yes!*

[60] Saunders and Harkins, *UFOs? Yes!*

[61] Craig, *UFOs*.

[62] Paul McCarthy, *Politicking and Paradigm Shifting,* unpublished PhD thesis, University of Hawaii, 1975, CUFOS files; David Saunders to J. Allen Hynek, 29 November 1967, CUFOS files.

[63] Robert Low, audiotaped lecture to the JPL at Caltech, October 1967, CUFOS files.

[64] Colorado Project, memorandum: meeting on 13 November 1967, APL archives.

[65] Daniel Gillmor (ed.), *Final Report of the Scientific Study of Unidentified Flying Objects*, 1968.

[66] Dan Culberson, unlabelled note from Dan Culberson to Edward Condon, c. Summer 1968, APL archives.

[67] Paul McCarthy, *Politicking and Paradigm Shifting*.

[68] Peter Michelmore, "The Flying Saucer Chasers," *Sydney (Australia) Sun-Herald*, 26 November 1967, CUFOS files.

[69] James McDonald to Robert Low, 31 January 1968.

[70] Saunders and Harkins, *UFOs? Yes!*

[71] Paul McCarthy, *Politicking and Paradigm Shifting*.

[72] Paul McCarthy, *Politicking and Paradigm Shifting*.

[73] Mary Lou Armstrong to Edward Condon, 24 February 1968, CUFOS files.

[74] Edward Condon to Dean T. E. Manning, 13 May 1968, University of Colorado archives, Boulder, CO; and James McDonald, file memos: phone calls to Richard Hall, February and March 1968, Richard Hall files.

[75] McCarthy, *Politicking and Paradigm Shifting*.

[76] Thornton Page to Edward Condon, 16 February 1968, APL archives.

[77] Edward Condon, memo to Files, 1 March 1968, APL archives; James McDonald, file memos: phone calls to Richard Hall, February and March.

[78] McCarthy, *Politicking and Paradigm Shifting*; James McDonald: a) "UFOs and the Condon Report," University of Arizona Colloquium, 30 January 1969, CUFOS files; and b) "Science in Default: 22 years of Inadequate UFO Investigations," paper given as addendum to his talk at the AAAS Symposium of 1969, CUFOS files.

[79] (Colorado Project), file: "UFO: Scientific Interest" (containing letters from scientists to Condon), APL archives.

[80] John Fuller, "Flying Saucer Fiasco," *Look*, 14 May 1968: pp. 58-63.

[81] McCarthy, *Politicking and Paradigm Shifting*.

[82] William Marvel, "UFO Project Is Called a Cloudy Caper," *Rocky Mountain News*, 1 May 1968.

[83] (Colorado Project) "S.L. file," a collection of letters relating to the Saunders-Levine charges and dismissals and legal problems, APL archives; "Libel suit may develop from UFO hassle," *Scientific Research*, 13 May 1968: pp. 11-12.

[84] Frank Drake to Frederick Seitz, 13 May 1968, APL archives.

[85] Edward Condon. Letter to Dean T. E. Manning, 29 May 1968. APL archives.

[86] Philip Boffey, "UFO Project: Trouble on the Ground," *Science*, 26 July 1968: pp. 339-342.

[87] (U.S. Congress) *Hearings, Symposium on Unidentified Flying Objects. House Committee on Science and Astronautics, July 29, 1968.*

[88] Edward Condon to Dean T. E. Manning, 31 May 1968.

[89] Edward Condon to Urner Liddell, 22 July 1971.

[90] William Hartmann, Draft of Photo Analysis chapter, APL archives.

[91] J. Allen Hynek, "The Condon Report and UFOs," *Bulletin of the Atomic Scientists*, April 1969: 39-42; James McDonald, "UFOs and the Condon Report," University of Arizona Colloquium, January 30, 1969; Peter Sturrock, "Evaluation of the Condon Report on the Colorado UFO Project," *SUIPR Report #599*, Stanford University, October 1974.

[92] Robert Hippler to Edward Condon, 16 January 1967, APL archives.

[93] Robert Low to Robert Hippler, 27 January 1967, APL archives.

[94] "Most UFOs Explainable, Says Scientist," *Elmira Star-Gazette*, 26 January 1967, CUFOS files.

[95] National Academy of Sciences, *Review of the University of Colorado Report on Unidentified Flying Objects by a Panel of the National Academy of Sciences. AD 688 541*, 1969.

[96] "A Sledgehammer for Nuts," *Nature 221*: 899-900, 8 March 1969.

[97] Fred Whipple to J. Allen Hynek, 7 May 1969, CUFOS files.

[98] Fred Durant to Charles Gibbs-Smith, 26 February 1970, "Record Unit 398," General Correspondence 1940-1980 and undated, Box 15, Smithsonian archives, Washington, DC.

[99] J. Allen Hynek to Jennie Zeidman, 19 June 1970, CUFOS files.

[100] Thornton Page and Carl Sagan (eds.), *UFOs: a Scientific Debate*, 1972.

[101] "UFOs: an Appraisal of the Problem," *Astronautics and Aeronautics*, November 1970: 49-51.

[102] David Jacobs, *The UFO Controversy in America*.

Chapter 15: After the Close of Blue Book

The Air Force breathed its sigh-of-relief and closed Project Blue Book. What had they lost by doing so? Were UFOs no longer to be looked at? The answer to that is, of course, obviously "No." Unidentified Flying Objects are exactly what the term says. If an object is unidentified and it is flying in U.S. airspace, the Air Force, by definition and by duty, *must* have concern about the security threat potential of any such object. This is not speculation. Documents and policy-making publications state this.

The best document to illustrate how the Air Force viewed the situation is the one that recommended termination of Blue Book itself. This memorandum, dated 20 October 1969, is known in UFO history circles as the "Bolender Memo,"[1] after the Air Force officer who signed it.[2] Brigadier General Carroll H. Bolender was a technical wizard (he had managed Lunar Module construction for NASA) and Deputy Director of Development for the Air Force's Research and Development Command (AFRDC). To cooperate with the University of Colorado Project, Blue Book had been shifted in the Air Force's structure to AFRDC. Now it was AFRDC's job to terminate it. The action officer responsible for writing the memo, a Major Espey, fulfilled his mission. After thumbnail histories of Blue Book and Colorado, supported by a number of documents which have not yet been found, Espey said that elimination of the Project would have no deleterious effect on national security and "that the defense function could be performed within the framework established for intelligence and surveillance operations without the continuance of a special unit such as Project Blue Book." Furthermore, to make it perfectly clear: "reports of unidentified flying objects which could affect national

Brigadier General Bolender

security are made in accordance with JANAP 146 or Air Force Manual 55-11, and are not part of the Blue Book system." And later: "as already stated, reports of UFOs which could affect national security would continue to be handled through the standard Air Force procedures designed for this purpose."

Few of the documents supporting this decision have been made available to historians. The original staffing document is one of the exceptions, although the staff comments and input and the enclosure have not been found. None of the AFRDC files concerning Project Blue Book during AFRDC's stewardship have been made available despite numerous attempts to find such material via the Freedom of Information Act.

For the historian, the message is simple. The Air Force will continue to do its job, and JANAP 146 is not going anywhere just because Blue Book is disappearing. One phrase in the memo *is* interesting, as it supports Allen Hynek's impression that he and Blue Book were not receiving the best cases.[3] This is the phrase that reports of UFOs which could affect national security are *not* part of the Blue Book system. This indicates how much things had changed from the early years when SIGN was a full-fledged part of the national security function of the Air Force. Probably there were always *some* Top Secret events that were not passed on to Blue Book.

It is important at this juncture to explain the history behind JANAP 146 and UFOs. Originally, JANAP/CIRVIS was a peacetime reporting system reworked from a joint United States and United Kingdom intelligence reporting procedure established in World War 2. It was called Communication Instructions for Reporting Enemy Sightings (CIRES). The initial attempt to establish the procedures in

336

peacetime did not include UFOs. They were added in 1948. When the system became fully operational in 1951, it created an unintended consequence: it split the UFO reporting channels. Some UFO reports were sent through the CIRVIS to Air Defense Command (ADC) and some through intelligence reporting channels to Air Technical Intelligence Center (ATIC). Attempts to fix this problem were made to ensure all CIRVIS UFO reports reached ATIC. These attempts were only partially successful. Over the years the system evolved into sending a copy to ADC and another to the Pentagon, and from there, in a timely fashion, to Blue Book. The Bolender Memo confirms that there was no need to send certain reports to Blue Book. Allen Hynek thought that, increasingly, cases were being stopped at higher offices, and Blue Book dealt mainly with the dregs. For the purposes of this chapter, we note that, of course, the Air Force continued (and continues) to pay attention to UFO reports. NORAD's job has not changed. Neither has the CIA's for that matter. Sensitive intrusions are going to be noticed. JANAP 146 did not go away. Only a publicly-known office, a source of constant irritation, went away.

But was *anything* lost at all? Maybe, maybe not. The elimination of Project Blue Book meant that no place was designated to keep a large active file of non-military UFO cases. Did the Pentagon or NORAD take up the slack? We do not know if there was, or is, a dedicated "UFO desk" anywhere. Probably the Air Force realized that the mass of UFO reports was too big to keep track of anyway, and could well have decided to give up that idea (Blue Book had already done that). Would a "UFO officer" anywhere in the intelligence community lose historical awareness and readiness to function well if a UFO-related situation came up? Probably. That may even have happened, given how the Air Force bungled a response to the Congress-inspired GAO investigation of the Roswell, New Mexico, alleged crash, which will be discussed later in this chapter.

Barry Greenwood

Edward Markey

The rest of the chapter will attempt to illustrate the continuing interest of the government in UFOs using incidents that have leaked out, despite a policy of secrecy. Much of the inspiration for this chapter comes from the ground-breaking book, *Clear Intent*,[4] written by Lawrence Fawcett and our colleague, Barry Greenwood. Greenwood, by the way, wrote his congressman (Edward Markey of Massachusetts) in 1977, asking him about the current Air Force policy. Congressman Markey passed along the Air Force's reply which stated:

JANAP 146 E (1977 edition) states that:

a. Sightings within the scope of this chapter, as outlined in paragraphs 102b(1), (2), (6) and (7), are to be reported as follows:

(1)   While airborne and from land based observers.

        (a) Hostile or unidentified single aircraft or formations of aircraft which appear to be directed against the United States or Canada or their forces.

        (b) Missiles.

        (c) Unidentified flying objects.

        (d) Hostile or unidentified submarines.

        (e) Hostile or unidentified group or groups of military surface vessels.

        (f) Individual surface vessels, submarines, or aircraft of unconventional design, or engaged in suspicious activity, or observed in a location or on a course which may be interpreted as constituting a threat to the United States, Canada, or their forces.

(g) Any unexplained or unusual activity which may indicate a possible attack against or through Canada or the United States, including the presence of any unidentified or other suspicious ground parties in the Polar Region or other remote or sparsely populated areas.[5]

Unidentified flying objects were still prominently listed and, as stated in *Clear Intent*, JANAP distinguishes them from aircraft and missiles. Lt. Colonel John Farr, who authored the reply to the congressman, admitted that standard policy *would* result in reports of UFOs, but "they would be transient in nature with no permanent record or file maintained." Farr was essentially saying that the Air Force not only had closed Blue Book but did not maintain a "desk" or ongoing file. Therefore, he says, the files of reports are quickly destroyed. One can choose to believe or disbelieve that claim, but knowing the intelligence community's predilection for *retaining* materials, one might suspect that a significant number of files exist.

The Freedom of Information Act (FOIA) was established by Congress in 1966 to organize and facilitate citizen access to government information.[6] In 1974, it was upgraded to make requests more likely to be filled. Somehow, in 1977, the rarely-to-be-trusted *National Enquirer* had gotten information about UFO incidents at Air Force bases in 1975. Responsible UFO researchers (like Greenwood) not knowing what to believe about this story, sent FOIAs to the Air Force, giving locations and dates as stated by the *Enquirer*. Somehow the Office of the Assistant Secretary of Defense and the Office of the Joint Chiefs of Staff decided to release 24 informative documents on these intrusions.[7] UFOlogists today still shake their heads in wonder at how this unusually helpful event happened. Since then FOIA requests have rarely been treated with this degree of cooperation.

A review of the FOIA releases relevant to the 1975 air base events for both the phenomenology and what might be learned about the military response is noteworthy. The first event was at Loring AFB, Maine, on October 27, 1975. At 7:45 p.m., a Security Police Squadron saw a red light with a white strobe light near the munitions dump. They naturally thought the lights were connected to an aircraft. The control tower picked the object up on radar. Attempts to communicate with the "plane" failed. The object began circling low (c. 150 feet) and came within 300 yards of the nuclear storage area. The base then went on alert. (This was a full hour into the incident.) The object circled further from the base and then suddenly disappeared from the radar screen. Servicemen and vehicles were now all over the base. No air support had been approved by NORAD for reasons unknown. (This would not be the first time that we have seen commanders of other air bases refuse to send up fighters during incidents that they were not "seeing" themselves.) Ground searchers found nothing unusual. The intruder was last seen visually heading towards Grand Falls, New Brunswick. Local police were involved in checking private aircraft, and nothing was found in the vicinity. Ultimately, it was felt that a wayward helicopter of unknown ownership must have strayed over the base.

The next evening, at the same time, it happened again. This time it was an amber light associated with a white flashing light. It did not approach as closely as the day before, but caused another alert, nonetheless. Again it was observed for a long period both visually and on radar. This time, however, members of a B-52 bomber crew on the ground at the time got a better look at it (a stretched-out football) and after witnessing a jumping, jerky, sometimes hovering, weird flying show, the crew commandeered their truck and drove after it. Coming around a turn, the crew now saw that the object was 300 feet ahead and only five feet off the ground. It was red-orange and as long as four cars.

The object looked like all the colors were blending together, as if you were looking at a desert scene. You see waves of heat rising off the desert floor. This is what I saw. There were these waves in front of the object and all the colors were blending together. The object was solid and we could not hear any noise coming from it.[8]

Suddenly it seemed like every military vehicle on the base was headed their way, sirens blaring. Sometime shortly thereafter, the object shut off its lights. There is no description as to how it disappeared. Radar, however, *did* track something heading for Grand Falls. Once again, the brass decided that this must be some kind of helicopter and requested their on-station helicopter to chase it when it returned. Some people even thought that this had something to do with drug running. The following evenings there were numerous reports of the intruder but the interceptor helicopter team never spotted anything, even when allegedly right on top of it. During this time the Strategic Air Command sent the following message to ten air bases from Washington State to New Hampshire:

> The past two evenings at one of our northern tier bases, an unidentified helicopter has been observed hovering over and in the near vicinity of the weapons storage areas. Attempts to identify this aircraft have so far met with negative results. In the interest of nuclear weapons security, the action addresses will assume Security Option 3 during hours of darkness until further notice. Actions also should be taken to re-establish liaison with local law enforcement agencies that could assist your base in the event of a similar incident. Bases should thoroughly review and insure all personnel are familiar with actions to take in association with the helicopter denial portion of your 207-xx plan.[9]

There is much more to this story which is detailed in *Clear Intent*. For our purposes, the Loring incidents indicate that the Air Force continued to have difficulties with UFO-type encounters and continued to respond aggressively if the encounter involved a sensitive area. What is unusual and unexpected is that the documents covering this and other incidents were released. This did not fit in with how the Air Force handled UFO reports after Blue Book's demise.

When the Air Force placed an interceptor helicopter on duty, the personnel assigned included civilian police. One member of the crew had to be Canadian because the intruder in both cases seemed to disappear across the Maine border to New Brunswick, making it an international concern. Negotiations had to take place to allow the Loring-based helicopter to cross the international line in pursuit if necessary. With civilians now officially involved, the press got involved as well. Reporters were already badgering both the FBI and the Royal Canadian Mounted Police. Out of that came enough information for the *National Enquirer* to ask specific questions of the Secretary of the Air Force. Because those questions were phrased in terms of helicopters (despite contrary evidence), the Secretary's Office may have been willing to provide brief answers. When a FOIA was finally submitted by Greenwood et al., it is possible that the FOIA officer(s) decided that so much of the story was out that no purpose would be served by a denial-of-request. This liberality would not have occurred in most Blue Book years, perhaps not even Ruppelt's era.

In the rest of the "Overflights" release were reports of several incidents over other northern U.S. air bases. These are all interesting UFO events, and the reader should consult sources such as *Clear Intent* and Richard Hall's *UFO Evidence, Volume II*[10] for detailed accounts. They show sometimes spectacular UFO intrusions in the Fall of 1975, a very serious military response, secrecy towards the public, information leaks, and finally the FOIA release. The Malmstrom AFB incidents in Montana seem to include radar as well as visual sightings of a huge, football-field-sized disk, and unexplainable tampering with critical elements of the missile launch systems. Many citizens reported UFO sightings in the area throughout October and into November of that year. One after another, bases in the northern tier of the U.S. experienced incidents, and those incidents continued into Canada. The events involved objects of greatly differing descriptions, but the Air Force tried to integrate them into one kind of event. As usual, they took liberties with witness testimony in an attempt to force-fit a conventional explanation. No solutions were ever obtained.

This is an appropriate place to mention something about history. It becomes dangerous to write history that is too close to the present. Historical understanding requires distance, which enhances objectivity. It gives a commonsense perspective and can remove some of the bias resulting from personal involvement. We have tried to be as objective as possible in writing this book while maintaining the narrative. Still, despite our investment in the subject and the discovery of the raw material, we feel that *some* mention of the post-Blue Book years needs telling.

Another incident involving a significant UFO encounter, a serious military response, and a lucky release of information occurred on September 19, 1976.[11] This event began with citizens calling in an unknown object to Mehrabad Airport in Tehran, Iran. A supervisor ultimately saw the rectangular light himself (with a small red light circling it). After an hour he called the Iranian Air Force Command. The Base Commander sent up an F-4 Phantom. The pilot spotted the brilliant object easily. At a distance of 29 miles from the object, however, all of his instrumentation (including communications) cut out. He abandoned the mission and turned away. After he had flown a bit further, his equipment functioned normally again. The Base Commander ordered a second jet up. The pilot, Lieutenant Parviz Jafari, quickly established radar lock-on. Visually, the object was a brilliant rectangular/cylindrical shape which seemed composed of

Lieutenant Parviz Jafari

flashing strobe lights sequencing blue, green, red, and orange. Suddenly this big object (estimated to be the size of a Boeing tanker) emitted a small object, which flew directly towards the jet. The pilot began to arm and fire at it when his control panel simply went off and his communications systems died. The pilot initiated a violent evasive turn and flew away. Again, after achieving distance from the bogey, his systems returned to normal. The emitted object rejoined the larger one , but another small object was released and it flew downwards, apparently landing. Lights flashing on both the big one and the one on the ground appeared to the pilot to be signaling of some kind. Other minor events occurred thereafter, but these are the more spectacular elements of the case.

How did we get the report? The case was leaked apparently by the Iranian Air Force or IAF personnel. As early as October 1, the *Iran Times* published a blow-by-blow account of certain aspects of the event, taken directly from a tape recording in real time. This was the proverbial "horse was out of the barn," which seems to be the primary motivation for the release of modern case materials. In August 1977, a request for U.S. documents about the case was honored by the Defense Intelligence Agency. The DIA document confirmed all the major elements of the event described above.[12] It also said that the information was "Confirmed by other sources" and that the value of the case was "High (Unique, Timely, and of Major Significance)." In the section labeled Remarks, it said:

An outstanding report. This case is a classic which meets all the criteria necessary for a valid study of the UFO phenomenon:

a) The object was seen by multiple witnesses from different locations (i.e., Shamiran, Mehrabad, and the dry lake bed) and viewpoints (both airborne and from the ground).

b) The credibility of many of the witnesses was high (an Air Force general, qualified aircrews, and experienced tower operators).

c) Visual sightings were confirmed by radar.

d) Similar electromagnetic effects (EME) were reported by three separate aircraft.

e) There were physiological effects on some crew members (i.e., loss of night vision due to the brightness of the object).

f) An inordinate amount of maneuverability was displayed by the UFOs.[13]

In 1981, the National Security Agency (NSA) admitted that the Tehran information had been passed on to one of their operatives, Captain Henry S. Shields (also a U.S. Air Force officer and a DIA analyst) for use in an article in the (classified-Secret) *MIJI Quarterly*.[14] MIJI is short for Meaconing, Intrusion, Jamming, and Interference, and is obviously part of NSA and DIA business. Meaconing means a system that receives signals from enemy navigational aids, then rebroadcasts them on the same frequencies to interfere with the enemy's ability to fly (sort of "messing with your beacons"). The Tehran case included navigation control interference as well as communications interference. NSA judged it appropriate for an *MIJI* article. The surprise in the article is the introduction:

> Sometime in his career, each pilot can expect to encounter strange, unusual happenings which will never be adequately or entirely explained by logic or subsequent investigation. The following article recounts just such an episode as reported by two F-4 Phantom crews of the Imperial Iranian Air Force during late 1976. No additional information or explanation of the strange events has been forthcoming: the story will be filed away and probably forgotten, but it makes interesting, and possibly disturbing, reading.

Well … what can one say? UFOs? Yes. UFOs "common"? Apparently so.

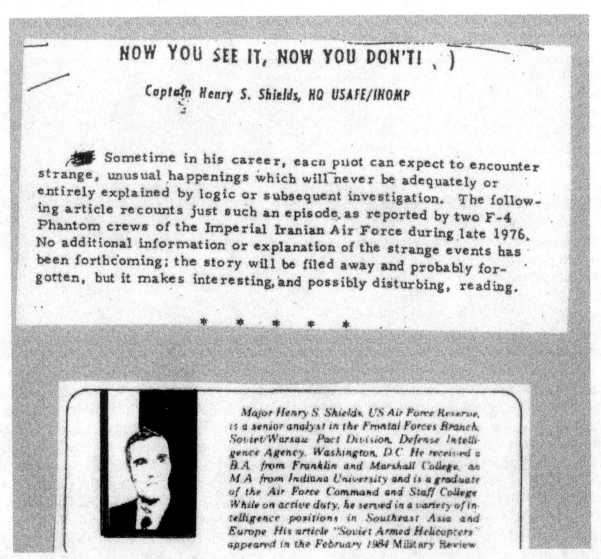

Article by Captain Henry S. Shields

Moving forward into the 1980s, we leave history behind and approach current events. These years belong to future historians to document as necessary materials emerge. Still, during the last thirty years several high profile public cases occurred in the United States, as well as a few other government involvements such as the Roswell GAO investigation. We will proceed in this chapter by making some thumbnail remarks about some of the high profile cases and then address the Air Force's *Roswell Report*.

In late 1980, two women and a young boy encountered something strange over a roadway near Huffman, Texas. This incident became known as the Cash-Landrum Affair after the names of the women. All three witnesses received radiation burn damage by the diamond-shaped "whatever-it-was." The medical records in this case are extensive and incontrovertible; even the military agrees to that. Because the object was surrounded by a large number of (apparently) military helicopters, the UFO investigators made that their primary target. Initially there was no cooperation. Then, after a blitz of media coverage including television, congressional inquiries woke up the Pentagon. An Air Force officer was assigned to the case, and responsibility soon shifted to the Army as the likely helicopter owner. An Army officer worked *very* hard and tried to track the helicopter activity; however at one point the most likely military base (Ellington) announced that all their records for that period were destroyed. The search dried up and no conclusions were drawn. A legal suit for help with the health damages was denied in federal court.[15]

On November 17, 1986, over Alaska, Japanese Airlines commercial flight JL1628 encountered three objects, one of them dwarfing the JAL plane. Records of the pilot's transmissions to ground controllers and radar data were made and preserved by the Federal Aviation Administration. The JAL pilot, Captain Kenju Terauchi, indicated that he had traffic visible at the 11 o'clock position and on the plane's radar. The FAA contacted the Military Regional Operational Control Facility and they confirmed that they had a target at the 10 o'clock position and 8 miles from the Japanese airliner.[16] Initially, everything was handled by the local FAA people. The Public

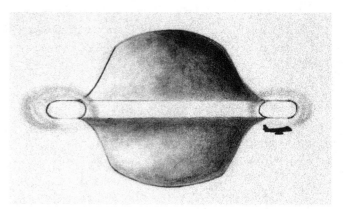

Drawing by Captain Terauchi comparing object to his JAL jet

Information Officer (PIO), however, began to get snowed under by news media requests for detailed information. He found that one of the radar operators was being cooperative with reporters. The PIO told the radar operator to shut up and direct all inquiries to him. Ultimately, the PIO solved some of his workload by preparing a huge packet of materials for the snappy price of $194. Meanwhile FAA HQ in Washington D.C. was bombarded as well. The records were sent there for analysis, and the public report issued about the radar returns was ingeniously non-committal, its explanation being a (bogus) split-signal and a clear separate (UFO) return. We do not know what else went on in DC. However, the FAA's Division Chief of the Accidents, Evaluations, and Investigations Division, John Callahan, has since made a statement about what happened. We have only his word for these details. Callahan says that the UFO radar targets were good and matched what the pilot and ground radio transmissions indicated. He said that he and FAA Administrator Admiral Engen were asked to come to the President's office and brief him and his science advisors, and that the CIA attended. He said that the CIA officials said to consider this as a secret event not to be discussed. Asked why not, the CIA gave the familiar "Robertson" answer that the public could not handle it and would panic.[17]

In 1994, the West Coast of Michigan had a UFO flap. The main elements involved a close encounter (with a lighted disk) by several people in Holland, Michigan, and then an on-air tracking of UFOs by a Muskegon weather station radar operator. It was "on air" because the Holland 911 emergency operator had called him and received his excited blow-by-blow descriptions over the beeper phone. This phone call generated tremendous national attention. The National Oceanic and Atmospheric Administration (NOAA), the agency in charge of the weather station, was scared to death of being involved in a UFO case and would let no one interview station personnel. Through a negotiation with NOAA HQ, it was decided that, to allay charges that NOAA was covering up, they would allow one local university science professor (in fact, Dr. Michael Swords, along with one long-time UFO field researcher who was a close friend) to visit the facility. Everyone there was extremely cooperative and Swords made elaborate diagrams of the radar returns' progression. These diagrams pleased the station administrator and copies of them became the center of the UFO file on this case, which was sent to NOAA's Washington D.C. headquarters. Amusingly, when the Air Force was sent a FOIA about the case, they had no file. They asked NOAA if it had a file, and NOAA dug out their materials and sent them over. FOIA requests for secret documents on this case are now satisfied by the receipt of materials originally drawn by a UFO historian. Funny as that is, it may indicate that for citizen, or at least non-military, UFO sightings, the Air Force really *was not* paying much attention anymore.[18]

In 1997, the nation became excited over a series of claims, apparently backed up with spectacular videos, about UFOs seen over Phoenix, Arizona. The episode quickly got the nickname of The Phoenix Lights. The situation was rife with confusion. The actual UFO sightings were probably of a single large triangular object coming from the direction of Nevada down towards Phoenix and then onward in an uncertain path. These sightings occurred in the approximate period of 8:00 p.m. to 8:30 p.m. About two hours later, several Phoenix residents witnessed and videotaped a series of bright lights that manifested in the sky to the South. These latter sightings probably have a conventional explanation, a military exercise involving flares, and have served to muddy the waters greatly. They have been consistently used as the focus of the conversation and the explanation of the case, despite being seen at least an hour after the anomalous sightings of the triangle. The Air Force appears to have been happy to encourage this confusion.[19]

The early sightings had a prominent witness, the governor of Arizona, Fife Symington. At the National Press Club in 2007, he described it as:

> ...a massive delta-shaped craft silently navigating over the Squaw Peak Mountain Preserve in Phoenix, Arizona . . . it was a solid structure, dramatically large with a very distinctive leading edge including embedded lights.[20]

Symington decided to keep the sighting to himself until later that evening when the coincidental southern flare-dropping exercise caused local and then national excitement. Symington, on his own judgment, called a press conference wherein his chief of staff dressed up like an alien, and everyone "made fool" of the occurrence. Some people were outraged. Symington later explained himself thusly:

> I think as a public figure you have to be very careful about what you say because people can have pretty emotional reactions. And I said my goal wasn't to try to stir the pot.

> The growing hysteria intensified when the story broke nationally. I decided to lighten the mood of the state by calling a press conference where my chief of staff arrived in an alien costume. We managed to lessen the sense of panic but at the same time, upset many of my constituents.

> I would like now to set the record straight. I never meant to ridicule anyone. My office did make inquiries

as to the origin of the craft, but to this day, they remain unanswered. Eventually the Air National Guard claimed responsibility stating that their pilots were dropping flares. This is indicative of the attitude from official channels. We get explanations that fly in the face of the facts. Explanations like weather balloons, swamp gas and military flares.

I was never happy with this silly explanation. There might very well have been military flares in the sky later that evening, but what I and hundreds of others saw had nothing to do with that.[21]

The governor quietly attempted to use his office to find out what he had seen. These efforts went nowhere. This frustrated him. In 2007, Symington (now safely in retirement) said:

We want the US government to stop perpetuating the myth that ALL UFOs can be explained away in down-to-earth, conventional terms. Instead, our country needs to re-open its official investigation that it shut down in 1969. The US government can no longer shun an international dialogue about this, and we invite the government to work in cooperation with the countries represented at this table.

When it comes to events of this nature dealing with the great unknown, we deserve more openness and a serious pursuit of the facts by our government.[22]

In early 2000, there occurred an incident in southern Illinois with no apparent military interest that was wonderfully researched by civilian investigators. Their report tells of a large delta-shaped craft that was monitored step-by-step across southern Illinois by state policemen. The sighting terminated near Scott AFB. As stated, the investigative work was unusually solid, creating an impressive timeline of multiple, credible witnesses over about an hour of flight. As there was some indication that the object remained in the vicinity of Scott AFB, the base was contacted for comment. The spokesperson said that they knew nothing about it. This fellow was not very good at his job as he gave a detail in response to a question that indicated he *was* aware of the case. He also said that the base had no active radars. This may have only been a half-lie, since the base does have radars, but they may have turned them off (as it was between 4 a.m. to 5 a.m.). These sorts of misdirections are, of course, no surprise anymore, and are indicators that old Air Force information policies are still in effect. The *active* debunking in this case came via rather vicious comments in the news media by "scientists." There is no indication, however, that their statements were inspired by anyone other than themselves, for whatever reasons motivate such behavior.[23]

One of the more tantalizing UFO events of recent history occurred near the town of Stephenville, Texas. It became known as the "Stephenville Lights." This incident touches on the Air Force fumbling in their attempt to remain aloof from the UFO phenomenon.

It was 6:10 p.m. and just after sunset on January 8, 2008. A truck driver, traveling east towards Stephenville saw two stationary and adjacent lights directly ahead. He described the lights as similar in brightness to welding arcs. The two lights split apart and moved rapidly away from each other to the north and south at such a high rate of speed that the witness, Harlan Cowan, could not specify their exact location from each other when they disappeared.[24]

Approximately five minutes later, private pilot Steve Allen and three other witnesses five miles to the southeast of Stephenville, near Selden, Texas, observed a similar event. Allen said four lights similar in intensity to burning magnesium came out of the northeast at a speed many times faster than a military jet. Although he had nothing to compare against, he estimated the lights were spread out over a one-mile area. The rapidly moving lights suddenly slowed to a stationary position

Pilot Steve Allen

northwest of his location. The four lights then shifted from a horizontal position to seven lights in a vertical position, emitted a bright white flame, and while still stationary, simply disappeared.[25]

Sightings such as these continued at different locations between 6:10 p.m. until 9:30 p.m. Over thirty witnesses came forward including a former air traffic control operator, a constable, a private pilot, three Stephenville policemen, and a chief of police from a neighboring county. These witness cases are very well documented and are shown not to have been explainable by any known aircraft, meteor, stellar objects, etc.[26] So what was the government reaction to this sudden explosion of unknown objects in the sky?

Photo rendering of Steve Allen sighting

The Air Force broke their normal code of silence on UFOs. Perhaps this error was caused by a major not familiar with AF procedures for providing information on UFOs and by the honest investigative tactics of a Stephenville newspaper reporter, Angelia Joiner. Mrs. Joiner had grown up in the local community, knew that the locals were familiar with F16 aircraft overflights, and felt that the large number of reports of an unknown object by local citizens merited a forthright investigation. She telephoned Major Karl Lewis of the nearby Naval Air Station Joint Reserve Base (NASJRB) in Ft. Worth, formerly known as Carswell Air Force Base. The normal response that the Air Force gives to UFO sightings is that they no longer investigate UFO reports and have no comment. But this time was different. Two days after the sightings, the Major told reporter Joiner that he might be able to solve the mystery in a couple of days.[27]

On January 11, less than 72 hours after the sightings, Major Lewis had an explanation for the Stephenville reporter. Mrs. Joiner described the Major's phone voice as friendly, helpful, and cheerful. He stated, "I think it was a consortium of lights. It sounds like sun reflection of an aircraft traveling at high altitude." Never mind that reports came in many hours after the sun had set and the difficulty of reflected aircraft light being seen by witnesses from different locations and different times; this theory seemed to satisfy the Major. When asked about witness reports of military aircraft in the area that night, he replied, "There were no F16s from this unit (the 301st Fighter wing) operating and no other pilots from our unit reported a UFO."[28] Not only did the Major have an explanation, he had done what the Air Force rarely does in modern times. He had discussed whether Air Force aircraft had been operating in the area and whether Air Force pilots had seen UFOs.

On January 16, eight days after the incident, a FOIA was sent to the FAA by Glen Schulze that requested the raw radar data from all radar sites in the area of Stephenville. This information would allow for the identification of all military aircraft and unknown objects in the area as well as precise measurements of their location at points in time.[29] The Air Force has access to the FAA data through the Joint Surveillance System. Whether this request to the FAA resulted in the Air Force's next statement is unknown, but it is interesting.

A terse news release was made on the afternoon of January 23 (two weeks after the sightings) from the Air Force:

> In the interest of public awareness, Air Force Reserve Command Public Affairs realized an error was made regarding the reported training activity of military aircraft. Ten F-16s from the 457th Fighter Squadron were performing training operations from 6 to 8 p.m., Tuesday January 8, 2008, in the Brownwood Military Operating Area (MOA), which includes the airspace above Erath County.

Major Karl Lewis, a spokesman for the 301st Fighter Wing at the Naval Air Station Fort Worth Joint Reserve Base, blamed the earlier erroneous release on "an internal communications error."[30] Further communication attempts by Mrs. Joiner to reach the Major resulted in unreturned phone calls. But Mrs. Joiner persisted and finally reached the Major. His demeanor on the phone had changed. Gone was his gregarious personality and helpfulness. Every question that was asked received the same reply: "I'm sorry, Mrs. Joiner. All I can say is…" and the Major would begin to read the press release.[31] Major Lewis had broken normal Air Force operating procedures related to UFOs and he was not going to repeat that mistake again. The Air Force stopped talking and newsworthy information about the Stephenville sightings began to slow.

In February, responses to FOIAs that were sent to ten different military bases and federal agencies by Robert Powell and Glen Schulze began to arrive. The FOIA requests for radar or any other information regarding unknown aircraft in the area of Stephenville on January 8, 2008, were met with almost identical FOIA responses from all the military bases: "We have found no records responsive to your request." This response is hard to believe since there are radar facilities at multiple military bases in the area. Despite this, success was achieved with one of the FOIAs. The FAA released raw radar information in mid-February. By early July, Powell and Schulze had completed their analysis of the 2.8 million radar returns.[32]

The radar results were detailed and striking in regards to the Air Force activity in the area of interest. Radar had recorded the location and time transit of every F-16 within 100 miles of Stephenville. It was clear that the unknown lights seen by the witnesses were not related to the F-16s. The amount of Air Force activity was unusual. Ten F-16s and an apparent AWACS jet showed up on FAA radar and made figure 8s over the area of interest from 4 p.m. to 8 p.m. At 7:30 p.m. two F-16s that were training in a Military Operating Area (MOA) 200 miles to the north of Stephenville in Oklahoma left their MOA. They did not proceed directly back to their point of origin at NASJRB in Ft. Worth, which was 150 miles southeast of their location. Instead they proceeded 200 miles to the south and directly towards the area where the unknown lights were seen. They did not travel into the MOA, which was only a few miles farther to the south. Instead, their route took them directly over Stephenville on their out-of-the-way journey back to Ft. Worth.[33] Was that flight diversion a coincidence, a planned diversion, or was it ordered on the spur of the moment because of the unknown object near Stephenville? Only the Air Force knows the answer to that question, as those records were not released. Whatever the reason, the Air Force activity in the area was exceptional that day.

But the radar results showed more than just the Air Force activity that day. At 6:15 p.m., the approximate time that Steve Allen had reported the extremely fast moving object moving from northeast of his position to the northwest, radar made contact with an object four miles north of Allen and then twenty seconds later it was twelve miles northwest of his position. The calculated speed from radar was 2100 mph. And there were more radar confirmations of witness testimony.[34]

At 7:20 p.m., two separate radar sites picked up another unknown object that matched the time and location of Constable Lee Roy Gaitan's sighting. The Constable described a silent and stationary reddish-orange light above the tree line and to the south of his home. The object was the visual size of the moon and he estimated the time to be around 7:15 p.m. He went inside to tell his wife and when he returned about thirty seconds later the reddish-orange light was gone and had been replaced with nine strobing and flashing white lights that appeared smaller and much higher up. He described them as covering much of the sky, moving randomly to each other, and dancing around. As he watched them with binoculars,

Constable Lee Roy Gaitan

the lights suddenly moved in tandem and disappeared at an extremely high rate of speed to the northeast of his home. Radar confirmed the Constable's story. Beginning at 7:20 p.m. radar made contact nine times with an object 2.8 miles to the south of his home. At 7:26 p.m. radar indicated the object moved suddenly to the north at a speed of 1900 mph.[35]

A most interesting radar track began at 6:51 p.m. What makes it interesting is the Air Force's "response" and "lack of response." An unknown object, *without a transponder signal*, was tracked with FAA radar for over an hour. (A drawing of the radar track is shown below.) It was a real object as two different radar systems (one near Ft. Worth and one near Temple) made contact with the object 187 times as the object covered a distance of about fifty miles on a constant trajectory to the southeast. Its speed varied from stationary, to accelerating to 532 mph in thirty seconds, to de-accelerating from 532 mph to 49 mph in ten seconds. The unknown radar bogey without a transponder was traveling on a direct course to President George W. Bush's Western White House in Crawford, Texas.[36] At 8 p.m. it was ten miles from Crawford Ranch and would be directly over the ranch in a few more minutes. Two witnesses riding bikes about two miles from Crawford Ranch reported a bright object in the direction of the president's ranch that slowly descended and then suddenly made a ninety degree angle turn and accelerated out of sight within one to two seconds.[37] This was restricted and sensitive air space. The no-fly zone was restricted to a twenty mile radius when the president was present and a six mile radius when he was not present. Once an aircraft violates that controlled air space, a response from military aircraft will occur. Previous intrusions by aircraft into this same no-fly zone resulted in pursuit of the aircraft by F16 jets and handcuffing of the trespassing pilot after landing.[38] What was the military's response in this incident? (The object was observable on FAA radar located 70 miles away, so it must have shown up on the F16s' radar that came within two miles of the object at one point in time, the AWACS radar, and radar at Ft. Hood only thirty miles distant.) But the response from the Air Force

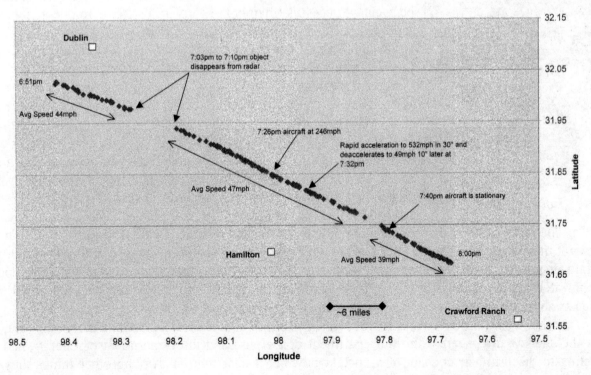

Radar track of unknown approaching Crawford Ranch

was zero. Analysis of the FAA radar data showed no attempt by any of the F16s in the area to divert and investigate an unknown aircraft, without a transponder, closing in on the president's ranch.

Due to the lack of response from the Air Force, a letter was sent in November of 2008 by Robert Powell to General Renuart, the Commander of NORAD, and Michael Chertoff, the Secretary of Homeland Security, with copies to the FAA and the ranking chairmen of the Senate and House Committees on Homeland Security. The letter asked for an investigation into the violation of restricted air space by an "unknown aircraft" in light of the tragic events of September 11, 2001. A response was received and it came from Major General John Bordelon, the Chief of Staff of NORAD. As might be expected, the Air Force claimed no knowledge of an unknown aircraft in the area on that date even though they had access to the same FAA radar data through the Joint Surveillance System. Surprisingly, General Bordelon called the "unidentified aircraft" a UFO. He even referred the author to the FAA guidelines for UFO reports as well as Peter Davenport's National UFO Hotline. Powell called the object on radar an *unknown aircraft* yet the

Major General John Bordelon

General chose to refer to it as a *UFO*.[39] (See the appendix for a copy of the letter to NORAD as well as General Bordelon's response.) One wonders if this was a slip of the tongue that perhaps epitomizes the Air Force approach to the investigation of this phenomenon.

As we approach the end of this chapter on U.S. governmental involvement in the UFO phenomenon, it is appropriate that we comment on the Freedom of Information Act requests, the basic

Robert Todd

tool that provided UFO researchers information on the government's reaction to this phenomenon in the 1940s and 1950s, but also in the post-Blue Book era. Since the late 1970s, FOIA requests had occasioned spectacular successes (mainly the early 1947-1953 era documents which made this book possible) but normally were a "grind it out" labor done by "heavy lifters" such as Robert Todd, Barry Greenwood, and Jan Aldrich. Many others threw their oars into the waters and were occasionally rewarded. An unusual cooperation came from the U.S. Navy (one of, if not *the*, most *uncooperative* agencies of government) when in 1990 its Naval Space Surveillance Center released records on hundreds of unidentified orbiting objects.[40] Whether any of these can be claimed to be anything other than human-launched space junk is another matter, but it points to a vast quantity of unanalyzed data that probably exists in all surveillance system records. It also disputes the brush-off insinuation that no telescopes or sky surveillance systems ever see

UFOs. The fact is, rather, that so many unknowns are tracked that one cannot follow them all. This still does not mean that any of these tracks are UFOs in the sense usually referred to in this book; only that certain dismissive arguments cannot in honesty be made. The same situation was found in both the Moonwatch and Ground Observer Corps programs of the 1950s and 1960s. On the other hand, FOIA requests along these lines to NORAD meet with, essentially, no cooperation.[41]

In another FOIA misadventure, it was NASA's turn to be embarrassed when a story leaked in 1992 that the agency, in concert with the Department of Defense and the Department of Energy, had been meeting to discuss their concept of a nuclear-powered Lunar Station. Among other things they were worried about FOIAs from a meddlesome public. NASA prepared a document, "Suggestions for Anticipating Requests under the Freedom of Information Act." The document is all about destroying meeting notes, rewriting them with the public's looking-over-one's-shoulder in mind, using filing and sequence-ordering tricks to "render any information released significantly less meaningful," printing (rather than hand-writing) to make identification of authorship difficult, and no cross-referencing to point requesters to deeper documents. A Congressional subcommittee uncovered this document, NASA was called onto the Congressional carpet about the outrageousness of the manipulative secrecy, and the NASA administrator (Richard Truly) vowed that they would behave in the future. The precise subject of this aside has nothing to do with UFOs. It *does* however have everything to do with government agency policies about the acceptability of misleading the public and hiding information.[42]

Government agencies continued to be interested in the UFO phenomenon, as we have seen. A further example of this was discovered (c. 1986) by a relative of a prominent Massachusetts researcher (Jim Melesciuc) and passed on to Barry Greenwood who knew him well. The relative was in the library of the FBI Academy (Quantico, Virginia), reading the microfilm collection, when he discovered example after example of press coverage of UFOs going back many years. Deciding to mine the resource, he filled five file folders (amounting to hundreds of articles) with materials from 1978, and continuing additions from future visits to 1991. This was obviously an active subject file, maintained for some long-term yet current reason. The collection appears to be some attempt to inform future FBI agents about aspects of the phenomenon. We will remember that early in 1947 J. Edgar Hoover and the Bureau saw dangers in the phenomenon related to possible manipulation of it (or the public's beliefs in it) by, in those years, Soviet spies. What the current threat-related intent of the file could be, we do not know.[43]

FOIAs were not always required to obtain interesting government information on the UFO phenomenon. Sometimes the government stepped right into the middle of the muck without any coercion from historians.

During August 1997, information about an unusual article was released. In that year's Spring Quarterly issue of the CIA publication *Studies in Intelligence,* author Gerald Haines penned a piece titled, "CIA's Role in the Study of UFOs: 1947–1990." Haines, a historian for the National Reconnaissance Office (NRO), sought to summarize the CIA's UFO involvement based upon internal CIA paperwork, the first time this had been done on an official basis. His conclusion in a nutshell was that the CIA was only intensely involved with UFOs until the early 1950s with the Robertson Panel. After that, interest was only sporadic.

What was peculiar about this article was Haines' claim that more than half of all UFO reports from the mid-1950s through the 1960s were due to observations of high-altitude flights by U-2 reconnaissance aircraft and the SR-71 "Blackbird." Haines calls the latter "Project OXCART" but OXCART should more correctly include the A-12 aircraft, a predecessor to the SR-71. The article noted that after test flights of the original U-2 began there was a large increase in UFO reports from commercial pilots and air traffic controllers. Haines also claims that the Air Force's Project Blue Book investigators were aware of this, having consulted with the CIA's U-2 project staff in Washington to coordinate dismissive explanations for UFO sightings.

In essence, what we were being told was that the CIA verified that the Air Force lied about more than half of all UFO reports logged from August 1955 on to protect the secrecy of the flights of spy aircraft, certainly an extraordinary claim. The problem was that not a single instance of linkage of a reconnaissance flight to a UFO report was provided in the article to support such a conclusion. Neither does one appear in Haines' source for this information, the once classified book, *The Central Intelligence Agency and Overhead Reconnaissance: The U-2 and OXCART Programs: 1954-74,* by Gregory Pedlow and Donald Welzenbach (CIA, 1992). A grand total of two pages of this book were devoted to the discussion.

For Haines' officially sanctioned statement on UFOs to be valid, there should be a paper trail. Which cases were U-2/OXCART flights and which were not? Someone in both the CIA and the Air

Force had to sit down and figure this out. Where is the case material with the conclusions or the documentation for staffing it between two separate government entities? If one accepts the official article by Haines, there must have been a huge "dark file," an underground Project Blue Book that existed which substantiated the U-2/OXCART explanations. To quantify this, there were 9,070 UFO cases in Project Blue Book from August 1, 1955, (the first test flights of the U-2) through 1969 when the Air Force announced the end of Blue Book. There had to have been more than 4,535 cases jointly inspected by the alleged CIA/Air Force cooperative effort for which spy flights were responsible. In a statement to researcher Joel Carpenter, Dino Brugioni, a CIA member of the U-2 program, said that he was the go-between with the Air Force Blue Book people. The way it worked, he said, was that whenever Blue Book suspected a U-2 was responsible for a sighting, they would call Brugioni to check for flights that may have been responsible. No paper records were created from the interchange. The Air Force, not prepared to reveal secret projects in their assessments, would skimp on the explanation for such reports.

CIA Agent Dino Brugioni

It seems likely that there was no such deep consideration of Blue Book UFO cases as spy aircraft since there is no evidence of such large-scale discussions between the Air Force and the CIA. Certainly a percentage of old sightings may have been of U-2 or A-12/SR-71 aircraft, but the extreme extrapolation of "more than 50%" is a frivolous figure, given the lack of documentation, and an easy way to reject a large block of UFO incidents as anything unusual. But, as in many official statements from the previous years, this latest governmental dismissal of the UFO phenomena was open to charges of sloppiness and deceit, a continuation of the now-legendary UFO cover-up.

Before ending the story of the American government's involvement with the UFO phenomenon, we must discuss the Air Force's more recent actions related to the Roswell Incident. Our concern here is not whether the story of a crashed spacecraft is true or not. It is the manner in which the Air Force dealt with the public's interest in this event and the actions that were taken that makes one wonder if this phenomenon will ever be dealt with seriously and scientifically by any U.S. government organization.

On July 8, 1947, the *Roswell Daily Record* published a report that the Roswell Army Air Field had "come into the possession of a flying disc"; just a few hours later, the commander of the Eighth Army Air Force at Ft. Worth, General Roger Ramey, "emptied the Roswell Saucer" by announcing that what had been found was the remains of a weather balloon and radar reflector. There the matter essentially rested for thirty-one years; as Jerome Clark has noted, if ufologists knew about Roswell at all, they "saw no reason not to credit the official explanation."[44] This perception changed for many when retired Major Jesse Marcel began to talk to UFO investigators in 1978. Major Marcel told a story about the Army's retrieval of a large amount of material possibly from an extraterrestrial vehicle. This story, given to ufologist Stanton T. Friedman, was compared with a tale also told him by a woman, who had worked at an Albuquerque radio station in 1947, about the transmission of a story about a crashed saucer and the bodies of little men being squelched by the government.[45] These accounts were connected with the mostly-forgotten Roswell event, spawned a search for more witnesses, and resulted

Major Jesse Marcel

in a 1980 book by William L. Moore and Charles Berlitz. That book caused a sensation, and a series of investigators converged upon the general area around the former Roswell Army Air Field, with more books, articles, films, and videos soon to follow. The "Roswell Incident" became a piece of twentieth-century folklore as new witnesses and new variants of the initial story emerged, including accounts of multiple crash sites, government conspiracies, and alien bodies, dead and alive.

It is our general opinion that the story of government involvement with the UFO phenomenon is intelligible with or without a "Roswell," whether that event was a secret government project, an extraterrestrial crash with alien bodies, or something in between. The Air Force response to the revived Roswell sensation, whatever the original event was, is a prime example of information management that had been prescribed and practiced as early as the Robertson Panel recommendations and confirmed or perhaps reinforced for once and for all by the Colorado Project.

In the 1990s the UFO community tried to generate Congressional interest in Roswell. Among these efforts was a petition initiative called "The Roswell Declaration," drafted by Kent Jeffrey and promoted by the J. Allen Hynek Center for UFO Studies, the Fund for UFO Research, and the Mutual UFO Network. The Roswell Declaration went far beyond seeking the uncovering of the events at Roswell in 1947, however, asking for "*an Executive Order declassifying any information regarding the existence of UFOs or extraterrestrial intelligence*" [italics in the original].[46] Perhaps more significantly, and in line with what we have seen most concerned the Air Force, a Congressman became involved.

Though his New Mexico Congressional district did not include the Roswell area, Representative Steven Schiff tried to get answers for his constituents and others about what exactly had occurred at Roswell. In the fall of 1993, Schiff mentioned his frustrations in these attempts to Charles A. Bowsher, the Controller of the Government Accounting Office, and matters moved forward. On January 12, 1994, Schiff announced that he was requesting a GAO investigation. Richard Davis, Director of the National Security Analysis group at the GAO, wrote in a letter of February 9, 1994, to William J. Perry, Secretary of Defense, that the GAO "is initiating a review of DOD's policies and procedures for acquiring, classifying, retaining, and disposing of official governmental documents dealing with weather balloon, aircraft, and similar crash incidents. In the course of this review, the GAO will test whether various military agencies have 'followed the proper procedures to ensure government accountability over such records.'"[47] Although the task did not single it out, it was clear that the focus was on the U.S. Air Force, the agency most often accused of hiding information and records on Roswell.

Steven Schiff

The Director, Security and Special Program Oversight, Office of the Secretary of the Air Force (SAF/AAZ), had anticipated that the GAO would involve the Air Force,[48] and in late January this unit directed its research/declassification team to find any official records bearing upon the Roswell matter. When the formal GAO contact with the Air Force came, "the Secretary of the Air Force directed that a complete record search identify, locate, and examine any and all information available on this subject."[49] The result of these efforts, *The Roswell Report: Fact versus Fiction in the New Mexico Desert*, was released by the Air Force to the GAO and Congressman Schiff on July 27, 1994, well before the GAO investigation itself was to be concluded.

USAF Roswell Report

The Project Mogul Explanation – July 27, 1994

The Roswell Report, subsequently released to the public on September 8, was brief, but had numerous attachments; when published in 1995 by the U.S. Government Printing Office, it was an approximately 1,000 page, 2½ inch thick tome dubbed the "Phone Book" by ufologists. The portion authored by Col. Richard L. Weaver, the "Report of Air Force Research Regarding the 'Roswell Incident'," with "Memorandum for the Secretary of the Air Force," was 23 pages long. First Lieutenant James McAndrew's "Synopsis of Balloon Research Findings, with Memorandum for SAF/AAZ, Att: Colonel Richard L. Weaver," was only 15 pages long—the next-to-last and 32nd attachment to the Weaver work—but itself contained 11 attachments and 25 appendices. The attachments and appendices were mostly comprised of memos dealing with the Air Force requests of its departments for whatever records they had, statements and interviews with some persons connected with Project Mogul, and New York University progress reports on the Constant Level Balloon project. Project Mogul was a secret program to send, to appropriately high altitudes, instrumentation designed to detect the artifacts from expected Soviet atomic atmospheric testing; Mogul piggybacked on the unclassified Constant

Project Mogul Balloon

Level Balloon project, which researched the feasibility of maintaining balloons and their payloads at consistent and high altitudes over long periods of time. The lack of Air Force records bearing upon the events of early July 1947 at Roswell Army Air Field, and of records specifically linking Project Mogul with the "flying disc" story, is remarkable.[50] About 95% of *The Roswell Report* as published was only tangentially germane to the issue of whether an alien spacecraft had crashed at Roswell; it was, in effect, mostly padding.

What does emerge from *The Roswell Report* is the claim that nothing of importance occurred in New Mexico in early July of 1947. All-but-ignoring the *Roswell Daily Record* article of July 8 that announced the possession of a "flying disc," *The Roswell Report* extensively repeats from the second article of July 9, emphasizing those characteristics of the debris that it wishes to use to support its contention: that a secret Project Mogul balloon train had crashed and its remains discovered on June 14; that somehow a local rancher had mistaken its debris as a possible "flying disc," but had waited until he went to Roswell on July 7 and mentioned it to the local Sheriff; that the Roswell Army Air Field intelligence people visited the crash site and collected the debris; and that the material confused almost everyone at the base including its head, Colonel Blanchard,[51] who then authorized (though this activity is not stressed) the issuance of the surprising press release. It was only after some or all of the material was flown to Eighth Army Headquarters at Fort Worth that its commander, Brigadier General Roger Ramey, got suspicious and had the material properly identified as having come from a weather balloon combined with a radar tracking target. Admittedly, some prevarication was in order because Ramey is said to have hidden a piece of equipment[52] to avoid uncomfortable questions that would have compromised the secrecy of the Mogul project.

What these conclusions are correct or not, *The Roswell Report* attempted to make the issue more clear-cut than it perhaps was and has several weaknesses as an objective research report. The selection of a limited number of witnesses, most of whom were Mogul balloonists and had no claim to direct information about the retrieval and subsequent events, is troubling in the face of a commission to bring to light all the facts of the case.[53] There are also a number of internal inconsistencies in *The Roswell Report*.[54] Further, the *Report* goes beyond an objective focus on the Roswell Incident and a refutation of the mistakes and faulty methods of previous researchers. It lumps all people who have looked into the matter of Roswell into one category as enthusiasts, although it does record disagreements on many points,[55] and casts aspersions on the motives of researchers by saying "many of the persons making the biggest claims of 'alien bodies' make their living from the 'Roswell Incident.'"[56] While recognizing stories about alien bodies as a major facet of the Roswell mythos, the *Report* does little in the way of investigating those claims.[57]

Besides being at variance with much of the other witnesses' stories, the Mogul theory espoused by *The Roswell Report* lacked strong documentary support. "The Air Force was unable, except through speculation and inference, to produce a document confirming the connection or to link the wreckage with any specific balloon flight."[58] Some will regard this absence of records as proof of a cover-up, but as our colleague Jan Aldrich has noted, "Most agencies do not devote high priorities or many resources to records preservation. Huge amounts of records are destroyed every day. The treatment of records during military drawdown periods may sometimes not be in compliance with regulations."[59] We will note later on further support for Aldrich's observations. In the end, the most that a careful researcher can say regarding the lack of key records is that the Air Force could provide no solid documentary evidence to support its claims, nor does the lack of documentation refute those assertions.

It was unusual for a government agency under current investigation by the General Accounting Office to release a report to the public as well as to the GAO, long before the GAO inquiry was complete.[60] The late Karl Pflock claimed that *The Roswell Report*'s real purpose was to get the AF position out well before the GAO's conclusions, possibly to convince the GAO and Congressman Schiff, as well as the media and American public, that there was nothing more to be learned; to confuse many in the public into believing that theirs, not the GAO's report, was what Congressman Schiff had sought; and to be used as the "Roswell-specific, Condon Report-style excuse" for future inquiries.[61] Pflock's opinions carry all the more weight because he had dealt with the GAO when he was a deputy assistant secretary of defense in the Reagan administration, was one of the few Roswell investigators regarded favorably enough to be acknowledged by name in *The Roswell Report*,[62] and is generally regarded as a Roswell debunker by the UFO community.

So what do we make of *The Roswell Report*? In fairness to authors Weaver and McAndrew, it is clear that many pro-UFO-crash people would reject the *Report*'s conclusions and its authors' motives, no matter how good the research and well-reasoned the presentation. However, the GAO Entrance Conference for Assignment Code 701034 had instructed the preparers to "Determine the 'OFFICIAL' explanation of what has become known as the 'Roswell Incident,'"[63] and in the *Report* Colonel Weaver himself stated that "It is recommended that this document serve as the final Air Force report related to the Roswell matter, for the GAO, or any other inquiries."[64] Yet McAndrew later had to admit[65] that this *Report* did not do the whole job.

The initial media response to the "Phone Book" was perhaps predictable. An AP wire story of September 9 was generally favorable, as was *New York Times* writer William J. Broad's September 18 article "Wreckage in the Desert Was Odd but Not Alien."[66] Most of those who had believed that unidentified flying objects were extraterrestrial and that Roswell had been an alien crash continued to so believe, seeing the "Phone Book" as more of the cover-up; after all, the Air Force admitted that it had come up with three explanations, and that one of them at least was a lie. Roswell skeptics overlooked or discounted the *Report*'s inconsistencies, lacunae, and other evidences of poor production and felt their opinions were justified. To them Mogul was a sufficient excuse for the inconsistent Army Air Force press releases. We do not know exactly how the American citizenry felt about the specifics of the Roswell Incident, but about UFOs in general it seems to have tilted more towards the "believer" camp than to the skeptical side—a Gallup Poll indicated that 71 percent of Americans as a whole believed the Government knew more about UFOs than it was telling.[67]

The GAO Investigation – 1994-1995

The General Accounting Office investigation was not designed to explore the Roswell Incident *per se*; it was intended to understand how and where the government had been spending our tax dollars—whether they were being spent efficiently and according to proper legal procedures. And the GAO's usual practice was not to collect all records it could, but to review "samples of relevant records . . . to look for patterns and evidence for government action or inaction." Those relevant records would include documents about the Roswell Incident.[68]

GAO Report

The review was conducted from March 1994 to June 1995, and its report was given to Congressman Schiff and then released by his office on July 28, 1995. The *Results of a Search for Records Concerning the 1947 Crash Near Roswell, New Mexico* was only twenty pages long, of which half were attachments providing the responses of government departments to the GAO's request for information. Following are the highlights of the "Results in Brief"[69] section that summarized the GAO investigation's findings:

1. No air accidents were reported by the Army Air forces or Navy in New Mexico in July on or before July 8, and the Air Force was not required to prepare reports on weather balloon crashes.
2. Some records covering Roswell Army Air Field activities from the time period in question had been destroyed, namely administrative records from March 1945 through December 1949, and outgoing messages from October 1946 through December 1949. What organization destroyed them, who authorized the destruction, and when that occurred were unknown, although the supposition is that the destruction occurred over 40 years before the GAO investigation.
3. A July 1947 history report of the combined 509th Bomb Group noted the recovery of a "flying disc" that was later identified as a weather balloon, and an FBI teletype message stated that the military had reported that an object resembling a high altitude weather balloon with a radar reflector had been recovered near Roswell. The FBI teletype said the disc was "hexagonal in shape and was suspended from a ballon [sic] by a cable, which ballon [sic] was approximately twenty feet in diameter" and that the material was being sent to Wright Field for further examination. Both these documents were already familiar to UFO researchers.
4. Other government records that were reviewed, including previously classified records, and executive branch agency responses to the GAO letters of inquiry, turned up nothing on the Roswell crash.

In a press release accompanying his release of the GAO report, Congressman Schiff pointed out that the lost outgoing messages from Roswell Army Air Field "would have shown how military officials in Roswell were explaining to their superiors exactly what happened."[70] However, the GAO report noted that "the records management regulations for the retention and disposition of records were unclear or changing during the period we reviewed."[71] Indeed, the Chief Archivist at the National Personnel Records Center "stated that from his personal experience, many of the Air Force organizational records covering this time period were destroyed without entering a citation for the governing disposition authority," and the GAO investigators' review of other records supports that view.[72]

So what was the impact of the GAO investigation and its report? Those who argued against an extraterrestrial crash at Roswell, New Mexico, were unsurprised by the lack of any documents coming to light that indicated something truly unusual. Those who espoused an alternative viewpoint of course thought otherwise. Congressman Schiff said "At least this effort caused the Air Force to acknowledge that the crashed vehicle was no weather balloon."[73] The media generally ignored the report.[74] But the Roswell story had at least one more turn to take.

The 1997 Air Force Explanation

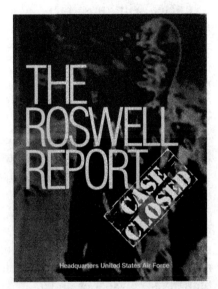

USAF Final Report

We are uncertain what prompted the AF to spend more taxpayer money on another attempted explanation, just two years after publication of the supposed "final Air Force word" on the matter. Perhaps the answer is provided by the author of the next report himself, Captain James McAndrew, co-author of the first Air Force effort: "Some persons may legitimately ask why the Air Force expended time and effort to respond to mythical, if not comedic, allegations of recoveries of 'flying saucers' and 'space aliens'." In *The Roswell Report: Case Closed*, which was released on June 24, 1997, McAndrew's answer was fourfold:

1. The Air Force had been asked to respond to a request from the GAO.
2. Air Force projects and personnel had been misrepresented as part of the Roswell Incident, and denied their due tribute as a result.
3. The Air Force has the duty to challenge those who try to exploit the human tragedies that are often encountered in its service.
4. Misrepresentation of Air Force activities as an extraterrestrial "incident" misleads the public "and is simply an affront to the truth."[75]

McAndrew's "Introduction" to *The Roswell Report: Case Closed* offers that "The issue of bodies was not discussed extensively in the 1994 report because there were not any bodies connected with events that occurred in 1947."[76] McAndrew then adds: "Subsequent to the 1994 report, Air Force researchers discovered information that provided a rational explanation for the alleged observations of alien bodies associated with the 'Roswell Incident'."[77] Released on the 50th anniversary of Kenneth Arnold's sighting that began the modern UFO era, *Case Closed* retained *The Roswell Report's* Project Mogul explanation for what was retrieved from the New Mexican desert in 1947. To explain the accounts of alien bodies, the new report offered that witnesses had misinterpreted both human accidents and anthropomorphic dummies that were carried on U.S. Air Force high altitude balloons. Since the balloon ascensions did not begin until 1953 and the human tragedies that *Case Closed* links most closely to the Roswell Incident until later still, the witnesses had to have erred in linking their experiences to 1947. Some of those who watched the press conference, which was held to announce the findings of the release, were certain that the briefing officer, Colonel John Haynes, was uncomfortable with what the report concluded; others were certain that the colonel had not even read the document.[78]

The Roswell Report: Case Closed was as padded as the 1994 report had been, but here the appendices took up a smaller percentage of the whole and were generally more relevant to the subject at hand; it was the *Report* itself that evinced the most fluff. Irrelevant-but-interesting material such as biographies and historical excursions pertaining to the Air Force's various high altitude balloon programs take the reader's attention away from discussions more relevant to the unfinished business of addressing questions about Roswell. Large font is used throughout, particularly with the "Notes," themselves set off in a separate section at the end, and overgenerous margins abound. The same pictures and charts are used multiple times.[79] Certain elements in *Case Closed* cast doubts upon the objectivity of the research and the report, although the Air Force congratulates itself for such an objective review.[80] Captain McAndrew's team still made no effort to interview all the then-living witnesses of the 1947 events, at variance with the charge "to find all the facts and bring them to light." The author claims that "a large number of accounts were eliminated by applying previously established facts to the testimonies"[81] to eliminate the need to look further at those witness testimonies that conflicted with those facts in some important degree. The established facts were that the Army Air Forces had *not* recovered an extraterrestrial craft and crew; that reports of bodies were *not* associated with Project Mogul; and that the actual events, if any, that inspired such reports of bodies did *not* happen in 1947. Indeed, *Case Closed* seems to use witness accounts very selectively, glossing over portions of those witnesses' reports that speak about truly unearthly things or of being told to forget everything they saw, but accepting other features of their testimony that support their interpretation of the overall events.[82]

A key element to the Air Force report of 1997 is that, beginning in the mid-1950s, witnesses mistook anthropomorphic dummies for living beings, human or otherwise. Much is made of the fact that, like the radar reflectors on the Mogul balloon train, anthropomorphic dummies were a new sight to the New Mexican residents of the 1950s and 1960s.[83] Yet, *Case Closed* also claims that "Air Force projects that used anthropomorphic dummies and human subjects were unclassified and widely publicized in numerous newspaper and magazine stories, books, and television reports [that began by 1951]. . . . The intense public interest . . . also resulted in a 1956 Twentieth Century Fox full-length motion picture, *On the Threshold of Space*."[84]

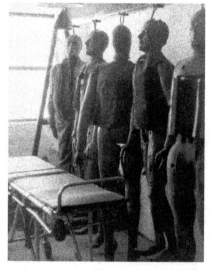

Anthropomorphic Dummies

The McAndrew team set itself another goal besides providing a final answer to the Roswell Incident: that of assuring that the brave men and women of the Air Force, and their sacrifices, received their just dues. Praiseworthy as this task may be on its own, this went beyond the boundaries of the initial commission and detracts from *Case Closed*'s original intended purpose, while incidentally inflating the document to make it more impressive. Further, this is used as a weapon in the document to hammer those who have "confused" the Roswell events with an extramundane origin. The work attempts to heap opprobrium upon "those who have attempted to exploit these human tragedies."[85] Perhaps unsurprisingly, the desire for money is to be inferred as an evil driver behind independent investigators' activities.[86] As with *The Roswell Report*, UFOlogists are generally lumped together into the same unsavory category of "UFO enthusiasts" or "flying saucer enthusiasts."[87] There is the claim that "the Aztec story [of a 1948 UFO crash and recovery in Aztec, New Mexico] is still revered by UFO theorists,"[88] a generalization that from a charitable perspective seems to betray a lack of familiarity with the literature. (And as the so-called Aztec Crash is regarded by essentially all serious UFO researchers as a shameful hoax, this is simply another falsity entered into McAndrew's narrative.) Yet, as had *The Roswell Report*, *Case Closed* does mention cases where its research agrees with that of independent UFO investigators.[89]

Released as it was on June 24, 1997, *Case Closed*'s publicity blocked out press attention towards the 50th anniversary of the Kenneth Arnold sighting of 1947.[90] *New York Times* writer William Broad lauded the report, calling it "detailed and intriguing" and, echoing the rhetorical question McAndrew had himself posed in the report's conclusion,[91] wrote:

> Some critics fault the Government for addressing the topic of alien visitations, dismissing it as ludicrous. But other experts say the United States' obsession with unidentified flying objects has never been greater and praise efforts to combat what they view as a dangerous mania. . . . Not surprisingly, true believers in Roswell are unshaken, seeing the new report as evidence of the most egregious Government cover-up of all time.[92]

Whether hardened UFO "conspiracy theorists" would ever have been satisfied by anything the Air Force could have done or said about Roswell is problematic but moot, as the two Air Force responses were not fully satisfactory. We are left with the image of a Herblock cartoon showing a crash dummy on a parachute, the manikin holding a sign with the words "Roswell Report: Latest Final Explanation; Case Closed Again Until Next Time."[93]

Beyond the U.S. Government Involvement with UFOs

With this presentation of the recent USAF response to the Roswell "problem," we finish our reporting of the U.S. government's activities in regards to the UFO phenomenon, and turn the book over to discussions of how some of the non-U.S. military and foreign intelligence communities reacted to the phenomenon. There are many nations whose governments investigated, or are still investigating, the UFO phenomenon. It is a worldwide phenomenon and is not unique to any particular nation. What is unique is how each nation addressed the phenomenon. The UFO investigative programs of nations identified in the remainder of this book were chosen based on their policies being significantly different to that of the U.S.(unlike similar policies to the U.S. conducted in Great Britain and Canada).

Notes

[1] The use of the word "memo" shows the confusion and basic misunderstanding of the operation of the military and how decisions are reached. Prior to issuing a major decision, policy, or directive a commander or major staff agency head designates an action officer to provide a discussion of the proposed action with background information. Then members of the staff will give their input, usually within the area of their expertise. If the proposed action affects other commands, others with those jurisdictions' inputs will be invited to make inputs. During this period, problems with the proposed action, conflicts with regulations or U.S. laws or treaties in the cases where the action will affect oversea commands, and improvements or changes are proposed with concurrence or objections. After the staffing input has been resolved, the decision is presented to the commander or approving authority for final action, which may be approval, further study with changes, or tabling the proposed action.

[2] C. H. Bolender, memorandum, subject: Unidentified Flying Objects (UFO), 20 October 1969, FOIA (USAF).

[3] J. Allen Hynek, personal communication (Hynek stated this to many UFO colleagues, and in some of his speeches on the subject).

[4] Lawrence Fawcett and Barry Greenwood, *Clear Intent*, 1984. (This chapter owes a great deal to Fawcett and Greenwood's book throughout.)

[5] Fawcett and Greenwood, *Clear Intent*, p. 3.

[6] Fawcett and Greenwood, *Clear Intent*, pp. 4-5.

[7] Fawcett and Greenwood, *Clear Intent*, 6; and Citizens Against UFO Secrecy, *Documents Describing UFO/Helicopter Overflights of USAF Bases in 1975,* Center for UFO Studies: Chicago, IL , date: 1981?

[8] Fawcett and Greenwood, *Clear Intent*, 6; and Citizens Against UFO Secrecy, *Documents Describing UFO/Helicopter Overflights*, p. 19.

[9] Major Medaker, SAC/SP message, subject: Defense Against Helicopter Assault, 29 October 1975, FOIA (USAF); and ongoing story via Fawcett and Greenwood, *Clear Intent*.

[10] Richard Hall, *The UFO Evidence, Volume Two,* 2000.

[11] Fawcett and Greenwood, *Clear Intent*; and Hall, *UFO Evidence, Volume Two*; and FOIA (DIA).

[12] FOIA (DIA), document 6846DI3976 (all characters difficult to read). (This is the coversheet for the incident report.) September 1976.

[13] FOIA (DIA), document 6846DI3976.

[14] Captain Henry S. Shields, "Now You See It, Now You Don't!" *MIJI Quarterly*: 32-34 (magazine date not on document, apparently third quarter 1978), FOIA (DIA).

[15] John Schuessler, *The Cash-Landrum Incident*, 1998.

[16] FAA Memorandum of 18 December 1986 written by Quentin J. Gates.

[17] Bruce Maccabee, "The fantastic flight of JAL 1628," *International UFO Reporter*, March-April 1987; and Marguerite del Giudice, "The UFO that can't be Explained," *The Philadelphia Inquirer Magazine*, 24 May 1987: pp. 14-17, 24-27; and John Callahan, *Testimony to the National Press Club*, 9 May 2001.

[18] Michael D. Swords, "The Holland, Michigan, Radar-Visual Case, 1994," *International UFO Reporter*, Fall 1999: pp. 3-7.

[19] The "Phoenix Lights" sightings are covered extensively on the Internet (see sites such as "nicap.org" and "ufoevidence.org").

[20] Governor Symington's remarks at the National Press Club on 21 March 2007 were widely covered, for example: CNN Newscast of interview with Symington by Gary Tuchman (21 Mar 2007).

[21] CNN Newscast of interview with Symington by Gary Tuchman.

[22] CNN Newscast of interview with Symington by Gary Tuchman.

[23] David B. Marler, Illinois State Director, MUFON Journal No. 383 (March 2000). The southern Illinois case was also investigated by Robert Bigelow's National Institute for Discovery Science, a well-funded civilian organization.

[24] Robert Powell and Glen Schulze, *Stephenville Lights: A Comprehensive Radar and Witness Report Study,* July 2008, pp. 31-32 (henceforth "Robert Powell and Glen Schulze, *Stephenville Lights*.") a copy of this report is located at http://www.theblackvault.com/encyclopedia/documents/MUFON/Files/MUFONStephenvilleRadarReport.pdf

[25] Robert Powell and Glen Schulze, *Stephenville Lights*, p. 32; *Stephenville Empire Tribune*, 10 January 2008.

[26] Robert Powell and Glen Schulze, *Stephenville Lights*, pp. 20-45.

[27] *Stephenville Empire Tribune*, 11 January 2008.

[28] *Stephenville Empire Tribune*, 13 January 2008.

[29] Robert Powell and Glen Schulze, *Stephenville Lights,* p. 73, FOIA copy.

[30] Jeffrey Weiss, "Military says fighter jets were in area; witnesses don't buy explanation," *Dallas Morning News*, 24 January 2008.

[31] Statements from Angelia Joiner to Robert Powell, November 2008. Her statements were related to her late January conversation with Major Karl Lewis after the Air Force retracted the statement that there were no F16s in the air on January 8, 2008.

[32] Robert Powell and Glen Schulze, *Stephenville Lights,* pp. 8-18.

[33] Robert Powell and Glen Schulze, *Stephenville Lights*, pp. 26.

[34] Robert Powell and Glen Schulze, *Stephenville Lights*, pp. 35-36.

[35] Robert Powell and Glen Schulze, *Stephenville Lights*, pp. 44-46.

[36] Robert Powell and Glen Schulze, *Stephenville Lights,* pp. 41-43.

[37] Recorded interview by Robert Powell of two witnesses on August 27, 2008.

[38] *The Wall Street Journal*, "Don't Go There: President Takes a No-Fly Zone Wherever He Goes," 22 August 2002.

[39] Powell letter to NORAD and Homeland Security dated 5 November 2008, and General Bordelon letter of 22 December 2008.

[40] FOIA (USN) (Documents not seen by this author; described and example exhibited in *JUST CAUSE 24*, June 1990: 1-4.)

[41] FOIA (USN) (Documents not seen by this author; described and example exhibited in *JUST CAUSE 24*, June 1990: 2.)

[42] NASA Lewis Research Center, "Suggestions for Anticipating Requests Under the Freedom of Information Act," November 1989 (Reported in *Common Cause*, April-June 1992.)

[43] Barry Greenwood, "FBI Academy Records Revealed," *UFO Historical Review 13*, September 2009.

[44] Jerome Clark, "Crashes and Retrievals of UFOs in the Twentieth Century," *The UFO Encyclopedia*, 264-267.

[45] See Stanton T. Friedman and Don Berliner, *Crash at Corona: The U.S. Military Retrieval and Cover-Up of a UFO: The Definitive Study of the Roswell Incident*, 2004, for Friedman's description of the initial investigations.

[46] "Roswell Declaration 1994," printed in *I.U.R.* vol. 19, #2 (March/April 1994): 21.

[47] Mark Rodeghier, "Roswell and the GAO Investigation," *I.U.R.* vol. 19, #2 (March/April 1994) [henceforth "Roswell and GAO"]: 3.

[48] Colonel Richard L. Weaver, "Report of Air Force Research Regarding the 'Roswell Incident': Executive Summary" in Colonel Richard L. Weaver, USAF, and 1st Lieutenant James McAndrew, USAFR, *The Roswell Report: Fact versus Fiction in the New Mexico Desert*, 1995 [henceforth *The Roswell Report*, Executive Summary], p. 10.

[49] 1st Lieutenant James McAndrew, USAFR, "Introduction" in Colonel Richard L. Weaver, USAF, and 1st Lieutenant James McAndrew, USAFR, *The Roswell Report: Fact versus Fiction in the New Mexico Desert* [henceforth, *The Roswell Report*, Introduction], p. 1.

[50] See, for example, *The Roswell Report*, Executive Summary, 20: "The research revealed only one official AAF document that indicated that there was any activity of any type that pertained to UFOs and Roswell in July, 1947."

[51] "The unusual combination of experimental equipment did not encourage easy identification." (*The Roswell Report*, Introduction, 3.) Then-Captain McAndrew would later characterize the delay in the identification in Captain James McAndrew, *The Roswell Report: Case Closed*, 1997 [henceforth *Case Closed*], 5, as "following some confusion at Roswell Army Air Field, the 'flying disc' was soon identified by Army Air Force officials as a standard radar target."

[52] *The Roswell Report: Fact versus Fiction in the New Mexico Desert*, "Photograph Section," picture of Brig. Gen. Roger M. Ramey, "Ramey withheld only the components that would have compromised the highly sensitive project." If indeed the Roswell debris came from New York University flight #4 of 4 June 1947, as the Air Force (*Case Closed*, 37) and Professor Charles B. Moore (with Benson Saler and Charles A. Ziegler, *UFO Crash at Roswell: The Genesis of a Modern Myth*, 1997, 86) claimed, then this does not comport well with Moore's remarks that "We never recovered any of the equipment from that flight, in part because we had not made any advance arrangements to chase it. We had not equipped it with reward tags; . . . because we had no need to recover the expendable equipment." Why would General Ramey hide something that was not intended to be hidden from public eyes? On the matter of prevarication, *New York Times* writer William Broad called the Air Force's identification of the Roswell debris a "white lie"; see "Wreckage in the Desert Was Odd but Not Alien," *New York Times*, 18 September 1994, online at http:///www.nytimes.com/1994/09/18/us/wreckage-in-the-desert-was-odd-but-not-alien.htm....

[53] Yet Philip J. Klass called the Air Force effort a "rigorous investigation," in Philip J. Klass, *The Real Roswell Crashed-Saucer Coverup*, 1997, p. 114.

[54] See Mark Rodeghier and Mark Chesney, "The Air Force Report on Roswell: An Absence of Evidence," *I.U.R.* vol. 19, No. 5 (Sept/Oct 1994) [henceforth "The Air Force Report"]: pp. 22-23 for some of these.

[55] *The Roswell Report*, Introduction, 1, speaks of those for whom "the belief in or study of UFOs has assumed the dimensions of a religious quest." For disagreements between "pro-UFO groups," see *The Roswell Report*, Executive Summary, 30.

[56] As noted in Karl Pflock, "Roswell, the Air Force, and Us" in *I.U.R.* vol. 19, #6 (Nov./Dec. 1994): p. 5.

[57] See Karl Pflock, "Roswell, the Air Force, and Us": pp. 4-5.

[58] Clark, *Encyclopedia*, 266.

[59] Jan Aldrich, "The Search for Records on Roswell," *Project 1947*, http://www.project1947.com/roswell/rosearch.htm

[60] "The Air Force Report," p. 3.

[61] Karl Pflock, "Roswell, the Air Force, and Us": p. 5.

[62] *The Roswell Report*, Executive Summary, p. 28.

[63] Richard Davis, GAO, to William J. Perry, DOD, GAO Code 701034, in *The Roswell Report*, Attachment 2 of "Attachments to Colonel Weaver's Report of Air Force Research."

[64] *The Roswell Report*, Executive Summary, p. 31.

[65] *Case Closed*, iii.

[66] As noted in Philip J. Klass, *The Real Roswell Crashed-Saucer Coverup*, p. 137.

[67] Harmon, Amy, "Flying Saucer Buffs to Mark Half Century of Hazy History," *The New York Times*, 14 June 1997.

[68] "Roswell and GAO," *I.U.R.* vol. 19, #2 (March/April 1994): p. 3.

[69] *Report to the Honorable Steven H. Schiff, House of Representatives: Government Records: Results of a Search for Records Concerning the 1947 Crash Near Roswell, New Mexico* [henceforth *GAO Report*], p. 3.

[70] Quoted in Mark Rodeghier and Mark Chesney, "What the GAO Found—Nothing about Much Ado," *I.U.R.* 20, No. 4, (July/August 1995) [henceforth "What the GAO Found"]: p. 3.

[71] *GAO Report*, p. 7.

[72] *GAO Report*, 4; cf. Jan Aldrich, "The Search for Records on Roswell," *Project 1947*, http://www.project1947.com/roswell/rosearch.htm

[73] Congressman Steven Schiff press release, 28 July 1995, quoted in "The GAO Report: Results of a Search for Records Concerning the 1947 Crash Near Roswell, New Mexico," in *I.U.R.* vol. 20, #4 (July/Aug 1995): p. 7.

[74] "What the GAO Found": p. 7.

[75] *Case Closed*, p. 125.

[76] *Case Closed*, p. 1.

[77] *Case Closed*, p. 2. On this score one might question why researchers had continued to research, when the 1994 book was to be the final and official last word on the subject?

[78] Mark Rodeghier and Mark Chesney, "Who's the Dummy Now? The Latest Air Force Report" [henceforth "Who's the Dummy"], *I.U.R.* vol. 22, No. 3 (Fall, 1997): p. 7.

[79] The same image of Colonel John P. Stapp occurs on page 27 and just 5 pages later; the same photograph of the Roswell Museum can be found on pages 3 and 75; and a more-than-half-page map of anthropomorphic dummy flight take-off and landing sites (Fig. 82, page 68) was repeated as full-page illustrations on pages 24 and 156.

[80] *Case Closed*, p. 123.

[81] *Case Closed*, pp. 12-13.

[82] See, for instance, *Case Closed*, 57-58. Note also page 48 challenging claims that witnesses felt they had been threatened by the military, the challenges coming from the flat position that soldiers never act that way to civilians. Later on, McAndrew does speak of "misunderstandings" that occurred in the 1970s and 1980s (page 50), and allows (pages 67-68) that in some instances, civilians may have been told to leave areas where they were not supposed to be. One could assume that some firmness would be expected in such situations, which of course could be misunderstood.

[83] "In the 1950s, anthropomorphic dummies were not widely exposed outside of scientific research circles and easily could have been mistaken for something they were not. . . . During the 1950s when the U.S. Air Force dropped the odd-looking test devices from high altitude balloons . . . public awareness and stardom were decades away." (*Case Closed*, 17).

[84] *Case Closed*, p. 26; see page 27 for the 1951 *Popular Mechanics* cover. See also "Who's the Dummy," pp. 9-10.

[85] *Case Closed*, p. 125.

[86] *Case Closed*, pp. 117-118. In another off-point sidebar on "The 'Red-headed Captain' and Dr. J. Allen Hynek," it is noted that Dr. Hynek's "reversal in philosophies led to numerous commercial endeavors." One might note that the McAndrew team had not done well by the "Red-headed Captain" (Captain Kittinger), incorrectly spelling his name as "Kittenger" several times in the "Witness Statements" they took for the record; see the interviews with Dan Fulgham and Bernard D. Gildenberg in Appendix B.

[87] *Case Closed*, p. 12. The term "unsavory" in the text is used advisedly, for page 123 speaks of "The usual unsavory accusations of UFO proponents of cover-up, conspiracy, intimidation, etc." Some of these ufologists make "shameless attempts" to exploit tragedies such as the Mantell accident (see page 96).

[88] *Case Closed*, p. 85.

[89] *Case Closed*, p. 81, notes that Air Force findings regarding the name and even existence of "Naomi Maria Selff" agreed with previous efforts of several "pro-UFO researchers." Selff was an Army nurse whom Roswell mortician Glenn Dennis claimed to have seen alien bodies that were being autopsied at the Roswell base hospital. When investigations failed to sustain the reality of this person, Dennis claimed that he had intentionally provided a false name. *Case Closed* devotes considerable effort to uncovering nurses from the forties and fifties who might possibly have figured in an altered memory scenario caused by the "fog of time."

[90] "Who's the Dummy": p. 7.

[91] *Case Closed*, p. 125.

[92] Broad, William J., "Air Force Details a New Theory in U.F.O. Case," *The New York Times*, 25 June 1997, at www.nytimes.com/1997/06/25/us/air-force-details-a-new-theory-in-ufo-case.html?sc...

[93] "Who's the Dummy": p. 7.

Chapter 16: The Swedish Military's UFO History

The very first indication that the Swedish military had an interest in unknown objects flying over Swedish territory came late in 1933 as an increased number of sightings of unidentified aircraft poured in from the North of the country. The reports often described what most likely were airplanes observed during conditions that made the observations difficult, but many of the sightings were of lights in the sky interpreted as searchlights mounted on an unknown aircraft.

One of the first reported sightings occurred in late November 1933 near Lake Fjosokken not far from the town of Sorsele. Just after sunset a lone observer could see what he thought was an aircraft land on the ice covered lake, before taking off and circling the lake for an hour, during which time it seemed to be directing a powerful searchlight towards the ice. But the newspaper story was slightly embellished, and after the witness was questioned by the local police the observation turned out less dramatic—a bright light had been moving near the horizon exactly where Venus was situated at the time.[1]

The publication of this observation triggered more newspapers to write about the subject that soon became known as the Ghost Flier, a name that was first used in late December.[2] Other names used for the unknown aircraft were "The Ghost Machine" and "The Flying X."

What is generally considered to be the first UFO wave over Sweden, and large parts of northern Norway and Finland as well, had its peak during the winter of 1933-1934. A lesser wave occurred in 1936-1937.

Local military authorities started to interview witnesses before the end of 1933. At first the Ghost Flier was thought to be smuggling liquor into Sweden and caught the attention of Swedish customs, which on December 30 sent a request for air support to the head of the Swedish Air Force, General Eric Virgin.[3]

Early January 1934 saw a new and powerful person entering the scene. General Pontus Reuterswärd, head of the armed forces in the North of Sweden and situated in Boden, in a letter to the county administration in Luleå, requested them to ask the Air Force for assistance. Conducting air surveillance was not an easy task since the areas over which the Ghost Flier had been reported were vast, covering more than one third of the Swedish territory. The nearest air force base was situated 600 kilometers from Boden and the aircraft were slow and ill equipped.

The county administrator, Mr. Bernhard Gärde, was initially reluctant to make a request to the Air Force for assistance, not knowing that the Air Force itself had started a surveillance mission on its own. In an interview Mr. Gärde described the reports as "vague and unreliable," an opinion he formed from interviews made by local police on his behalf.[4] Air Force commander Eric Virgin recognized that the air force did not have enough information to evaluate if the

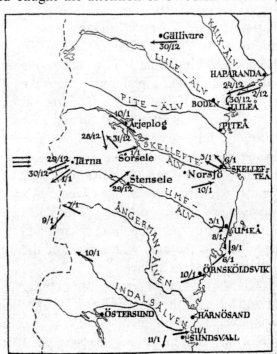

A map published in the newspaper Dagens Nyheter on January 12, 1934, showing reports of Ghost Flier activities.

Ghost Flier was a threat or not and wanted to wait before sending more air support to the North.[5] It was not until February 12 that the county administration requested air assistance from the government.[6]

During this first winter, sighting reports of actual aircraft or a body of a craft were scarce. Many reports consisted of bright lights or the sound of an engine heard from the sky, in some instances both. Venus and Sirius were prominent in the southern sky during the entire winter and continued to cause reports in the press and to the military. It is worth mentioning that more than fifty percent of the reports were made between 5 p.m. and 7 p.m., when Venus was low over the horizon.

That a foreign intruder would carry bright lights, or any other lights, on its aircraft was something that Air Force commander Eric Virgin ruled impossible: "It should be obvious for everyone that no pilot trying to intrude over populated areas would use a searchlight or carry its marker lights," said General Virgin in an interview. His opinion was later seconded by the former Swedish military attaché to London, Erland Mossberg, in another interview.[7]

The Ghost Flier reports of the first winter were used by several newspaper editors to campaign for a stronger defense and to place at least some aircraft in the north of Sweden. Many suspected that Russia was behind the intrusions, while others pointed to Germany.

The reports were not only coming from Sweden but from all parts of northern Scandinavia, and one newspaper pointed out that "The Ghost Flier is everywhere at the same time."[8] The sheer mass of reports made the Air Force suspect that they were dealing with some form of mass hysteria, which they also indicated in interviews. But after a report of a sighting of a Ghost Flier over one of Sweden's most sensitive and secret military installations, the fortress of Boden, on January 22, General Pontus Reutersvärd wrote a letter published in several newspapers that established as fact that the Ghost Flier had flown over restricted military areas.[9]

The day after General Reutersvärd's letter was published, the leader of the right wing party in the Swedish Parliament, MP Arvid Lindman, put a question to Prime Minister Per Albin Hansson, asking what kind of action the government was planning to take regarding the Ghost Flier.[10] The answer came some days later, on February 2, in front of a fully seated public gallery. The Prime Minister stated that while most reports were misidentifications or fantasy, others were unsolved. Air surveillance had been taking place since early January, and three more aircraft had been sent to the area where most of the sightings had taken place.[11]

Swedish military fighter pilot Gösta Svanlund at the wreckage of his Bristol Bulldog J7 near Pilgrimstad after returning from a chase for the Ghost Flier Feb. 24, 1934

On March 4, with reports still pouring in, the hunt for the Ghost Flier was cancelled. Even though 24 airplanes participated, no Swedish pilot was able to see the unknown aircraft. Soldiers on the ground did occasionally report sound from a motor or lights moving in the sky but, standing on hilltops, they could do nothing more than report their observations.[12]

One of the soldiers, interviewed in 1989, described the problems:

> Standing there it was easy to see all kind of things. It happened that soldiers were reporting the Big Dipper as something out of the ordinary. As a matter of fact this happened several times. But sometimes

we did hear sounds from an engine but we were never able to see the actual aircraft.[13]

When the hunt stopped in March, 96 reports had been filed by the Swedish military, but the total of sightings published in the newspapers was many times that figure. In Finland, the military had received 157 reports and in Norway 234; in total 487 reports were sent through official channels. The result of the investigation was a harsh statement: "There have never been any Ghost Fliers." The total cost for the Swedish hunt stopped at 12,667 kronor or about 51,000 USD in today's value.[14]

Not everyone agreed. General Pontus Reuterswärd published his own statement a couple of weeks later, summarizing the reports in a different way. According to the general, several reports during January had been of real but unidentified aircraft. "It could not be denied that a violation of our nation's air space has been going on," he said.[15] In his personal files, now at the Swedish War Archives in Stockholm, are several written reports from hearings with witnesses and summaries about the Ghost Flier made by his staff.[16] The general was met with heavy criticism from a member of the parliament and of the defense commission, MP Elof Lindberg, who accused the general of not being competent enough to draw such conclusions.[17]

In another twist, the Swedish military, through its Chief of Staff, published its final report on the Ghost Flier in early July 1935, more than a year after the wave had ceased. After concluding that 42 of the 487 reports investigated by the three countries were of actual aircraft violating the borders, the General Staff now admitted that the Ghost Flier was real. "It must be concluded that aircraft whose nationality has not been established have flown over Northern Scandinavia during the winter of 1933-1934," the report said.[18]

A close inspection of the press reports that were widely published, and the original investigations made by the military, shows that very few, if any, of the sightings were similar to modern UFO sightings. However, many of the reports show the same kind of misidentifications of known objects (i.e. Venus, Sirius) as today's observers make.

When the Ghost Flier, or at least reports of it, returned over Sweden, Norway, and Finland in the early winter months of 1936, the pattern was in many ways repeated: mostly lights in the sky mixed with some reports of aircraft. This time the sightings started to get more frequent. In late January 1937, a light was seen wandering near the horizon East of Umeå; a light brighter than a headlight was reported from a community near Dorotea; and a light similar to position lights on an aircraft flew over a village outside Stensele.[19]

The new sightings again prompted General Pontus Reuterswärd to write to the Minister of Defence, Ivar Vennerström, stating that the intruders were real and probably spies. New sightings near the Fortress of Boden on January 4 had made the situation even more acute, according to the general. Again, his remarks made the Ghost Flier a topic of discussion in the Swedish Parliament.[20]

General Reuterswärd's conclusions were again met with criticism from a member of the Parliament, this time from Social Democrat MP Elof Lindberg who demanded that a commission with civil experts, not military, should investigate the intrusions. MP Lindberg and others suspected that the military had embellished the reports for their own purpose, namely to direct more resources to the Northern regions and to the Air Force in general.[21]

But Elof Lindberg's demand for a new commission was rejected. An answer from the Minister of Defence made it clear that no new facts had surfaced and few new observations had been reported.[22]

During early 1937 it was obvious that the Swedish reports were used for German propaganda and appeared in several German newspapers controlled by information minister Joseph Goebbles. The printed articles pointed out that the aircraft over Sweden most likely were Russian.[23]

As the Ghost Flier slowly vanished from the Scandinavian skies, it did so as part enigma and part mass hysteria. Real or not, one direct result did come out of the chase and the agitated debate: in 1939, two years after General Pontus Reuterswärd demanded a stronger defense in the North, a new Air

Force base was being built in Luleå just 30 kilometers from Boden. The F21 AFB is still an important base more than 70 years after the last Ghost Flier left the Swedish skies.

The four files containing several thousand pages of investigations about the Ghost Rockets was found by Archives for UFO Research's Anders Liljegren at the Swedish War Archives in 1986. They were still classified but are now open to the public.

The Ghost Rockets

During six months in 1946, the first year of peace after the Second World War, Swedish skies again were the scene of unknown intruders. These Ghost Rockets, as they were called, were taken very seriously by the Swedish military, which formed a special and secret commission to chase them down. The story of the Ghost Rockets has been described in more detail in Chapter 2 of this book.

Even though the Ghost Rockets never were positively identified, the reports made the Swedish military aware of how vulnerable the country was to foreign aircraft and missiles. The name Ghost Rockets or Space Projectile, often used during the 1946 wave, was sometimes used by military investigators and the media in 1947 and 1948 to describe different unknown objects or lights in the sky. During 1948 and 1949, the Swedish military on several occasions tried to buy radar equipment from the U.S. manufacturer Bondis Corporation to address sightings of unknown missiles but was denied an export license by the State Department.[24]

The 1950s

During the 1950s the Swedish Defence staff not only collected but also investigated hundreds of alleged sightings of unidentified flying objects from all over Sweden. Extensive archives, now at the Defence Research Institute, show a dedicated staff making a great effort to solve the many reports.

"We did get reports from several sources—the general public, the local military organizations in different parts of Sweden, and from the central air control," says Per Sundh, who from October 1951 until October 1954 was head of a unit at the Defence Staff responsible for investigating reports about UFOs. During this time his department handled 6,000 reports, of which 400 were investigated and around 40 remained unexplained.[25]

A typical report came via telephone or mail. A first interview with the witness was conducted, after which a contact with a professor in astronomy at the Stockholm Observatory, Bertil Lindblad, was made to rule out misidentifications of astronomical objects. If the object was still unidentified, the staff called the local police to see if the witness was known to them and to get an

From October 1951 until October 1954, Per Sundh was the head of a unit at the Defence Staff that held responsibility for investigating reports about UFOs.

evaluation of the credibility of the witness. If the report remained interesting, experts at the Defence Research Institute could be used for a more thorough investigation.

Even though they never found any report that indicated a technology that could not be explained through misidentifications, hoaxes, foreign technology, or natural phenomena, Per Sundh says that he and his personnel always took even the weirdest observations seriously:

> We always tried to verify the reports, make a thorough interrogation and never had a superior attitude towards the witnesses. Even when we took the reports higher up in the hierarchy, no one laughed at the concept of aliens or flying saucers. There were always these five to ten percent that we never could explain.[26]

One of the observations that drew attention from the public during the 1950s was made by a Swedish airline pilot and former pilot in the Royal Air Force during the Second World War, Ulf Christiernsson, and his flight mechanic, Olle Johansson. On December 15, 1953, while en route in a Transair DC-3 from Bulltofta airport in Malmö to Bromma airport in Stockholm, they encountered an object that would soon make headlines—and not only in Sweden. The incident found its way to the CIA, which translated the newspaper reports for distribution in an eight-page-long memorandum.[27] The aircraft's proximity to the Baltic area and the object's possible likeness to a Russian weapon drew the attention of both the international news wires and the Agency.[28]

Captain Christiernsson told the military investigators and the press how he and Olle Johansson, while flying on autopilot, at 2:37 p.m. local time near Hässleholm, encountered "a completely unorthodox, metallic, symmetric, round object which was unlike anything I have seen before." For less than ten seconds, the men in the cockpit saw this unknown object closing in and passing, they later estimated, 600 meters under the aircraft, flying at an altitude of 2,150 meters.

The incident was taken seriously, and Commander in Chief General Bengt Nordenskjöld called in reports from all relevant Swedish radar stations in an attempt to identify the object. The military investigators made several interviews with both the pilots and other persons involved and even conducted their own reconstructions of the event. Per Sundh and his fellow investigators at the Defence Research Institute spent many hours recreating the circumstances during the observation, building a model with a balloon, and taking pictures from different angles.[29]

Even though the observation never received a definitive conclusion, the answer may have come from an owner of a local perfume company. In an interview less than a week after the incident, the owner confessed to having released 300 hydrogen filled balloons south of Hässleholm in an advertising campaign two hours before the object was observed from the aircraft.[30]

Documents from the files of the Swedish General Staff show that the Swedish military kept itself informed of the American Air Force's Project Blue Book and was influenced by the way the Americans made their investigations. During the late 1950s and early 1960s, copies of AFR 200-2, an Air Force Regulation from 1958 detailing how to deal with UFO reports, were sent to the Swedish Air Attaché in Washington, DC, as were several Blue Book press releases. The documents were forwarded to the General Staff's Foreign Division in Stockholm. Several underlinings and

General Bengt Nordenskjöld was the first Commander in Chief of the Swedish Air Force who was also a pilot.

notes on the documents show that they were treated with great interest.[31] Even though most Swedish investigators were skeptical about the reports having anything to do with alien technology, others privately were interested in that hypothesis. One of them was the Swedish Deputy Naval Attaché, Nils Dellgren, who during his time in Washington met with prominent UFOlogist Donald Keyhoe and also traveled to California to meet with contactee George Adamski at his home on the way to Mt Palomar.[32]

Although the Swedish investigators were aware of the word "UFO" and worked with "UFO reports," they never used that acronym but called the objects "sound- and light-phenomena" or "space phenomena." A special form with this heading was used to gather information from witnesses. A modified version of this form is still in use today.

The investigations were always taken seriously. "We spent the time we needed," says Per Sundh, and experts were contacted if the investigation so demanded.[33] But some reports were more sensitive than others. When in the early hours of December 5, 1951, His Royal Highness Prince Carl Bernadotte Jr. entered the headquarters of Stockholm Criminal Investigation Department (CID) together with a friend to report that they had just witnessed a "flying saucer," it created a stir amongst the police, who after interviewing the men sent their report to the Security Police who then informed the UFO investigators at the General Staff. The report was instantly classified, even though the object observed was nothing more than a bright light in the sky. According to the Prince and his friend, director Berl Gutenberg, the UFO had lit up the sky and caused the Prince, who was driving, to stop the car and open a door to listen for sounds. That the two men minutes earlier had been discussing flying saucers may have contributed to their reaction, since the observation most probably was of a bright fireball. "I met with the Prince and Mr. Gutenberg but did not find the report worth investigating," says Per Sundh. Very few investigations were classified during the 1950s, and those that were had been assessed as possible intrusions by foreign aircraft or missiles, a decision that was made by the head of General Staff or officers immediately under him. The Swedish military did not want intruders to know that they had been spotted.

If the UFO Desk suspected that a report had its source in another country, it was sent to the State Department, says Kurt Johansson, who worked at the desk in 1955–1956. Other reports turned out to be more mundane: "Sometimes we got flocks of migrating birds on radar that at first looked like aircraft, but after a while we learned to recognize them," Johansson states. "We did not know that before, so that was a novelty for us."[34]

According to Kurt Johansson, the Defence Staff investigators never tried to explain reports if they did not believe in the explanation themselves. "Of course we had the ambition to find out what kind of object an observer had seen, but I do not think that we gave any explanations that we couldn't stand for," he says. "We did realize that people saw things that we, with our resources, did not have the ability to identify."[35]

One of the most complicated and highly publicized reports that Swedish authorities investigated was made by two young men, Stig Rydberg, 30, and Hans Gustafsson, 24, who claimed to have met alien beings and had fought with them. Early on a Saturday morning on December 20, 1958, Rydberg and Gustafsson arrived back at their home in Helsingborg in the South of

UFO investigator Sven Schalin together with MD Ingeborg Kjellin and the two witnesses, Hans Gustafsson and Stig Rydberg, in a picture from January 7, 1959. This case was probably the first in the world where a UFO witness was put under hypnosis.

Sweden. They were obviously scared and told a story about coming upon a landed flying saucer in a clearing north of the city where they had to fight for their lives against several alien creatures trying to bring them onboard. The story soon reached the newspapers, and Stig Rydberg and Hans Gustafsson became nationwide celebrities. Their story interested the local CID and the Defence Staff in Stockholm who sent investigators to the site documenting the clearing and the traces said to have been left by the flying saucer. Criminal investigators interrogated the men and even put a hidden microphone in one of the interrogation rooms after leaving the two men to themselves. Early in January 1959, a medical doctor, Lars-Erik Essén, put the men under a kind of light hypnosis. This was probably the first time in history that hypnosis was used on a UFO witness. But the men managed to keep themselves awake and in full control, and fooled doctor Essén, who himself was a believer in alien visitations. The story was later shown to be a hoax.[36]

The very reason for the military's involvement was explained in a communiqué from the Defence Staff that referred to "the rapid technical development in aircraft and weaponry as the main cause for their interest in this spectacular case." They also wrote: "This could not entirely rule out the suspicion that it could have something to do with some kind of spacecraft, missile or something similar."[37]

Not surprisingly the Domsten case caught the interest of the first emerging UFO groups and their members in Sweden—and the groups caught the interest of the military. On the 19th of November 1959 the Danish chairman and founder of Syd-Jysk UFO Investigation (now Skandinavisk UFO Information, SUFOI), H. C. Petersen, talked in front of the members of the Stockholm based UFO group Ifologiska sällskapet. Mr. Olle Nord from the Defence Research Institute, FOA3, sat in the public meeting making notes. But Olle Nord, who worked with technical intelligence, did not find anything that merited a continuation of military interest into the groups and their activities.[38]

Members of the staff in Stockholm seldom left their offices to do on-site investigations. In most cases lower ranking officers from units in the area where the observation was made conducted the preliminary investigations and later reported to Stockholm. But the Domsten case was different and a military psychologist, MD Michael Wächter, met with the men and evaluated their psychological status. Even though the military suspected a hoax, it was not proven until 1989 when Clas Svahn and Anders Liljegren at Archives for UFO Research cracked the case.

The reports continued to reach the Defence Staff and its UFO desk, even though the conclusions echoed those of U.S. investigators. In an interview in August 1962, Colonel Bror von Vegesack stated that "in no instance has it been able to determine that the observer did see a real alien object." Colonel von Vegesack also estimated the amount of unknowns to be between 10 and 15 percent but stressed that most of them had not been able to undergo a thorough investigation since they were "too unspecific."[39]

The many years of analysis and investigations without finding any military significance in the reports led the Swedish General Staff to decide that some other body would be better equipped to handle UFO reports. On October 1, 1965, the General Staff transferred the responsibility for investigating UFO reports to the Defence Research Institute (Försvarets forskningsanstalt, FOA, now FOI) where it has remained. The official document states that the transfer had been decided since after nearly 20 years of systematic collection and processing of the reports, "no significant result of military value" had surfaced. FOA was ordered to continue to collect reports from the public, but as soon as an observation with possible military implications was reported, it should be sent to the Defence Staff. On the other hand, the Defence Staff should, "after screening," send observations that were reported from military units to FOA.[40]

Few of the observations in the files were sensitive enough to be stamped secret, but as late as December 2009 a file of previously unknown secret reports was found at FOI.[41] "Observations made by civilians were never filed as secret," says Bengt Hindsefeldt, who was in charge of the UFO reports at the Defence Staff from 1964–1966. "The few they considered secret were from military sources."[42]

But even such reports were seldom assessed as secret. A report had to meet at least one of three criteria to be filed away as secret: the contents could reveal positions or the technical performance of radar installations; they could expose a secret military exercise; or the content could affect the relationship with another country. A fourth condition could be added, even though it has seldom been used: the anonymity of the witness had to be protected, as in the case of Prince Bernadotte.

Ten years after the Defence Staff handed over the responsibility to FOA, the head of UFO investigations at FOA, Mr. Tage Eriksson, harshly summarized the situation in a report to the head of his section. During these ten years, 341 reported observations had reached his desk. But Tage Eriksson did not want to continue with this work, which took a lot of his time, and he wrote: "Nothing has emerged from the UFO reports, neither from a defense nor from a scientific point of view. For this reason there is no motivation that FOA should continue to deal with UFO reports." Tage Eriksson suggested that the task of receiving and investigating UFO reports should be transferred to the Defence Staff. His request was denied.[43]

Tage Eriksson took over the UFO files from the Defence Staff in 1965. He ran the UFO desk until 1976.

In April 1967, the acting Swedish Chief of Air Force, Lage Thunberg, made headlines when he said in an interview, "One should not laugh at things that you do not know anything about. Even I have chased a flying saucer once. It was in the 1940s, but I am sorry to say that we did not catch them. The saucers were too fast for us." Two years later he retracted the statement, when asked by UFO-Sweden, but the journalist still claims that the general really admitted to the chase during his interview.[44]

During the 1950s and 1960s Sweden did not have any nationwide UFO organization. Several smaller groups had emerged and all of them saw the military as their opponent. UFO-Sweden was formed in 1970 as the first nationwide organization. Through most of the early 1970s, the contacts between UFO-Sweden and the military UFO investigators were if not hostile at least not very cooperative. UFO-Sweden saw the military as a counterpart not willing to share information, and the military saw UFO-Sweden as an ET-proponent group not willing to discuss alternative explanations. In the early 1970s this situation started to change as UFO-Sweden, through its new chairman, Thorvald Berthelsen, began to make personal contacts with several high ranking officers. At one point Mr. Berthelsen and some other persons on the UFO-Sweden board could call military radar operators via a direct telephone number to get information regarding ongoing observations. This service ended in 1978 after Thorvald Berthelsen stepped down as chairman.

After Tage Eriksson left the UFO Desk at FOA in 1976, he was replaced by a fellow meteorologist, Sture Wickerts. Wickerts had been appointed to the Desk without his approval and, returning from a business trip, found himself with a job he did not want. In spite of this, Wickerts was to be one of FOA's most prominent UFO spokesmen. A typical year produced around 40 reports, most of them reported by the public through military sources and sent to FOA for investigation. The bulk of them were filed, some with follow up calls to astronomers or other experts.

During the mid-1980s a new approach was taken by UFO-Sweden to establish reliable contacts in the military services, especially through the Defence Research Institute. Visits to the FOA archives and personal contacts with Sture Wickerts created a new atmosphere, and Wickerts in 1988 decided to let

UFO-Sweden and Archives for UFO Research borrow and copy all of their UFO files. The files, thousands of reports, were returned after several weeks of copying and are now available at the Archives for UFO Research (AFU).

Wickerts was often depicted by Swedish UFOlogists as a front for a greater cover-up during his years at the UFO Desk. In reality, he had little interest in UFOs and put a minimum effort into the subject. Only once during his appointment as head of the UFO Desk (1976-1990) did he leave his office to investigate a report—he traveled to Målilla in Småland in October 1976 to supervise diving in a water-filled hole found in the woods, possibly connected to an observation of a light in the sky. Nothing was found but old logs.[45]

In October 1976 the head of the UFO desk at The Defence Research Institute, Sture Wickerts, conducted a search for an unknown object thought to have crashed in the woods near Målilla in the south of Sweden. Nothing was found.

Even though UFO reports seldom were classified on their own merits, it happened that through association with other events, they were hidden from the public. During a wave of reports indicating unknown submarines in Swedish waters during the 1980s and into the early 1990s, some observations of missile-shaped objects seen over land were put into the same secret files as indications of underwater activities since the military analysts thought the two phenomena had the same origin. Much of this material is still secret, which makes it impossible to know how many unidentified flying objects are hidden in these files.

Some UFO reports with military significance never turned up at the UFO Desk or in the FOA's open UFO files. According to the instructions from 1965, these kinds of observations were to be directed to other relevant departments within the military. In spite of this, some highly interesting observations did not find their way to the relevant investigators. One of these occurred on August 18, 1985, as four pilots flying in a Cessna in broad daylight encountered a small missile-shaped craft with delta-shaped wings north of Gävle. The pilots turned their aircraft and descended, trying to follow the unknown object, but could only see the "missile" follow a high-voltage power line, even as the line turned, before vanishing. After landing, the men contacted the Defence Staff but were advised to call the UFO Desk at FOA instead, in spite of the object looking very much like a cruise missile to all four. Much later one of the pilots mentioned the encounter to an officer at the regiment Ing 3 in Boden and was told to send a written report to the regional military staff, which he did nearly a year after the sighting. The local intelligence and security section concluded that "the report seems highly credible and should be investigated" and criticized the Defence Staff for not

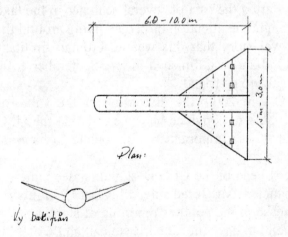

On August 18, 1985, four men, all with pilot licenses, met an unknown missile-like object while flying together in a Cessna 200 kilometers north of Stockholm. The object was never identified in spite of a long military investigation.

taking it seriously in the first place. After a year-long investigation at the Air Staff, the object, which left no trace on radar, was listed as an unknown and never identified.[46]

Reports like this never made paper trails at FOA. Had the chain of command worked, they should have been sent to the Defence Staff and their military intelligence and security services. During the years with Sture Wickerts, FOA primarily put reports in files.

In 1990 Sture Wickerts was replaced by a more enthusiastic and interested person, Arne Gjärdman, who held this position until 2000. During this period the number of reports sent to FOA dropped to 10-20 a year. Gjärdman and UFO-Sweden soon started to share information and ideas, and regular meetings between Gjärdman and the chairman of UFO-Sweden were held. This created an atmosphere of understanding and cooperation. In a 1994 letter to the Civil Department, Gjärdman wrote: "The activities of UFO-Sweden have been found to be a well functioning complement to FOA through their investigations of reports of unidentified flying objects. . . . FOA finds UFO-Sweden's work valuable."[47]

Arne Gjärdman, head of the Swedish military's UFO desk between 1990 and 2000. Here with some of the files of The Swedish Defence Research Institute.

Some reports never reached FOA at all. In an operation echoing the 1946 Ghost Rocket scare when objects crashed into lakes on several occasions, the Swedish military not only sent several search teams to a lake in the west of Sweden but also created a cover story to hide what they were doing.

On the 27th of July 1999, seven men and women witnessed the crash of an unknown object in a lake not far from the Norwegian border. The object was described as cigar shaped with wings and was seen in broad daylight and sunny weather from three different locations around Lake Backsjön not far from the small town of Arvika. On August 12, military divers started the first of several searches in the lake but could not find any trace of an object. The activities caught the attention of people living around the lake and the local media but were concealed by the cover story that this was an ordinary military exercise. The secret search was labeled Operation Sea Find and was finished in late September 1999 without any tangible trace of any craft going down in the lake to be found.[48]

In connection with Arne Gjärdman retiring from FOA in 2000, the discussion of the value of keeping this service at FOA started again. Gjärdman was able to convince his superiors that the UFO Desk was not a liability but an asset for FOA, and that it was important for the public to have an authority to call with their reports and questions.[49]

Karsten Jöred replaced Arne Gjärdman in 2000, the first head of the UFO Desk with a deep interest in astronomy, and also, like Gjärdman, a skilled mathematician. Mr. Jöred solved several UFO reports during his six years at the desk but also saw a slight decrease in the public's reporting of sightings. As did his predecessor, he stressed the importance for the public to have the authority to call and write: "It is important that people report their sightings, however strange the observation may seem to them," he later said in an interview.[50]

During recent years the cooperation between UFO-Sweden and the Swedish military, through the Defence and Research institute, has increased. Several new heads of the UFO Desk have continued the cooperation that started in the middle of the 1980s—space technology expert Sandra Lindström (2006-2009) and for just over a year from 2009 to early 2010 hydroacoustic expert Per Söderberg until he died suddenly from an illness in April 2010. The task is now handed over to yet another woman, Eva Bernhardsdotter, with experience from NASA and the Swedish Space Agency. In 2008, FOA, now renamed FOI, decided to share a database with UFO-Sweden to make all reports coming to FOI available to UFO-Sweden's Report central and their field investigators. This cooperation and sharing of information between a civilian UFO group and a military UFO Desk is unique.

The last twenty years have also seen a more open attitude from the military intelligence and security services toward UFO-Sweden. This has resulted in sharing radar data and expert help in some cases. During this time there has been a decrease in the public reports of UFOs to the military but UFO-Sweden still receives an average of one report per day from members of the public.

Notes

[1] *Norrbottens-Kuriren*, 12 and 13 December 1933; *Dagens Nyheter*, 13 December 1933.

[2] *Dagens Nyheter*, 28 December 1933.

[3] *Dagens Nyheter*, 2 January 1934.

[4] *Dagens Nyheter*, 11 January 1934; *Norrbottens-Kuriren*, 12 January 1934.

[5] *Stockholmstidningen*, 11 January 1934.

[6] *Dagens Nyheter*, 13 January 1934.

[7] *Norrbottens-Kuriren*, 12 January 1934; *Norrbottens Allehanda*, 15 January 1934.

[8] *Dagens Nyheter*, 26 January 1934.

[9] *Norrbottens-Kuriren*, 26 January 1934; The Swedish War Archives, Pontus Reuterswärd, volume III.

[10] *Norrbottens-Kuriren*, 27 and 29 January 1934.

[11] *Norrbottens-Kuriren*, 3 February 1934; *Dagens Nyheter*, 3 February 1934.

[12] *Norrbottens-Kuriren*, 5 March 1934; *Dagens Nyheter*, 4 March 1934; *Nationen [Norway]*, 3 November 1936; *Dagens Nyheter*, 23 September 1934.

[13] Sven Karlsson, interview made by the author (Clas Svahn), 18 December 1989.

[14] *Dagens Nyheter*, 4 March 1934; *Dagens Nyheter*, 23 September 1934.

[15] *Norrbottens-Kuriren*, 30 April 1934; *Dagens Nyheter*, 30 April 1934.

[16] The Swedish War Archives, Pontus Reuterswärd, volume III.

[17] *Norrbottens-Kuriren*, 9 May 1934.

[18] *Dagens Nyheter*, 9 July 1935.

[19] *Dagens Nyheter*, 30 January, 3 and 6 February 1937.

[20] *Aftonbladet*, 12 February 1937.

[21] *Piteå-Tidningen*, 15 February 1937.

[22] *Dagens Nyheter*, 19 May 1937.

[23] *Dagens Nyheter*, 18 February 1937.

[24] Air Intelligence Information Report numbers IR pp. 115-48 and pp. 47-49.

[25] Per Sundh, interview made by the author, 24 April 1990; "Kanske ett tefat?" *Industria* No. 10, 1954.

[26] Per Sundh, interview made by the author, 24 April 1990.

[27] CIA Information from foreign documents or radio broadcasts Report No: 00-W-29745.

[28] The New York Post (18 December 1953) carried the UPI story "Swedes report 'Flying Saucer' near Reds' secret Baltic bases," but many other newspapers covered the story as well.

[29] *Expressen*, 3 February 1954; personal interview with Per Sundh, 24 April 1990.

[30] *Dagens Nyheter*, 20 December 1953.

[31] Letters from the Swedish Air Attaché in Washington DC, 21 July 1959, 11 August 1960, and others.

[32] Nils Dellgren, interview made by the author on 1 December 2009.

[33] Per Sundh, personal interview, 24 April 1990.

[34] Kurt Johansson, personal interview with the author, 27 November 1990.

[35] Kurt Johansson, personal interview with the author, 27 November 1990.

[36] "Domstensfallet—En svensk närkontakt 1958" by Clas Svahn and Anders Liljegren, Archives for UFO Research 1989, ISBN 91-7970-577-4.

[37] *Teknikens Värld*, March 1959.

[38] Olle Nord, interview made by the author on the 27th and the 28th April 1990 and 5th July 1992; Olle Nord's notes and his reports to Lennart Bunke, 20 November 1959.

[39] *Året Runt* No. 34, 22 August 1962.

[40] Fst/Sekt IV, 27/9 1965 nr 8101.

[41] FOI to the author, private communication, 2 December 2009.

[42] Bengt Hindsefeldt, personal interview by the author, 29 June 1987.

[43] Tage Eriksson Inst 3 to C FOA2, 14 April 1975.

[44] *Göteborgs-Tidningen* 12 April 1967; letter from Carl-Axel Jonzon to Lage Thunborg 29 April 1969 and his answer some days later; letter from the author to Lage Thunberg and his answer 2 July 1986; interview with Monica Frime 11 February 1987.

[45] "Ny Målillagrop förbyllar FOA," *Göteborgs-Posten*, 29 October 1976.

[46] A former secret document held by Milo ÖN 25 May 1986, Und/säk H 810:338; interviews with the four pilots made by the author in 1995; interview with Gunno Gunnvall, the former head for radar analysis at MUST, the military intelligence and security services, 12 November 1999.

[47] Arne Gjärdman to Civildepartementet, FOA 94-3837/S, 27 July 1994.

[48] "Genomförande av Operation Sjöfynd", mellersta mlitärområdet, Rapport 1999-10-01 10390; interviews by the author; "Cigar-Shaped UFO at Lake Backsjön, Sweden, July 27 1999," *International UFO Reporter*, Fall 2000: 16-18.

[49] Arne Gjärdman, personal interview with the author, 10 May 2000.

[50] "Det händer mer än jag trodde," *UFO-Aktuellt* No 2, 2006: 26.

Chapter 17: The Australian Military and the Official Government Response

The year 1969 was a watershed year for official UFO investigations because the most prominent official investigation—the USAF's Project Blue Book—was terminated in the wake of the Condon Committee report. With the U.S. investigation officially and publicly at an end, countries around the world also conducting investigations were at a turning point.

The Australian military had conducted an investigation on a smaller scale almost as long as the USAF, but rather than leap at the opportunity of Blue Book's termination and end their involvement with the UFO problem, they instead continued throughout the 1970s and into the 1980s. In 1984 the Royal Australian Air Force (RAAF) substantially shifted focus, stating they would only investigate cases that "suggest a defence or national security implication." It was an inevitable outgrowth of a slow decline in the determination of the RAAF to engage the UFO problem, while at least giving the appearance of being a serious "official governmental examiner" of UFO reports. Still, they were not officially out of the UFO business. That "swan song" came in 1993 when official RAAF policy finally determined that the RAAF would no longer accept reports or investigate UFOs.

Why did the RAAF Stick with UFO Investigations after 1969?

Why was the Australian response far different from that of the United States? A portion of the answer was in "the ties that bind," namely Australia's relationship with its major defense partners—the United States and the United Kingdom. While Australia routinely followed the lead from the much larger scale UFO investigations of the U.S. Air Force, the government also took stock of the approach of the UK. Despite the releases from the UK Ministry of Defence (MOD) UFO files in recent years, this sort of openness on the part of the UK MOD is only a recent development. Through the 1970s and 1980s, the UK's position was defined by secrecy and an unwillingness to take their general population into their confidences.

The Australian response was more of a middle ground. Part of the answer for the longer duration of the Australian official dance with the UFO controversy involved specific local circumstances, not the least being a major UFO wave playing out in the country during 1969. The rest of the answer was an internal "UFO war" taking place within the secret world of military intelligence, pushed along by a scientist with long and deep connections with the issue. That such events took place at a time when the defense and intelligence communities were undergoing extensive reviews and reorganizations was also significant and not without consequences. The UFO problem would remain an issue that would surface regularly, and the RAAF would continue its reluctant embrace.

A 1969 RAAF UFO Review Document

A framing document at this critical juncture came in the form of a review of official Australian UFO policy undertaken by RAAF officer Flight Lieutenant K. Jordan. The document drew together an inside picture of how the Directorate of Air Force Intelligence (DAFI) participated in the official UFO scene. Flt. Lt. Jordan's review of "UFO Investigation in the RAAF"[1] highlighted that:

...research into this subject has come up with some unrewarding answers, firstly the enquiry can not go back any further than the 11th November 1953. The cause of this blockage is the loss of Part 1 of file 114/1/197 (ex SEC CD2/2) in the move of the Department from Melbourne to Canberra. Two searches through records and the archives have failed to trace this file. One search was carried out in March 1966 and the other on 15th and 16th July 1969. As the first UFO report was received in America in July 1947, there would be up to six years of correspondence dealing with UFOs unaccounted for. A further hinderance [sic] was the reference to four different files dealing with UFO policy, however after rationalization of the files in 1966 there is now only one current file on this subject (554/1/30).

The July 1969 search facilitated Flt. Lt. Jordan's undated review document, which appeared in the latter part of 1969. The document divided policy considerations into three sections—Australian government policy, RAAF investigation policy, and overseas observations. The review also included a special section focusing on an investigation carried out by Mr. O. H. Turner in 1954. Flt. Lt. Jordan's review was cursory and brief. It captured the basic directions of the RAAF's UFO investigations. He stated, "the first recorded statement by [a] Government minister was by the Minister for External Affairs (Richard Casey, via a copy of a letter to the press dated January 28, 1954). The statement suggests a connection between UFO sightings and periods of intense meteorite activity."

Lord Richard Casey

The Devil in the Detail

Flight Lt. Jordan's statement was not correct. Casey, the Minister for External Affairs and the Minister for the CSIRO (the Commonwealth Scientific and Industrial Research Organisation—the government's premier scientific establishment), had made a statement back in May 1952, suggesting the "saucers" were one of three things—products of the imagination, meteors, or sunlight glinting off planes at high altitude. But Casey's views would change. He developed something of an obsession with "flying saucers" using his ambassadors to brief him on developments in other countries. He also used CSIRO scientists to give him assessments of key information, even getting one of them to review Donald Keyhoe's book *Flying Saucers from Outer Space* soon after it had appeared.

More clandestinely, Casey used his powerful intelligence connections, particularly Alfred Brookes, the head of the foreign intelligence service ASIS (Australian Secret Intelligence Service), to secure intelligence on the subject. Casey's man in Rome, Paul McGuire, even secured diplomatic intelligence from the American ambassador, Clare Boothe Luce, and her Air Attaché, Major General Emmett Cassady. McGuire attributed to Cassady the following information:

> The (Italian) sightings (of 1954) are constantly increasing and are up to 50 "unexplaineds" a week. The reports are now sufficiently consistent to establish the prime type as cigar or clipped-cigar shaped, about 70 metres long. They are recorded by various instruments, sufficiently to establish a physical object: i.e. to remove the assumption that they are all effects of atmospheric disturbances, or such. He says that two senior Air Generals of the U.S. Forces have met a saucer in flight. Mrs. Luce mentioned a third General. She says that her brother-in-law saw one closely while walking in New England, and "he hasn't been the same man since"; though he refuses to talk for publication.[2]

Emboldened somewhat by the McGuire communication, Casey wrote to his Chief of the Division of

Radiophysics CSIRO in Sydney, Dr. E. G. Bowen, on November 15, 1954, enclosing "a can of worms." Casey revealed:

> I am sending you copy of a small book...You'll probably have a fit when you see it. It is called "Flying Saucers from Outer Space." The cover is enough to put anyone off. It was given to me—
> and I had the greatest reluctance even to start it, but I found that I became strangely interested in it. Maybe you would have the same experience. One naturally regards the title with every skepticism—if not something stronger.
>
> I have seen one or two official U.S. Air Force statements about "Unexplained Air Objects," which are always carefully worded and are at pains to explain that the greater part of the "sightings" are explainable as natural phenomena or on some other grounds. But the inference is that there is a percentage that are not so explainable. It is with this small minority of these things that this fellow Keyhoe deals in this book...It appears to be honestly written (although rather journalistically)—and he quotes a number of Pentagon people by name—not that they endorse his theory, but they never wipe it or indeed even discount the possibility of it.
>
> Anyhow, I think you will not be as nauseated when you read the book, as you will undoubtedly be from the look of the cover. And when you have read it—if you can bring yourself to do so—I'd be interested to know your reaction.[3]

The letter was marked "PERSONAL," but of course it was from Casey, Dr. Bowen's Federal minister and political master. A reply would eventually come, which may have been a turning point in Casey's descent into the flying saucer controversy.

Dr. E. G. Bowen replied to Casey's letter:

> Mr. Dear Minister, I found the book by Major Keyhoe intensely amusing and entertaining...I must say, however, that I am far from convinced by any of the anecdotes or arguments.[4]

Bowen cited inadequate evidence and Keyhoe's intent to trap the U.S. Air Force into "saying something they obviously were not going to say." He then highlighted "a whole range of atmospheric reflection phenomena in which it is possible to see mock suns, sun dogs etc.," as well as "radar reflections from meteors" (of which he said, "These are real visitors from outer space and there is no mystery about what they consist of or how they behave"), and "a large number of radar-echo phenomena which can arise from refraction or reflection of radio waves in the atmosphere."

Bowen then launched into a negative analysis of Keyhoe's book, indicating that all the radar sightings were quite unconvincing, and so too the visual sightings. However he did surrender one point: "One thing which I most decidedly cannot understand is simultaneous visual and radar sightings of high speed objects in the lower atmosphere." Bowen wrote:

> I know many of the scientists concerned with defence matters in the United States and know that they completely discount the suggestions made in Keyhoe's book. I also know several of the Canadians, but I do not know W. B. Smith. His ideas on rotating magnets are wild in the extreme and I suspect from his other answers that he is either being misreported or is a rather irresponsible member of the scientific community.[5]

He agreed "that the Air Force have not behaved particularly well on this question," especially on the question of hiding explanations, such as the involvement of Skyhook balloons in the death of Captain Mantell back in 1948. Mantell was involved in an attempted intercept of a flying saucer, which Bowen believed was caused by the classified Skyhook program. Dr. Bowen concluded:

The whole thing can be put down to hysteria and mass suggestion. People certainly see phenomena which they cannot explain. In the old days they put it down to witches and sorcerers; now it has simply changed to saucers from outer space. In this respect books like that of Keyhoe will, of course, do a great deal of good. Like people who used to predict the end of the earth, they build up suspense, made out, as he does, that 1954 is the fateful year—and then nothing happens. The public gradually becomes disillusioned and forgets the whole thing. This, I think, is what will happen in the present case. There will, no doubt, be saucer scares in other parts of the world but I doubt whether we will hear much more about them from the U.S.A.[6]

Well, he certainly got that one wrong.

This myopic response had an effect on Richard Casey. He responded, "Both my wife and I have read your letter with the greatest interest. It puts Keyhoe's theories into proper perspective—and I can well believe that your reaction to it is the right one—although it removes a rather romantic conception that had intrigued both my wife and myself."

Dr. Bowen's November 1954 letter was wrong on a number of accounts, but more through a lack of knowledge of what was going on around him, even in his own country. In late August 1954 a spectacular radar-visual aircraft encounter occurred near Goulburn, New South Wales. It leaked out in a sensational way in December 1954 and created widespread media publicity. Meanwhile another physicist, Harry Turner, secretly assessed the DAFI UFO files. He, too, considered Donald Keyhoe's book *Flying Saucers from Outer Space* but came to very different conclusions. We will return to Turner's assessments in a moment.

The RAAF's Minister Buckets UFOs

The RAAF's own direct minister, the Minister for Air, William McMahon (a future Australian Prime Minister), had also made a statement prior to the 1954 Casey comments highlighted by Flt. Lt. Jordan. McMahon stated facetiously in parliament on August 14, 1952, that the "flying saucer" reports were "probably based on flights of imagination," but indicated he would "cause a thorough investigation to be made."[7] One day later Flight Lieutenant William H. Scott, the chief test pilot for the Government Aircraft Factories, a person not given to "flights of imagination," had his own encounter while flying in a Vampire aircraft between 35,000 and 36,000 feet near Rockhampton, Queensland. He observed something he could not explain. Looking east, towards the coast, Scott saw a large circular light at a lower elevation, which could not be estimated due to bad ground haze. The light was the color of an ordinary incandescent light globe. After approximately one minute, a number of small lights (six to ten) appeared to come from the main light. The smaller lights appeared to surround the bright light for about two

William McMahon

minutes before disappearing. After a further two minutes, the big light also disappeared. That report did not become public knowledge. It might have been embarrassing for the Minister if it had. The report remained classified until found in Department of Civil Aviation UFO files and examined at the offices of the Bureau of Air Safety Investigations during November 1982.[8]

It was not until November 20, 1953, that the Minister of Air, William McMahon, conveyed a more considered response to parliament, saying:

I still think that the problem is one more for psychologists than for defence authorities. The Royal Australian Air Force has received many reports about flying saucers, as have the Royal Air Force and the Royal Canadian Air Force, but the phenomena have not yet been identified...The Royal Australian Air Force has informed me that, so far, the aerodynamic problems relating to the production of flying saucers have not been solved. It is possible to produce a flying saucer aircraft and to fly it in a circular manner by means of ram jet engines. Aircraft of that type may be developed in the future, but I do not think there is any immediate need for them.[9]

To facilitate minister McMahon's parliamentary response, a November 20, 1953, "Note of Action" indicated that "...all reports are still being investigated closely and recorded as an aid to further research into future reports of this nature." In reality the RAAF were conducting a more ad hoc response and resisted investigating all sighting reports.[10]

Such material did not appear in Flt. Lt. Jordan's 1969 review. It is surprising that the Jordan review did not list these ministerial position statements, as it was often these statements to parliament which drove the development of RAAF DAFI policy on UFOs.

Early Efforts

Although there are many omissions in the Jordan review, it is best to use its initial references to the earliest files as a starting point. Part 1 of file 114/1/197 was seemingly the earliest DAFI UFO file and was closely tied to the controversial 1953 Drury film affair. The DAFI file registry reveals that the original 114/1/197 file was opened on October 30, 1953, with the title "Photographs of Unexplained Aerial Object over New Guinea forwarded by Mr. T. C. Drury." As revealed by Flt. Lt. Jordan's 1969 review document, this file was "lost" for many years despite searches for it in 1966, 1969, and 1982-84. The title of this file series soon became "Reports on Flying Saucers and other Aerial Objects."[11] For much of its involvement, the RAAF Directorate of Air Force Intelligence UFO files evolved into three types of file series, namely sightings, enquiry, and policy files. There was, however, a rather ad hoc adherence to these file distinctions. Following the paper trail became a convoluted art form requiring patience and determination.

The Federal Government Air Board issued, on January 16, 1951, a standard pro forma to cover the collection of flying saucer/UFO data by all RAAF units. The form "Report on Aerial Object Observed" was revised in January 1952, and November 1953. The January 1951 communication from the Chief of Air Staff to HQs Southern Area; Eastern Area; North Eastern Area; North Western Area and Western Area, indicated:

A number of reports have been made by Areas regarding unusual sightings which have been brought to the notice of various authorities. In order to standardise the reports made about these occurrences, the attached pro-forma has been drafted. ...It would obviously be unwise to draw any publicity towards Service interest in these reports, and persons making the reports should be asked to treat Service interest as Confidential.[12]

At least one other Government agency, the Department of Civil Aviation (DCA), was active in the collection and collation of reports during the early 1950s. It appeared the DCA wanted to establish a special bureau to gather information about flying saucers. Part of the reason for this was because civilian pilots were prominent in reporting UFO sightings, such as Australian National Airways (ANA) pilot Captain Bob Jackson and the crew of another ANA aircraft near Mackay.

The Jackson sighting was one of the more striking Australian cases from this early period. ANA pilot Captain Bob Jackson was flying near Sydney, New South Wales. He delayed revealing his experience during that flight for fear of ridicule, and only did so after other experienced pilots described their own encounters. He stated:

> I was flying towards Mascot, near Worinora Dam, about 11 p.m., when suddenly I saw a flash of light. I watched the thing with an orange coloured light at the tail flash past toward the coast, near Wollongong. Naturally the first thing I did was call Mascot control to ask if any other planes were in the vicinity. They replied that their radar proved negative. About two minutes later the thing appeared again. It made a complete circle around us and vanished again towards the coast at a terrific speed. I can't explain it. All I know is it was nerve wracking. I mentioned to control that if their radar failed to pick up an object—and it was a definite object—then it must be a flying saucer. They laughed, so I've kept quiet about it.[13]

The "Mackay Incident" of May 10, 1953, involved not only the crew of an ANA DC-3 aircraft but also Mackay airport personnel. At 6:08 p.m. on May 10, Captain B. L. Jones was piloting an ANA DC-3 airliner just south of Mackay. He radioed the local DCA control tower that a "strange object like a lighted glass dome" was maneuvering around his plane. Captain Jones said that he and his co-pilot observed the object for about five minutes during which time it had climbed and dived, yet not erratically. The object's speed varied between 200 mph and 700 mph during the sighting. No vapor trails or sparks were observed. Finally the object crossed the path of the aircraft and disappeared travelling fast towards the

Boeing DC-3

west.[14] A previously classified RAAF document describes the UFO as a "light like [a] star," first seen in the east, which then circled north, west, and south, before disappearing above the plane. The formerly "Secret" 1954 Report categorized the observation as being a "U.F.O." It added:

> The description given by Captain Jones is indicative of a U.F.O. Anticipatory vectoring on an internal light reflection may possibly have produced the circling movement, but it would not give the impression of flashing overhead. In any case, a pilot is well aware of illusions produced by light reflections and there was ample time to check various possibilities as to the origin of the light.[15]

The control tower at Mackay Airport confirmed that there were no other aircraft in the vicinity. Mr. W. Overell, the officer in charge at the tower, said he saw the light apparently climbing from about 4,000 or 5,000 feet in the west, at a terrific rate, until it vanished. Captain Jones, who still had the light under sight at that point, said that it crossed his path again, near Freshwater Point southeast of Mackay.

When Dr. Shaw of the DCA visited Captain Jones in Brisbane, he obtained an official report of the Mackay incident. Other DCA officials in Brisbane confirmed that they knew of no other aircraft that might have been in the Mackay area at the time of Captain Jones' eventful flight. Frank Hines, a radio operator, saw a similar light at 3 o'clock in the morning following Captain Jones' observation. It was first sighted over the sea. When Mr. Hines switched off the lights of the radio room in order to see better, the light shot straight upwards at terrific speed and vanished.[16]

It was reasonable to expect the DCA to get involved in the Australian UFO mystery, but it soon became apparent that the Australian government wanted to centralize the official investigations and viewed the incident as in the domain of national security. Ultimately the DCA's investigations were supplanted by the RAAF's involvement. The period from 1952 to 1954 was the high point for the DCA. It would continue in a limited way into the 1960s.

The 1954 Secret Turner UFO Study

A secret study by the DAFI provided the most coherent picture of the early period of RAAF/DAFI investigations from 1950 to 1954. The DAFI asked Melbourne University professor O. H. (Harry) Turner to undertake a classified "scientific appreciation" of the official reports held in files. In his detailed report, Turner recommended greater official interest and specific interest in radar-visual reports. His most profound conclusion was: "The evidence presented by the reports held by RAAF tend to support the...conclusion...that certain strange aircraft have been observed to behave in a manner suggestive of extra-terrestrial origin."[17]

In studying the RAAF/DAFI UFO files, Turner also utilized retired Marine Corps Major Donald Keyhoe's USAF reports described in his best-selling book *Flying Saucers from Outer Space*, and suggested the RAAF seek official USAF confirmation of the legitimacy of Keyhoe's data. Turner said of Keyhoe's USAF data that "if one assumes these Intelligence Reports are authentic, then the evidence presented is such that it is difficult to assume any interpretation other than that UFOs are being observed."

The disposition of Harry Turner's controversial report is a revealing indictment of the official handling of the UFO controversy. Faced with his provocative conclusions and Keyhoe's data as one cornerstone, the Director of Air Force Intelligence (RAAF) did seek out official confirmation from America. The Australian Joint Service Staff (intelligence) in Washington wrote to him saying:

> I have discussed with the USAF the status of Major Keyhoe. I understand that his book is written in such a way as to convey the impression that his statements are based on official documents, and there is some suggestion that he has made improper use of information to which he had access while he was serving with the Marine Corps. He has, however, no official status whatsoever and a dim view is taken officially of both him and his works.[18]

After considering Turner's classified report, the Department of Air concluded: "Professor Turner accepted Keyhoe's book as authentic and based on official releases. Because Turner places so much weight on Keyhoe's work, he emphasized the need to check Keyhoe's reliability. [The Australian Joint Service Staff communication] removes Keyhoe's works as a prop for Turner's work so that the value of the latter's findings and recommendations is very much reduced." In the light of the discrediting of Keyhoe's data, Turner's findings, including one in which he recommended the setting up of a scientific investigating panel, were found to be impractical and not justified.[19]

The main problem with the Department of Air's conclusion was that it was based on an act of either conscious or unconscious misrepresentation on the part of the U.S. Air Force. They were engaged in a campaign to undermine the popularity of Donald Keyhoe's books. While Keyhoe may have slightly overstated his USAF data, the intelligence reports quoted by Keyhoe and used by Turner to support his conclusions to DAFI were authentic. Eventually the USAF admitted that the material Keyhoe used was indeed from official Air Force reports. Political myopia, from both the U.S. and Australian military, effectively scuttled Australia's first serious flirtation with the scientific investigation of UFOs.

The Sea Fury Encounter

One of the most controversial radar-visual reports of the fifties occurred on August 31, 1954. The story leaked out in December 1954, and made front page headlines. The official Navy file on the event remained classified until the Directorate of Naval Intelligence released a copy in 1982.[20] During his 1973 visit to Australia, Dr. Hynek was able to interview the pilot involved in this famous incident, which became known as the "Sea Fury" encounter.

Lieutenant J. A. O'Farrell was returning to Royal Australian Navy Air Station Nowra in a Sea Fury aircraft. After contacting Nowra at about 1910 hours, O'Farrell saw a very bright light closing fast at one o'clock. It crossed in front of his aircraft and took up position on his left side, where it appeared to orbit. A second and similar light was observed at nine o'clock. It passed about a mile in from of the Sea Fury and then turned in the position where the first light was observed. According to O'Farrell, the apparent crossing speeds of the lights were the fastest he had ever encountered. He had been flying at 220 knots. O'Farrell contacted Nowra, which in turn confirmed that they had two radar "paints" in

Lieutenant J.A. O'Farrell

company with him. The radar operator, Petty Officer Keith Jessop, confirmed the presence of two objects near the Sea Fury on the G.C.I. remote display. The two lights reformed at nine o'clock and then disappeared on a north easterly heading. O'Farrell could only make out "a vague shape with the white light situated centrally on top." The Directorate of Naval Intelligence wrote that O'Farrell was "an entirely credible witness" and that he "was visibly shaken by his experience, and remains adamant that he saw these objects." The unidentified technology generated serious concern since the Sea Fury aircraft was one of the fastest planes in Australian skies in 1954, and the unidentified flying objects (UFOs) made the Sea Fury look as though it was standing still.[21]

The JIB Gambit

The UFO subject was laden with problems that went far beyond the ambit of intelligence. The RAAF Directorate of Air Force Intelligence attempted to divest itself of the UFO problem, despite Harry Turner's secret "scientific appreciation" report. When Group Captain A. D. Henderson, the Director of Air Force Intelligence, learned that the JIB (Joint Intelligence Bureau) had a scientific intelligence division, he wrote to JIB director Harry King. In a letter dated April 1, 1957, Henderson indicated that "[DAFI] ... frequently receives reports direct from civilians, or passed on by other departments, of unidentified flying objects. We also receive requests for assistance and advice from various Flying Saucer Research societies." He further elaborated, "Many of these reports presumably cover such mundane things as meteorological and astronomical phenomena," and in an interesting internal admission Henderson added, "Others appear to be inexplicable." He lamented:

> Most of them are outside the aeronautical field. As your branch has now established a scientific Intelligence Section, it would appear that these reports could best be investigated and evaluated by one of your Scientific Research officers, who will have a broader background of knowledge of this type of phenomena than anyone in this Directorate. If you agree that you can accept this commitment, I will be glad to make available all the papers which we have acquired, to date, on this subject.[22]

Harry Turner, who would later become a JIB scientist and their liaison man with DAFI, told Bill Chalker that JIB rejected the RAAF overture. The clandestine side of JIB did not want "a bar of it," as they believed they would then be caught up in a complex conjectural matter, which might drag them into the limelight—the last thing an intelligence organization would want. The reality was that JIB's resources were very limited. Harry King appointed Bob Mathams as the first Australian scientific intelligence analyst in May 1955. His initial tenure ended in mid-1957. In October 1958, he rejoined

JIB as the first head of their Scientific Intelligence Branch. In 1982, Bob Mathams recounted in correspondence with Chalker that his Directorate of Scientific and Technical Intelligence (DSTI)

> ...had only a marginal interest in UFOs; our analytical resources were limited and I had to take the position that we could not afford to become too involved in investigation of UFO sightings until we had reasonable grounds for believing that they were of foreign—as opposed to alien—origin. We relied on DAFI to make the initial investigations and, at times, assisted in the interpretation of the resulting data.

He also recalled that his:

> ...interest (as DSTI) in UFO sightings was aroused only when there was sufficient evidence to suggest that they may have been connected with or caused by foreign scientific or technological developments. There were only one or two that fitted that category. We never really decided who would take responsibility for further investigation if it were shown, convincingly, that a UFO sighting in Australia was of extra-terrestrial origin. [23]

This perspective was the primary template JIB applied to the UFO material it decided to evaluate. Generally there had to be an aspect that suggested the possibility of a foreign earthly power, such as the Russians. This attitude comprised JIB's flirtations with the UFO subject until Harry Turner re-entered the picture.

Big Science & Someone Else's

Ivan Southall, a popular writer and former RAAF pilot during World War Two, was given special access to the restricted Woomera rocket testing site. His book *Woomera* appeared in 1962. UFOs got a mention, and Southall indicated he had an indirect personal experience with UFOs during the war.

> Members of my air crew, from different gun turrets and the astro-dome, observed several dozen unidentified lights over the Bay of Biscay on the night of 10th-11th August 1944, and kept them under observation for 40 minutes. Our aircraft, Sunderland P/461, was the only machine of Allied or Axis origin in the area, though I did not know it at the time. As pilot, on a strict patrol, and frankly not anxious to make contact with so numerous a force, I saw nothing. I was facing in the wrong direction. [24]

Ivan Southall's reference to flying saucers at Woomera is startlingly at odds with the reality of the secret record of UFOs events that took place there in 1954. He wrote in 1962:

> Woomera, perhaps better fitted than any other place on earth to observe and track these mysterious manifestations, cannot produce a single item of documentary or photographic evidence to prove that they are real or unreal. [Chief Defence scientist William] Butement says: "Flying saucers representing something extraterrestrial are extremely unlikely. I think we have to look to the earth for the answers." J. D. [the Principal Officer, Ranges Group], too, points out that Woomera has been in a unique position to secure the evidence during the period of maximum sightings, but has failed to do so, and not from any desire to turn a blind eye. The flying saucer theory has its adherents in Woomera and any one of them would have given a month's pay to prove it. Among the operators there are a few who have observed puzzling phenomena, but none can state dogmatically, "this was a flying saucer or this was not." [25]

Defence Scientist Harry Turner advocated attempts to secure more radar cases. Radar at the restricted Woomera rocket range facility in South Australia picked up a UFO on May 5, 1954. Turner's report indicated that at about 1630 hours three witnesses saw a misty grey disc at a 355 degree bearing, at some 35 miles distance and at an altitude of more than 60,000 feet. The object appeared to have an apparent diameter of about ten feet. The visual observation, which lasted five minutes, was aided by binoculars. The object travelled south then west. The radar echo confirmed a speed of 3,600 mph! Turner later revealed details of the case which impressed him the most while studying the DAFI UFO files that led to his classified 1954 report. The case, originally classified Secret, describes the UFO event over Woomera as witnessed by an English Electric (EE) scientist and a radar operator. The EE scientist was outside talking to the radar operator when the radar confirmed the presence of a UFO. The scientist watched the object with binoculars. Since one of the scientist's functions at Woomera was to monitor rocket tests, he was experienced in observing movement in the sky. The UFO was moving in formation with a Canberra bomber whose crew could not see the UFO. Both the plane and the UFO were confirmed on radar. This allowed confirmation of the UFO's distance and size. The radar tracked the UFO until it went out of range.[26]

Skylark rocket launch from Woomera in 1957

The official case file has now become available and supplies the supporting evidence:

> 5 May 1954 Woomera SA app 1630hrs 5 mins 3 wits
> Three relevant documents were found, being statements by the two men involved and a covering letter forwarding the statements, from the Superintendent Long Range Weapons Establishment Range, Woomera, to the "Chief Superintendent." This letter included the statement: *"The persons reporting were separated by a distance of approximately three hundred yards and give corroborative accounts of what each observed."* [27]

One statement, dated 6 May 1954, read:

> Post "R"
> RE: UNIDENTIFIED TARGET OBSERVED ON RADAR 5TH MAY, 1954
>
> Sir,
> At about 1600 on 5th May, an unidentified Target was observed on radar AA Number 4 Mk. 6.
> The target appeared on High Beam at a range of about 60,000 yards Brg 355 degrees approaching 'R', described a Hyperbols [sic] over 'R' and went out at a bearing of approx. 90 degrees. On its way out it passed behind Spotting Tower, S2." I timed it over 15,000 yards 10 seconds which would make its speed approximately 3600 M.P.H. Cfn. KEANE observed this occurrence with me. Since the target was followed to 70,000 yards on High Beam the height would be greater than 60,000 feet. See Diagram on next page.

The diagram referred to was not located in the examined file.[28] A statement, dated 7 May 1954, from Vickers-Armstrong, read:

> REPORT ON A FLYING OBJECT SIGHTED ON 5TH MAY, 1954
>
> I was at Range R1 (Post R1), the Radar Post, standing by the Security Officer's Hut, and looking towards the radar Post at approximately 1645 hours, observing one of our trials through binoculars.

This object appeared to be travelling towards me or directly across a path of the approaching Canberra. When it got to the path of the Canberra it turned to my right and was going in the direction from which the Canberra had just come.

When it got directly over the Canberra it slowed down. During this time I found it very hard to believe what I was seeing, so I shut my eyes and then looked again through the binoculars and the object was still stationary over the flight path of the Canberra.

Since it appeared to be the same relative size as the Canberra through the binoculars, I thought it would be possible to see it with the naked eye. However, when I looked over the top of the binoculars the object had either gone or I could not see it with the naked eye, and when I looked again through the binoculars I could not pick it up.

The object appeared to be travelling about three times as fast as the Canberra, but of course it is impossible to estimate, since I did not know what height it was. It was perfectly circular all the time and a dark grey colour, and gave the appearance of being translucent. It did not glisten at all when it turned or was it shiny.[29]

The Boianai Visits According to the RAAF

In 1959 Papua New Guinea was still a territory of Australia. June of that year saw the spectacular entity sightings of Reverend Gill and members of his Boianai mission. A brief retelling of this series of events is warranted to illustrate the sort of "high strangeness" sightings the government had to confront. That year Papua New Guinea was experiencing a spate of sightings of mainly unusual lights, but also disk shaped objects. Near the Anglican mission and medical facility at Boianai, the assistant of Father William Gill reported seeing a hovering disk with what appeared to be a human crew standing on the deck. Father Gill was extremely skeptical. A few evenings later, a disk very much like that described by the assistant appeared near the mission and this time Gill saw it himself. The fact that there was a low cloud cover added to this mystery as that eliminated anything but a low, hovering, mechanical vehicle. Gill thought that the only thing it could be was an American aircraft. The next evening the disk appeared again under more clear skies. At that time both Gill and a second assistant waved to the "humans" and the humans waved back. Waving of different hands produced imitative responses (i.e. one hand/one wave back; two hands/two hands waved back). This imitative action eliminated any sort of rare mirage or optical illusion. Gill was certain that he and 38 others at the mission had seen a discoid vehicle silently

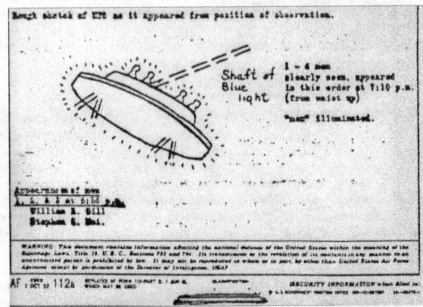

Drawing of the Father Gill sighting from a USAF Air Intelligence Information Report; January 21, 1968

parked in the sky two nights in a row. As Gill and others subsequently mused about the characteristics of this extremely well-witnessed and strange aircraft, it came to almost everyone's mind that even the advanced technologies of the United States could not duplicate this performance—the lengthy silent hovering and subsequent fast speed getaway through the clouds—with no apparent engines nor exhausts. It was, and has remained, a great mystery. The major civilian groups of the day, in a spirit of newfound cooperation inspired by the significance of the Boianai observations, distributed copies of Reverend Gill's own sighting report to all members of the House of Representatives of Australia's federal parliament. A letter accompanied the report, signed by the presidents of the participating civilian UFO groups, urging members of parliament to press the Minister for Air for a statement about the attitude Air Force Intelligence had about the New Guinea reports.

On November 24, 1959, in federal parliament, Mr. E. D. Cash, a Liberal politician from Western Australia, asked the Minister for Air, Mr. F. M. Osborne, whether his department (specifically Air Force Intelligence) had investigated "reports of recent sightings of mysterious objects in the skies over Papua and New Guinea." The Minister's reply did not address this question but instead focused on the general situation. He indicated that most sightings were explained and "that only a very small percentage—something like three percent—of reported sightings of flying objects cannot be explained."[30]

Air Minister F.M. Osborne waving

Peter Norris, president of the Victorian Flying Saucer Research Society (VFSRS), was advised by the Directorate of Air Force Intelligence that the Department was awaiting "depth of evidence" on the New Guinea sightings. However, the department had not even interviewed Father Gill. Given the growing political fallout, the Minister for Defence requested a report on the alleged sightings of UFOs in the Boianai area of New Guinea by Rev. W.B. Gill. The RAAF finally visited Rev. Gill on December 29, 1959. Rev. Gill's recollections of the visit were that the two RAAF officers from Canberra talked about stars and planets and then left. He indicates that he heard no more from them. The interviewing officer, Squadron Leader F. A. Lang, AI1 DAFI, concluded after what could have only been best described as a cursory investigation that:

> Although the Reverend Gill could be regarded as a reliable observer, it is felt that the June/July incidents could have been nothing more than natural phenomena coloured by past events and subconscious influences of UFO enthusiasts. During the period of the report the weather was cloudy and unsettled with light thunder storm. Although it is not possible to draw firm conclusions, an analysis of rough bearings and angles above the horizon does suggest that at least some of the lights observed were the planets Jupiter, Saturn and Mars. Light refraction, the changing position of the planet relative to the observer and cloud movement would give the impression of size and rapid movement. In addition varying cloud densities could account for the human shapes and their sudden *appearance and disappearance.*[31]

A close analysis of the reports argues powerfully that the RAAF explanation of "either known planets seen through fast moving cloud, or natural phenomena" was unsatisfactory.

The civilian groups stood at the end of the fifties in a position of strength: unified, and galvanized into action, by the quality of the Gill reports. The extraordinary reports of UFO visitants over Boianai, Papua New Guinea, during 1959, were remarkable testimony from "credible observers of relatively incredible things" (as the director of USAF intelligence, Major General John Samford, referred to the witnesses of the minority of unknown and unidentified reports, back in 1952). The Anglican Church missionary, Reverend William Gill, provided civilian groups with remarkable testimony of unknown "interlopers." It was in stark contrast to the silliness that punctuated the claims of the "contactee" absurdities during much of the fifties. Buoyed by substantial data, the civilian groups were ready to face what would prove to be the turbulent sixties.

In contrast, the RAAF began a retreat from their original open-minded position. By then the growing number of sightings had turned into *the UFO problem*—a public relations problem with uncertain and controversial military and political dimensions. Public controversy about possible unknown interlopers in our airspace could not be tolerated, and officialdom was moving towards effectively managing "the problem." The scientific approach never really got off the ground. Science had been effectively pushed aside with the rejection of nuclear physicist Harry Turner's secret study of the DAFI UFO files. The military and political ethic had begun its long march of dominating the official approach to the UFO controversy. The decades to follow would prove to be controversial and exciting as the Australian UFO controversy continued its evolution.

The 1960s and the 1970s were periods that saw UFO accounts of "high strangeness." Considerable intrigue and energetic debate marked the search for answers from both the perspective of the civilian researcher and that of the clandestine world of official investigations. Occasionally such activities came together in curious ways, but generally official investigations remained the stuff of secrecy.[32]

The Cressy Affair and the RAAF

The Cressy area of Tasmania became the center of a spectacular wave of sightings in October and November, 1960. An entirely credible witness was at the center of the story. Once again, an Anglican priest reported that he had seen a UFO. The Reverend Lionel Browning and his wife witnessed a fantastic sight from the dining room of the Cressy Anglican rectory on October 4, 1960. A detailed account appeared in the *Launceston Mercury* of October 10 headlined "FLYING SAUCER SEEN AT CRESSY. Mysterious ships in the sky." A succession of media stories followed, elevating the sighting into national prominence.

Again, because of the undeniable credibility of the witness, the RAAF were in a difficult position in their efforts to contain the rapidly escalating public clamour.

Wing Commander Waller interviewed Reverend Browning and his wife on November 11, at their Cressy home. Waller's report provided a description of the event based on Reverend Browning's written statement:

> He and his wife were standing in the dining room...looking out through the window at a rainbow over some low hills approximately 8 miles to the east. The hills, the highest of which are approximately 800 feet, were partly obscured by low cloud and rain. ... (His) wife drew his attention to a long cigar shaped object which was emerging from a rain squall.

> The object was a dull greyish colour, had 4 or 5 vertical dark bands around its circumference...and had what looked like a short aerial array which projected outwards and upward from the northern facing end of the object. The object seemed to be slightly longer than Viscount aircraft which Mr. Browning frequently sees flying in that area and he therefore estimated the object's length as about one hundred feet. The outline of the object was well defined and was even more so a little later when it had as a backdrop the tree covered slopes of a rain free area of the hills...

> The object after emerging from the rain squall moved on an even keel in a northerly direction at an estimated speed of sixty to seventy MPH and at a constant height of approximately four hundred feet. ...

[It] moved approximately one and a half miles north...and then abruptly stopped. Within seconds it was joined by five or six small saucer like objects which had emerged at high speed from the low cloud above and behind...[They] stationed themselves at positions around the cigar shaped object at a radius of one half of a mile and then, after an interval of several seconds the cigar shaped object accompanied by the smaller objects, abruptly reversed back towards and then into the rain squall from which it had emerged...In all, the cigar shaped object had been visible for approximately one minute...[33]

The Brownings watched the area for several more minutes but the objects did not reappear. Another person, a Mrs. D. Bransden, also witnessed the spectacle, describing it as like "a lot of little ships flocking around a bigger one."[34]

In a memorandum dated November 14, 1960, the Director of DAFI (operations) reported to the Australian government's Minister of Air's staff officer that "a preliminary analysis of the available information indicates that this sighting was some form of natural phenomena associated with the unsettled weather conditions."[35]

Wing Commander Waller, in a letter to American researcher Dr. James McDonald, indicated that the couple "impressed me as being mature, stable, and mentally alert individuals, who had no cause or desire to see objects in the sky other than objects of definite form and substance."[36] Such comments by the RAAF investigative officer are difficult to reconcile with the Air Force Intelligence statement released a few days after Wing Commander Waller's interviews. It dismissed the observation

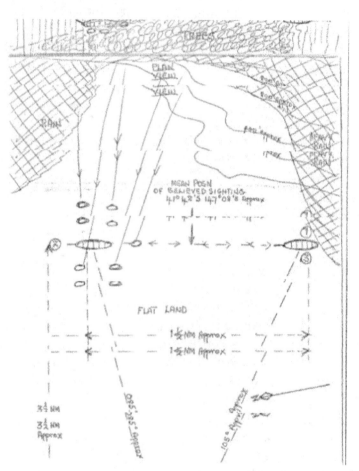

Drawing of sighting made by Reverend and Mrs Lionel Browning near Cressy, Tasmania

as "a phenomena (caused by) a moon rise associated with meteorological conditions at the time." The intelligence report further stated, "The presence of 'scud' type clouds, moving in varying directions due to turbulence in and around a rain squall near where the objects were sighted, and the position of the moon or its reflections, produced the impression of flying objects."[37]

Reverend Browning indicated that at no time during the 90-minute Air Force intelligence interview was he asked about clouds. He added:

At no time was there cloud or scud when I saw the objects. The mountain was not the backdrop to what I saw. The rain cleared in front of us although it was still raining near the mountains. I saw the objects in the sky where there was no rain and the rain near the mountains provided the backdrop...[38]

Dr. McDonald, an acknowledged international expert in meteorology and atmospheric physics, concluded "the official suggestion...seems entirely out of the question."[39]

The RAAF's attempts to explain the Cressy sighting away were rather hollow, particularly given another intriguing sighting report buried in the DAFI UFO files. On November 15, 1960, some 50 kilometers north of Cressy, a United States Air Force JB57 aircraft, operating out of East Sale RAAF base, encountered a UFO. The USAF pilot's report in the RAAF UFO files stated:

> Approximately 1040 LCL while flying on a mission track 15 miles north of Launceston. My navigator __ called out an aircraft approaching to our left and slightly lower.
>
> Our altitude at the time was 40,000 feet, TAS of 350 knots, heading of 340 degrees.
>
> I spotted the object and immediately commented to __ (the navigator) that it was not an aircraft, but looked more like a balloon. We judged its altitude to be approximately 35,000 feet, heading 140 degrees and its speed extremely high.
>
> From a previous experience I would say its closing rate would have been in excess of 800 knots.
>
> We observed this object for five or seven seconds before it disappeared under the left wing.
>
> Since it was unusual in appearance, I immediately banked to the left for another look, but neither of us could locate it.
>
> The colour of the object was nearly translucent somewhat like that of a "poached egg." There were no sharp edges but rather fuzzy and undefined. The size was approximately 70 feet in diameter and it did not appear to have any depth.[40]

The Cressy affair had a sequel in Australia's federal parliament. Rev. Browning's federal member, Mr. Duthie, asked the following question on October 20, 1960:

> Mr. Duthie: Has the Minister for Air read the reports of unidentified flying objects sighted in Australia in the last two years, especially the detailed description of such an object at Cressy in my electorate by the Reverend Lionel Browning and his wife two weeks ago, and twice last weekend? Incidently, the reverend gentleman was my Liberal opponent at the 1951 and 1954 elections. Does the Minister accept responsibility for investigating these sightings? Has the Minister any information about them that may be of interest to the people of Australia?

The Minister for Air, Mr. Osborne, responded with an answer that would form the basis of RAAF policy for more than a decade to come.

> Mr. Osborne: I have read the press reports of these sightings in Tasmania, and in accordance with the usual practice, all the information that is available concerning them has been furnished to my department and is now being examined. The Department of Air does obtain information about all well reported cases of unidentified flying objects. The department not only receives information about them but also exchanges it with the Royal Air Force and the United States Air Force. There is a regular exchange of information on these matters. I can tell the honourable member from Wilmont that although reports of this sort have been investigated very carefully for years, nearly all of them are explainable on a perfectly normal basis. Sometimes they are found to be weather balloons, high-flying aircraft or even stars. On one occasion, it was established that a reported spaceship was the moon. Of all these reports, only 3 per cent, or 4 per cent, cannot be explained on the basis of some natural phenomenon, and nothing that has arisen from that 3 per cent or 4 per cent of unexplained cases gives any firm support for the belief that interlopers from other places in this world, or outside it, have been visiting us.[41]

The Gill "entity" reports of 1959 and the Browning "mothership" report at Cressy in 1960 provided substantial dilemmas for official UFO investigations. In both cases Anglican ministers were the primary witnesses and press coverage was extensive and positive. A confidential briefing paper prepared by DAFI to the RAAF Staff Officer to the Minister of Air concluded after cursory investigations:

> A preliminary analysis of the available information indicates that (the Cressy) sighting was some form of natural phenomena associated with the unsettled weather condition. You will recall that the sighting by Reverend William Gill in the Boianai area of New Guinea, which also received wide publicity, was very similar and occurred under almost identical weather conditions. On that occasion, after investigation, we concluded that the sightings were either known planets seen through fast moving cloud, or natural phenomena. The notable difference between the reports is that objects observed by the Reverend Browning were dull grey in colour, while those seen by the Reverend Gill were brightly lit and, in one case, allegedly contained humanoid beings.[42]

The Brownings in the case of Cressy impressed the investigating RAAF officer as "mentally alert individuals who had no cause or desire to see objects in the sky other than objects of definite form and substance." In the case of the Gill reports, the investigating officers' opinions on the main witness's character were also most favourable. Despite the impact of the Boianai and Cressy reports and the apparent incongruity of the official explanations, the prevailing controversy failed to shift the official stance on UFOs that "nothing that has arisen from the 3 or 4 per cent of unexplained cases gives any firm support for the belief that interlopers from other places in this world or outside it have been visiting us." A close analysis of both cases (Boianai and Cressy) argues powerfully that the RAAF "explanations" are unsatisfactory.

The Classic Willow Grove Encounter

At 7 a.m., February 15, 1963, Charles Brew bore witness to a classic close encounter. Brew was at work in the milking shed on their farm, "Willow Grove," near Moe, Victoria, with his 20-year-old son, Trevor. It was daylight, but rain clouds lay overhead. Charles Brew was standing in an open area with a full view of the eastern sky. It was from that direction that he saw a strange object appear and descend very slowly towards the milk shed. The object's approach was coincident with the cattle and a pony reacting violently. The two farm dogs fled. A local newspaper even reported that the cows turned somersaults, a suggestion the Brews denied.

The UFO descended to an apparent height of between 75 and 100 feet, and hovered over a large Stringy-Bark tree. The UFO was about 25 feet in diameter and nine-to-ten feet high. The top section appeared to be a transparent dome of a glass-like material, from which protruded a five-to-six foot high mast or aerial. The "aerial" appeared to be as thick as a broom and resembled bright chrome. The top portion of the disc was battleship grey in color and appeared to be of a metallic lustre. The base or underside section glowed with a pale blue color and had "scoop-like protuberances about 12 to 18 inches apart around the outside edge." This section rotated slowly at about one revolution per second. This spinning motion apparently caused the protuberances to generate a swishing noise, somewhat like a turbine noise, that was clearly audible not only to Brew but also to his son Trevor, who was inside the shed near the diesel-powered milking machines.

Charles Brew described how he felt his eyes were drawn towards the object, "as though beams of magnetic current" were between it and him. He also experienced a peculiar headache that came on with the approach of the object. Even though Brew normally did not suffer migraines, the use of tablets did not subdue the headache.

After hovering for a few seconds, the object began to climb at roughly a 45 degree angle, continued on its westward course, and passed up into the cloud deck again. Trevor did not see the UFO, but confirmed the unusual sound, like a didgeridoo or bullroarer—aboriginal artifacts which can produce a pulsating wind rushing noise.[43]

Flight Lieutenant N. Hudson and Squadron Leader A. F. Javes of the RAAF interviewed Charles Brew on site on March 4, 1963. While impressed with his credibility, the weather at the time of the sighting—heavy continuous rain with very low cloud and poor visibility, and with a fresh wind in an easterly direction—caused them to focus on weather related explanations. Their report describes the basis of their somewhat extraordinary explanation for the incident:

> On 6th March, Dr. Berson and Mr. Clark (of the CSIRO—Commonwealth Scientific & Industrial Research Organisation—Meteorological Physics division) were interviewed to see if clouds give this type of phenomenon. They agreed that a tornado condition could give this effect. The direction of rotation of Brew's report of the object was consistent with known facts for the Southern Hemisphere. The blue-ish colouring has been reported previously and is probably due to electric discharge and there would be a smell of ozone. The only difference in Brew's report was that the object moved from East to West because all previous reports to the CSIRO Met section of this nature have been from West to East. Mr. Brew stated that the wind was fresh from an easterly direction. However, (a) meteorological report states that wind was westerly at 8 knots.

The report notes that the meteorological report was from a Yallourn observer, which is about 20 kilometers away; therefore local variations in the weather would not have been unusual.

Despite this lack of rigor in determining the relevance of their hypothesis, the RAAF officers' report concluded:

> There is little doubt that Brew did witness something, and it is most likely that it was a natural phenomenon. The phenomenon was probably a tornado. There was no reported damage along its path; therefore one could assume that it was weak in nature.[44]

The Department of Air responded to a civilian UFO group enquiry about the incident with the following statement:

> Our investigation and enquiries reveal that there are scientific records of certain tornado-like meteorological manifestations which have a similar appearance in many ways to whatever was seen by Mr. Brew. The information available is such however, that while we accept this is a possibility, we are unable to come to any firm conclusion as to the nature of the object or manifestation reported.[45]

The official sighting summaries removed any such doubt. By then the possible cause was listed as a "tornado like meteorological manifestation." In correspondence with the Victoria Flying Saucer Research Society, the CSIRO's Dr. Berson indicated "we are unable to come to any firm conclusion as to the nature of the object or manifestation reported." The RAAF were largely parroting the CSIRO's conclusions and taking things a little further without any realistic justification.

Dr. Berson and an associate visited Charles Brew at the Willow Grove property. According to Brew, Dr. Berson was interested in the headache that he had, and indicated that Berson had said that it tied in with their theory of a possible electromagnetic nature of the incident. The CSIRO's field investigation had in fact preceded that of the RAAF by about a week. There was evidently extensive interest from the military and government scientists. Brew indicated that the RAAF officers told him that the object he saw was similar to those seen overseas, and that it was the best sighting they had looked at.

What the Department of Air referred to as a "tornado like meteorological manifestation" elicited the following emotive description from Charles Brew; it mirrors the striking nature of his encounter with the unknown object. He said, "I wished it would come again. It was beautiful. I could feel the life pulsating from it."[46]

Dr. James McDonald visited Charles Brew during his 1967 Australian trip and interviewed him at the site of the 1963 incident. McDonald concluded, "Like that of many other UFO witnesses, it is extremely difficult to explain in present-day scientific or technological terms."[47]

Despite the extraordinary nature of the Willow Grove incident and the high level of official interest in it, the sighting was listed in a subsequently released *Summary of Unidentified Aerial Sightings reported to Department of Air, Canberra, ACT, from 1960* as having a possible cause of "tornado like meteorological manifestation."

The Electromagnetic Light Wheel near Groote Eylandt

According to this summary, the first official "unknown" in the RAAF DAFI files occurred on January 23, 1964. For a list of "Aerial sightings," it is unusual because it was reported as located in water. The summary states:

> Seen at sea by crew of a vessel NE Point of Groote Eylandt, WA. Large lights in water, made compass go "Haywire." Shadow in center of lights rotated clockwise, causing lights to pulsate.[48]

The complete report noted an unusual sighting made by the crew of the landing craft "Loellen/M." The incident was located between Cape Grey and the north east point of Groote Eylandt, a large island on the western side of the Gulf of Carpentaria, Northern Territory. The official summary incorrectly lists the incident as occurring in "WA" (Western Australia). The report mentions that the vessel encountered a number of submarine "light patches":

> C. W__ turned on the compass light and found the vessel approx 60° off course. The compass went 'Haywire.'

> As soon as he had corrected the vessel as best he could, he switched off the compass light and found the un-natural light was about 6 ft on the starboard side. The light was in the water. It was described as a ghostly white light, in the centre was a shadow which rotated in a clockwise direction causing the light to pulsate. The light appeared to draw away to the stern. It is estimated that it was miles across and a few hundred yards through....

> The light on the water passed about 100 yds to port. As the barge began to return to course, another light was seen coming at the barge at an angle of about 45° which [sic—with?] the bow. It came to within inches of the starboard side and appeared to rebound at 45° with the stern and moved away. It disappeared in a few seconds....

> All lights were the same colour, with this strange rotating shadow, causing the lights to pulsate. The pulsations timed at 12 for 9 seconds, then completely irregular, then settled down to 12 for 9 seconds.

> The compass swung out of control, but became worse as the light approached...[49]

This is a fascinating report, but its origins may lie in some form of extraordinary bioluminescence.

The RAAF in the Lion's Den

A major turning point in civilian UFO research in Australia occurred on February 27, 1965, at Ballarat, Victoria. What was billed as Australia's first convention of UFO groups provided a focus for elevating the respectability of the UFO subject. Unfortunately, in hindsight it also started a process that, while initially encouraging, would eventually divide some UFO groups and lay the seeds of group political warfare that would resound for years to come.

Air Marshall Sir George Jones

The occasion was one of great euphoria for those researchers, investigators, and enthusiasts who attended. The conference had been arranged by W. Howard Sloane, of the Ballarat Astronomical Society, with the aim of removing the stigma of ridicule from research into UFOs. Not only did representatives of most existing Australian groups attend, but so did several witnesses to some of Australia's most famous cases, including the Reverend William Gill and Charles Brew, who spoke about their experiences. Former Air Marshall Sir George Jones attended and was outspoken in his support for serious UFO research. The RAAF was represented by Mr. B. G. Roberts, Senior Research Scientist of the Operational Research Office, Department of Air, Canberra. The presence of a scientific consultant of the RAAF, along with two RAAF officers manning a hardware display, was an unprecedented step for the Australian government.

B.G. Roberts gave a presentation that addressed the term UFO and some objections to it, official assessments of aerial sightings, and the identification of sightings. Roberts argued the term "unidentified aerial sightings" (UAS) was a more appropriate one than UFO, the latter term having long since been regarded as just another term for flying saucers. He indicated that:

> ...the assessment of reports of unidentified aerial sightings in Australia and the territories is the responsibility of the Department of Air at Canberra. There is no hidden implication in this allocation of responsibility. The Department is simply the most appropriate authority for the task, which is performed to determine whether or not a threat to the security of the nation is involved.

Roberts highlighted that nine out of ten sightings are explainable.

In terms of unidentified sightings Roberts stated:

> The number of sightings which the Department is unable to identify from the information available has remained fairly consistent at around two a year. Indeed, given sufficient time and effort, the number of unidentified sightings probably could be reduced further. One has to assess, however, whether the required additional time and effort is warranted. The Department of Air believes that there is, and always will be, a small number of sightings (due to high altitude phenomena, which are strange to the untrained eye) for which the available information will never be sufficient to enable an identification to be made. In other words it is just not possible to achieve a 100% record of successful identification. The ideal can be approached but not achieved, simply because the inaccuracies inherent in this type of work militate against its achievement.

Roberts indicated:

> The number of unidentified sightings each year in Australia does not warrant such great effort or expense. Only where there is evidence that a threat to the security of the nation is involved (e.g. the

possibility of foreign aircraft infringing our air space) would this attitude be reversed. The Department of Air believes that there always will be aerial sightings of high altitude phenomena which are strange to the untrained eye and that of these some will not be identified.

Finally, I would like to make it clear that the Department of Air never has denied the possibility that some form of life may exist on other planets in the universe. ...However, the Department has, so far, neither received nor discovered in Australia any evidence to support the belief that the earth is being observed, visited or threatened by machines from other planets. Furthermore, there are no documents, files or dossiers held by the Department which prove the existence of "flying saucers."[50]

The civilian UFO researcher audience at the Ballarat convention was skeptical of the claimed lack of compelling UFO photos in the RAAF files. They were interested in Mr. Roberts' knowledge on the holy grail of Australian ufology, namely the photographic evidence secured by Papua New Guinea DCA Deputy Director, Tom Drury, back in August, 1953. Peter Norris, President of VFSRS, asked Roberts if he was aware of the film. Roberts said he was not. Fred Stone indicated that four stills from the Drury film had been supplied to him by the RAAF in 1954. Roberts clearly was uninformed about this famous case and even remarked, "I feel a bit like Daniel in a lions' den!" Civilian researcher Andrew Tomas indicated he had seen the film in the hands of Edgar Jarrold, the pioneer Australian researcher and director of the Australian Flying Saucer Bureau. There is evidence that Jarrold did eventually receive prints of individual frames, some 94 prints, but not the actual film. Tomas told the convention that the RAAF sent the film to Dayton, Ohio, and then researchers lost track of it.

Former RAAF Air Marshall Sir George Jones also challenged Mr. Roberts. While questioning the value of photographs as evidence of the reality of UFOs, he nevertheless insisted on keeping an open mind towards reports such as those of Charles Brew at Willow Grove, Victoria, and Rev. William Gill and others in Papua New Guinea. Sir George said to Mr. Roberts, "You leave me with an impression that everything can be explained away given sufficient time and effort. I don't know how they (RAAF) get on with those things (meaning reports like those of Charles Brew and Rev. Gill)."[51]

The RAAF and the UFO Problem

A Department of Air memorandum, dated February, 1966, revealed that there were "no written responsibilities for (RAAF) Operational Command in the UFO field." It indicated that the writer (Squadron Leader _____ AI-2) had "reviewed the current 'Ad Hoc' system in the practice of processing U.F.O. reports and with minor criticisms," found that it appeared "to be working satisfactorily, entailing the minimum of work by this Directorate [Directorate of Air Force Intelligence]." After much discussion, a DAFI directive was issued to both Commands (Operational and Support Commands) in March 1966. Group Captain I. S. Podger (for the Chief of the Air Staff) wrote in it:

The main purpose of the investigation of any UFO is to establish whether or not the subject of the report poses a threat to the security of Australia. The identification of the cause of the UFO report and its classifications as aircraft, balloon, missile, astronomical body or phenomena etc, is of minor importance and mainly for the benefit of members of the public whose interest may have been aroused by the report.

The directive also specified:

No attempts should be made to answer public enquiries at unit or command level. Requests by members of the public for information on UFOs in Australia and for the RAAF assessment of their origin etc should be referred to the Department of Air where they will be dealt with by the Directorate of

Public Relations.[52]

It was not long before a conflict arose between the Directorates of Air Force Intelligence and Public Relations. It came to a head when the director of the Directorate of Public Relations (DPR) forwarded a detailed memorandum to DAFI, dated August 16, 1966. It was entitled "UFOs—RAAF HANDLING OF PROBLEM." The conflict was over whether to cease "the distribution to interested members of the public of the *Summary of Unidentified Aerial Sightings Reported to Department of Air from 1960*." The DAFI was keen to soft-pedal the UFO business and gave "the reason for this cessation [as] the undesirability of whetting the interest of the public in UFOs." DPR's reaction was terse and to the point:

> The "Summary" grew out of a requirement for certain statistical UFO information to provide material for a ministerial reply to a parliamentary question.
>
> DPR willingly undertook to draft an answer for the Minister (a task which entailed folio-for-folio research through some four or five parts of the relevant file), because it felt that the otherwise burdensome task had some distinct side-benefit, namely, the collation of an unclassified and innocuous summary of UFO "sightings" in Australia for the past five years.
>
> DPR envisaged the day when it would be able to reply to all public UFO enquiries by the mere despatch of the "summary" covered, if thought necessary, by a letter in which we explain that we are not prepared to engage in any subsequent disputation [i.e. take our "Summary" or leave; we have told you all we know].
>
> In order to keep this "Summary" current, D/DAFI [Ops] was good enough to agree to provide DPR with the basic information which DPR would expect to have been security cleared for general release before adding the information to the "Summary."

The DPR director made "a plea to remove the present restriction on the sharing of our unclassified UFO information with the public. ..." The DPR director said:

> In summary: by continuing with the old policy of playing our UFO cards close to the chest, we only foster the incorrect (but nevertheless widely held) belief that we have much vital information to hide. On the other hand, by maintaining a current "Summary" (which DPR is prepared to do, with your continued help) we dispose in one blow, of the UFO enthusiasts' belief that:
> (a) he is not being taken into the RAAF's confidence; and
> (b) the RAAF is desperately determined to suppress UFO information to prevent
> national panic...

The Director of Public Relations concluded his memorandum to the Director of Air Force Intelligence, by stating, "While security is not DPR's affair, our relations with the general public (cranks and all) certainly are and I feel strongly, from the PR point of view, that we are handling this whole UFO business in an unnecessarily rigid and unimaginative way." [53]

This theme was continued in another Department of Air memorandum, entitled "Unidentified Flying Object—RAAF policy" and dated 12th October 1966. It emerged following a request from author Richard Tambling, who had requested permission to publish B. G. Roberts' Ballarat UFO conference presentation as an official view. DAFI were not inclined to do this. The memorandum confirmed that uncertainty and confusion were keynotes in RAAF UFO policy during 1966—hallmarks that would continue right up to today. It stated:

> There appears to be some confusion concerning Departmental policy over UFOs... on file... there is a ministerial statement to the effect:

"Anyone who is interested in sightings of
UFOs can apply to the Department of Air
for information on the subject and is
welcome to a synopsis of UFO sightings
which includes a very brief assessment of
the probable causes."

This statement was made in answer to ministerial representation. It would appear, however, that the policy represented by this statement may not have reflected the view of DAFI, despite earlier, although inconclusive evidence of this concurrence.

...DAFI has proposed to DGPP [Director General Plans & Policy] who in turn referred to DCAS that our approach to UFO reports be liberalised. It does not appear that either DGPP or DCAS were aware of the Minister's statement. In my opinion we must either comply with the terms of that statement or inform the minister of our "new" approach, if it is not intended to provide the synopsis of sightings and on this I am not at all together clear from reading the files.

It would, however, seem that agreement has not been reached that DPR is to handle all enquiries for information, however, it does not appear that DPR has been consulted on the extent of the liberalisation proposed by DAFI in answer to his [DPR] submission [the August 16, 1966, minute paper] and could DPR indicate his views.

It would also appear that there is some need for rationalization of our files on this subject. There are at least 4 different files which contain a confusion of policy, reported sightings and requests for information. Three of these files are classified, two of which are SECRET although there appears to be nothing in the files consistent with this classification. Could DAFI and DPR consider rationalising these files please...?[54]

The "Summary" did indeed become the public front of the RAAF involvement in the Australian UFO controversy. By the end of the sixties, the "Summary" crystallized as a largely annual affair. "Summary No. 1" covered reports from 1960 to 1968; "Summary No. 2" covered 1969 accounts; while 1970 and 1971 reports appeared in "Summary No. 3." From 1972 to 1977 inclusive, the summaries appeared somewhat erratically, covering each year with Numbers 4 to 9. The RAAF had embarked on a course that locked them into a bureaucratically orchestrated formula for handling the "UFO problem."[55]

The Emergence of an "Invisible College," "Down Under"—the RAAF "Helps Out"?

The RAAF files also held a copy of a detailed 1967 report written by Dr. Michael Duggin, of the CSIRO National Standards Laboratory, Division of Physics. It was a report about a striking close encounter in the Sydney suburb of Canterbury. The report was sent by Dr. Duggin to Dr. Allen Hynek. Duggin, an Australian physicist, had recently joined Hynek's informal international "invisible college" of collaborating scientists. Dr. Duggin had secured a letter of introduction from Dr. Hynek dated November 16, 1966. It stated:

Dr. M. Duggin is collecting information on UFOs and is part of an International effort to collate information on this phenomenon from

Dr. Michael Duggin

several countries. For many years I have acted as a scientific monitor on this scientifically vexing problem of UFOs, and a number of colleagues and I have agreed to act as a "clearing house" for the investigation of which Dr. Duggin is a part. Any cooperation which may be extended to Dr. Duggin would be greatly appreciated.

Sincerely yours, J. Allen Hynek, Director, Dearborn Observatory.

Dr. Duggin contacted Squadron Leader Baxter of the RAAF in his initial attempts to get official cooperation. In a December 20, 1966, letter to Sqd. Ldr. Baxter he wrote:

I would like to add a few details to today's telephone conversation. Dr. Vallee, an astronomer at the University of Chicago and Professor J. A. Hynek, whom I saw in Chicago a few weeks ago, are very interested in the UFO phenomenon from the point of view of a scientific investigation. So am I and so are many other scientists in other countries. These gentlemen have carefully documented files on many (about 6000) sightings in many different countries. Many of these sightings are doubtful but there are a large number which it has not so far been possible to explain in terms of natural phenomena. These are the cases of interest.

Dr. Vallee has at his disposal a computer program for an automatic question-answering system (which was originally developed for stellar astronomy). He has asked Dr. O. Fontes in Brazil, Professor [sic] Michel in France, myself and several other scientists in different countries to collect data on sightings and where possible interview those who originate the report in order to determine its reliability and so weight it for future statistical analyses. This information will be coded, so that it can be punched onto an IBM card and later fed onto a magnetic library tape for use with the question-answering system.

Present investigations have indicated the existence of certain patterns in this phenomenon but unfortunately much more data is required before great reliance can be placed on the results of such an investigation. Several reports from isolated observers, contiguous in time and consistent in description, would appear to suggest that perhaps some observations are made sequentially along great circle routes. Again more data is needed.

"Landing" reports have been quite frequent in South America and, I believe, in the Southern hemisphere as a whole.

What is needed is information, (1) as soon as it is turned in, so that the case can be correlated with other information, if possible, at Dearborn Observatory, (2) results of the follow-up.

I would like to investigate cases myself where possible and would be very willing to be of any help I can.

Dr. Hynek is the scientific advisor on UFOs to the U.S. Air Force. I am enclosing a letter from him to substantiate my request. I stress that this is a scientific investigation and that although my interest is extracurricular, I feel that it is very necessary to subject those unexplained phenomena to scientific investigation.

The DAFI reviewed Dr. Duggin's request. A Department of Air Memorandum from Wing Commander N.G. Marshall, D/DAFI (Ops) to DAFI addressed the issue, and made a fascinating admission that the RAAF actually had unexplained UFOs:

You will note that one of the scientists involved in this UFO investigation is Dr. Hynek who is stated to be the scientific advisor on UFOs to the United States. Dr. Duggin, however is acting in an extracurricular capacity.

You will note that these scientists are mainly interested in *the unexplained UFOs,* but as far as I can make out they would like information on all sightings. As you know, we already have an official arrangement with CSIRO whereby we can pass to them any report on which we would like their assistance, so it would really be only a question of stretching this arrangement slightly to pass them a copy of all reports. However, Dr. Duggin's interest is un-official as far as CSIRO is concerned and this may cause embarrassment.

These scientists, with all the documents and facilities available to them, are obviously in a position to assist us in this matter, and though I am not keen on releasing the details of the RAAF investigations or anything which may increase the interest of the general public in this field, I think we should give these scientists the information they require. However, although they would like the information as soon as possible, I recommend that we stick to our present system for UFO investigations, i.e. the nearest RAAF Base investigates the report and passes it up through Command Headquarters to Department of Air. If we change the system to allow CSIRO to get a copy of the report before it has completed the RAAF process, we may get two concurrent investigations of the same report.

Annotations to this memo indicated, "Seen by DAFI who agrees." Other file folios indicated that CSIRO were asked if all reports could go to Dr. Duggin and that CSIRO agreed to Dr. Duggin acting in an unofficial capacity.[56]

Thus Dr. Duggin's report to Dr. Hynek on an impressive close encounter in 1967 was an extension of the process that had been put into play. The RAAF were sanctioning, albeit sometimes in a token fashion, the activities of the "invisible college."

A Secret Military "Rapid Intervention" Team

By 1968, Harry Turner, who prepared the classified 1954 report on the DAFI UFO reports, was working in the Directorate of Scientific and Technical Intelligence of the JIB. At the end of 1954, Turner, a University of Western Australia trained physicist, went to England, where he worked at Harwell—the British atomic energy research establishment. He returned to Australia in 1956 and until 1964 was stationed at Maralinga. There he was the Australian Health Physics Representative during the controversial atomic bomb trials. When he joined DSTI, Turner functioned as a JIB liaison with DAFI and used the connection to try to once again encourage serious UFO research within the secret world of Defence Science and Intelligence.

As early as August 1968, Turner drafted a memo for the JIB director entitled "U.F.O. Investigations with respect to DAFI, JIB and the future NIO" (generic designation for National Intelligence

Left: physicist Harry Turner
Right: Bill Chalker

Organisation), which highlighted that, "DAFI is not anxious to retain responsibility for UFO analysis but would be prepared to continue collation responsibility. The main problems are: (a) lack of scientific capability, (b) no specific position has been established for UFO work which means additional duties for personnel allocated to other duties." He elaborated, "Many of the explanations offered by DAFI, usually under political pressure, impose a considerable scientific credibility gap." Turner recommended tentative explorations of ways to mount a limited assessment of the subject.

Harry Turner requested access to DAFI's UFO reports. This was granted. In May 1969, at Turner's suggestion, a new RAAF UFO report form was devised that intended to give the reports a more scientific slant. At this time Turner was working with other scientists to set up a rapid intervention team to scientifically investigate cases of UFO physical evidence. A firm proposal was developed with the team to operate within the Defence Science and Technical Organisation (DSTO). The team was to consist of four or five scientists, with its mainstay to be rapid intervention into UFO landing events, for which an aircraft was to be on standby. Turner, in a memo dated November 8, 1969, to the Director of JIB, indicated that he had recruited Dr. Morton from Australian National University (ANU), Dr. John Symonds from the Australian Atomic Energy Commission, and Dr. Mike Duggin, then of the National Standards Laboratory. George Barlow of Defence Science and Technology (DST) had also offered the help of his group. Turner indicated that Arthur Wills, then Chief Defence Scientist, "had agreed to this." The plans for the scientific team had been almost completed and authorization to proceed appeared imminent. However, Fate had already intervened.[57]

Sub Rosa Fallout in Western Australia

In the middle of 1969, a major flap broke out in Western Australia. It was centered in Perth. One of the reports included an impressive radar-visual event at Cloverdale that was tracked on Kalamunda radar on May 23. The Director of Air Force Intelligence felt that things had gotten out of control and made an appeal for the Defence intervention group to assist. Unfortunately the group had not been finalized, and Harry Turner was tasked to help out. Turner described the radar-visual incident in his report as follows:

> On the 23rd May, 1969, (Mrs. C__'s) 13 year old son, who has an interest in the night sky, noticed from the front door of their house...that to the south and about 10 degrees above the horizon, there was a moving light which he first took to be an aeroplane. As it approached to the SE of the observer, it became apparent to him that its behaviour pattern differed considerably from that of an aircraft. He called his mother who observed...in an easterly direction a steady red light on top of a more diffused blue-white light, and darting haphazardly in a zig-zag pattern, but in general travelling towards a northerly direction until it disappeared behind the house. The two witnesses proceeded to the NW side of the house where they observed a luminous object stationary against the clear starry sky, at an elevation between 10 and 15 degrees and at a bearing of 015 degrees.

> The light observed was circular—about half the diameter of a full moon. It was steady in position and intensity for some 15-20 minutes. It no longer had a red light on top and had the brightness of a fluorescent street light. The edge was not clean cut but was somewhat hazy, even though the night air was perfectly clear. The time at which the object was first sighted was estimated as being 1835 hours. ...Shortly before 1900 hours the object moved at extremely high velocity, away from the observers in a general N to NE-ly direction.

> Mrs. C___ ...telephoned the shift operator on site. (He) was still talking to Mrs. C___ when a request came from the meteorological radar situated near Perth Airport as to whether he could check out an unidentified echo seen on the meteorological radar.

> The Kalamunda radar operator had not been watching his screen as no aircraft were in the vicinity, but on checking the radar P.P.I. screen, he observed a large echo some 9 miles away at 300 degrees from his position which placed the echo some 2 1/2miles north of Mrs. C___'s position. Initial contact was made at 1901 hours and held for only 30 to 40 seconds. The echo which reappeared for short durations on 5 further occasions was twice the size of a large aircraft at that position. The echo has not been seen since it finally disappeared at 1942 hours.

> One unusual feature of the Kalamunda report is that the radar is equipped with Moving Target Indicator (MTI) which suppresses all permanent echoes and all targets moving at speeds less than an estimated 6 knots...The night in question was clear and calm and there is no justification for an MTI break-through in the region of the target. Despite the operation of MTI, the unknown target was clearly visible, even

though there was no noticeable displacement of its position. The operator had never before met an apparently stationary target that was recorded so clearly despite the operation of MTI. [The operator] paid particular attention to this echo over the whole period of 41 minutes that it occurred, because it was a potential traffic hazard, to two aircraft in circuit at about that time, and they had to be warned to avoid the area of the unknown target. ...The operator is quite sure... that the echo's appearance never lasted more than a minute at any one time. ...

...Just before 1900 hours the object moved away from the observer, disappearing from sight in a fraction of a second, and it is possible that it correlates with the stationary echo on radar at 1901 hours. The unusual features of the radar echo are:
(a) size;
(b) the fact that it was seen despite the operation of MTI; and
(c) the spasmodic appearance.
It is not possible to readily conceive of an explanation for these observations. All observers were obviously sincerely puzzled individuals with an aversion to publicity. ...

Harry Turner concluded the metrology returns were possibly prosaic and unrelated to the main event, and that "Neither the Kalamunda radar observation nor Mrs. C__'s sighting can be readily explained by conventional objects or phenomena." His report also criticized the DAFI system's lack of assistance to the "on the spot" Air Force Intelligence officer. The DAFI empire was under threat. The Air Force did not take kindly to criticism, particularly when it came from what DAFI saw as an outsider—a JIB scientist. The outcome of this was that Harry Turner's access to the DAFI UFO files was withdrawn.[58]

UFO Impact and the JIB

The plan for the rapid intervention team was dropped. It is obvious that political considerations had again frustrated attempts to undertake official scientific UFO research in Australia. For a number of years, Turner tried unsuccessfully to encourage JIB or DSTO to undertake a serious scientific investigation into UFOs.[59]

This unfortunate turn of events was not helped by the lack of interest that the then Director of Air Force Intelligence, Group Captain R. S. Royston, had in pursuing the subject. Royston's attitude was described in a July 1971 memo:

> Although I am directly concerned with any possible threat to Australian security, I am not particularly interested in the subject of UFOs, even though my directorate devotes valuable time to this problem. I accept the US assessments without question and consider that it would be a complete waste for we here in Australia to spend valuable time and money in further detailed investigations. However, should the Department of Supply wish to undertake such studies the records of this directorate would be freely available. It would have to be pointed out to Supply, however, that the RAAF could provide no additional assistance in the matter and Supply would have to undertake all the facets of the further investigations.[60]

Captain R.S. Royston

Harry Turner's JIB superior was Bob (R. H.) Mathams, the Director of Scientific Intelligence and author of the book *Sub Rosa—Memoirs of an Australian Intelligence Analyst (1982)*. Mathams later said that he did not encourage Turner's UFO interests, and his access to DAFI (RAAF) materials was an informal liaison agreement, which became more unworkable in the environment of Defence restructuring.

There was uneasiness in JIB's dance with UFOs. The interest was almost entirely driven by Turner's interest. If Turner had not been there, it is doubtful that the matter would have come up. Turner wrote numerous papers and memos in the period 1969 to 1971 in an attempt to get the "UFO ship" afloat. During early 1970, there were exchanges between the JIB deputy director and DSTI head Bob Mathams about Turner's persistent *sub rosa* UFO crusade.

In January 1970, Harry Turner even utilized Dr. Jacques Vallee's listing of 1,000 worldwide UFO landing or near-landing reports (appended in Vallee's book *Passport to Magonia*) to highlight to JIB the potential military threats involved:

> The information suggests the existence of 3 "weapon systems" – (1) a device to interfere with electrical circuits, (2) a device to induce paralysis, (3) a heat ray. Turner indicated, "There is circumstantial evidence that these weapons are at times used deliberately, although mostly in a defensive role. A number of reports allege that a lone car at night has been followed, and after being stopped by a beam, some kind of interaction has developed between the car occupants and the landed craft occupants. Information is included which deals with residual effects on the environment of the landed craft. It is these residual effects which offer the greatest potential reward to scientific investigation at this stage."
> [61]

Even reports of this nature that went to the heart of defense issues failed to get Turner's proposed study off the ground. The status quo prevailed.

The JIB deputy director wanted to know, "Should we maintain an incipient capacity in this field?" Mathams replied:

Robert H. Mathams 1940

> I have discussed the paper...with Mr. Turner and have told him that my views on the subject of UFOs, from a scientific intelligence point of view, are as follows:
> (a) ...There is no surplus research capacity within the (DSTI) establishment that could be diverted to problems such as the investigation of UFO reports.
> (b) I am not convinced that there is a sufficient scientific intelligence component in the UFO problem such as to warrant any diversion of Australia's very limited resources for scientific intelligence research.
> (c) It is evident that there is still considerable controversy concerning UFOs and this will undoubtedly continue until the subject is fully examined by some competent authority. Such an examination, however, would require a considerable effort to collect information on UFO sightings, to investigate reports of such sightings and to examine all information in an objective, scientific manner.

The deputy director responded to Bob Mathams:

> I have by now (February 1970) read a considerable amount of material on this subject. I am sure that there is an area for investigation that should be pursued by some authority. That authority, however, would need very considerable resources indeed. I have considered carefully whether a part of the subject might be undertaken by us, but this approach doesn't seem practicable. I am forced, therefore, whilst agreeing that the subject should be studied somewhere, to decide that JIO cannot be that somewhere. Without considerable back-up we would be wasting our time and the RAAF have apparently cancelled out the little that they were doing.

Harry Turner persisted in his efforts and even convinced the Joint Intelligence Organisation (the reorganized JIB) director, R. W. Furlonger, to sign off on a May 1971 memorandum on the

"Investigation of UFO Sightings" directed to the Deputy Secretary of Defence. The memo recommended passing on responsibility for the investigation of UFOs from the RAAF to the Department of Supply (namely DSTO—Defence Science & Technology Organisation—as distinct from DSTI). The memo focused on a limited number of select cases (perhaps six per year) over a two to three year period, after which JIO could make a better determination if a strategic intelligence interest exists. Despite some support from DSTO, Turner was unable to maintain sufficient momentum in his *sub rosa* UFO campaign.

It was clear Turner was not going to succeed within JIO—too limited resources and the subject was not within the primary mission of JIO, but DSTO was seen by Turner as the best fit. The timing and the prevailing politics, driven by the state of flux of the Defence Science realm, played against the "UFO problem" coming under DSTO. The UFO subject interested people like George Barlow (Defence Science No. 2) and Dr. John Farrands, the Chief Defence Scientist, but not enough though to rock the boat, as much as Turner tried.

As a potentially related point of interest: The JIO maintained a secret BOLIDE file, which seemed to be anchored to the premise that UFOs could involve the chance of retrieval of Soviet hardware and therefore contribute some useful intelligence. It appeared JIO had a rapid intervention capability, as they were able to institute prompt widespread ground searches in suspected hardware crashes. They did this through special access channels. A specific example occurred in October 1979, when reports of a fireball over the Esperance area of Western Australian had JIO's DSTI branch investigate "through special access channels a search over a 1,500 nautical mile radius of Esperance and covering the time frame of the reported sightings, but with zero results."

The *sub rosa* JIO involvement in the UFO controversy could have been a good stepping stone towards the application of some solid science to the UFO mystery. Instead the situation was frustrated by perceptions of limited resources and politicking—a lost opportunity.

The role of the Australian Joint Intelligence Organisation and now the Defence Intelligence Organisation (DIO) is a complex one. JIO emerged in 1970 and the DIO in 1989. The original JIB had emerged by 1947, but its intelligence activities were limited. Critical to our story was the expansion of its spheres of interest to scientific and technical intelligence in 1957.

An important JIO UFO file was released to investigator Keith Basterfield in May 2008. There was very little new information beyond what was already known or suspected. Some of Harry Turner's material was in that JIO file release. Some was not. Indeed it was the apparent absences in the released file that were perhaps of more significance than the released contents.

There was no material about the important 1954 Sea Fury radar-visual case. The pilot involved, James O'Farrell, had stated that two JIO files were made available to him in 1973 by Arthur Tange, the powerful and influential Defence Secretary, to refresh his memory of the episode so that he could discuss the event with Dr. Allen Hynek during his 1973 Australian visit.

The JIO file that Keith Basterfield had managed to get released contained some, not all, of Harry Turner's extensive memos and papers. One surprising omission was his detailed report on the 1969 Kalamunda Perth radar-visual case. Turner's report on the case was largely instrumental in closing the door on his access to the Directorate of Air Force Intelligence UFO files, because he was critical of the lack of DAFI support for the DAFI officer on the ground. The officer was under-resourced and overwhelmed by the UFO outbreak. The Director of Air Force Intelligence was not interested in ensuring a fully resourced UFO investigation by his own people, and was also not interested in supporting other efforts, such as Harry Turner's attempts to establish a rapid intervention team with the DSTO.

Other omissions in the JIO file released to Basterfield may have been due to typical file attribution effects and file borrowings, sensitivities about the material, or other matters, rather than any inherent substantial content. For example, there is a Department of Supply internal memorandum from the

Radar and Electronic Group, "Regarding Recent Symposium on UFOs," which discusses the *1971 ANZAAS UFO* symposium. Another describes a sighting by the crew of an Australian National Lines ship off Pipon Island in 1966.

There is no material in the JIO UFO file release on the classified BOLIDE file, which indicates that JIO had special access channels for rapid wide-search investigations. These were generally anchored in the premise of attempts to retrieve foreign technology, as Bob Mathams, the former head of DSTI in JIO, stated.[62]

Intruder at Woomera

In the wake of Harry Turner's abortive efforts, the scientific investigation of UFOs at an official level had all but disappeared; the primary goal had become the resolution of any defense and/or political implications.

This attitude can be seen in the Woomera intrusions in late 1971. Prior to the launch of a Black Arrow rocket, an unidentified aircraft was observed by a trained site-meteorology observer over Woomera prohibited airspace. Another sighting led to a Department of Supply letter to the Director of Air Force Intelligence, dated January 7, 1972, which stated that:

> this sighting appears to be sufficiently authenticated, yet there is no official knowledge of any military or civil aircraft that could have intruded into the Woomera air space. It is therefore now a matter of speculation that some foreign aircraft passed through a Restricted Flying Area on December 20th, 1971 without the knowledge of the appropriate authorities and this is cause for concern.

Rather than accept that maybe the Soviets or perhaps something else entirely was the problem, it was more politically expedient for DAFI to suggest an alternative. They suggested that a more plausible explanation was re-entering space debris, even though this was impossible to confirm.

RAAF UFO "Counter-Intelligence" in South Australia

The unidentified intrusions during sensitive Woomera rocket launches created a state of ferment. The Australian and New Zealand Association for the Advancement of Science (ANZAAS) and "invisible college" scientists engaged in attempts to understand the puzzling and frustrating phenomenon, but the RAAF did not. They were too busy trying to assert their official responsibility to investigate UFOs. The RAAF UFO files contain documents prepared by RAAF Edinburgh Base South Australia personnel that address their frustration with the "UFO problem." Their documents carried the extraordinary title of "COUNTER-INTELLIGENCE—UNIDENTIFIED FLYING OBJECTS." The documents did not indicate classic counter-intelligence activities. The choice of title therefore is either, unfortunate, inappropriate or sinister. An extract from one of the documents gives an insight into the UFO milieu:

6/32/Air(10)
Headquarters
RAAF Base
EDINBURGH SA 5111
29th May 1972

Department of Air (Attention: D/DAFI IR)
For Information:

Headquarters Operational Command

COUNTER-INTELLIGENCE -
UNIDENTIFIED FLYING OBJECTS

1. Enclosed is an UFO report forwarded to this Headquarters by "The Australian Flying Saucer Research Society - (Adelaide)," together with an accompanying letter from Mr John Burford which, inter alia, outlines recent moves to amalgamate the various UFO "research" societies in South Australia...

2. As on many occasions in the past, the report arrived at this Headquarters too late to make an investigation possible without considerable embarrassment and possible adverse publicity. The various UFO societies in this State, while aware of the RAAF's responsibility to investigate UFO sightings in an official capacity, are nonetheless reluctant to pass on information on UFO sightings to the RAAF until they have "picked the bones clean." Every attempt has been made by this Headquarters to elicit the co-operation of local UFO organisations, and in particular the AFSRS, in an endeavour to gain some first-hand information on UFO sightings....

4. Also enclosed for your information is a list of alleged sightings investigated by the AFSRS alone in 1971. It is significant that of the 112 sights, not one was reported to this Headquarters in the first instance. Indeed, it was only at the personal whim of Mr. Norris that the RAAF received copies of investigations (without "findings") in the long term. It would appear that, in spite of sparse and rather patronising publicity by the mass media to the effect that the RAAF is the responsible UFO-reporting organisation, and arrangements with the police to have any individual sighting a UFO contact this Headquarters, the public at large in this State remains either ignorant of the correct procedure, or chooses to contact the more glamorous - and credulous – "flying saucer" society. Furthermore, we are not aware of any effort on a national scale by higher authority to inform the public of the RAAF position in this matter, which is very active in South Australia.

5. From the foregoing, it can be seen that, if the proposed amalgamation of UFO groups in this State comes to pass, and timely reports of UFO sightings are passed to this Headquarters as indicated by Mr. Burford's remarks, the volume of work involved in investigating and processing such sightings will increase considerably. In fact, it is doubtful whether the Officer-in-Charge of UFO's at this Headquarters (a secondary appointment) would be able to cope with such an increase, without significant and non-acceptable inroads being made into his primary role.

(E.T. PICKERD) Air Commodore, Officer Commanding[63]

DEFCON 3 to Top Secret UMBRA—A National Security Crisis with a UFO Connection in 1973

On a narrow west coast peninsula, over one thousand kilometers to the north of the main centers of population in Western Australia, stands an enigmatic monument to the military ethic. It is a remote spot even for a country as immense and thinly populated as Australia. A vast array of antennas and towers stands out in stark contrast to the harsh natural beauty of the

U.S. Naval Communication Station Harold E. Holt

surrounding terrain. The facility is divided into three principal sites—Areas A, B and C. Area A lies on the northernmost tip of the peninsula. Rising to a dizzying height of 387 meters is Tower Zero—the central structure of an enormous arrangement of towers. Another twelve towers stand in two concentric rings around it. The towers support large spider webs of wire—the Very Low Frequency (VLF) antenna array covering one thousand acres—the largest in the world. A few kilometers to the south is Area B. It consists of the facilities headquarters and the High Frequency transmitter site. Area C—the main receiver site of this secretive facility—is located 60 km further to the south.

Collectively the three sites function as a window into an extraordinary world that few of us are privy to enter. This is the vast world of military intelligence. The site is officially called U.S. Naval Communication Station Harold E. Holt. It is more popularly known as North West Cape. In the enormous scheme of facilities that make up the worldwide U.S. intelligence gathering network, North West Cape, until recently, played an important and acutely sensitive role. It was never very far from the drama and controversy that pivoted around the fears of possible nuclear war between the superpowers.

In his 1980 book, *A Suitable Piece of Real Estate*, Dr. Desmond Ball, senior research fellow in the Strategic and Defence Studies Centre at the Australian National University, wrote, "NW Cape...is presently one of the most important links in the U.S. global defence network." Its main function was "to provide communication for the U.S. Navy's most powerful deterrent force—the nuclear powered ballistic missile submarine." Dr. Ball further stated: "The National Security Agency (NSA) is the principal U.S. intelligence agency operating in Australia; ...Compared to the CIA in Australia, the NSA has a much larger presence, is more important, more secret, and closer to Australia's own intelligence organisations." It is responsible for all "the various activities associated with Signals Intelligence (SIGINT)—electronic intelligence, communications intelligence, radar intelligence, electronic counter intelligence and signal security."[64]

The NSA operates at the NW Cape base through its Naval Security Group component. The base acted as a ground station for the Big Bird "spy in the sky" satellites.[65] The North West Cape base, along with other U.S. bases around Australia (such as Pine Gap and Nurrungar), have long been a matter of acute political sensitivity, specifically related to the assertion that such sites would be prime nuclear targets during a major outbreak of hostilities between the superpowers.

While that threat appears to have diminished in recent years, due to the collapse of the old Soviet empire, during October 1973 as humanity staggered towards the edge of nuclear brinkmanship, NW Cape dragged Australia into the global arena as a naive and compromised sidelines player. Perhaps never were we so close to the brink of annihilation than during those harrowing days of the Yom Kippur Middle East war.

On October 11, 1973, five days after the Middle East War broke out, North West Cape along with other U.S. bases in Australia were put on full alert. According to Richard Hall, in his book *The Secret State* (1978), this alert status was to escalate dramatically due to "an NSA misreading of Arabic in a Syrian message to the USSR which led Kissinger and Nixon to believe that Soviet troops might be sent to the Middle East." This fiasco climaxed early on the morning of October 25, 1973, in Washington D.C. A full nuclear alert went out to all U.S. forces. North West Cape was used to communicate the alert to both conventional and nuclear forces in this region. The acute security alert status "Def Con 3" was reached. Local time at North West Cape was early evening.

Something else intruded into the crisis-charged atmosphere over North West Cape that evening. At about 1915 hours, on that fateful Thursday, Lt. Commander M_____ (USN) observed "a large black, airborne object" at a distance of approximately 8 kilometers to the west at an altitude estimated at 600 meters. Lt. Cmdr. M_____ was driving south from the naval communication station towards the support township of Exmouth, along Murat Road. The officer indicated in a written statement that "After about 20-25 seconds the craft accelerated at unbelievable speed and disappeared to the north." The officer, who had "never experienced anything like it," said the craft made "no noise or exhaust."

403

He saw it "hovering at first, then accelerating beyond belief."

At the base, Fire Captain (USN) Bill L____ also saw the extraordinary craft. He provided the following statement:

> At 1920 hrs, I was called by the POW to close the Officers club. I proceeded towards the club in the Fire Dept. pick-up 488, when my attention was drawn to a large black object, which at first I took to be a small cloud formation, due west of Area 'B' [in the vicinity of Mount Athol—B. C.]. Whilst travelling towards the Officers club I couldn't help but be attracted by this object's appearance. On alighting from pick-up 488, I stood for several minutes and watched this black sphere hovering. The sky was clear & pale green-blue. No clouds were about whatsoever. The object was completely stationary except for a halo around the centre, which appeared to be either revolving or pulsating. After watching it for approx. 4 minutes, it suddenly took off at tremendous speed & disappeared in a northerly direction, in a few seconds. I consider this object to have been approx. 10 metres in diameter, hovering at 300 metres over the hills due west of the base. It was black, maybe due to looking in the direction of the setting sun. No lights appeared on it at any time.

This was an extraordinary incident. In hindsight of its broader implications, it is incredible that people outside the world of military intelligence were made privy to this report.

A classified NSA affidavit released to U.S. UFO researchers, stated that some UFO material was collected related to intercepted communications of foreign governments (or SIGINT operations) and therefore was properly classified. A date appears in the heavily censored report:

> NSA-originated reports—
> Thirty-eight documents are the direct product of NSA SIGINT operations and one document describes classified SIGINT activities. These documents can be further described as follows:
>
> _____
> b. One record is a 1973 report which _____
>
> _____

The rest of the five line paragraph is censored. Given the SIGINT based coincidence with the UFO presence over North West Cape during a nuclear alert on October 25, 1973, it is reasonable to suspect that the censored paragraph refers to this event. The final telling point was that the Australian Whitlam Labour government was not even promptly informed of the DEFCON 3 nuclear status emanating from Australian soil. This led Whitlam to say the U.S. bases in Australia were no longer sacrosanct, a position that had him completely at odds with the U.S. intelligence community. All this and a provocative UFO report in the middle of it![66]

Despite such obvious national security concerns with UFO sightings, DAFI regularly tried to downgrade their UFO activities. Occasional opportunity arose to breathe life into the RAAF UFO program but these seemed more like mere tokenism.[67] One such example occurred with Dr. Allen Hynek's visit to Australia in 1973. A "Record of Discussion" dated August 24, 1973, revealed "an unofficial meeting" held between Dr. Hynek, Dr. M. Duggin, Harry Turner, and DAFI. The DAFI memo indicated:

> Each member was present in a private capacity to discuss certain procedures of investigation into unusual aerial Sightings in Australia and throughout the world, in an endeavour to expand the scientific relationship to the problem.

The memo concluded on an upbeat note:

All present agreed that the scientific aspects were of prime importance. DAFI suggested that CSIRO or the Department of Science...seemed to be logical agencies to conduct greater in depth investigation in Australia...Any such study should be low key and not known to the lunatic fringe of ufologists.

A week later a memo from Defence HQ Support Command to DAFI concluded that "...unidentified flying objects are not a defence threat. It is therefore suggested that UFO investigation be discontinued." However, the idea of closing the UFO effort also fizzled out.[68]

Strangeness Near Nebo—The RAAF Takes a Look

During March 1975, the RAAF investigated a report that involved physical traces found in a roadside gravel storage area in proximity to the small town of Nebo, Queensland. This was the location of a frightening encounter experienced by five people. The group of two young men and three girls had returned from walking livestock on the night of March 22 along the new Mount Flora to Dingo beach road. At about 10:30 p.m. and some 90 km from Nebo, the group noticed a strange light amongst the timber ahead on the left-hand-side of the road. As they drew closer, the group made out a rather curious object in a gravel storage area just off the road.

The object appeared to consist of a row of flashing dull white-to-yellow lights, attached to a large box-like mass about one meter above ground level, with a circular mass situated directly above. This sphere, some three meters wide, consisted of several concentric rings of non-flashing bluish-green lights, with a central black disc. Some of the witnesses noticed a *pole* connecting these two masses and four legs faintly discernible at the base of the complex. The whole object was about 2.5 meters high and three meters wide.

As they drew level with the strange object and stopped the car, a tremendous bang emanated from the object. The noise was likened to the sound heard when in close proximity to a shot gun being fired. The vehicle seemed to shake in response, and the suddenness of the sound frightened the group. They drove further down the road. Some of the witnesses saw that the upper circular mass "seemed to be watching us," as if "they were keeping us under observation." The driver turned the vehicle around and then, once they were level with the object again, stopped. This time there was no loud noise. The two men wanted to get out, but all three girls in the back seat were terrified. They locked the car doors and pummelled the driver with their fists, imploring him to drive away.

The group drove 15 km and stopped when they found a road construction crew, and proceeded to describe the frightening spectacle. The two men convinced one of the construction workers to accompany them back to the area. The girls were too frightened and waited at the camp. The trio found that the object was no longer at the storage area, but they confirmed the presence of unusual indentations at the spot. The shaken party then returned home.

The next day they reported the event to the Nebo police. One of the officers accompanied them back to the site. His report highlights the impact of their experience:

Whilst at the scene I mentioned to Caroline, aged 12 years, that if we waited for a bit, the UFO might return. The child became quite upset and was obviously frightened. She continued to be disturbed whilst at the location and constantly looked all around as if she expected something to return.

Caroline's written statement concludes: "I *never* want to see one of them again."

On March 25, an investigating officer from Townsville RAAF base and an RAAF photographer examined the site of the unusual incident. The RAAF officer's report states:

The unusual marks on the ground consist of: three oval shaped areas; one roughly circular area; and a rectangular area. ...The impact appeared to be very recent with no weathering of the particular areas in question. Some gravel in the areas...was freshly fragmented. ...This was quite obvious to the eye as the bright colours of the unweathered exposed centres of the gravel, stood out among the surrounding weathered stones in the immediate vicinity...

Samples were taken and a number of Townsville RAAF officers were asked to examine the samples. Without exception, all agreed that the stones appeared to be freshly broken when compared with the weathered sample from the surrounding areas. No test for residual radiation was conducted at the site. The investigating officer indicated that the compressed ground had been produced by a heavy weight or pressure. He wrote that he was "unable to explain the nature of the alleged object, or the cause of the unusual ground markings..."[69]

1978 and the RAAF

The RAAF were not prepared for 1978. When the year ended, some 30 incidents remained classified as unknowns, giving a percentage unknown figure of 25.4%. The year before, although lower in actual numbers of reports, also yielded a similar figure of 24.0%. Previous years had been as low as 3.0% and the previous all time high of 12.6% occurred in 1972. It is not surprising that the Department of Defence ceased publishing the annual Summaries with the appearance of Summary No.9 in 1977.

The year 1978 was unusual based on the holdings in the official RAAF files. Some of the highlights included an extraordinary phenomenon seen in a cane field east of Mandurana, Queensland, for three hours on December 6; a UFO sighting by the crew of the *HMAS Adroit* on April 11; an apparent "electromagnetic case" north of Goulburn, New South Wales, on October 22, which left the car speedometer broken; a daylight disc seen near Laverton Air Force base on December 27; a very close encounter between a mini-bus like UFO and a taxi driver in Wavell Heights, Aspley, Queensland, on October 10, 1978; and a large disc-shaped UFO with portholes, one of which allegedly had a shadow or silhouette behind it, at Heathcoate Road, near Menai, New South Wales, on the 29th of October.[70]

On April 11, 1978, the crew of the *HMAS Adroit*, operating out of Darwin in the Timor Sea, observed, at a bearing of 285 degrees, a UFO:

...rise and hover and sink to the horizon several times before finally disappearing beyond the horizon. This object appeared very large and bathed with bright red lights and at one stage appeared to close (on) the ship...The light also appeared at one stage to flicker on and off. This phenomenon lasted several minutes...

The Royal Australian Naval officer who reported the sighting stated: "There is no possibility that sighting was the moon setting and I believe [it] to have [been] caused by a UFO." The event is officially listed as unknown.[71]

The RAAF'S UFO Dance in Decline

The RAAF's enthusiasm for the UFO controversy appears to have diminished sharply after 1977 and 1978. The problem had become unwieldy and unmanageable. Controversy rather than resolution was at every turn. It was difficult to obtain information from the RAAF during those years. Letters were either not answered or replies skirted the substance of enquiries.

A letter, written to the RAAF in April 1980, drew the following internal exchanges:

11/4 A/ADRR -
Re reply, I believe there is a policy of not providing information on UFOs—Is this true?

A/ADPR (Press):
Could you please get a policy sorted out with DAFI in [sic?], whether we should continue to answer such enquiries? I think we are obliged to, particularly when FoI comes in [a reference to the Australian Freedom of Information Act], but I think you were going to discuss the matter with [unclear] at one stage.

DAFI:
I still presume we are still in the UFO business. If so, could I have a suitable reply to pass on to Mr. Chalker, please (14.4.80).

A reply was not forthcoming for another five months. Bill Chalker persisted with efforts to get direct access to the RAAF DOD UFO files. A May 26, 1981, memo from DAFIS (Director of Air Force Intelligence) to DCAS addressing "Investigation of Unusual Aerial Sightings (UAS)" continued the RAAF's occasional lamentations about the toxic political nature of the UFO problem. DAFIS revealed:

My Directorate is charged with the responsibility for UAS investigation and reporting. It has been a contentious issue for many years with opinion varying from a questioning of the need for monitoring such sightings, to the organisational area most appropriately placed to deal with them...The only advantage I see in retaining UAS investigation responsibilities are:
a. it allows a security oversight of unusual events which, on the odd occasion, may bear some military implication
b. it provides "cover" if we wish to investigate some incident, not necessarily related, in more details, and...
...I seek your views on whether the RAAF should continue to carry the responsibility for the investigation of UAS...

It is intriguing to note here that the internal memo was describing *cover* opportunities with regard to UFO events. The Chief of Air Staff replied:

We spoke. While I agree with you in principle, the practicalities suggest we will continue to wear the responsibility. You should, however, ensure that the impact of this chore does not unduly impede our normal business.[72]

Despite this, the end game was quickly approaching.

The next major wave of sightings occurred in the middle of 1983. There was a flurry of nocturnal light sightings, supported in some cases by photos, around Bendigo and Ballarat, Victoria, during May. A spate of activity, including some close encounters, occurred in New South Wales, during June and early July, against a backdrop of radar returns at Sydney airport. The RAAF initiated, with perhaps tongue in cheek, what their UFO files called "Operation Close Encounter," which led to RAAF aircraft being on standby to pursue any verified radar returns. They finally concluded the returns were probably spurious.

In June and July 1983, there was a rash of puzzling radar "paints" from Sydney Airport (Mascot). More than 30 unidentified radar returns were recorded. None were correlated with any visual sightings. When word about the radar returns leaked out, widespread media attention occurred.

The UFO wave of 1983 saw the RAAF remarkably public in their role of examining UFO sightings, indeed at a level virtually unprecedented in the history of the Australian controversy. An uncharitable interpretation of these developments is that the RAAF wanted to be seen as doing its job.[73]

The RAAF'S Change in UFO Policy

The RAAF used the lack of a coherent threat in their 1983 "Operation Close Encounter" to finally resolve their ongoing dilemma—how to eliminate their public involvement in the UFO controversy that fell outside of the RAAF's military/security domain. What of the breaches at North West Cape in 1973 and at Rockbank in 1983? Both incidents had clear links to the clandestine world of military intelligence. Predictably it was not long before the RAAF changed its UFO policy.

The Defence News Release of May 2, 1984, carried the details:

WEDNESDAY. MAY 2 1984 NO. 80/84
UNUSUAL AERIAL SIGHTINGS - RAAF CHANGE IN POLICY

The RAAF in the future will investigate fully only those Unusual Aerial Sightings (UAS) which suggest a defence or national security implication.

The Minister for Defence, Mr Gordon Scholes, said today that while the RAAF would continue to be the first point of contact, UAS reports not considered to have a defence or security implication would not be further investigated. Instead they would be recorded and the UAS observer would be given the address of civilian UAS research organisations if the observer wished to pursue the matter further.

Mr Scholes said that in the past the RAAF's investigation of all UAS reports had often proved time consuming, unproductive and had led to many man-hours of follow-up action by the RAAF and other agencies such as the Department of Aviation and the Bureau of Meteorology.

He said that procedures for investigating UAS reports had remained unchanged for many years. The vast majority of reports submitted by the public had proven not to have a national security significance.

Gordon Scholes

The RAAF news release sparked an inevitable response from the nation's media, with headlines like:

"Gordon's blow: No UFOs" (*Daily Telegraph, Sydney*)
"No go for the average UFO" (*Courier mail, Brisbane*)
"RAAF resets UFO targets" (*Canberra Times*)
"RAAF gives up chase for UFOs" (*West Australian, Perth*)
"UFO reports now have low rating" (*Hobart Mercury*)
"RAAF turns back on UFO Investigations" (*The Australian*)

Bill Chalker responded to the RAAF's policy change with a letter-to-the-editor of *The Sydney Morning Herald*, one of Australia's leading newspapers of record, which was published on May 19, 1984:

RAAF now has correct UFO policy

SIR: The Defence Ministers recent announcement of the RAAF's "new" policy on UFOs (or UASs) ("Stay in

Touch," May 3) is a logical and inevitable expression of the RAAF's 34 year involvement in the UFO controversy.

As the first civilian to have been permitted direct access to the entirety of the RAAF's UFO files, I can confirm that the whole history of the RAAF's activity in this area has been based on two criteria—logically, national security and, predictably, political expediency.

In the main, the RAAF UFO investigations have served their publicly stated purposes. That is, they may have allayed possible fear and alarm by the general public and satisfied the Government that there is no apparent defence implications.

The RAAF has stated "nothing that has arisen for the 3 or 4 per cent of unexplained cases gives any firm support for the belief that interlopers from other places in this world or outside it have been visiting us." It is my contention, having examined many of those unexplained cases, that surprisingly many of them contain extraordinary details which do not lend themselves to easy explanation. These deserve to be the stuff of scientific scrutiny.

In the great majority of cases that make up this unexplained residue, national security implications were not clearly apparent. However in a few, violations are apparent. For example, on October 25, 1973, a UFO hovered near the sensitive North West Cape US Naval Communications base. It was observed by a U.S. Lt-Commander and a base fire captain, before it "accelerated at unbelievable speed and disappeared to the north." The U.S. experience is similar. For example an alleged UFO ostensibly showed "clear intent" (according to previously classified documents) when observed hovering near a weapons storage facilities at Loring Air Force Base late in 1975.

Therefore, I believe the recent change in policy is an appropriate one for the RAAF to adopt. It will allow the RAAF to weed out those rare occasions in which national security violations are suggested and also allow civilian groups to attempt scientific investigations of the infrequent "close encounters" that the RAAF prefers to ignore.

The month of September 1984 saw an embarrassing incident for the government's new UFO policy. Having down-graded their interest, due to an alleged lack of national security impact, a delta-winged aircraft that startled golfers and trail bike riders at Cunnamulla, in southwest Queensland, put the RAAF into a flap. The UFO was described as having no tail, no windows, and no apparent sound. One witness reported it had "beautiful rainbow colours" and "seemed to zigzag like it was out of control" for a short time before disappearing. The object ostensibly remained unidentified. The RAAF denied ownership. The matter was raised in the Senate of Australia's parliament. This led the senator representing the Defence Minister in the Senate to confirm that the RAAF advised there had been no known delta-winged aircraft operating in the vicinity at that time. "Beryl flying off course" was supplied as the only suggestion—a flippant reference to the Queensland's premier pilot, Beryl Young.

Since then the RAAF have taken a relatively low profile in the UFO controversy, but civilian researchers have benefited in that reports coming to the RAAF have been passed on to them. Even RAAF officers have contacted civilian researchers to report their own UFO sightings.[74]

1987—UFO Intrusion at a SAS Exercise

The Australian UFO Research Association's (AURA) Disclosure project uncovered information about a fascinating case that involved Special Air Services Commando units.

UAS report—9 Jun 1987 Learmouth WA 1900hrs 10mins 2M NL

Report form 1—2SASSQN SASR Age 36 Witness A
At RAAF airstrip Learmouth. North/south runway. 9 Jun 1987. 1900-1910hrs. Wispy thin cloud at 10,000 feet. Nil ground wind. Visibility good. First observed East at 1600mils 45 deg el. Last seen NE at 800mils 45 deg el. Initially object at 5000 feet then moved up into cloud at 10,000 feet. Used naked eye and binoculars. One white light changing/pulsating to amber. About 5m in diameter. Round. Like a bright star. Zig zag movement from E to W. Nil sound. Approx speed 200km plus slowed to 80km. Disappeared with great speed.

Approached from E towards the strip. Strip lights were on. It zigzagged to left and right of its axis at 5000 feet. Arrived over the strip (northern end) and went into hover and remained stationary for 6-7 minutes. Light changed colour from white to amber, then it moved upwards into light cloud. Moved NE slowly, then at great speed.

Part 3 of the pro forma is investigating officer's evaluation.
14 Jul 87 at SASR RHQ. Witness has stable personality and is reliable. "Cause is unknown." "It would not appear to have been an aircraft."

Witness A was setting up a DZ for a night free-fall descent. At 1855K was at the W side of the strip opposite civilian terminal. At 1900K the light came from the East. The C130 aircraft involved in the exercise was still on the ground. It became airborne at 1915hrs. Once aircraft airborne tried to establish VHF comms. Two VHF radios used—could not communicate. Fresh batteries in radios. When activity finished witness spoke to pilot of C130. Aircraft had tried to communicate with no success. This was the first time 3-9 Jun 1987 that comms ground to air failed.

Report form 2 Witness B age 26

Same details as witness A. Witness B is a medic. No connection with any UFO organisation. Stable and well balanced.[75]

An Insider Reveals the RAAF Paranormal Experience

It came as a great surprise to many when the RAAF Senior Public Relations Officer in Canberra, Ken Llewelyn, wrote a book about "incredible true stories of airmen on the earth plane and beyond"— *Flight into the Ages*. The book, released in February 1992, carried the disclaimer that it did not represent the official view of the RAAF on paranormal activities. It described ghost encounters, past lives, psychic experiences, and most interestingly of all, as far as this history is concerned, accounts of UFO experiences. Ken Llewelyn covered the highly publicized Valentich disappearance and its alleged UFO connections.[76] He also described Shamus O'Farrell's classic radar-visual encounter and recounted a number of other less well known accounts.

One of Ken Llewelyn's sources was former RAAF pilot Dave Barnes. He gave details of an extraordinary event that took place at Amberley RAAF Base in the late 1970s. More than 20 airmen saw "a large UFO hovering above the runway" at about 5:00 a.m. The object was described as being an inverted cone shape. Barnes also indicated he had spoken to aboriginal elders near the Maralinga atomic bomb test site about their dreamtime and the Min Min lights. The aboriginals had often seen high speed lights north of Maralinga.[77]

Another of Ken Llewelyn's prominent sources was Group Captain Tom Dalton-Morgan. He had been part of a combined Royal Air Force and United States Air Force committee in the late 1940s investigating UFO sightings. It had concluded that most reports could be explained except for three percent which remained unexplained. Dalton-Morgan was the Officer in Charge of Range Operations at Woomera between 1959 and 1963. In the late 1950s, shortly before the test firing of a Black Night rocket, he received a radio call from Percy Hawkins, the Recovery Officer, who reported an exceptionally bright light at about 5,000 feet, travelling at high speed directly towards the test site. Dalton-Morgan and his team, who were 80 to 90 miles southeast of Hawkins' position, were able to view the incoming light from their elevated control building position. They watched it fly in from the northwest, then orbit around the range buildings some five miles to the south. When the UFO was east of the control building, it accelerated and climbed very steeply away to the northeast. Dalton-Morgan concluded:

> I am unable to conceive of any object, plane or missile during my posting to Woomera that was able to perform the manoeuvres seen by my team. Observers at the control tower and the launch site all agreed on the brilliant white-greenish light; the high degree of manoeuvrability, including rate and angle of climb; complete lack of sound; the lack of positive identification of the vehicle fuselage because it was a dark moonless night; and the exceptionally high speed of which it was capable.[78]

Ken Llewelyn said that his book was like *Lady Chatterley's Lover* in official circles—a popular underground book even at high levels. When asked about the perennial charges of cover-ups, he said he had such regular and sufficient contact at high levels in the RAAF to be certain that there was no evidence of hidden cells of high power involvement in the UFO mystery. He appreciated that many people, particularly a lot of UFO researchers and enthusiasts, did not believe this position. He indicated that as of 1992, the current intelligence head was emphatic that there had been no real interest since 1984 and even prior to that year. It was felt that manpower and resources were lacking, and there was no really compelling material to sustain high level interest.[79]

Despite the O'Farrell encounter, the numerous reports of military personnel, such as the 1978 *HMAS Adroit* report, sightings from witnesses of the calibre of Dalton-Morgan and others, and the high level interest of scientists like Harry Turner (JIB), Dr. John Farrands and George Barlow (DSTO), and Dr. Michael Duggin (CSIRO), the military ethic was entrenched and the inevitable termination was well underway. The RAAF's exorcism of the "UFO problem" was at hand.

The RAAF UFO "Swan Song"?

During December 1993, the RAAF formally concluded its long love-hate relationship with UFOs, or "Unusual Aerial Sightings" (UAS) as they preferred to call them. The Department of Defence "swan song" was dryly expressed in Enclosure 1 to Air Force file AF 84 3508 Pt 1 folio 18—RAAF POLICY: UNUSUAL AERIAL SIGHTINGS. In correspondence dated January 4, 1994, civilian UFO groups around Australia were informed by now-Wing Commander Brett Biddington (of the 1983 "Operation Close Encounter" caper fame), on behalf of the Chief of Air Staff, that "The number of reports made to the RAAF in the past decade had declined significantly, which may indicate that organisations such as yours are better known and are meeting the community's requirements."

The new policy, which was an inevitable outgrowth of the downgrading of the RAAF's role back in 1984, stated:

> For many years the RAAF has been formally responsible for handling Unusual Aerial Sightings (UAS) at the official level. Consideration of the scientific record suggests that, whilst not all UAS have a ready explanation, there is no compelling reason for the RAAF to continue to devote resources to recording, investigating and attempting to explain UAS.
>
> The RAAF no longer accepts reports on UAS and no longer attempts assignment of cause or allocation of

reliability. Members of the community who seek to report a UAS to RAAF personnel will be referred to a civil UFO research organisation in the first instance...

Some UAS may relate to events that could have a defence, security, or public safety implication, such as man-made debris falling from space or a burning aircraft. Where members of the community may have witnessed an event of this type they are encouraged to contact the police or civil aviation authorities.[80]

Given the rich history of political and military machinations that quite often effectively prevented opportunities for real science, the policy statement alluding to the "scientific record" is particularly perplexing. Some scientists who have examined in detail the RAAF record can state with some certainty that their record was not particularly scientific and was largely defined by two criteria—national security and political expediency. This appeal to the "scientific record" is particularly galling as the RAAF regularly highlighted that national security, not scientific investigation, was their main focus. For example, in a December 6, 1968, memo from DAFI to HQSC in 554/1/30 Part 2, DAFI mentions, "As you are probably aware the Department of Air (later DOD (Air Office)) is concerned solely with any possible threat to Australian security and *does not go into detailed scientific investigation of UFO reports.*" The evidence in the history written here indicates that science rarely was utilized, despite courageous and persistent efforts by scientists like Harry Turner and Michael Duggin.

But the Department of Defence had a sense of an efficient burial of the "UFO problem," someone had forgotten to inform the alleged corpse. The UFO phenomenon has never really passed away. Remarkable events continue to occur, providing a challenging testament for the legitimacy of the UFO phenomenon.

This concludes the summary of the Australian government's interaction with the UFO phenomenon. The following additional information concerns specific information related to the chronology of Australian disclosure efforts as well as statistical data related to RAAF UFO sighting reports.

Appendix I: The Chronology of Australian Disclosure Efforts

In one of the earliest "disclosure" or access efforts, pioneer flying saucer researcher Edgar Jarrold (from Sydney) had a meeting with DAFI Sqd. Ldr. Peter Birch in Melbourne during 1954. This was a discussion-style meeting; Jarrold did not get any access to files. Fred Stone, a researcher from South Australia, had a similar experience. The CAPIO (Commonwealth Aerial Phenomena Investigation Organisation), formed in 1965 as a united civilian front, also only received limited information.

1965-1977. Period covered: 1960 to 1977. Archives released: Sighting summaries 1-9 released: 1,048 reports summarised. Comments: The first of the summaries appeared in 1965, listing events from 1960 to 1965. This format continued until 1968. The year 1969 marked the first of the annual summary formats, which largely continued up to 1977. These summaries became the form of "public disclosure." A few groups and researchers such as VUFORS and Bill Chalker got some actual case reports, but those reports did not detail any of the material they apparently received.

1982-1984. Period covered: 1950 to 1984. Archives released: 63 files examined by Bill Chalker, which included more than 1,610 reports mainly from RAAF DOD files and limited amount from DoA (Dept.

of Aviation) files. Sighting summary No. 9 (1977 reports) was the last publicly released. Summaries 10 to 12 covering 1978, 1979 and 1980 (a total of 210 summarised reports) were released to Bill Chalker in 1982. Chalker published extensively on this access and made a set of file papers available to the UFO Research Australia Network (in view of the decline of the Australian Centre for UFO Studies). Comments: 18 RAAF files were examined in Chalker's first 1982 visit. The total examined through 1984 were the 63 files mentioned.

1999. Period covered: 1953-1955 (the missing first DAFI file 114/1/197), 1952-1955 (the Casey UFO papers), 1954 (Sea Fury case file), 1952-1957 (CSIRO file), 1952-1960 NSW DoA UFO files. Archives released: Bill Chalker examined 114/1/197 file and CSIRO file in Canberra NAA office. Jason Cowland, then a Victoria-based researcher, facilitated Chalker's access to the Casey papers and the Sea Fury case file; the latter duplicated a RAN (Royal Australian Navy) file released to Chalker in 1982. (During this period Keith Basterfield started using the Archives Act under the 30 year rule to get full copies of early DOD file series.)

2000. Period covered: 1968-1973 (JIB/JIO DOD UFO files). Archives released: Government intelligence files copies given to Bill Chalker from private files of Harry Turner, retired Defence scientist.

2001. Period covered: 1952, 1969. Archives released: 1952 file re: NSW sightings which precipitated Government minister Richard Casey's entry into the UFO controversy.

By 2003 the first of the digitized government UFO files began to appear on the NAA website.

2003-2008. Period covered: 1950 to 1991. Archives released: 151 files examined by the AUFORN auspiced Disclosure Australia project undertaken by the AURA group, co-ordinated by Keith Basterfield. There is an uncertain quantity of reports beyond 1610, mainly RAAF files, but also including CSIRO, Department of Supply, DoA, JIB/JIO (now DIO-Defence Intelligence Organisation), ASIO and other agencies. Details on the AUFORN website in the Disclosure Australia archive: http://www.auforn.com/

Disclosure and Destruction of Official Australian UFO Files

The Australian Disclosure Project, supported by the Australian UFO Research Network (AUFORN) and carried out by AURA is a worthy and excellent effort that has made much of the official UFO history more readily identified and accessible.

The Disclosure project, however, identified one disturbing action on the part of the Australian Department of Defence. The DoD had destroyed a substantial part of their UFO files for little more reason than cleaning house. The Disclosure project had John Peterson, case officer, FOI unit for the DoD in 2004 confirm that the AF 529/1/3 series and AF84/3265 Part 1 files were destroyed in accordance with NAA Disposal Authority GDA 14. These represent the RAAF UFO (or UAS) sightings files from 1974 to 1982. The Department of Defence had destroyed eight years of official sighting files.[81]

Appendix II: The RAAF UFO Data

More than 1,612 reports were received by the RAAF between 1950 and June, 1984. The actual figure is somewhat greater due to incomplete records and scattered omissions from the Summary reports periodically produced by the RAAF between 1965 and 1980. Accurate figures for the period 1950 and 1954 are not possible, due to the loss of the original files.

It is possible to give a rough statistical breakdown of the RAAF's total investigations from 1950 to June 1984. This needs to be broken up into four periods, due to different sources of information and lack of official "unknown" percentages outside the period from 1960 to 1990 inclusive. The following tables represent a breakdown of RAAF UFO investigations.

PERIOD 1 (1950-1954)

YEAR	No. Reports	No. "unknown"	Percent "unknown"
1950	3	0	0
1951	4	2	50.0%
1952	5	0	0
1953	13	2	15.4%
1954	38	8	20.0%

Records for this period are incomplete with the only surviving records being the previously secret "1954 Report on 'Flying Saucers'" prepared for the Directorate of Air Force Intelligence (DAFI) at their request by nuclear physicist Harry Turner as a "scientific appreciation" of their reports. Some of the reports from this period survive in the old DCA UFO files, which were examined by Bill Chalker during November 1982, at the Melbourne offices of the Bureau of Air Safety Investigation. The total for 1954 consists of 35 from the "1954 Report" plus three additional reports, namely two from the Ballarat School of Radio and the classic radar visual event over Goulburn, NSW, involving a Naval Sea Fury aircraft. Only the latter is included as an "unknown," in addition to those cited in the "1954 Report."

PERIOD 2 (1955-1959)

YEAR	No. Reports	No. "unknown"	Percent "unknown"
1955	3	0	0
1956	9	1	11.1%
1957	14	2	14.2%
1958	7	1	14.3%
1959	24	2	8.3%

Records for only the latter part of 1955 are present in the extant DAFI files Chalker examined. Reports for 1956 to 1959 appear to be somewhat incomplete. The "unknown" figures are Chalker's own estimates and therefore should not be regarded as official figures.

PERIOD 3 (1960-1980)

YEAR	No. Reports	No. "unknown"*	Percent "unknown"	Source of Information
1960	20	0	0	Summary No. 1
1961	14	0	0	Summary No. 1
1962	25	0	0	Summary No. 1
1963	17	0	0	Summary No. 1
1964	17	1	5.9%	Summary No. 1
1965	52	2	3.9%	Summary No. 1
1966	74	1	1.4%	Summary No. 1
1967	95	0	0	Summary No. 1
1968	101	0	0	Summary No. 1
1969	94	2	2.1%	Summary No. 2
1970	37	4	10.8%	Summary No. 3
1971	52	6	11.5%	Summary No. 3
1972	87	11	12.6%	Summary No. 4
1973	193	4	2.1%	Summary No. 5
1974	67	2	3.0%	Summary No. 6
1975	39	4	10.2%	Summary No. 7
1976	39	4	10.2%	Summary No. 8
1977	25	6	24.0%	Summary No. 9
1978	118	30	25.4%	Summary No. 10
1979	45	15	33.3%	Summary No. 11
1980	47	10	21.3%	Summary No. 12
TOTAL	1258	102	8.1%	

* Some "unknowns" are not included due to low weight status, i.e. insufficient information or the possible explanation provided was probable.

This is the only period for which official "unknown" figures can be supplied, as based on the Unusual Aerial Sighting Summaries, nos. 1 to 12. Summaries nos. 10, 11 and 12 were not generally released but were supplied to Bill Chalker, during his file review in 1982, by the RAAF.

PERIOD 4 (1981-1984)

YEAR	No. Reports	No. "unknown"	Percent "unknown"
1981	44		
1982	56		
1983	117		
1984	15*		

(* up to June 1984)

Only the total numbers of reports on file with the RAAF can be supplied based on personal file inspections and DAFI advice.

Appendix III: The Civilian UFO DATA

To put the RAAF data into proper perspective, consider the following. From 1950 to 1984, the RAAF dealt with more than 1,612 reports, and 1,258 from 1960 to 1980. One of the best civilian groups in Australia, the Tasmanian UFO Investigation Centre (TUFOIC), has been keeping valuable statistics on their investigations for years. For one small Australian state alone, they dealt with 2,131 reports up to and including 1980. The period 1960 to 1980 has been chosen for display here as it is the only period for which the RAAF have published data. The following table compares the data.

Organization	Total No. of Reports	Total No. of "unknowns"	Percent "unknowns"
RAAF	1,258	102	8.1%
TUFOIC	1,681	390	23.2%

It is quite apparent that compared to civilian UFO research groups, the RAAF has far less claim to having legitimately and comprehensively examined the UFO problem.

Notes

[1] RAAF UFO Policy File Series 554/1/30 Part 3.

[2] External Affairs File Series M1148.

[3] External Affairs File Series M1148.

[4] External Affairs File Series M1148.

[5] External Affairs File Series M1148.

[6] External Affairs File Series M1148.

[7] Hansard Parliamentary Record, August 14, 1952.

[8] DCA file series 21/1/387 Part 1.

[9] Hansard Parliamentary Record, November 20, 1953

[10] RAAF UFO Policy File 554/1/30 Part 1.

[11] Indeed the second part of the 114/1/197 series, opened on 16 September 1955, was renumbered to become the 554/1/30 Part 1—the beginning of the long running file series devoted to DAFI material on flying saucers, UFOs and ultimately their favoured nomenclature UAS—Unusual Aerial Sightings. There were 35 parts to this file series running from 1955 to about 1974, when it was replaced by yet another UFO sightings file, series 529/1/3, which lasted until 1983 with 15 parts. Another file series, 114/1/201 (related to the 1950s 114/1/197 series), evolved into the policy file series 554/1/30 by 1953 and had three parts up to 1984. Because UFO enquiries directed to the RAAF from a variety of parties including civilians were included in the early parts of this file series, yet another file series, namely Enquiry Files, developed by the 1960s with 574/3188 evolving then into series 529/1/4.

[12] RAAF File Series 5/6/Air Part 1 "Training Command Headquarters Reports on Unusual Activity & Aerial Phenomena."

[13] *Melbourne "Sun"* newspaper, January 5, 1954.

[14] Captain Jones' own detailed account, as described in his official report to a Dr. Shaw of the DCA, was present in the earliest DCA UFO files I was permitted to examine in November 1982. Here is how Captain Jones described his experience:

> On the evening of the 10th, whilst setting course for Mackay, I wish to report that I witnessed a phenomenon.

Whilst climbing out of Mackay, on a heading of 114 magnetic, at an altitude of 2,000 feet, I observed due east of us, a light the size and comparative intensity of the star Sirius and the same colour right above the horizon.

This light levelled off at approximately 4000 ft. and headed in a northerly direction and then back to the northwest. This light climbed at an angle of approximately 70 degrees to a height of approximately 8,000 ft, described a large orbit and passed over us heading north approximately 1,000 feet above us. At this time we were heading south at a height of 5,000 feet. The time was 1811 hours EST (6:11 pm AEST). We had this light in view continuously for 5 minutes. Both myself and the second pilot and the Tower operator saw this light. The sun had been set for some minutes. There was a strong red glow in the west and the horizon to the east was still discernible. As soon as it levelled out heading north when I first saw it, the intensity decreased to that of a faint star. There were no abrupt changes of courses and altitude apart from the climb. The speed varied from initially 200 mph to 700 mph.

[15] O.H. Turner's report located in RAAF UFO Policy file series 554/1/30 Part 1.

[16] DCA file series 21/1/387 part 1.

[17] O.H. Turner's report located in RAAF UFO Policy file series 554/1/30 Part 1. In 1999 I was reviewing the current status of the Canberra UFO file holdings at the National Archives via a web search. I was surprised to see a listing for a 114/1/197 file with a date range of October 1953 to April 1955. This predated the earliest file I had examined during my file review between 1982 and 1984. That file started in 1955. I soon established that it was the long missing 114/1/197 file. I immediately travelled to Canberra to examine the file in October 1999. It contained, as expected, information on the famous 1953 Drury film, further information on the background to Harry Turner's classified examination and report on the DAFI UFO files of 1950 to 1954. The file also contained interesting "intelligence" about man-made "flying saucer" rumours and anecdotes, as well as early pre-1955 flying saucer and UFO events.

[18] RAAF UFO Policy File Series 554/1/30 Part 1.

[19] Ibid.

[20] DNA file released to the current author in 1982. The Sea Fury is also duplicated in DAFI files.

[21] In a 2JJJ Australian radio interview (circa 1995), "Shamus" O'Farrell described the incident:

I said, "Nowra, this is 921. Do you have me on radar?"

And a few seconds later they came back and said, "Affirmative 921. We have you coming in from the west. We have another two contacts as well. Which one are you?"

I said, "I think I'm the central one." And so they said, "Do a 180...for identification." So I did a quick 180 and then continued on around and made it a 360 back to where I was going.

They said, "Yes, we've got you. You're the centre aircraft." I said that's correct. They then said to me, "Who are the other two aircraft," and I said, "I don't know. I was hoping you would tell me, because I didn't think there was anyone up here." They said, "Well there shouldn't be, and they certainly shouldn't be that close to you."

So the conversation went on like this and I was very pleased to be talking to somebody because it gave me a lot of reassurance. With that these two aircraft came in quite close to me and I could really see the dark mass and that they were quite big, but I couldn't make out any other lights or any other form of an aircraft. With that they took off and headed off to the north east at great speed.

I was about to press the button and tell them at Nowra that the two aircraft were departing when Nowra called me up and said, "The other two aircraft appear to be departing at high speed to the north east. Is that correct?" and I said, "Yes!" And they said, "Roger, we'll see if we can track them." They tracked them for a while and then lost them.

I came in and landed at 7:30 (1930) and when I got there, there were quite a few people waiting for me. I thought it was a bit strange and so they came over, and they said, "You sure you had aircraft out there!" and I said yes. The Surgeon Commander came over and spoke to me. He said did I feel sick, or was I upset. I said no. He ran his hand over my head to see whether I had any bumps. He had a look at me and decided I was okay. So then he said, "Perhaps you'd like to come to the sick bay after you've changed and we'll do an examination." So after I was finished I went up to sick bay and he gave me a more thorough medical, and said, no, I appeared to be alright. I found out later, they at the same time, they checked to make sure I hadn't been drinking before I took off and all that sort of thing.

During this interview, Dr. Hynek's involvement came up:

> This man [Hynek]—a professor—had made a study of thousands of sightings all around the world and he had decided my sighting was one of those that he had not been able to explain away by other means. Any way I had a talk with him. He was a very interesting chap and he made the comment that there were about 13 or 15, I don't remember, sightings that he was aware of over the years that were like mine and could not be explained away. The interesting thing he said was that all of these sightings had been made by professional people in aviation. By that he meant they were military pilots, military air crew, civil aviation operators, air traffic controllers, and the like, or airline pilots. These were the ones he was now (1973) going around meeting the people themselves and investigating. All the others he had written off and had been able to explain down to some other phenomena. It came to the point where he said, "Your sighting cannot be explained away." And he left it at that. To this day I wouldn't know where it came from or where it went.

I have had the opportunity to talk extensively with Shamus O'Farrell. I was particularly interested in how the interview with Dr. Hynek in 1973 came about:

> It was done through Sir Arthur Tange, who was secretary of the Department of Defence at the time. Hynek contacted him direct. Prior to that the Victorian group (VUFORS) had written to me and asked me for the details, which I sent to them. I didn't care...I had some correspondence. They spoke with me about it. Sometime after that Sir Arthur Tange contacted me and said Hynek was coming out. He had written to him, through the U.S. Embassy, to set up a meeting. I think they (VUFORS) were trying to bask a bit in his glory when he was out here at the time. He may have seen them for all I know. They certainly wrote to me and asked for the full details of the story which I did. They sent me back a lot of gobbledygook. It was all wrong. They hadn't done much work on it themselves, even for an organisation meant to be specialising in it. Anyway, I didn't worry about it. And the next thing I knew I had a telephone call one day from Sir Arthur Tange saying that Hynek was coming and he would like me to met him. I said, well, I haven't got all the facts, they're all a bit hazy. So he sent me the two Defence Department files over to read, to refresh it all.

I said, "That seems to indicate a high level of interest in Hynek's visit at the time?"

> Yes, well, I don't think so. All that happened was that it was more of a courtesy because he was a very important guy, Hynek, and they wanted to show him the courtesies etc. As far as Defence was concerned it was dead and forgotten but they had not got rid of the files. They kept them. Normally when files like that are written off they are either decided they'll put them in Archives or dispose of them and destroy them. But they had done neither. They had remained in the JIO. They'd kept them. I don't know what they had in mind about it, I never questioned it. I just used them as a means to refresh my memory.

> Later the guy who became the chief Defence scientist, John Farrands, was very interested in it too, and he had done a lot of early investigations in most of the reports when he was chief defence scientist and in the period just before he became chief defence scientist. He had a talk with me. I was a friend of his. I used to meet with him at lunch. He went over it in great detail. He knew it all. He agreed it was something that couldn't be refuted. No matter how hard they tried, and they tried very hard to knock it all back. They checked everything from medical, down to when was the last time I had had a drink...

I said, "That must have been a bit of a concern to you?"

> Well, I wanted to hush it all up. That sort of investigation made me look a bit of a fool. I was worried it wasn't going to do my career any good. (Apart from the radar witness) it locked in a sighting over the NDB (non directional beacon) at Narulan, at the same time. There happened to be a guy working on the NDB. It was down at the time. He had gone to repair it. He happened to look up at the time because he saw these lights fly overhead. Also the air traffic control officer in the tower at Mascot saw them approaching him. It was all investigated by the then RAAF guy who did it and later it was also investigated by the Joint Intelligence Bureau.

[22] RAAF UFO Policy file series 554/1/30 Part 1.

[23] Letters to the current author (1982) from R. Mathams. During 1966 Bob Mathams drove out with three CIA staff to a location west of Alice Springs for a celebratory wine toast for the selection of a site for "Merino," the codename for what was to become Pine Gap (see *The Wizards of Langley* by Jeffrey Richelson (2001), page 109). So it shouldn't be surprising if Mathams' DSTI group in JIB/JIO would occasionally forward UFO reports to the CIA. They were, after all, "brothers in arms," tied together through the UKUSA agreement (See *The Ties that Bind* by Richelson & Ball (1985). More interesting perhaps is the CIA's role in examining the 1953 Drury film. Art Lundahl's CIA NPIC group was apparently involved, just as it had been in other famous films of the same saucer era, such as the Great Falls and Tremonton footages.

[24] Ivan Southall, "Woomera" (1962), p. 250.

[25] Ibid.

[26] Bill Chalker "The OZ Files – the Australian UFO Story" (1996), p. 85.

[27] Department of Supply file series SA 5281, letter dated 20 May 1954.

[28] Department of Supply file series SA 5281.

[29] Department of Supply file series D174 "Unusual Occurrences Flying Saucers at Woomera (1952 – 1955).

[30] Hansard Parliamentary record, November 24, 1959.

[31] RAAF file 580/1/1 (folio 22A) located in policy file 554/1/30 Part 1.

[32] Bill Chalker "The OZ Files – the Australian UFO story" (1996) pp. 91-98.

[33] RAAF UFO Sightings file series 580/1/1 Part 2.

[34] See also "Cressy Revisited" Tasmanian UFO Investigation Centre (TUFOIC) report and media reports also held at 580/1/1 Part 2.

[35] RAAF UFO Sightings file series 580/1/1 Part 2.

[36] James McDonald, "UFOs – an international scientific problem" presented at Canadian aeronautics & Space Institute, Astronautics Symposium, Montreal, Canada, March 12, 1968.

[37] RAAF UFO Sightings file series 580/1/1 Part 2.

[38] Media reports also held at 580/1/1 Part 2, particularly the Launceston Examiner.

[39] Ibid, McDonald.

[40] RAAF UFO Sightings file series 580/1/1 Part 2

[41] Hansard Parliamentary Record, October 20, 1960.

[42] RAAF UFO Policy File series 554/1/30 Part 2.

[43] Bill Chalker, "The OZ Files – the Australian UFO Story" (1996) pp. 106 – 109.

[44] RAAF UFO Sightings file series 580/1/1 Part 4.

[45] RAAF UFO Sightings file series 580/1/1 Part 4.

[46] Media account quoted in James Holledge "Flying Saucers over Australia" (1965) p. 58.

[47] Ibid.' McDonald.

[48] "Summary of Unidentified Aerial Sightings reported to Department of Air, Canberra, ACT, from 1960." See "The RAAF and the UFO problem" section for the background and evolution of the "UAS" summaries. The RAAF started referring to the reports as "*Unusual* Aerial Sightings" rather than "Unidentified Aerial Sightings," removing from summary documentation the cover reference to "unidentified." Within these summaries identifications of events with a "possible cause" of "unknown" evolved to denote "the small percentage of UAS reports that remained unresolved because of insufficient information being supplied, late receipt of report denying timely investigation, remoteness of sighting location, and insufficient current scientific knowledge being available to provide an explanation ..." (Letter to current author from Director of Public Relations (Department of Defence (Air Office), 1980).

[49] RAAF UFO Sightings file series 580/1/1 Part 4 (also RAAF (Darwin) file series BS5/6/Air (91).

[50] The Roberts' paper is held in the RAAF UFO Policy file series 554/1/30 Part 2. See also Bill Chalker, "UFO Sub Rosa Down Under" re the 1965 Ballarat UFO convention for further background, and Australian Flying Saucer Review (UFOIC Edition), No. 8, 1965.

[51] Australian Flying Saucer Review (UFOIC Edition), No. 8, 1965.

[52] RAAF UFO Enquiry file series 574/3/88 Part 1 and Policy file series 554/1/30 Part 2.

[53] RAAF UFO Enquiry file series 574/3/88 Part 1 and Policy file series 554/1/30 Part 2.

[54] RAAF UFO Enquiry file series 574/3/88 Part 1 and Policy file series 554/1/30 Part 2.

[55] Bill Chalker, "UFO Sub Rosa Down Under."

[56] RAAF Policy file series 554/1/30 Part 2.

[57] Based on JIB memos by O.H. Turner made available to the current author.

[58] File copy supplied by O.H. Turner to the current author, plus discussion with O.H. Turner.

[59] Chalker, "The OZ Files" & "UFO Sub Rosa Down Under."

[60] Department of Defence JIO file series 3092/2.

[61] JIB memo by O.H. Turner made available to the current author.

[62] Bill Chalker "The Joint Intelligence Organisation (JIO) and UFOs – A Matter of History" UFO History Keys column, Ufologist magazine, Vol. 11, No.4, Nov-Dec, 2007. See also "Unusual Aerial Sightings – A search through the Australian Government's records systems" compiled by Keith Basterfield, AURA, 2008, available on line through AURA & AUFORN. The Department of Defence JIO file series 3092/2 was referred to the Turner memos supplied to the current author in 2000. The incomplete JIO file 3092/2 was released to Keith Basterfield in 2008.

[63] RAAF file series 6/32/Air (RAAF Edinburgh, SA) located in RAAF UFO Enquiries file series 574/3/88. The second document in the same file also forwarded to Headquarters Operational Command was dated 20th June, 1972:

COUNTER-INTELLIGENCE - UNIDENTIFIED FLYING OBJECTS

Reference: ....

1. ...peculiar ground markings discovered on a farming property at Tooligie Hill, Eyre Peninsula, in late December 1971.

2. The matter first came to the notice of this Headquarters through the "Day by Day" column of "The Advertiser" on 27th January 1972 (which mentioned the markings)

> "...sighted by Eyre Peninsula farmer Robert Habner in the middle of a wheat paddock.
> "Farmer Habner found it while he was reaping. No tracks led to or from it. Peter is investigating."]

... This Headquarters' OIC UFOs...contacted the Peter Powell referred to in the clipping and... received assurances of co-operation. Mr. Powell stated that considerable interest in the Tooligie Hill "phenomenon" was being evinced by local UFO groups and added that a meeting of several of the groups, including the Australian Flying Saucer Research Society (of Colin Norris notoriety), was to be held that Sunday (30th January 1972)...At this juncture it became apparent that a belated RAAF investigation of the "phenomenon" would attract unwanted publicity, and would in any case probably be paralleled by simultaneous investigations by civilian groups. The question of "co-operation" between the RAAF and local UFO groups would then be a matter for speculation and individual interpretation by the media. This Headquarters therefore deemed it prudent not to initiate an on-site investigation into the incident at the time.

4. ...(Newspaper accounts referred to) a projected "safari" to Eyre Peninsula to investigate the "phenomenon"....

> Flt. Lt. King (O i/c UFOI) minuted the following:
> "This morning I received a phone call from Mrs. Habner of Tooligie Hill. She said that Messrs Ianson and Mackereth (of AFSRS) had arrived and were investigating the "phenomenon" on the Habner property. As might be expected, Mr. Norris had arranged the usual publicity and the ABC, 5KA and the Advertiser, according to Mrs. Habner, were on the scene or on tap. She said that she had not expected so much publicity and in any case it was Peter Powell who was supposed to be doing the investigating. His "safari" is due to arrive on Saturday and she had tried to contact him without success to tell him that he had been pre-empted. I informed Mrs. Habner that there was nothing the RAAF could do about the situation and offered my condolences. Mrs. Habner seemed surprised that this HQ had not been informed officially of the "phenomenon" in the first instance as she had reported it to the police in the area.
> "ORWO this morning noticed a leave application submitted by Cpl. A___ of Catering Section. The address given on the application for the week's leave was c/o the Habner property. I interviewed Cpl A____ who said he had answered an advertisement inserted in the local newspapers by Peter Powell for people to accompany him to Eyre Peninsula to investigate the finding. I briefed him on the "no-publicity" requirement and asked him to keep me informed of events."

The airman referred to (above) was also mentioned in our (message) to your department. On his return from leave he was again interviewed by OIC UFOs. The "safari" had taken soil samples and photographed the markings, and also interviewed a number of people in the district, but after a week on the site had not made any findings. Present on the Habner property at the same time were two members of the Australian Flying Saucer Research Society, who also fossicked without discovering the origin of the markings.

5. ...(Mrs. Habner wrote to Flt. Lt. King):

"I am sending you, as promised, some slides and information on the mark we found in our paddock on December 28th 1971. This mark was made in the middle of a wheat crop, with no tracks or marks leading in or out. The diameter of the rim-shape which is spun into the clay soil is approximately 7 feet. 2 feet from the outer edge of the mark the crop was laid flat in an anti-clockwise spinning motion, and in the centre, which measures 45 inches across, the crop was cut to a height of 9 inches.

"The crop was also laid flat (anti-clockwise again) in a small crescent which joins onto one side of the mark. About 12 feet away from the main mark is the same shaped marking spun into the wheat straw, but not with as much force as the main mark. This mark was just on the top of the straw and not cut into the ground. We can only think that whatever tried to land here was put off because of a small mallee stump, and, wanting a smoother place to land, rose up and hovered over to finally land on the main 'site.'

"One family in our district say they saw a strange light which would have been in that position. They saw this on Christmas Eve. We were away from home all that evening.

"We have had approximately 200 visitors from surrounding districts to see it and they all wonder what could have made this mark.

"The cut out circle is still there and will be until we plough it up for seeding. There are still markings of the spun down straw etc. too, although they are not as clearly defined as they were when fresh...."

6. (Attached) is a letter from this Headquarters to the Commissioner of Police, dealing with the incident,

"Dear Commissioner,

"....A telephone conversation between my Officer-in-Charge of UFOs and Mrs. Habner reveals that police authorities in the area were informed of the incident and indeed visited the Habner property prior to the 'phenomenon' becoming public knowledge....

"I am sure you will agree that, as this Headquarters was not informed of the incident in the first instance, any post-event official RAAF investigation of the incident, with attendant publicity, would prove not only unfeasible but also embarrassing to some extent.

"In view of the above, I would appreciate your once again bringing to the notice of your staff the necessity of referring all UFO reports to this Headquarters with the minimum of delay.

Yours faithfully,

(E.T. Pickerd)

Air Commodore"

and (also enclosed) is the Commissioner's reply

"Dear Air Commodore Pickerd,

"...I enclose copy of a report furnished by Inspector R. A. Schlein of Port Lincoln.

"It appears that there was no actual sighting of a U.F.O. at Tooligie Hills in December last, and although the Inspector was aware of strange markings in a field, he did not consider there was sufficient evidence at that time to connect them with a U.F.O. Moreover, as there was already growth from the dislodged wheat heads, it seemed that some time must have elapsed since the disturbance.

"...we are sorry that you have been hindered or embarrassed by the lack of an earlier report.

"Although members generally are already aware of the necessity to report such matters for your information, a further instruction will be issued by a notice in the Police Gazette.

Yours sincerely,

(J.G. McKinna)

Commissioner of Police."

and a copy of a report by Inspector Adolf Schlein of Port Lincoln Police.

7. For your information.

(B.G. KING)

Flight Lieutenant
For Officer Commanding

For something generally dismissed by the RAAF all this seems to be a great amount of effort and activity, either in the name of bureaucracy or "counter-intelligence." Think about it. The two documents were classified RESTRICTED.

[64] Desmond Ball, *A Suitable Piece of Real Estate—American Installations in Australia*, Hale & Iremonger, 1980.

[65] Some of the NSA's operations are described in James Bamford's books *The Puzzle Palace* (1982) and *Body of Secrets* (2001).

[66] Bill Chalker "The UFO Connection – Startling Implications for North West Cape and Australia's security," Omega Science Digest, March, 1985. The 1973 NW Cape RAAF UFO files were made available to the current author's UFO group UFOIC circa 1976. The files in question had not to my knowledge been located in the current available files.

[67] By tokenism I mean the Australian Macquarie Dictionary definition: "the policy of avoiding a real resolution to a problem by a superficial gesture intended to impress and to distract attention from the real issues."

[68] RAAF UFO Policy file series 554/1/30 Part 3.

[69] RAAF files made available to Bill Chalker following request for physical trace data circa 1980.

[70] Chalker, "UFOs Sub Rosa Down Under."

[71] RAAF UFO File series 529/1/3 (1978).

[72] RAAF UFO Policy file series 554/1/30 Part 3

[73] Chalker, "The OZ Files" & "UFO Sub Rosa Down Under."

[74] Chalker, "The OZ Files" & "UFO Sub Rosa Down Under."

[75] RAAF file 5/6/1/Air part 15 (UFO-reports).

[76] The October 1978 disappearance of Cessna & pilot Frederick Valentich in the wake of an apparent UFO encounter over Bass Strait has been extensively documented and discussed. See for example the current author's 1996 book "The OZ Files – the Australian UFO Story." Specific books include Kevin Killey & Gary Lester's "The Devil's Meridian" (1980) and Richard Haines' "Melbourne Episode – Case study of a missing pilot" (1987).

[77] "Min Min lights" are the Australian generic term given to "ghost light" reports. The term originally emerged from reports in the late 19th century and early 20th century located near the old Min Min pub (bar in American parlance) near Boulia in Western Queensland. The area has become a famous landmark for the Min Min light sightings and the term has extended to similar sightings around Australia. See for example Bill Chalker "The Min Min Light revealed – Nature Unbound?" Australian Ufologist Magazine, 2002 and "The Mystery of the Min Min Light" by Maureen Kozicka (1994).

[78] Ken Llewelyn, "Flight into the Ages" (1992).

[79] Interview with Ken Llewelyn by the current author (1992).

[80] Enclosure 1 to RAAF file AF 84 3508 Pt 1 folio 18—RAAF POLICY: UNUSUAL AERIAL SIGHTINGS.

[81] The FOI decision maker in this extraordinary destruction of important UFO case material was Group Captain G. MacDonald, Director of Coordination-Air Force. This unfortunate and extremely short-sighted decision needs to be closely scrutinised and forcefully addressed to avoid any further destruction of official Australian UFO files.

Chapter 18: UFO Secrecy and Disclosure in Spain

UFO Policy in Spain

In November 1967, the Air Force Staff drafted the first internal memo on UFOs. The presence of unidentified flying objects in the national air space was considered "indubitable." The memo proposed to the Chief of Staff that an Information and Analysis Center be created for this purpose within the Air Defense Command. The note was returned to the files without further comments or action.

In 1968, a typical wave of UFO sightings occurred in Spain, with many incidents reported by newspapers and other news media. As a response, in December 1968, the Air Ministry's press office released a communiqué inviting citizens to report cases to the authorities. Days later, 2nd Air Force Chief of the Staff General Mariano Cuadra Medina issued the first regulations on how to handle UFO observations. The information was rated as Confidential.[1]

At this time, Ministry authorities in Spain labeled UFOs as a "delicate issue" and did their best to provide objective information to the public while avoiding cause for alarm. During 1974, another UFO "wave" shook Spain, and early in 1975 the official procedures for dealing with UFO information were updated by General Cuadra, then Minister of the Air.

Copying what journalist J.C. Bourret did in France in 1976 (securing permission from the *Gendarmerie* to have access to its UFO archives), reporter J.J. Benítez requested access to the Spanish Air Force UFO files in October 1977, and he was granted *General Mariano Cuadra Medina*

summaries for twelve reports, which he published immediately in a sensationalist and commercially-oriented book that violated the signed agreement he had reached with the Air Force Chief of Staff. This kind of mismanagement of official UFO information spoiled normal relationships between the Air Force and UFO researchers in Spain for 15 years. The Air Force stated in an internal memorandum:

> This journalist made an indiscriminate use of this information and exploited it for their own benefit, publishing a book and several articles, which have led to the legend of the Secret UFO Archives of the Air Force.[2]

During the 33rd meeting of the United Nations General Assembly, held on October 12, 1978, in New York City, agenda item #126 discussed the "Establishment of an Agency or a Department of the United Nations for Undertaking, Coordinating and Disseminating the Results of Research into Unidentified Flying Objects and Related Phenomena," a proposal addressed by Grenada's Prime Minister, Eric Gairy. (Grenada is a tiny Caribbean island country located northeast of Venezuela.) Subsequently, in the 35th meeting of the UN's Special Political Committee held on November 27, 1978, pursuing the same subject, Dr. Jacques Vallee, among others, spoke for the delegation of Grenada. No positive resolution was made regarding this resolution.

As a consequence of this resolution, the permanent ambassador of Spain to the United Nations wrote to the Spanish Ministry of Foreign Affairs to inform him that during the session devoted to

UFOs "a French scientist from the delegation of that country [sic] made reference to a recently published study by the Armed Forces of Spain on this issue."

This letter was relayed to the Ministry of Defense, which in turn wrote to the Air Force Staff. JEMA (Chief of the Air Staff) replied on January 16, 1979, to say that whenever a UFO sighting was reported to the authorities, an Informing Judge was appointed by the corresponding Air Region to proceed with a proper investigation, according to the norms currently in force. (See appendix: JEMA letter to Ministry of Defense, January 16, 1979) The missive follows:

> According to the records and reports of the Informing Judges held by this Staff, concerning alleged UFOs, some of the phenomena have been motivated by natural causes and others have not been determined accurately, considering the latter as unidentified aerial phenomena. Excluding these investigations, a general study on this topic has not been carried out.[3]

It was obvious that the French scientist (either Dr. Vallee, or Claude Poher who also attended as part of the Grenada delegation) had certainly alluded to the newly-marketed book by Benítez that publicized the set of twelve UFO report summaries he had obtained from the Spanish Air Force.

In January of 1979, the Barcelona-based UFO organization CEI (Center for Interplanetary Studies) solicited the King of Spain for his mediation to gain access to the UFO information collected by the Air Force, Army, Navy and Police. Don Juan Carlos handed this request to the Chief of the Air Staff (JEMA). As a result, on January 25, 1979, the JEMA recommended that the Minister of Defense discontinue the classification of UFO information (See appendix: Ministry of Defense letter, March 26, 1979). The consequence was a meeting held by the Joint Chiefs of the Staff on March 3, 1979, where it was decided to formally define UFO information as Classified, rather than Confidential.

There is little written information disclosing the thoughts of the successive heads of the Air Force regarding the UFO issue. On July 1981, Joan Plana wrote to the Air Space Section (SESPA) posing several conceptual questions. Internal correspondence from the Second Chief of Staff to the Office of Public Affairs established the criteria for a potential (but never-sent) reply to Plana, as follows:

> ...the setting of standards to follow for the appropriate inquiries about the appearance of UFOs in the Spanish airspace, as [well as] the interest the Air Force has on the subject, do not indicate any recognition of the existence of such UFOs as manned or alien spacecrafts, but rather the responsibility that this Air Force has in the environment of the national territory against risks which these Unidentified Flying Objects might cause on air navigation.[4]

This internal document also stressed that this subject was not secret because of the UFO sightings, but because of the related information concerning radar surveillance, detection, and air defense system issues.

During the decade of the 1980s Vicente-Juan Ballester Olmos developed a catalogue of UFO observations by military and police personnel.[5] The plan was to have access to all the UFO information produced by the Armed Forces. This program generated a lot of correspondence with multiple government agencies. The program's working objective was reshaped by focusing it to ensure that the Air Force would deliver its UFO files to the public at large, as these were the most extensive and elaborate records by orders of magnitude. In May 1991, an "Informative Note" (NI) was sent to the Chief of the Air Staff entitled "The UFO Archive and its Possible Release." (See appendix: Flight Safety Section NI, May 22, 1991.) This NI request was the result of meetings and correspondence between Ballester Olmos and both the head of the Air Force Public Affairs Office, Major Ramón Alvarez Mateus, and the head of the Flight Safety Section of the Air Staff, Colonel Alvaro Fernández Rodas. The latter unit was where the UFO archive was kept.

This NI is essential because it explained the current situation of the files. After describing the efforts towards a full declassification, it disclosed two interesting facts:

> What has been filed at Flight Safety [55 records] has become aged. Since 1980 no investigation has been made and, as noted before, since 1988 cases are not even archived.

> The contents of our archive do not reveal any mystery, nor does it clear up doubts to whoever may have them. Investigations have not been made by professionals or by [UFO] phenomenon specialists.[6]

This document is very important because it started a process that would end in the total release of the UFO files in the coming years. The NI recommended that the UFO archives be declassified. Prompted by Ballester Olmos' suggestion, in July 1991 the Chief of the Staff passed instructions to the Air Regions in order to centralize all UFO registers into Madrid Air Force Headquarters. Consequentially, records increased to 62 files. (See appendix: Second Chief of Staff letter to Air Regions, July 26, 1991)

The next step was taken in January 1992, when all the UFO archives were transferred to the Air Operative Command (MOA is the Spanish acronym) at Torrejón AFB (Madrid). This order by General Ramón Fernández Sequeiros, Chief of the Air Staff (JEMA), is a milestone in the history of the Spanish Air Force handling of the UFO phenomena. (See appendix: Chief of Air Staff letter to MOA, January 15, 1992):

General R. Fernández Sequeiros

> I inform you that upon receipt of this letter you will be responsible for the management and handling of all matters related to unidentified flying objects (UFOs), for which the existing documentation at the Air Force Staff is attached.

> After analyzing the documentation submitted, you must draft and submit for approval of my authority the management procedures it deems appropriate, which will include rules to follow on the classification and declassification of records that are generated.

> Once these procedures are approved, declassification will proceed, consistent with the standards adopted in the documents submitted.[7]

At the time this new directive was released, MOA's commander-in-chief was General Alfredo Chamorro Chapinal, who during the next several years would carry out the order with the utmost professionalism and rigor.

Within the MOA structure, the newly added responsibility was placed in the intelligence section, commanded by Lt. Col. Ángel Bastida, a first class officer who years later reached the rank of general, before he died prematurely. He was a key figure in the management of the declassification process, and a great friend with whom Ballester Olmos would work hundreds of hours in the succeeding years.[8]

General A. Chamorro Chapinal

During a hectic pair of months in March and April of 1992, MOA's intelligence produced several official notes and papers: a proposal for UFO files management, the Air Force's UFO archival history from 1962-1992, the existing military rules and regulations, an inventory of all letters addressed to UFO authorities on UFOs since the late 1960s, the first computerized listing of the Air Force UFO files, and finally the draft of IG-40-5— the future procedure for investigation of UFO claims. A proposal for full UFO disclosure was the final result of the working papers prepared by Lieutenant Colonel Bastida for his commander in chief, General Chamorro,

Lt. Colonel A. Bastida and V.J. Ballester

who signed and forwarded it to the Air Force Chief of Staff, General Fernández Sequeiros. (See appendix: MOA's commander-in-chief to JEMA, April 13, 1992)

On April 14, 1992, the Joint Chiefs of the Staffs (JUJEM) supported Fernández Sequeiros' proposal and downgraded the classification level to mere Internal Reserve, its practical significance being that the Air Force Chief of Staff was empowered to fully declassify and release the UFO files at his discretion. (See appendix: Letter from JEMA's chief of cabinet, April 29, 1992)

UFO Procedures Currently in Force

"Instrucción General 40-5" (General Instruction No. 40-5) is the present 28-page procedure used for investigations of UFO sightings by the Air Force, issued March 31, 1992, by the Chief of the Staff and distributed to the units in June of 1992. As Lieutenant Colonel Bastida later admitted, it was inspired by several UFO questionnaires that Ballester Olmos had supplied to the Air Force, including those used by the USAF.

IG 40-5 states that as soon as a UFO report is communicated to the Air Force, it will be reported to both MOA and the regional Air Command with some primary information on the event, accompanied with a statement from the nearby Air Force unit advising whether or not an investigation should be carried out. If the regional Air Command decides to start an inquiry, a Reporting Officer will be appointed. MOA may also appoint an Investigating Officer from the Intelligence Section. Following the issued procedures, a Confidential File will be created. When the investigation is finished, MOA will either recommend that JEMA declassify it or to send it to the JUJEM for higher classification.

As internal documentation, the IG protocol is not declassified itself, but the Air Force is indulgent in allowing UFO researchers to have access to it. (See appendix: Cover of IG 40-5, issued March 31, 1992) Since the inception of the IG 40-5, only three times has this been activated, two in 1993 and one in 1995. In all cases, it generated files of some 100 pages in length, which soon were declassified in their entirety. It is expected that any future release of reports will continue to be complete.

The UFO Disclosure Process

As soon as the classification downgrading took place, MOA's Intelligence Section (Bastida) started the hard work of reviewing all 62 files. Only people's names were deleted from the documents, and for every file a declassification proposal was submitted to the authority of JEMA on a routine basis.

Stamped with the Chief of Air Staff signature, the files were sent to the Library of the Air Force Headquarters (Madrid) for free consultation and reproduction for the public. The first UFO file was declassified in September 1992. This process lasted seven more years up to 1999, when finally 84 files (covering 122 events reported from 1962 to 1995) were disclosed. In 1993, Lt. Col. Bastida left the MOA due to a promotion and was replaced by Lt. Col. Enrique Rocamora Aniorte, who followed-up the process until its termination, utilizing serious and high working standards. Bastida released 22 files between 1992 and 1993, and Rocamora released 62 files between 1993 and 1999.

Lieutenant Colonel E. Rocamora

The design structure of a typical declassified file includes the cover sheet (one or more pages), with several box headings: MANDO OPERATIVO AÉREO (Air Operative Command) later renamed as MANDO AÉREO DE COMBATE (Air Combat Command), ESTADO MAYOR - SECCIÓN DE INTELIGENCIA (Staff-Intelligence Section), and the general subject description AVISTAMIENTO DE FENÓMENOS EXTRAÑOS (Sighting of Strange Phenomena).

It is followed by seven brief sections that summarize the file contents.

EXPEDIENTE (file): file number representing the event date as year, month, day (e.g., 791111 for 11 November 1979) or any other indicative like the source and reception date (e.g., MACAN NOV92)

LUGAR (location)

FECHA (date)

RESUMEN (abstract)

ÍNDICE DE DOCUMENTOS (index of documents)

CONSIDERACIONES (comments). In every case it reads: "There are no issues that require maintaining the status of "classified matter")

PROPUESTA DE CLASIFICACIÓN (proposal for classification). In every case it reads: "Declassified"

The cover sheet is then dated in Torrejón (a town on the outskirts of Madrid where the Air Force Base is located) and signed by the MOA/MACOM intelligence officer in charge. The rest of the file is the body of the report and the attachments. Once JEMA approves the proposal, a DESCLASIFICADO (declassified) stamp is printed on the document. (See appendix: Example of declassified file, cover pages 1 and 2)

When the process was finished, 84 files had been compiled and all of them were made fully public. The disclosed files and the 122 actual UFO events they represent (i.e., individual reports, some files containing several cases) consist of:

78 (*Case*) files comprising 122 different events, 1962-1995

4 (*Bis*) files with supplementary information found for cases previously declassified

1 (*Directive*) file to release an assortment of historical regulations

1 (*Catalogue*) file containing 4 Air Force UFO report lists created over time

UFO Monographs at the Air School

Not unexpectedly, over the years the UFO subject has been the motif for several academic monographs delivered to fulfill academic requirements in the Superior Air School of the Spanish Air Force ("Escuela Superior del Aire"). In fact, three such papers devoted to the UFO phenomenon have been presented. In February 1967, Captain Antonio González de Boado wrote the text (in Spanish) "Unidentified Flying Objects" to qualify in the 73rd Training Course for rank upgrading. Captain Boado believed in the factual reality of UFOs, and his 19-page essay was a simple, personal overview of the existing flying saucer evidence. This ahead-of-his-time Air Force captain died in 1969 in a flight accident.

The second monograph was prepared in September 1981 by Lt. Col. Antonio Muñoz Ferro-Sastre, as a requirement for the 37th Staff Course. It was entitled "Methodology Used Between 1974 and 1977 in the UFO Investigations in the Air Zone of the Canary Islands." Lt. Col. Muñoz spoke from the extensive experience he had gained as an instructing judge appointed to investigate several UFO sightings reported in this Spanish region located in the Atlantic Ocean. The full text of this monograph, plus introductory notes by this author, is available online.[9] An analysis of the so-called UFO sightings in the Canary Islands area, revealed years later, their man-made nature as U.S. Navy ballistic missiles.[10]

In September 1998, Lieutenant Colonel Enrique Rocamora, who had been in charge of declassification from 1993-1999, entered the 57th Staff Course. Along with consultations and contributions from Ballester Olmos, he created a massive monograph under the title "The Process of Declassification of UFO Documentation in the Air Force," with ten chapters and 16 attachments amounting to 296 pages. (See appendix: Cover of UFO monograph by Lt. Col. Enrique Rocamora. Unfortunately, most works by alumni of Staff Courses are not available to the public, but may be released over time.)

Cooperation with Air Force Intelligence on UFOs

Before the disclosure process started, Vicente-Juan Ballester Olmos, who at the time was the Director of Research for CEI, was contacted by Lt. Col. Bastida of MOA Intelligence. No precedent existed for a UFO researcher to receive a request to brainstorm with a member of the military intelligence community. Bastida was found to be a thoughtful and open-minded military man. As a result, a sincere friendship coupled with a smooth working relationship and fruitful trading of ideas soon developed. Bastida was able to glean useful information on serious UFO studies from an experienced civilian, even to the point of using one of his books[11] as a reference work for his duties at the MOA.[12] Ballester Olmos in turn learned first-hand of the Air Force's declassification plans and database.

During the years the declassification process lasted, Ballester Olmos assisted MOA Intelligence, first through Bastida, then with Rocamora, in the study of the reports to be declassified and in many aspects of its development. This assistance was official and backed by MOA's top command. The possibility of a more formal collaboration agreement with the Ministry of Defense was once considered, but eventually both parties decided to keep it as a simple but highly efficient "gentleman agreement." The agreement was established on November 16, 1992, and it produced many long working meetings with MOA Intelligence over the years (See appendix: Lt. Col. Bastida letter to author, November 16, 1992).

This extraordinary cooperation allowed Ballester Olmos to personally view, handle, and copy the original case files located in the filing cabinets of MOA/MACOM, and what was more important, to oversee the entire declassification process as an insider. It insured that all reports in official custody were released; increased the momentum of the process; secured copies of all related UFO documentation (additional to case files) such as policy statements, internal notes and letters, mail from and to citizens; and instigated further searches for missing information. The latter was most effective, and uncovered, among other items, an important set of color slides for a March 5, 1979, missile case.

Essentially, in practice, Ballester Olmos performed loose quality control and audit functions during the entire UFO declassification process. All objectives were accomplished. It should be emphasized that this eight-year-long cooperation was totally *gratis et amore*.

Public knowledge of this process generated some controversy in the sensationalist Spanish UFO press, but a similar technique was used later during the British disclosure and transfer of UFO files from the British Ministry of Defense to their National Archives. Dr. David Clarke played a similar role as Ballester Olmos had earlier in Spain.[13]

After the archives were deposited at MOA, there were 62 files with 87 UFO cases by then. Since 1992, the incremental evolution of the official archives was mostly influenced by initiatives prompted by Ballester Olmos. For example, on November 17, 1992, and July 11, 1994, MOA produced requisitions to all units in the Air Force system demanding a search for, and the submission of, any existing documents on UFOs for centralization and disclosure.[14] Consequently, 16 additional files were created, containing 35 new cases, including three applying the new IG 40-5 procedures. These made up the 122 known UFO events.

The reason why the Spanish disclosure process lasted eight years (1992-1999) for just 84 files lies in the fact that this was not a high-priority job in the daily routine of the Intelligence Section of the Air Operative/Air Combat Command. The good fortune that they requested civil cooperation allowed follow up, increased the rate of progress, and recovered important materials and case reports lost, misplaced, or located elsewhere.

Summing up, all UFO reports in the custody of the Spanish Air Force Staff have been disclosed to the last page. It is also certain that, over the years, potentially interesting information was not submitted to the central depository

Col. Bastida (left), Lt. Col. Rocamora (right) and author.

(Air Staff) because it was considered irrelevant to the air safety or defense viewpoint by the local command. Later, such information was destroyed following the standard time rules for inactive files (five years on average).

Review of the Defense UFO Files

The first UFO claim officially reported to the Air Force authority occurred in 1962 and the last entry was in 1995. From the first to the last, a total of 122 different UFO events are counted. In the 34 intervening years, six of them had zero entries, and peak years appeared in 1968, 1975, 1978-1979, and 1986. This is the yearly tabulation of 122 UFO events included in the 84 AF archives:

1962:	3	1973:	1	1984:	3	1995: 2
1963:	0	1974:	2	1985:	5	
1964:	0	1975:	8	1986:	6	
1965:	2	1976:	3	1987:	0	
1966:	1	1977:	7	1988:	1	
1967:	3	1978:	11	1989:	3	
1968:	23	1979:	12	1990:	0	
1969:	7	1980:	7	1991:	2	
1970:	1	1981:	1	1992:	1	
1971:	2	1982:	1	1993:	3	
1972:	0	1983:	1	1994:	0	

UFO sightings in Spain are in excess of 7,000. However just a tiny fraction of these (< 2%) have been reported to the Air Force. Probably people do not know that they can make reports to the Air Force, or they are unfamiliar with how to make the reports. In fact, when this option was publicized, the population did report their sightings, as it was demonstrated when the Ministry of the Air released four press communiqués in March, September, and December 1968, and April 1969. These announcements to the public ("authorities are concerned with UFO sightings, please report to us") elicited responses that gave rise to the peaks in the yearly distribution of sightings in the custody of the Air Force (See appendix: Relationship of number of UFO cases reported to the Air Force and Air Ministry press releases, 1968-1969).

Of those actually investigated, many of the UFO reports in the Spanish Air Force files were merely descriptive; no conclusions were furnished. In a number of events, the AF didn't have complementary information saved in the private archives of civilian ufologists. During the eight years the declassification process lasted, Ballester Olmos had all events scrutinized and evaluated by a group of experts. The statistics discussed in the following paragraphs reflect the findings of this research. These are not official Air Force figures or statistics, which do not exist as such, other than as mere inventory lists of available files. Most of the declassified AF files have no conclusions, as the Air Force never saw fit to play the researcher's role in this context.

The magnitude of reports to the Air Force decreased dramatically over the decades. In the 1960s, wave year 1968 had 23 real-life accounts reported; in the 1970s, peak year 1979 had 12 (half); in the 1980s, year maximum was 1986 with only six cases reported (half again); and in the 1990s, peak year of 1993 showed barely three, once again half. Since 1995, no formal, direct request has been addressed to the Spanish Air Force to generate any new investigation. In the following years—beyond the closure of the process—there had been occasionally some internal correspondence related to UFO sightings, for example concerning the November 27, 1999, re-entry of a Chinese rocket.[15] However, the information lacks the expected characteristics needed to generate the activation of IG 40-5, the Air Force procedure for investigation of UFOs.

Out of 122 cases analyzed by the international team directed by Ballester Olmos,[16,17] 99 had conventional causes, 14 had insufficient data for evaluation, and 9 were considered potentially unidentified. The 23 unexplained and 99 explained cases are tallied in a comparison following a modified Hynek classification:

	Unexplained	Explained	Total
Nocturnal lights	9	59	68
Daylight discs	0	14	14
Radar-Visual	7	13	20
Radar tracks	4	5	9
Close encounters	3	8	11
Total	23	99	122

Over half of the total cases concerned distant lights in the night sky, and most are explained as misperceptions of short-lived lights in the sky (astronomical and aerospace). In the daylight disc class, there are no cases of typical "flying saucers" seen in plain daylight as all such incidents had conventional solutions (mostly aircraft). Radar-visual incidents represent, obviously, the highest score in terms of aeronautical strangeness; typically these are uncorrelated tracks matching the sighting of an anomalous object in the atmosphere. Although most such reports lie in the explained category, there are a few unknown phenomena as well. In the group of radar-only cases (no human-witness involvement), we find a relatively high number of unexplained events. Basically it is due to the fact that most records lack additional data, being just a few lines in terms of documentation, taken from military radar logbooks with no follow-up or investigation ever done. These are mostly candidates for false echoes, and the lack of information precludes any proper analysis. Finally, close encounters also score high in strangeness but include a higher incidence of psychological and hoax causes; yet a few such incidents survived preliminary study.

As in civilian ufology, sometimes one observes an unwillingness to accept that a given UFO experience can be solved. On November 4, 1968, Iberia pilot commander J. Lorenzo Torres was flying from London to Alicante, through Barcelona, when at 18:23 hours (GMT) the pilot reported to Barcelona control tower the sight of a "very big light...a central light with two lateral lights...it is like a UFO." The light was seen in front of the plane making an up and down motion. In a press interview months later, he stated: "We thought it could not be Venus, as I had read something in this regard, and I was convinced after thinking carefully, that it was not that planet." Questioned about what it could have been, the pilot replied: "Perhaps the reflection of a star, there are many problems of reflection. I do not believe it was a flying saucer." Analysis of the incident has revealed a match of the space-time position of planet Venus with the UFO source. To this day, the pilot continues to reject this explanation (in spite of the fact the he himself considered it during the sighting, meaning we are talking about a stellar-sized light). He never reported having seen Venus and the UFO at the same time, as what should have occurred given the nearby placement if two different light sources ever existed.

The former pilot stated that when the Air Force learned of this occurrence, they said he had seen the planet Venus. Unlike other case investigations of the period, the AF files contained no paper trail of any inquiry made regarding this observation (as has been confirmed by Ballester Olmos), except the transcript of conversations between ground control and the airplane, a two-page document that was duly declassified. A manuscript note in the transcript's first sheet (erased in the released version) reads: "Commander Lorenzo: careful!" This note is open to interpretation. A conservative one is that the pilot was perceived as prone to problems by the military. Conspiracy lovers may think otherwise, of course.

This pilot has reported recently that when he arrived back at Barcelona airport, he was told that radar had detected three objects, that he was given the radar records, and that these were later confiscated. However, the actual Air Force archives retain no information whatever about this UFO observation other than the air control's conversation and no radar records at all. The official files of the time were rather extensive, with good field investigations on other UFO sightings of the same time frame, but in this case the pilot's assertions cannot be checked or proven.

Coming back to Venus, the period November 1968–February 1969 was very rich in UFO misidentification with this planet, and several of the UFO cases in the official repository vouch for this, either by the original AF inquiry or by independent fresh re-investigations.

There is another episode of alleged confiscation of records by the military. On May 1968, there was a wave of sightings of flying triangles of large size at high altitudes in Spain; they were seen both from the ground and the air. To make a long story short, it turned out to be a flood of tetrahedron-shaped stratospheric balloons launched by CNES (French Space Center) from a location near the north of Spain. The evidence to support this explanation is considerable and is both national and international. One of the released files, dated May 15, 1968, covers two observations from Madrid and Barcelona.

The file included a report by the Defense Command. It related that a passenger filmed one such object near Madrid during the inaugural Iberia flight from Tenerife (Canary Islands) to Paris. The report writes: "COC controller suggested Madrid ground control, in touch with the airplane, asks the captain to get hold of the film, something that he had already done by himself in order to furnish it to the Defense Command, the passenger freely agreeing to cooperate. It should be noted that the passenger had entered the pilot cabin, where he was asked to film the object. The film was submitted to Madrid Control, which in turn mailed it to the Ministry of the Air's chief of the National (Air) Control Service, who in turn dispatched it to this (Defense) Command."

The archived file contains a letter from the Defense Command to the Minister of the Air dated May 31, 1968, saying it is attaching a report and the film. But the film did not arrive. The incoming letter, entry-stamped June 1, 1968, contains a manuscript note stating that the film was not included in the submission. In 1992, Lt. Col. Bastida tried his best to find the film everywhere, unsuccessfully. All this information is part of the declassified file.

Stories like this (the "severe" loss of a four-minute film of a sounding balloon in flight), cooked in a sensationalist prose, have been used to cast doubts about the honorability of what has been a transparent and comprehensive disclosure process.

A note on missing files seems to be in order. The UFO policy by the Air Force in Spain has been loose. There was never a department focused on UFO claims and UFO sightings as it represented a low priority subject. No rules even existed until 1968 when the first rules were drafted and disseminated within AF circles. When new cases arose in 1975, the 1968 rules were reinforced to cope with the investigations of those sightings. In consequence, a number of UFO sightings originally reported to regional units, airdromes, Air Force bases, or radar stations (either by military personnel or civilians) were never submitted to the Air Staff and never found their way into the UFO archive. These reports were irretrievably lost, with a number of these missing reports being known to ufologists. In addition to not being listed in any internal catalogue of UFO case resources in the Air Force Staff, these reports are not present in the original files in MOA/MACOM facilities.

Furthermore, over a 30-year period, with so many different persons handling the centralized information in the Operations Division of the Air Staff (Air Space/Flight Safety section), the loss and destruction of correspondence, reports, films, etc, was inevitable. This is the normal result of a low-profile activity with no specialists or continuing work program.

True UFO Cases

Only nine out of the 122 cases collected by the Air Force resisted a full explanation. This is the judgment of a group of civilian specialists and scientists under the coordination of Ballester Olmos. They evaluated the information that was received directly from MOA. Lastly, these nine reports described incidents that seemingly defied explanation as known objects or phenomena, and occurred between 1975 and 1985. The first four cases were inland but the last five were maritime sightings over areas of the Mediterranean Sea and the Atlantic Ocean (heavy airborne and seaborne traffic areas). There have been no "true" UFO cases reported to the Air Force since 1985 (and no actual reports beyond 1995). It seems to be that many of the apparent high-strangeness accounts refer to old-time episodes when, presumably, investigative techniques were not as sophisticated as they are today, or the access to background or environmental information was much more restricted or difficult to obtain. One cannot avoid thinking whether this conclusion—the best cases are old cases—can be generalized to other countries as well.

The case abstracts that follow serve to illustrate the type of raw unknown phenomena found in the Spanish Air Force records.

January 1, 1975, Quintanaortuño, Burgos: At 6:25 in the morning four soldiers were driving from Santander to the Army Engineers Academy at Burgos after a New Year's Eve celebration on their Christmas leave. When they were 14 km from their destination, the driver stopped the car after seeing a high-speed light in the sky moving in a parabolic course. Then, they all saw in the fields a very intense light. Intrigued, they got out of the car, crossed the highway, and saw some 400 meters away a luminous body, shaped like a truncated cone and hovering some two meters above the ground. It was about two meters in height by three meters across the base. It emitted a yellowish light, and on the bottom it had some luminous spurts aimed at the ground. Suddenly, the phenomenon faded. Almost immediately a row of four objects appeared in its place. After two minutes, the nervous witnesses decided to continue their trip. They realized that two other cars had also stopped. About one kilometer further, they stopped again, now seeing only two lights in the distance. Some three minutes later they resumed their trip. The Army inquiry, including a field trip and an overflight of the area by plane, revealed no visible traces of the incident. Days later, a magazine took the soldiers and their officers to the alleged landing location and several burnt spots were discovered on the site.

The Army (not the AF) inquiry revealed some ambiguity in the witnesses' accounts (in fact, some of the data above come from complementary sources other than the official report). The Army also advanced the hypothesis of an optical illusion caused by a reflection of moonlight on metallic parts of a nearby high power line coupled with some prior suggestion. This case looks very interesting but was not expertly investigated; therefore it is an unidentified rather than an unidentifiable phenomenon.

In some ways this incident is reminiscent of the narrative of a Canadian farmer who, on September 1, 1974, just four months before the Spanish event, also saw four similar objects which produced swirl marks on his fields in Langenburg, Saskatchewan.[18] UFO research certainly demands exercises in comparative ufology, but, most importantly, such exercises should be based on *bona fide* cases.

January 2, 1975, Bárdenas Reales firing range, Navarra: At 22:55 hours a soldier on duty near the main tower of this Air Force firing range in northern Spain saw a motionless bright red light at ground level. He called the Corporal guard, who went out in the company of three soldiers. The light seemed to be from two to five kilometers away. After five to ten minutes, it rose up to 25 to 50 meters from the ground and flew slowly in the direction of an auxiliary tower. When the light reached the tower, it changed course and increased speed and height, moving towards the main tower. Very rapidly, it disappeared to the northwest.

At 23:10 hours the Corporal reported the sighting by telephone to the Sergeant on duty, who went out to a mound and through binoculars he saw an object similar to an "inverted cup," with white lights on top and bottom, and with pulsed amber and white lights around it. It was in the same position as the initial sighting. Its size was compared to a long truck. The object illuminated the environment over an area of 100 meters in radius. As before, the light rose up and flew towards the auxiliary tower, disappearing this time to the northeast 15 minutes later. Five soldiers standing by the main tower guard post also saw the object, but they could not identify any shape. The following morning, the Civil Guard called the military facility and asked if any aircraft had crashed in the area, as sightings of lights over the range had been reported to the police post of the nearby town of Tudela.

The Air Force inspection of the site found no traces of any type. Radar did not detect any abnormal tracks. The military inquiry was superficial and did not offer any conclusion. The Lieutenant General of the III Air Region wrote a "personal interpretation" of the facts and addressed it to the Minister of Air. He rejected the possible landing of UFOs in the area and concluded: "The lights or light effects observed may have been produced by the Moon halo, the light from any star, or by any nearby farm tractor, when crossing some of the fog layers or mist that intermittently cross the Range, thus provoking an optical effect that caused the appearance of a lighted object in motion." This was a hasty opinion based on personal prejudice and the desire to close the case. A helicopter is a possibility, but it cannot be proven. This interesting case demands a professional re-investigation. (A drawing of this event at the Bárdenas Reales Firing Range is displayed in the appendix.)

July 14, 1978, Mazarrón, Murcia: This is not an Air Force report. During a dawn exercise performed by an Army unit, where a military group attempted to perform an outflanking maneuver on a number of camped soldiers, they observed for two hours an unfamiliar group of lights. They described them as a red light (vanishing on occasion), two greenish-white lights (that shone sporadically) and four white lights that appeared irregularly and flew without any specific formation. Initially, the first light was sighted near a pond for 15 minutes, at an uncertain distance, oscillating from right to left. Back at their camp, they saw a red light hovering less than ten meters over the road, which was then joined by two white lights. They continued in the direction of this group of lights. The lights also moved forward, leaving the road and moving around obstacles like houses or hills, then coming back to the road in front of the group of soldiers. Height over the terrain was estimated between 4 and 30 meters. A reconnaissance of the area on the following night did not reveal anything unusual, except the antenna of a meteorological station. The observers insisted they could not have been confused by it.

This is one of the few UFO reports from the Spanish Army, and it was submitted to the Air Force (Intelligence) for information purposes. The editing of the report, prepared by a Captain, is quite poor and the event description unclear. The case has not been investigated and it remains poorly documented.[19]

The Army report from Mazarrón was one of the cases not originally filed in the Flight Safety (SEGVU) Section of AF Headquarters where all UFO documents were under custody. As mentioned before, Ballester Olmos' first contacts with Air Staff officers included the boss of SEGVU, Colonel A. Fernández Rodas. He was the author of the May 22, 1991, memo which recommended UFO disclosure and which commenced the process. In 1993 his job position was changed and he was appointed head of the Intelligence Division. It was there that some old UFO files were found, and he rushed to send them to MOA to be added to the declassification plans. Had it not been for his commitment to the idea, these would have become part of the missing UFO reports.

Based on his consulting arrangement with the military, Ballester Olmos received for review the Mazarrón report from the MOA Intelligence Section in 1993. Years later, by April 1998, he realized that the UFO declassification process was slowing down, so to expedite the process Ballester Olmos typed up the standard cover memorandum himself, along with the summary of the information and the list of the attachments, and sent it all off to the MOA. As a result of this initiative, the file was declassified one month later.

July 20, 1978, Agoncillo airdrome, La Rioja: A soldier was on duty at the main gate of this military airfield when he observed a strange object in the air. It was 01:20 hours when he informed the guard post. A Second Lieutenant and a Corporal went to the site in time to observe for five minutes a flying object moving from east to west some 1,000 meters above the ground. The object's flight was slow and noiseless. Two of the witnesses described it as lozenge-shaped, while the other two said it had the shape of a triangle. All agreed that there was an intense white light flashing at one second intervals in the very center of the structure, while they differed in the number of additional white lights which were placed on every apex of the object's body, i.e., three in the triangle and four in the rhombus. The object continued to fly steadily until it disappeared from sight.

This sighting was unknown to the AF Staff until 1991, when it arrived at Headquarters from the corresponding Air Region in response to the centralization query activated by Colonel Fernández Rodas, therefore an investigation never occurred in the first place. An airplane or a helicopter could explain the observation but the information is too limited to conclude anything for certain.

September 9, 1978, Mediterranean Sea, 142 km East Barcelona: This is an incident where most of the available information comes from civilian sources. A transcript of air-to-ground conversations between some airline pilots and personnel from the Barcelona Air Control Center described lights seen at 20:35 hours that the pilots could not identify in the environment of aeronautical point *India*. Whether or not they were stationary or moving, at sea level or above, we do not really know. The Barcelona Control radar did not register any abnormal echo, but a civil aviation report mentions that contact was established with *Pegaso* Defense radar center in Madrid.

With this background, in 1992 Ballester Olmos requested that MOA Intelligence look for any reference to it in the secret control logbooks of this underground facility at Torrejón AFB. A short annotation was all that was recorded (it was declassified in 1997). From it we know basically what Barcelona Control was reporting about calls being received from several pilots describing unknown luminous activity over the Mediterranean Sea (apparently it lasted 35 minutes in total). Defense noted that at no time was any signal detected on their radar screens. There was no Air Force or Civil Aviation investigation, other than the conversation transcript. Presently, this event is under independent, private analysis.

February 25, 1979, Atlantic Ocean, Southeast of Gran Canaria (Canary Islands): This is another example of recovered information. For the third time MOA was convinced to request once more that certain records be searched for lost UFO information. Successfully, the CAMO, or Circulación Aérea Militar Operativa (Operative Military Air Traffic), radar unit in the Canary Islands replied by sending a number of entries copied from logbooks in the time span of 1977-1991. An 11-line annotation was found describing how at 2 a.m and for 35 minutes CAMO radar—as well as the major military W-8 radar station—detected one unidentified track located 84 km to the southeast, flying at an altitude of 4,400 meters. An Iberia airplane in the area was alerted, and the pilot reported having seen above his position an intense, elongated light. Information acquired from the W-8 local radar site disclosed that the radar echo transmitted *squawk*, which is a signal emitted by the transponder of an airplane. This is the most probable explanation, but one that cannot be confirmed due to the brevity of the information at hand. This information was declassified in 1997.

March 13, 1979, Mediterranean Sea, Balearic Islands to Alicante: In an underground secret bunker called Pegaso, placed within the facilities of Torrejón AFB (Madrid), lies the major surveillance center to coordinate all radar sites in Spain. In this key Operations Center of the defense system, just before 11:00 am. an uncorrelated echo was detected north of Algeria, over the Mediterranean Sea. It was traveling at 840 knots (1,556 km/hour) on a northwest course, in an incoming direction to Spain. The track was code-named KL-553 and it was classified as unknown. Three minutes later, a scramble was ordered and a Mirage III aircraft took off from Manises AFB (Valencia) to identify the trace, but before it could be intercepted, the trace vanished from the radar screen. It had traveled 115 km during that time. Four minutes later, the echo reappeared in another position; this time it was apparently motionless. It was now thought to be a ship's reflection. In spite of this, the military aircraft was vectored towards that point.

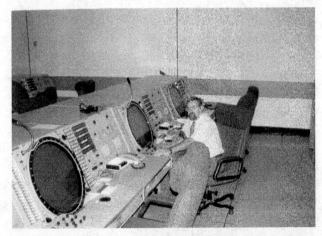

Juan-Vicente Ballester Olmos at Pegaso control room, the mainframe Defense center.

When the interceptor jet was at 15 km distance from the track, the radar echo started to move in a northwest direction again. It accelerated to 730 knots (1,352 km/hour) climbing to a height in excess of 24,000 meters. Six minutes later, the track had changed its route to the northeast and in two minutes it was lost. There was never visual contact by the Mirage III pilot. (The appendix contains a radar overlay of the March 13, 1979, sighting.)

The brief information available makes it difficult to decide whether or not it could have been an advanced foreign aircraft, a false echo, or anything else. In consequence, in absence of an established solution, this qualifies as a true UFO report.

May 22, 1980, Atlantic Ocean, South Gran Canaria (Canary Islands): At 23:05 hours the Air Transit Control Center at Gando airport (Gran Canaria) detected some unidentified traffic on a 210° course (SSW) at a speed of 600 knots (1,110 km/hour), moving away from the Berriel airdrome, located to the south of the island. A few minutes later, an aero-taxi pilot flying on a 231° course reported a bright object pass on his left and descend towards the sea (See appendix: May 22, 1980, UFO and airplane courses as well as a drawing by the instructing judge).

An officer experienced in UFO inquiry investigated this case. He concluded that it was an unknown object. Independently, however, we have determined that the position of the light observed by the pilot matched the position of the planet Venus at that time and place. Because the object was not also tracked from the W-8 radar station on the island, the possibility of a false echo also exists. This continues to be classified as a UFO as of today.

December 23, 1985, Atlantic Ocean, Las Palmas to Arrecife (Canary Islands): The merchant vessel *Manuel Soto*, owned by Transmediterránea Co., was sailing from Las Palmas to Arrecife, two islands of the Canary archipelago, when at 03:10 hours the third officer on duty observed on the horizon by the prow what seemed to be the rising of a heavenly body. Initially, he identified it as the star Antares. Ten minutes later, he confirmed that the light's position corresponded neither with Antares nor with any other star or planet. The officer took measurements of height and azimuth of the light, which remained stationed in the same spot for 15 minutes, after which it started to move quickly.

Other members of the crew came to view the light as well; the second officer, the radio operator, the steersman, and the deck's guardian. The light was approaching the ship, reaching the vessel's zenith two minutes later. At that moment, all witnesses could perceive the object's profile, which did not resemble that of a familiar airplane or helicopter. The object had a very intense white light at its center, a weaker red light near it, and another soft white light set apart. The separation between lights made the witnesses think that the object was flying low, yet no noise was heard.

The shipping company delivered the logbook annotations to the Spanish Navy, which in turn submitted this information to the Air Force. No records of anything uncommon in this time frame were found in the Canary Island sentry systems. The sighting details might be compatible with the approach of an airplane from the horizon, flying at a constant altitude; however, lack of investigation precludes any conclusion other than unidentified.

These cases serve to illustrate the magnitude and relevance of the unexplained episodes managed by the Air Force. While these reports have some potential, the evidence does not force us to re-examine current paradigms or mainstream concepts. These are either intrinsic mysteries, or mysteries due to a lack of proper field investigation and competent event analysis.

The information collected does not indicate military ownership of this problem, nor does it prove any threat to homeland security; therefore it is understandable that there exists no long-standing philosophy towards UFOs from the defense perspective in Spain.

UFOs, as a class of phenomenon reported as flying objects, fell naturally under the jurisdiction of the Air Force. Therefore the subject was handled by Air Space (SESPA) or Flight Safety (SEGVU) sections within the Air Staff from 1968 to 1992. When it was transferred to the MOA/MACOM, since it was unrelated to Operations, Telecommunications & Electronic War, or Logistics, UFO case management was assigned to Intelligence. But true intelligence work was performed on the UFO question as one might expect. No consultations with scientists, exchanges with foreign governments, review panels, analysis of reports, or the like were undertaken. History shows that UFO accounts were approached (if at all) with little forethought and then simply filed away.

Conclusions

For decades (early 1960s to early 1990s), the Spanish Air Force response to the UFO phenomenon was to collect information on UFO events when reported to the authorities and submit them for investigation following simply-designed protocols, the output of which was a function of the competence and interest of the appointed investigator (called a "judge"). In general, no preconceived opinions existed other than the personal bias of the investigator, sometimes pro, sometimes con. Inquiries were not followed-up or scientifically tested, and when finished they were simply filed away and forgotten.

The level of secrecy (actually called confidentiality or reserve) officially applied to UFO-related documents was first established in 1968. These were "Confidential" and this lasted from 1968 to 1979. They were then upgraded to "Classified" in 1979, and finally downgraded to "Internal Reserve" in 1992. This variability over time was due to reactions from external pressures.

In 1976, a poorly handled release of summaries for twelve Air Force UFO files to a journalist unfortunately stifled the potential openness of the Air Staff. Beginning in 1990, Ballester Olmos succeeded in pushing forward what later became the start of a full disclosure of the UFO archives accumulated from 1962. Between 1992 and 1999, all records in the possession of the Air Force entered the public domain.

Norms for a methodical investigation of UFO cases (field inquiry, use of standard questionnaires, etc.) were enacted in 1968 and 1975, and then superseded by modern procedures published in 1992 (IG 40-5).

Historically speaking, two stages are distinguished in the performance of the Spanish Air Force in the UFO business: (a) secrecy (1962-1990) and (b) disclosure (1990-1999.) The "secrecy stage" shows a concern based in the ignorance of the nature of the UFO phenomenon and the understanding that it posed a potential threat to national security. The motivation for the "disclosure stage" mirrored the conduct of other governments, and it recognized the evidence that no real threat had become apparent since 1947, coupled with the acknowledgement that the UFO problem really belonged to scientists, not to the military.

This contemporary vision is shared by many governments[20] that are declassifying and releasing their UFO archives, all clearly implying that "this is not our cup of tea" (UK, Australia, Canada, New Zealand, Brazil, Denmark, Sweden, Italy, and Spain.). Others (France, almost exclusively) continue with a staffed, albeit minimal, structure to cope with the study of UFO sightings. From this perspective, the situation in the United States seems to be unique.

Notes

[1] Circular No. 9266-CT, issued December 26, 1968.

[2] Internal note from the Public Affairs Office of the Air Force, January 15, 1979.

[3] Memo from Chief of the Air Staff to the Ministry of Defense, January 16, 1979.

[4] Memo from Second Chief of the Air Staff to the Office of Public Affairs, October 1981.

[5] Vicente-Juan Ballester Olmos, "Spanish Air Force UFO Files: The Secret's End," in *MUFON 1993 International UFO Symposium Proceedings*, Walter H. Andrus, Jr. and Irena Scott (eds.), Mutual UFO Network, Inc. (Seguin, Texas), July 1993, pp. 127-168.

[6] Informative Note of Flight Safety Section (SEGVU), May 22, 1991.

[7] Chief of the Air Staff to Chief of Command, MOA, January 15, 1992.

[8] Vicente-Juan Ballester Olmos, "Ángel Bastida: El hombre del MOA," @nomalía (II), 9, June 2008 (CD edition). http://tinyurl.com/bastida-fotocat

[9] Vicente-Juan Ballester Olmos, "Documentos oficiales online (I): La monografía de Antonio Munáiz Ferro-Sastre," http://www.ikaros.org.es/g035.htm

[10] Vicente-Juan Ballester Olmos and Ricardo Campo Pérez, "¡Identificados! Los OVNIS de Canarias fueron misiles Poseidón," *Revista de Aeronáutica y Astronáutica*, March 2001, 200-207. http://www.ikaros.org.es/misiles.htm Translation: "Navy Missiles Tests and the Canary Islands UFOs," *International UFO Reporter*, 29:4, July 2005, pp. 3-9 and 26.

[11] Vicente-Juan Ballester Olmos and Miguel Guasp, *Los OVNIS y la Ciencia*, Plaza y Janés (Barcelona), 1989.

[12] Ángel Bastida Freijedo, "Los OVNIS y el Ejército del Aire," *Revista de Aeronáutica y Astronáutica*, August-September 1992, pp. 655-659.

[13] David Clarke, *The UFO Files: The Inside Story of Real-Life Sightings*, The National Archives (Kew, Surrey, UK), 2009.

[14] Vicente-Juan Ballester Olmos, "Monitoring Air Force Intelligence: Spain's 1992-1997 UFO Declassification Process," in *MUFON 1997 International UFO Symposium Proceedings*, Walter H. Andrus, Jr. and Irena Scott (eds.), Mutual UFO Network, Inc. (Seguin, Texas), July 1997, pp. 139-178 .

[15] Vicente-Juan Ballester Olmos and Matías Morey Ripoll, "27 noviembre 1999: ¿La última reentrada del milenio?", http://www.ikaros.org.es/271199.pdf See additional information in http://fotocat.blogspot.com/2009_10_21_archive.html

[16] Vicente-Juan Ballester Olmos, "Declassification! Military UFO Records Released: The Spanish Experience," in *UFO 1947-1997. Fifty Years of Flying Saucers*, Hilary Evans and Dennis Stacy (eds.), John Brown Publishing Ltd. (London), May 1997, pp. 177-184. http://www.ikaros.org.es/declass.htm. The full paper is available in Spanish: http://www.ikaros.org.es/desclasificacion.pdf

[17] Vicente-Juan Ballester Olmos, *Expedientes insólitos*, Temas de Hoy (Madrid), 1995, pp. 153-236. (Epilogue: Dr. Jacques Vallee.)

[18] Jerome Clark, *The UFO Encyclopedia, Volume 3. High Strangeness: UFOs from 1960 through 1979*, Omnigraphics, Inc. (Detroit, Michigan), 1996, pp. 280-282.

[19] Vicente-Juan Ballester Olmos and Manuel Borraz, "Encuentro de clase militar en Mazarrón," http://www.ikaros.org.es/mazarron.pdf

[20] Vicente-Juan Ballester Olmos, "State-of-the-Art in UFO Disclosure Worldwide," http://www.tinyurl.com/3b3qh5q

Chapter 19: UFOs and France—Beginnings of a Scientific Investigation

Government investigations of Unidentified Flying Objects or OVNI (Objet Volant Non-Identifié) by France began after the Second World War. These sightings were collected by the French Air Force in the Office of Long-Term Studies.[1] The French Air Force's interest in UFOs was similar to that of the United States. Both governments' military organizations were mostly concerned with the protection of national security. Perhaps for a myriad of reasons, the American flirtation with the phenomenon was more extravagant and public than the French. The creation of Blue Book initiated a high profile era for the U.S., while the French investigation of the 1950s and 1960s was more subdued. The view of the French Air Force during this era was expressed by Lieutenant Colonel Alexis of the Office of Prospective Studies in 1976 when he stated:

> The role [of the French Air Force] is extremely limited. It is a matter of looking through the evidence to see if there are any interesting connections or not for the National Defense. At present, one could say that since 1951, no evidence calls into question the French Defense or the French Air Space. As you can see by a number of statistics, we have not seen any aggressive cases, nor any particular location of OVNI [UFO], be it on military sites, industrial zones, cities, etc. In short, these observations remain very random. As it is clear, through this evidence, that the National Defense is not involved, you can imagine that it would not be easy for the military to judge the nature of the phenomenon....this phenomenon is absolutely harmless to the French people, send it to the scientists so that they may do their work, that is to say, search for and reveal the origin of these phenomena.[2]

The French colonel was direct. He was very clear in his view that the UFO phenomenon was not of a concern to the national security of France. This is the same conclusion drawn at varying times by the U.S. Air Force. The colonel did not deny or confirm the existence of the UFO phenomenon. However, he did part ways with the U.S. Air Force in a key aspect: how to deal with this enigma. He suggested that the investigation of this phenomenon should be handled by *scientists*. This is exactly what the French government would soon do.

The Birth of GEPAN (1974 – 1978)

Perhaps the impetus for the investigation of the phenomenon was a wave of UFO sightings over France in 1973. This UFO wave attracted the media's interest and caused France's Defense Minister, Robert Galley, to comment about the military's knowledge of the phenomenon when he stated on national radio in February of 1974:

> There has been an extremely impressive increase in the number of visual sightings of luminous phenomena, sometimes spherical, sometimes ovoid, traveling at extraordinarily high speeds... My own profound belief is that it is necessary to adopt an extremely open-minded attitude towards these phenomena. Man has made progress because he has sought to explain the inexplicable...[3]

Left: French Defense Minister Robert Galley
Right: U.S. Sec of Defense James Schlesinger

The man in charge of running all of France's military had stated that the phenomenon was real and that an *open-minded* attitude should be employed in the investigation of the phenomenon.

France laid the groundwork for their scientific study of the UFO phenomenon in 1974. The government's decision to systematically investigate the phenomenon was placed at the doorstep of a military organization: the National Gendarmerie. This was a natural progression since the Gendarmerie had already begun to record UFO sightings from the public in the 1950s.[4] Gendarmes were already stationed throughout France. Their reach extended from the largest cities to the smallest villages. No other nation has put resources

The National Gendarmerie headquartered in Paris

into the study of this enigma as well as the French. To understand this resource commitment, it is necessary to understand a little about the Gendarmerie.

The National Gendarmerie is part of the French Armed Forces and came into existence in the late 18th century.[5] It is a military institution in charge of public safety with police duties among the civilian population. There are more than 105,000 persons involved with this military branch, and a general is placed in charge of each of the various French defense zones. The Gendarmerie also has forensic science units, which conduct investigations whenever a case exceeds the abilities of the local authorities.[6] The number of gendarmes distributed throughout France, their investigative training, and their capability to analyze physical evidence makes the French approach to the investigation of the UFO phenomenon unique.

The Gendarmerie is a serious organization and has never been taken lightly. A road-mender reported to the gendarmes that he saw a flying cigar land in a field, and he claimed that the object paralyzed him with a strange light. He told the gendarmes that the object created three holes in the ground where it landed. The gendarmes immediately investigated and determined that the man had made the holes himself. The gendarmes picked him up a couple of days later and held him for disciplinary action.[7] This is not an organization that one would want to hoax.

The Gendarmerie provided the investigative backbone for the new organization, and on May 1, 1977, Yves Sillard, President of CNES (Centre National d'Études Spatials – the French National Center for Spaces Studies), the French equivalent to NASA, created the research arm. Protocols were signed between the CNES and the Gendarmerie Nationale, the French Air Force, the National Civil aviation department, and National Meteorology. GEPAN (Groupe d'Etudes des Phenomenes Aerospatiaux non-Identifies – Unidentified Aerial Phenomena Study Group) was born. Their mission was to research the UFO phenomenon with scientists. GEPAN had the support of leading government scientists

CNES; The French National Center for Space Studies

from multidisciplinary fields. This included the National Center for Scientific Research, the Astrophysical Institute, and the National Meteorological Services. A dozen scientists outside of CNES and a dozen CNES engineers were expected to participate. Their work would be reviewed and judged by a scientific board acceptable to the president of the French national space center. One must admire the French for their combination of scientists and an investigative arm such as the Gendarmerie. The first scientist to head up this new organization was Dr. Claude Poher.[8,9]

Poher was well suited to direct French scientists in GEPAN's mission. His PhD was in astrophysics and he was an experienced member of the Scientific Projects Division of CNES. His resume also included experience as a pilot, and he was a former chief of the CNES Rocket Sounds Division in Toulouse. Poher had already begun to study the UFO reports prior to the formation of GEPAN, and in 1973 he had completed a statistical analysis of the phenomenon that he presented at a 1975 meeting of the American Institute of Astronautics and Aeronautics with Jacques Vallee.[10] In 1976, the National Defense Institute of Higher Studies (IHEDN) recommended that a technical group be created for the study of UFOs. Poher was one of the key individuals involved in the creation of GEPAN, as well as its first leader.[11]

Dr. Claude Poher

GEPAN's first task was to establish data collection procedures, conduct statistical analysis of sightings, and investigate previously reported cases prior to the formation of GEPAN. They had initially been given over 300 reports, mostly from the Gendarmerie.[12] Their initial review of those cases led them to three conclusions:

1. Those events that remain unexplained after careful analysis are neither numerous nor frequent.

2. The appearance of some reported phenomena cannot readily be interpreted in terms of conventional physical, psychological, or psychosocial models.

3. The existence of a physical component of these phenomena seems highly likely. [13]

As a result of this evaluation, a more rigorous approach to the analysis of this aerial mystery was developed.

Scientists at GEPAN put together a plan with a detailed and highly structured scientific procedure for future investigations. This procedure identified all of the key variables to record in each case, allowed for statistical analysis of the database, established a high-level coding system, and provided a framework for evaluation of the data. GEPAN intended to study the phenomenon in a scientific manner.

A detailed document to record all the key variables was created for use by the gendarmes. This document included everything from ranking the quality of witnesses, to photographing the site, longitude and latitude coordinates, and observational details such as a detailed description, luminosity description, apparent size in degrees, elevation, azimuth, and trajectory/speed. The entire list of variables is completely documented in an 80-page report issued by the National Space Center. All of this information was formatted so that it could be easily analyzed with computers. This enabled GEPAN to produce a myriad of tables and graphs that examined everything from correlations of "witness profession" vs. "UFO shape" to "number of reports" based on "geographic location."[14] The use of an organization such as the Gendarmerie allowed them to consistently obtain these criteria from case to case. There is yet to be a thorough scientific investigation of the UFO phenomenon that meets this level of scrutiny.

Once the data was collected and evaluated, the reports were classified into one of four different categories:

Type A: The phenomenon is fully and unambiguously identified.

Type B: The nature of the phenomenon has probably been identified, but some doubt remains.

Type C: The report cannot be analyzed since it lacks precision, so no opinion can be formed.

Type D: The witness testimony is consistent and accurate but cannot be interpreted in terms of conventional phenomena. [15]

The Type D reports were the reports of most interest when evaluating the phenomenon.

GEPAN needed a scientific methodology for the evaluation of the rare and randomly occurring UFO phenomena: a methodology that would allow for the analysis of phenomena that could not be repeated in a laboratory environment. Similar examples of known phenomena that are now understood are random meteorite strikes and ball lightning. GEPAN developed a method that was approved by its scientific council. A tetrahedron was used to represent a complex set of basic variables that all had the potential to interact with each other. These variables were:

1. Witnesses: physiology, psychology, etc.

2. Witness testimony: accounts, reactions to questions, general behavior, etc.

3. The physical environment: weather, air traffic, photographs, radar data, traces left in the environment, etc.

4. The psycho sociological environment: readings and beliefs of witnesses, possible influence of the media and various groups on these witnesses, etc. [16]

These basic variables and their interaction affect how the data is interpreted. In the past, scientists have long remained committed to a strict definition of the concept of objectivity, linked to the complete independence of the observer and the observed. This concept has long been known as false in medicine and psychology. More recently, the concept of the independence of the observer and the observed has been shown as false in quantum mechanics. In its study of UFOs, GEPAN took into account the *possibility* that the observer and the observed might not be independent.

Clearly, the methods chosen by GEPAN to study the UFO phenomenon were designed to provide a scientific evaluation without preconceived notions and without ridicule of the subject matter at hand. Perhaps their study of the phenomenon is best summarized by Dr. Jean-Pierre Rospars, a neurobiologist, author of 70 articles, and an original member of the GEPAN team, *"There is no subject unworthy of science, but only methods unworthy of science."*[17]

There was one last unique decision made by GEPAN during its first year of operation. The organization's technical open-mindedness was extended to its willingness to collaborate with civilian UFO organizations. This was the first time a government body had extended a hand in the study of this enigma. In October of 1977 and within months of its creation, GEPAN reached out to the Center for UFO Studies (CUFOS), the largest U.S. organization with a computerized databank of over 60,000 UFO reports, and asked for their cooperation.[18] Less than a year later, GEPAN organized a meeting of more than 100 people that encompassed more than 40 civilian UFO groups. This latter effort was too cumbersome to manage and was of short duration.[19]

In 1979, Claude Poher took a one year sabbatical from GEPAN. He had another goal that needed fulfillment. He had a built a boat himself and wanted to sail around the world with his family. Before he left GEPAN, Poher told the organization's Scientific Council that he believed UFOs were real.[20]

The Growth of GEPAN (1979 – 1983)

With the departure of Poher, a young engineer named Dr. Alain Esterle took over leadership of GEPAN. Alain Esterle received his engineering degree from the prestigious Ecole Polytechnique in Paris and his PhD in Applied Mathematics from the University of Washington in 1976. (Esterle's career had just begun and he would go on to be very active in the French space program; he would work at the French Ministry of Defense and for the General Secretary of National Defense.)[21] At GEPAN, he continued the scientific evaluation of the phenomenon as laid out by his predecessor.

Esterle expanded the resources of GEPAN and began publishing detailed technical notes on the progress of the organization. There were 18 of these technical papers published between October 1979 and May 1983. The papers are available on the website of the French National Center for Space Studies.[22] He also suggested the development of a diffraction gradient that could be easily adapted to any camera lens and that could be manufactured quite cheaply. This allowed for the capture of light spectrum of any unknown light source. These devices were made available to the gendarmes.[23]

Two of the most important UFO sightings occurred during the time that Esterle led GEPAN. These cases were presented publicly in 1983. The first involved physical traces and occurred in Trans-en-Provence in January 1981. The second incident involved the purported landing of a small UFO in a garden near Nancy, France, in October of 1982. This case involved effects on nearby plants and is sometimes called L'Amarante after the name of the plant affected. It is appropriate to spend some time reviewing these two unique sightings.

On the afternoon of January 8, 1981, a retiree became witness to a very unusual event on his farm in Trans-en-Provence. The witness' attention was caught by a low whistling sound. He turned and saw an egg-shaped craft in the air near the top of the trees. There were no flames or smoke emanating from the craft. The object descended rapidly from that height and set down on four landing legs. It was no more than 70 meters from the man. He described the object as shaped like two inverted plates with a rib-like configuration between the plates. It landed close to familiar structures on his farm so that he was able to estimate its width as two and

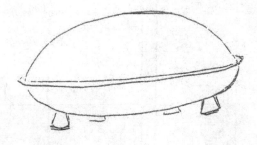

Witness' drawing of the craft

a half meters across and its height as about one and three quarter meters. He watched it sit motionless on the ground for several seconds. He saw no windows or openings. No method of propulsion was visible. After a few seconds the object rose vertically a few meters, hovered briefly, and then departed silently in an upwardly diagonal path at a very high rate of speed. The witness felt no heat, vibration, or sound as it departed. All of this happened over a period of 30 to 40 seconds.[24]

The next morning, the man saw an imprint in the ground at the location where the object had landed. He had told his wife and a neighbor about the incident. They recommended that he call the Gendarmerie, which he did. The same day, January 9, two gendarmes arrived to investigate at 11:30 a.m. They took witness reports from the man and his wife. Their investigation of the purported landing site revealed two concentric circles. The outer circle was 2.4 meters in diameter and the inner circle was 2.2 meters. Between the circles is a crown about ten centimeters thick. Along this crown were two diametrically opposed areas about 80 centimeters long that contained black scraped areas. The gendarmes took a soil sample from between the concentric circles and from alfalfa plants just outside the circle.[25]

Soil and plant samples were sent to laboratories for analysis. The Gendarmerie alerted GEPAN on January 12. On January 23 additional alfalfa samples were taken 20 meters from the landing site as controls. On February 17 a control sample of earth was taken four meters away from the central point. Additionally, eight more alfalfa samples were taken at radiating distances from the center point. The testing done was exhaustive. The soil samples were analyzed at four different labs with the use of optical microscopes, electron microscopy, electron diffraction, and mass spectroscopy. The plant samples were

Emplacement de la trace (39 jours après t'observation)

LES POINTILLES INDIQUENT L'EMPLACEMENT DE LA TRACE

Photograph of imprint found by the witness

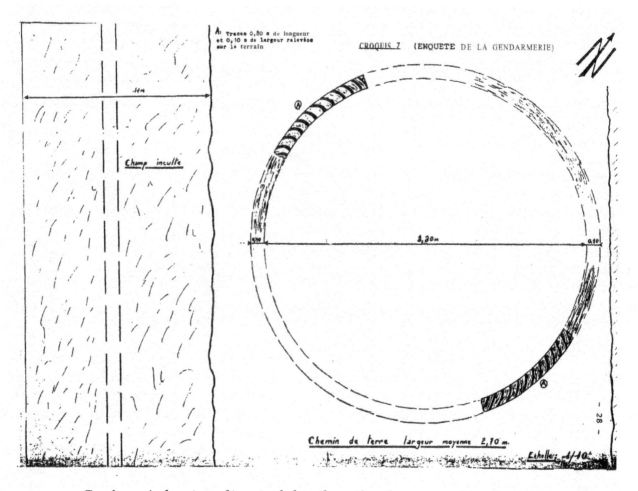

Gendarme's drawing of imprint left in the soil at the supposed landing site

sent to the biochemistry lab at the National Institute for Agronomic Research. Testing was done with chromatography followed by spectral analysis. GEPAN took this case seriously.[26]

What made this case interesting was the chemical and biological analysis that supported the witness' testimony. The soil analysis indicated that the dirt at the landing site was heavily compacted. Also, there were no traces of hydrocarbons in the soil, which eliminated the possibility that the compressed soil was caused by any type of heavy equipment. The conclusions from the laboratory were three-fold: strong mechanical pressure had been exerted on the soil, probably due to shock on the surface; there was a modified surface structure due to striations; any thermal heating of the soil was less than 600 degrees centigrade since the calcium carbonate in the soil had not changed. The plant analysis was equally interesting. Chlorophyll in the plants dropped off by 30% to 50% (depending on the type of chlorophyll) near the center point and linearly improved with increased distance from the landing site. The chlorophylls had decomposed into their oxidized forms. Based on their experience with radiation studies that had been done previously, the laboratory theorized that some type of electromagnetic field had caused the degradation in the chlorophyll, perhaps a pulsed electromagnetic field in the high frequency microwave range.[27]

GEPAN and the Gendarmerie had committed the resources to analyze the anomaly at Trans-en-Provence as no government agency had done before. Clearly, something very unusual had occurred. The answer is not yet known, but the scientific data had been taken. In less than two years, GEPAN would have the opportunity to again display its skills of analysis. The next occasion would be in northeastern France.

Just after 12:30 on the afternoon of October 21, 1982, a 30-year-old cellular biologist living in the French Department of Nancy was surprised by "something bizarre"[28] that descended from a cloudless southeastern sky and came to hover about one meter above his small ornamental garden. The object was oval in shape, about 1.5 meters in diameter and 80 cm in height; its lower portion appeared metallic gray blue like polished beryllium, and the upper half had a wide lateral band separating the top and bottom which were both of a bluish green color that the witness would later associate with the depths of a lagoon. No rivets or seams indicative of a manufactured product could be discerned. No noise, heat or cold, radiation, magnetism, or particular odor was noticed by the witness. Since the man eventually approached within about a half-meter of the object, this negative data may be of value.

For about 20 minutes the thing hovered above the man's garden, during which time the witness viewed the object from several different positions, fetched his camera, and tried to take a photograph, but the camera jammed (he admitted that it was not in perfect working order). Then the ovoid took off extremely rapidly and straight upwards, as if, according to the witness, it was drawn up by a strong suction. The apparatus produced a small brilliance like the sun as it rose and vanished as a small brilliant point. The bizarre object left no visible marks on the ground—no charred nor flattened grass, but the grass directly beneath the object did stand straight up briefly the moment the craft departed.

The witness went to the local Gendarmerie that evening and gave a statement. When the man and his wife returned home, he noticed that the leaves of the foxtail amaranth bushes,[29] which were near where the object had hovered, had withered, while amaranths more distant from that afternoon's events were unaltered. In fact, those parts of the affected plants that were above ground were dehydrated, while their roots were apparently unaffected. The color of the affected plants had changed from a reddish-brown to a sienna-earth hue.[30] This discovery led him to call the gendarmes, who collected samples of the withered and non-withered amaranth on the 22nd and 27th of October.

Although this was a single-witness case, GEPAN/SEPRA investigated the event, given the possibility of doing laboratory analyses on the presumed effects on the vegetation, the abundant and precise testimony, the good observation conditions (closeness and long duration of observation), and the absence of interference by the media and private groups.[31] GEPAN interviewed the witness and collected more amaranth samples, as well as samples of the grass and other vegetation on the 29th. A

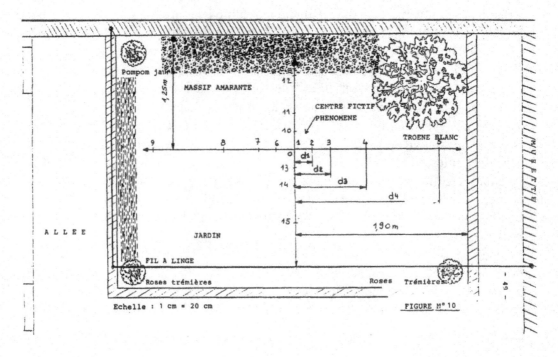

Drawing of vegetation sampling plan made by the Gendarmes

two-pronged investigation considered extensively both the technical aspects of the witness' description, and the behavioral aspects of the witness. Weather and soil conditions were noted, and local air traffic on the day of the sighting was assessed, with no significant anomalies noted.[32] The witness did not claim any particular interest in UFOs nor science fiction, showed no tendency towards fantasy, and indeed was very precise in his descriptions. He was annoyed that he was the sole witness to the event. He indicated no lasting physical effects due to his experience, though he admitted to having been stressed initially by the episode,[33] nor any change in his overall outlook on life.[34] The GEPAN study concluded that there was no reason to reject the witness' testimony. Previous studies suggested that an electrical field of at least 30 kV/m (kilovolt per meter) would have been necessary to make the blades of the biologist's grass stand up the way they were said to have done, while a field well in excess of 200 kV/m would have been needed to create the desiccation on the amaranth bush.

Laboratory analyses were carried out on withered and control samples that had been collected on the 22nd of October, as they had been gathered nearest in time to the strange event.[35] Differences were noted between control and withered amaranth plants in water content,[36] and the seeds comprising the amaranth clusters of the affected plants "were literally cooked."[37] But the conditions of sampling and storage (not at a low enough temperature) did not allow plant biochemistry to verify a hypothesis of strong electrical fields generating the vegetal damage, to explain the difference in the appearance observed between "control" and "withered" plants. The lab report suggested that certain parts of the amaranth bed could have been withered due to weather and their location in the garden near to a gate, and that differential fertilizing and parasitic activity could have caused some of the differences measured. The laboratory analysis therefore ended up raising more questions than answers.[38] The Amaranth Case did lead to suggestions on how to improve sample-taking procedures and a call for data on other cases that might make it possible to link electrical field activity to the withering of some of the amaranth plants.

446

The Demise of GEPAN (1984 – 1988)

GEPAN was criticized by both proponents and antagonists of France's examination of the UFO phenomenon. UFO advocates such as physicist Jean-Pierre Petit argued that GEPAN was used as a government cover up. Petit charged that GEPAN,[39]

> ...was created in order to serve as an interface with the private research groups and with the few rare scientists who possessed concrete and exploitable ideas about the UFO Phenomenon. The aim in creating it was not to promote research, but to scoop up as quickly as possible what the civilian population knew about the UFOs in order to feed it to the Military GEPAN.

The UFO critics were just as unappreciative. They despised the use of government resources on a subject that they believed was undeserved of scientific inquiry. This criticism occurred even though GEPAN's work and papers were overseen by a governing scientific council. There were complaints related to cost, despite the fact that it garnered a very small fraction of France's overall space budget. GEPAN's budget near the height of its activity in 1980 was only 500,000 francs.[40] Nonetheless, rumors began to circulate in late 1982 and early 1983 that GEPAN would soon be shut down.[41]

Despite GEPAN's success at scientifically analyzing UFO sighting reports, the organization's funding was reduced in the early 1980s. This reduction caused a drastic reduction in both resources and personnel available for analysis of the data collected by the Gendarmerie. Esterle saw the writing on the wall and left the organization for a different post in France's space agency. His assistant, statistician Jean-Jacques Velasco replaced him on September 1, 1983.[42]

GEPAN was reorganized and its power diminished. It no longer reported directly to CNES. Its reporting structure was transferred under ESO (Environnement Spatial Terrestre—Earth Space Environment). Technical notes and papers were no longer published. The seven members of GEPAN's scientific council were transferred into other areas of CNES. These actions bothered Velasco to the point that in 1984 he privately complained to one of GEPAN's critics Jean-Pierre Petit, "We have no scientific

Left: Michael Swords
Right: Jean-Jacques Velasco

structure behind GEPAN." Velasco had become the caretaker of the stripped-down organization until it was discretely closed in 1988.[43]

While GEPAN battled for survival, the gendarmes remained busy investigating cases. On March 24, 1984, the gendarmes of the Gers section in southwestern France received an early morning phone call. A Mother Superior and four nuns witnessed a very unusual event at 5:50 a.m. that morning. From the first floor of the convent's balcony, they saw a very bright oval object that was five meters long and two meters tall. The object changed its motion from standing still to moving up and down and right to left at a speed the nuns described as "at the speed of lighting." The oval object came to a stop about 30 meters above the cemetery and 100 meters away from the nuns. There was no sound. Then the object left in the direction from where it had originated. The phenomenon was close enough to make misidentification a moot point, and it is difficult for anyone to doubt the veracity of four nuns and a Mother Superior. The gendarmes listed the case as unknown.[44]

SEPRA (1988 – 2004)

SEPRA (Service of Expertise on the Atmospheric Re-entry Phenomena) was created in November of 1988 to succeed GEPAN. Jean-Jacques Velasco continued his previous role, but as the director of the new organization. The title of this new group no longer referred to unidentified aerial objects but instead to the study of satellite and rocket debris. Velasco himself suggested this name. He wanted quiet discretion in future investigations of the phenomenon. Velasco had salvaged UFO research at CNES, at least temporarily.[45]

SEPRA was reduced in size. Although Velasco had only a research assistant and a secretary, he continued UFO research. The agreements that allowed for cooperation with the Gendarmerie, the Air Force, and civil aviation were still in effect, so new UFO cases were still made available to SEPRA and a flow chart of that process is shown below. All of the investigative methodologies developed under GEPAN were still in force; the analytical capabilities of the organization had been weakened. But Velasco was determined to be successful and without his dedication it is difficult to discern if there would have been sufficient momentum to continue the study of UFOs.

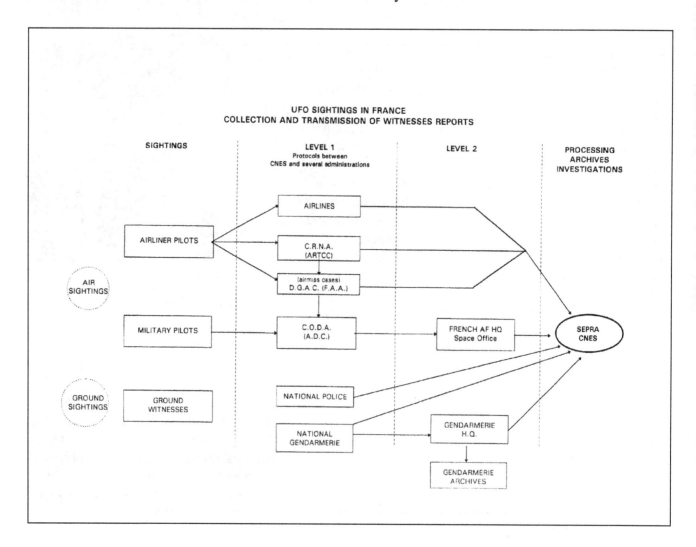

Flow chart of information from the field for GEPAN and it successor, SEPRA

The reduced size of SEPRA and its low-profile policy brought forth accusations of wanton debunking from UFO proponents. These claims were erroneous. A careful reading of the SEPRA case files shows no prejudicial treatment of the phenomenon. In fact, Velasco stated that there was a physical reality to UFOs, and he believed that UFOs most likely had an extraterrestrial origin. In 1993 he co-authored a book entitled, *OVNI: La science avance* (*UFOs: Science Advances*), and published his conclusions. He emphasized that the book represented his personal position and not necessarily that of CNES. However, he did have CNES' approval to publish the book. His book was also endorsed by Jean-Claude Ribes, an astrophysicist and the president of the French Astronomical Society.[46]

With reduced resources, Velasco was surely busy in the years 1993 and 1994, which brought forth the busiest two years in SEPRA's history. These two years accounted for the largest increase in UFO reports since the peak years of 1979-1981. The number of unexplainable cases also peaked at 31 during that timeframe.[47] One of the most interesting cases of this time frame involved the gendarmes themselves as witnesses.

Three gendarmes witnessed a bright set of lights in the night sky. It was June 24, 1994, and the time was 2:40 a.m. The location was La Ferte Sous Jouarre, which is 40 kilometers east of Paris. The gendarmes drove slowly towards the lights to investigate. As they approached the lights, they soon could see that the source was a stationary object with three yellow-white lights. Its underside was triangular in shape with a central pyramid spire that pointed downwards. The gendarmes stopped their patrol car, and the object moved slowly towards them until it stopped directly above their vehicle. There was no noise, smoke, or odor. As soon as the gendarmes began to move, the object headed west at a breakneck speed and was a speck on the horizon within a second. The total time involved from when the three men first saw the object was ten minutes. The gendarmes noted that their radios stopped functioning, and it was very hot even though their

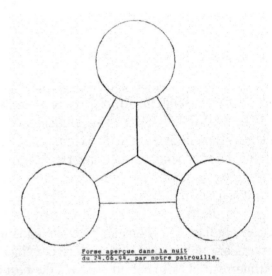

Forme aperçue dans la nuit du 24.06.94. par notre patrouille.

The Gendarmes' drawing of the craft that they encountered

vehicle windows were open. The temperature that night was between 55 and 57 degrees Fahrenheit. This case is listed as unknown in SEPRA's records.[48]

A few years prior to the termination of SEPRA, an important event in the annals of French UFO history occurred with the release of a 90-page UFO report entitled *UFOs and Defense* by a group called COMETA (Committee for In-Depth Studies). This group was *not* a government sanctioned organization and the French government did not endorse the report. However, it is important to briefly discuss this report because so many of its authors were high level French military personnel involved in France's investigation of the UFO phenomenon.

COMETA was comprised of former "auditors" of a high-level military think-tank, the IHEDN, and various other experts. This is the same organization discussed earlier, which was instrumental in France's creation of GEPAN. The members of COMETA studied the GEPAN and SEPRA cases in detail as well as, superficially, the UFO phenomenon in other countries. The credentials of the authors of the report were impressive. They included:[49]

General Bernard Norlain of the Air Force and former Director of IHEDN, France's military think-tank; former Commander of Air Defense Command, Officer of the Legion of Honor;

General Bruno Le Moine of the Air Force and former auditor of IHEDN;

Dr. André Lebeau, the former president of CNES, the French space agency; Officer of the Legion of Honor;

Major General Denis Letty of the Air Force and former auditor of IHEDN;

Pierre Bescond, Engineer for General Armaments and Quality Director for CNES;

Admiral Marc Merlo and former auditor of IHEDN;

Denis Blancer, Chief National Police and superintendent at the Ministry of the Interior;

Dr. Michel Algrin and former auditor of IHEDN;

Christian Marchal, chief engineer of the National Corps of Mines and Research Director at the National Office of Aeronautical Research;

Dr. Alain Orszag, PhD in physics and armaments engineer.

Other contributors included Jean-Jacques Velasco of SEPRA at CNES; François Louange, President of Fleximage, specializing in photo analysis; and General Joseph Domange, of the Air Force.

The COMETA Report was published on July 16, 1999. Although the report was not sanctioned by the government, it is difficult to ignore the thoughts of French generals who were part of France's study of the UFO phenomenon. The report gives a brief history of France's study of the phenomenon, highlights some of the more inexplicable French cases, provides testimonies from French fighter pilots, and discusses the implications of UFO contact for the military, the public, and the media. There is too much in the report to properly cover its pros and cons in this chapter. The more salient parts of the report are its conclusions and recommendations. The authors concluded that although only 5% of UFO reports are unexplained, they were convinced that UFOs have a physical reality. They argued that the extraterrestrial (ET) hypothesis was the best explanation for the source of UFOs. The recommendations that they advanced were inexpensive to carry out and seemed to be logical steps. They recommended that the physical existence of the UFO phenomenon be acknowledged, boost resources to SEPRA, create a worldwide scientific group to study the phenomenon, use space surveillance systems for detection, put together a reaction plan for the possibility of alien contact, and urge the United States to share its knowledge of the phenomenon with the rest of the world. Perhaps the last recommendation was based on the COMETA authors' experience with the phenomenon or perhaps it was driven by French suspicions and apprehensions toward their old crony but cultural nemesis. But one fact is certain: The recommendation to boost SEPRA's resources so that the phenomenon could be more fully investigated was in vain.[50]

In January of 2004, CNES terminated SEPRA. This was done in spite of the results of an audit requested by the new director of CNES, Gérard Brachet. The audit was completed in 2002 by François Louange, an outsider and expert photo analyst. It was a favorable report that recommended that SEPRA be more fully supported with resources. The report was picked up by the French press. The major newspaper, *Le Figaro*, noted in November 2002 that, "UFOs: The state must give more resources for their study." Perhaps the decision to close SEPRA was hastened by its director's decision to publish a book that featured his opinion on the UFO enigma. In April of 2004, Jean-Jacques Velasco published *UFOs: The Evidence*. This title was a play on words as the word "évidence" in French means the same as the word "obviousness." Velasco's work at GEPAN and SEPRA had led him to the conclusion that UFOs were a physical reality, and he supported the COMETA Report in his book as an advocate of the ET hypothesis.[51]

GEIPAN

In July of 2005, Yannick d'Escatha, the new director of CNES, made the decision to reactivate France's study of unknown aerial phenomenon. SEPRA was reborn under the new name of GEIPAN (Groupe d'Études et d'Informations sur les Phénomènes Aérospatiaux Non-identifiés – Unidentified Aerospace Phenomenon Research and Information Group). Jacques Patenet was appointed the director of the new organization. Patenet had an extensive career in France's space program with the Ariane rocket program. Like GEPAN of the past, GEIPAN was placed under the control of the CNES hierarchy at the Toulouse Space Center.[52]

Monsieur Yannick d'Escatha

GEIPAN's mission is the same as GEPAN of old. The organization was and still is overseen by an independent and external steering committee, which guides and monitors its work. The committee is headed by former CNES Director General Yves Sillard and has 15 members that represent French civil and military authorities as well as the French government research departments.[53]

Monsieur Yves Sillard

The steering committee's first meeting was held on September 22, 2005. Among those present was Yves Sillard who was the former General Manger of CNES, the Deputy Manager of the Toulouse Space Center, the CNES Director of Education and Public Affairs, and representatives of the Air Force, the National Gendarmerie, Civil Aviation, and the National Police Force. At that meeting the committee renewed the agreements between all the organizations to allow for the continued flow of cases to GEIPAN. It required the person in charge of GEIPAN to submit semi-annual reports to the committee, and the committee also emphasized the need for a transparent policy on the phenomenon.[54] The French government was still serious about its investigation of the UFO phenomenon, and it was just as serious about the public "right to know."

Exactly one week after the committee meeting, Yves Sillard was interviewed on Radio France International. That was a very telling interview, but to properly appreciate its significance, one needs to know a little about the man who spoke. Yves Sillard studied as an engineer at France's prestigious Polytechnic Institute and its School of Aeronautical Engineering. He led France's Ariane rocket launch program in 1971 and was the head of France's space program (CNES) from 1976 to 1982. He later worked for the French Ministry of Defense and was President of the Institute for Research and Exploitation of the Sea. And in 1998 he represented France as the Secretary General of NATO. Yves Sillard was very prominent in France's space program and scientific community.[55]

Rather than paraphrase the interview, here are some of the key questions and answers as they were broadcast over Radio France in 2005. The following is a translation of a portion of the original French broadcast:[56]

> Vincent: Yves Sillard, your record is impressive. You worked on the Concorde jet program, you were one of the fathers of Ariane, you directed the CNES, and later became a General Manager of the Armament. If one asked you how to direct this committee on the observation of UFOS, is it a serious topic?

Sillard: It is a subject which it is necessary to tackle with rigor, seriousness, and without any preconceived ideas. Besides, it is a very interesting subject.

Vincent: There is a question of reactivating a structure which already existed to study the UFO Phenomenon, GEPAN. Why was GEPAN created in 1977 and then later terminated?

Sillard: Listen, this is a phenomenon, the phenomenon of Unidentified Aerospace Phenomena, which is very serious. It involves multiple honest witnesses who have made statements and expect, rightly, answers to their questions.

Sillard: Going back a little... To me, it is the role of CNES to try to meet these expectations, although in some cases, the answer is not easy to find. As you just mentioned, I created GEPAN for this purpose in 1977 when I was the Director General of CNES. And GEPAN worked perfectly. Unfortunately, this subject requires, as we just mentioned, to be approached with full scientific rigor. It is very often the subject of passionate responses both "for" and "against". There are campaigns of misinformation that try to destabilize, even ridicule, those who treat the subject seriously. In recent years, say the last 15 years, CNES has yielded somewhat to the campaigns of misinformation. An audit was done in the years 2001-2002, which involved hearing many people who recommended GEPAN restore the normal means of operation—without giving it means of course—and to oversee and guide its activities through a steering committee involving all the different agencies concerned with the study of this phenomenon. And so these recommendations were accepted and followed by Yannick d'Escatha, who is the current president of CNES.

Vincent: So, precisely, is the observation of these aerospace phenomena intellectually, scientifically, I guess, stimulating? Does it excite?

Sillard: It is exciting and it should be. But you know that a number of scientists refuse, saying "it is not possible, so it does not exist"...this does not seem a very scientific attitude. On the other hand, if you take the trouble to look, to look seriously and objectively, all these cases, some of which are not only cases with visual observations by witnesses but also some with radar echoes recorded by airplanes, by airborne radar or ground radar and, in some cases, traces of landings and damage to vegetation...this raises some extremely serious questions. And today, obviously, we cannot understand all of this, but can only make hypotheses and assumptions.

Vincent: Last question, Yves Sillard. Did America "invent" the UFO phenomenon a little...today do they still continue their research? You hear about it much less...

Sillard: Officially, the Americans have abandoned any UFO research after completing a report called the Condon Report in 1969. If I may have a minute, I can simply say that within the body of the report there curiously appears that 30% of the observed phenomena were completely inexplicable but the report concluded by saying that there was no interest in the continuation of the study [of UFOs]. There was a discrepancy between the findings and the body of the report. In fact, I think the American effort on the subject—in which they expended, I am sure, greater efforts to investigate than those of any other country—is deliberate and orchestrated disinformation. So, for what purpose? Is it a fear of the loss of supremacy if one day they find themselves facing a much more advanced civilization from the outside? Is it a concern to keep for themselves potential acquired technology, or is it some other explanation...we do not know.

The French government's open study of the UFO phenomenon was back on track.

France's study of the phenomenon has continued to make headlines. In January of 2006 Jacques Patenet announced that GEIPAN would make its UFO files available to the public worldwide. The files would be placed on the CNES website. This revelation was taken seriously and was announced in many newspapers around the world.[57] On March 22, 2007, GEIPAN kept its promise. France opened its files on UFOs and their website posted dozens of scientific papers and more than 1,600 sightings covering the last five decades. The public interest was so intense that the website crashed due to heavy usage.[58]

GEIPAN is expected to continue it role as France's research arm for the study of the UFO phenomenon through the foreseeable future. On January 1, 2009, Yvan White took over the role of director from Jacques Patenet, who continued with GEIPAN as an advisor to the new director.[59] Research and analysis of case reports continues, and as of November 2011, GEIPAN's website showed 22% of 1,170 fully investigated cases as Type 'D': an unidentifiable phenomenon.

The support provided to GEIPAN by the French government illustrates the significance that one of the world's major powers places upon the scientific understanding of the UFO phenomenon. French scientists openly investigate the phenomenon without stigma and have cooperated in an international fashion with scientists from Norway and Italy on the Hessdalen Project.[60] This cooperation and open scientific research is in stark contrast to that of the United States, whose public policy is to define the UFO phenomenon as not a "national security" issue and "unworthy of scientific study." If this mystery is someday to be understood, the answer may come from GEIPAN. As Robert Galley, the French Minister of Defense stated in 1974: "…it is necessary to adopt an extremely open-minded attitude towards these phenomena. Man has made progress because he has sought to explain the inexplicable…"

Notes

[1] Gildas Bourdais. *IUR*. Winter 2000-2001. "From GEPAN to SEPRA: Official UFO Studies in France." p. 10.

[2] French to English translation of an Interview by R. Roussel and F. Buchi. *Rhedae Magazine*. 1976. Lieutenant Colonel Alexis, director of the Office of Prospective Studies of the Air Force.

[3] G. Creighton, "French Minister Speaks on UFOs," *Flying Saucer Review*, Vol. 20, No. 2 (1974), p. 3. Based on an interview by J.C. Bourret.

[4] Gildas Bourdais. *IUR*. Winter 2000-2001. "From GEPAN to SEPRA: Official UFO Studies in France." p. 11.

[5] Clive Emsley. *Gendarmes and the State in Nineteenth-Century Europe*. Oxford: Oxford University Press. 1999. pp. 288.

[6] *Gendarmerie Nationale*, "Au labo de criminalistique." http://www.defense.gouv.fr/gendarmerie/a-la-une/au-labo-de-criminalistique/%28language%29/fre-FR#SearchText=science%20recherche#xtcr=1.

[7] *New York Herald Tribune*, Paris edition. October 6, 1954.

[8] Personal letter from Dr. Claude Poher at the Toulouse Space Center to Dr. Allen Hynek at CUFOS. May 27, 1977.

[9] Jean-Jacques Velasco. Short chronology, "Official Interest and Research on UFOs in France." May 28, 1999.

[10] Poher and Vallee. "Basic Patterns in UFO Observations." AAIA 13th Aerospace Meeting. Pasadena, California. January 20-22, 1975.

[11] David Rossoni, Éric Maillot, Éric DéGuillanume. *Les OVNI du CNES: 30 ans d'études officielles 1977-2007*. December 2007. Published by book-e-book. p. 44.

[12] Gildas Bourdais. *IUR*. Winter 2000-2001. "From GEPAN to SEPRA: Official UFO Studies in France." p. 12.

[13] Peter Sturrock. *The UFO Enigma*. Statements from François Louange and Jean-Jacques Velasco. Warner Books. 2000. p. 132.

[14] Centre National D'Etudes Spatiales. *No.1 Technical Report*. Toulouse October 29, 1979. "Encoding Rules" by Jacques Duval p. 9-22.

[15] Peter Sturrock. *The UFO Enigma*. Statements from François Louange and Jean-Jacques Velasco. Warner Books. 2000. p. 133.

[16] Institute of Higher Studies for National Defense (IHEDN). *Cometa Report*. "UFOs and Defense: What Should We Prepare For." July 1999. p. 31.

[17] Centre National D'Etudes Spatiales. *No.1 Technical Report*. Toulouse October 29, 1979. p. 79.

[18] Press Release, Center for UFO Studies, October 6, 1977.

[19] Gildas Bourdais. *IUR*. Winter 2000-2001. "From GEPAN to SEPRA: Official UFO Studies in France." p. 12.

[20] Gildas Bourdais. *IUR*. Winter 2000-2001. "From GEPAN to SEPRA: Official UFO Studies in France." p. 12.

[21] European Commission web site.
http://ec.europa.eu/information_society/policy/ipv6/docs/experts/bios/alain_esterle_bio_en.pdf

[22] Centre National D'Etudes Spatiales. *No.18 Technical Report*. Toulouse March 15, 1983. "Le Point sur l'Utilisation des Reseaux de Diffraction," pp. 5-6.

[23] J. Allen Hynek. *IUR*. 1980. "France's Official UFO Agency." p. 7.

[24] Centre National D'Etudes Spatiales. *No.16 Technical Report*. Toulouse March 1, 1983. "January 1981 Trace Analysis" pp. 16-25.

[25] Centre National D'Etudes Spatiales. *No.16 Technical Report*. Toulouse March 1, 1983. "January 1981 Trace Analysis" pp. 4-29.

[26] Centre National D'Etudes Spatiales. *No.16 Technical Report*. Toulouse March ', 1983. "January 1981 Trace Analysis" pp. 4-38.

[27] Centre National D'Etudes Spatiales. *No.16 Technical Report*. Toulouse March 1, 1983. "January 1981 Trace Analysis" pp. 39-66.

[28] Centre National D'Etudes Spatiales. *No.17 Technical Report*. CNES, March 21, 1983. "L'Amarante," p. 37.

[29] Jean-Jacques Velasco, "Amaranth Investigation," *Workshop on Physical Evidence*, materials describing the GEPAN/SEPRA program, circa 2000, p. 25.

[30] Centre National D'Etudes Spatiales. *No.17 Technical Report*. CNES, March 21, 1983. "L'Amarante," p. 45.

[31] Centre National D'Etudes Spatiales. *No.17 Technical Report*. CNES, March 21, 1983. "L'Amarante," p. 4.

[32] Centre National D'Etudes Spatiales. *No.17 Technical Report*. CNES, March 21, 1983. "L'Amarante," p. 59.

[33] Centre National D'Etudes Spatiales. *No.17 Technical Report*. CNES, March 21, 1983. "L'Amarante," p. 41.

[34] Centre National D'Etudes Spatiales. *No.17 Technical Report*. CNES, March 21, 1983. "L'Amarante," p. 38.

[35] Centre National D'Etudes Spatiales. *No.17 Technical Report*. CNES, March 21, 1983. "L'Amarante," p. 67.

[36] Centre National D'Etudes Spatiales. *No.17 Technical Report*. CNES, March 21, 1983. "L'Amarante," p. 61.

[37] Jean-Jacques Velasco, "Amaranth Investigation," *Workshop on Physical Evidence*, p. 25.

[38] Centre National D'Etudes Spatiales. *No.17 Technical Report*. CNES, March 21, 1983. "L'Amarante," p. 68.

[39] Jerome Clark. *UFO Encyclopedia, 2nd Edition*. 1998. p. 462.

[40] Yves Sillard, Letter from Director General of CNES, April 14, 1980. Appendix of CNES Work Document #4. "Study of Unidentified Aerospace Phenomena 1977-1981—Results and Perspectives. December 18, 1981. p. 32

[41] Jerome Clark. *UFO Encyclopedia, 2nd Edition*. 1998. p. 462.

[42] Gildas Bourdais. *IUR*. Winter 2000-2001. "From GEPAN to SEPRA: Official UFO Studies in France." p. 13.

[43] Jerome Clark. *UFO Encyclopedia, 2nd Edition*. 1998. p. 462.

[44] CNES-GEIPAN Case Observations. Sarmon (32) 1984. http://www.cnes-geipan.fr/index.php?id=202&cas=1984-03-01023

[45] Gildas Bourdais. *IUR*. Winter 2000-2001. "From GEPAN to SEPRA: Official UFO Studies in France." p. 13.

[46] Gildas Bourdais. *IUR*. Winter 2000-2001. "From GEPAN to SEPRA: Official UFO Studies in France." p. 13.

[47] CNES-GEIPAN web site. Graph of UFO cases by year. Last updated August 4, 2010.
http://www.cnes-geipan.fr/index.php?id=295.

[48] CNES-GEIPAN Case Observations. La Ferte Sous Jouarre (77) 1994. http://www.cnes-geipan.fr/index.php?id=202&cas=1994-06-01360.

[49] *COMETA Report*. "Les OVNI et la Defense." July 1999. pp. 7-9.

[50] *COMETA Report*. "Les OVNI et la Defense." July 1999. pp. 12-88.

[51] Gildas Bourdais. "On the Death & Rebirth of Official French UFO Studies: 2004-2007." January 19, 2008. pp. 4-5.

[52] Gildas Bourdais. "On the Death & Rebirth of Official French UFO Studies: 2004-2007." January 19, 2008. p. 5.

[53] CNES-GEIPAN web site. "New unit, broader mandate." http://www.cnes.fr/web/CNES-en/5040-new-unit-broader-mandate.php.

[54] CNES Press Communiqué. Paris, September 28, 2005, CP 075 – 2005.

[55] *Le Monde*. "Yves Sillard, Secretary General of NATO." December 13, 1997.

[56] Radio France International. Vincent Roux interview of Yves Sillard. September 29, 2005.

[57] Gildas Bourdais. "On the Death & Rebirth of Official French UFO Studies: 2004-2007." January 19, 2008. p. 6.

[58] AFP (French Press Agency). March 22, 2007.

[59] CNES-GEIPAN web site. "Change of Direction for GEIPAN." December 10, 2008. http://www.cnes-geipan.fr/index.php?id=181&no_cache=1&tx_ttnews[backPid]=211&tx_ttnews[pointer]=3&tx_ttnews[tt_news]=75.

[60] CNES-GEIPAN web site. "Scientific Campaign Analysis of Luminous Phenomena Observed in the Valley of Hessdalen

Norway." November 29, 2010 http://www.cnes-geipan.fr/index.php?id=181&no_cache=1&tx_ttnews[tt_news]=98.

The Hessdalen Project was initiated by Østfold University College in Norway in 1983. Hessdalen is a small valley in central Norway whose residents have experienced many strange light phenomena. . Between 1981 through 1984, residents of the valley became concerned after strange, unexplained lights appeared at many locations throughout the valley. Hundreds of lights were observed. At the peak of activity there were about 20 reports a week. This number has declined to about 20 reports per year. In August of 1998 an automatic measurement station was put in place that captures both data and photographs of the phenomena. More can be learned of the joint Norwegian-French-Italian science research on this phenomenon at the project's website http://www.hessdalen.org/index_e.shtml.

Chapter 20: Glimpses of Episodes in Other Countries

Belgium: 1989-1991

Belgium had a very public UFO flap between November 1989 and August 1990.[1] Twenty years after the United States closed Project Blue Book and indicated that they would no longer investigate UFOs, the Air Force of Belgium still took the subject seriously. This is one of many nations that continue to investigate legitimate UFO phenomena when they occur. Their air force worked with the civilian population, with the police, with NATO, and they maintained open communications. If this event had occurred in the United States, one would seriously doubt that such openness would have occurred. This begs the question, "Does the United States truly ignore the UFO phenomenon with its ability through satellites to monitor every flying object in the earth's atmosphere?"

While an early case awakened the interest of the civilian investigating group, SOBEPS, on November 7, 1989, the entire country's interest was piqued by a November 29 incident. A total of 143 sightings were reported, involving approximately 250 people, including several police officers. Some of these sightings occurred at very short distance; in some cases the witnesses were directly beneath the craft. The policemen first saw the craft at 5:20 p.m. and described it as a triangular platform with three lights and emitting a very light humming noise. They estimated an altitude of 500 feet with a wingspan of 110 feet. The policemen followed the craft to a lake where it remained immobile during more than 30 minutes. During those 30 minutes, the policemen witnessed the craft repeatedly emit two red light beams with a red ball at the spearhead of both beams. The red balls returned to the center of the vehicle after which another cycle started. A full cycle lasted several minutes. Then at 8 p.m., two other policemen also spotted a triangular craft near a monastery. The craft emitted "a red light ball" that headed downward toward the policemen. The light ball moved around the monastery before disappearing. Subsequently, the craft began to move and passed directly over the policemen's vehicle and departed to the northeast.[2]

With this case and its publicity, the Belgian Air Force found itself the recipient of increasing numbers of phone calls. According to Colonel Wilfred de Brouwer, the Air Force had never had an internal organization assigned to the study of UFOs[3] (this is despite the fact that Belgium has had many UFO cases over the years, including a very intense, one-day, flap on July 4, 1972).[4] Auguste Meessen, a physics professor at the Catholic University of Louvain, joined SOBEPS' UFO investigation in early December of 1989 and immediately sent inquiries to the Belgian Air Force.[5] At the other end of the inquiry was Colonel de Brouwer, Air Force Chief of Operations. De Brouwer had a problem. He had no funding and no personnel to dedicate to a full-scale UFO investigation, yet he believed that whatever this intruding phenomenon was, it required examination. He and Meessen began an ongoing communication.

Wilfred de Brouwer

Although the Belgian gendarmerie refused to cooperate with SOBEPS[6] on a December 18 incident, Meessen's relationship with de Brouwer convinced people in the Ministry of Defense that the civilian researchers could be helpful. Shortly thereafter, the Ministry of the Interior sent out a directive that instructed gendarmerie to send SOBEPS their reports.[7] On December 21, the Minister of Defense made a public statement that there had been many UFOs reported and that the Ministry and the Army had no idea what they were.[8] The statement did say that the Ministry was certain that they were *not* ultralight air vehicles, remotely-controlled military vehicles, US stealth planes, nor AWACS aircraft.

Reports of UFOs were sporadic until March 30 and 31 of 1990, when sightings occurred again. Radar returns resulted in the Air Force scrambling two F-16 jet planes, an action which, as usual, was to no avail except that one pilot had photographic records of the radar responses from his instruments.[9] De Brouwer notified Meessen of the case early, and Meessen volunteered, with other scientists associated with SOBEPS, to analyze the radar data. The Air Force agreed. De Brouwer's public statement was that the Air Force "was unable to identify the nature nor the origin of the phenomena."[10]

In an attempt to identify these unknown craft, the Air Force agreed with SOBEPS to set up four night watches for the triangular-shaped objects in mid-April around the Easter holiday.[11] Both civilians and military participated side-by-side in the watches, and the Air Force provided a standby jet to intercept any bogey reported. (Somewhere around this time, the U.S. Defense Intelligence Agency received intelligence on de Brouwer's actions and statements, and transmitted this on to the other intelligence agencies and offices such as the White House and the State Department.[12])

Due to military procedures, it was not until June 22 that SOBEPS personnel were able to examine the radar data from the March 30 case. Meesen and his colleagues began their radar analysis.[13] Simultaneously, Major P. Lambrechts of the Air Force General Staff produced and released an official report on the incident to the press.[14] In that report, Lambrechts excluded well-known explanations for UFOs, including optical illusions, astronomical objects, weather balloons, atmospheric inversions, and holographic projections. The report was of the opinion that the performance characteristics of the objects, particularly with regards to their speed in change-of-altitude, and a lack of a sonic boom, precluded their identification with known aircraft.

De Brouwer was cleared for two further public appearances on the subject. One was a frank and detailed interview for the popular magazine *Paris-Match*. This interview was published in the July 5, 1990, issue.[15] On July 11, he also gave a talk at NATO headquarters in Brussels.[16] A large contingent of the public was present. In the talk, de Brouwer asserted that the events of March 30 and 31 were highly unusual, witnessed by several gendarmes (among others), and occasioned the scrambling of two F-16 fighters. Although his statements would be vigorously argued against in later publications by skeptics,[17] de Brouwer said that the target was detected by radar and conformed to ground visual observation. He stated that the objects remain unidentified. The study of the radar data by a joint SOBEPS/Air Force team would not report until much later, and that analysis also produced controversy from skeptics. In October, an Air Force team at its training school (Ecole Royal Militaire) began a computer analysis of photos that had been taken at about the same time period as the event of the jet scramble.[18] These photos, *not* simultaneous with the F-16 event, are generally considered unrevealing at best.

The point of all this is not whether the Belgium Triangle Wave was a series of incidents that involved unexplainable technology or not. The point is rather that the Belgian military took the events seriously and took the serious *civilians* seriously. Working with professionally-minded people, the military collaborated in the pursuit of information about UFO-like reports. In doing so, they also trusted the public generally, releasing with much of the relevant information once they had digested it. It was the sort of transparency and cooperation that American UFO researchers have hoped for and not seen. Belgium continued to view unknown overflights as a security issue of interest not only to themselves, but also to the European Union as a whole. Between 1991 and 1993, the idea of creating a Euro Centre to coordinate investigation into such reports was brought before the European Parliament ten times.[19] Belgium supported the concept; Great Britain vetoed it.

After his retirement as a Major General in the Belgian Air Force, Wilfred de Brouwer issued the following statement, summarizing his views as the central military figure involved in these episodes:

My name is Wilfred De Brouwer. I am a retired Major General of the Belgian Air Force and I was Chief Operations in the Air Staff when an exceptional UFO wave took place over Belgium. Indeed, during the evening of 29 November 1989, in a small area in Eastern Belgium, approximately 140 UFO sightings were reported. Hundreds of people saw a majestic triangular craft with a span of approximately 120 feet, powerful beaming spot lights, moving very slowly without making any significant noise, but, in several cases, accelerating to very high speeds.

The following days and months, many more sightings would follow. The UFO wave would last more than one year during which a Belgian UFO organization conducted more than 650 investigations and recorded more than 400 hour of audio witness reports. On one occasion, a photograph revealed the triangular shape and four light beams of the object.

Belgium had no official focal point for reporting UFO observations. Nevertheless, in my function of Chief Operations, I was confronted with numerous questions about the origin and nature of these craft. In the first instance, and in consultation with other NATO partners, I could confirm that no flights of stealth aircraft or any other experimental aircraft took place in the airspace of Belgium. In addition, the Civil Aviation Authorities confirmed that no flight plans had been introduced. This implied that the reported object(s) committed an infraction against the existing aviation rules.

The Belgian Air Force tried to identify the alleged intruder(s) and, on three occasions, launched F 16 aircraft. On one occasion, two F 16 registered rapid changes in speed and altitude which were well outside of the performance envelope of existing aircraft. Nevertheless, the pilots could not establish visual contact and the investigation revealed that specific whether conditions may have caused electromagnetic interferences and false returns on the radar screens. The technical evidence was insufficient to conclude that abnormal air activities took place during that evening.

In short, the Belgian UFO wave was exceptional and the Air Force could not identify the nature, origin and intentions of the reported phenomena.[20]

Soviet Union: The Gindilis Study

Any official government involvement in UFOs by the former Soviet Union remains, at this writing, a highly controversial matter and the source of much speculation. This history will doubtless be written, based on responsible government documents, some day, but it is, at the moment, premature. Nonetheless, it seems reasonable to present a description of one known Soviet study. The inclusion of this study in this current volume is merely to indicate that despite what rumors have occasionally suggested, there was, at least in this instance, interest in the phenomenon at high levels of government.

The work we will discuss came to the attention of the West when a document was given to NASA's Richard Haines. Dr. Haines, a physiological psychologist working at the NASA-Ames (CA) laboratories, and also a Russian scholar, was able to read and translate it. The document is entitled: "Observations of Anomalous Atmospheric Phenomena in the USSR-Statistical Analysis."[21] It was authored by L. M. Gindilis, D. A. Men'kov, and I. G. Petrovskaya. Gindilis was a well-known astronomer and interested in the Search for Extraterrestrial Intelligence using radio telescopes and other approaches. The study was sanctioned by the USSR Academy of Sciences' Institute of Space Research (PR #473), and dated 1979. For short, it goes by the name of the "Gindilis Report."

L.M. Gindilis

Whether one wishes to view the Gindilis Report as relevant to the "military or government response" to the UFO phenomenon is up to individual evaluation. In most countries, this report would be considered a scientific or academic report with no particularly close relationship to government. But this was the Soviet Union. Because the central government exercised such strict controls over the systems of the body politic in that country, and the Presidium Academy of Sciences was no exception, the publication of this work must be viewed as at least approved by the government in some sense. Given the fact that in early years the Soviet Press was not allowed to publish UFO news at all,[22] this is at a minimum a change in attitude. The report opens with this remark, indicating a type of high sanction:

> The work is published by decision of the Section of General Physics and Astronomy, Presidium Academy of Sciences USSR.

> Preparatory processing and formalization of the initial observational material was carried out by I. G. Petrovskaya (Institute of Space Research).[23]

Skeptics in the United States have argued that the majority of the incidents in the study were misidentifications of secret Soviet weapons systems.[24] This assertion certainly is not proven. But the identity of the cases' stimuli is not the issue here anyway. The point is merely that Soviet interest in the UFO phenomenon produced a study by high-ranking scientists, and that study was approved by the government-monitored Presidium Academy.

The Gindilis study did statistical analyses on 256 reports. Two-thirds of these were gathered from a single year (1967). A large number of these (perhaps one-fourth, but, given interpretation of witness testimony, maybe up to a third) were of crescent-shaped objects. This is an unusual shape in UFO reports and, when combined with the dates, gives some credence to the idea that *these* cases (not everything in the study) might be observations of a new weapons system warhead on re-entry.[25] Nevertheless, there are still between two-thirds and three-quarters of the cases not of the "crescent" variety. With or without the misidentification of Soviet weaponry, the USSR *could* have been experiencing a UFO flap in 1967, just as the United States and other areas of the world were. Due to this, there seems to have arisen some breakage of the public silence about UFOs, and people became openly interested.[26] Two professors, Felix Y. Zigel and Yuri A. Fomin, made an appeal for persons to send witness reports to them for private (i.e. not government-related) analysis. This appeal took place via an appearance on Soviet Central Television. This is another form of tacit government approval. It is apparently true that the large number of reports elicited by this appeal formed the basis for a 1968 monograph by Zigel, entitled *Unidentified Flying Objects in the Union of Soviet Socialist Republics.*[27] The text of the Zigel monograph describes between 178 and 191 cases, depending upon whether one counts the brief thumbnails added on just before printing. This number is in the ballpark of the 256 ultimately included by Gindilis, and gives confidence to his statement that the cases for his study were received from Zigel (about ten years later). This is mentioned to avoid a false impression that Gindilis et al. went out on a UFO-case gathering survey as part of their task. This was a statistical analysis of already-existing reports.

The Gindilis Study showed surprising awareness of the state of U.S. and French UFO investigations, quoting J. Allen Hynek, Jacques Vallee, Claude Poher, and David Saunders. Spain's V. J. Ballester-Olmos was also referred to for his statistical analysis expertise.[28] The study's conclusions were, as to be expected, mixed. Some reports are errors; some do not seem to be.

> A conclusion as to the nature of the observed phenomena can be drawn from available data. Some of them possibly can be due to atmospheric optics effects. However, in the overwhelming majority of cases, they evidently are of a completely different nature. The large percentage of independent

observations made simultaneously at different points hundreds of kilometers apart indicates this, in particular.

A certain portion of the observations may be due to various technical experiments in the atmosphere and space near the earth, to observations of space technology objects, in particular. However, the kinematic characteristics exclude the possibility of such an explanation for at least one third of the cases. It also is difficult to match data on the shapes of the objects and other characteristics noted above with such an explanation. Finally, observations made long before 1957, i.e., before the start of the space age, must be considered.

Obviously, the question of the nature of the anomalous phenomena still should be considered open.

To obtain more definite conclusions, more reliable data must be available. Reports on observations of anomalous phenomena have to be well documented. The production of such reports must be organized through the existing network of meteorological, geophysical, and astronomical observation stations, as well as through other official channels.

Here, a mechanism for the verification of incoming reports, both from the point of view of their adequacy with respect to the phenomena actually observed, and from the point of view of determination of the possible nature of the phenomena (astronomical and geophysical phenomena or engineering experiments in the atmosphere and space near the earth), must be provided.

The question of setting up special instrument observations must be carefully thought out.

In our opinion, the Soviet and foreign data accumulated so far justifies setting up such studies.

Continuation of statistical analysis of the available material, as well as study the physical parameters of the anomalous phenomena is proposed.[29]

The Gindilis Study considered a significant portion of the cases to be anomalous, and suggested on-going formal study, including instrumentation arrays and statistical work. Whether any positive action resulted from this is doubtful. Some observers say that, if anything, the government tightened controls on UFO-related public comment shortly thereafter. We do know that this did not stop academic interest in the USSR. Dr. Gindilis is still interested in both SETI and UFOs today, and is an advisor to a prominent UFO group (RIAP) directed by Vladimir Rubtsov.

Brazil

Brazil has had many spectacular UFO events over the years, some of these occurring quite early in the history of the phenomenon. The history of the government's response has not really been documented, but perhaps, as the country releases its UFO files, it may soon be possible to do so. Despite what may seem to be a premature status, there are a few worthwhile remarks about early Brazilian UFOlogy that might be useful at this time.

As an important element of the political stage for the handling of UFOs, it should be noted that the Brazilian Air Force (FAB) was highly dependent upon the USAF during the 1950s. The USAF could either sanction or veto the transfer of air technology to the Brazilians, and at least in one case did so (to maintain the strategic power balance in the region, they claimed). Both the types of planes and the initial training of crews were to a significant extent controlled by the Americans. The FAB and the USAF were "close," and the USAF opinions about things made a difference.

An early example of this occurred in 1952 when a series of photos were taken at Barra de Tijuca.[30] These photos have a controversial back-and-forth life even today. At the time, the photos were presented to the FAB by the two men who took them (one a prominent journalist who played a role in Brazilian UFOlogy for years, Joao Martins, and the other, Ed Keffel, a press photographer). The FAB took them quite seriously as is shown by both early news stories of officials examining photos with Martins and Keffel, and by a released file that showed attempts to gauge a potential flight path for the object.[31] The FAB sent personnel, including a civilian photographer that they used as a consultant, Almiro Barauna, to see if they could fake the photos using a model. They determined that it was not easy to do so. FAB brought the case to the attention of the USAF early on.

For much of the 1950s, the FAB and the government were silent on UFOs, seeming to follow the American lead. But there were frequent stories in the press that indicated leaks.[32] Normally, without official documents, commenting upon these matters would be too unfounded for this book, but an exception is being made here. This is because in the middle 1950s there existed three outstanding Sao Paulo professionals (a pilot, a lawyer, and a science professor) of great credibility and well-connected to inside information. Two of these, Auriphebo Simoes and J. Escobar Faria, published highly sensible and conservative UFO newsletters, and corresponded with U.S. researchers. The third, Flavio Periera, was president of the British Interplanetary Society, among his other science activities. All had connections with the FAB, often serving on committees with military officers. Simoes, Faria, and Periera are our checks on the validity of otherwise poorly-documented facts. (The most famous name in Brazilian UFOlogy, however, was the medical doctor,

J. Escobar Faria

Olavo Fontes. Fontes resided in Rio de Janeiro rather than Sao Paulo, and only gradually came to know and collaborate with the Big Three. All of them seemed to like Fontes and admire his energy and intelligence, but, whereas Faria felt Fontes was regularly on the mark with his analyses, Simoes thought him a bit naïve.)[33]

A telling moment in the Brazilian handling of UFO cases came with the 1954 flap that hit Brazil right along with Venezuela, but without the "little men" cases being prevalent. The major incident in the flap occurred on October 24, 1954, at Gravatai AFB.[34] The manifestation at the air base took place over an extremely long period of time (approximately 1 p.m. to 4:30 p.m.) and was seen by more than a hundred people. Because the military presented a detailed report to the public, a few weeks later we can repeat some of the specifics with some assurance of accuracy. The following is a direct transcript of the words of a chief military witness, Lieutenant H. Ferraz De Almeida, jet pilot:

> On October 24, 1954, I was the only duty officer at Gravatai Air Force Base near Porto Alegre, Rio Grande do Sul. It was about 1:00 p.m. when a sergeant called me to see a flying saucer that was flying over the base. I said, "Good, I want to get a look at this thing." We left the office, crossed the airport and approached some buildings around the base soldiers' quarters. Then he pointed to the sky. I looked and saw an object hovering over the base. It was silver-dull in color, like the aluminum-dull color of our jets, and reflected in the sunlight. It appeared to be moving in a very strange way. The movements were circular but, at the same time, it maneuvered from one side to another in an erratic "zig-zag" course. To the observers on the ground these motions seemed to be slow. But, as a jet pilot, I know that a supersonic jet plane flying at the altitude the object appeared to be, between 40,000 and 45,000 feet, would give the impression of a very slow motion. For this I am induced to believe that the object's speed was tremendous, far beyond anything known to me. It was hard to believe but I was not alone. Ten sergeants and the same number of soldiers were now at my side witnessing the sighting. But I understood it would be wise to call for the opinion of more skilled observers. In so doing, I found Major Magalhaes and reported, "Major, there is a body over the base. I would like you to have a look at it and give me your opinion." We agreed and I drove him to a place where he could see the object.[35]

Major-Aviator J Magalhaes Mota witnessed the same object and its antics. It was reported to him that there were no balloons aloft. He was also told that there were many civilian observers on the base.

As he watched, a second object rapidly came across the sky, closed in on the first object, and then stopped beside it. At this point, the two were very high overhead. Then the second object moved again very rapidly, abruptly reversed course, and flew off in an arc. The officers were stunned by the speed. When the object was in motion, it was surrounded by a misty halo. When it stopped, the halo disappeared. The more it increased speed, the more strongly apparent was the halo. Characteristics such as this, of course, appeal to pilots and technologists, as they look for signs of propulsion. Mota's full statement and that of Lieutenant Ferraz De Almeida agreed precisely. A major UFO event had occurred over the base and had been witnessed by a hundred personnel and civilians.

The reports went to FAB headquarters with a request for a full investigation. Somewhat extraordinarily, a call went out to the citizenry to report similar sightings to FAB.[36] A promise was made by FAB command to release an official report after all the information was examined. It was reported that the Chief of FAB intelligence, Colonel Joao Adil de Oliveira, would head the investigation, and, given later developments, that was probably true. Adil de Oliveira was personally interested in UFO reports and had been evaluating reports for some time.[37] Simoes, Faria, Periera, et al. knew of de Oliveira, and said that he was convinced that some UFO cases were real, true mysteries. Perhaps because of his attitude, perhaps just due to a different feeling about UFOs, Brazilian policy was to not (normally) make official statements about UFOs, but if interested pilots wanted to, they were free

Colonel Oliveira

to do so. Lots of loose talk took place, therefore, alongside such events as Gravatai.

U.S. historians would probably be surprised to find that the Brazilian military did as it promised. They laid their report about Gravatai on the table on the 2nd of December.[38] Colonel de Oliveira was there to present it and so was Major Mota of Gravatai. Mota and two other Gravatai witnesses described the event in detail. De Oliveira gave a tour-de-force general presentation on UFOs, including even Project Blue Book data. Here were his concluding remarks:[39]

1. Evidence shows that the saucers are real. No government could afford to ignore the reports about UFO's and all investigations should be made to determine the identity of any UFO sighted over the country. The problem could be of military interest.

2. The saucers appear to be some kind of revolutionary aircraft. They are not conventional phenomena or illusions. There are too many responsible people involved to say that the whole thing was a hallucination.

3. We don't know where they come from, and we don't know the purpose of their survey. I hope some day we can solve the riddle and know the answers.

To close the session, a FAB aero-technologist, Brigadier General Guedes Muniz, said, "We military technicians and aeronautic engineers have not tried in the past to discuss the technological and scientific probability of these space vagabonds. And we are not trying to discuss it now."[40] He went on to say that there is no use trying to figure out how these things fly any more than we could figure out how the horn-beetle manages it. Everything about the horn beetle seems to be aerodynamically wrong by current knowledge. "But the horn beetle, knowing nothing of this, is still flying." Thus, the UFOs; and thus, our ignorance. Surely the conference attendees were stunned.

All of this was presented to the U.S. Air Force Attache, who reported back to the Pentagon.[41] He told of the flap and the military sightings. He had either spoken to Mota or read the formal Gravatai report. He said that the FAB authorities were convinced that the sightings were credible, but that the cases are merely read and filed away. He stated that the FAB has no idea what to do with them. If he was honest and frank, he would have said that the FAB and the USAF had the identical problem.

462

During the mid-1950s, the government tended to mimic the U.S. policy of "officially" rendering negative statements, but with a much gentler hand. As stated, military personnel were free to talk about their cases. When an investigation took place, everything was not automatically confiscated. (In the case of what became known as the Campinas "Tin Rain," an alleged fall of metal from a flying saucer, only a small sample was taken by the military.)[42] Many civilian cases were ignored. If any military involvement existed (even with an officer non-directly part of an encounter but somehow related to the case as consulted or quoted), then FAB *did* investigate. Such a situation occurred with a famous "contactee" claimant, where Dr. J. Freitas Guimaraes was speaking of meeting with extraterrestrials and bringing a message of peace to humanity.[43] Guimaraes, by the way, was a legitimate college teacher. According to Simoes and Faria, he was willing to rationalize his fabrication of the story because of the truth of the message itself for the world. The FAB operated at least two focus points for UFO cases: one in Rio de Janeiro (Colonel Oliveira's office) and one in Sao Paulo (Major Taborda's office).[44] Taborda, who according to Simoes and Faria did not believe in the anomalousness or mysteriousness of UFO reports, told them that the result of the "Tin Rain" analysis was that it was pure tin.[45] This comment is a) wrong based on analysis done in the U.S.—it was a rather mundane alloy; and b) surprisingly loose-lipped, as such a comment could not help defuse public excitement over UFOs.

Then in 1958 came the Ilha de Trindade incident.[46] Trindade is a large piece of volcanic rock about ten square kilometers in area, 740 miles from the Brazilian coast. It has always been uninhabited, except for military and scientific personnel (in modern times it has housed about 30 personnel). In the post-World War Two era, the Brazilian Navy's Division of Hydrography and Navigation had set up a permanently manned station there to do both meteorological and oceanographic research.[47] In 1957, the island's facilities became a national focus for experiments in conjunction with the International Geophysical Year (IGY). One element assigned to these duties was the Navy ship *Saldanha da Gama*. This was formerly a cadet instruction vessel, now refitted as an IGY research ship. It carried a laboratory, a military crew, and both civilian and military scientists and technicians. One of these civilians was considered to be an expert on submarine (underwater) photography, with whom the military had worked before. This was Almiro Barauna, the same photographer that the FAB had asked to help with the Barra de Tijuca photos investigation.

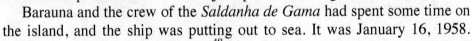

Almiro Barauna

Barauna and the crew of the *Saldanha de Gama* had spent some time on the island, and the ship was putting out to sea. It was January 16, 1958. Barauna, according to testimony,[48] was preparing to shoot some photos of this disembarkation, when his attention was drawn to an object approaching the island at apparently relatively low altitude. A

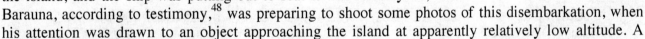

retired FAB officer, Captain J. Teobaldo Viegas, saw the object and Barauna hurriedly taking pictures of it.[49] Many others were on deck and witnessed the object, according to the statement by the Navy Ministry.[50] Barauna was able to take four photographs before the object flew well away. At that point, Captain Viegas (and, according to the formal Navy statement, Captain Bacellar, the commander of the Oceanographic Station) hustled Barauna off and supervised the immediate development of the film. Once the processing had taken place, the negatives were given to Bacellar, who testified that he was able to see the shape of the object on

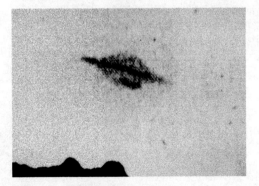

"Trindade Disk"

them at that time. Positive prints were, of course, being produced, and they showed four stages of what the personnel said was the object's approach, circling, and flyaway from the island. The images showed a "Saturn-shaped" object (a flattened spheroid with a ring around its major horizontal axis). Many UFO researchers have evaluated these pictures and consider them to be among the most interesting UFO photographs.[51]

Possibly because of the civilians on board, and possibly just due to the government's loose policy regarding individuals talking about UFO events, information about this sighting (and the rumor of photographs) spread widely. Barauna, after a brief sequestering of the film by Captain Bacellar, was returned the film at the completion of the IGY sailing, and he worked to bring out the images from the dark negatives.

By late February, the Navy Minister, Admiral Antonio Alves Camara, publicly vouched for not only the occurrence of the event but also for the authenticity of the photographs.[52] He said that the President of Brazil, Juscelino Kubitschek, had also seen the photographs and vouched for them. The Minister said, somewhat cryptically: "The Navy has a great secret which it cannot divulge because it cannot be explained." This has always been the dilemma of the military. What does a government say to its civilians when there is nothing definitive to say? Colonel de Oliveira and Captain Viegas also talked with the press, but the actual photos still were not to be divulged.[53] The Navy, for one, did not want to make the case a featured focus of news, since they were aware (as Bacellar had reported) that there had been several UFO reports by Trindade civilian scientists prior to the day of the pictures.[54] Why this bothered them is not stated. Perhaps they merely did not want the press harassment which would follow.

The photos *were* divulged, though. How this happened is anecdotal and may be a mere legend, but according to J. Escobar Faria,[55] President Kubitschek was being visited by a prominent journalist when he spotted the prints on Kubitschek's desk. The journalist asked to see them, and was permitted to do so. The journalist then badgered the President until he said that he would order their release to the public. This, then, happened over the Navy's objections. Barauna was then allowed to make a deal with the Rio newspaper *O Globo*, for first publication. Also, by February 22, copies had already been sent to the Pentagon through the U.S. Embassy Attache.[56] After Kubitschek's order, the Navy did a beautiful job of saving face and walking a middle line with the following release:[57]

President Kubitschek

ABOUT THE NEWS SPREAD BY THE PRESS IN WHICH WAS SAID THAT THE BRAZILIAN NAVY HAS BEEN AGAINST THE DISCLOSURE OF ALL THE FACTS DEALING WITH THE APPEARANCE OF AN OBJECT OVER TRINDADE ISLE, THIS CABINET MUST DECLARE THAT SUCH PRESS INFORMATIONS ARE NOT TRUE. THIS CABINET CONSIDERS THAT THERE IS NO REASON TO FORBID THE DISCLOSURE OF ALL PHOTOGRAPHS TAKEN BY SR. ALMIRO BARAUNA, WHO WAS A NAVY GUEST ON THE TRINDADE ISLE, AND BEFORE THE PRESCENCE OF NUMEROUS PERSONNEL OF THE NAVY SHIP "SALDANHA DA GAMA," ABOARD OF WHICH THE SNAPSHOTS WERE TAKEN. EVIDENTLY, THIS CABINET COULD NOT GIVE A STATEMENT ABOUT THE OBJECT WHO [sic] WAS SEEN OVER TRINDADE ISLE DUE TO THE FACT THAT SUCH PHOTOGRAPHS DO NOT EXHIBIT A DEFINITE EVIDENCE.

Colonel de Oliveira, in keeping with his previous statements about Gravatai et al., stated: "At present, it's impossible to doubt the flying saucers' existence."[58] Despite all of this, the official United States Air Force position was that the photographs were a hoax.[59] This was during the George

Gregory/Lawrence Tacker era, when the solutions to UFO cases were the most improbable in Blue Book Project history.

The release of the Trindade photos did not usher in a Brazilian age of openness to the phenomenon. In fact, due apparently to the surprise the military felt over all the emotions the release had caused, the military created a tighter policy.[60] By the end of 1958, FAB Air Minister Brigadier General Melo Correia was quoted as saying that he did not believe in flying saucers but did believe that the *idea* of flying saucers was engineered by a well-planned publicity campaign.[61] He also said: "Besides, the FAB has more serious things to do than to talk about flying saucers." That latter comment could just as easily have been said by the USAF's Harold Watson or Curtis LeMay.

But the "back door" of inside information between the military and certain civilians never closed, and may even have become more formalized. Due to the hard work of Flavio Periera, assisted by Simoes, Faria, and others, various scientific boards were created, which had both civilian and military personnel. In 1958, Periera, through the Brazilian Interplanetary Society, initiated a "Brazilian Assembly on UFOs," which consisted of himself, Faria, Simoes, Fontes, Joao Martins, Hulvio Aleixo, and several others, including "a top officer in the Brazilian Air Force" (one would suspect de Oliveira).[62] Later, in 1959, Periera again using the Interplanetary Society, initiated a committee on Interplanetary Law that also involved Air Force officials.[63] Finally, he laid the foundations for a "Brazilian Committee for Confidential Research in UFOs," consisting of civilian researchers and military members.[64] It began meeting in the fall of 1959 and looked forward to incorporation and financial backing by a Brazilian Foundation. How long this organization and this type of cooperation went on is unknown, as the formal state of Brazil's military UFOlogy becomes quite murky after that time. Recently (c. 2009) the government has released many pages of UFO files. Perhaps the fuller story will soon be known.

Notes

[1] The *Paris-Match* article (see reference #15) is a good overview of these events; see also Auguste Meessen, "The Belgian Sightings," *International UFO Reporter*: May-June 1991.

[2] Major General Wilfred de Brouwer, *MUFON 39th International Symposium Proceedings*: July 2008, pp. 140-142.

[3] Major General Wilfred de Brouwer, statement: National Press Club, 12 November 2007.

[4] SOBEPS, Special Report, "Cette Annee Encore, Des 'Objets' Mysterieux Ont Survole A Diverses Reprises 'La Belgique'," 2 May 1973, CUFOS files.

[5] Meessen, "The Belgian Sightings," *International UFO Reporter 16:3*, May-June 1991, pp. 4-11, 22, 24.

[6] Meessen, "The Belgian Sightings."

[7] See Marie-Therese de Brosses, "A UFO on the F16's Radar," *Paris-Match*, 5 July 1990 (henceforth "de Brosses, *Paris-Match* article." English translations abound: example, Robert Durant, trans., *MUFON UFO JOURNAL 268*: August 1990; also, SOBEPS report to various UFO groups, c. June-July 1990.

[8] See de Brosses, *Paris-Match* article; also, SOBEPS report to various UFO groups, c. June-July 1990; and Meessen, "The Belgian Sightings"; news article (ex. *La Wallonie*, December 22, 1989).

[9] See de Brosses, *Paris-Match* article; and, Col. W. de Brouwer to A. Victorian, letter with enclosures, 6 August 1991.

[10] Col. W. de Brouwer, letter with enclosures, 6 August 1991; and de Brouwer, *MUFON 39th International Symposium Proceedings*: July 2008, pp. 140-142.

[11] Bob Pratt and Patrick Ferryn (SOBEPS), "The Belgium UFO Flap," *MUFON UFO JOURNAL 267*: July 1990; and widespread press (ex. *Financial Times*, London, 18 April 1990; Joel Mesnard, "Belgium Haunted by Huge Triangular Craft," *Flying Saucer Review*, Dec. 1990).

[12] Evaluated Intelligence Report, subject: Belgium and the UFO Issue, 30 March 30, 1990 (mentions the USAF had made no overflight requests for Stealth aircraft), FOIA (DIA); also, Meessen, "The Belgian Sightings."

[13] Meessen, "The Belgian Sightings."

[14] Major P. Lambrechts, "Report Concerning the Observation of UFOs during the Night of March 30 and 31 1990," Belgian Air Force, 22 June 1990.

[15] de Brosses, *Paris-Match* article.

[16] Wim Van Utrecht, "The Belgian 1989-1990 UFO Wave," in Hilary Evans and Denis Stacy, eds., *UFOs: 1947-1997*, 1997, pp. 165-176.

[17] Meessen, "The Belgian Sightings"; Marc Hallet, "The So-Called 'Belgian UFO Wave': a Critical View," *Revue Francaise de Parapychologie 1*(1): 5-24, 1992 (translation: CUFOS files); and Maj. Gen. De Brouwer, *MUFON Symposium Proceedings*: July 2008, pp. 140-142.

[18] Colonel W. de Brouwer, comment to Tom Walker for the *Wall Street Journal*, "Belgian Scientists Seriously Pursue a Triangular UFO," 10 October 1990.

[19] Wim Van Utrecht, "The Belgian 1989-1990 UFO Wave," in UFOs: *1947-1997*.

[20] Major General Wilfred de Brouwer, *39th International MUFON Symposium Proceedings*: July 2008, pp. 140-142.

[21] L. M. Gindilis, D. A. Men'kov, and I. G. Petroskaya, *Observation of Anomalous Atmospheric Phenomena in the USSR* (translated), CUFOS: Chicago, 1980.

[22] This alarmed early U.S. Psychological Warfare analysts. See chapters 5 and after passim.

[23] Gindilis, Men'kov, and Petrovskaya, *Observation*.

[24] James Oberg, "The Great Soviet UFO Cover up," *MUFON UFO JOURNAL #176*: October 1982 (republished widely on the internet).

[25] Vladimir Rubstov of the post-Soviet UFO organization RIAP published a statement such as this on www.paranormalnews.com/article.asp?articleid=24.

[26] This thumbnail history is taken from Felix Zigel, *Unidentified Flying Objects in the Union of Soviet Socialist Republics*, 1968 (translation: CUFOS files), and is agreed to by both skeptics and UFO sympathizers.

[27] Felix Zigel, *Unidentified Flying Objects in the Union of Soviet Socialist Republics*.

[28] V. J. Ballester-Olmos, *A Catalogue of 200 Type-I UFO Events in Spain and Portugal*, 1976.

[29] Gindilis, Men'kov, and Petroskaya, *Observation*.

[30] Brazilian government UFO document release, "Occurrencies Traflego Hotel 6SC Comdabra," undated; and Auriphebo Simoes, *The Flying Saucer #9*: December 1957.

[31] Brazilian government UFO document release, "Occurrencies Traflego Hotel 6SC Comdabra," undated.

[32] Auriphebo Simoes, *The Flying Saucer 6*: June 1957. In both this and Faria's newsletter are many examples of stories wherein Brazilian military talked "on their own" to the press (ex. See Faria's bulletin of 1959, re: B-29 encounter).

[33] Auriphebo Simoes, *The Flying Saucer*, remarks passim.

[34] Olavo Fontes, "Flying Saucers Are Real says Brazilian Air Force Official Report on Unidentified Flying Objects," *Flying Saucer Review* (Seattle), May 1956. This, and the following several references, refer to the report at the 2 December 1954 press conference.

[35] Olavo Fontes, "Flying Saucers Are Real," quoted; these materials also exist in NICAP files as translations from Spanish language (Venezuela) newspapers by Alexander Mebane.

[36] Olavo Fontes, "Flying Saucers Are Real."

[37] Olavo Fontes, "Flying Saucers Are Real"; and Auriphebo Simoes, UFO lecture, CSI:-New York, 21 October 1957 (audiotape), CUFOS files. (Lecture mentioned also in *CSI: NY Newsletter #9:* 1 November 1957.

[38] Olavo Fontes, "Flying Saucers Are Real"; and Auriphebo Simoes, UFO lecture, CSI:-New York, 21 October 1957 (audiotape), CUFOS files; extensive notes from this conference were taken by reporters and used widely in Brazilian newspapers such as *O Cruzeiro*, 2 December 1954. A packet of these notes exists in Loren Gross' files.

[39] Quoted: Olavo Fontes, "Flying Saucers Are Real."

[40] Quoted: Olavo Fontes, "Flying Saucers Are Real."

[41] Mickel Bougard, "Le Dossier Photo d'Interspace" (Barra da Tijuca, Brazil, 7 May 1952), *Inforespace 18*, 1974.

[42] J. Escobar Faria, *UFO-Critical Bulletin II*, Jan-Feb, 1958; and J. Escobar Faria, *UFO-Critical Bulletin III*, no. 4, Jul-Aug, 1959.

[43] J. Escobar Faria, *UFO-Critical Bulletin I*, no. 9-10, Sept.-Oct. 1957; and Auriphebo Simoes, UFO lecture, CSI-New York; 21 October 1957 (audiotape). CUFOS files.

[44] J. Escobar Faria, *UFO-Critical Bulletin III*, no. 1, Jan-Feb, 1959.

[45] J. Escobar Faria, *UFO-Critical Bulletin II*, no. 1, Jan-Feb, 1958.

[46] J. Escobar Faria, *UFO-Critical Bulletin II*, no. 2, Mar-Apr; 1958; and several documents released by Brazil's Department of the Navy dated Feb. 6, Feb. 13, Feb. 21, and Feb. 25, and particularly Mar. 3, 1958.

[47] J. Escobar Faria, *UFO-Critical Bulletin II*, no. 2, Mar-Apr; 1958; and several documents released by Brazil's Department of the Navy dated Feb. 6, Feb. 13, Feb. 21, and Feb. 25, and particularly Mar. 3, 1958.

[48] Barauna's testimony is referred to in the Department of the Navy Summary (see reference 53). His recollections also appear *in International UFO Reporter VIII* (4): July-August, 1983.

[49] J. Escobar Faria, *UFO-Critical Bulletin II*, no. 2, Mar-Apr; 1958.

[50] "Brazil Has a Secret; Can't Explain It," news story in *Los Angeles Times*, 26 February 1958 (AP: dateline, Rio de Janeiro, Feb. 25); also reported by Faria.

[51] See website: www.nicap.org for an excellent overview of this case.

[52] Department of the Navy (Brazil), subject: Clarification of the Observation of unidentified flying objects sighted on the island of Trindade in the period of 12/5/57 to 1/16/58 (this report, slightly differently titled, seems equivalent to the 3 March 1958 report by the Department).

[53] J. Escobar Faria, *UFO-Critical Bulletin II*, no. 2, Mar-Apr; 1958.

[54] J. Escobar Faria, *UFO-Critical Bulletin III*, no. 1, Jan-Feb, 1959.

[55] J. Escobar Faria, *UFO-Critical Bulletin II*, no. 2, Mar-Apr, 1958.

[56] Auriphebo Simoes to Alexander Mebane, 23 February 1959; and Captain S. N. Sunderland, Naval Intelligence Information Report, 11 March 1958, subject: Brazil Navy Flying Saucer Photographed from Almirante Saldanha. Blue Book Microfilm.

[57] J. Escobar Faria, *UFO-Critical Bulletin II*, no. 2, Mar-Apr, 1958.

[58] J. Escobar Faria, *UFO-Critical Bulletin III*, no. 2, Mar-Apr, 1959.

[59] "UFO Photo Certified by Brazilian Navy Labeled a Hoax by USAF," *UFO Investigator 1* (10): July-August 1960; and (letters) Colonel Lawrence Tacker to Richard Hall, 8 July 1960, and Commander J. G. Brady to Coral Lorenzen, 10 October 1960.

[60] J. Escobar Faria, *UFO-Critical Bulletin III*, no. 1, Jan-Feb, 1959.

[61] J. Escobar Faria, *UFO-Critical Bulletin I*, no. 9-10, Sept-Oct., 1957; and Auriphebo Simoes, *The Flying Saucer 6*, June 1957.

[62] J. Escobar Faria, *UFO-Critical Bulletin II*, no. 3, May-June, 1958.

[63] J. Escobar Faria, *UFO-Critical Bulletin III*, no. 3, May-June, 1959.

[64] J. Escobar Faria, *UFO-Critical Bulletin III*, no. 5, Sept-Oct. 1959; and Flavio Pereira and J. Escobar Faria letter to Donald Keyhoe, 3 November.

Epilogue

This book, long and difficult as it was to complete, is at its close. It was created by a group of people sympathetic to the idea that the UFO phenomenon is a true mystery, not a trivial one. Some would say that all true scholarship requires skepticism in the researcher. We agree. The UFO History Group is not composed of "skeptics" in the often misused sense of deniers. We consider ourselves "analysts" who are willing to take any and all information as it comes. If that information requires the rejection of an idea or a claim, then rejection is the appropriate response. In this we are "skeptics." In the book, this trait is expressed in what might be considered our "first commandment" to scholarship (and to the wider community): Remain true to the sources. We hope that we have accomplished at least this.

We do not imagine that the story of UFOs and government is simple and obvious. History is, rather, difficult and complex, particularly when all the important information has not been made available. Like any complicated history, we will have made errors. Despite our many internal debates and clarifications, such things inevitably occur. We can only say to that: we have tried to present as solid a document as we could, and believe that the general flow of fact and description will stand the test of time. We welcome corrections. That is the lifeblood of all scholarship.

And so, what does this book demonstrate? Most importantly, we believe that it gives an accurate depiction of how governments, and particularly the United States Government, responded to the UFO phenomenon and why they did so. Although people familiar with intelligence communities would not be surprised, many others might be stunned to realize that such responses would rarely be based on anything but "national security." This would include even the issue of whether the phenomenon was real or not. Most of us, who live our lives in the general world outside of the national security communities, naturally feel that whether something (particularly something fascinating) is real or not would be a scientific priority. It is not. Nothing which is not germane to national security is important in a national security context. This is almost embarrassingly obvious when stated that way, yet so many of us have not understood it. Things which may be sacrificed to the higher goal of national security might, in certain instances, include science and even Truth. Not to understand that fact has been our naïveté. This book, we believe, demonstrates that principle of intelligence community behavior over and over again. This, in itself, is not a criticism of intelligence community behavior. It is simply recognition of what was done.

As applied to the problem of the UFO phenomenon, this natural form of governmental behavior expressed itself, almost immediately, by focusing on the danger to the body politic, in the sense of psychological warfare and the potential inducement of mass hysterical responses in the public. These dangers were judged as rating a significantly higher priority than exploration and discovery of what the phenomenon was. Consequently, discouragement of such interests in the non-governmental elements of the body politic was judged appropriate, even in the extreme. The targets for this discouragement were, of course, science, academia, and the media, and generally the public itself. Such a strategy was nearly an inevitable result of the government's primary beliefs. For any encouragement of belief in and investigation of the mystery by these public elements ran precisely counter to the goals of blunting the threats of psychological warfare and mass hysteria. With rare exceptions, the source documents portray a continual strategic manipulation of what the public should hear from government authorities about the phenomenon. Sometimes this manipulation was blundered and not effective. But it was in the main consistent in its intent: keep the subject on a non-serious level regarding public interest and concern. This assessment takes no speculative reading between the lines. Several documents, and most explicitly the CIA's 1953 Robertson Panel Report, state exactly that.

468

Epilogue

What then does this say about the phenomenon itself? It does not explain it. That simple sentence is worth noting. It does NOT explain it. What the intelligence communities did, and what was voiced to the public by governments around the world, did not explain the UFO phenomenon. In fact, one of the strongest conclusions that a researcher can come to upon reading the intelligence communities' documents is that they never could explain this phenomenon and knew that they had not. To explain the phenomenon was not their goal, especially in any scientific sense. Despite the choices of dismissive language in many of their public pronouncements, explanation, in the sense of Truth, was not the intent of those pronouncements, nor the work which went on behind them. This, of course, required continual clever crafting of these non-explanations and occasionally created a great deal of embarrassment due to the inevitable unbelievability of the words.

So what are UFOs? This too was not the focus of this book. We cannot, standing on the information presented here, make many detailed conclusions about the nature of UFOs. Indeed, because of the continuous elusiveness of the phenomenon, it is probably true that no one can make such detailed conclusions. But that is the point. We feel that the governmental handling of the phenomenon demonstrates that they themselves could not come to such conclusions. Their strongest remarks to the public were driven by policies characterized not by transparency nor intellectual honesty about what was really known. And often, as when Project Blue Book operatives changed case incident conclusions from "unknown" to a prosaic "known," and these changes were made by individuals having nothing to do with the earlier investigations but rather who were pursuing a policy to lower the percentage of listed unknowns, that dishonesty was deliberate.

However, we believe that, even without this being our focus, the book amply demonstrates that a large number of UFO incidents eluded every attempt by the intelligence community to explain them. These failures left them only with denial and fabrication as a public resort. We believe that these cases stand unexplained to this day. This does not allow us to conclude that such incidents were the product of non-human technologies. It would, however, be intellectually dishonest to merely discard such a hypothesis a priori. This is exactly our conclusion: many UFO incidents have occurred and are documented in the governmental sources for which no obvious explanation was, nor is, available. Such incidents, plus a very large case count of similar reports which have been investigated by the civilian UFO research community, constitute the UFO mystery. It is a mystery which the government did not solve, despite its public claims to have done so. And we have seen why such false statements were made. As such, a proper attitude towards the UFO phenomenon should be that it has been a robust part of our recent history, and it is a proper subject for investigation still.

A significant point of interest in this history is why the French government, in more recent times, took a different position on UFO case investigation than any other country in the world. This too is a question which cannot be answered, at least in any simplistic way. For the most part, the French government acted as did the United States, the British, and most other countries: with secrecy and denial. The different element arose when, in the 1970s, the French Space Agency became involved. The direction given by CNES did not demand focus on national security, but on scientific investigation. Without national security dominating the policy process, procedures could be initiated that involved public elements of the nation state and, most significantly, the cooperation of universities and their laboratory facilities. But none of this could have occurred had not some very senior scientist, placed in a perfect position of authority, chosen to make it so. Dr. Yves Sillar and his colleague Dr. Claude Poher were able to use their scientific standing and position within the space agency (at the right moment in history) to go counter to decades of governmental programming and academic ignorance and hostility. No such person(s), and no such success, arose anywhere in other countries. As we have seen, from the point of view of seeking answers to the UFO mystery, the French program was, at least on paper, a proper philosophical approach. Even underfunded and understaffed, it produced some interesting results. Most importantly, it presented a proper *attitude* to the public and to academia.

That attitude was: Why not explore this? This is a mystery. This is not solved. This is what Science does. It is, in fact, what Human Beings do when they are neither afraid nor otherwise restricted. It is, indeed, what the earliest investigators of the U.S. Air Force's Project SIGN wanted to do.

Why have there not been more willing scientists like Drs. Sillar and Poher? Why has academia been so "incurious" and even hostile towards this phenomenon? That is another very large and complex question, the answer to which is almost entirely sociological rather than "scientific." Dr. Charles Emmons has made a fine attempt at interviewing academics about involvement in UFO research and has found, as one would expect, that there are essentially no rewards for doing so, and a great deal of professional risk. His book, *At The Threshold: UFOs, Science, and the New Age,* is an insightful telling of at least part of this story. This rejection of personal involvement, at least publicly, arises in an environment of derision, perhaps not deliberately a goal of the intelligence community policies, but certainly supported by the public statements coming from them. When Dr. Hynek did his survey of astronomers for Project Blue Book in the 1950s, he noted that even astronomers who themselves had seen a UFO would not discuss that fact in the presence of co-workers. Even when Hynek left the Air Force consultancy and began his own Center for UFO Studies, his close friends and colleagues called themselves "The Invisible College." As an academic interested in UFOs, it was much safer professionally to be "invisible." Without active scholars publishing on the subject, there were no authorities who had actually done anything substantive with which a newly interested scholar could defend one's interest in the field. This profound academic ignorance of the subject makes the level of negative opinion voiced by academics that much more astonishing. This situation continues to exist today. Some interested parties get UFO researchers to swear to never mention their names. Others are told that their career will be hurt if they continue their publicly known interest. Others publish under pseudonyms.

Such are the complicated forces that have come together to create the "common knowledge" about the UFO phenomenon which is in place today. This common knowledge is the result of a formidable array of negative sociology and policy, dramatically at odds with what the intelligence documents tell us. This book is intended to unravel part of that array. But, even if this current piece of scholarship is in some small way successful at its task, and even with the presence of the French Government program as a light in the darkness, this common knowledge will not soon change. The decades-long, inbred negative attitude has been so thoroughly shot through the culture that only some utterly unexpected activity by the phenomenon itself might change things in any short time period. No one in the serious UFO scholarly community expects that to occur. We have been chasing this tricky mystery for sixty years.

So why continue the quest at all? Everyone knows the answer to that as soon as the question is broached. It is what we do. It is what we humans are. We are questers and we are discoverers. And it is a shame whenever we get in our own way.

But what *can* we do? It would be nice if the governments of the world would make a better effort, and have a better policy, to release all their relevant documents. This book is entirely the offspring of those documents already at hand. There could be many more documents, many more offspring, and many more understandings possible. That is the least that we can do. Any reader can participate in these adventures. Any reader can visit archives or seek intelligence through the Freedom of Information Act. Sifting the low-grade ore occasionally uncovers a nugget of gold. Then, please publish it so all of us will know.

The governments of the world could imitate in some form the French research office. And they could cooperate more fully with civilian researchers needing radar or satellite data, or other data from their dispersed detection arrays. No one is asking for security violations, just specific data for specific real-time incidents as may be available. The civilian researchers, despite being unpaid and forced to act like hobbyists, work hard at the task, but can only do as well as the information they are allowed to receive. Such information is usually minimal indeed.

And what might academia, and for that matter the media, do? The UFO community sympathizes with academic scientists interested in the subject, considering the barriers that they are up against. We realize that they have neither the time nor the reward system to dedicate any of their careers to the subject. As this insures a near total ignorance of the information resident in the field, the UFO community knows that little help can be expected from academia. But there is one thing that this intelligent but unknowing group could do: admit their ignorance. Reflect on what it means to be a scientist. Reflect on what it means to have earned an opinion about something. Particularly, reflect on what it takes to have earned a learned one. And then, get out of the way.

A pervasive attitude of derision projected by opinion makers in the sciences, and couched in false confident assertion, is definitely "in the way." And it is, ironically, deeply anti-scientific. Though not driven by precisely the same forces, the media suffers from the same disastrous combination of not knowing the subject but presenting strong attitudes about it. It is a shame and a burden that we are struggling along a pathway of hard-won and piecemeal discoveries and clarifications with little help and much rock throwing by media, science, and the government. There is a great book on human sociology and psychology to be written about our species in all of this.

Until that book is written, well, the Sun will still rise in the morning, and we will go about our lives at work and school, and laugh and love, and maybe even learn something that will one day enable us to tackle this great UFO mystery.

"Credible people have seen incredible things."
—Major General John Samford, Chief of Intelligence, United States Air Force

APPENDIX

Chapter 3 page 34
Memo from Tactical Air Command; June 28, 1947

SUBJECT: Report of Unusual Celestial Phenomena

TO: Assistant Chief of Staff, A-2
        Headquarters Tactical Air Command
        Langley Field, Virginia

1. The following report is submitted concerning an unusual occurrence observed by the following AAF Personnel at Maxwell Field, Montgomery, Ala. on the night of 28 June 1947:

        CAPT. WILSON H. KAYKO, 0-38841, Hq, TAC
        CAPT. JOHN H. CANTRELL, 0-255404, Hq, TAC
        1ST LT. THEODORE DEBEY, 0-2094172, Hq, TAC
        CAPT. REDMAN, Randolph Field, Texas

2. At approximately 2120 Central time, a light, with a brilliance slightly greater than a star, appeared from the West. It was first noted above the horizon of a clear moon-light night, traveling in an easterly direction at a high rate of speed. There was no audible sound and it was impossible to determine the altitude, except that it appeared to be at great height. It traveled in a zig zag course with frequent bursts of speed, much like a water bug as it spurts and stops across the surface of water. It continued until it was directly overhead and changed course 90° into the south. After traveling in the above manner for approximately five (5) minutes, it turned southwest and was lost in the brilliancy of the moon. At 2145 Central it was no longer possible to observe it.

3. A call was placed to Maxwell Field operations reference this phenomena and inquiry made if any experimental aircraft were scheduled for a flight in the vicinity. The reply was negative.

4. No plausible explanation is offered for the unusual action of this source of light, which acted contrary to any common aerodynamical laws. This report is submitted upon request, in view of the many recent reports reference unusual aerial objects observed throughout the U. S.

5. Two of the above noted observers are rated pilots and the other two are air intelligence officers. All observers were cold sober.

Chapter 3 page 39
Lt. Colonel George Garrett's Draft Estimate on Flying Disks

<u>FLYING DISCS</u>

30 July 1947

For purposes of analysis by AFBIR-CO, eighteen reported sightings of "Flying Discs" were selected for breakdown into detailed particulars. Each report was assigned a number and each number appears in the left-hand column of the data on the following pages.

One report, Number 7, has not yet been received and therefore no information is included other than Date, Name of Observer, and Location. The Fourth Air Force is attempting to secure a statement from this observer.

- Four reports, Numbers 2, 4, 17, and 18, have not been analyzed.

The subject headings on which the breakdown has been made are:

Date
Hour (Local standard Time)
Location
Observer's Name
Observer's Occupation
Observed from Ground or Air
Number of Objects Sighted
Altitude
Direction of Flight
Speed
Distance Covered
Length of Time in Sight
Deviation from Straight Flight
Color
Size
Shape
Sound
Trail
Weather
Manner of Disappearance
Remarks

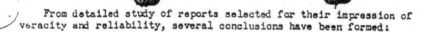

From detailed study of reports selected for their impression of veracity and reliability, several conclusions have been formed:

(a) This "flying saucer" situation is not all imaginary or seeing too much in some natural phenomenon. Something is really flying around.

(b) Lack of topside inquiries, when compared to the prompt and demanding inquiries that have originated topside upon former events, give more than ordinary weight to the possibility that this is a domestic project, about which the President, etc. know.

(c) Whatever the objects are, this much can be said of their physical appearance:

1. The surface of these objects is metallic, indicating a metallic skin, at least.

2. When a trail is observed, it is lightly colored, a Blue-Brown haze, that is similar to a rocket engine's exhaust. Contrary to a rocket of the solid type, one observation indicates that the fuel may be throttled which would indicate a liquid rocket engine.

3. As to shape, all observations state that the object is circular or at least elliptical, flat on the bottom and slightly domed on the top. The size estimates place it somewhere near the size of a C-54 or a Constellation.

4. Some reports describe two tabs, located at the rear and symetrical about the axis of flight motion.

5. Flights have been reported, from three to nine of them, flying good formation on each other, with speeds always above 300 knots.

6. The discs oscillate laterally while flying along, which could be snaking.

Chapter 3 page 42
Lt. General Nathan Twining's memo on "Flying Discs"; September 23, 1947

By __#GLewis__ NARA, Date 3/13/86 .

TSDIN/HMM/is/6-4100

SEP 2 3 1947

TSDIN

AMC Opinion Concerning "Flying Discs"

Commanding General
Army Air Forces
Washington 25, D. C.
ATTENTION: Brig. General George Schulgen
AC/AS-2

1. As requested by AC/AS-2 there is presented below the considered opinion of this Command concerning the so-called "Flying Discs". This opinion is based on interrogation report data furnished by AC/AS-2 and preliminary studies by personnel of T-2 and Aircraft Laboratory, Engineering Division T-3. This opinion was arrived at in a conference between personnel from the Air Institute of Technology, Intelligence T-2, Office, Chief of Engineering Division, and the Aircraft, Power Plant and Propeller Laboratories of Engineering Division T-3.

2. It is the opinion that:

    a. The phenomenon reported is something real and not visionary or fictitious.

    b. There are objects probably approximating the shape of a disc, of such appreciable size as to appear to be as large as man-made aircraft.

    c. There is a possibility that some of the incidents may be caused by natural phenomena, such as meteors.

    d. The reported operating characteristics such as extreme rates of climb, maneuverability (particularly in roll), and action which must be considered evasive when sighted or contacted by friendly aircraft and radar, lend belief to the possibility that some of the objects are controlled either manually, automatically or remotely.

    e. The apparent common description of the objects is as follows:-

    (1) Metallic or light reflecting surface.

U-39552

Incl #2

476

By ___.GLewis___ NARA, Date _8/13/86_ .

SECRET

Basic Ltr fr CG, AMC, WP to CG, AAF, Wash. D. C. subj "AMC Opinion Concerning "Flying Discs".

(2) Absence of trail, except in a few instances when the object apparently was operating under high performance conditions.

(3) Circular or elliptical in shape, flat on bottom and domed on top.

(4) Several reports of well kept formation flights varying from three to nine objects.

(5) Normally no associated sound, except in three instances a substantial rumbling roar was noted.

(6) Level flight speeds normally above 300 knots are estimated.

    f. It is possible within the present U. S. knowledge — provided extensive detailed development is undertaken — to construct a piloted aircraft which has the general description of the object in subparagraph (e) above which would be capable of an approximate range of 7000 miles at subsonic speeds.

    g. Any developments in this country along the lines indicated would be extremely expensive, time consuming and at the considerable expense of current projects and therefore, if directed, should be set up independently of existing projects.

    h. Due consideration must be given the following:-

(1) The possibility that these objects are of domestic origin - the product of some high security project not known to AC/AS-2 or this Command.

(2) The lack of physical evidence in the shape of crash recovered exhibits which would undeniably prove the existence of these objects.

(3) The possibility that some foreign nation has a form of propulsion possibly nuclear, which is outside of our domestic knowledge.

3. It is recommended that:-

    a. Headquarters, Army Air Forces issue a directive assigning a priority, security classification and Code Name for a detailed study of this matter to include the preparation of complete sets of all available and pertinent data which will then be made available to the Army, Navy, Atomic Energy Commission, JRDB, the Air Force Scientific Advisory Group, NACA, and the RAND and NEPA projects for comments and recommendations, with a preliminary report to be forwarded within 15 days of receipt of the data and a detailed report thereafter every 30 days as the investi-

SECRET
-2-

477

Basic Ltr fr CG, AMC, WF to CG, AAF, Wash. D.C. subj "AMC Opinion Concerning "Flying Discs"

gation develops. A complete interchange of data should be effected.

4. Awaiting a specific directive AMC will continue the investigation within its current resources in order to more closely define the nature of the phenomenon. Detailed Essential Elements of Information will be formulated immediately for transmittal thru channels.

N. F. TWINING
Lieutenant General, U.S.A.
Commanding

SECRET

Chapter 3 page 43
"Flying Disc" Information Request to European Command"; October 1947

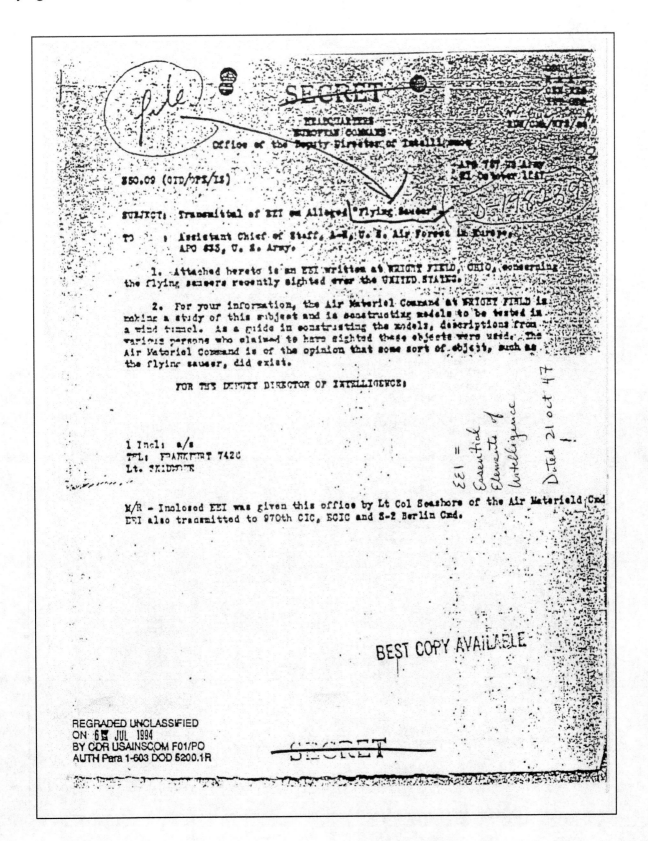

AIR INTELLIGENCE GUIDE

for

ALLEGED "FLYING SAUCER" TYPE AIRCRAFT

An alleged "Flying Saucer" type aircraft or object in flight approximating the shape of a disc has been reported by many observers from widely scattered places, such as the United States, Alaska, Canada, Hungary, the Island of Guam, Japan, etc. This object has been reported by many competent observers. Sightings have been made from the ground as well as from the air.

Commonly reported features that are very significant and which may aid in the investigation are as follows:

a. Relatively flat bottom with extremely light reflecting ability.

b. Absence of sound except for an occasional roar when operating under super performance conditions.

c. Extreme maneuverability and apparent ability to almost hover.

d. A plan form approximating that of an oval or disc with a dome shape on the top surface.

e. The absence of an exhaust trail except in a few instances when it was reported to have a bluish color like a Diesel exhaust which persisted for approximately one hour. Other reports indicated a brownish smoke trail that could be the results of a special catalyst or chemical agent for extra power.

f. The ability to quickly disappear by high speed or by complete disintegration.

g. The ability to suddenly appear without warning as if from an extremely high altitude.

h. The size most reported approximated that of a C-54 or Constellation aircraft.

i. The ability to group together very quickly in a tight formation when more than one aircraft are together.

j. Evasive action ability indicates possibility of being manually operated, or possibly by electronic or remote control devices.

k. Under certain power conditions, the craft seems to have the ability to cut a clear path through clouds - width estimated to be approximately one-half mile. Only one incident indicated this phenomenon.

UNCLASSIFIED

The first sightings in the U.S. were reported around the middle of May. The last reported sighting took place in Toronto, Canada, 14 September 1947. The greatest activity in the U.S. was during the last week of June and the first week of July.

This strange object or phenomenon may be considered, in view of certain observations, as a long-range aircraft capable of a high rate of climb, high cruising speed (possibly subsonic at all times) and highly maneuverable and capable of being flown in very tight formation. For the purpose of analysis and evaluation of the so-called "Flying Saucer" phenomenon, the object sighted is being assumed to be a manned aircraft, of Russian origin, and based on the perspective thinking and actual accomplishments of the Germans. There is also a possibility that the Horten Brothers perspective thinking may have inspired this type of aircraft particularly the "Parabola", which has a crescent plan form. Records show that a glider version only was built of this type aircraft. It is reported to have been built in Heiligenberg, Germany, but was destroyed by fire before having ever been flown. The Horten Brothers latest trend of perspective thinking was definitely toward aircraft configurations of low aspect ratio. The younger brother, Reimar, stated that the "Parabola" configuration would have the least induced drag which is a very significant statement. The theory supporting this statement should be obtained.

The German High Command indicated a definite interest in the Horten type of flying wing and were about to embark on a rigorous campaign to develop such aircraft toward the end of the war. A Horten design known as the IX which was designated as the Go-8-229 and Go-P-60 (night fighter) was to be manufactured by the Gotha Plant. It is reported that a contract of fifty such aircraft was planned but only three or four were built. This plant is now in the hands of the Russians. A recent report indicates that the Russians are now planning to build a fleet of 1800 Horten VIII (six engine pusher) type flying wing aircraft. The wing span is 131 feet. The sweepback angle is 30 degrees. The Russian version is reported to be jet propelled. Answers to the following questions, therefore, are requested:

a. What German scientist had a better than average knowledge of the Horten Brothers work and perspective thinking; where are those scientists now located, and what is their present activity? Contact and interrogate them.

b. What Russian factories are building the Horten VIII design?

c. Why are the Russians building 1800 of the Horten VIII design?

d. What is their contemplated tactical purpose?

e. What is the present activity of the Horten Brothers, Walter and Reimar?

UNCLASSIFIED

2

f. What is known of the whereabouts of the entire Horten family, particularly the sister? All should be contacted and interrogated regarding any contemplated plans or perspective thinking of the Horten brothers and any interest shown by the Russians to develop their aircraft.

g. Are any efforts being made to develop the Horten "Parabola" or modify this configuration to approximate and oval or disc?

h. What is the Horton perspective thinking on internal controls or controls that are effective mainly by streams of air or gas originating from within the aircraft to supplant conventional external surface controls?

For any aircraft approximating that of an oval, disc or saucer, information regarding the following items is requested:

a. Boundary layer control method by suction, blowing, or a combination of both.

b. Special controls for effective manouverability at very slow speeds or extremely high altitudes.

c. Openings either in the leading edge top and bottom surfaces that are employed chiefly to accomplish boundary layer control or for the purpose of reducing the induced drag. Any openings in the leading edge should be reported and described as to shape, size, etc. This investigation is significant to justify a disc shape configuration for long-range application.

d. Approximate airfoil shape in the center and near the tips.

e. Front view and rear view shape.

Items of Construction

a. Material whether metal, ferrous, non-ferrous, or non-metallic.

b. Composite or sandwich construction utilizing various combinations of metals, plastics, and perhaps balsa wood.

c. Unusual fabrication methods to achieve extreme light weight and structural stability particularly in connection with great capacity for fuel storage.

Items of Arrangement

a. Special provisions such as retractable domes to provide unusual observation for the pilot or crew members.

UNCLASSIFIED

3

b. Crew number and accomodation facilities.

c. Pressurized cabin equipment.

d. High altitude or high speed escapement methods.

e. Methods of pressurization or supercharging from auxilliary units or from the prime power plant.

f. Provisions for towing especially with short fixed bar and for refueling in flight.

g. Provisions for assisted take off application.

h. Bombay provisions, such as dimensions, approximate location, and unusual features regarding the opening and closing of the doors.

Landing Gear

a. Indicate type of landing gear whether conventional, tricycle, multiple wheel, etc.

b. Retractable, and jettison features for hand gear.

c. Provisions for takeoff from ice, snow, or water.

d. Skid arrangements for either take-off or landing.

Power Plant Item

a. Information is needed regarding the propulsion system used in the aircraft. Possible types of engines that could be employed include:

(1) Reciprocating (piston type) engine or gas turbine. Either or both of these could be used to drive propellers of conventional or special design, rotating vanes, ducted fans or compressors.

(2) Jet propulsion engines including turbo jets, rockets, ramjets, pulse jets or a combination of all four.

(3) Nuclear propulsion (atomic energy). Atomic energy engines would probably be unlike any familiar type of engine, although atomic energy might be employed in combination with any of the above types. Aircraft would be characterized by lack of fuel systems and fuel storage space.

The power plant would likely be an integral part of the aircraft and could possibly not be distinguished as an item seperate from the aircraft.

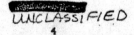

UNCLASSIFIED

4

If jet propulsion is used, large air handling capacity characterized by a large air inlet area and large exhaust nozzle should be evident. The size of entrance and exit areas would be of interest.

It is possible that the propulsive jet is governed or influenced for control of the aircraft. The presence of vanes or control surfaces in the exhaust or methods of changing the direction of the jet should be observed.

Information desired on the propulsion systems pertains to the following items:

a. Type of power plant or power plants.

b. General description.

c. Rating (thrust, horsepower, or air flow).

d. Type of fuel.

e. Catalytic agents for super-performance or normal cruising power.

UNCLASSIFIED

5

Chapter 3 page 43
USAF Directorate of Intelligence Statement on Reality of Disks

DECLASSIFIED PER EXECUTIVE ORDER 12356, Section 3.3, NND 863511

By __WGLewis__ NARA, Date 8/13/86.

MEMORANDUM FOR RECORD

18 December 1947

PROBLEM:

1. To prepare for signature of the Director of Intelligence an R&R for the Director of Research and Development outlining available information and recommendations concerning problems proposed by "flying discs."

FACTS AND DISCUSSION:

2. At the request of the Chief, Air Intelligence Division, an earlier memorandum dated 6 October 1947, Subject: "Recommendations Relative to Unidentified Flying Objects," was reanalyzed and rewritten as a memorandum.

3. This memorandum together with a letter from Headquarters, Air Materiel Command, Subject: "AMC Opinon Concerning 'Flying Discs'," dated 23 September 1947, were attached to an R&R addressed to the Director of Research and Development. Note was made in this R&R that the Director of Intelligence concurred with the recommendations of AMC concerning a specific project to study the "flying disc" situation.

ACTION:

4. R&R forwarded for signature of Major General MacDonald.

COORDINATION:

Colonel J. F. Olive, Chief, Air Intelligence Division - Ext. 2542
Lt. Colonel J. E. Thomas, Offensive Air Branch - Ext. 6625

DECLASSIFIED PER EXECUTIVE ORDER 12356, Section 3.3, NND 863511

By ..GLewis   NARA, Date 3/13/86 .

AFOAI-OA

Written: 18 Dec. 1947

"Analysis of 'Flying Disc' Reports"

Director of Research and Development

Director of Intelligence

22 DEC 1947

Lt.Col.Thomas/mau/6625.

1. Attached are two papers, one prepared by the Directorate of Intelligence, USAF, Subject: "Analysis of 'Flying Disc' Reports," and one prepared by the Air Material Command, Subject: "AMC Opinion Concerning 'Flying Discs'."

2. The Directorate of Intelligence paper summarizes present information and observations concerning 'flying discs' and indicates the lines of investigation which have been pursued since the first sightings were reported.

3. As part of these investigations the AMC was requested to make an independent study, and the attached reply indicates that "it is possible within the present U. S. knowledge---provided extensive detailed development is undertaken---to construct a piloted aircraft which has the general description ... (of the flying discs) ... which would be capable of an approximate range of 7,000 miles at subsonic speeds."

4. The AMC report recommends the issuance of "a directive assigning a priority, security classification and code name for a detailed study of this matter to include the preparation of complete sets of all available and pertinent data" which would be made available to all interested agencies.

5. In view of the conclusions reached as a result of the study of the problem made in this office, the Director of Intelligence concurs in the AMC recommendation and forwards it for your consideration and reply to the CG, AMC. Request reply be coordinated with this Directorate.

2 Incls.
   1. Subj:"Analysis of
      'Flying Disc' Reports."
   2. Subj: "AMC Opinion Con-
      cerning 'Flying Discs',"
      dtd Sep.23 1947.

GEORGE C. McDONALD
Major General, USAF
Director of Intelligence

FILE COPY - DIRECTORATE OF INTELLIGENCE

~~SECRET~~

"ANALYSIS OF 'FLYING DISC' REPORTS"

1. Summary of Information

a. During the past six months reports from several areas of the world have indicated that unidentified flying objects, variously identified as flying discs, lights, smoke trails, etc., have been observed by separate and unrelated sources.

b. Sightings of "flying discs" in the United States occurred principally in the far west. Observers have been indicated to be reliable and in some instances several observers have corroborated separate observations of the same phenomenon at the same time.

c. Outside the continental United States, an object and its trail were seen over Newfoundland; a light which had the appearance of a twin ram-jet was observed near Necker Island from an aircraft en route between Midway and Honolulu; a flying disc reputedly larger than a DC-3 was sighted near Bethel, Alaska.

d. In the Far East, three radar intercepts of rapidly moving, unidentified objects were made by United States radars operating in Japan.

e. No connection has been indicated between the "ghost rocket" sightings in Sweden, some of which conceivably might have been the result of guided missile operations, and the unidentified flying objects sighted in the United States and Pacific areas.

2. Discussion of Reports

a. Study of the various reports describing unidentified flying objects, lights, and smoke trails discloses that certain features are common to many of the observations as follows:

(1) In shape the objects are a thin disc, rounded on top and flat on the bottom, perhaps approximating a C-54 in size. The front half of the disc is often circular, sweeping back to a square tail across the full width.

(2) The surface is described as metallic or light reflecting.

(3) Extreme maneuverability, coupled with high lateral stability, is noted. Speed is high, with a snaking motion or a lateral oscillation. A few reports indicate an ability to hover; to appear suddenly as if from a dive; to disintegrate or to disappear, perhaps by

1

increasing speed; to group quickly in a tight formation, and to take evasive action. Good control of flight is indicated.

(4) Trail is absent, except in a few instances when the object apparently is operating under high performance conditions. The trail, when seen, seems to be very hot, as indicated by night observations of a glowing trail, and a daytime observation of a trail that cut a wide, clean swath in a cloud.

(5) Sound is normally not associated with the sightings, although a hum or rumbling roar was heard in two or three instances. No connection between sound and trail is indicated.

(6) Estimated level speed is normally greater than 300 knots.

(7) Formation flights of three to nine objects are reported by several observers.

(8) During one night observation, a change in glow from blue-white when approaching to a reddish glow when withdrawing was observed. This could indicate ram-jets.

b. The following are typical reports of observations of discs, and indicate the type and variety of the sources of information:

(1) On 7 July, 1947, five Portland, Oregon, police officers saw varying numbers of discs flying over different parts of Portland. All observations were made within a minute or two of 1305 hours.

(2) On 7 July, 1947, William Rhoads of Phoenix, Ariz., saw a disc in the glow of sunset and took two photographs. The resultant picture showed a round front and square tail in plan form.

(3) On 10 July, 1947, a Mr. Woodruff, PAA mechanic, observed a circular object flying at high velocity and leaving a trail. The sighting occurred near Harmon Field, Newfoundland. Two other persons also saw the trail.

(4) On 11 July, 1947, three persons at Cedroy, Newfoundland, saw a disc flying at high velocity and leaving a smoke trail.

(5) On 29 July, 1947, Kenneth Arnold, while flying near Tacoma, Washington, saw a formation of flying objects. His sketch of their shape corresponds closely to that shown in the photographs made by Mr. Rhoads. On the same day, two United States Air Force pilots at Hamilton Field, Calif., saw two flying discs trailing a P-80, following it toward Oakland, Calif.

2

SECRET

(6) On 4 August, 1947, the pilot and co-pilot of a DC-3, flying for Al Jones, were near Bethel, Alaska, when they saw a flying disc larger than their DC-3. Their airplane was flying 170 mph, but the disc flew out of sight in four minutes.

(7) On 12 November, 1947, two flying discs trailing jet-like streams of fire were sighted from the bridge of the tanker Ticonderoga, according to Second Officer Claude Lee Williamson. The Ticonderoga was 20 miles off the Oregon shore. Williamson said the two discs were in sight 45 seconds, moving at a speed estimated at 700-900 mph out of the north horizon and curving westerly in a long, low arc.

c. Typical of the observations made of lights and trails rather than discs or objects, are these three:

(1) On 28 June, 1947, four USAF officers observed a light from some object which did not fly like a conventional aircraft. The light was sighted over Maxwell Field, Alabama.

(2) On 6 July, 1947, several persons, including a USAF sergeant, saw a strangely moving light over Birmingham, Alabama. A photograph was taken.

(3) On 12 September, 1947, the pilot and co-pilot of a Pan American aircraft, passing Howker Island at 0558 GCT, en route from Midway to Honolulu, saw a blue-white light approaching, changing to a reddish glow upon withdrawal. The pilot estimated speed of the light at about 1,000 knots.

d. The three United States radar intercepts of unidentified radar targets flying near or over Japan are as follows:

(1) On 1 July, 1947, a GCA radar at Chitose AAB, Hokkaido, Japan picked up a target at 16 miles, speed in excess of 500 mph. This target split up into two targets, each larger than a P-51.

(2) On 28 August, 1947, a MEW radar at Fukuoka, Japan picked up a target at 26 miles in instrument weather. Target withdrew in a climb to 34 miles before it faded.

(3) On 16 September, 1947, the same MEW radar at Fukuoka, Japan picked up a target at 59 miles and tracked it in to 19 miles, where it faded. Speed was 840 to 900 miles per hour. This observation indicates use of a homing receiver; fading at short range further indicates the possibility of good radar evasion techniques. The speed measurement is believed accurate, since it was made by a good crew, through a 70-mile long track.

SECRET

DECLASSIFIED PER EXECUTIVE ORDER 12356, Section 3.3, NND 863511

By __GLewis_____ NARA, Date 3/13/86 .

~~SECRET~~

3. **Investigations made**

    a. In addition to analyzing the reports concerning flying discs and other phenomena observed both in the United States and elsewhere in the world, the Directorate of Intelligence, USAF, has taken the following action:

    (1) Requested the Air Material Command to conduct an independent investigation. The results of this study are contained in a Headquarters, AMC letter, Subject: "AMC Opinion Concerning 'Flying Discs'," dated 23 September 1947, which includes recommendations for further study of this problem.

    (2) Sought information from appropriate agencies to determine whether the phenomena might be the result of highly classified project being conducted under United States auspices. Responses to date have not indicated existence of any American developmental work which might explain the reported observations.

    (3) Submitted to a group of scientists the question whether the "flying saucer" observations might be the result of some natural phenomenon, such as falling meteors. While it was admitted there was a possibility some few of the incidents could have been caused by natural phenomena, the scientists concluded that such phenomena could not have been responsible for all of the observations.

    (4) Requested the Federal Bureau of Investigation to check the possibility that the "flying saucer" episodes might be the result of a deliberately planned subversive effort to create mass hysteria, possibly Communist-inspired. Backgrounds of the first four persons who had reported sightings of flying disc were investigated by the FBI, with negative results in each case.

    (5) Forwarded to the Air Weather Service a list of the first ten sightings reported by responsible persons for comparison with dates and locations of the release of meteorological balloons. The resultant check indicated there was no connection, or coincidence, between meteorological balloons aloft and the times, dates, and locations of the selected sightings.

    (6) Investigated the possible existence of foreign aircraft projects which might be related to these observations. Of interest in this regard are two German designs that could be under current exploitation by the U.S.S.R.

    (a) The Horten Brothers' "Parabola," a flying wing of low aspect ration and a very low induced drag. The plan forms of this design were crescent shaped.

4

(b) The XF-130, a long range bomber, was a flying wing design that could satisfy the few indicated features of the "flying discs."

(7) Analyzed the possibility that the flying objects were operated or controlled by representatives of a foreign nation—perhaps for photo reconnaissance purposes, or to ferret out our defensive capabilities, or to test the American psychological reaction. Principal sightings were near the borders of the United States, which lends credence to a foreign source of origin. Sightings were not reported, however, at or near the principal strategic target areas of the United States. Moreover, it is difficult to conceive why any foreign nation, if it possessed such an unconventional aircraft or missile, would risk sending it near or over the United States for anything short of an attack. Even if the disc contained a self-destroying device, any crash landing would disclose a certain amount of information which the nation possessing such an aircraft or missile would desire to keep secret. This would be particularly true if the form of propulsion was one outside American knowledge. The final answer still has not been obtained from this line of inquiry.

4. Conclusions

a. Flying discs, as reported by widely scattered observers, probably represent something real and tangible, even though physical evidence, such as crash-recovered exhibits, is not available. While a portion of the observations may be the result of natural phenomena, such as meteors, or may have other conventional explanation, the likelihood that some observers actually saw disc-shaped objects sufficiently large to be compared in size with known aircraft cannot be dismissed.

b. Considering the described conduct of these disc-like objects when sighted, it must be considered a possibility that they may have been humanly controlled, either manually or remotely, or by pre-set automatic controls.

c. On the basis of presently available information, if these discs actually exist they are foreign in origin, so investigation of the possible country of development and the place of origin should continue.

d. The Directorate of Intelligence, USAF, will continue to collect and analyze all reports of sightings of flying objects, lights, trails, etc., in an effort to develop an answer to the puzzling problem which they present.

Chapter 4 page 58
Rand Project to study UFOs

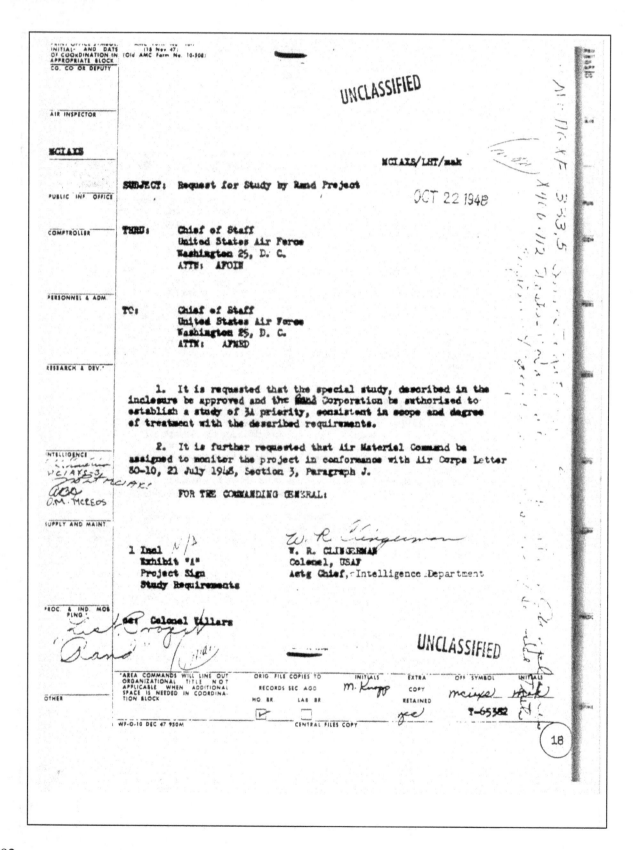

UNCLASSIFIED

MCIAXS/LHT/mak

SUBJECT: Request for Study by Rand Project

OCT 22 1948

THRU: Chief of Staff
United States Air Force
Washington 25, D. C.
ATTN: AFOIN

TO: Chief of Staff
United States Air Force
Washington 25, D. C.
ATTN: AFMED

1. It is requested that the special study, described in the inclosure be approved and the Rand Corporation be authorized to establish a study of 3A priority, consistent in scope and degree of treatment with the described requirements.

2. It is further requested that Air Material Command be assigned to monitor the project in conformance with Air Corps Letter 80-10, 21 July 1948, Section 3, Paragraph J.

FOR THE COMMANDING GENERAL:

1 Incl
Exhibit "A"
Project Sign
Study Requirements

W. R. CLINGERMAN
Colonel, USAF
Actg Chief, Intelligence Department

UNCLASSIFIED

PRINT OFFICE SYMBOL, AMC Form No. 10-7
INITIALS AND DATE   (18 Nov 47)
OF COORDINATION IN (Old AMC form No. 10-508)
APPROPRIATE BLOCK

CG, CO OR DEPUTY

AIR INSPECTOR

PUBLIC INF OFFICE

COMPTROLLER

PERSONNEL & ADM.

RESEARCH & DEV.

INTELLIGENCE

SUPPLY AND MAINT

PROC & IND MOB
PLNG

OTHER

UNCLASSIFIED

EXHIBIT "A"

Project Sign Study Requirements

The possibility that some of the unidentified aerial objects
that have been reported both in the United States and in foreign
lands may have been experimental spaceships, or test vehicles for
the purpose of assisting in the development of spaceships, has been
given consideration by this Command.

If such craft actually have been sighted, it is believed more
likely that they represent the effort of a foreign nation, rather
than a product from beyond the Earth.

Present world knowledge, techniques and resources are probably
adequate to meet the requirements for spaceship construction, or at
least to establish the preliminary experimental foundation for such
an accomplishment in the near future.

In any case, the design and performance parameters of the craft
would necessarily be in conformance and consistent with the established
principles of our sciences.

To assist in the collection of information, relating to unidentified aerial objects that may possibly represent spaceships or spaceship
test vehicles, and to assist in the analysis and evaluation of such reported craft, technical information that includes the distinguishing
design and performance parameters for spaceships is considered necessary.

While such information is contained outright, or implicitly, in
the series of Rand Project reports, it would be of such value to this
Command to have a list of the special design and performance characteristics that are believed to distinguish spaceships, together with
any further scientific clues that might assist in their detection
and identification, prepared by Rand scientific personnel.

UNCLASSIFIED

T-65382

"AREA COMMANDS WILL LINE OUT   ORIG FILE COPIES TO   INITIALS   EXTRA   OFF SYMBOL   INITIALS
ORGANIZATIONAL   TITLE   NOT
APPLICABLE   WHEN   ADDITIONAL   RECORDS SEC AGD   COPY
SPACE IS NEEDED IN COORDINA-
TION BLOCK   HQ BR   LAB BR   RETAINED

WF-O-10 DEC 47 950M   CENTRAL FILES COPY

Chapter 4 page 65
Colonel McCoy's "Estimate" of Unknown Flying Objects sent to General Cabell

UNCLASSIFIED

Basic ltr fr Hq USAF, 3 Nov 48 to CG, AMC, "Flying Object Incidents in
the United States"

1st Ind   MCIAT/AED/amb

Hq AMC, Wright-Patterson Air Force Base, Dayton, Ohio. 8 Nov 48

TO: Chief of Staff, United States Air Force, Washington 25, D. C., ATTN:
AFOIR

1. In attempting to arrive at conclusions as to the nature of unidentified flying object incidents in the United States, this Command has made
a study of approximately 180 such incidents. Data derived from initial reports have been supplemented by further information obtained from check
lists submitted by mail, from interrogations of other field agencies, and
by personal investigation by personnel of this Command in the case of incidents that seem to indicate the possibility of obtaining particularly
significant information.

2. The objects described fall into the following general classification groups, according to shape or physical configuration:

    a. Flat disc of circular or approximately circular shape.

    b. Torpedo or cigar shaped aircraft, with no wings or fins visible
in flight.

    c. Spherical or balloon shaped objects.

    d. Balls of light with no apparent form attached.

3. Some of the objects sighted have definitely been identified, upon
further investigation, as weather or upper air scientific balloons of some
type. A great many of the round or balloon shaped objects indicated in
paragraph 2c above are probably of the same nature, although in most cases,
definite confirmation of that fact has been impossible to obtain.

4. Some of the objects have been identified as being astro-physical
in nature. For example, in daylight sightings, the planet Venus has been
reported as a round, silvery object at extremely high altitude. Action is
being taken to obtain the services of a prominent astro-physicist as a consultant, to study all of the incidents to determine whether some can be
identified as meteors, planets or other manifestations of astral bodies.

5. Arrangements for accomplishing a study of the psychological problems
involved in this project are being made in coordination with the Aero-Medical
Laboratory at this Headquarters. The possibility that some of the sightings
are hallucinations, optical illusions or even deliberate hoaxes has been considered.

2

T-73017

UNCLASSIFIED

25

1st Ind

Basic ltr fr Hq USAF, 3 Nov 48 to CG, AMC, "Flying Object Incidents in the United States".

6. Although explanation of many of the incidents can be obtained from the investigations described above, there remains a certain number of reports for which no reasonable everyday explanation is available. So far, no physical evidence of the existence of the unidentified sightings has been obtained. Prominent scientists, including Dr. Irving Langmuir of the General Electric Company, have been interviewed to determine whether they could advance any reasonable explanation for characteristics exhibited by the objects sighted. In an early interview, Dr. Langmuir indicated that these incidents could be explained, but insufficient data were available at that time on which to base definite conclusions. It is planned to have another interview with Dr. Langmuir in the near future to review all the data now available, and it is hoped that he will be able to present some opinion as to the nature of many of the unidentified objects, particularly those described as "balls of light."

7. All information that has been made available to this Headquarters indicates that the discs, the cigar shaped objects, and the "balls of light" are not of domestic origin. Engineering investigation indicates that disc or wingless aircraft could support themselves in flight by aerodynamic means. It is probable that the problems of stability and control could also be solved for such aircraft. However, according to current aerodynamic theory in this country, aircraft with such configurations would have relatively poor climb, altitude and range characteristics with power plants now in use.

8. The possibility that the reported objects are vehicles from another planet has not been ignored. However, tangible evidence to support conclusions about such a possibility are completely lacking. The occurrence of incidents in relation to the approach to the earth of the planets Mercury, Venus and Mars have been plotted. A periodic variation in the frequency of incidents, which appears to have some relation to the planet approach curves, is noted, but it may be purely a coincidence.

9. Reference is made to "The Books of Charles Fort" with an introduction by Tiffany Thayer, published 1941, by Henry Holt & Co., New York, N. Y. It appears that similar phenomena have been noted and reported for the past century or more.

10. In view of the above, the following conclusions are drawn:

a. In the majority of cases reported, observers have actually sighted some type of flying object which they cannot classify as an aircraft within the limits of their personal experience.

3

UNCLASSIFIED

1st Ind

Basic ltr fr Hq USAF, 3 Nov 48 to CG, AMC, "Flying Object Incidents in
the United States"

b. There is as yet no conclusive proof that unidentified flying
objects, other than those which are known to be balloons, are real aircraft.

c. Although it is obvious that some types of flying objects have
been sighted, the exact nature of those objects cannot be established until
physical evidence, such as that which would result from a crash, has been
obtained.

11. It is not considered advisable to present to the press information
on those objects which we cannot yet identify or about which we cannot present any reasonable conclusions. In the event that they insist on some
kind of a statement, it is suggested that they be informed that many of
the objects sighted have been identified as weather balloons or astral
bodies, and that investigation is being pursued to determine reasonable
explanations for the others.

12. A report, summarizing the results obtained from analysis of the
data and a technical investigation of the engineering aspects of the objects
described, is nearly complete, and a copy will be forwarded to your Headquarters in the near future.

FOR THE COMMANDING GENERAL:

H. M. McCOY
Colonel, USAF
Chief, Intelligence Department

UNCLASSIFIED

4

T-73017

Chapter 5 page 79
Dr. Theodore von Karman's letter of concern on "green fireballs"

CONFIDENTIAL

THEODORE VON KÁRMÁN
1501 SOUTH MARENGO AVENUE
PASADENA, CALIFORNIA

11 February 1949

Major General C. P. Cabell
Director of Intelligence
Office, Deputy Chief of Staff, Operations
Headquarters, United States Air Force
Washington 25, D. C.

Dear General Cabell:

Dr. Joseph Kaplan, a member of the Scientific Advisory Board to the Chief of Staff, USAF and Professor of Physics at the University of California, Los Angeles, called my attention to a report of the 17th District Office of Special Investigations (Inspector General, USAF), Kirtland Field, New Mexico, subject: (UNKNOWN) Aerial Phenomena, file number 24-8, dated 19 January 1949.

This report deals with extraordinary observations of certain aerial phenomena. These observations concern so-called "fireballs" of unusual color, size and speed. The report also contains the observations of Dr. Lincoln LaPaz, Director of the Institute of Meteoritics, University of New Mexico, Albuquerque.

I always have been, and am yet, extremely skeptical about flying discs, saucers, fireballs and related effects. In this case, however, the personality and prestige of the observer and the number of apparently reliable people who saw the phenomena, makes me think it might be worthwhile to give more serious attention to the matter.

I wonder whether it would not be desirable to set up a kind of project in Albuquerque, which would give an opportunity for Dr. LaPaz to obtain adequate equipment and personnel for continuous, well planned observations. It seems to me that intelligent speculation on the nature of the phenomena can only begin when one has scientifically correct determination of size, altitude, speed, shape and color. Director LaPaz, who is an authority on meteoritics, definitely states that at least one of the observed "fireballs" could not be of heavenly origin. As far as my technical judgement goes, I believe it is highly improbable that the phenomena originates as a man made missile. Never-the-less, the fact is there, observed by competent and reliable people. Therefore, I believe the scientific approach is necessary, at least in order to secure exact and objective measurements.

I submit the question to you, as I am aware that such a project can be successful only if it is kept secret and is set up with the cooperation of trained experts in the Intelligence Division. I believe you can easily procure the subject report, providing it is not already in your hands. I would appreciate your reaction and advice.

CONFIDENTIAL

Chapter 6 page 101
Memo to Watson on Cabell's Directive to continue investigating UFOs; July 7, 1950

DECLASSIFIED PER EXECUT: DER 12356, Section 3.3, NND 841508
By W G Lewis   ARS, Date Jan 29, 1985.

SECRET
AUTH CS...USA

SECRET

7- 7-50

MEMORANDUM FOR COLONEL H.E. WATSON, AMC

1. I am sending this by Major Pianitza hoping to save the
bother of an officially coordinated directive. Gen Cabell's views
regarding the "Flying Saucer" project are in substance as follows:

   a. He feels that it probably was a mistake to abandon
the project and to publicly announce that we are no longer interested.
However, the decision having been made, he feels that it was
incumbent upon him not to overrule, at least for the time being.

   b. Our instructions, which rescinded a long list of
letters to numerous agencies, were published in an unnumbered HQS,
USAF letter, file AFOIR-CO 7 dated 12 January 1950, Subject: "Reporting
of Information on Unconventional Aircraft". The last paragraph of
this letter requested all recipients to continue to treat information
and observations received as intelligence information and to continue
the processing in a normal manner. We have continued to receive from
many USAF sources a number of reports of this nature.

   c. Gen Cabell's views are that we should reinstitute, if it
has been abandoned, a continuing analysis of reports received and he
expects AMC to do this as part of their obligation to produce air
technical intelligence. He specifically desires that the project, as
it existed before, be not fully re-implemented with special technical
teams traveling around the country interviewing observers, etc., and
he is particularly desirous that there be no fanfare or publicity
over the fact that the USAF is still interested in "flying saucers".

   d. Gen Cabell desires that we place ourselves in a position
that, if circumstances require an all-out effort in this regard at
some future time, we will be able to announce that we have continued
quietly our analysis of reports without interruption.

   e. Under this philosophy then, we will continue to receive
from USAF sources reports of "flying saucers" and we will immediately
transmit these reports to AMC. You will be at liberty to query, through
AFOIC-CC normal channels, the USAF reporting source for more information.
We will also be scanning State, CIA, Army, and Navy incoming reports
for pertinent information which will be relayed to AMC. You may also
address queries regarding specific reports of this nature to AFOIC-CC
in the normal manner.

   f. Ordinary newspaper reports should be analyzed without
initiating specific inquiry. Information received direct from non-USAF

SECRET

SECRET

Memo to Col Watson

individuals may be acknowledged and interrogated through correspondence. Where geographically convenient, specific sightings may be investigated quietly, at your discretion, by AMC depot personnel, and requests for investigation may be filed with your local OSI office.

    g. Queries from news agencies as to whether USAF is still interested in "flying saucers" may be given a general answer to the effect that AMC is interested in any information that will enable it to produce air technical intelligence - and just as much interested in "flying saucer" information as it would be in any other significant information. Work in the "flying saucer" field is not receiving "special" emphasis because emphasis is being placed upon all technical intelligence fields.

    2. The foregoing probably is in more detail than is necessary. If, after reading this you are still uncertain as to what to do, give me a call. If this clarifies your questions, go ahead under A MC's general directive to produce air technical intelligence.

/S/ Col. Barber
AFOIC

SECRET

Chapter 6 page 102
Memo from Brig Gen Moore on responding to press question about a UFO sighting; October 18, 1950

DECLASSIFIED PER EXECUTIVE ORDER 12356, Section 3.3, NND 841508
By _W G Lewis_ _____ NARS, Date _Jan 29, 1985._

CONFIDENTIAL

OCT 1 - '50

AFOIV-TC

SUBJECT: (Restricted) Releasing Results of Analysis and Evaluation
of "Unidentified Aerial Objects" Reports

TO: Commanding General
           Air Material Command
           Wright-Patterson Air Force Base
           Dayton, Ohio
           ATTENTION: Chief, Intelligence Dept

1. This headquarters is cognizant of press interests in the so-
called "flying saucers" reports, referred to by this headquarters as
"unidentified aerial objects." Your headquarters has previously been
advised as to the release of information concerning Air Force interest
in this subject. Your attention is invited to USAF PIO release of 6
September 1950 and Hq USAF letter, subject "Reporting of Information
on Unconventional Aircraft," dated 8 September 1950.

2. In a recent telephone conversation between Colonel Watson,
Hq AMC and Colonel Harris, this headquarters, Colonel Watson requested
guidance in the matter of releasing results of investigation, analysis,
and evaluation of incidents brought to his attention. This headquarters believes that release of details of analysis and evaluation of
incidents is inadvisable, and desires that, in lieu thereof, releases
conform to the policy and spirit of the following:

"We have investigated and evaluated _____ incident
and have found nothing of value and nothing which would change
our previous estimates on this subject."

3. Results of analysis and evaluation of incidents possessing
any intelligence value will be forwarded to this headquarters for information and for any action relative to possible press releases.

BY COMMAND OF THE CHIEF OF STAFF:

                                    S/
                                    E. MOORE
                                    /Brig. Gen., USAF
                                    Assistant for Production
                                    Directorate of Intelligence

OUT OCT50

VX COO.76 GENERAL - Press Release

OFFICE SYMBOL	1 AFOIV	2 AFOIA	3 AFOIN	4 AFOIC	5 AFOIP	6 AFCPR
SIGNATURE OF RESPONSIBLE OFFICER	Col				Col.	
INTERNAL OFFICE COORDINATION		CUSAF		Brannon		

16—20042-1   U. S. GOVERNMENT PRINTING OFFICE

500

Chapter 7 page 127
Captain Ruppelt's notes on General Cabell's meeting demanding seriousness regarding UFOs; 1951

When the briefing was rolling the General asked Jerry to give a
resume of what had been taking place on Project Grudge. Jerry told me
that he looked at Rosy and got the OK sign, so he cut loose. He told
how every report was taken as a huge joke; that at the personal direction of Watson, Rogers, Watson's #1 stooge, was doing everything to
degrade the quality of the reports; and how the only analysis consisted
of Roger's trying to think up new and original explanations that hadn't
been sent to Washington Before. Rogers couldn't even find half of the
reports.

The General then got on his horse. He said, "I want an open mind,
in fact I order an open mind. Anyone that doesn't keep an open mind
can get out, now. As long as there is any element of doubt, the Project will continue."

About this time one of the General's staff suggested that since
there were industry observers present, maybe the remarks should be
kept objective or that the industry people chouls leave. This got
the Old Man and he said that he didn't care how embarrassing it was,
he wasn't ashamed to give people the devil in front of strangers.

He said that the apparent disregard of his orders were a source
of concern. He complimented Cummings and Rosy by saying that he was
glad to "Get action."

The General asked about the results of the investigations of
several other good sightings but a telephone check to ATIC showed that
they had been lost, no one ever could find them.

His next question was: "Why do I have to stir up the action?

Anyone can see that we do not have a satisfactory answer to the saucer question."

Cabell went on to say that he wanted some action. He wanted the Project reorganized and he wanted all of the directives reissued because, he said, it was obvious that they were not being followed.

Then, Jerry told me, the General looked at his staff of colonels for about 45 seconds and said, "I've been lied to, and lied to, and lied to. I want it to stop. I want the answer to the saucers and I want a good answer." He started in on the Mantell Sightings and said that he had never heard such a collection of contradictory and indefinite statements. He said that he thought that he had a big activity operating and found out the only man, and apparently incompetent one at that, fumbling around trying to make excuses.

Col Porter (whom I considered to be one of the most totally incompetent men in the Air Force for reasons other than the UFO Project) was his old stupid self and said that he still thought that the project was a waste of time. The General's reply was that he didn't consider himself a crackpot or impressionable person and that he had a great deal of doubt in his mind that the saucers were all "hoaxes, halucinations or the misinterpretation of known objects". He took a swing at the famous Grudge Report by saying that it was the "most poorly written, unconclusive piece of unscientific tripe" that he'd ever seen.

The General ended up the meeting by giving a pep talk and saying that he thought that things would change and that the saucers would become respective. He said that he was going to keep an open mind and that he wanted the same from his staff.

Chapter 9 page 175
Chadwell memo to Director of CIA WB Smith on UFO assessment

7 Sept 1952

MEMORANDUM FOR: Director of Central Intelligence

THRU   : Deputy Director (Intelligence)

SUBJECT   : Flying Saucers

1. PROBLEM

To determine:

a. Whether there are national security implications in the problem of "unidentified flying objects" i.e. flying saucers;

b. Whether adequate study and research is currently being directed to this problem in its relation to such national security implications; and

c. What further investigation and research should be instituted, by whom, and under what aegis.

2. FACTS BEARING ON THE PROBLEM

a. OSI has investigated the work currently being performed on flying saucers and has found that:

(1) The only unit of Government currently studying the problem is the Directorate of Intelligence, USAF, which has charged the Air Technical Intelligence Center (ATIC) with responsibility for investigating the reports of sightings.

(2) At ATIC there is a small group consisting of a reserve Captain, two Lieutenants and two secretaries to which come all reports of sightings through official channels, and which conducts investigation of the reports either itself or through consultation with other Air Force officers or with civilian technical consultants.

(3) A world-wide reporting system has been instituted and major Air Force bases have been ordered to make interceptions of unidentified flying objects.

(4) The research being carried on is strictly on a case basis and appears to be designed solely to attempt a satisfactory explanation of each individual sighting as it occurs.

(5) ATIC has concluded an arrangement with Battelle Memorial Institute for the latter to establish a machine indexing system for official reports of sightings.

(6) Since 1947, ATIC has received approximately 1500 official reports of sightings plus an enormous volume of letters, phone calls and press reports. During the month of July 1952 alone, official reports totaled 250. Of the 1500 reports, Air Force carries 20% as unexplained and of those received January through July 1952 it carries 20% unexplained.

3. DISCUSSION

a. OSI entered into its inquiry fully aware that it was coming into a field already charged with partisanship, one in which objectivity had been overridden by numerous sensational writers, and one in which there are pressures for extravagant explanations as well as for oversimplification. The OSI Team consulted with a representative of Air Force Special Studies Group; discussed the problem with those in charge of the Air Force Project at Wright field; reviewed a considerable volume of intelligence reports; checked the Soviet press and broadcast indices; and conferred with three OSI consultants, all leaders in their scientific fields, who were chosen because of their broad knowledge of the technical areas concerned.

b. OSI found that the ATIC study is probably valid if the purpose is limited to a case-by-case explanation. However, the study makes no attempt to solve the more fundamental aspect of the problem which is to determine definitely the nature of the various phenomena which are causing these sightings, or to discover means by which these causes and their visual or electronic effects may be immediately identified. Our consultant panel stated that these solutions would probably be found on the margins or just beyond the frontiers of our present knowledge in the fields of atmospheric, ionospheric, and extraterrestrial phenomena, with the added possibility that our present disposal of nuclear waste products might also be a factor. They recommended that a study group be formed to perform three functions:

(1) Analyze and systematize the factors of information which form the fundamental problem;

(2) Determine the fields of fundamental science which must be investigated in order to reach an understanding of the phenomena involved; and

(3) Make recommendations for the initiation of appropriate research.

Dr. Julius A. Stratton, Vice President of the Massachusetts Institute of Technology, has indicated to OSI that such a group could be constituted at that Institute. Similarly, Project Lincoln, the Air Force air defense project at MIT, could be charged with these responsibilities.

- 2 -

4. CONCLUSIONS

a. The flying saucer situation contains two elements of danger which, in a situation of international tension, have national security implications. These are:

(1) Psychological - With world-wide sightings reported, it was found that, up to the time of our investigation, there had been in the Russian press no report or comment, even satirical, on flying saucers, though Andre Gromyko had made one humorous mention of the subject. With a State-controlled press, this could result only from an official policy decision. The question, therefore, arises as to whether or not these sightings:

    (a) Could be controlled,

    (b) Could be predicted, and

    (c) Could be used from a psychological warfare point of view either offensively or defensively.

The public concern with the phenomena, which is reflected in the United States press and in pressure of inquiry upon the Air Force, indicates that there is a fair proportion of our population which is mentally conditioned to the acceptance of the incredible. In this fact lies the potential for the touching-off of mass hysteria and panic.

(2) Air Vulnerability - The United States Air Warning System will undoubtedly always depend upon a combination of radar screening and visual observation. We give Russia the present capability of delivering an air attack against us, yet at any given moment now, there may be current a dozen official unidentified sightings plus many unofficial. At any moment of attack, we are now in a position where we cannot, on an instant basis, distinguish hardware from phantom, and as tension mounts we will run the increasing risk of false alerts and the even greater danger of falsely identifying the real as phantom.

b. Both of these problems are primarily operational in nature but each contains readily apparent intelligence factors. From an operational point of view, three actions are required:

(1) Immediate steps should be taken to improve identification of both visual and electronic phantom so that in the event of an attack, instant and positive identification of enemy planes or missiles can be made.

- 3 -

(2) A study should be instituted to determine what, if any, utilization could be made of these phenomena by United States psychological warfare planners, and what, if any, defenses should be planned in anticipation of Soviet attempts to utilize them.

(3) A national policy should be established as to what should be told the public regarding the phenomena, in order to minimize risk of panic.

c. Intelligence problems include:

(1) The present level of Russian knowledge regarding these phenomena.

(2) Possible Soviet intentions and capabilities to utilize these phenomena to the detriment of US security interests.

(3) The reasons for silence in the Soviet Press regarding flying saucers.

d. Intelligence responsibilities in this field as regards both collection and analysis can be discharged with maximum effectiveness only after much more is known regarding the exact nature of these phenomena.

e. The problem transcends the level of individual departmental responsibilities, and is of such importance as to merit cognizance and action by the National Security Council.

f. Additional research, differing in character and emphasis from that presently being performed by Air Force, will be required to meet the specific needs of both operations and intelligence.

5. RECOMMENDATIONS

It is recommended that:

a. The Director of Central Intelligence advise the National Security Council of the security implications inherent in the flying saucer problem with the request that, under his statutory coordinating authority, the Director of Central Intelligence be empowered to initiate through the appropriate agencies, either within or without the Government, the investigation and research necessary to solve the problem of instant positive identification of "unidentified flying objects"

b. CIA, under its assigned responsibilities, and in cooperation with the psychological strategy board, immediately investigate possible offensive or defensive utilization of the phenomena for psychological warfare purposes both for and against the United States, advising those agencies charged with U. . internal security of any pertinent

- 4 -

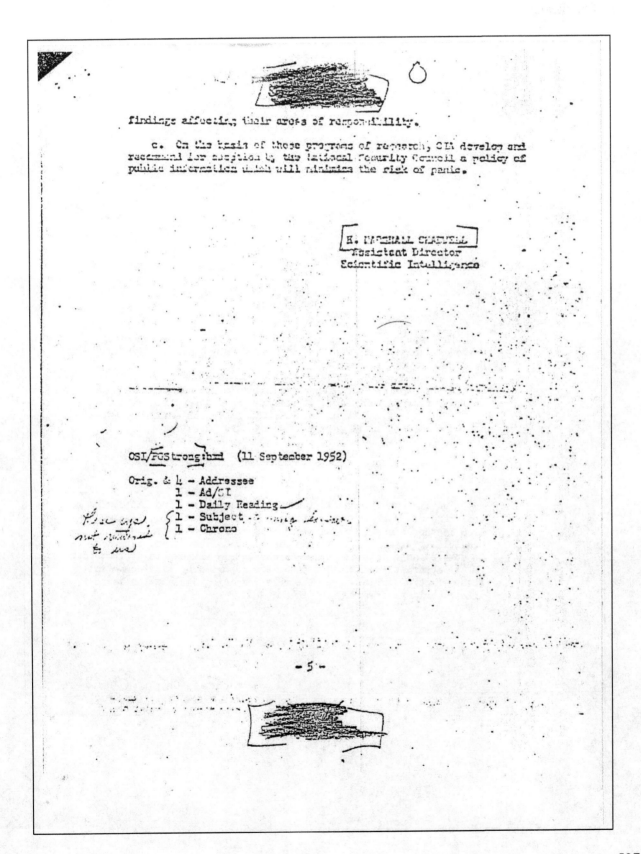

findings affecting their areas of responsibility.

c. On the basis of these programs of research, CIA develop and recommend for adoption by the National Security Council a policy of public information which will minimize the risk of panic.

H. MARSHALL CHADWELL
Assistant Director
Scientific Intelligence

OSI/FGStrong:bml (11 September 1952)

Orig. & 4 - Addressee
        1 - Ad/SI
        1 - Daily Reading
        1 - Subject
        1 - Chrono

- 5 -

Chapter 11 page 216
Al Chop's Letter of Endorsement from the Back Cover of Maj. Donald Keyhoe's book *Flying Saucers from Outer Space*

DEPARTMENT OF DEFENSE
OFFICE OF PUBLIC INFORMATION
WASHINGTON 25, D. C.

26 January 1953

Henry Holt & Company
383 Madison Avenue
New York 17, N.Y.

Dear Sirs:

This will acknowledge your letter of recent date regarding a proposed book on "flying saucers" by Major Donald E. Keyhoe, U. S. Marine Corps, retired.

We in the Air Force recognize Major Keyhoe as a responsible, accurate reporter. His long association and cooperation with the Air Force, in our study of unidentified flying objects, qualifies him as a leading civilian authority on this investigation.

All the sighting reports and other information he listed have been cleared and made available to Major Keyhoe from Air Technical Intelligence records, at his request.

The Air Force, and its investigating agency, "Project Bluebook," are aware of Major Keyhoe's conclusion that the "Flying Saucers" are from another planet. The Air Force has never denied that this possibility exists. Some of the personnel believe that there may be some strange natural phenomena completely unknown to us, but that if the apparently controlled maneuvers reported by many competent observers are correct, then the only remaining explanation is the interplanetary answer.

Very Truly Yours

Albert M. Chop
Air Force Press Desk

Chapter 13 page 272
Dewey Fournet's statement that he had read the ET Estimate and had authored the UFO motion study

CONFIDENTIAL: For Release to NICAP Officials Only

At the request of Major Keyhoe, I would like to confirm the existence of two USAF documents which were recently denied by an official USAF representative. These are:

1. An intelligence summary on UFOs prepared in 1948 by the organization which later became the Air Technical Intelligence Center at Wright-Patterson AFB.

2. An intelligence analysis on specific aspects of UFO data which I prepared in 1952 while acting as UFO program monitor for Headquarters USAF, Washington, D.C.

Since both documents were classified when I last saw them, I am not at liberty to reveal their contents. I would also like to add a qualification about #2: I completed it in rough form just a few hours before my departure from Washington (following my release from active duty) and turned it over to one of my associates in the Directorate of Intelligence. Therefore, I never saw it in its published form. However, since I had prepared it - as well as other reports which I recorded on tape - at the specific request of my Branch and Division Chiefs, I am certain that it was published.

Another word of caution is necessary on the latter document: I prepared it primarily as a weapon for use against the apathy and/or bias on the subject which prevailed in certain official quarters. Although the processes of logic employed would stand up under ordinary circumstances, they become somewhat tenuous and difficult to defend completely when applied to the task in question. The important point should be, therefore, that such a document did exist - not that it did or did not establish anything about UFOs.

There is also a question about the report prepared by the panel of civilian scientists convened in January 1953 to examine the UFO data. I met with this panel during part of its deliberations; this was during the week when I was being processed off active duty. Since I had departed by the time the panel adjourned, I did not see any report which it may have prepared. However, since it was convened for the specific purpose of reviewing all available data and making recommendations on the UFO program, it must necessarily have left some sort of report, undoubtedly written. (I have since been informed that it did, although let me repeat that I never saw it.)

Dewey J. Fournet, Jr.
Baton Rouge, La.
May 4, 1958

509

Chapter 15 page 348
Letter to NORAD requesting information on unknown aircraft picked up on radar

November 5, 2008

Robert Powell

███████████████████

Secretary Michael Chertoff
U.S. Dept of Homeland Security
Washington, DC 20528

General Victor Renuart, Jr.(USAF)
United States Northern Command
250 Vandenberg, Ste. B-016
Peterson AFB, CO 80914-3808

Subject: Request for Dept of Defense and Dept of Homeland Security Response to Unknown Aircraft without Transponder Beacon near the No Flight Zone of Crawford Ranch, Texas on Jan.8, 2008

Dear Sir:

This request is being sent to the Dept. of Defense and Homeland Security with copies to the FAA and heads of the Senate and House Committees on Homeland Security. As a U.S. citizen and the Director of Research at the Mutual UFO Network, I am formally requesting an explanation regarding an unidentified aircraft that was detected by FAA radar and that flew into the "No Flight Zone", without a transponder beacon, towards Crawford Ranch, Texas, on January 8, 2008, at about 8pm.

Glen Schulze, an electrical engineer with experience on Army radar at White Sands Proving Grounds, and myself, obtained radar data from the FAA's Ft. Worth center for the night of January 8, 2008. Upon analyzing the radar data, an unidentified aircraft was determined to have been traveling on a direct course towards the President's ranch near Crawford, Texas.

The unidentified aircraft in question first appeared on radar at 6:51pm to the southwest of Dublin, Texas. The aircraft continued on a southeasterly course at varying speeds but with an average speed of about 47mph. At 7:32pm radar data indicates that the aircraft accelerated to 532mph and then drops back in speed to less than 50mph. By 8:00pm the object is 10 miles from Crawford Ranch. The aircraft was already within the No Flight Zone used when the president is present at his ranch and within 5 minutes it would have been within the No Flight Zone used when the president is away from his ranch. A copy of the unidentified aircraft's path on radar is enclosed. All of the radar information supporting these claims is available from the FAA branch in Ft. Worth, Texas.

In light of the tragic events of September 11, 2001 this type of situation should be of grave concern to the U.S. government and the U.S. public. This is a formal request to the Dept. of Defense and Homeland Security to explain what occurred on the night of January 8, 2008. Hopefully, there is a simple explanation to the event that occurred. The Air Force should have the necessary information to explain the event. There were 10 F-16s in the area at the time, so there should be radar data available from the Air Force to explain what occurred on January 8th. (It is noted, however, that the FAA radar data showed no attempt by any of the F-16s to investigate or intercept the unknown aircraft.) There is also a radar installation at Ft. Hood that should have been able to pick up the unidentified aircraft.

Page 1

I look forward to your response. Thank you for your time and consideration.

Sincerely,

Robert Powell

cc: Sen. Joseph Lieberman, Ranking Majority Chairman of the Senate Committee on Homeland Security and
Governmental Affairs
Sen. Susan Collins, Ranking Minority Chairman of the Senate Committee on Homeland Security and
Governmental Affairs
Rep. Bennie Thompson, Ranking Majority Chairman of the House Committee on Homeland Security
Rep. Peter King, Ranking Minority Chairman of the House Committee on Homeland Security
FAA, Asst. Administrator for Regions & Center Operations

Page 2

Chapter 15 page 348
NORAD reply from Major General John H. Bordelon

 NORTH AMERICAN AEROSPACE DEFENSE COMMAND

DEC 2 2 2008

Major General John H. Bordelon
Chief of Staff, NORAD
250 Vandenberg Street, Suite B016
Peterson AFB CO 80914-3804

Mr. Robert Powell

Dear Mr. Powell

This letter is provided in response to your request for information regarding an unknown aircraft in the vicinity of Waco, Texas on the night of 8 Jan 08. An exhaustive search of 601 Combined Space and Air Operations Center (CAOC) and Western Air Defense Sector (WADS) forensic data files was conducted and no information was found concerning the unidentified aircraft in question.

Regarding the establishment of a "No Flight Zone," this would only occur if a FAA VIP Temporary Flight Restriction (TFR) was in place. On 8 Jan 08, an active FAA VIP TFR was not in place in the vicinity of Crawford, TX. Given the absence of an active TFR, the 10 F-16s conducting flight operations in the area that night were neither controlled nor monitored by the 601 CAOC or the WADS.

To assist your research, here is other information you may find helpful. FAA procedures JO 7110.65S, Air Traffic Control, Section 8, Unidentified Flying Objects Reports, Page 9-8-1, states that information submission or requests should be made to the UFO/Unexplained Phenomena Reporting Data Collection Center:

- The National UFO Reporting Center Hotline: 206-722-3000
- The National Institute for Discovery Science: ww.nidsci.org/reportform.php

Bottomline - we could find no tactical or technical information that would corroborate this event in the area of Waco, Texas on 8 Jan 08.

Sincerely

JOHN H. BORDELON
Major General, USAF

FOR THE COMMON DEFENCE   POUR LA DEFENSE COMMUNE

Chapter 18 page 424
JEMA letter to Ministry of Defense, January 16, 1979

ESTADO MAYOR DEL AIRE
DIVISION DE OPERACIONES
SECCION ESPACIO AEREO

34   15.12.78.   S.4.7.

Informe Fuerzas Armadas sobre OVNIS.

Excmo. Sr.:

Conforme a lo interesado en su escrito de referencia,
tengo el honor de informar a V.E., que se han notificado
varios casos de supuesta aparición de objetos voladores
no identificados (OVNIS), habiendo sido nombrados por lo
Jefes de Región o Zona Aéreas para la investigación de
cada uno de ellos, un Juez Informador, de acuerdo con
las normas dictadas por el Estado Mayor del Aire.

Según los antecedentes e Informes de los Jueces Infor
madores que obran en este Estado Mayor, sobre presuntos
OVNIS, algunos de los fenómenos han sido motivados por
causas naturales y otros no han podido ser determinados
con exactitud, considerándose estos últimos como fenóme
nos aéreos no identificados.

Fuera de estas Informaciones, una de las cuales se
adjunta, no se ha realizado ningún otro estudio general
concerniente al tema citado.

Dios guarde a V.E. muchos años.
Madrid, 16 de Enero de 1979.
EL GENERAL JEFE DEL ESTADO MAYOR
DEL AIRE.

ESTADO MAYOR DEL AIRE
Base de operaciones
16 ENE. 1979
REGISTRO
SALIDA
Núm. SGG.DU

EXCMO. SR. SUBSECRETARIO DE DEFENSA.
(SECRETARIA GENERAL PARA ASUNTOS
DE POLITICA DE DEFENSA).   MADRID.-

Chapter 18 page 424
Ministry of Defense letter, March 26, 1979

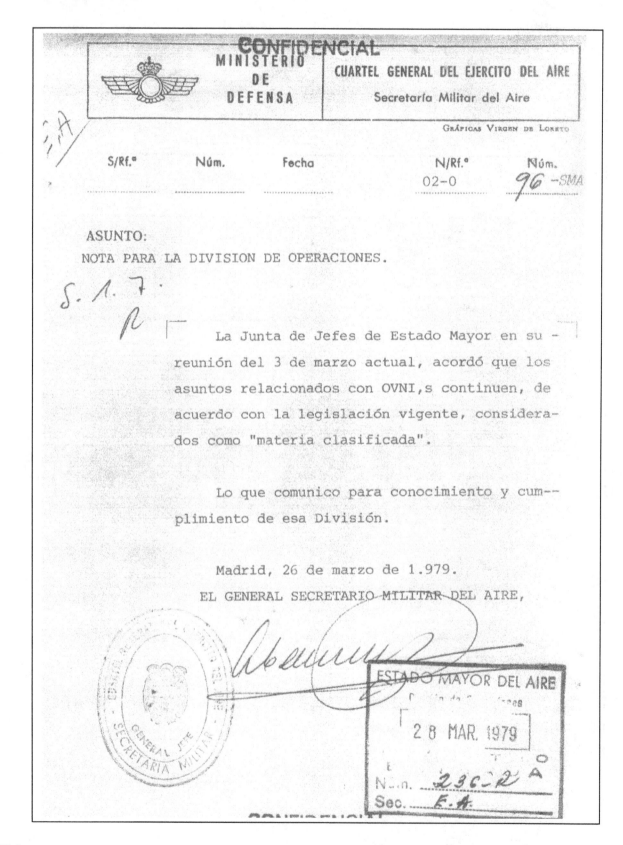

CONFIDENCIAL

| MINISTERIO DE DEFENSA | CUARTEL GENERAL DEL EJERCITO DEL AIRE |
| | Secretaría Militar del Aire |

GRÁFICAS VIRGEN DE LORETO

| S/Rf.º | Núm. | Fecha | N/Rf.º | Núm. |
| | | | 02-0 | 96 -SMA |

ASUNTO:

NOTA PARA LA DIVISION DE OPERACIONES.

La Junta de Jefes de Estado Mayor en su — reunión del 3 de marzo actual, acordó que los asuntos relacionados con OVNI,s continuen, de acuerdo con la legislación vigente, considerados como "materia clasificada".

Lo que comunico para conocimiento y cum--plimiento de esa División.

Madrid, 26 de marzo de 1.979.

EL GENERAL SECRETARIO MILITAR DEL AIRE,

ESTADO MAYOR DEL AIRE

2 8 MAR. 1979

Núm. 23602

Sec. E.A.

Chapter 18 page 424
Flight Safety Section NI, May 22, 1991

SEGVU / DOP / EMA

NOTA INFORMATIVA

ASUNTO: EL ARCHIVO DEL TEMA OVNI Y SU POSIBLE DESCLASIFICACION

Un investigador del fenómeno OVNI, el Sr. Ballester Olmos, pertenecien
te a un grupo privado que trata, según manifiesta, de explicar la lógi
ca de estos fenómenos, ha tenido diversos contactos con este Cuartel
General, a través de la Oficina de Relaciones Públicas, de la División
de Logística y de Seguridad de Vuelo. Unas veces personalmente y otras
por correo.

El interés del Sr. Ballester, puede resumirse en los dos aspectos si-
guientes:

a) La desclasificación del archivo de expedientes de casos OVNIs que
   posee el EA, y

b) La cumplimentación de un cuestionario de preguntas.

1. CON RELACION A a)

En este EMA -SEGVU/DOP- hay archivados 55 expedientes de casos
OVNI. Algunos han tenido una amplia (que no necesariamente profunda)
investigación, otros no tanto, otros ninguna y algunos no son más que
un parte o una leve referencia.

Los 55, con mención de su fecha, lugar, tipo de observación y clase de
informe realizado, figuran en la relación del ANEXO 1. Constan desde
el año 1962 hasta el de 1988, aunque realmente no se estudian en abso-
luto desde 1980. Como referencia de su volumen, el conjunto ocupa dos
carpetas-caja de archivo.

Para estudiar la posible desclasificación de este material debe consi-
derarse el origen de su clasificación y el caracter real de secreto o
confidencial que hoy se considere debe tener.

La clasificación se remonta a 1968, cuando se difundieron por la Ofici
na de Prensa del Ministerio del Aire unas normas para el tratamiento
del tema y se consideraba éste confidencial. En marzo de 1979 la JUJEM
clasificó los asuntos OVNI como "materia reservada". Ver ANEXO 2.

Pero hoy:

-Lo archivado en SEGVU se ha quedado viejo. No se investiga desde 1980
 y, como se ha señalado, ni siquiera se archivan casos desde 1988.

-La nueva legislación sobre competencia de la jurisdicción militar qui
 ta al EA de la responsabilidad de hacer esas investigaciones, salvo
 que se viera directamente involucrado o amenazado. Tal vez este argu
 mento es el que se ha venido considerando para que las investigaciones se hayan interrumpido; aunque también, pero para continuar con
 ellas, cabría el argumento de su posible repercusión en la seguridad
 de vuelo e incluso en la nacional.

-El contenido de nuestro archivo no revela ningún misterio ni despeja
 dudas a quien las tenga, seguramente porque las investigaciones no
 están hechas por profesionales o estudiosos del fenómeno.

Chapter 18 page 425
Second Chief of Staff letter to Air Regions, July 26, 1991

ESTADO MAYOR DEL AIRE

DIVISION DE OPERACIONES

SEGURIDAD DE VUELO

SEGVU
Z13

Stdo. remision documentación sobre OVNI's

        Ruego a V.E. remita, a la mayor brevedad posible,
toda la documentación que posean, tanto Mandos como
Unidades, relativa a Objetos Voladores No Identificados
(OVNI's).

            Madrid, 26 de julio de 1991
        EL JEFE DEL ESTADO MAYOR DEL EJERCITO DEL AIRE

                    De Orden de S.E.
            EL GENERAL 2.ª JEFE DEL E. M. AIRE

                    CARLOS GOMEZ COLL

DESTINATARIOS:

- EXCMO. SR. GENERAL JEFE DEL MANDO AEREO DEL CENTRO/MADRID. ——— no
- EXCMO. SR. GENERAL JEFE DEL MANDO AEREO DEL ESTRECHO/SEVILLA. solo Aznalcollar 74 (refe)
- EXCMO. SR. GENERAL JEFE DEL MANDO AEREO DE LEVANTE/ZARAGOZA. Sí, varios
- EXCMO. SR. GENERAL JEFE DEL MANDO AEREO DE CANARIAS/LAS PALMAS. — Sí (reples)
- EXCMO. SR. GENERAL JEFE DEL MANDO OPERATIVO AEREO/MADRID. — no
- EXCMO. SR. GENERAL JEFE DEL MANDO DEL APOYO LOGISTICO/CASA. ——— no
- EXCMO. SR. GENERAL JEFE DEL MANDO DE PERSONAL/CASA.
- EXCMO. SR. GENERAL JEFE DE LA AGRUPACION DEL CUARTEL GENERAL/CASA.

Chapter 18 page 425
Chief of Air Staff letter to MOA, January 15, 1992

MINISTERIO DE DEFENSA
EJERCITO DEL AIRE
ESTADO MAYOR DEL AIRE

DIVISION DE OPERACIONES
SECCION DE ESPACIO AEREO

S/Rf.ª	Núm.	Fecha	N/Rf.ª	Núm.
			SEGVU	061

ASUNTO: Rtdo. documentación OVNI's.

Comunico a V.E. que a la recepción del presente escrito deberá hacerse cargo de la gestión y tramitación de todos los asuntos referentes a los objetos volantes no identificados (OVNI), para lo cual se adjunta la documentación existente en el Estado Mayor del Ejército del Aire.

Una vez analizada la documentación que se remite, deberá redactar y someter a la aprobación de mi Autoridad los procedimientos de gestión que considere oportunos, en los que se incluirá la normativa a seguir sobre la clasificación y desclasificación de los expedientes que se generen.

Una vez aprobados estos procedimientos se procederá a la desclasificación, consecuente con las normas aprobadas, de los documentos remitidos.

Madrid, 15 de enero de 1992
EL JEFE DEL ESTADO MAYOR DEL EJÉRCITO DEL AIRE

RAMON FERNANDEZ SEQUEIROS

ESTADO MAYOR DEL M.O.A.
17 ENE 1992
REGISTRO
ENTRADA
Núm. 59-C
Sección

MOA – CUARTEL GENERAL
FECHA   Nº REG 59-C
SG SEM

V-f. 17-1-92

EXCMO. SR. COMANDANTE EN JEFE DEL MANDO OPERATIVO AÉREO
BASE AÉREA DE TORREJON   (M A D R I D)

CONFIDENCIAL

Chapter 18 page 426
MOA's commander-in-chief to JEMA, April 13, 1992

MINISTERIO DE DEFENSA	ESTADO MAYOR
EJERCITO DEL AIRE	
MANDO OPERATIVO AEREO	INTELIGENCIA

CONFIDENCIAL

S/Rf.ª	:	Núm.	Fecha		N/Rf.ª	Núm.

ASUNTO: PROPUESTA DE DESCLASIFICACION DE EXPEDIENTES RELATIVOS A "AVISTAMIENTOS DE FENOMENOS EXTRAÑOS EN EL ESPACIO AEREO NACIONAL"

En relación con el tema del Asunto, y en cumplimiento de las instrucciones verbales recibidas de V.E., adjunto tengo el honor de remitir la Nota Informativa elaborada por la Sección de Inteligencia del Estado Mayor de este Mando Operativo Aéreo.

Como Anexos a dicha Nota Informativa se incluyen la Normativa Militar española sobre OVNIs y la relación y fichas de los expedientes sobre avistamiento de fenómenos extraños que han sido recibidas en este MOA.

Madrid, a 13 de Abril de 1.992

EL COMANDANTE EN JEFE DEL MOA

- Alfredo Chamorro Chapinal -
Teniente General

CONFIDENCIAL

- ECMO.SR. GENERAL JEFE DEL ESTADO MAYOR DEL EJERCITO DEL AIRE

Chapter 18 page 426
Letter from JEMA's chief of cabinet, April 29, 1992

MINISTERIO DE DEFENSA	
EJERCITO DEL AIRE	GABINETE DEL JEMA

SECRETO

S/Rf.ª	Núm.	Fecha		N/Rf.ª	Núm.
				02-0 (16/84)	/C

ASUNTO: DESCLASIFICACION EXPEDIENTES OVNI,s.

De orden del JEMA, comunico a VE. que en la JUJEM cele-
brada el pasado 14 de abril se acordó desclasificar los expedientes relacionados con asuntos OVNI,s., facultando al JEMA para
tratar estos temas como materia objeto de "reserva interna" y
elevar a la JUJEM para su clasificación, aquellos expedientes
que, a su juicio lo requiera.

Madrid, 29 de abril de 1.992
EL JEFE DEL GABINETE DEL JEMA

JULIO ROCAFULL GARCIA

M.O.A. — CUARTEL GENERAL

Nº REG. ENTRADA W-S FECHA 0 4 MAYO 1992

S3	SEM	SS0	1ª	2ª	3ª	4ª	GRUPO MAC
				X			

EXCMO: SR: GENERAL SEGUNDO JEFE DEL ESTADO MAYOR DEL AIRE
EXCMO: SR: COMANDANTE EN JEFE DEL MANDO OPERATIVO AEREO.   B.A. DE TORREJON

SECRETO

Chapter 18 page 426
Cover of IG 40-5, issued March 31, 1992

Instrucción General

I.G. : 40-5   Fecha Emisión : 31/03/92

Descripción de la Instrucción General

Emisor	MOA
Materia	Información
Propósito	Establecer las normas que determinen los cauces de recepción de información, sea cual fuere su procedencia, relativa a avistamientos de fenómenos extraños dentro del Espacio Aéreo Nacional, nombramiento de Oficial Informador, procedimiento de elaboración de los Informes, y clasificación, tramitación y custodia de los mismos.
Anexos	ANEXO A: Cometidos de los Oficiales Informadores e Investigadores

NORMAS A SEGUIR TRAS LA NOTIFICACION DE AVISTAMIENTOS DE FENOMENOS EXTRAÑOS EN EL ESPACIO AEREO NACIONAL

PROPOSITO

Establecer las normas que determinen los cauces de recepción de información, sea cual fuere su procedencia, relativa a avistamientos de fenómenos extraños dentro del Espacio Aéreo Nacional, nombramiento de Oficial Informador, procedimiento de elaboración de los Informes, y clasificación, tramitación y custodia de los mismos.

ORGANO ORIGINADOR

El órgano originador de la presente Instrucción General es el Mando Operativo Aéreo. Dicho Mando velará por su cumplimiento y permanente actualización.

FECHA DE ENTRADA EN VIGOR

La presente Instrucción General entrará en vigor a su recepción.

DISPOSICIONES AFECTADAS

Esta Instrucción General anula y sustituye a la Circular 9266-C-T CONFIDENCIAL del JEMA, de fecha 26 de Diciembre de 1968, así como su actualización en 1974 por el Ministro del Aire, y todas aquellas disposiciones de igual o inferior rango, en cuanto a ella se opongan.

INDICE

- 1 -

520

Chapter 18 page 427
Example of declassified file, cover page 1

MANDO AÉREO DE COMBATE	ESTADO MAYOR SECCIÓN DE INTELIGENCIA

AVISTAMIENTO DE FENÓMENOS EXTRAÑOS

EXPEDIENTE: - MACAN NOV92

LUGAR: - EVA-21

FECHA: - 20 de Marzo de 1992

RESUMEN:

-        El 17 de Noviembre de 1992 CJMOA solicita al GJMACAN información acerca de 26 casos ocurridos en su Espacio Aéreo y de los que se tenía constancia por su aparición en los medios especializados para que, en la medida de lo posible, se intentara la búsqueda de alguna información acerca de los mismos.

-        GJMACAN contesta a CJMOA informando que toda la documentación referente a temas OVNI había sido ya solicitada por JEMA el 26 de Julio de 1991 (escrito 8690/SEGVU) y se había remitido al EMA el 13 de Agosto de ese mismo año (escrito 666/INL).

-        Posteriormente a estas comunicaciones y a pesar de esa centralización en el EMAIRE y debido a las acusaciones vertidas en los medios de comunicación acerca de ocultismo de datos, CJMOA remitió MSGID nº 708-C del 110830Z JUL94 al GJMACAN nuevo listado de casos con el ruego de remisión a las unidades afectadas para la búsqueda de información. La información remitida por el MACAN mediante escrito 17388/SINTE de fecha 10 de Agosto de 1994, en contestación a la solicitud de CJMOA, fue DESCLASIFICADA por JEMA a la propuesta MACAN JUL94 mediante escrito 3.1/2.1 SESPA con fecha 15 de Julio de 1997.

-        De los 26 casos relacionados en la presente propuesta existe contestación/anotaciones de 15 de ellos, ya desclasificados en el escrito de SESPA anteriormente citado. Posteriormente aparece en los archivos del MOA, el documento nº 0006 de la actual propuesta, en la que se refiere a dos casos ya desclasificados y uno mas, el correspondiente al 20 de Marzo de 1992, en el que la traza fue calificada como DESCONOCIDA, y que da pie a la presente propuesta de desclasificación.

-1-

521

Chapter 18 page 427
Example of declassified file, cover page 2

INDICE DE DOCUMENTOS

Documentos 0001
y 0002:   Oficio nº 1254-C de fecha 17 de Noviembre de 1992
                           de CJMOA dirigido a GJMACAN adjuntando listado de
                           casos de los que se solicita información.

Documentos 0003
al 0005:   Escrito 25763 de fecha 26 de Noviembre de 1992
                           por el que el GJMACAN contesta a CJMOA referente
                           a la solicitud anterior, adjuntando los oficios
                           de solicitud de remisión de documentación OVNI
                           por parte de JEMA (8690/SEGVU) y escrito de
                           GJMACAN contestando lo solicitado (666/INL.).

Documento 0006:   Resumen de las anotaciones habidas en el Grupo de
                           Alerta y Control referente a tres casos de los
                           listados anteriormente citados.

CONSIDERACIONES:

No se aprecian aspectos que hagan aconsejable mantener la condición
de "MATERIA CLASIFICADA".

PROPUESTA DE CLASIFICACIÓN: | DESCLASIFICADO |

Torrejón, 04 de septiembre de 1997
EL OFICIAL DE INTELIGENCIA DEL MACOM

DESCLASIFICADO

ESCRITO	NUM.	REFERENCIA	FECHA
EMA/DOP	5768	SESPA	23-9-9?

OBSERVACIONES:

Chapter 18 page 428
Cover of UFO monograph by Lt. Col. Enrique Rocamora

ESCUELA SUPERIOR DEL AIRE

57º CURSO DE CAPACITACIÓN
PARA EL ASCENSO A GENERAL
DE BRIGADA

EL PROCESO DE DESCLASIFICACIÓN DE LA DOCUMENTACIÓN ACERCA DE
OVNLs EN EL EA

TCOL. ENRIQUE ROCAMORA ANIORTE

14-SEPTIEMBRE-1998

Chapter 18 page 428
Lt. Col. Bastida letter to author, November 16, 1992

Torrejón, 16 de Noviembre de 1.992

VICENTE J. BALLESTER OLMOS

Guardia Civil, 9 D-16
46020 - V A L E N C I A
VALENCIA - ESPAÑA

[handwritten greeting]

Te escribo esta carta por encargo expreso del Teniente General
Chamorro, como continuación a la que él mismo te remitió con fecha 20
de Agosto del presente año, relativa a tu amable oferta de colabora-
ción en el proceso de desclasificación de los expedientes OVNI del
Ejército del Aire.

Como muy bien sabes, el Ejército del Aire solamente se dedicó a la
investigación OVNI en aquellos casos y aspectos que pudiesen afectar
a la Defensa Nacional, a nuestro Espacio Aéreo o a la seguridad de las
personas. Consiguientemente, no se recopilaron y analizaron todos los
casos de avistamientos ocurridos en España, sinó solo aquellos en que
se vieron involucrados medios, establecimientos o personal del Ejército del Aire, o que fueron notificados por escrito a alguna Autoridad
Aérea.

Como consecuencia, en algunos casos, a la hora de elaborar un
"cover memorandum" que complemente, con un punto de vista mas actual,
los análisis realizados en su día, se echa en falta una "visión global" que pueda proporcionar un marco mas esclarecedor de los hechos.
La experiencia y los archivos del CEI, pueden ayudar a esa visión de
conjunto, difícilmente extrapolable de un archivo como el nuestro, con
un número de avistamientos muy limitado.

En ese sentido, pienso que los contactos directos entre nosotros
sería el modo mas lógico y rápido para exponerte las necesidades de
información que vayan presentándose a medida que avanza el proceso de
desclasificación.

En cuanto un determinado expediente haya sido desclasificado, te
informaré de ello para que me indiques si te interesa que te envíe
copia de alguno de los documentos que lo integran.

[handwritten closing]

[signature]

- Angel Bastida Freijedo -

Chapter 18 page 430
Relationship of number of UFO cases reported to the Air Force and Air Ministry press releases, 1968-1969

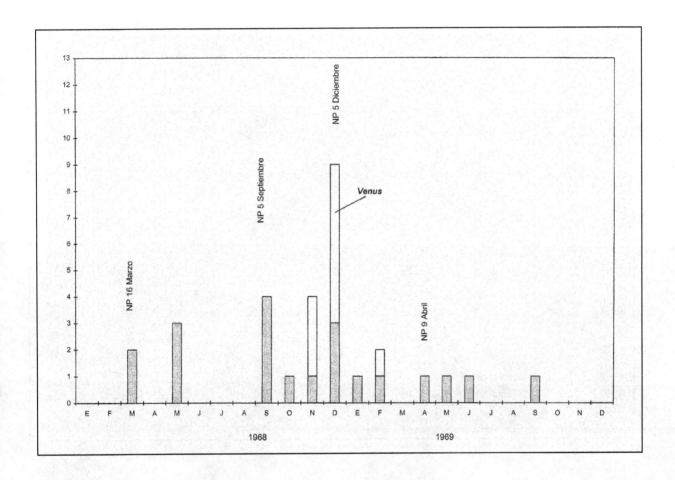

Chapter 18 page 434
January 2, 1975, sighting drawing, Bardenas Reales Firing Range

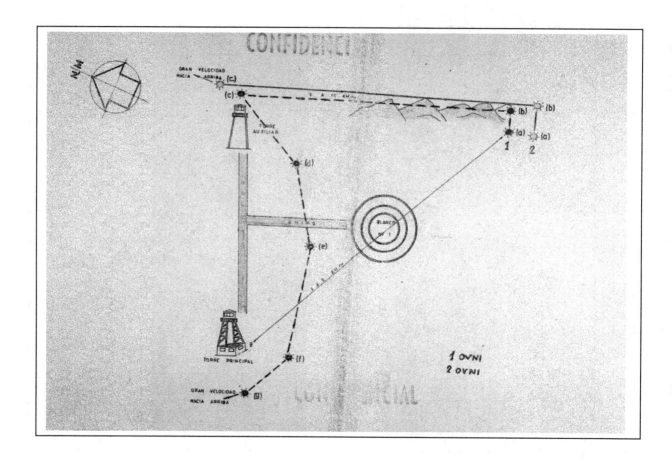

Chapter 18 page 435
Radar overlay for March 13, 1979 sighting

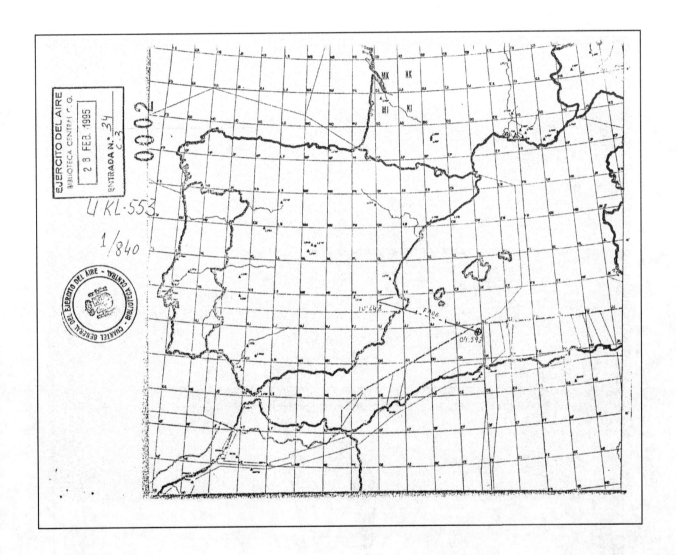

Chapter 18 page 436
Attachment 15: May 22, 1980, UFO and airplane courses

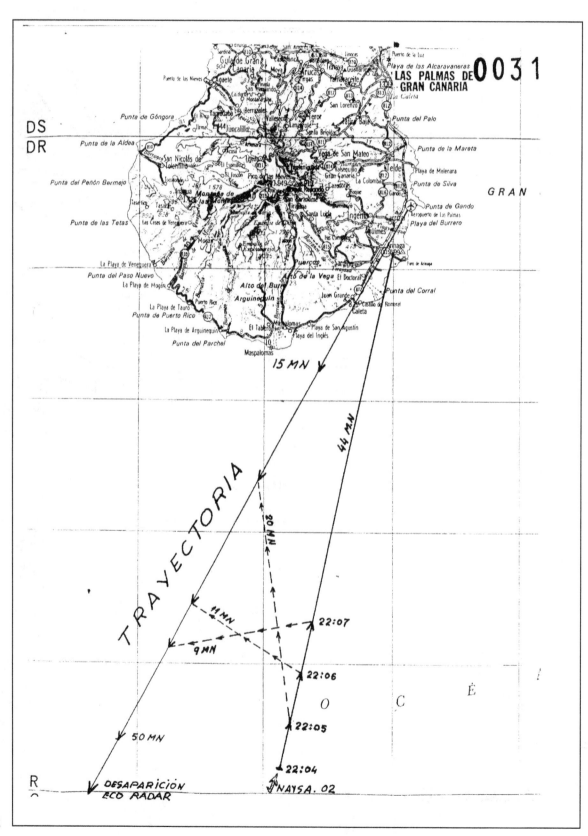

Appendix

Chapter 18 page 436
May 22, 1980, drawing by the instructing judge

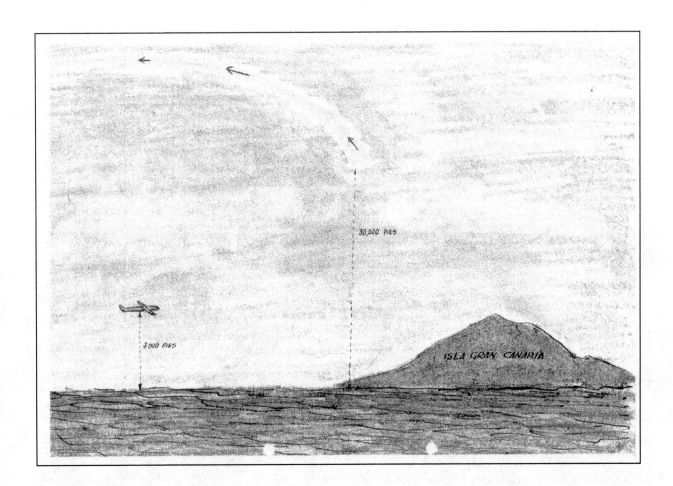

Illustration and Photography Credits

39   FBI agent S.W. Reynolds. Courtesy of the F.B.I.
40   Garrett's estimate written to Air Force Research and Development. United States Air Force.
41   Loedding's disk patents. U.S. Patent Office.
42   Albert Deyarmond and Howard McCoy. Courtesy of the Howard McCoy family and the United States Air Force.
42   General Nathan Twining. United States Air Force.
43   Lt. Col. Malcolm Seashore. United States Air Force.

Chapter 4

49   Generals Hoyt Vandenberg and Charles Cabell. United States Air Force.
51   Captain Mantell. United States Air Force.
52   Skyhook balloon. United States Navy.
52   Joint Research and Development Board. United States Air Force.
53   Cover to *Amazing Stories*. Wizards of the Coast, LLC.
53   Cover to *Fate*. Courtesy of Fate Magazine and their website at http://www.fatemag.com
54   German lenticular model craft. United States Air Force.
55   Dr. Irving Langmuir. Public Domain.
55   Dr. Theodore von Karman. National Aeronautics and Space Administration.
56   Dr. Lincoln La Paz. Courtesy of Ohio State University Archives.
56   Dr. J. Allen Hynek. Courtesy of the J. Allen Hynek Center for UFO Studies.
57   Sergei Korolev. National Aeronautics and Space Administration.
60   Captains Chiles and Whitted drawings. U.S.A.F. Bluebook.
60   Drs. Ludwig Prandtl and von Karman. United States Army.
61   AMC T-2 meeting with Colonel McCoy. United States Air Force.
63   Top Secret document regarding Swedish flying saucers. U.S. National Archives.
64   General Cabell letter to Wright Patterson. U.S. National Archives.
65   Air Force Science Advisory Board. United States Air Force.
67   National Security Council Meeting. Courtesy of the Truman Presidential Library.
67   Brigadier General Moore. United States Air Force.

Chapter 5

72   Dr. George Valley. United States Air Force.
73   Generals Vandenberg, Spaatz, LeMay, and Colonel McCoy. United States Air Force.
75   Major Donald Keyhoe. Courtesy of the National Investigations Committee on Aerial Phenomena (NICAP).
75   Walter Winchell. Department of Defense.
76   General Cabell and Colonels Schweizer and Allen. United States Air Force.
77   Lt. Colonel Doyle Rees. United States Air Force.
78   Dr. Lincoln LaPaz. Courtesy of the Center for UFO Studies (CUFOS).
79   Dr. Joseph Kaplan. Courtesy of Toplitt Studio and the Emilio Segrè Visual Archives.
79   Theodore von Karman. National Aeronautics and Space Administration.
79   Norris Bradbury. Los Alamos National Laboratories.
79   Dr. Edward Teller. Lawrence Livermore National Laboratories.
80   Dr. Allen Hynek. Courtesy of the Center for UFO Studies (CUFOS).
81   Clyde Tombaugh. Courtesy of the New Mexico State University; Archives and Special

Chapter 8

132   General Lionel Chassin. N.A.T.O.

139   Dr. J. Allen Hynek. Courtesy of the Center for UFO Studies (CUFOS).

140   Lieutenant Howard Smith. United States Air Force.

141   General Cabell, Colonel Schwizer, Major Boggs, Colonel Watson, Captain James, General Garland, Major Fournet, and Colonel Dunn. All courtesy of the United States Air Force.

141   General Samford. Courtesy of the Fortean Picture Library.

141   Captain Ruppelt. Ruppelt files. Courtesy of the UFO Research Coalition.

142   Memo from General Garland to General Samford regarding continued concern about UFOs. Courtesy of the United States Air Force.

144   Capt. Ruppelt, Lt. Olsson, and Lt. Rothstein. United States Air Force.

145   General LeMay, Richard Russell, and Roger Ramey. United States Air Force.

148   Two Project Blue Book aides, 1952. United States Air Force.

149   Delbert Newhouse. United States Navy.

149   Tremonton UFOs. United States Air Force.

150   William Fortenberry and William Nash. Public Domain.

150   Dr. Stefan Possony. United States Government Printing Office.

151   Charles Moore. Courtesy of the Center for UFO Studies (CUFOS).

152   Dewey Fournet, Al Chop, and Edward Ruppelt. Courtesy of National Investigations Committee on Aerial Phenomena (NICAP).

152   Dr. Donald Menzel. American Institute of Physics, Courtesy of the Emilio Segrè Visual Archives.

156   General Robert Landry and President Harry Truman. Courtesy of the Truman Presidential Library.

156   Al Chop. United States Air Force.

157   USAF pilots during the Washington scramble. United States Air Force.

158   Radar simulation. Ruppelt files. Courtesy of the UFO Research Coalition.

159   General Nathan Twining. United States Air Force.

160   Samford Conference in Washington, D.C. © Corbis and the Bettman Archives.

161   General John Samford. Courtesy of the National Security Agency.

163   Donald Keyhoe. Courtesy of National Investigations Committee on Aerial Phenomena (NICAP).

165   Secretary of the Navy Dan Kimball and Admiral Arthur Radford. United States Navy.

165   Admiral Delmar Fahrney and Admiral Calvin Bolster. United States Navy.

165   Arthur Lundahl. Courtesy of the Lundahl Family.

166   Dr. James McDonald. Collection MS412 Box21. Courtesy of University of Arizona Libraries, Special Collections.

166   Admiral Roscoe Hillenkoetter. United States Navy.

Chapter 9

170   Frederick Durant. Smithsonian Institution.

170   Walter Bedell Smith. Courtesy of the Truman Presidential Library.

172   Assistant CIA Director, Dr. H. Marshall Chadwell. Courtesy of Tufts University Archives.

173   Major Dewey Fournet. Courtesy of National Investigations Committee on Aerial Phenomena (NICAP).

Chapter 10

Chapter 11

Chapter 12

Chapter 13

296   Major Melden LeRoy. Courtesy of the Red Bluff Daily News.
296   Walter Webb. Courtesy of Walter Webb.
297   William Coleman. Courtesy of William Coleman.
298   Major Hector Quintanilla. United States Air Force.
298   Hallett Station, Antarctica. Courtesy of the government of New Zealand.
301   Edward J. Ruppelt. Ruppelt files. Courtesy of the UFO Research Coalition.

Chapter 14

306   Quintanilla seated with Blue Book team. United States Air Force.
307   Congressman Gerald Ford. Courtesy of the LBJ Presidential Library.
307   Secretary of the Air Force Harold Brown. United States Air Force.
308   NACA Special Committee on Space Technology. National Aeronautics and Space Administration.
308   Walter Cronkite. Library of Congress.
308   Kelly Johnson. Lockheed Martin Corporation.
308   Art Lundahl. National Security Agency.
309   Mr. Robert Low and Dr. Ed Condon. Courtesy of the University of Colorado.
310   Dr. Stuart Cook, Dr. Franklin Roach, Dr. David Saunders. Courtesy of the University of Colorado.
312   Scott, Condon, Low, Cook and Wertheimer. Courtesy of the University of Colorado.
313   Dr. Michael Wertheimer. Courtesy of the University of Colorado.
314   Dr. Edward Condon. Courtesy of the University of Colorado.
315   Dr. Norman Levine. Courtesy of National Investigations Committee on Aerial Phenomena (NICAP).
316   Dr. Roy Craig. Courtesy of the Texas A&M Cushing Memorial Library.
316   Dr. Edward Condon. Courtesy of the University of Colorado.
317   Dr. Donald Menzel. American Institute of Physics, Courtesy of the Emilio Segrè Visual Archives.
318   Dr. Richard Feynman. Public domain.
320   Betty and Barney Hill. Courtesy of their niece, Kathleen Marden.
326   McMinnville UFO. © Corbis and the Bettman Archives.
328   James McDonald. Collection N-6995. Courtesy of University of Arizona Libraries, Special Collections.
329   Frank Drake. Public domain.
332   Philip Morrison. Los Alamos National Laboratories.
332   AIAA Subcommittee Panel. Courtesy of the Center for UFO Studies (CUFOS).

Chapter 15

336   Brigadier General Bolender. Courtesy of the U.S. National Archives, photo no. 342-B-12-015-4.
337   Barry Greenwood. Courtesy of Barry Greenwood.
337   Edward Markey. Collection of the U.S. House of Representatives.
340   Lieutenant Parviz Jafari. Iranian Air Force.
341   Article and photo of Captain Henry S. Shields. U.S. Government Printing Office.
342   Drawing by Captain Terauchi. Courtesy of the Center for UFO Studies (CUFOS).
344   Steve Allen. Courtesy of Steve Allen.

Chapter 16

Chapter 17

Chapter 18

Chapter 19

Chapter 20

Bibliography

Archival Sites

Air Technical Intelligence Center, Wright-Patterson AFB, Dayton, OH. (Project Blue Book and Project Grudge status reports, Project Blue Book Special Report #14, and other referenced documents)

American Philosophical Library Archives, Philadelphia, PA. (Papers of Donald Menzel, papers related to the "University of Colorado Study of UFOs," and other referenced documents)

Archives for UFO Research, S-600 11, Norrkoping, Sweden. (One of the most exhaustive archives of UFO research documents from throughout Europe)

California Institute of Technology Archives, Pasadena, CA. (Papers of H.P. Robertson)

Cushing Library Archives, Texas A&M University, College Station, Texas. (Papers of Roy Craig)

Georgetown University Library, Special Collections Division, Washington, D.C. (Papers of Stefan Possony)

National Academy of Sciences, Springfield, VA.

National Archives and Records Administration, Washington, D.C. (United States Air Force, *Project Blue Book and Project SIGN,* microfilm, as well as other referenced documents)

National Archives of Australia, Canberra, Australia. (RAAF UFO Policy File Series, External Affairs File Series, DCA files, and the Dept of Supply files)

National Investigations Committee On Aerial Phenomena files held at the Center for UFO Studies, Chicago, IL.

Smithsonian Archives, Washington, D.C. (Papers of Frederick Durant and other referenced documents)

Swedish War Archives, Krigsarkivet, Banérgatan 64, 115 88 Stockholm, Sweden.

Tasmanian UFO Investigation Centre, South Hobart, Tasmania, 7004, Australia.

UFO Research Coalition, Ruppelt papers held at Center for UFO Studies, Chicago, IL.

University of Arizona Archives, University of Arizona, Tucson, Arizona. (Papers of James McDonald)

University of Colorado Libraries, Western Historical Collections, Boulder, Colorado. (Papers of Edward Condon)

Articles

"AF General Warns UFOs Serious, Will Increase," *UFO Investigator 1* (9), March 1960, p. 3.

"Air Force General Admits UFO Sightings Kept from Public," *The UFO Investigator 1* (3), January, 1958, pp. 1, 3.

"Artificial Meteors," *Army Ordnance,* July/August 1947, pp. 157-163.

"A Sledgehammer for Nuts," *Nature 221,* March 8, 1969, pp. 899-900.

"CIA releases documents -- GSW prevails in FOIA lawsuit," *Just Cause* 1 (7), January 1979, pp. 1-2.

"Cigar-Shaped UFO at Lake Backsjön, Sweden," *International UFO Reporter,* Fall 2000, pp. 16-18.

"CSI To Go On Standby Status," *Civilian Saucer Investigation Quarterly Bulletin 1*(III), July 1953, pp. 5-6.

"Det händer mer än jag trodde," *UFO-Aktuellt 2,* 2006, pp. 26.

"Flying Saucers -- The Real Story," *U.S. News and World Report,* April 7, 1950, pp. 13-15.

"If You're Seeing Things in the Sky," *U.S. News & World Report,* November 15, 1957, pp. 122, 124, 126.

"It Keeps Up," *Le Courrier de l'Ouest,* October 19, 1954. Translated news story, CSI-NY files.

"Libel suit may develop from UFO hassle," *Scientific Research,* May 13, 1968, pp. 11-12.

"Mystery Object Sighted by Pilots over Victorville," *The Lockheed Star 20* (6), March 19, 1953, pp. 1, 5.

"Navy Missiles Tests and the Canary Islands UFOs", *International UFO Reporter* 29 (4), July 2005, pp. 3-9, 26.

"New Angle on Armstrong Show," *Confidential NICAP Bulletin,* April 4, 1958, p. 4.

"New Board Members Announced," *The UFO Investigator* 1 (1), July 1957, pp. 1-2, 30-31.

"No Evidence for Saucers," *Science News Letter,* November 16, 1957, p. 307.

"Out of the Past," *International UFO Reporter,* January-February 1985.

"Psychoanalyzing the 'Flying Saucers'," *Air Force,* February 1950, pp. 15-19.

"Recent UAO Radiation Cases," *APRO Bulletin,* March 1958, p. 6.

"Roswell Declaration 1994," *International UFO Reporter* 19 (2), March-April 1994.

"Russia Claims Saucers Never Seen over USSR Territory," *The UFO Investigator* 1 (2), August-September 1957, p. 15.

"Saucer Blue Book," *Time,* November 7, 1955, p. 52.

"Senator Goldwater Reveals Interest in UFO Problem," *The UFO Investigator* 1 (2), August-September 1957.

"The 1962 Occupants Case," *APRO Bulletin,* September-October 1972.

"The GAO Report: Results of a Search for Records Concerning the 1947 Crash Near Roswell, New Mexico," *International UFO Reporter* Volume 20 (4), July-Aug 1995.

"Two Huge UFOs Sighted by Baltimore Astronomer," *UFO Investigator 1 (5)*, August-September 1958, pp 1-3.

"UFO Photo Certified by Brazilian Navy Labeled a Hoax by USAF," *UFO Investigator 1* (10), July-August 1960.

"UFOs: an Appraisal of the Problem," *Astronautics and Aeronautics*, November 1970, pp. 49-51.

Aldrich, Jan, "Investigating the Ghost Rockets," *International UFO Reporter* 23 (4), Winter, 1998, pp. 9-14.

Alexis, Lieutenant Colonel (Director of the Office of Prospective Studies of the Air Force), French to English translation of an interview by R. Roussel and F. Buchi, *Rhedae Magazine,* 1976.

Amazing Stories 22 (4), April, 1948. Editor, Raymond Palmer.

Året Runt 34, August 22, 1962.

Australian Flying Saucer Review 8, 1965.

Baker, Robert M.L., "Observational Evidence of Anomalistic Phenomena," *Journal of the Astronautical Sciences XV* (1), Jan.-Feb. 1968, pp. 31-36.

Baker, Robert M.L., "Photogrammatic Analysis of the 'Montana' Film Tracking Two UFOs," Santa Monica, CA: *Douglas Aircraft*, March 1956, pp 14.

Ballester Olmos, Vicente-Juan, "Ángel Bastida: El hombre del MOA." @*nomalía* (II), 9, June 2008 (CD edition).

Ballester Olmos, Vicente-Juan, "Monitoring Air Force Intelligence: Spain's 1992-1997 UFO Declassification Process," MUFON 1997 International UFO Symposium Proceedings, July 1997, pp.139-178.

Ballester Olmos, Vicente-Juan, "Spanish Air Force UFO Files: The Secret's End," MUFON 1993 International UFO Symposium Proceedings, July 1993, pp. 127-168.

Bernstein, Carl, "The CIA and the Media," *Rolling Stone*, October 20, 1977.

Boffey, Philip, "UFO Project: Trouble on the Ground," *Science*, July 26, 1968, pp. 339-342.

Bougard, Mickel, "Le Dossier Photo d'Interspace," *Inforespace 18*, 1974.

Bourdais, Gildas, "On the Death & Rebirth of Official French UFO Studies: 2004-2007," January 19, 2008.

Bourdais, Gildas, "From GEPAN to SEPRA: Official UFO Studies in France," *International UFO Reporter*, Winter 2000-2001, p. 10.

Bryan, Joseph, III, Open letter to National Investigations Committee on Aerial Phenomena, The UFO Investigator III (8): 5, May-June 1966.

Carpenter, Joel, "The Lockheed UFO Case, 1953," *International UFO Reporter*, Fall 2001, pp. 3-9, 33-34.

Chalker, William, "The UFO Connection—Startling Implications for North West Cape and Australia's Security," *Omega Science Digest*, March 1985.

Chamberlain, Jo, "The Foo Fighter Mystery," *The American Legion Magazine,* December, 1945, pp. 43-47.

Clarke, Arthur C., book review of Edward Ruppelt's *Report on Unidentified Flying Objects, Journal of the British Interplanetary Society 15* (5), Sept.-Oct. 1956, pp. 289-290.

Clarke, Terry, "The Day All Roads Led to Alamogordo," *Writer's Digest*, December 1957, pp. 24-5, 27-31.

Coleman, William, interview with *TV Guide*, June 10, 1978.

Common Cause, April-June 1992, reporting on the NASA Lewis Research Center, "Suggestions for Anticipating Requests Under the Freedom of Information Act," November 1989.

Considine, Bob, "The Disgraceful Flying Saucer Hoax," *Cosmopolitan*, January 1951.

Creighton, G., "French Minister Speaks on UFOs," *Flying Saucer Review 20 (*2), 1974, p.3. Radio France Inter broadcast, February 21, 1974.

Darrach, H.B., and Robert E. Ginna, "Have We Visitors from Space?," *Life Magazine*, April 7, 1952, pp. 80-96.

de Brosses, Marie-Therese, "A UFO on the F16's Radar," *Paris-Match*, July 5, 1990.

de Brouwer, Wilfried, Major General (retired), "The Belgian UFO Wave," *MUFON 39th International Symposium Proceedings: July 2008,* pp. 137-152.

del Giudice, Marguerite, "The UFO that Can't be Explained," *The Philadelphia Inquirer Magazine*, May 24, 1987, pp. 14-17, 24-27.

Delaney, William P., and William W. Ward, "Radar Development at Lincoln Laboratory," *Lincoln Laboratory Journal 12* (2), 2000, pp.147-166.

Durfield, Yvonne S., "The Eyewitness Report of the Incredible UFO Invasion of Antarctica," *Ideal's UFO Magazine 2, 1978, pp.* 44-50.

Edwards, Frank, "Guest Editorial," *Flying Saucers (CSI-NE) 5* (2), Fourth Quarter 1957, pp. 1-4.

Faira, J. Escobar, *International UFO Reporter VIII* (4), July-August 1983.

Faria, J. Escobar, *UFO-Critical Bulletin I*, (9-10), September-October 1957.

Faria, J. Escobar, *UFO-Critical Bulletin II* (2), March-April 1958.

Faria, J. Escobar, *UFO-Critical Bulletin II*, January-February 1958.

Faria, J. Escobar, *UFO-Critical Bulletin III (*1), January-February 1959.

Faria, J. Escobar, *UFO-Critical Bulletin III (*4), July-August 1959.

Faria, J. Escobar, *UFO-Critical Bulletin III (*5), September-October 1959.

Fate 1 (1), Spring, 1948. Editor, Robert N. Webster.

Fontes, Olavo, "Flying Saucers Are Real says Brazilian Air Force Official Report on Unidentified Flying Objects," *Flying Saucer Review*, May 1956.

Fournet, Dewey, Major, "Inside the Early Days of Project Blue Book: an exclusive interview by Antonio Huneuus," *UFO Universe*, November 1988, pp. 14-17.

Francis, Devon, "New Balloons Explore Roof of the Airways," *Popular Science*, May 1948, pp. 98-104.

Freijedo, Ángel Bastida, "Los OVNIS y el Ejército del Aire," *Revista de Aeronáutica y Astronáutica*, August-September 1992, pp. 655-659.

Fuller, Curtis, "Report on the Flying Saucers," *FATE Magazine*, May 1954, pp. 18-19.

Fuller, John, "Flying Saucer Fiasco," *Look*, May 14, 1968, pp. 58-63.

Gindilis, L.M., D. A. Men'kov, and I. G. Petroskaya, "Observation of Anomalous Atmospheric Phenomena in the USSR," (translated), March 2, 1958, Center for UFO Studies: Chicago, 1980.

Greenwood, Barry, "FBI Academy Records Revealed," *UFO Historical Review 13*, September 2009.

Greenwood, Barry, and Lawrence Fawcett, "First Official Foo-Fighter Records Discovered," *Just Cause* (32), June 1992 and September 1992 (entire bulletins).

Greenwood, Barry, ed., "Were Most of 1947s Flying Discs Meteors?," *U.F.O. Historical Revue*, #4 (April, 1999), p. 3.

Greenwood, Barry, ed., *U.F.O. Historical Revue*, #8 (February, 2001), pp. 4-7.

Gross, Loren E., "A New Look at the Robertson Panel," *FOCUS 3*(4), pp. 1, 3-5.

Haines, Gerald K., "CIA's Role in the Study of UFOs, 1947-1990," *Studies in Intelligence (1),* 1997, pp. 67-83.

Hall Richard, "NICAP: The Bitter Truth," *MUFON UFO Journal 145*, 1980, pp. 11-12.

Hall, R. Cargill, "Early U.S. Satellite Proposals," *Technology and Culture* IV (4), Fall 1963, pp. 412-434.

Hallet, Marc, "The So-Called 'Belgian UFO Wave': a Critical View," *Revue Francaise de Parapychologie 1* (1), 1992, pp. 5-24. (translation: Center for UFO Studies, Chicago, IL.)

Hickman, John C., et al. "Fewer Sightings in the National Press: Content Analysis in *The New York Times*, 1947-1995," *Journal of UFO Studies n.s.6*, 1995-6, pp.213-225.

Hull, Joe, "Men in Motion: Obituary of the Flying Saucers," *AIR LINE PILOT 22,* September 1953, pp. 13-14.

Hynek, J. Allen, "Are Flying Saucers Real?," *Saturday Evening Post*, December 17, 1966.

Hynek, J. Allen, "France's Official UFO Agency," International UFO Reporter, 1980, p. 7.

Hynek, J. Allen, "The Condon Report and UFOs," *Bulletin of the Atomic Scientists*, April 1969, pp. 39-42.

Hynek, J. Allen, "Unusual Aerial Phenomena", *Journal of the Optical Society of America 43*(4), April 1953, pp. 311-314.

JUST CAUSE 24, June 1990, pp. 1-4

Karig, Walter, Captain, "Operation UFO," *The American Weekly*, November 22, 1953, pp. 4-5.

Karth, Joseph, letter to Donald Keyhoe, *The UFO Investigator II* (2), October 1981, pp. 1-2.

Keyhoe, Donald, "Flying Saucers Are Real," *True*, January 1950, pp. 11-13, 83-87.

Keyhoe, Donald, "Flying Saucers from Outer Space," *Look*, October 20, 1953, pp 114-120.

Keyhoe, Donald, "Head of NACA Backs Down on Flying Saucer Claim," *NICAP Special Bulletin*, April 22, 1957.

Keyhoe, Donald, "The Captain Ruppelt Letters," *The UFO Investigator II* (2), October 6, 1961.

Kociver, Ben, "Is This the Real Flying Saucer?," *Look,* June 14, 1955, p. 44.

Lang, Daniel, "A Reporter at Large: Something in the Sky," *New Yorker,* September 6, 1952, pp. 64, 66-82.

Langmuir, Irving, "Pathological Science," Technical Information Series #G8-C-035. General Electric Research and Development Center, Schenectady, NY, April 1968.

LeBlanc, N., *German Flying Wings Designed by Horten Brothers*. Document #: F-SU-1110-ND. Headquarters Air Materiel Command, Wright Field, Dayton, OH, July 5, 1946.

Liddel, Urner, "Bogies at Angels 100," *Research Reviews,* Office of Naval Research, March 1951.

Lorenzen, Coral, "The New Mexico Story," *The APRO Bulletin*, November 1957, pp 1-2; 5.

Lorenzen, L.J., "The Stokes Case," *The APRO Bulletin,* January 1958, pp. 2, 6.

Maccabee, Bruce, "The fantastic flight of JAL 1628," *International UFO Reporter*, March-April 1987.

Markowitz, William, "The Physics and Metaphysics of Unidentified Flying Objects," *Science 157,* 1967, pp. 1274-1279.

Marler, David B., "Illinois police officers track UFO near Scott AFB," *MUFON UFO Journal,* March 2000, pp. 3-8.

Maurer, Stephen M., "Idea Man," *Beamline*, Winter 2001, pp. 21-27.

McDonald, James, "The 1957 Gulf Coast RB-47 Incident," *Flying Saucer Review*, May-June 1970, pp. 2-6.

McDonald, James, "UFOs—an international scientific problem," Canadian Aeronautics & Space Institute, Astronautics Symposium, Montreal, Canada, March 12, 1968.

McDonald, James, "Science in Default: 22 years of inadequate UFO Investigations," paper given as an addendum to the AAAS Symposium of 1969.

McDonald, James, "The Problem of the Unidentified Flying Objects," summary of a talk given to the District of Columbia Charter of the American Meteorological Society, October 19, 1966.

McLaughlin, Robert, "How Scientists Tracked a Flying Saucer," *True*, March 1950, pp. 25-27, 96-99.

McNamara, Lt. Colonel James, "Angel's Hair," *Pageant*, November 1954, pp. 52-56.

Meessen, "The Belgian Sightings," *International UFO Reporter 16 (*3), May-June 1991, pp. 4-11, 22, 24.

Mesnard, Joel, "Belgium Haunted by Huge Triangular Craft," *Flying Saucer Review*, December 1990.

Michael D. Swords, "David Griggs and the Foo Fighters," *International UFO Reporter* 31 (1), 2007, pp.17-19. Center for UFO Studies: Chicago, Illinois.

Moore, Charles B., letter to Adie Suehsdorf, *This Week Magazine*, December 31, 1949.

Moorehouse, Frederick, "The Case of the Flying Saucers," *Argosy*, July 1949, pp. 26.

Murray, Daniel C., "The Avro VZ-9 Experimental Aircraft: Lessons Learned," paper AIAA 90-3237 at the AIAA / AHS / ASEE Aircraft Design, Systems and Operations Conference, Dayton, OH, September 17-19, 1990.

Nash, William and William Fortenberry, "We Flew Above Flying Saucers," *True*, October 1952, pp. 65, 110-112.

Oberg, James, "The Great Soviet UFO Cover up," *MUFON UFO Journal #176*, October 1982.

Oberth, Hermann, "Flying Saucers Come From a Distant World," *The American Weekly*, October 24, 1954, pp 4-5.

Oberth, Hermann, "Lecture Notes," *Australian UFO Bulletin*, September 1991.

Orlov, Vadim, interview by Professor Valery Burdakov, in AURA-Z, No. 1 (March 1993), p. 11.

Perry, Robert L., "The Atlas, Thor, and Titan," pp. 466-477 in Emme, Eugene M., ed., "The History of Rocket Technology," special dedicated edition of *Technology and Culture*, Fall, 1963.

Pflock, Karl, "Roswell, the Air Force, and Us," *International UFO Reporter* 19 (6), November-December 1994.

Poher, Claude, and Jacques Vallee, "Basic Patterns in UFO Observations," AAIA 13th Aerospace Meeting, Pasadena, California, January 20-22, 1975.

Powell, Robert, and Glen Schultz, "Stephenville Lights: A Comprehensive Radar and Witness Report Study," July 2008. Copy at John Greenwood's, *The Black Vault*, http://www.theblackvault.com/encyclopedia/documents/MUFON/Files/MUFONStephenvilleRadarReport.pdf. Accessed February 17, 2012.

Pratt, Bob and Patrick Ferryn (SOBEPS), "The Belgium UFO Flap," *MUFON UFO Journal 267*, July 1990.

Putt, D.L., *German Developments in the Field of Guided Missiles*. Document #: F-SU-1122-ND. Headquarters Air Materiel Command, Wright Field, Dayton, OH. 12 July 1946.

Redfern, Nick, "Operation Espionage," *The Anomalist* 12, 2006, pp. 46-73.

Rodeghier, Mark, "Roswell and the GAO Investigation," *International UFO Reporter* 19 (2), March-April 1994.

Rodeghier, Mark, and Mark Chesney, "The Air Force Report on Roswell: An Absence of Evidence," *International UFO Reporter* 19 (5) September-October 1994.

Rodeghier, Mark, and Mark Chesney, "What the GAO Found – Nothing about Much Ado," *International UFO Reporter* 20 (4), July-August 1995.

Rodeghier, Mark, and Mark Chesney, "Who's the Dummy Now? The Latest Air Force Report," *International UFO Reporter* 22 (3), Fall 1997.

Ruppelt, Edward, "What Our Air Force Found Out About Flying Saucers," *True*, May 1954, pp. 19-20, 22, 24, 26, 30, 124-134.

Ruppelt, Edward, letter to Donald Keyhoe, August 3, 1954, printed in *UFO Investigator II (2)*, October 1961, p.6.

Samford, John A., General, interview, "Flying Saucers -- the last word," *SEE*, March, 1953, pp. 30-32.

Shalett, Sidney, "What You Can Believe About Flying Saucers (Part 1)," *Saturday Evening Post*, April 30, 1949, pp. 20-21, 136-139; and Part 2, May 7, 1949, pp. 36, 184-186.

Shields, Henry S., Captain, "Now You See It, Now You Don't!," *MIJI Quarterly*, October 1978, pp. 32-34.

Simoes, Auriphebo, "Occurrencies Traflego Hotel 6SC Comdabra," *The Flying Saucer 9*, December 1957.

Simoes, Auriphebo, *The Flying Saucer 6*, June 1957.

Smith, H.W., Lieutenant, and Mr. G.W. Towles, Unidentified Flying Objects: Project "Grudge" (Project No. XS-304). Technical Report 102-AC 49/15-100. Air Materiel Command, Dayton, Ohio. August 1949.

Spruch, Grace, "Reporter Edward Condon," *Saturday Review*, February 1, 1969, pp. 55-8, 62.

Sturrock, Peter, "Evaluation of the Condon Report on the Colorado UFO Project," *SUIPR Report #599*, Stanford University, October 1974.

Sundh, Per, interview by Clas Svahn, "Kanske ett tefat?," *Industria* No. 10, 1954. April 24, 1990.

Swords, Michael D, "The Holland, Michigan, Radar-Visual Case, 1994," *International UFO Reporter*, Fall 1999, pp. 3-7.

Swords, Michael D., "Project Sign and the Estimate of the Situation," *Journal of UFO Studies*, N.s. Vol. 7, 2000, pp. 27-64.

Swords, Michael, "Fun and Games in the Desert near Las Cruces," *International U.F.O. Reporter 30 (3)*, 2006, pp. 20-21.

Teknikens Värld, March 1959.

Tokaty, G.A., "Soviet Rocket Technology," in Eugene Emme (ed.)," pp. 515-28, "The History of Rocket Technology," a special dedicated magazine edition of *Technology and Culture*, Fall 1963.

Truettner, L.H., and A.B. Deyarmond, "Unidentified Aerial Objects: Project 'SIGN'." Technical Intelligence Division, Air Materiel Command, Technical Report No. F-TR-2274-IA. February, 1949.

UFO Bulletin 1 (4), March 1958. UFO Investigations Center, Sydney, Australia.

Velasco, Jean-Jacques, "Amaranth Investigation," *Workshop on Physical Evidence*, materials describing the GEPAN/SEPRA program, circa 2000, p. 25.

Velasco, Jean-Jacques, short chronology, "Official Interest and Research on UFOs in France," May 28, 1999.

von Braun, Werner, "The Redstone, Jupiter, and Juno," pp. 452-465 in Emme, Eugene M., ed., "The History of Rocket Technology," special dedicated edition of *Technology and Culture*, Fall, 1963.

Webb, Walter N., "Allen Hynek as I Knew Him," *International UFO Reporter,* January-February, 1993, pp. 4-10, 23.

Wilson, Richard, "A Nuclear Physicist Exposes Flying Saucers," *Look Magazine,* February 27, 1951.

Wood, Robert H., "Saucers, Secrecy, & Security," *Aviation Week*, February 19, 1951.

Yves Sillard, Letter from Director General of CNES, April 14, 1980. Appendix of CNES Work Document #4. "Study of Unidentified Aerospace Phenomena 1977-1981—Results and Perspectives. December 18, 1981. p.32

Zechel, Todd, "NI-CIA-CAP or NICAP," *MUFON UFO Journal* 133, January-February 1979.

Books

Baker, David, *The Rocket.* Crown Publishers: NY, 1978.

Ball, Desmond, *A Suitable Piece of Real Estate—American Installations in Australia.* Hale & Iremonger: 1980.

Ballester Olmos, Vicente-Juan, *A Catalogue of 200 Type-I UFO Events in Spain and Portugal.* Center for UFO Studies: Evanston, IL, 1976.

Ballester Olmos, Vicente-Juan, Expedientes Insólitos. Ediciones Temas de Hoy: Madrid, 1995.

Ballester Olmos, Vicente-Juan, Los OVNIS y la Ciencia. splugues de Llobregat, Plaza & Janés Editores: Barcelona, 1989.

Bamford, James, *Body of Secrets: Anatomy of the Ultra-secret National Security Agency.* New York, NY: Doubleday, 2001.

Bamford, James, *The Puzzle Palace: A Report on America's Most Secret Agency.* Houghton Mifflin: Boston, 1982.

Bloecher, Ted, *Report on the UFO Wave of 1947.* National Investigations Committee on Aerial Phenomena: Washington, D.C., 1967.

Bush, Vannevar, *Modern Arms and Free Men.* Simon and Schuster: New York, NY, 1949.

Cabell, Charles P., *A Man of Intelligence.* Edited by Charles P. Cabell, Jr. Impavide Publications: Colorado Springs, CO, 1997.

Cantril, Hadley, *The Invasion from Mars.* Princeton University Press: Princeton, NJ, 1940.

Chalker, William, *The Oz Files.* Duffy and Snellgrove: Potts Point, NSW, 1966.

Chester, Keith, *Strange Company.* Anomalist Books: 2007.

Citizens Against UFO Secrecy, *Documents Describing UFO / Helicopter Overflights of USAF Bases in 1975.* Center for UFO Studies: Chicago, IL, 1981.

Clark, Jerome, *The UFO Encyclopedia,* 2nd ed., 2 vols. Omnigraphics, Inc: Detroit, MI, 1998.

Clarke, David, *The UFO Files: The Inside Story of Real-Life Sightings.* The National Archives: Kew, Surrey, UK, 2009.

Craig, Roy, *UFOs.* University of North Texas Press: Denton, TX, 1995.

Dick, Steven J., *The Biological Universe.* Cambridge University Press: Cambridge, UK, 1996.

Dulles, Allen, *The Craft of Intelligence.* Harper and Row: New York, NY, 1963.

Durant, Robert J., *The Fitzgerald Report.* UFO Research Committee of Akron: Akron, OH, 1958.

Emenegger, Robert, *UFOs, Past, Present, and Future.* Ballantine: New York, NY, 1974.

Emsley, Clive, *Gendarmes and the State in Nineteenth-Century Europe.* Oxford University Press: Oxford, 1999.

Bibliography

Evans, Hilary and Dennis Stacy, *UFOs, 1947-1997.* John Brown Pub.: London, 1997.

Fawcett, Lawrence, and Barry Greenwood, *Clear Intent.* Prentice-Hall: Englewood Cliffs, NJ, 1984.

Fuller, John, *The Interrupted Journey.* Dial: New York, NY, 1966.

Gillmor, Daniel, (ed.) *Final Report of the Scientific Study of Unidentified Flying Objects.* Bantam Books: New York, NY, 1968.

Gross, Loren, *Charles Fort, the Fortean Society, and Unidentified Flying Objects.* Loren Gross: Fremont, California, 1976.

Gross, Loren, *UFOs: A History,* including monographs and supplements for 1947-1963. Loren Gross: Fremont, California, 2000.

Guieu, Jimmy, *Flying Saucers Come from Another World.* Hutchinson: London, 1956.

Haines, Richard F., *Melbourne Episode: Case Study of a Missing Pilot.* L.D.A. Press: Los Altos, CA, 1987.

Hall, Michael D., and Wendy A. Connors, *Alfred Loedding and the Great Flying Saucer Wave of 1947.* Rose Press: Albuquerque, New Mexico, 1998.

Hall, Richard, "Bridging 50 Years of UFO History," in Hilary Evans and Dennis Stacy (eds.), *UFOs 1947-1997,* John Brown: London, England, 1997.

Hall, Richard, *The UFO Evidence, Volume Two.* Scarecrow Press: Lanham, MD, 2000

Hall, Richard, *The UFO Evidence.* National Investigations Committee on Aerial Phenomena: Washington, D.C., 1964.

Hanson, Terry, *The Missing Times.* Xlibris Corporation, 2000.

Hogan, Michael J., *A Cross of Iron: Harry S. Truman and the Origins and the National Security State 1945-1954.* Cambridge University Press: New York, NY, 1998.

Holledge, James, *Flying Saucers over Australia.* London: Horwitz Publications, 1965.

Hynek, J. Allen, and Jacques Vallee, *The Edge of Reality.* Henry Regnery: Chicago, IL, 1975.

Hynek, J. Allen, *The Hynek UFO Report.* Dell: NY, 1977.

Jacobs, David, *The UFO Controversy in America.* University of Indiana Press: Bloomington, IN, 1975.

Keyhoe, Donald, *Aliens from Space.* Doubleday and Company: Garden City, NY, 1973.

Keyhoe, Donald, *Flying Saucer Conspiracy.* Henry Holt: New York, NY, 1955.

Keyhoe, Donald, *Flying Saucers from Outer Space.* Holt: New York, NY, 1953.

Keyhoe, Donald, *Flying Saucers: Top Secret.* G.P. Putnam: New York, NY, 1960.

Keyhoe, Donald, *The Flying Saucers are Real.* Fawcett Publications: New York, NY, 1950.

Killey, Kevin, and Gary Lester, *The Devil's Meridian.* Lester-Townsend Publications: Sydney, AU, 1980.

Klass, Philip J., *The Real Roswell Crashed-Saucer Coverup.* Prometheus Books: Amherst, New York, 1997.

Klass, Philip, *UFOs: the Public Deceived.* Prometheus: Buffalo, NY, 1983.

Kleinknecht, Kenneth, entry in Emme, Eugene (ed), *The History of Rocket Technology,* "The Rocket Research Airplanes." Wayne State University: Detroit, MI, 1964.

Kozicka, Maureen, *The Mystery of the Min Min Light.* Mt. Molloy Qld.: M. Kozicka, 1994.

Lieser, Robert A., unpublished work, *The Troubled Background of CIA's UFO Venture.*

Liljegren, Anders, and Clas Svahn, "The Ghost Rockets," in H. Evans and J. Spencer, *UFOs: 1947-1987.* Fortean Times: London, U.K.

Llewelyn, Ken, *Flight into the Ages.* Felspin Pty Ltd: Warriewood, N.S.W., 1991.

Lore, Gordon, and Harold Deneault, *Mysteries of the Skies.* Prentice Hall, Inc.: Englewood Cliffs, NJ, 1968.

Lorenzen, James and Coral Lorenzen, *The Great Flying Saucer Hoax.* William-Frederick: New York, NY, 1962.

Lorenzen, James and Coral Lorenzen, *UFOs Over the Americas.* Signet: New York, NY, 1968.

Manno, Jack, *Arming the Heavens.* Dodd-Mead: New York, NY, 1984.

McDonald, James, *UFOs: The Greatest Scientific Problem of Our Time?,* personally published and distributed. April 22, 1967.

Menzel, Donald, and Lyle Boyd, *The World of Flying Saucers.* Doubleday and Co.: NY, 1963.

Menzel, Donald, *Flying Saucers.* Harvard University Press: Cambridge, MA, 1953.

Michel, Aimé, *Flying Saucers and the Straight Line Mystery.* Criterion: New York, NY, 1958.

Michel, Aimé, *The Truth About Flying Saucers.* Criterion: New York, NY, 1956.

Miller, Max, *Flying Saucers.* Trend: Hollywood, CA, 1957.

Montague, Ludwell Lee, *General Walter Bedell Smith as Director of Central Intelligence.* Pennsylvania State University Press: University Park, PA, 1992.

Moore, Charles B., Benson Saler, and Charles A. Ziegler, *UFO Crash at Roswell: The Genesis of a Modern Myth.* Smithsonian Institution Press: Washington D.C., 1997.

Moore, Patrick, *Guide to the Planets*. Eyre and Spottiswoode: London, UK, 1955.

Page, Thornton, and Carl Sagan (eds), *UFOs: A Scientific Debate*. Cornel University Press: Ithaca, NY, 1972.

Pflock, Karl T., *Roswell: Inconvenient Facts and the Will to Believe*. Prometheus Books: Amherst, NY, 2001.

Quintanilla, Hector, "Project Blue Book's Last Years," in Hilary Evans and Dennis Stacy (eds.), *UFOs, 1947-1997*, John Brown: London, England, 1997.

Randle, Kevin, and Donald Schmitt, *UFO Crash at Roswell*. Avon Books: New York, NY, 1991.

Rodeghier, Mark, *UFO Reports Involving Vehicle Interference*. Center for UFO Studies: Evanston, IL, 1981.

Rossoni, David, Éric Maillot, and Éric DéGuillanume, *Les OVNI du CNES: 30 ans d'études officielles 1977-2007*. Valbonne: Éd. Book-e-book.com, 2007.

Rullán, Antonio, *The Levelland Sightings of 1957*. 2000.

Ruppelt, Edward J., *The Report on Unidentified Flying Objects*. Doubleday and Company: Garden City, NY, 1959 (second edition).

Ruppelt, Edward, *The Report on Unidentified Flying Objects* (uncorrected draft). Ruppelt files, held by the UFO Research Coalition.

Samuel, Wolfgang W.E., *American Raiders -- The Race to Capture the Luftwaffe's Secrets*. University Press of Jackson, 2004.

Saunders, David and Roger Harkins, *UFOs? Yes!*. World Publishing: New York, NY, 1968.

Schmidt, Reinhold, *Edge of Tomorrow: A True Account of Experiences with Visitors from Another Planet*. The author: Hollywood, CA, 1963.

Schuessler, John, *The Cash-Landrum Incident*. Geo-Graphics: LaPorte, Texas, 1998.

Scully, Frank, *Behind the Flying Saucers*. Henry Holt: NY, 1950.

Shrader, Welman, *Fifty Years of Flight*. Eaton Manufacturing: Cleveland, OH, 1953.

Simpson, Christopher, *The Science of Coercion, Communication Research, and Psychological Warfare*. Oxford University: Oxford, UK, 1994.

Southall, Ivan, *Woomera*. Angus and Robertson: Sydney, AU, 1962.

Stefan Possony, *Strategic Airpower*. Infantry Journal Press, 1949.

Strentz, Herbert, *A Survey of Press Coverage of Unidentified Flying Objects*, University of Northwestern Ph.D. dissertation, Evanston, IL, 1970.

Sturrock, Peter, *The UFO Enigma*. Warner Books: New York, NY, 2000.

Swords, Michael D., compiler; *The Levelland, Texas, Incidents, November 2-3, 1957, and Coincident Events of the Early November 1957 Wave*. Center for UFO Studies: Chicago, IL, October 1992.

Tacker, Lawrence, *Flying Saucers and the U.S. Air Force*. Van Nostrand: Princeton, NJ, 1960.

Valle, Jacques, *Anatomy of a Phenomenon*. Henry Regnery: Chicago, 1965.

Van Utrecht, Wim, "The Belgian 1989-1990 UFO Wave," in Hilary Evans and Denis Stacy, eds., *UFOs: 1947-1997*, pp. 165-176.

von Karman, Theodore, and Lee Edson, *The Wind and Beyond*. Little, Brown and Co.: Boston, MA, 1967.

W. Patrick McCray, *Keep Watching the Skies! The Story of Operation Moonwatch and the Dawn of the Space* Age. Princeton University Press: 2008.

Winkler, David F., *Searching the Skies*. USAF Air Combat Command: Langley Field, VA, 1997.

Government Documents

Australian Parliament, Hansard Parliamentary Records, August 14, 1952, November 20, 1953, November 24, 1959, and October 20, 1960.

Brazil's Department of the Navy, *Clarification of the Observation of unidentified flying objects sighted on the island of Trindade in the period of 12/5/57 to 1/16/58*. (English translation in the papers of the late Dr. Edward U. Condon at the American Philosophical Society in Philadelphia.)

Central Intelligence Agency, Frederick C. Durant, *Report on Meetings of Scientific Advisory Panel on Unidentified Flying Objects Convened by Office of Scientific Intelligence, CIA, January 14-18, 1953*. Washington, D.C., 1953.

Centre National D'Etudes Spatiales, No.1 Technical Report, *Analyse du problème du pré-traitement des données*. Toulouse, October 29, 1979.

Centre National D'Etudes Spatiales, No.16 Technical Report, *Analyse d'une Trace*. Toulouse, March 1, 1983.

Centre National D'Etudes Spatiales, No.17 Technical Report, *L'Amarante*. Toulouse, March 21, 1983.

Centre National D'Etudes Spatiales, No.18 Technical Report, *Le Point sur l'Utilisation des Reseaux de Diffraction*. Toulouse, March 15, 1983.

Bibliography

Cometa Report, "UFOs and Defense: What Should We Prepare For"Institute of Higher Studies for National Defense," July 1999.

Congressional Record-House Vol. 104, pt. 9, Roland V. Libonati, "Flying Saucers," remarks for Wednesday, June 18, 1958.

Congressional Record, Appendix, Vol. 96, part 17, September 20, 1950, p. A6711.

Department of Defense, *General John A. Samford Press Conference*. Director of Intelligence, U.S. Air Force, July 29, 1952.

Department of Defense, Joint Chiefs of Staff, *JANAP 146 (C): Communicating Instructions for Reporting Vital Intelligence Sightings from Airborne and Waterborne Sources.* Joint Communications-Electronics Committee: Washington, D.C., March 1954.

Department of Defense, News Release. January 22, 1959.

Department of Defense, Office of Public Information News Release, *Fact Sheet: Air Force's 10 year Study of Unidentified Flying Objects.* November 5, 1957.

The National Security Act of 1947, title 1, Sev 101[U.S.C.402] (Public Law No. 235, 80th Congress, 61 Stat. 495, 50 U.S.C. ch.15).

U.S. Congress, House. Committee on Science and Astronautics, *Symposium on Unidentified Flying Objects*. 90th Cong., 2nd sess., July 29, 1968.

U.S. Government Printing Office, Michael Donald, Brookings Institution Project Director, *Proposed Studies on the Implications of Peaceful Space Activities for Human Affairs.* Washington, D.C., 1961.

United States Air Force Research and Development, Louis Elterman, *Project Twinkle: Final Report*, November 21, 1951. Washington, D.C., December 11, 1951.

United States Air Force, *Air Force Regulation No. 200-2*: "Intelligence: Unidentified Flying Objects Reporting." August 26, 1953.

United States Air Force, Albert P.Simpson, *Mission Report No. 11-327. Headquarters VII Bomber Command, 2 May 1945,* Director of Intelligence. Washington, D.C.: Headquarters United States Air Force, January 22, 1953.

United States Air Force, Colonel Richard L. Weaver and 1st Lieutenant James McAndrew, *The Roswell Report: Fact versus Fiction in the New Mexico Desert.* Washington, D.C.: Headquarters United States Air Force, 1995.

United States Air Force, *Grudge Report.* Air Materiel Command, Wright-Patterson AFB, Dayton, Ohio, August 1949.

United States Air Force, Harold Steiner, *Special Report of the USAF Scientific Advisory Board Ad Hoc Committee to Review Project Blue Book.* March 1966.

United States Air Force, National Military Establishment Office of Public Information, *Project "Saucer."* Washington, D.C., April 27, 1949.

United States Air Force, *The Roswell Report: Case Closed.* Washington, D.C.: Headquarters United States Air Force, 1997.

United States General Accounting Office, *Report to the Honorable Steven H. Schiff, House of Representatives: Government Records: Results of a Search for Records Concerning the 1947 Crash Near Roswell, New Mexico.* Gaithersburg, MD, 1995.

United States Navy, Directorate of Intelligence and Office of Naval Intelligence, *Air Intelligence Report 100-203-79: Analysis of Flying Object Incidents in the U.S.* December 10, 1948.

Government Internal Communications

"Conference on Aerial Phenomena," report of a February 16, 1949, meeting at Los Alamos, with cover letter by Commander Richard Mandelkorn, USN, reporting for Sandia base. Obtained from the USAF through a Freedom of Information Act request.

Adams, William A., Colonel, memorandum (written by Dewey Fourney) to Office of Public Information, subject: "Inquiry from *Baltimore Evening Sun*," April 17, 1952. Obtained from the USAF through a Freedom of Information Act request.

Air Defense Command, general directive 200-1 to all commands, subject: "Unconventional Aircraft," April 11, 1951. Obtained from the USAF through a Freedom of Information Act request.

Allen, Brooke, Colonel, memorandum to Chief of Air Intelligence Division, October 11, 1948. Obtained from the USAF through a Freedom of Information Act request.

Anderson, S.E., memorandum to Director of Intelligence, subject: "Flying Discs," March 3, 1948. Obtained from the USAF through a Freedom of Information Act request.

Arcier, Francis A., memorandum to George Gregory, subject: "UFO Program," February 1, 1957. Obtained from the USAF through a Freedom of Information Act request

Author unidentified, Air Force memorandum of record, subject: "Temporary duty travel to Europe," April 29, 1952.

Obtained from the USAF through a Freedom of Information Act request.

Author unidentified, FBI internal memo, subject: "Unidentified Aerial Phenomena," May 19, 1950. Document is listed as "UFO Related Information from FBI Files: Part 7," *MUFON UFO Journal*, November-December 1978, p. 12. Obtained from the FBI through a Freedom of Information Act request.

Author unidentified, minutes of Branch Chief's meeting, August 11, 1952. Obtained from the CIA through a Freedom of Information Act request.

Author unidentified, office memorandum from Chief, Contact Division to Assistant for Operations, OSI, Subject: "California Committee for Saucer Investigation," February 9, 1953. Obtained from the FBI through a Freedom of Information Act request.

Author's name illegible, memorandum of record for General Charles P. Cabell, subject: to prepare response to Far East Air Force, July 31, 1950. Obtained from the USAF through a Freedom of Information Act request.

Author's name illegible, memorandum to director of the FBI, received at FBI on May 22, 1950. Document reported by Bruce Maccabee in "UFO Related Information from FBI Files: Part 7," MUFON UFO Journal, November-December 1978, p. 12. Obtained from the FBI through a Freedom of Information Act request.

Barber, Colonel, memorandum for Colonel Harold E. Watson, Air Materiel Command, July 7, 1950. Obtained from the USAF through a Freedom of Information Act request.

Belmont A., to L. Boardman, memorandum subject: "Flying Saucers," November 4, 1955, quoted in Gross, *UFOs: A History (1955, Sep.-Dec.)*. Loren Gross: Fremont, California, 2000.

Belmont, A., memorandum to L. Boardman, subject: "Flying Saucers," October 18, 1955, quoted in Gross, *UFOs: A History (1955, Sep.-Dec.)*. Loren Gross: Fremont, California, 2000.

Belmont, A.H., memorandum to Mr. Ladd, subject: "Flying Saucers," October 19, 1950. Obtained from the FBI through a Freedom of Information Act request.

Belmont, A.H., to V.P. Keay, memorandum, October 27, 1952. Obtained from the FBI through a Freedom of Information Act request.

Blair, W.D., Jr., of the *Baltimore Evening Sun*, letter attached to memorandum from Major Edwin G. Jane, AF Press Desk, to Directorate of Intelligence, Technical Capabilities Branch, April 9, 1952. Obtained from the USAF through a Freedom of Information Act request.

Boggs, Major J., memorandum of record, subject: "AEC request for Grudge files," May 24, 1950 (original request March 14, 1950).

Bolender, Carroll, H., Brigadier General, memorandum of record, subject: "Unidentified Flying Objects (UFO)," October 20, 1969. Obtained from the USAF through a Freedom of Information Act request.

Cabell, Charles P., General, draft of letter and notes to Air Force Air Intelligence Division, November 28, 1948, and November 30, 1948. Obtained from the USAF through a Freedom of Information Act request.

Cabell, Charles P., General, letter to Air Materiel Command, November 3, 1948. Obtained from the USAF through a Freedom of Information Act request.

Cabell, Charles P., General, memorandum to Commanding General Air Materiel Command, subject: "Flying Objects Incidents in the United States," November 3, 1948. Obtained from the USAF through a Freedom of Information Act request.

Cabell, Charles P., General, note to Air Force Office of Air Intelligence on redraft of response, April 21, 1949. Obtained from the USAF through a Freedom of Information Act request.

Carey, George G., memorandum to Deputy Director (Intelligence), subject: "USSR and Satellite Mention of Flying Saucers," August 22, 1952. Obtained from the CIA through a Freedom of Information Act request.

Chadwell, H. Marshall, memorandum of record, subject: "British Activity in the Field of UFOs," December 18, 1952. Obtained from the CIA through a Freedom of Information Act request.

Chadwell, H. Marshall, memorandum of record, subject: "Flying Saucers," December 3, 1952. Obtained from the CIA through a Freedom of Information Act request.

Chadwell, H. Marshall, memorandum to Deputy Director (Intelligence), subject: "Approval in Principle—External Research Project Concerned with Unidentified Flying Objects," No date. Obtained from the CIA through a Freedom of Information Act request.

Chadwell, H. Marshall, memorandum to Director of Central Intelligence, subject: "Flying Saucers," September 17, 1952. Obtained from the CIA through a Freedom of Information Act request.

Chadwell, H. Marshall, memorandum to Director of Central Intelligence, subject: "Flying Saucers," October 2, 1952 Obtained from the CIA through a Freedom of Information Act request.

Chadwell, H. Marshall, memorandum to Director of Central Intelligence, subject: "Flying Saucers," September 24, 1952. Obtained from the CIA through a Freedom of Information Act request.

Chadwell, H. Marshall, memorandum to Director of Central Intelligence, subject: "Unidentified Flying Objects,"

December 2, 1952. Obtained from the CIA through a Freedom of Information Act request.

Chadwell, H. Marshall, memorandum to Secretary of Defense, Subject: "Unidentified Flying Objects (Flying Saucers)," No date. Obtained from the CIA through a Freedom of Information Act request.

CIA memorandum, Deputy Chief Requirements Staff to Deputy Director Plans, subject: "Flying Saucers," August 20, 1952, quoted in Gerald K. Haines, "CIA's Role in the Study of UFOs, 1947-1990," *Studies in Intelligence 1*: 68, 1997.

Clark, Ralph I., memorandum to Robert Amory, Jr., July 29, 1952. Obtained from the CIA through a Freedom of Information Act request.

Clingerman, W.R., (AMC/ATIC), memorandum to Chief of Staff, USAF, Washington, D.C., subject: "Request for Study by Rand Project," October 22, 1948. Obtained from the USAF through a Freedom of Information Act request.

Cook, Eugene, Lt. Colonel, letter to Air Coordinating Committee, Dept. of Commerce, December 26, 1950. Obtained from the USAF through a Freedom of Information Act request.

Cybulski, J., Captain, "Unidentified Flying Objects (UFOB)," 3rd Commander's Conference, Ent AFB, CO, undated, but c. November 1954. Obtained from the USAF through a Freedom of Information Act request.

Dept of Defense document to multiple parties including the Sec of Def, Joint Chiefs of Staff, and the White House, Document 6846D13976, September 1976. Available at the National Security Agency website, http://www.nsa.gov/public_info/_files/ufo/joint_chiefs_staff_report.pdf.

Draft of the Preface to Project Blue Book No.14, undated. Obtained from the USAF through a Freedom of Information Act request.

Drain, Richard D., minutes of the Intelligence Advisory Committee, December 4, 1952. Obtained from the CIA through a Freedom of Information Act request.

Dunn, Frank L., Colonel, memorandum (written by Ray W. Taylor) to AFOIN-A, attn. Brig. Gen. Garland, subject: (Unclassified) "Declassification of Project BLUE BOOK Material," March 31, 1952. Obtained from the USAF through a Freedom of Information Act request.

Dunn, Frank L., memorandum (written by James J. Rodgers) to Assistant for Atomic Energy, subject: "Unconventional Aircraft," November 15, 1950. Obtained from the USAF through a Freedom of Information Act request.

Earnest, Lt. Colonel, memorandum to higher officers and Commands, September 8 [?], 1950. Obtained from the USAF through a Freedom of Information Act request.

Eiseman, Douglas W., Lt. Colonel (Executive, Air Intelligence Requirements Division), letter to Commanding General, Air Materiel Command, attention MICA [should be MCIA].

Eiseman, Douglas W., Lt. Colonel, memorandum to AGAO, subject: "Information Regarding the Flying Disks," July 21, 1947. Obtained from the USAF through a Freedom of Information Act request.

Eriksen, John G., Colonel, draft of letter to Colonel T.R. Johnson, July 5, 1956. Obtained from the USAF through a Freedom of Information Act request.

Eriksen, John G., Colonel, memorandum to Lt. Colonel T.R. Johnson, Director of Intelligence Office, subject: "UFO Movie," June 1, 1956.

Erikson, J.G., Colonel, memorandum to General Samford, subject: "Evaluation of News Articles Concerning Observation of Flying Saucers," March 4, 1952. Obtained from the USAF through a Freedom of Information Act request.

Evaluated Intelligence Report, subject: "Belgium and the UFO Issue, 30 March 30, 1990," Obtained from the DIA through a Freedom of Information Act request.

Evans, Philip G., Colonel, memorandum to Lt. Colonel Lawrence Tacker, subject: "Congressional Request for Summary of UFO Sighting (Mr. Robert Smart, House Armed Services Committee)," November 18, 1960. Obtained from the USAF through a Freedom of Information Act request.

Evans, Philip G., memorandum to HQ, USAF, Chief of Intelligence, "Unidentified Aerial Phenomena," December 27, 1960. Obtained from the USAF through a Freedom of Information Act request.

Fitch, E.G., memorandum to D.M. Ladd, subject: "Flying Discs," August 19, 1947. Obtained from the FBI through a Freedom of Information Act request.

Garland, William N., General and Colonel Harry J. Kieling, memorandum of record (written by Lt. Colonel Sterling), April 2, 1952. Obtained from the USAF through a Freedom of Information Act request.

Garland, William N., General, memorandum for General Samford, subject: "(Secret) Contemplated Action to Determine the Nature and origin of the Phenomena Connected with Reports of Unusual Flying Objects," January 3, 1952. Obtained from the USAF through a Freedom of Information Act request.

Garret, George, Lt. Colonel, draft summary, "Flying Discs," July 30, 1947, 7 pp. Obtained from the FBI through a Freedom of Information Act request.

Garrett, Lt. Colonel, analysis report, AFBIR-CO: "Flying Disks," July 30, 1947. Obtained from the FBI through a Freedom of Information Act request.

Gates, Quentin J., FAA memorandum to Manager, Air Traffic Division, AAL-500, December 18, 1986. Obtained from the USAF through a Freedom of Information Act request.

Gilbert, H.K., Colonel, to Commander 1006th Air Intelligence Service Squadron, (undated, c. mid-April 1958). Obtained from the USAF through a Freedom of Information Act request.

Glover, Colonel, memorandum of record, subject: "Reporting of information on unidentified flying objects," October 15, 1951. Obtained from the USAF through a Freedom of Information Act request.

Gordon, Ray A., memorandum of record, "The Air Force Stand on 'Flying Saucers'," briefing on August 22, 1952. Date otherwise unlisted. Obtained from the CIA through a Freedom of Information Act request.

Gregory, George, memorandum to Dr. Miley and Mr. Arcier, subject: "Preface to Project 'Blue Book' Nr. 14," July 12, 1957. Obtained from the USAF through a Freedom of Information Act request.

Gregory, George, memorandum to Major Byrnes, subject: "False Charges by NICAP regarding Air Force Findings in Oxnard and Other Cases," October 1, 1957. Obtained from the USAF through a Freedom of Information Act request.

Group Captain, D. Ops. (signature illegible), memorandum to Director of Air Force Intelligence, February 15, 1956.

Harris, Colonel, memorandum to higher officers, subject: reply to Colonel Watson regarding "proper procedure for handling unidentified aerial object reports," October 12, 1950. Obtained from the USAF through a Freedom of Information Act request.

Headquarters European Command, memorandum to Counter Intelligence regions, subject: "Essential Elements of Information," October 20-28, 1947. Obtained from the USAF through a Freedom of Information Act request.

Hennrick, C.E., memorandum to A.H. Belmont, subject: Frank Scully -- Security Matter, October 20, 1950. Obtained from the FBI through a Freedom of Information Act request.

Intelligence Report, Office of Chief of Naval Operations, Navy Department, subject: "Unidentified Phenomena," February 10, 1950. Obtained from the FBI through a Freedom of Information Act request.

Irholm, Gunnar, Lieutenant, report, "med rapport om flygande projektil to Försvarstabens Luftförsvarsavdelning," August 14, 1946.

Johnson, Dave, telegram transcript to Lt. General George E. Stratemeyer, Air Defense Command, Mitchell Field, New York, November 18, 1947. Obtained from the USAF through a Freedom of Information Act request.

Johnson, Lyndon, letter to the War Department, July 8, 1947. Obtained from the USAF through a Freedom of Information Act request.

Joint Chiefs of Staff (Joint and Allied Communications Publications), *JANAP 146B*, "Communications Instructions for Reporting Vital Intelligence Sightings from Aircraft (CIRVIS)," September 6, 1951.

Kaplan, Joseph, letter to Major General Charles P. Cabell, July 13, 1949. Obtained from the USAF through a Freedom of Information Act request.

Kieling, Harry J., Colonel, draft letter to Commanding General of the Far East Air Force, July 31, 1950. Obtained from the USAF through a Freedom of Information Act request.

Kieling, Harry J., Colonel, letter (written by Lt. Colonel Willis) to 1009th Special Weapons Squadron, subject: "Unconventional Aircraft," January 5, 1951. Obtained from the USAF through a Freedom of Information Act request.

Kieling, Harry J., Colonel, memorandum (written by Dewey Fournet) to Directorate of Research and Development, subject: (Unclassified) "Project Twinkle," March 4, 1952. Obtained from the USAF through a Freedom of Information Act request.

King, Kenneth, Colonel, (Counter Intelligence Division, Office of Special Investigations) memorandum to Deputy Chief of Staff of Development, subject: "Dr. Anthony O. Mirarchi, former AFCL Employee -- Violation of AFR 205.1.," September 2, 1953. Obtained from the USAF through a Freedom of Information Act request.

Ladd, D.M., memorandum to the Director of the FBI, subject: "Flying Saucers," March 26, 1950. Obtained from the FBI through a Freedom of Information Act request.

Lambrechts, P., Major, preliminary report, subject: "Report Concerning the Observation of UFOs during the Night of March 30 and 31 1990," June 22, 1990. Belgian Air Force.

Lamphire, Wallace R., memorandum to Richard M. Bissell, subject: "Unidentified Flying Saucers (UFO)," June 11, 1957. Obtained from the CIA through a Freedom of Information Act request.

LaPaz, Lincoln, letter to Colonel Doyle Rees, subject: "Anomalous Luminous Phenomena, Sixth Report," August 17, 1949. Obtained from the USAF through a Freedom of Information Act request.

LeMay, Curtis, note to Air Intelligence Requirements Division, subject: "Flying Saucer Phenomena," August 29, 1947. Obtained from the USAF and FBI through a Freedom of Information Act request.

Leo, Stephen F., memorandum to Director of Intelligence, subject: "Flying Saucer Story," April (day unreadable), 1949. Obtained from the USAF through a Freedom of Information Act request.

Lexow, W.E., (Chief, Applied Science Division, Scientific Intelligence) memorandum of record, subject: "Meeting with Air Force Personnel Concerning Scientific Advisory Panel Report on Unidentified Flying Objects dated 17 January

1953 (Secret)," May 16, 1958. Obtained from the USAF through a Freedom of Information Act request.

Mandelkorn, Richard, USN, transcript of "Conference on Aerial Phenomena," (Sandia) February 16, 1949. Obtained from the USAF through a Freedom of Information Act request.

McCoy, Howard M., Colonel (Chief of Intelligence), letter to Chief of Staff, United States Air Force, attention: Lt. Col. George Garrett, January 23, 1948.

McCoy, Howard M., Colonel, memorandum to Chief of Staff, November 8, 1948. Obtained from the USAF through a Freedom of Information Act request.

McCoy, Howard M., Colonel, memorandum to Chief of Staff, USAF, object: "Project Status Report on Project 'SIGN'," February 9, 1949. Obtained from the USAF through a Freedom of Information Act request.

McCoy, Howard M., Colonel, memorandum to Chief of Staff, USAF, subject: "Flying Object Incidents in the United States," November 8, 1948. Obtained from the USAF through a Freedom of Information Act request.

McCoy, Howard M., Colonel, memorandum to Chief of Staff, USAF, subject: "Project 'SIGN'," April 23, 1948. Obtained from the USAF through a Freedom of Information Act request.

McCoy, Howard M., Colonel, memorandum to Chief of Staff, USAF, subject: "Transmittal of Project 'SIGN' Incident Summaries," December 6, 1948. Obtained from the USAF through a Freedom of Information Act request.

McCoy, Howard M., Colonel, memorandum to Commanding General, Army Air Forces, Washington, D.C., subject: "Flying Disk," September 24, 1947. Obtained from the USAF through a Freedom of Information Act request.

McCoy, Howard M., Colonel, memorandum to Commanding General, USAF, November 18, 1947. Obtained from the USAF through a Freedom of Information Act request.

McCoy, Howard M., Colonel, memorandum to Lt. Colonel George Garrett, subject: "Flying Discs," January 16, 1948. Obtained from the USAF through a Freedom of Information Act request.

McCoy, Howard M., letter to Central Intelligence Agency, subject: "Project 'SIGN'," October 7, 1948. Obtained from the USAF through a Freedom of Information Act request.

McCoy, Howard, M., memorandum to Chief of Staff, USAF, subject: "Interview of Brig. Gen. Erik N. Nelson," date of memo not readable. Obtained from the USAF through a Freedom of Information Act request.

McDonald, George (but written by Lt. Col. Thomas), letter to Director of Research and Development, subject: "Analysis of 'Flying Disc' Reports," December 22, 1947.

McDonald, George C., memorandum to Director of Research and Development, subject: "Analysis of 'Flying Disc' Reports," December 22, 1947. Obtained from the USAF through a Freedom of Information Act request.

McSwain, C.C., memorandum to J. Edgar Hoover, subject: "Flying Saucers Observed over Oak Ridge Area," January 10, 1949. Obtained from the USAF through a Freedom of Information Act request.

Medaker, Major, SAC / SP message, subject: "Defense Against Helicopter Assault," October 29, 1975. Obtained from the USAF through a Freedom of Information Act request.

Memorandum of record for Director, FBI, subject: "Detroit Flying Saucer Club. Espionage-X," undated, Obtained from the FBI through a Freedom of Information Act request.

Moore, Ernest, Brigadier General, letter to Air Materiel Command, attention Chief of Intelligence Department, subject: "(Restricted) Releasing Results of Analysis and Evaluation of Unidentified Aerial Objects. Reports," October 18 [?], 1950. Obtained from the USAF through a Freedom of Information Act request.

Moore, Ernest, Brigadier General, memorandum of record (written by Major Aaron Boggs), re: "Flying Saucer Story" release, April 21, 1949. Obtained from the USAF through a Freedom of Information Act request.

Moore, Ernest, Brigadier General, memorandum of record (written by Major de La Vigne), subject: "Proposed Magazine Article by Sidney Shalett," March 2, 1949. Obtained from the USAF through a Freedom of Information Act request.

Moore, Ernest, Brigadier General, memorandum of record, (prepared by the Air Force Office of Air Intelligence), subject: "Prepare response to Walter Winchell's comments of 3 April 1949," April 4, 1949. Obtained from the USAF through a Freedom of Information Act request.

Moore, Ernest, Brigadier General, memorandum to Chief: Evaluation Division, Chief: Air Targets Division, and Chief: Estimates Division, subject: "Unidentified Objects," July 1, 1950. Obtained from the USAF through a Freedom of Information Act request.

Moore, Ernest, General, memorandum of record to Air Force Air Intelligence Division, November 24, 1948. Obtained from the USAF through a Freedom of Information Act request.

Newburger, Sidney, Security Operations Branch, USAF, memorandum to Carroll L. Tyler, OSI, subject: "Aerial Phenomena," November 30, 1949. Obtained from the USAF through a Freedom of Information Act request.

Nuckols letter to Colonel [Sory] Smith, [Director, Air Information Division, Directorate of Public Relations] April 6, 1949. Obtained from the USAF through a Freedom of Information Act request.

O'Conner, Robert E., message to Commander 4602nd AISS, March 27, 1957. Obtained from the USAF through a Freedom of Information Act request.

Odarenko, Todos M., memorandum to Acting Asst. Director for Scientific Intelligence, subject: "Unusual UFOB Report," July 12, 1955. Obtained from the CIA through a Freedom of Information Act request.

Odarenko, Todos M., memorandum to Assistant Director, Scientific Intelligence, subject: "Current Status of Unidentified Flying Objects (UFOs) Project," December 17, 1953. Obtained from the CIA through a Freedom of Information Act request.

Odarenko, Todos, memorandum to Director of Scientific Intelligence, subject: "Unidentified Flying Objects," August 8, 1955. Obtained from the CIA through a Freedom of Information Act request.

Office of Naval Intelligence, Op-322F2-Weekly Briefing Topic, April 4, 1950. Obtained from the USN through a Freedom of Information Act request.

Office of the AC of S, G-2, Headquarters, Fourth Army, memorandum and summary of information, subject: "Unconventional Aircraft," January 13, 1949. Obtained from the USAF through a Freedom of Information Act request.

O'Keefe, Richard J., Major General (Deputy Inspector General, USAF), Operations and Training Brief, subject: "UFOs – Serious Business," December 24, 1959.

Quarles draft letter to Congressman Moss, memorandum from Colonel T.R. Johnson discussing desired contents of letter, June 25, 1956. Obtained from the USAF through a Freedom of Information Act request.

Reber, James Q., to Deputy Director (Intelligence), subject: "Flying Saucers," October 13, 1952.

Rees, Doyle, Lt. Colonel, memorandum and letter to Director of Special Investigations, Office of the Inspector General, subject: "Unknown (aerial phenomena)," USAF, Washington, D.C., May 12, 1949. Obtained from the USAF through a Freedom of Information Act request.

Roach, R.R., memorandum to A.H. Belmont, September 23, 1957. Obtained from the FBI through a Freedom of Information Act request.

Roach, R.R., memorandum to A.H. Belmont, subject: "Unidentified Flying Object Reported on September 20, 1957," Intelligence Advisory Committee, Watch Committee, September 23, 1957. Obtained from the CIA through a Freedom of Information Act request.

Rochlen, A.M., letter to Brigadier General Harold E. Watson, April 16, 1956, quoted in Gross, *UFOs: A History (1956, Jan.-Apr.)*. Loren Gross: Fremont, California, 2000.

Rogers, Colonel, Deputy for Intelligence for the Commanding General of the Far East Air Force, memorandum to Director of Intelligence USAF, subject: "Unidentified Object," June 8, 1950. Obtained from the USAF through a Freedom of Information Act request.

Russell, Richard B., letter to Thomas K. Finletter, Secretary of the Air Force, February 21, 1952. Obtained from the USAF through a Freedom of Information Act request.

Ryan, Thomas S., Lt. Colonel, Air Intelligence Information Report, subject: "Observations of a Traveller in USSR," October 14, 1955, quoted in Gross, *UFOs: A History (1955, Sep.-Dec.)*. Loren Gross: Fremont, California, 2000.

SAC San Francisco to D.M. Ladd, Subject: "Flying Disks," July 28, 1947. Obtained from the FBI through a Freedom of Information Act request.

Sanford, Lindsey J., letter to Air Materiel Command, subject: "Request for reports," March 10, 1950. Obtained from the USAF through a Freedom of Information Act request.

Schulgen, George F., General, to Director, Federal Bureau of Investigation, September 5, 1947. Obtained from the FBI through a Freedom of Information Act request.

Schweizer, John, Colonel, memorandum for a draft letter to Director of Intelligence, United States Army, August 19, 1949. Obtained from the USAF through a Freedom of Information Act request.

Schweizer, John, Colonel, memorandum of record (written by Major Aaron J. Boggs), June 28, 1949. Obtained from the USAF through a Freedom of Information Act request.

Schweizer, John, Colonel, memorandum of record (written by Major Aaron J. Boggs), June 16, 1949. Obtained from the USAF through a Freedom of Information Act request.

Scoville, Herbert, memorandum to Acting Director, Central Intelligence, subject: "Unidentified Flying Object Reported on 20 September, 1957," September 21, 1957. Obtained from the CIA through a Freedom of Information Act request.

Scoville, Herbert, memorandum, subject: "Interview with (deleted)," October 27, 1955, quoted in Gross, *UFOs: A History (1955, Sep.-Dec.)*. Loren Gross: Fremont, California, 2000.

Simpson, Albert P. (Chief, USAF Historical Division, Maxwell AFB, Alabama), letter to Major General John A. Samford, Director of Intelligence, Headquarters USAF, January 22, 1953.

Stattler, C.J., Lt. Colonel, memorandum to AFOIC, subject: "Special Instruction, for preparing a letter to all major commands," August 29, 1950. Obtained from the USAF through a Freedom of Information Act request.

Strong, P.G., memorandum to Assistant Director, Scientific Intelligence, subject: "Report on Book Entitled 'Flying Saucers from Outer Space'," December 8, 1953. Obtained from the CIA through a Freedom of Information Act request.

Tauss, Edward, memorandum to Deputy Assistant Director/SI, subject: "Flying Saucers," August 1, 1952. Obtained from the CIA through a Freedom of Information Act request.

Taylor, Robert (written by Lt. Col. Garrett), letter to Deputy Chief of Air Staff for Research and Development, subject: "Flying Saucer phenomena," August 22, 1947. Obtained from the USAF through a Freedom of Information Act request.

Taylor, Robert, to Deputy Chief of Air Staff for Research and Development, subject: "Flying Saucer Phenomena," August 22, 1947. Obtained from the USAF through a Freedom of Information Act request.

Taylor, Robert, memorandum to Director of Public Relations, subject: "Flying Discs," December 11, 1947. Obtained from the USAF through a Freedom of Information Act request.

Twining, N.F., General, memorandum (written by Colonel Howard McCoy) to Commanding General, Air Materiel Command, Wright Field, Dayton, Ohio, subject: "Reported Sightings of Flying Discs," September 21, 1947. Obtained from the USAF through a Freedom of Information Act request.

Twining, Nathan F., General, (written by Major Turk) memorandum for Secretary Finletter, subject: "Evaluation of Observation of Unidentified Object in the Far East," March, 1952. Obtained from the USAF through a Freedom of Information Act request.

U.S. Army Intelligence, 111th CIC Detachment, Knoxville, TN. "Summary of Information," October 21, 1950, quoted in Gross, *UFOs: A History* (1950, Aug.-Dec.). Loren Gross: Fremont, California, 2000.

United States Air Forces in Europe (USAFE) 14, IT 1524, Top Secret, USAFE document. November 4, 1948.

von Karman, Theodore, letter to General Charles P. Cabell, February 11, 1949. Obtained from the USAF through a Freedom of Information Act request.

Watson, Harold E., Colonel, letter to Director of Intelligence, April 23, 1951. Obtained from the USAF through a Freedom of Information Act request.

Welch, Clare, Colonel, Air Materiel Command, letter to Brigadier General Ernest Moore, November 1, 1950. Obtained from the USAF through a Freedom of Information Act request.

Willis, Lt. Colonel, memorandum of record, subject: "To prepare a non-military letter to Mr. Robert B. Sibley for signature of the DI/USAF," January 28, 1951. Obtained from the USAF through a Freedom of Information Act request.

Wing Commander, RAAF Intelligence (signature illegible), letter to Director of Air Force Intelligence, subject: "Flying Saucers," October 19, 1955.

Wright, Edward K., memorandum to President Harry Truman, subject: "Ghost Rockets Over Scandinavia," August 1, 1946. Obtained from the USAF through a Freedom of Information Act request.

Wynn, Edward, Colonel, memorandum to Secretary of Air Force, subject: "Congressional Committee Staff Member Visit," August 16, 1961. Obtained from the USAF through a Freedom of Information Act request.

Media

"Meet the Authors", WOR-TV broadcast, October 21, 1962.

"*UFOs: Friends, Foes or Fantasy,*" CBS Reports, hosted by Walter Cronkite, May 10, 1966.

Callahan, John, testimony to the National Press Club, May 9, 2001.

CNES Press Communiqué, CP 075-2005, Paris, September 28, 2005. *CNES* website, http://www.cnes.fr/automne_modules_files/pPressReleases/public/r549_81_r390_pr075-2005-unidentified_aerospace_phenomena.pdf. Accessed February 19, 2012.

de Brouwer, Wilfred, Major General, statement before the National Press Club, November 12, 2007.

Sillard, Yves, interview by Vincent Roux, Radio France International, September 29, 2005.

Symington, Fife, CNN Newscast of interview by Gary Tuchman, re: remarks at the National Press Club, March 21, 2007.

Taylor, Henry, "The Flying Saucer," *Your Land and Mine* radio program, Dallas, Texas, March 27, 1950.

The Case of the Flying Saucer, hosted by Edward R. Murrow, CBS television documentary, April 7, 1950.

The UFO Oral History Project, Thomas Tulien Producer, James Bittick interview by Thomas Tulien, Minneapolis, MN, October 28, 2002.

The UFO Oral History Project, Tomas Tulien Producer, Frank E.Baker interview by Thomas Tulien, Minneapolis, MN, October 20, 2002.

The UFO Oral History Video Project, video cassette, created by Tom Tulien. Video: July 2000 "J.J. Kaliszewski."

Unidentified Flying Objects, movie production by Greene, Clarence, and Russell Rouse, United Artists, 1956.

Newspapers

"100 Mystery Flying Objects Spotted Here," *Wilmington* [DE] *Morning News*, July 9, 1954.

"15% of Saucer Reports Are Labeled Mystery," United Press news story, dateline: Dayton, OH, July 17, 1952.

"AF Stifles Saucer Reports of Civilians, Ex-Admiral Says," *New York World-Telegram*, January 19, 1957.

"Air Force Denies It Hides Hunks of Flying Saucers," Associated Press, dateline: Washington, D.C., March 23, 1954.

"Air Force Explains Mysteries: Strange Flying Objects Held Hoaxes or Sightings of Natural Phenomena," *Washington Post*, November 16, 1957.

"Air Force Set to Study 3 of 46 Objects," *Washington Post and Times Herald,* November 7, 1957, from Associated Press news story, dateline: Colorado Springs, CO, November 7, 1957.

"Arkansas Has Its Share; Pilot Sticks to His Story," *Arkansas Gazette*, July 24, 1955.

"Army says what Disks are NOT," *New York Times*, July 8, 1947.

"Brazil Has a Secret; Can't Explain It," *Los Angeles Times*, February 26, 1958

"Cal Tech Expert Also Denies Weapons Story," Associated Press, in *Long Beach Press-Telegram*, April 5, 1950.

"Condon, UFO Agnostic, Should Keep Sparks Flying," *Denver Post*, October 19, 1966.

"Disks Discounted: Blandy Waits to See Disks before his Eyes," *New York Times*, July 8, 1947.

"Doolittle skall bara prata bensin – har hört om spökbomber," *Expressen*, August 21, 1946.

"Doolittle studerar bara bruket av vår ekoradio," *Dagens Nyheter,* August 14, 1946.

"Eight Officers Report Seeing Flying Saucers," *Red Bluff* [CA] *Daily News,* August 15, 1960.

"Expert Debunks 'Saucer' Stories," *Chicago American*, January 31, 1956.

"Expert Forms Unit to Study Space Objects," *Washington Post and Times-Herald,* January 17, 1957, Associated Press wire story, dateline: January 17, 1957, Washington, D.C.

"Experts Up in Air Over Sky Phantom," *Chicago Tribune*, July 29, 1960.

"Fjärrdirigerade bomber spökar lite varstans," *Morgon-Tidningen*, May 26, 1946.

"Floating Mystery Ball is New Nazi Air Weapon," *New York Times*, December 14, 1944.

"Flying Disc — Astronomer Views Sky Visitor," United Press, dateline: Flagstaff, AZ, May 23, 1950.

"Flying Discs Book Declared Closed," *Pendleton East Oregonian*, January 31, 1948, quoted in Loren Gross, *UFOs: A History, 1948*. Loren Gross: Fremont, California, 2000.

"Flying Saucer Radar, Spotter, Posts Are Urged," United Press news story, dateline: Scituate, MA, February 26, 1951.

"Flying Saucer Scare Solved: Gen. Mills Chief in L.A. Tells Research," *Los Angeles Herald Express*, October 4, 1954.

"Flying Saucers Are Real, Lear Says," *Grand Rapids Herald,* AP news story, dateline: Bogota, Colombia, February 2, 1955.

"Flying Saucers Not Just Balloons, Says Scientist," AP news story, February 26, 1951.

"Former CIA Chief Urges UFO Investigation," *Jersey Journal*, Jersey City, NJ, May 21, 1960.

"Gen. Ramey Empties Roswell Saucer," *Roswell Daily Record,* July 9, 1947.

"I Saw Flying Disc, Rep. Engel Asserts," United Press news release, dateline: Washington, D.C., April 5, 1950.

"Jerome Teachers, Students Watch Strange Occurrence in the Sky," *Marysville* [OH] *Evening Journal-Tribune*, October 25, 1954.

"Londoners Panicked by TV 'Invasion' Play," UPI News story, dateline: London, U.K., February 21, 1959.

"Mars Acts Up: Strange Formations Seen on Planet," Associated Press news release, dateline: Osaka, Japan, April 10, 1950.

"'Mars Raiders' Cause Quito Panic; Mob Burns Radio Plant, Kills 15; QUITO PANIC CAUSED BY 'MARS RAIDERS'," New York Times, February 14, 1944, front page.

"'Martian Invasion' Terrorizes Chile," *New York Times*, November 14, 1944, front page.

"Men of Mars May Replace Flying Saucers," Associated Press story, dateline: Portland, Oregon, July 26, 1948, cited in Loren Gross, *UFOs: A History, 1948*. Loren Gross: Fremont, California, 2000.

"Meteorregn över Västerbotten," *Umebladet*, February 22,1946.

"Missile Aide Tells of Seeing Flying Fireball," Associated Press news story, dateline: Lubbock, TX, November 4, 1957.

"Missiles Expert 'Convinced' Flying Saucers From Planets," *Christian Science Monitor*, February 23, 1950.

"Most UFOs Explainable, Says Scientist," Elmira Star-Gazette, January 26, 1967.

"Mystery 'Flying Discs' Sighted Over No. Japan," *San Francisco Call,* Associated Press, dateline: Northern Japan, January 21, 1953.

"Mystiskt ljus över Malmö," *Norra Västerbotten*, January 8, 1946.

Bibliography

"New Aerial Mystery," Associated Press story, dateline: Yakima, Washington, July 25, 1948, cited in Loren Gross, *UFOs: A History, 1948*. Loren Gross: Fremont, California, 2000.

"Ny Målillagrop förbyllar FOA," *Göteborgs-Posten, October 29, 1976.*

"RAAF [Roswell Army Air Force] Captures Flying Saucer On Ranch in Roswell Region," *Roswell Daily Record*, July 8, 1947.

"Rickenbacker Says Saucers Not From Mars," Associated Press news release, dateline: Indianapolis, IN, June 12, 1950.

"Scientist Raps Saucer Report: AMC Here Continues Study," Associated Press news story, dateline: Scituate, MA, February 25, 1951.

"Shoot to Kill: Pacific Navy Fliers Ordered to Engage Saucers," *Fullerton [CA] News-Tribune,* July 26, 1956.

"Sighting 'Shakes' Scientists," *El Paso Times*, November 7, 1957.

"Spyglasses Search Through the Southwest Sky But Great What-was-it Keeps Out of Sight," *Louisville [KY] Courier-Journal,* January 9, 1948.

"Swedes report 'Flying Saucer' near Reds' secret Baltic bases," *The New York Post,* December 18, 1953.

"White House Pooh-poohs 'Secret Weapon' Saucers," Associated Press, dateline: Key West, FL., April 4, 1950.

AFP (French Press Agency). March 22, 2007.

Aftonbladet, February 12, 1937, and May 28, 1946.

Allen, Robert B., "AEC Wants Info on Flying Saucers Seen Near A-Plants," *The Oak Ridger* [Oak Ridge, TN] , October 12, 1950.

Alsop, Joseph, and Stewart Alsop, "Problems of Scientific Developments," dateline: Washington, D.C., February 20, 1952.

Amarillo Times, July 10, 1947, quoted in Loren Gross, *UFOs: A History, Supplemental Notes for 1947, July 7th - July 10th*. Loren Gross: Fremont, California, 2000.

Associated Press news story, dateline Kelowna, British Columbia, November 10, 1957.

Associated Press news story, dateline: Dayton, Ohio, October 5, 1948, cited in Loren Gross, *UFOs: A History, 1948*. Loren Gross: Fremont, California, 2000.

Barry, Bob, "12 Years of Flying Saucers," open letter to media outlets, June 24, 1959.

Blakeslee, Alton, "Flying Saucers Are Explained," Associated Press news story, February 13, 1951.

Bridwell, Lowell, "Aerial Experts Still Mystified By Stories of 'Flying Saucers'," *New York World-Telegram*, August 3, 1953.

Broad, William J., "Air Force Details a New Theory in U.F.O. Case," *The New York Times*, June 25, 1997.

Broad, William J., "Wreckage in the Desert Was Odd but Not Alien," *New York Times*, September 18, 1994.

Chapman, Ralph, "Flying Saucer Sightings Still Get Air Force Study", *New York [NY] Herald Tribune*, March 1, 1959.

Chicago Daily Tribune, July 7, 1947, quoted in Loren Gross, *UFOs: A History, Supplemental Notes for 1947, June 24th - July 6th*. Loren Gross: Fremont, California, 2000.

Clifford, Craig, "Saucer Sightings Making AF Weary," Scripps-Howard wire story, Dayton, OH, November 7, 1957.

Considine, Bob, "Air Force Insists Imagination, Reflections have Tricked Public," International News Service column, dateline: New York, November 16, 1950.

Dagens Nheter, December 28, 1933 and January 2,11,13,26, 1934 and February 3, 1934 and March 4, 1934 and September 23, 1934 and July 9, 1935 and January 30, 1937 and February 3,6,18, 1937 and May 19, 1937 and July 29, 1946 and December 20, 1953.

Dayton (OH) *Journal-Herald*, February 15, 1951, article quoted in toto by Gross, *UFOs: A History, 1951* supplement pp. 15-16. Loren Gross: Fremont, California, 2000.

Denver Colorado Post, July 4, 1947, quoted in Loren Gross, *UFOs: A History, Supplemental Notes for 1947, June 24th - July 6th*. Loren Gross: Fremont, California, 2000.

Dittmer, Dean, "See Flying Spheres," United Press news release, February 19, 1952.

Downing, Lord, "I Believe in Flying Saucers," *London Sunday-Dispatch,* July 11, 1954.

Ellis, Paul, "Those Flying Saucers Are Here Again," United Press release, [NY], March 8, 1950.

Financial Times, London, April 18, 1990.

Gordon, Sam, "Flying Saucer Probe Is Asked," *Washington [D.C.] Daily News*, April 4, 1956.

Göteborgs-Tidningen, April 12, 1967.

Harmon, Amy, "Flying Saucer Buffs to Mark Half Century of Hazy History," *The New York Times*, June 14, 1997.

INS news story, July 28, 1952, dateline: Washington, D.C.

Joiner, Angelia, *Stephenville Empire Tribune*, January 10, 11, 13, 2008.

Kaliszewski, J.J., comments reported in United Press news story, dateline: Minneapolis, Minnesota, April 12, 1952.

Key, William, "Sky Devil-ship Scares Pilots," *Atlanta Journal,* July 25, 1948.

Larsen, Douglas, "U.S. Air Force Has Flying Disc Debunker," NEA news release, dateline: Washington, D.C., April 4, 1950.

Larsson, Kurt, telephone interview, October 7, 1984; *Norrbottens-Kuriren*: "Ytterligare en rymdprojektil ner i Norrbottenssjö" July 22, 1946.

Latham, Sally, "Jax Mayor Has Near-Miss With Wednesday's flying Whatsis," *Fort Pierce* [FL] *News Tribune*, 26 March 1961.

Lawrence, David, "Flying Saucer 'Mystery' Solved Officially At Last," *New York Herald Tribune*, November 2, 1955.

Le Monde. "Yves Sillard, Secretary General of NATO". December 13th, 1997.

Lester, John, "Flying Saucer Captured, U.S. Aide Claims," *Newark* [NJ] *Star-Ledger*, December 23, 1958.

Lester, John, "Pilots Call Air Force Secrecy on Flying Saucers 'Ridiculous'," *Newark* [NJ] *Star-Ledger*, December 22, 1958.

Lester, John, "Radar Experts Track Mysterious Flying Objects," *Newark* [NJ] *Star-Ledger*, December 19, 1958.

Leviero, Anthony, "Air Force Remains Calm while the 'Saucers' Fly," *The New York Times*, December 19, 1954.

Leviero, Anthony, "President Discounts 'Saucer' from Space," *New York Times,* December 16, 1954.

Loedding, Alfred, quoted in "Princeton Engineer Believes Flying Saucers Real Thing," *Trenton [*NJ] *Times-Advertiser*, October 10, 1954.

London Daily Telegraph, June 26, 1958, dateline: Lisbon, Portugal, quoted in Loren Gross, UFOs: A History, Supplemental Notes for 1958, May-June. Loren Gross: Fremont, California, 2000.

Lucas, Jim G., "5 to 10 'Saucers' Reported Nightly by Airline Pilots," *Rocky Mountain News*, Denver, CO, Scripps-Howard, dateline: Washington, February 12, 1954.

Lucas, Jim G., "Flying Saucer Sightings Increase," Scripps-Howard, dateline: Washington, D.C., February 13, 1954.

Lynam, Marshall, "Did Space Ship Visit Levelland?," *The Fort Worth [*TX] *Press*, November 17, 1957.

Marvel, William, "UFO Project Is Called a Cloudy Caper," *Rocky Mountain News,* May 1, 1968.

Matador Texas Tribune, July 3, 1947; quoted in Loren Gross*, UFOs: A History, Supplemental Notes for 1947, June 24th - July 6th*. Loren Gross: Fremont, California, 2000.

Melbourne Sun, January 5, 1954.

Michelmore, Peter, "The Flying Saucer Chasers," Sydney [Australia] Sun-Herald, November 26, 1967.

Miles, Marvin, "U.S. Officers Report Seeing Flying Disks," *Los Angeles Times*, August 30, 1949, p. 1.

Mirarchi, Anthony, interview in the *Quincy* (ME) *Patriot Ledger*, February 27, 1951.

Nationen [Norway], November 3, 1936.

New York Herald Tribune, Paris edition. October 6th, 1954.

Newark [NJ] *Star-Ledger*, December 21, 1958.

Newark [NJ] *Star-Ledger*, December 24, 1958.

Norrbottens-Kuriren, December 12-13, 1933 and January 12, 26, 27,29, 1934 and February 3, 1934 and March 5, 1934 and July 30, 1946.

Pearson, Drew, "Worried About Flying Saucers?," syndicated column, Washington, D.C., March 31, 1950.

Phelan, James, "U.S. Saucer Expert Debunks 'Em,"*Long Beach* [CA] *Independent*, October 9, 1953.

Pillsbury, Fred, "Soviet Saucers Spied on Atom Tests, Expert Says," *Quincy* [ME] *Patriot Ledger*, February 27, 1951.

Piteå-Tidningen, February 15, 1937.

Riley, Albert, "Atlanta Pilots Report Wingless Sky Monster," *Atlanta Constitution,* July 25, 1948.

Roswell Morning Dispatch, July 1, 1947, quoted in Loren Gross, *UFOs: A History, Supplemental Notes for 1947, June 24th - July 6th*. Loren Gross: Fremont, California, 2000.

San Francisco Examiner, July 4, 1947, dateline: Wright Field, Ohio, July 3, 1947.

Stair, Joseph, "Saucers May Be Just That," *Detroit* [MI] *Times*, February 26, 1959.

Stockholmstidningen, January 11, 1934.

Sweeney, Dick, "Air Force Uncertain About Flying Disks, Says Santa Monican," *Santa Monica* [CA] *Evening Outlook*, October 13, 1953.

Troconis, Guillermo, "Brazilian Air Force Affirms Existence of Flying Saucers," translation of a South American news story by Alexander Mebane of CSI-NY (National Investigations Committee on Aerial Phenomena files), December 20, 1954.

Walker, Tom, "Belgian Scientists Seriously Pursue a Triangular UFO," *Wall Street Journal*, October 10, 1990.

Wall Street Journal, "Don't Go There: President Takes a No-Fly Zone Wherever He Goes," August 22, 2002.

Bibliography

Weiss, Jeffrey, "Military says fighter jets were in area; witnesses don't buy explanation," *Dallas Morning News*, January 23, 2009.

Wells, Bob, "Flying Disks Pure fantasy to USAF; Ex-Chief of 'Saucer' Survey Urges Inquiry," *Long Beach* [CA] *Independent*, November 7, 1957.

Williams, Brad, "Scribe Finds Tracking 'Saucer' Confusing Job," *Portland* [OR] *Journal*, March 5, 1955.

Wydem, Peter, interview with Captain Ruppelt, *St. Louis Post-Dispatch,* March 8, 1953.

Wydem, Peter, *St. Louis* [MO] *Post-Dispatch*, March 8, 1953.

Wylie, C.C., "Saucers Not Seen by Astronomers," news story, dateline: Iowa City, IA., June 4, 1952.

Websites

Aldrich, Jan, *Project 1947*, "The Search for Records on Roswell," http://www.project1947.com/roswell/rosearch.htm. Accessed on February 17, 2012.

Aldrich, Jan, *Project 1947*, "UFOs Sub Rosa Down Under—The Australian Military and Government Role in the UFO Controversy," http://www.project1947.com/forum/bcoz1.htm. Accessed on March 6, 2012.

Ballester Olmos, Vicente-Juan, *UFO Fotocat Blog*, "¿La última reentrada del milenio?," by Vicente-Juan Ballester Olmos and Matías Morey Ripoll. http://www.anomalia.org/272299.pdf, subtitle "Appendix II for this Blog:" November 27, 1999. Accessed February 18, 2012.

CNES, "New unit, broader mandate." http://www.cnes.fr/web/CNES-en/5040-new-unit-broader-mandate.php. Accessed February 19, 2012.

CNES-GEIPAN, "Number of Observations per Year." Last updated January 2012. http://www.cnes-geipan.fr/index.php?id=295. Accessed February 19, 2012.

CNES-GEIPAN, "Change of Direction for GEIPAN," December 10, 2008. http://www.cnes-geipan.fr/index.php?id=181&no_cache=1&tx_ttnews[backPid]=211&tx_ttnews[pointer]=3&tx_ttnews[tt_news]=75. Accessed February 19, 2012.

CNES-GEIPAN, "Scientific Campaign Analysis of Luminous Phenomena Observed in the Valley of Hessdalen Norway," November 29, 2010. http://www.cnes-geipan.fr/index.php?id=181&no_cache=1&tx_ttnews[tt_news]=98. Accessed February 19, 2012.

European Commission, "Alain Esterle." http://ec.europa.eu/information_society/policy/ipv6/docs/experts/bios/alain_esterle_bio_en.pdf. Accessed February 19, 2012.

Gendarmerie Nationale, "Au labo de criminalistique." http://www.defense.gouv.fr/gendarmerie/a-la-une/au-labo-de-criminalistique/%28language%29/fre-FR#SearchText=science%20recherche#xtcr=1.

Morey, Matiás, *Fundación Anomalía*, "Declassification! Military UFO Records Released: The Spanish Experience," by Vicente-Juan Ballester Olmos. http://www.anomalia.org/declass.htm. Accessed February 18, 2012.

Morey, Matiás, *Fundación Anomalía*, "Encuentro de clase militar en Mazarrón," by Vicente-Juan Ballester Olmos and Manuel Borraz. http://www.anomalia.org/mazarron.pdf. Accessed February 18, 2012.

Morey, Matiás, *Fundación Anomalía,* "La monografía de Antonio Munáiz Ferro-Sastre," by Vicente-Juan Ballester Olmos. http://www.anomalia.org/g035.htm. Accessed February 18, 2012.

Morey, Matiás, Fundación Anomalía, "State-of-the-Art in UFO Disclosure Worldwide," by Vicente-Juan Ballester Olmos. http://www.anomalia.org/disclosure2.pdf. Accessed February 18, 2012.

Morey, Matiás, *Fundación Anomalía*, "¡Identificados! Los OVNIS de Canarias fueron misiles Poseidón", by Vicente-Juan Ballester Olmos and Ricardo Campo Pérez, *Revista de Aeronáutica y Astronáutica*, March 2001, pp. 200-207. http://www.anomalia.org/misiles.htm. Accessed February 18, 2012.

Project Hessdalen, Østfold University College, Norway. http://www.hessdalen.org/index_e.shtml.

Ridge, Frances L., *National Investigations Committee on Aerial Phenomena,* Thomas Kirk testimonies to Francis Ridge. http://www.nicap.org/571105sebago_dir.htm. Accessed February 17, 2012.

Ridge, Frances L., National Investigations Committee on Aerial Phenomena. http://www.nicap.org/search/search.pl?Match=1&Realm=All&Terms=Trindade. Accessed February 20, 2012.

Ridge, Francis L., *National Investigations Committee on Aerial Phenomena,* "Grumman Proposal for Optical Surveillance of the Retrograde Satellite," circa 1961. http://www.nicap.org/grummanreport.htm. Accessed February 16, 2012.

Ridge, Francis L., *National Investigations Committee on Aerial Phenomena,* "1958 UFO Chronology," December 15, 1997. http://www.nicap.org/waves/1958fullrep.htm. Accessed February 15, 2012.

Ridge, Francis L., *National Investigations Committee on Aerial Phenomena,* "The Chop Clearance List," letter to Donald Keyhoe. http://www.nicap.org/chop.htm. Accessed February 4, 2012.

Rubstov, Vladimir, *Paranormal News*, "Post Soviet Ufology -- A View From The Inside." Accessed February 20, 2012.

United States Department of State, Office of the Historian, *Foreign Relations of the United States, 1950–1955, The Intelligence Community, 1950–1955*, documents 256-259, http://www.history.state.gov/historicaldocuments/frus1950-55Intel/ch2. Accessed February 2, 2012.

Wisner, Frank G., "Frank Gardiner Wisner" biography, December 21, 2007, *Arlington National Cemetery Website*, http://www.arlingtoncemetery.net/fgwisner.htm. Accessed February 2, 2012.

About the Authors

Jan Aldrich retired from the U.S. Army with over 25 years in field artillery and seven overseas tours. He has had 16-years experience in meteorology with the remaining time in intelligence, personnel, and safety positions. He received a Bachelor of Arts in History from University College, University of Maryland. Aldrich has visited more than 150 libraries, universities, archives, museums, and historical societies in 46 states and Canadian Provinces in his research of the UFO topic.

Bill Chalker has 25 years experience in laboratory management and quality control. He has a Bachelor of Science in Chemistry and Mathematics from the University of New England in Armidale, New South Wales, Australia. He is the author of *The OZ Files: The Australian UFO Story* and *Hair of the Alien: DNA and other Forensic Evidence of Alien Abduction.* Chalker has written many articles on the subject of UFOs and is also a contributing editor to the *International UFO Reporter*. During 1982 to 1984 he undertook a comprehensive review of official files at the Australian Department of Defence in Canberra.

Barry Greenwood is retired from the U.S. Postal Service and has been researching the UFO phenomenon for nearly 50 years. Since the 1970s, he has held memberships with the National Investigations Committee on Aerial Phenomena (NICAP), the Aerial Phenomena Research Organization (APRO), the Mutual UFO Network (MUFON), the British UFO Research Association (BUFORA), the Center for UFO Studies (CUFOS), and the Society for Scientific Exploration (SSE). He has spent thousands of hours in archival libraries locating obscure records on the topic of UFOs, and he specialized in research into government UFO involvement and the early history of strange aerial phenomenon. He was editor of the publication *Just Cause* for Citizens Against UFO secrecy (CAUS) from 1984 to 1998. He co-authored the book *Clear Intent*: *The Government Coverup of the UFO Experience* in 1984. He has been the editor of *U.F.O. Historical Revue* from 1998 to date.

Vicente-Juan Ballester Olmos is a retired financial analyst and manager for Ford Motor Company in Spain. He has a bachelor's degree from Colegio San José (Padres Jesuitas), Valencia, Spain. He has authored seven books on the UFO phenomenon and has received a scholarship for the study of UFO close encounter cases reported in Spain and Portugal, as well as several awards for his contributions in the study of UFOs. His close cooperation and work with the Spanish Air Force in the review of their UFO files helped open up those files to the public. Since the year 2000, Ballester Olmos has managed the FOTOCAT project, a computer-based databank compiling photographic UFO reports, i.e. cases where an image has been obtained in the form of a picture, slide, film, video, or digital mode. It currently has almost 11,000 entries.

Robert Powell is a retired Engineering Manager. He holds a Bachelor of Science in Chemistry from Southeastern Oklahoma State University. He managed a research and development lab working on nanotechnology, a state-of-the-art chemical laboratory in the semiconductor industry, and is a joint holder on four patents related to nanotechnology. Powell has been the Director of Research at the Mutual UFO Network since 2007 and is a member of the Society for Scientific Exploration. He co-authored an extensive paper on the Stephenville UFO incident of 2008 that included the correlation of witness reports to radar returns.

Steve Purcell works as a Field Engineer in the power industry. He has also worked in the nuclear, aviation and printing industries. He is a former Mutual UFO Network State Director for Tennessee and is a member of the Mutual UFO Network's STAR Field Investigative Team. Purcell has investigated hundreds of UFO cases and has been researching anomalous phenomena for more than 20 years.

Clas Svahn is a journalist at Sweden's largest morning newspaper, *Dagens Nyheter*. He is the author of eleven books and is a co-author or contributor to fourteen books on various topics from UFOs and cults to unusual natural phenomena and the paranormal. Svahn has studied the UFO phenomenon for more than 35 years and is chairman of the nationwide research organization UFO-Sweden and the vice chairman of Archives for UFO Research, the world's largest archive on unusual and unexplained phenomena.

Michael Swords is a retired college science professor. He has a Bachelor of Science in Chemistry from the University of Notre Dame, a Masters of Science in Biochemistry from Iowa State University, and a PhD in the History of Science and Technology from Case Western Reserve University. He taught at Western Michigan University for 30 years, retiring in 2000 as professor emeritus in Environmental Studies. Professor Swords is a long term board member of the J. Allen Hynek Center for UFO Studies, and edited the *Journal of UFO Studies* for six years. He is a member of the Coalition for UFO Research and the Society for Scientific Exploration. His published book, *GrassRoots UFOs,* describes the great number of UFO case reports received by former CUFOS treasurer John Timmerman from everyday citizens that he encountered in his travels with the Center's photo exhibit.

Richard Thieme is an author and professional speaker focused on the deeper implications of science, technology, and religion for twenty-first century life. He speaks professionally about the challenges posed by new technologies and the future, how to redesign ourselves to meet these challenges, and creativity in response to radical change. Thieme has keynoted hundreds conferences around the world with a focus on information security. He has a Bachelor of Arts with highest honors in Literature and Writing from Northwestern University, a Master of Arts in English Literature from the University of Chicago, and a Master of Divinity degree with honors from Seabury-Western Theological Seminary. He has written articles for numerous periodicals, including *Forbes*, *Salon,* and the *International UFO Reporter*, and has written two books and contributed chapters to several others.

Name Index

Subject Index

UFO Event Location Index

CPSIA information can be obtained
at www.ICGtesting.com
Printed in the USA
BVHW06s0042090718
521075BV00006B/40/P